Beginning PHP5

Beginning PHP5

Dave W. Mercer
Allan Kent
Steven D. Nowicki
David Mercer
Dan Squier
Wankyu Choi

with
Heow Eide-Goodman
Edward Lecky-Thompson
and Clark Morgan

WILEY

Wiley Publishing, Inc.

Beginning PHP5

Published by
Wiley Publishing, Inc.
10475 Crosspoint Boulevard
Indianapolis, IN 46256
www.wiley.com

Copyright © 2004 by Wiley Publishing, Inc., Indianapolis, Indiana

Published simultaneously in Canada

CIP Data available upon request.

ISBN: 0-7645-5783-1

Manufactured in the United States of America

10 9 8 7 6 5 4 3 2 1

No part of this publication may be reproduced, stored in a retrieval system or transmitted in any form or by any means, electronic, mechanical, photocopying, recording, scanning or otherwise, except as permitted under Sections 107 or 108 of the 1976 United States Copyright Act, without either the prior written permission of the Publisher, or authorization through payment of the appropriate per-copy fee to the Copyright Clearance Center, 222 Rosewood Drive, Danvers, MA 01923, (978) 750-8400, fax (978) 646-8600. Requests to the Publisher for permission should be addressed to the Legal Department, Wiley Publishing, Inc., 10475 Crosspoint Blvd., Indianapolis, IN 46256, (317) 572-3447, fax (317) 572-4447, E-Mail: permcoordinator@wiley.com.

For general information on our other products and services or to obtain technical support, please contact our Customer Care Department within the U.S. at (800) 762-2974, outside the U.S. at (317) 572-3993 or fax (317) 572-4002.

Wiley also publishes its books in a variety of electronic formats. Some content that appears in print may not be available in electronic books.

About the Authors

Dave W. Mercer

Dave W. Mercer has 15 years' experience in industrial and process engineering, and systems analysis, and is CTO for a B2B, responsible for the development and deployment of online automated business services. His entire site, hosting server, and the applications he builds for hosted clients are programmed in PHP using Postgres or MySQL as the database.

Allan Kent

Allan Kent is a PHP programmer who runs his own company and is a co-author of *Beginning PHP 4*. Allan has been programming seriously for the past dozen years and, other than the single blemish when he achieved a diploma in Cobol programming, is entirely self-taught.

Steven D. Nowicki

Steven D. Nowicki is Director of Software development at The Content Project, a Santa Monica, California–based consulting firm currently developing a massive enterprise resource planning and contact management system comprising more than 300,000 lines of OO PHP code. He has a decade of experience in large-scale software development and system architecture on all major platforms.

David Mercer

David Mercer is a PHP programmer and contributed to *Beginning PHP 4*. He has maintained a keen interest in all things open source ever since he managed to put together a working Beowulf cluster by nicking old computer parts from colleagues and assembling them under his desk. He has worked on Wrox open source titles about PHP, Perl, and Linux.

Dan Squier

Dan Squier is a longtime contributor to the Wrox community and a PHP programmer.

Wankyu Choi

Wankyu Choi is an accomplished PHP programmer and lead author of *Beginning PHP 4*. He holds a Master's degree in English/Korean interpretation and translation from the Graduate School of Translation & Interpretation.

Heow Eide-Goodman

Heow Eide-Goodman is a member of NYPHP and LispNYC who uses PHP in his day job to do Web sites, services, and back-office transformations among SQL Server, Interbase/Firebird, and MySQL.

Edward Lecky-Thompson

Edward Lecky-Thompson is the founder and director of Ashridge New Media, a professional new media technology consultancy based in Berkhamsted, just north of London, England. Self-described as "utterly obsessed with PHP," Ed has more than six years' experience in commercial software development and enterprise-level systems architecture across myriad platforms, with particularly strong exposure to PHP and Apache on Linux-based platforms.

Clark Morgan

Clark Morgan is an experienced programmer who creates and administers databases with Web sites using PHP and MySQL for Fusion Computing and Media.

This book has been a team effort and represents the efforts of many people. The current team of authors dedicates this book to the previous authors for their great introduction to earlier versions of PHP and to the editors and managers who worked so hard to help us build another great introduction to the new PHP5, especially Debra Williams Cauley, Maryann Steinhart, and David Mercer. We also thank the developers of PHP, the ZEND engine, and all the folks who've contributed the open-source software and code examples that make PHP the ideal scripting language for Web applications.

Credits

Acquisitions Editor
Debra Williams Cauley

Project Editor
Maryann Steinhart

Technical Editors
David Mercer
Heow Eide-Goodman

Production Editor
Eric Newman

Editorial Manager
Mary Beth Wakefield

Vice President & Executive Group Publisher
Richard Swadley

Vice President and Executive Publisher
Bob Ipsen

Vice President and Publisher
Joseph B. Wikert

Executive Editorial Director
Mary Bednarek

Contents

Introduction   xix

Chapter 1: Getting Up and Running   1

The Roots of PHP   1
Installing, Configuring, and Running PHP   2
    System Requirements   3
    php.ini, the PHP Configuration File   3
    Setting Up a Test Machine   4
    Network Connections   4
    Where Do You Start?   4
    Running PHP5   5
Installing PHP5 with Linux and Apache   6
    Choosing Your Installation Method   6
    Setting up Apache for PHP   16
Installing PHP5 on Windows 2000/Internet Information Server (IIS) 5   19
    Downloading PHP5   20
    php.ini and Extensions   22
Testing and Troubleshooting   26
Configuring PHP   28
    php.ini   28
    PHP Extensions   29
    Caching   29
Summary   29
Exercise   30

Chapter 2: Writing Simple Programs   31

Create a Simple PHP Program   31
    Explore Some Details   33
    How PHP Code Works   33
    How Online PHP Programs Run   36
Web Communications: Internet Protocols and HTTP   36
    TCP/IP   37
    The HTTP Protocol   37

Contents

Using Variables in PHP   **41**
Issues Concerning Creating Variables   41
Defined Constants   45
Operators and Expressions   **46**
PHP Operators   46
PHP Expressions   47
Operator Types   47
Arrays   58
Summary   **62**
Exercises   **62**

Chapter 3: PHP, HTML, and State   63

HTML Primer   **63**
The HTML Document Type Definition   65
The Form and Input Elements   65
Accessing PHP and HTTP Data   **67**
Predefined Variables   67
Variables in HTTP Request and Response   69
SuperGlobal Arrays   69
Links   **72**
Query Strings   **73**
HTML (Web) Forms   **74**
HTML Form Elements   74
HTML Form Fields (Controls) and PHP   79
The Concept of State   **108**
State Maintenance   108
Native Sessions in PHP   116
Summary   **120**
Exercise   **120**

Chapter 4: Decisions, Loops, and Arrays   123

Designing PHP Program Logic   **123**
Problem Statement   123
Writing Pseudo Code   124
Boolean Logic   125
Conditional or Branching Statements   **127**
An Example of Branching   128
if Statements   129
switch Statements   140

Loops and Arrays   **145**
   Loops   145
   Arrays   161
Summary   **185**
Exercise   **185**

Chapter 5: Robust and Healthy Code   187

Testing and Debugging   **187**
   Values That Break Your Code   188
   Basic Error Types   189
Debugging PHP Script   **189**
   Understanding PHP Error Messages   189
   Syntax Errors   190
   Logic Errors   193
   Runtime Errors   193
Debugging and Handling Errors in PHP5   **198**
   Preventing the Display of Private Information   198
   Roll-Your-Own Debugging Tools   198
Form Validation   **199**
   Using the exit Statement   200
   String Validation and Regular Expressions   204
   Validating Data Entry   213
   Using Regexps to Check File Path Parameters   218
Handling Errors Gracefully   **220**
   Configuring PHP for Error Handling   220
   Try/Catch—New in PHP5   222
Summary   **229**
Exercise   **230**

Chapter 6: Writing High-Quality Code   231

Development Planning   **231**
   Formal Software Development Processes   232
   Optimizing Your Code   234
Using Coding Standards   **234**
Writing User-Defined Functions in PHP   **236**
   The Structure of Functions   237
   Switching Functions   243
   How Values Get Inside Functions   245

Contents

Scope of Variables   **247**
Global and Local Variables   247
Creating Static Function Variables   248
Nesting   251
Recursion   251
The Include and Require Statements   **254**
Things To Be Careful About with Include and Require   **257**
Summary   **257**
Exercise   **258**

Chapter 7: Files and Directories   **259**

File and Directory Handling   **260**
Working with Files   **260**
Opening and Closing Files   261
Getting Information About a File   264
Reading and Writing to Files   264
Reading and Writing Characters in Files   **269**
Reading Entire Files   **272**
Random Access to File Data   **274**
Getting Information on Files   **278**
Ownership and Permissions   **282**
Working with Files You Own   **287**
Splitting the Name and Path from a File   287
Copying, Renaming, and Deleting Files   288
Working with Directories   **290**
Other Directory Functions   292
Traversing a Directory Hierarchy   294
Creating a Directory Navigator   295
Building a Text Editor   **300**
Uploading Files   **307**
Summary   **312**
Exercise   **312**

Chapter 8: XML   **313**

What Is XML?   **313**
XML Document Structure   **315**
Major Parts of an XML Document   315
Well-Formed XML Documents   316
Using XML Elements and Attributes   317

Valid XML Documents: DTDs and XML Schemas	318
Web Services	322
PHP and XML	**322**
PHP4 XML Functions	**323**
XML Parsers	329
The Document Object Model	332
PHP5 XML Functions	**334**
The SimpleXML Extension	334
Changing a Value with simpleXML	338
Summary	**340**
Exercise	**341**

Chapter 9: An Introduction to Databases and SQL

	343
Storing Data	**344**
Databases and Databases	344
Database Architectures	345
Choosing a Database	346
Setting Up MySQL	**347**
Installing on Windows	347
Installing on Linux	348
Configuring MySQL	350
Relational Databases	**351**
Normalization	352
Talking to Databases with SQL	355
A Quick Play with MySQL	**360**
Starting the mysql Client Program	360
Selecting a Database to Use	361
Looking at Tables Inside a Database	362
Using SQL to Look at Data	363
Manipulating Data in a Database	364
Using GRANT and REVOKE Commands	365
Connecting to MySQL from PHP	**367**
PHP MySQL Connectivity	**368**
Basic Connection Functions	368
Handling Server Errors	371
Creating Databases and Tables from MySQL	**375**
Creating the Sample Database and Tables with PHP	379
Altering Tables	383
Inserting Data into a Table	385
Summary	**388**

Contents

Chapter 10: Retrieving Data from MySQL Using PHP   391

Retrieving Data Using PHP   **391**
SQL Statements for Retrieving Data   **394**
    Server Functions   394
    Retrieving Fields   395
    Getting Summaries   400
    More Complex Retrievals   401
Putting It All Together   **404**
    The common_db.inc File Contents   405
    The userviewer.php File Contents   407
    Using the User Viewer   414
Summary   **415**

Chapter 11: Using PHP to Manipulate Data in MySQL   417

Inserting Records Using PHP   **417**
    Special Characters   418
    htmlspecialchars()   419
Updating and Deleting Records in Tables   **420**
Working with Date and Time Type Fields   **422**
Getting Information on Database Tables   **426**
ENUM Options and Field Defaults   **431**
Creating a User Registration Script   **435**
    register.php   435
    Choosing Actions to Take   440
Creating an Access Logger Script   **442**
    auth_user.php   442
    access_logger.php   444
Creating a User Manager   **449**
    userman.php   449
    Choosing an Action to Take   457
Summary   **458**
Exercises   **459**

Chapter 12: An Introduction to Object-Oriented Programming   461

What Is Object-Oriented Programming?   **461**
Understanding OOP Concepts   **463**
    Classes   463
    Objects   464
    Inheritance   477

Interfaces   486
Encapsulation   489
Changes to OO in PHP5   **490**
Summary   **491**
Exercises   **491**

Chapter 13: Working with UML and Classes   493

The Unified Modeling Language   **493**
Why Would You Want to Use UML?   494
UML Software   494
Class Diagrams   495
Creating the Contact Manager   **496**
The Contact Manager UML Diagrams   496
Other Useful UML Diagrams   500
Creating the Entity Class   **503**
Putting it All Together   **509**
The PropertyObject Class   509
The Contact Type Classes   512
The DataManager Class   516
The Entity, Individual, and Organization Classes   517
Making Use of the System   525
Summary   **527**

Chapter 14: PEAR   529

What Is PEAR?   **529**
How Is PEAR Structured?   530
Recapping PEAR Standards   532
Installing PEAR Packages   **534**
Finding Your Way Around pear.php.net   534
Exploring PEAR Classes and Applications   534
Installing and Using the PEAR Package Manager   535
Using PEAR Packages   **545**
Building an Application Using Two PEAR Components   551
Summary   **566**

Chapter 15: PHP5 and E-Mail   567

E-Mail Background   **567**
Internet Mail Protocols   **568**

Contents

Structure of an E-Mail Message **568**

Sending E-Mail with PHP **570**

Using the mail() Function 570

Multipurpose Internet Mail Extensions 572

PEAR Mail Libraries 574

Building a Simple PHP E-Mail Application **575**

Summary **583**

Exercises **583**

Chapter 16: Generating Graphics **585**

Basics of Computer Graphics **585**

Color Theory 586

Coordinate Systems 586

Image Types 587

Working with Raster Images **588**

Creating a New Image 588

Allocating Colors 588

Basic Drawing Functions 589

Manipulating Raster Images **598**

Opening an Existing Image 598

Applying a Watermark 600

Creating Thumbnails 604

Using Text in Images **607**

Adding Standard Text 607

Using True Type Fonts 609

Summary **612**

Exercises **612**

Chapter 17: Case Study: A PHP Logging Agent **613**

Why a Logging Agent? **614**

Smarty 615

PHPUnit 620

Designing the Logging Agent **621**

The sitelogs.db Database 622

Using UML to Map Out the Logging Agent 624

Coding the Solution **628**

Miscellaneous Scripts 628

Data-Handling Scripts 632

Validation and Error-Handling Scripts 645

Presentation Scripts and Templates 651

Testing the Application   **654**
Working with the Logging Agent   **665**
    userlog.php   666
    Viewing the Logging Agent   666
Summary   **670**

Appendix A: Answers   **671**
Appendix B: PHP Functions Reference   **693**
Appendix C: Using SQLite   **765**
Appendix D: ODBC   **781**
Appendix E: PHP CLI   **795**
Appendix F: Configuring PHP5   **805**
Index   **829**

Introduction

PHP5 is the latest incarnation of PHP (PHP: Hypertext Preprocessor)—a programming language devised by Rasmus Lerdorf in 1994 for building dynamic, interactive Web sites. Since then, it's been evolving into a full-fledged language in its own right, thanks to the hard work of all the people who contribute to its development.

A sure sign that PHP is maturing as a technology is evidenced by its totally revamped and upgraded support for object-oriented programming (OOP) principles and improved support for XML. The Zend engine (the part that interprets and executes PHP code) now enables PHP5 developers to implement, among a host of other things, graceful application-wide error handling.

With all the new features and functionality that PHP5 provides, it's important for programmers to "upgrade" their understanding in order to best make use of this powerful Web scripting tool. And that's why it's important for you, the reader, to invest your time learning about the latest and greatest that the people developing PHP5 have to offer.

That's all well and good, but what exactly is PHP?

You know it's a language for writing computer programs, so the real question is "What *sort* of programs can you write with it?" In technical terms, PHP's main use is as a cross-platform, HTML-embedded, server-side Web scripting language. Let's take a moment to examine these terms:

❑ **Cross-platform:** Most PHP code can be processed without alteration on computers running many different operating systems. For example, a PHP script that runs on Linux generally also runs well on Windows.

❑ **HTML-embedded:** PHP code can be written in files containing a mixture of PHP instructions and HTML code.

❑ **Server-side:** The PHP programs are run on a server—specifically a Web server.

❑ **Web-scripting language:** PHP programs run via a Web browser.

This means you'll write programs that mix PHP code and HTML, run them on a Web server, and access them from a Web browser that displays the result of your PHP processing by showing you the HTML returned by the Web server. In other words, you can make your programs available for other people to access across the Web, simply by placing them on a public Web server.

You're probably already familiar with HTML (HyperText Markup Language)—it's the main language used to create Web pages, combining plain text with special tags that tell browsers how to treat that text. HTML is used to describe how different elements in a Web page should be displayed, how pages should be linked, where to put images, and so on.

Pure HTML documents, for all their versatility, are little more than static arrangements of text and pictures, albeit nicely presented ones. However, most of the sites you find on the Web aren't static but dynamic, even interactive. They can show you a list of articles containing a particular word in which you're interested, show you the latest news, even greet you by name when you log on. They enable you to interact, and present you with different information according to the choices you make.

You can't build a Web site like that using raw HTML, and that's where PHP comes in. What sort of things can you do with it? Well, you can program sites that

❑ Present data from a wide variety of sources, such as databases, files, or even other Web pages.

❑ Incorporate interactive elements, such as search facilities, message boards, and straw polls.

❑ Enable the user to perform actions, such as sending e-mail or buying something.

In other words, PHP can be used to write the sort of sites that those who regularly use the Web are likely to encounter every day. From search engines to information portals to e-commerce sites, most major Web sites incorporate some or all of these sorts of programming. Among other things in the course of this book, you'll use PHP to build

❑ A simple, online text editor

❑ A Web-based e-mail application

❑ An object-oriented contact manager application

❑ An object-oriented logging agent

So, PHP5 can be used for a diverse range of applications, from simple utilities such as a text editor to powerful Web applications such as the logging agent case study. This book equips you with the knowledge necessary to build any kind of Web site you want using PHP5. You'll learn some useful techniques along the way and perhaps pick up some ideas that you can incorporate into your own Web sites and applications.

> *Web scripting is certainly the mainstay of PHP's success, but it's not the only way to use the language. Command line scripting—using CLI (Command Line Interface), which was introduced in PHP4—is one of many popular applications of PHP. (CLI is covered in an appendix at the end of this book). Client-side graphical user interface application development using GTK (Gnome ToolKit) is another.*

Why PHP?

One of the best things about PHP is the large number of Internet service providers (ISPs) and Web hosting companies that support it. Today there are hundreds of thousands of developers using PHP, and it's not surprising that there are so many, considering that several million sites are reported to have PHP installed.

You already know that PHP is a cross-platform technology and that once you've written your Web page, it's easy to get it up and running on our Web server, but how does PHP compare with other technologies out there? Well, comparing PHP with Perl is a bit tricky because they were designed for different things. PHP was specifically designed to rapidly create dynamic Web content; Perl was not. As a result, Perl can sometimes be a complicated language that can become prohibitive for users who want to create Web pages. Comparing PHP with ASP is a more balanced comparison, but then you have to pay for ASP, and ASP doesn't work well on a variety of platforms—it needs to be used on other proprietary platforms for which you also must pay.

You may ask, "Is there a downside to PHP?" In the past, PHP has been criticized for the way it handled a number of things—for example, one of its main stumbling blocks was the way in which it implemented object support. However, PHP5 has taken stock of the downfalls of its predecessors and, where necessary, has completely rewritten the way in which it implements its functionality. Now more than ever, PHP is a serious contender for large-scale enterprise developments as well as having a large, consolidated base of small- to medium-sized applications.

Who This Book Is For

As you've probably guessed from its title, this book is intended for people who are just starting out with PHP5. That covers a pretty broad range of folks, from complete beginners who want to start writing programs for the very first time to experienced, battle-hardened developers who want to find out what's possible in the latest version of PHP.

We've tried wherever possible to make the book's content equally useful to readers all across the spectrum, but there are inevitably some sections that will be of more use to one group than they will to another. For example, people who already have PHP5 up and running on their machines could happily skip Chapter 1, which is all about just that—getting PHP up and running.

What This Book Covers

The main intention of this book is to ensure that the reader gains a broad understanding of PHP5 and its associated technologies and topics. A wide range of issues is discussed in the book, so you should consider looking at more focused books if you are concerned about specific issues only. For example, if you are mainly interested in how to use PHP5 and MySQL, you'll probably be best off looking at something that focuses specifically on that aspect of PHP. Further, if you are already well versed in all things PHP-ish, then you may want to consider looking at *Professional PHP5 Programming* (Wrox), which goes into more detail and covers more advanced topics.

Here's a quick list of some of the more important topics discussed in this book:

- ❏ Installation and setup
- ❏ Fundamentals—variables, loops, decisions, arrays
- ❏ Programming technique and good practices—creating and maintaining efficient, robust code
- ❏ Working with data
- ❏ File and directory handling
- ❏ XML
- ❏ PHP5 and databases—specifically MySQL and SQLite
- ❏ Object-oriented programming
- ❏ PEAR
- ❏ E-mail
- ❏ Graphics
- ❏ CLI

There's much more, of course, but this list should give you a good idea of what you can expect to get out of *Beginning PHP5*.

How This Book Is Structured

To provide you with an effective learning tool, every effort has been made to present all the information in a logical, consistent manner. This means that, unless absolutely necessary, you won't encounter new concepts or topics without having been introduced to them first. For example, if we're discussing how to create a class method, you will already have been introduced to the idea of functions, so that you won't have to waste time jumping from one place to another to understand the discussion.

To this end, the first few chapters provide a grounding in the fundamentals of PHP—how to get hold of it, how to get it working, and how to do some basic things with it. Afterward, a certain level of knowledge is assumed, and you move on to more advanced topics.

Here's a chapter-by-chapter breakdown to help you to decide whether to read the book cover to cover, or simply dip in here and there. If you're already PHP-savvy, of course, you'll just want to dive into those chapters that are of most interest to you.

Chapter 1 gets you up and running. A brief discussion of PHP is followed by step-by-step instructions for installing it on Linux or Windows platforms. You also learn how to install and configure a Web server (IIS or Apache), so that you can view your PHP5 pages from a Web browser. In the event that you run into problems during this setup and configuration stage, a helpful troubleshooting and debugging section is provided at the end of the chapter.

Chapter 2 presents a small PHP5 script in action. There's a discussion of Internet protocols and HTTP and how PHP relates to them; and with the example script as a base, you get a broad look at how PHP fits into the bigger picture. Then we start drilling down to the basics of the language: Variables, data types, and expressions all get introduced in the second half of this chapter.

Chapter 3 demonstrates how you can use the information supplied as part of HTTP requests and responses to collect useful data on a variety of programming environment aspects such as server information, GET and POST methods, cookies, and more. Plenty of practical examples later in the chapter show how you can use HTML forms and form elements to collect information for use in your PHP scripts. HTTP, sessions, and state are other topics in this chapter.

Chapter 4 deals with one of the most critical topics in any language: programming logic. You'll explore comparison and logical operators and the various statements, such as if and switch, that make use of them. Just as important are loops, which enable you to perform repetitive tasks with relative ease. With a good grasp of these fundamentals, you tackle the slightly more complex concept of arrays and learn how you can use loops, among other things, to manipulate the data contained within them.

Chapter 5 makes a pre-emptive strike at bad programming practices by discussing debugging and testing and how you can use PHP5 to handle errors gracefully. The chapter provides useful examples of how to maintain efficient, robust, and healthy code and also shows you how form validation can be used to keep your programs clear of erroneous or nonsensical data.

Chapter 6 is nominally related to the preceding chapter in that you explore good programming practices. You examine all the aspects involved in producing high-quality code, from code design, optimization and presentation, to modularization (writing user-defined functions) and important related concepts such as scope.

Chapter 7 deals comprehensively with PHP's capability to work with files and directories. Opening, closing, reading, and writing to files are all basic requirements of many PHP programs, and these, along with other important issues such as file ownership and permissions, are detailed here. You build a text file editor to demonstrate the functionality you learned through the course of the chapter.

Chapter 8 illustrates the exciting world of XML, which is rapidly becoming the most popular method for transmitting structured information wherever there's a need to transmit data. PHP5 is endowed with new functionality so that it works faster and more efficiently with XML. Plenty of practical examples ensure that you get all the requisite information to take full advantage of XML in your applications.

Chapters 9–11 provide an excellent guide to storing, manipulating, and retrieving data using PHP and an RDBMS (Relational DataBase Management System)—in this case, MySQL. You'll install MySQL and then use it to explore the fundamentals of relational database architecture. You'll learn the basic connection functions that PHP5 supplies in order to perform many of the necessary basic functions such as creating and connecting to databases and inserting, retrieving, updating, and altering information. You put your knowledge to work by developing related programs through these three data chapters.

Chapters 12 and 13 discuss one of the most important concepts in programming today: objects. Chapter 12 introduces you to the theory behind object-oriented programming (OOP) and examines important topics such as inheritance, encapsulation, and abstraction, providing examples to demonstrate how PHP5 supports these concepts. Chapter 13 then takes a more pragmatic approach and rounds off the OO topic by leading you through an object-oriented application designed with the aid of UML, the Unified Modeling Language, which is itself explained in some detail at the beginning of the chapter.

Chapter 14 introduces the excellent PHP Extension and Application Repository (PEAR). You learn to use PEAR to find and use the packages it provides to add functionality to your own applications. You'll develop a couple of applications that use PEAR packages to complete various tasks.

Chapter 15 delves into the topic of e-mail. After presenting a bit of background on e-mail and its associated protocols and technologies, the chapter shows you how PHP5 supports e-mail functionality. Multipurpose Internet Mail Extensions (MIME) messages are also discussed, and a sample application provides a good practical demonstration for enabling e-mail attachments using MIME.

Chapter 16 shows you how to make use of the GD image library to render graphics for your Web pages. You'll be creating and manipulating images, drawing shapes, and working with text in GD.

Chapter 17 pulls together everything you learned in the book and challenges you to use your knowledge to develop a larger application. It leads you through the entire process of building a complex solution like the logging agent case study that's created in the course of this chapter.

Appendix A provides the answers to the exercises presented in most chapters.

Appendix B presents a PHP5 function reference, which is sure to come in handy given the large amount of native PHP functions milling around.

Appendix C discusses the SQLite database that's bundled with PHP5. It includes practical examples of SQLite in action.

Appendix D gives you a rundown on Open Database Connectivity (ODBC)—what it is, what it does, and how you can use it to connect to the various SQL-based databases. Specifically, you look at setting up ODBC with MySQL and see how you can use PHP5's ODBC functions to connect to MySQL.

Appendix E explains how you can use the PHP Command Line Interpreter to perform non–Web-based tasks using PHP5. It enables PHP5 users to open the door to command-line jobs that were previously the domain of Perl, BASH, and DOS users.

Appendix F provides an in-depth look at the php.ini file, which contains all of the configuration settings for PHP5. This appendix is a useful reference for any of the more advanced settings (which aren't discussed in the book) that you may need to modify at some stage during the course of your programming.

What You Need to Use This Book

As already noted, PHP can be run on a broad range of different operating systems, including Windows, Linux, Mac OS X, and more. The first step is therefore to get a version of PHP that's suitable for your own OS. (You'll find full instructions for downloading and installing the correct version of PHP5 in Chapter 1.)

You'll need a text editor of some kind to create and edit your scripts.

You also need a Web server. Apache is always a good bet, particularly on UNIX machines (although, it works just fine on Windows, too). Apache is included with most Linux distributions and Mac OS X as well, and if you don't already have a copy, note that it's available for download from www.apache.org. Oh, and it's free.

Windows users may find it easier to work with Microsoft's own Web server, IIS (Internet Information Server), which is included with Windows 2000 and most versions of XP (not XP Home), although it won't necessarily be installed by default. If you're using Windows 98, there's a cut-down version of IIS called PWS (Personal Web Server), which does a perfectly adequate job for small projects. If you're aiming to build big, though, Apache's probably a better option in the long run. And if you're running Windows ME or XP Home edition (neither of which support PWS or IIS), Apache is definitely the way to go.

Using the Command Line

If you're using a Windows PC or Macintosh computer, it's quite possible that you won't be familiar with the command-line interface or "shell." This is a powerful tool for communicating with your system, and one that you'll be relying on in a number of chapters throughout the book.

Before rich graphical environments came into common use, and drag-and-drop interfaces were virtually unheard of, the only way to interact with computers was to type commands, one line at a time. You wanted to run a program? There was no icon to click—you typed the program's name.

Many programs still make use of the command-line interface. Why? For one thing, it's a lot simpler to write them that way, and even now, many powerful utilities and applications are written exclusively for use via the command line. For another, many people still find it easier to interact with the command prompt than with a mouse-driven windowed environment.

For example, when you begin looking at databases in Chapter 9, you make use of the MySQL database manager, which you configure by typing instructions at the command line.

So first of all, you need to access the command line interface:

❑   On Windows, look in the Start menu for an entry (normally under Programs ⇨ Accessories) named Command Prompt or MS-DOS Prompt. Alternatively, press Windows+R to call up the Run dialog, type cmd, and click OK.

❑   On UNIX (including variations such as Linux and Mac OS X), look for a program with a name such as console, terminal, konsole, xterm, eterm, or kterm. These are all widely used shell programs that can be found on a broad range of UNIX-based systems.

After you've called up the interface, you'll probably be confronted by a nearly blank screen, with just a snippet of text such as one of these:

```
$
%
C:/>
#
bash$
```

This is a *command prompt*, which is simply there to let you know that the interface is ready to receive instructions—prompting you for commands, in effect. It doesn't really matter what the prompt looks like, just that you recognize it when it appears. In this book, the prompt is designated this way:

```
>
```

Whenever you have to type instructions at the command line, we show those instructions immediately following the prompt (>), nearly always in the first line. What the computer generates by itself follows:

```
> mysqlshow
+-----------+
| Databases |
+-----------+
| mysql     |
| test      |
+-----------+
```

Conventions

To help you get the most from the text and keep track of what's happening, we've used a number of conventions throughout the book.

> **Boxes like this one hold important, not-to-be-forgotten information that is directly relevant to the surrounding text.**

Notes, tips, and asides to the current discussion are offset and placed in italics like this.

As for styles in the text:

- ❑ We *highlight* important words when we introduce them
- ❑ We show keyboard strokes like this: Ctrl+A
- ❑ We show file names, URLs, and code within the text like so: `persistence.properties`
- ❑ We present code in two different ways:

```
In code examples we highlight new and important code with a gray background.
```

```
The gray highlighting is not used for code that's less important in the
present context, or has been shown before.
```

Source Code

As you work through the examples in this book, you may choose either to type all the code manually or to use the source code files that accompany the book. All of the source code used in this book is available for download at www.wrox.com. At the site, simply locate the book's title (either by using the Search box or by using one of the title lists) and click the Download Code link on the book's detail page to obtain all the source code for the book.

Because many books have similar titles, you may find it easiest to search by ISBN; this book's ISBN is 0-7645-5783-1.

Once you download the code, just decompress it with your favorite compression tool. Alternatively, you can go to the main Wrox code download page at www.wrox.com/dynamic/books/download.aspx to see the code available for this book and all other Wrox books.

Errata

We make every effort to ensure that there are no errors in the text or in the code. However, no one is perfect, and mistakes do occur. If you find an error in one of our books, like a spelling mistake or faulty piece of code, we would be very grateful for your feedback. By sending in errata you may save another reader hours of frustration, and at the same time you will be helping us provide even higher quality information.

To find the errata page for this book, go to www.wrox.com and locate the title using the Search box or one of the title lists. Then, on the book details page, click the Book Errata link. On this page you can view all errata that has been submitted for this book and posted by Wrox editors. A complete book list including links to each's book's errata is also available at www.wrox.com/misc-pages/booklist.shtml.

If you don't spot "your" error on the Book Errata page, go to www.wrox.com/contact/techsupport.shtml and complete the form there to send us the error you have found. We'll check the information and, if appropriate, post a message to the book's errata page and fix the problem in subsequent editions of the book.

p2p.wrox.com

For author and peer discussion, join the P2P forums at p2p.wrox.com. The forums are a Web-based system for you to post messages relating to Wrox books and related technologies and interact with other readers and technology users. The forums offer a subscription feature to e-mail you topics of interest of your choosing when new posts are made to the forums. Wrox authors, editors, other industry experts, and your fellow readers are present on these forums.

At http://p2p.wrox.com you will find a number of different forums that will help you not only as you read this book, but also as you develop your own applications. To join the forums, just follow these steps:

1. Go to p2p.wrox.com and click the Register link.

2. Read the terms of use and click Agree.

3. Complete the required information to join as well as any optional information you wish to provide and click Submit.

4. You will receive an e-mail with information describing how to verify your account and complete the joining process.

You can read messages in the forums without joining P2P but in order to post your own messages, you must join.

Once you join, you can post new messages and respond to messages other users post. You can read messages at any time on the Web. If you would like to have new messages from a particular forum e-mailed to you, click the Subscribe to this Forum icon by the forum name in the forum listing.

For more information about how to use the Wrox P2P, be sure to read the P2P FAQs for answers to questions about how the forum software works as well as many common questions specific to P2P and Wrox books. To read the FAQs, click the FAQ link on any P2P page.

Getting Up and Running

PHP, which stands for HyperText Preprocessor, is widely used for creating programmed features for Web sites because it is easy to learn and also because PHP syntax is drawn from other widely used languages, making it familiar to many programmers. In this chapter we present a very brief history of PHP, and then discuss the nature of PHP as it relates to the Web.

Before you can get into the nitty-gritty of programming with PHP5, you need a clear understanding of how PHP programs work across the Web, and that obviously implies knowledge of the Web protocol called HyperText Transfer Protocol (HTTP). HTTP is the language or format for communications from browser to Web server and back, and is therefore fundamental to many aspects of PHP. HTTP gets some coverage in this chapter, and quite a bit more in Chapter 3.

You'll see how to properly setup PHP on a Linux server, and on a Windows server as well. PHP programs run in conjunction with Web pages, which in turn run (or are distributed by) Web server software (such as Apache or IIS), which in turn run on top of an operating system (such as Linux or Windows). Although it's not strictly necessary to know everything about network operating systems to build good PHP programs, there are many aspects of PHP that are controlled or affected by the Web server. If you're unfamiliar with server computers, Web servers, and the like, don't worry. You'll soon see how they work, and look at the requirements and process of installing basic Web server software.

This chapter leads you through installing PHP on a Red Hat Linux machine running Apache, and through installing PHP on a Windows 2000 machine running IIS. Just pick the one that's right for you.

You'll also examine the contents of the PHP configuration file php.ini with you, and test your PHP installation.

Obviously there's a lot of work for you in this chapter, so let's get started.

The Roots of PHP

PHP is a programming language designed to work with HTML, but unlike HTML, PHP has data processing capabilities. If you are familiar with HTML, you know that it is not really a programming language, but more of a rendering language—that is, HTML enables you to write Web pages using code that creates a pleasing (hopefully) display of text, graphics, and links within a browser. Although there are a few helpful features of HTML (such as the capability to cause a form submission), for the most part HTML does nothing programmatically. For example, there are no HTML commands that enable you to add two numbers together, or access a database.

If you remember the Web back in the early '90s, you may recall that early Web pages were made from HTML code written as plain text source files. When you made a connection to a Web site with your browser, the Web server software sent these plain text HTML files to be processed and rendered into Web pages. Your browser actually did the rendering process (and still does, to be sure), but if you clicked View ⇨ Page Source, you'd see the raw HTML code.

Javascript (and a few other almost unknown programming languages) improved the situation for Web designers in that it provided for programmatic functionality within Web pages. However, it was limited to programmatic functionality on the user's computer, not on the back-end (on the Web server), where all the really cool data processing and database access takes place. Practical Extraction and Reporting Language (PERL) was one of the first widely used languages for programming on the back-end, but has limitations of its own, such as an inability to be mixed in with HTML for easy in-page programming.

So where does PHP fit in with HTML? PHP began as PHP/FI, developed in 1995 by Rasmus Lerdorf from some Perl scripts he had created for tracking accesses to his online resume. Eventually, Rasmus wrote an implementation in C, released the source code to the public, and by the beginning of 1998 version 3.0 of PHP was released (written by Rasmus Lerdorf, Andi Gutmans, and Zeev Suraski), the first version that is very similar to the current releases of PHP.

The main goal of PHP is to enable users to easily develop dynamic Web pages. The difference between dynamic Web pages and static Web pages is that the content and structure of dynamic Web pages may change each time they are accessed (that's what the back-end programming is for) whereas the content and structure of static Web pages is fixed and does not change unless the designer manually changes them.

Unlike many other languages, PHP can be embedded directly into HTML, making it quite easy for those familiar with HTML to grasp how to add back-end, programmatic functionality to their Web pages. This single capability is one of the most important factors in PHP's usefulness, and thereby its popularity. But have no doubt that PHP is growing into a much more full-features language going well beyond the initial intentions of its authors. PHP intends to be the primary language for a great variety of online and offline applications, and PHP5 is showing every sign of doing just that.

And you shouldn't forget how well PHP works with HTTP (HyperText Transfer Protocol), the communications protocol (pre-agreed format for data communications) for Web. Whenever you click a link or enter a Web address into your browser, a request in HTTP format is sent to the Web server, which responds by sending back the Web page. If the Web page isn't found, you'll probably get the "404 Not Found" error. Sending back the correct page or sending an error if the page is not found are HTTP functions. We discuss HTTP thoroughly in Chapter 2 because several important aspects of PHP applications depend on HTTP.

Installing, Configuring, and Running PHP

Before you can write a PHP application that works with your Web pages, you need to have PHP installed and configured. Because you'll be writing a Web application, it's a given that you'll need a Web server and some Web pages (a short HTML primer is provided in Chapter 3, although it's assumed that you know or can easily pick up how to make basic Web pages). You'll also need to download, install, and configure PHP, so we provide complete instructions about how to do these things in the coming sections. Note that some configuration options for PHP are related to very specific application requirements (you don't need to worry about them unless you need them) so many of the options aren't discussed until you reach the appropriate chapter.

System Requirements

To run the code in this book you will need at least the following software:

- ❑ Server software (an operating system such as Windows 2000 or Linux)
- ❑ A PHP-compatible Web server (such as Apache or Internet Information Server (IIS)
- ❑ PHP5 (get the download from www.php.net)
- ❑ A relational database system (starting at Chapter 9, we use SQLite or MySQL)
- ❑ A Web browser (such as IE, Mozilla, and so on)
- ❑ A text editor, such as Notepad, Emacs, vi, BBEdit, and so on.

You shouldn't have to worry about hard drive space or RAM, unless you are working on a very old system, or one that is overloaded. PHP doesn't take up much room, and runs very efficiently.

You can run all of the software listed here on the same computer, for development purposes. If you have access to several networked computers, you may want to install all of your server software on one (typically either a UNIX or Windows NT/2000 computer), and use another networked computer as your client machine. For the purposes of this book, we will generally assume you are running all of the software on a single computer. This is the configuration used by most Web developers.

php.ini, the PHP Configuration File

There are two examples of PHP configuration files that come with PHP when you download it: php.ini-dist and php.ini-recommended. After you download and install PHP, there will be one file named php.ini strategically placed on your system, and each time PHP starts it will read this file and set itself up accordingly. The php.ini file can be written out by hand, but of course most of us just modify either the dist or recommended file to suit our needs, and then copy and rename it into the appropriate folder.

However, you should note the following lines in the top of the dist file:

```
; This is the default settings file for new PHP installations.
; By default, PHP installs itself with a configuration suitable for
; development purposes, and *NOT* for production purposes.
```

The settings in the dist file are used for nearly all of the examples in this book and we'll let you know whenever the configuration settings are changed. But you will want to use the recommended file when you complete your applications and copy them over to your production server, and you should be aware that you may need to rewrite your code a little bit to work properly with the recommended file's configuration settings. We'll discuss this more as we go along.

Setting Up a Test Machine

In this chapter, we'll walk through setting up PHP5 on a Red Hat Linux machine running the Apache Web server, as well as on a Windows 2000 machine running Internet Information Server (IIS). You can run PHP5 with many other operating systems and Web servers, so see the PHP5 documentation for installation and configuration on other servers. And there are a variety of installation methods you can use. For example, there is an automatic installer for the Windows version, whereas you can install the Linux version using RPMs (for some versions of Linux), and you can also download and compile the Linux versions from the original source code if you like. None of the installations are all that difficult if you follow procedures correctly, and the examples we provide are a good starting point for many of the installations available.

> *There are some third-party installers (often open-source and free) out there, if you want to look for them. For instance, you might try PHPTriad or Foxserv in Google.*

Network Connections

If you don't already know, a computer doesn't need to be attached to the Internet, or even to a network, to run Web server software. If you install a Web server on a computer, it's always possible to access that Web server from a Web browser running on the same machine, even if it doesn't have a network card or modem. Of course, to download and install the software you need, you have to have access to an Internet connection. But you don't need it to be active just because you're running your Web server.

Once you have a Web server installed and running, you'll install PHP5 alongside it. There's some configuration required to tell the Web server how to run PHP programs, and we'll walk through that process before we start PHP. There is an automatic installer to be found with most distributions of PHP; we'll use a primarily manual process to illustrate what's happening during installation.

> **What if it goes wrong?** The **README** and **INSTALL** files that are included in most PHP downloads, as well as the PHP manual at **www.php.net/manual/**, provide detailed information which may be more up-to-date than the information here, which covers the PHP5.0.2 release.

Where Do You Start?

There are two main installation paths from which to choose, and each simply depends on which operating system you're using:

❑   Installing PHP5 with the Apache Web Server on Linux (we use Red Hat Fedora Linux)

❑   Installing PHP5 with Microsoft Internet Information Server on Windows (we use Windows 2000)

PHP5 can be installed on a great variety of Web server/operating system combinations, including under Apache on Windows. The two systems we're using are the easiest to get working. If neither of them suits you, of course you can install whatever other configuration you want—you should still be able to run all of the examples in the book. Refer to the PHP5 manual for more general installation instructions.

Running PHP5

One of the basic choices to make when installing PHP5 with your Web server is whether to run it as a CGI binary or as a separate static or dynamic module. CGI (Common Gateway Interface) is a very useful way to run interpreters such as PHP5. Because of security risks (see the *"Running as a CGI"* section later in this chapter for more information), compiling PHP5 as a static or dynamic module is recommended under most circumstances. Our installations (on Linux and on Windows) load PHP as a separate SAPI (Server Application Programming Interface) module. On Windows, the ISAPI filter was used to run PHP as a SAPI module.

Although it is most common to run PHP in conjunction with a Web server, so that Web pages with a file extension such as .php are processed through the PHP interpreter before the finished page is sent back to the browser, there is also a command line utility that enables you to run PHP code from the command line. It is present from any of the installation types we demonstrate. You can find plenty of documentation about it on the PHP site (www.php.net).

Creating and running PHP Web applications in a satisfactory way implies that you are running (or have access to) a Web server upon which PHP is (or can be) installed, and that the installation has been tested and runs properly. It also implies that PHP has been (or can be) configured to support the needs of your PHP programs. There are a couple scenarios under which these requirements can be achieved:

❑ You are running a desktop or server machine, operating system, and Web server compatible with PHP, and PHP has been installed and configured.

❑ You are running a desktop or server machine connected to the Internet, with access to a Web hosting account supported by a Web server with which PHP has been installed and configured.

The vast majority of desktop machines run Windows 98, NT, 2000, 2003, and XP. In many cases you can get a free copy of Personal Web Server (PWS) and install it on a machine running one of these operating systems. PHP is compatible with PWS, so you can install and configure PHP on desktop machines running basic operating systems such as Windows 98. Server operating systems such as Windows NT, 2000, and 200, come with Internet Information Server (IIS). PHP is compatible with IIS, and you can install and configure PHP on these machines. Our Windows 2000 installation of PHP5 uses IIS as a Web server.

The majority of Web-hosting computers run some version of Linux, such as Debian, RedHat, FreeBSD, and so on. The Web server of choice for these machines is Apache. PHP is compatible with Linux and Apache, and you can install and configure PHP on these systems, but if you are not in charge of the Web-hosting computer (and many times you won't be) you'll probably have little control over the installation and configuration. If you find yourself in this position (for example, if you've been hired to work on an existing Web site running on someone else's server), you can simply verify the operating system, Web server software, and PHP version so you can cope with whatever you've have to work with as you develop your PHP programs.

Installing PHP5 with Linux and Apache

At the time of this writing, the very first release candidate of PHP5 was available, and that's the one we're using. But you may want to check the PHP site for more recent versions, and any notes about changes.

The combination of Linux, Apache, MySQL, and PHP is probably the most common production environment for running PHP Web servers. This combination of open-source software has been referred to by the acronym LAMP. If you run the same combination of software, you can benefit from the experiences of the many other people who've used this setup.

The PHP developers work very closely with the Apache and MySQL teams to ensure that advances in the three server systems are fully supported by the other components. However, at the time of this writing PHP5 is being distributed with SQLite rather than MySQL, because there is some concern about whether MySQL is still open source. This may not be a concern when you read this and begin developing, but it's worth noting.

Choosing Your Installation Method

As with other open-source software, you have the option of downloading the PHP and Apache source code (which, in both cases, is written in the C programming language) and compiling the programs yourself. If that sounds daunting (it's not actually as scary as it sounds), you can obtain precompiled versions in one of two forms: binary downloads, which are precompiled versions of the software that typically come with installation scripts to put all the required pieces into the necessary parts of your file system, and binary packages, which are available for systems that have a software package management system, such as the Red Hat Package Manager (RPM) for Linux, and are the easiest to install.

Here's a quick overview of the three methods:

Installation Method	Advantages	Disadvantages
Source	Most flexible solution for custom installations. Additional tests and examples are included in the source distribution	Needs to be compiled. Slightly more difficult than the other options. Harder to remove once it's been done
Binary (compiled)	No need to mess around with trying to compile the server. Takes less time to install	Less flexible than doing an installation from source
Binary RPMs	Fastest and easiest installation method. Very easy to uninstall or upgrade later	Must be using an RPM-based Linux distribution such as Red Hat. Least flexible installation method

An RPM Installation of PHP4

The version of Red Hat we're using is actually called Fedora, because Red Hat has split off development into two parts: Fedora and the enterprise version of Red Hat Linux. Currently, the Fedora site doesn't have an RPM for PHP5, so we'll provide the instructions for getting and installing the RPM for PHP4 here, and then show how to download and compile PHP5 for Fedora later. By the time you read this, in all likelihood there will be an RPM available for PHP5 for your Linux distribution, so the RPM installation presented here should provide good guidance for installing PHP5 via the RPM method.

A number of popular Linux distributions use the Red Hat Package Manager, including Red Hat, SuSE, Mandrake, Definite, TurboLinux, Caldera, and Yellow Dog. If your system uses an alternative package management system, such as Debian's deb packages, refer to your distribution's manual for installation instructions.

Obtaining RPMs

The best place to get RPMs is almost always the disks from which you installed your Linux system. Red Hat 7 and SuSE 7 both include PHP4 (although it isn't installed by default)—by the time you read this, the same should be true of most current Linux distribution versions.

If your distribution doesn't include PHP4, or it doesn't include all the required functionality or support RPMs, then the next place to check is your Linux distribution vendor's Web site, which should have a download area or FTP site from which you can obtain the latest RPMs.

Finally, www.rpmfind.net provides a comprehensive search service for RPMs. When you download RPMs, though, make certain that they are compatible with your Linux distribution and your computer hardware. Different distributions put important files in different places, and this can lead to RPMs from different vendors not working on other systems. Most RPMs are available compiled to run on the different hardware systems that Linux supports. The following table shows the most common abbreviations used in RPM names (you need the abbreviation to search on the rpmfind site):

Abbreviation	Compatible with
i386	PCs based on Intel and 100% compatible processors: Intel 80386, 486, Pentium, Pentium II, Pentium III, and Celeron; AMD 5x86, K-series, and Athlon; and Cyrix 6x86
i586	PCs based on Intel Pentium and 100% compatible processors: Intel Pentium II, III, and Celeron; AMD K-Series and Athlon; and Cyrix 6x86
PPC	Computers built around Motorola PowerPC (and compatible) chips, such as Apple's Power Macs, G3s, G4s, and iMacs. You can still only use the RPMs on Macintosh hardware with Linux installed, though
alpha	Servers and workstations running the Compaq Digital 64-bit Alpha processor
sparc	Servers and workstations running the processors which use the 64-bit SPARC architecture, such as Sun Microsystems' UltraSPARC
m68k	Computers built around Motorola's older 68000 series processors, such as Amigas, and older Apple Macintoshes, for which various Linux ports exist

Refer to your distribution's manual if you want to use the graphical installation tools that come with your specific distribution. These differ widely, so they can't all be covered here. However, any RPM-based system can be controlled using the rpm command-line tool, and you'll see how to install the required components using this interface.

Which RPM Packages Do You Need?

The RPM packages you will need are:

❑ zlib

❑ libpng

❑ libjpeg

❑ gd

❑ gd-devel

❑ apache

❑ mod_php4

You can find out which of them are already installed on your system by typing the following at a command prompt, substituting in the name of each of these packages in turn:

```
> rpm -q zlib
zlib-1.1.3-6-i386
> rpm -q libng
Package libpng is not installed
```

As you can see, if the package is installed, it gives you a random-looking string. If it isn't installed, you get a helpful error message. The string actually tells you which version of the software you installed using the package (1.1.3 in this case), which release of the package it is (this example has the sixth public release installed), and the architecture for which the RPM was compiled (Intel 386 compatible, which is just as well, because the package is installed on a Pentium III for this book).

Note which of the packages you already have, and which versions they are (the version number is more important than the release number).

Apache is at version 1.3.29 if you want to remain at the old versions of GD, or 2.0.48 if you want to be current with the latest version of GD. Of course, if you are installing PHP5, GD is now bundled with PHP and is up to version 2.0.17

Then locate suitably up-to-date versions of all the packages that you don't have already, or have old versions for. As suggested, try your install CDs, your distributor's Web site, and www.rpmfind.net.

Once you have current versions of all the packages you need, you can install them. The command for upgrading an existing installation or installing a package for the first time is exactly the same. Navigate your command prompt to the location of the files on the CD or the directory into which you downloaded the RPMs. As root, type:

```
> rpm -Uh libpng-1.0.5-3-i386.rpm
##################
```

For each package you need to upgrade or install, just substitute the name of the package file you downloaded. The line of # signs extends across the screen as each installation progresses.

If you install the packages in the order listed previously, you should find that all the prerequisite files are installed in the necessary order.

Installing PHP5 by Compiling from Source Files

The installation method we'll use for installing PHP5 on Red Hat Fedora running Apache is downloading the source files and compiling them. You use command-line commands in Linux, but also make use of some of the visual tools (such as Konqueror) included in your Red Hat installation. If you are running Linux visually (for example, with KDE), you get to the command prompt by going to the Red Hat button, and then choosing System Tools ➪ Terminal. Figure 1-1 shows the terminal window you'll see.

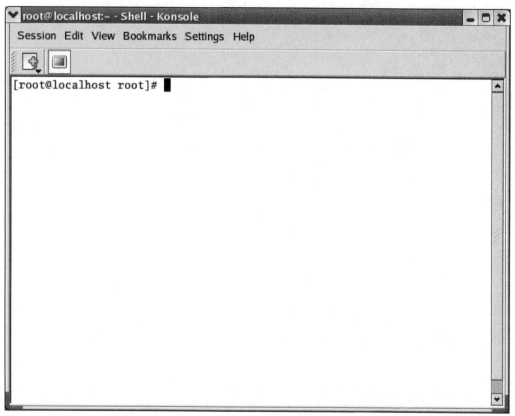

Figure 1-1

You must have a compiler installed (an ANSI C compiler). Sometimes such a compiler is installed as part of your Linux installation, but if you need one, a good one (and free), named gnugcc, can be found at www.gnu.org. Figure 1-2 shows the GNU Web site.

And Figure 1-3 shows a bit of the documentation for GCC.

With your compiler installed, download the source file from www.php.net. This file is archived as a tar file and compressed with gzip, so you will need to uncompress it. There is also a .bz2 file you can download, but you need only one of these files—either the gzip or a .bz2 file.

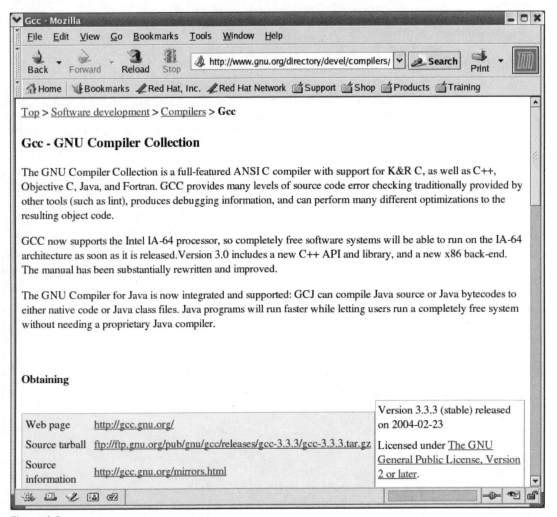

Figure 1-2

You can use the Konquerer file-management tool to view the contents of the compressed file. Figure 1-4 shows some of the contents in the tar file.

You also could use Konquerer to copy all of the compressed file's contents directly to another folder, but doing so will make your compilation fail cryptically (meaning you'll get strange error messages that won't help you figure out what's wrong). Instead, make sure to use the following command from the terminal (see Figure 1-5) to uncompress the files:

```
tar -xvzf php-5.0(insert the rest of the version number here).tar.gz
```

Next, use the cd command to change to the PHP5 distribution directory:

```
cd php-5.0(insert the rest of the version number here)
```

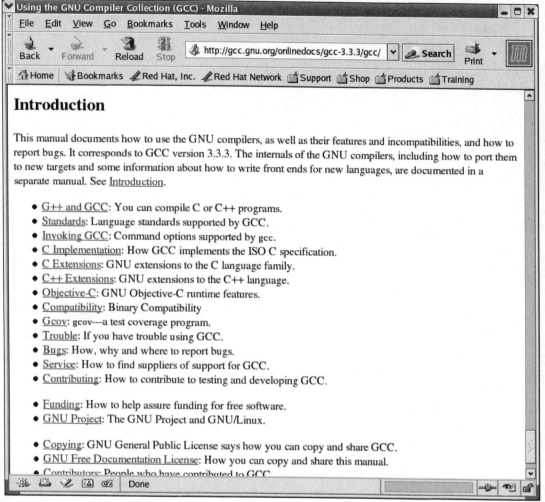

Figure 1-3

Now that you've cd'd to the `php-5.0.0RC1` folder, you'll see quite a few folders and files there. Open the `INSTALL` text file (see Figure 1-6) to find many of the instructions related to your installation.

Folder *and directory are equivalent terms and can be used interchangeably.*

For this book, PHP is installed as a Dynamic Shared Object (DSO), and that's what you'll also do, so that the entire Apache Server won't need to be recompiled.

The latest versions of Apache support DSOs, and shared objects can be used by other programs, such as PostGreSQL. Although you could compile PHP5 as a static module, that isn't recommended. If PHP is statically linked to, say, Apache or PostGreSQL, each of those programs would need to be recompiled before they would recognize PHP. The programs' configuration files can be easily changed in shared objects (DSOs) without any recompiling.

Chapter 1

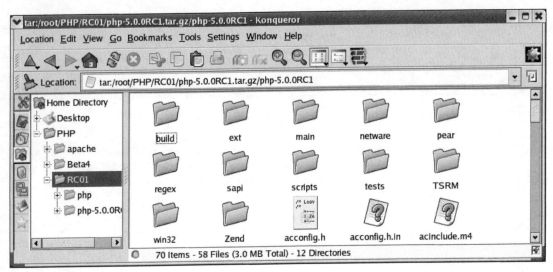

Figure 1-4

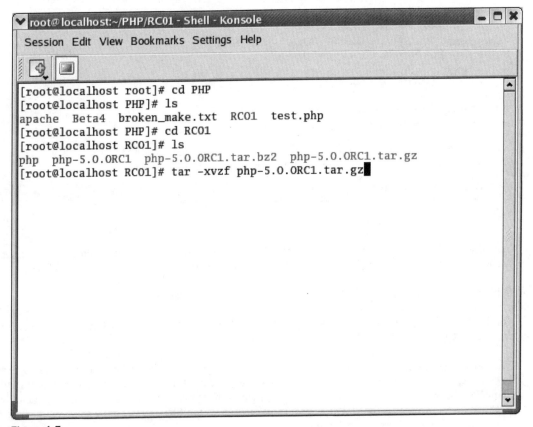

Figure 1-5

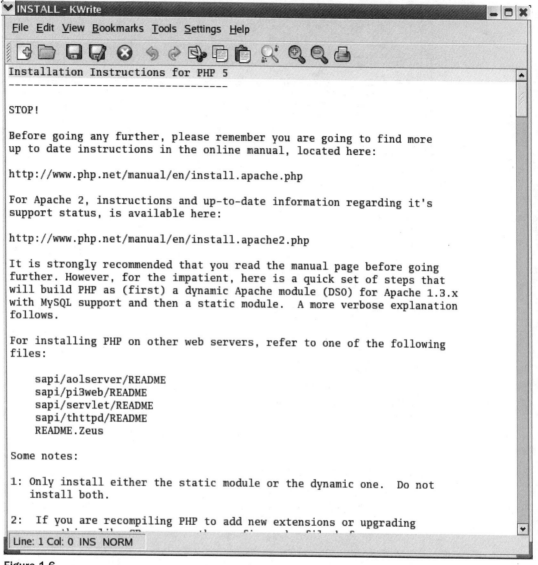

Figure 1-6

Checking Apache for DSO installation

You must have Apache installed and set up for dynamic modules before compiling PHP5 as a DSO. Use the following command from the terminal to make sure Apache is ready:

```
httpd -l
```

You see a terminal window like the one shown in Figure 1-7.

As long as mod_so.c is present, you're OK to proceed.

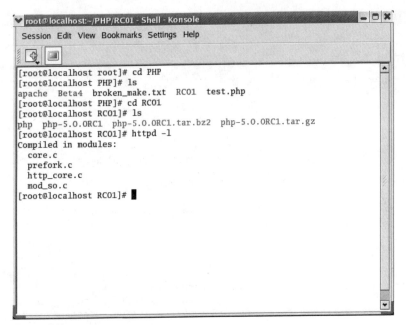

Figure 1-7

Running the configure Script

Within your PHP5 directory (probably named something like php-5.0.0RC1.), you'll find a shell script named configure. This script accepts arguments to control the features that PHP will support. You'll need to run this script to configure compilation, not PHP5 itself (PHP configuration with php.ini will come later).

Commands Available for the configure Script

The default configure is to compile PHP5 as a CGI binary. Use the –with-apache option to compile PHP5 as a static module; use the –with-apxs option to compile PHP5 as a DSO. For this installation, use the –with_apxs option (actually –with_apxs2 because you're running Apache 2).

Here are some of the command line arguments that you may use when you compile PHP5. The configure command is ./configure (the ./ lets it run) followed by a single space and then as many of the following options as you like:

❑ –enable-track-vars: Automatically populates associative arrays with values submitted as part of GET and POST requests or provided in a cookie.

❑ –with-gd = /path/to/directory: Enables support for the GD library that allows you to create dynamic GIF and PNG images from your scripts. You'll either want to compile with this or add this module later to do the graphics work in Chapter 16.

❑ –with-mysql = /path/to/directory: With MySQL support.

❑ –with-pgsql = /path/to/directory: With PostgreSQL support.

For your quick install use only –with-mysql and –with-apxs2. If you get any error messages telling you something couldn't be found, provide the full path to the folder in which the appropriate files can be found. For example, our configure command found the path to mysql. If it hadn't we would have provided the full path to mysql as part of the command to run the configure script.

Other Configure Options

There are many more command line arguments that you can use as well. For example, type in the command

```
./configure --help
```

and you'll see the complete range of arguments that you can use, along with their descriptions.

Performing the QUICK INSTALL (DSO)

The quick installation in the PHP INSTALL text file recommends starting with just two commands: –with-mysql and –with-apxs. Run the configure script like this for quick installation:

```
./configure --with-mysql --with-apxs2
```

You need to use –with-apxs2 rather than –with-apxs because you're running a later version of Apache. The script actually came back and informed me of this when it ran, which was very helpful. If you read through the commands that appear in your terminal as the script runs, you'll see that it does quite a few such checks as it gets ready for the make command.

After the configure script has run, you need to enter two more commands:

```
make
make install
```

Install makes a directory in /user/local/lib named php where it places a copy of PEAR (php Extension Add-on Repository) and the php.ini file. The Location bar on the screen in Figure 1-8 shows that the main panel's contents are in the php directory.

Running Additional Configure Options

You may use some of the other options of the configure script to compile PHP5 with enable_track_vars, with-gd, and with_pgsql. But if you'd like to use the configure options for gd (the graphics module) and pgsql (the database) you must make sure these programs are also loaded for everything to work properly, and you must provide the full path to the installations as required.

Running as a CGI

PHP5 is compiled as a module if you used the configure script with the –with-apache or —with-apxs2 options. It's compiled as a CGI executable binary file if you used the configure script without any reference to Apache or apxs. And if you compiled PHP5 as a CGI, then when you installed PHP5, it most likely put the actual binary in /usr/local/bin. Copy the CGI executable binary to your cgi-bin directory using:

```
cp /usr/local/bin/php /usr/local/apache/cgi-bin/php.cgi
```

This enables Apache users to run different PHP-enabled pages under different user-ids. However, CERT advisory CA-96.11 recommends against placing any interpreters (such as PHP5) into cgi-bin because

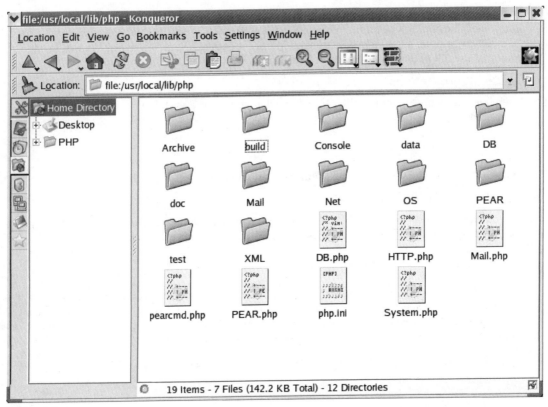

Figure 1-8

attacks such as accessing system files and Web documents can be launched against your server. When you compile PHP5 with the –with-apache option, you will have a Server Application Programming Interface (SAPI), which provides a higher level of performance and security over the CGI method.

Setting up Apache for PHP

To install Apache, use RPMs or download and compile the source code. But Apache probably comes with your Linux distribution, and may already be properly installed. On my Red Hat Fedora installation, Apache was already installed, and all that was needed to verify this was go to the Red Hat button, choose System Settings ⇨ Server Settings ⇨ Services, and look for httpd, as shown in Figure 1-9.

Httpd (all lowercase) means HTTP daemon, and daemon is the name of services running in the background on Linux machines. So httpd means the HTTP daemon running in the background, for example, the Web server.

If you're using Linux visually (running KDE, for example), click the httpd service to see whether it's running. If it isn't, start it, and then open your browser and enter http://localhost. You should see a Web page such as the one shown in Figure 1-10.

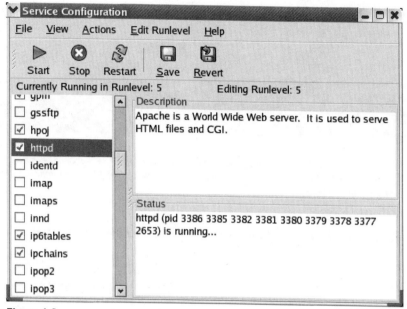

Figure 1-9

If Apache is not already installed and running, you can use these commands for installing it from the Terminal:

```
lynx http://httpd.apache.org/download.cgi
gzip -d httpd-2_0_NN.tar.gz
tar xvf httpd-2_0_NN.tar
./configure --prefix=PREFIX
make
make install
vi PREFIX/conf/httpd.conf
PREFIX/bin/apachectl start
```

You must replace the NN with the minor version number, and PREFIX with the correct path in which you'd like to install Apache (the default is /usr/local/apache2).

Configuring Apache to Run PHP5

If PHP5 is installed as a DSO (as the example installation was), you need to check the Apache configuration file (named httpd.conf) to make sure it has several entries. In the Fedora installation, you can find the httpd.conf file in the /etc/httpd/conf folder. Open any text editor and let's modify the httpd.conf file.

First, ensure that PHP is enabled on your Apache server. Look for a lot of lines that begin with the word LoadModule. Among them you should find a line like this:

```
LoadModule php5_module /usr/local/apache/lib/libphp5.so
```

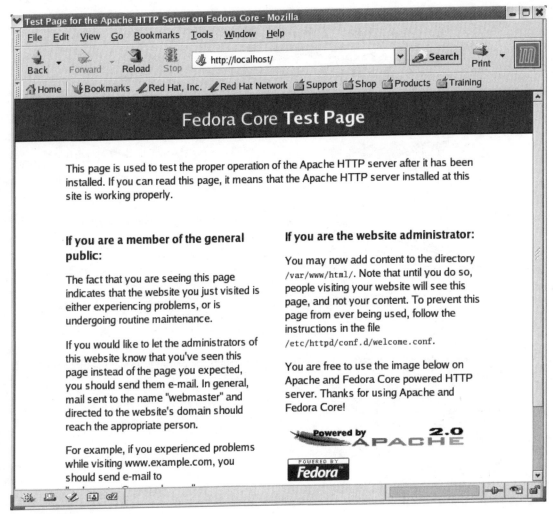

Figure 1-10

If there isn't such a line, you need to add one; or if the path is wrong, you need to correct it. Find out where the PHP compile put your `libphp5.so` file. Open Konqueror and choose Tools ⇨ Find file. My installation put the `libphp5.so` file in

```
/usr/lib/httpd/modules
```

You need this information to tell Apache how to run PHP scripts. In the Apache configuration file `httpd.conf`, add the `LoadModule` instruction to load PHP5. Put it after any of the other `LoadModule` lines, using the path you just obtained:

```
LoadModule php5_module      /usr/lib/httpd/modules/libphp5.so
```

Now that Apache knows how to load PHP5, you need to activate PHP5 in Apache. There's a section farther down the file consisting of a lot of lines beginning with `AddModule`. If you find a

`ClearModulesList` line in the file, you need to add the following line to the file. Although it doesn't matter where you put it, it makes sense to locate it near other `AddModule` lines for easy access in the future:

```
AddModule mod_php5.c
```

The `AddModule` line is not required unless you have a `ClearModulesList` line.

Finally, you tell Apache how to recognize a PHP program file by its extension. Further down the document are some directives that begin `AddType`. To the end of these, add the following line:

```
AddType application/x-httpd-php .php
```

This tells Apache that all files that end in `.php` are PHP programs. Now you're done, so save the file.

Starting or Restarting Apache

Check to see if Apache is running by going into Services once again and checking the httpd service. If it's not running, start it. Verify that it's running by opening the `http://localhost` test page. If everything seems to be working OK (and you're not also installing on Windows), move on to the *"Testing Your Installation"* section to test that PHP is working properly.

The majority of Web hosting computers runs some version of Linux, such as Debian, RedHat, FreeBSD, and so on. The Web server of choice for these machines is Apache. PHP is compatible with Linux and Apache, so you can install and configure PHP on these systems. However, if you are not in charge of the Web hosting computer (and many times you won't be) you'll probably have little control over the installation and configuration. If you find yourself in this position (for example, if you've been hired to work on an existing Web site running on someone else's server) you can simply verify the operating system, Web server software, and PHP version so you can cope with whatever you've got as you develop your PHP programs.

Installing PHP5 on Windows 2000/Internet Information Server (IIS) 5

Before beginning the installation process, let's take a look at IIS. If it's been properly installed using the default settings, it should already be running. Select Start ➪ Programs ➪ Administrative Tools ➪ Services and scroll down to World Wide Web Publishing Service to see if IIS is currently running. If it isn't, start it up

If you need to install IIS, go to Settings ➪ Control Panel and open Add/Remove Programs. Then click the Components button to find the list of components that can be installed in Windows 2000, including Internet Information Server. Select IIS and then click the Details button to see all the services (such as FTP, SMTP, and so on) that can be installed. Choose any you'd like, but be sure to include World Wide Web Publishing, and click the Finish button. IIS should be installed and running.

You can examine the installation of IIS by opening its documentation from your browser, using `http://localhost/iisHelp` as the URL. You should see something like Figure 1-11, which shows IIS 5.0 running on Windows 2000.

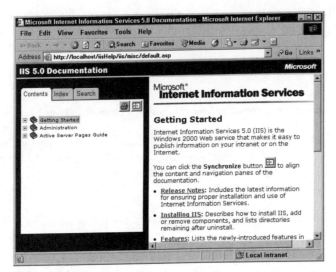

Figure 1-11

Now let's take a look at the Internet Service Manager, a console application for managing IIS, to see how IIS has been configured. Select Start ➪ Programs ➪ Administrative Tools ➪ Internet Services Manager. The IIS snap-in displays in Microsoft Management Console (MMC), as Figure 1-12 shows.

The MMC provides an easy way to examine and manage the services provided by IIS, as well as the Web sites and FTP sites set up under IIS. Figure 1-13 shows the hierarchical view of the default installation of IIS:

To do the installation of PHP you need to turn off Internet Information Services and then restart it after you're done making some changes. Right-click on the Default Web site and chose Stop from the short-cut menu. When you've got your installation of PHP files complete, you'll turn the Web server back on. For now, close the Internet Services Manager.

Downloading PHP5

To get the most recent version of PHP5, go to www.php.net and find the downloads section, as shown in Figure 1-14 (it may look a bit different by the time you read this).

Download the Windows binary file (it's zipped) and set it aside. Create a folder (such as C:\PHP5RC01) on your hard drive, put the downloaded file in the folder, and then unzip the file. You should end up with something like Figure 1-15 (as seen in Windows Explorer).

The filenames are current at the time of this writing, but of course may change by the time this book is published and in your hands. But the version of PHP5 that this book is using is very nearly ready for final release, so don't despair—your PHP5 installation should work just the same as the book's does. And while your installation of Windows may be on your C: drive, the book's is on the D: drive. You may have to change some of the path names to reflect your C: drive (or whatever drive Windows is loaded on) to make your installation work.

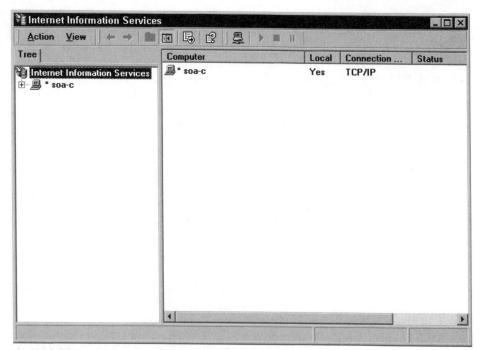

Figure 1-12

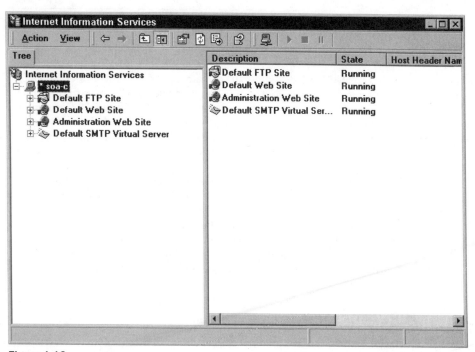

Figure 1-13

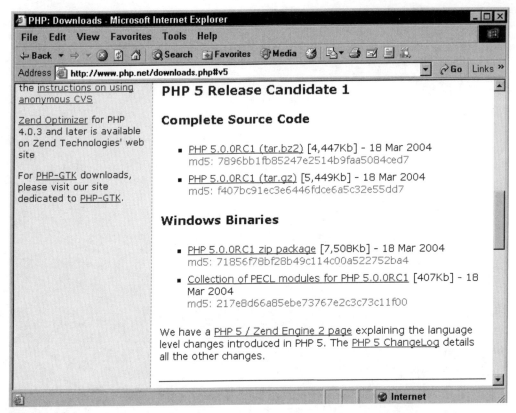

Figure 1-14

Now, the directory you created (such as PHPRC01) contains several subdirectories, and a few text files. It also contains a program file called php.exe, which you won't actually be using, and a library file called php5ts.dll (in the dev folder). Copy this .dll to your D:\WINNT\System32 directory (using the correct drive letter for your machine). Now copy the rest of the .dll files from here to your D:\WINNT\System32 directory as well. If Windows complains that you've already got a file by one or other of these names, then keep your old one—don't overwrite it with the newly downloaded files.

If you prefer not to copy all your .dlls into your System32 directory and you are installing PHP as an SAPI (like this book does), you may create another folder for them and make a change to your PATH environment variable so that they can be found. (A PATH environment variable contains a list of directories—paths—in which Windows will look for things, such as your .dlls. If, for example, you have a C:\php5\dlls directory, you'd add the string C:\php5\dlls to your variable, and then anything in that folder could be used by your Windows environment. To set the variable, select Start ⇨ Control Panel ⇨ System ⇨ Advanced ⇨ Environment Variables, and locate and set the PATH variable.)

php.ini and Extensions

As mentioned earlier, the php.ini file contains instructions to PHP such that, when it is running, certain configuration settings are in place and certain extensions to PHP are running. Configuration settings are

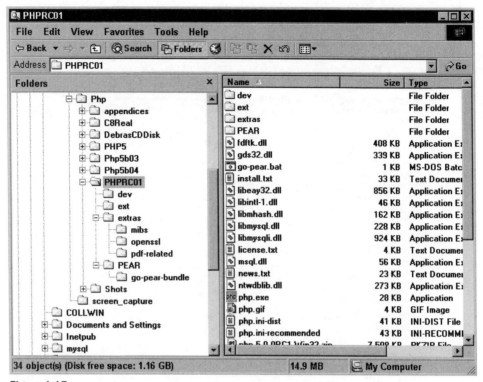

Figure 1-15

like switches, turning a variety of PHP behaviors on and off. Extensions provide added or enhanced built-in capabilities to PHP.

At the top of your PHP directory should be files called php.ini-dist and php.ini-recommended. Copy the php.ini-dist file to D:\WINNT (using the appropriate drive letter), rename it php.ini, and open it up with Notepad. Scroll down the document until you find a line that looks like:

```
extension_dir = C:\php\extensions ; directory in which the loadable extensions
(modules) reside
```

Make sure that this path is the correct path to the extensions directory of the unzipped PHP5 installation. If it isn't, change it to point to the right place (look for an ext folder under your unzipped PHP folder). The extensions directory is the one that contains a large number of files whose names begin with php_ and end with .dll.

The next section in your php.ini file tells PHP which extensions to load. There are semicolons at the beginning of all the lines that load extensions you don't need—a semicolon means that PHP will ignore the directive on that line. Remove the semicolon from extension=php_gd.dll, so that you have text like this:

```
;extension=php-filepro.dll
extension=php-gd.dll
;extension=php_mssql.dll
```

This gives you access to the functionality of the GD library, which enables you to generate images using PHP programs (you'll see how in Chapter 16, "*Generating Graphics*"). Save your modified php.ini file.

Again, select Start ➪ Programs ➪ Administrative Tools ➪ Internet Services Manager, and open the hierarchy of services. Right-click Default Web Site, and bring up its Properties (see Figure 1-16).

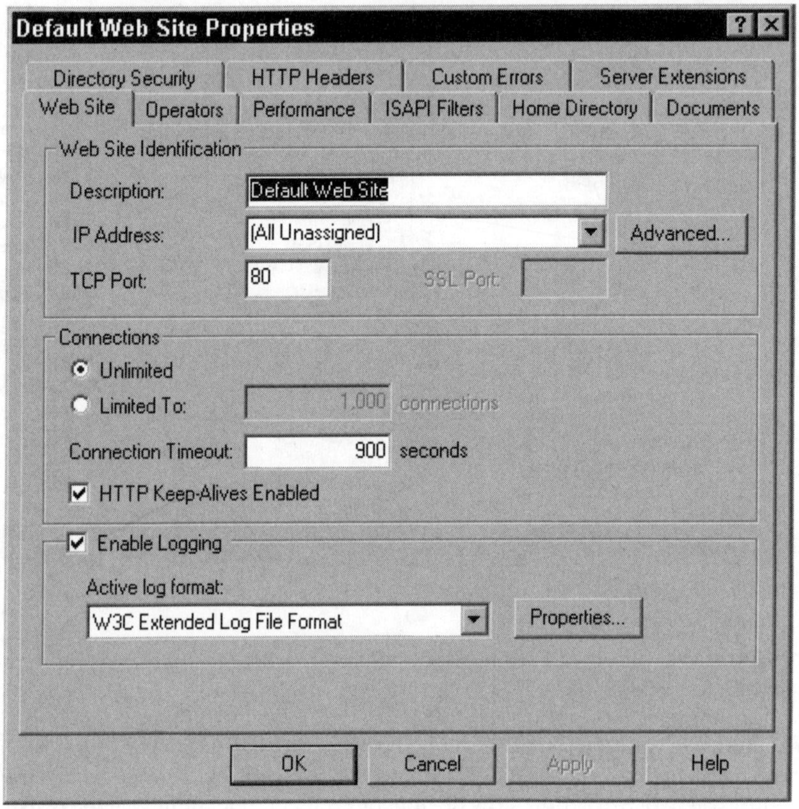

Figure 1-16

There are two changes to make. First, you need to register the PHP5 ISAPI filter, because you want to install PHP with its own SAPI rather than as a CGI binary. Click the ISAPI Filters tab. Click the Add button, and create a new filter called PHP. The folder of PHP files you downloaded contains php5isapi.dll, a PHP ISAPI filter, in the sapi directory. Put in the correct path for your php5isapi.dll file, as shown in Figure 1-17.

And second, you need to tell IIS which files to apply the PHP5 filter to. You want it to treat all files that end with .php as PHP programs. On the Home Directory tab, click the Configuration button. Click the Add button in the next dialog box, and the Add/Edit Application Extension Mapping dialog box opens (see Figure 1-18).

Click the Browse button and specify the path to php5isapi.dll. Tell IIS to apply it to .php files by entering .php in the Extension text box. Click OK, and then click OK again. Now you need to restart IIS. Close the Properties box, right-click the Default Web site, and choose Start from the shortcut menu.

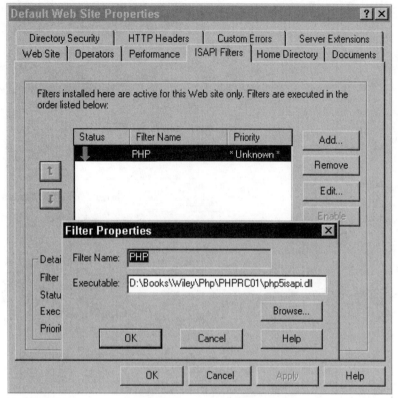

Figure 1-17

Provided the message in the MMC reports that the World Wide Web Publishing service was started successfully, you now have PHP5 installed. Remember the name of your Web site's root directory (the book's is D:\Inetpub\wwwroot).

Create a folder in the wwwroot folder. Name it anything you want (but something helpful, like php_files), and place files in it with a .php extension. These files will be processed through the PHP scripting engine when requested by a browser.

Now open your text editor and create a text file with the following code in it:

```
<?php
phpinfo();
?>
```

Save this file as test01.php (or something like that, so long as the filename extension is .php) in the folder you just created under the wwwroot folder. Open the file in your browser, using http://localhost plus the name of your new folder and the filename (for example, http://localhost/php_file/myfile.php). You should now see something like Figure 1-19 in your browser (although your PHP version number might be a bit different if you have a more recent release):

Assuming it works, you're now in business. If not, check out the following section.

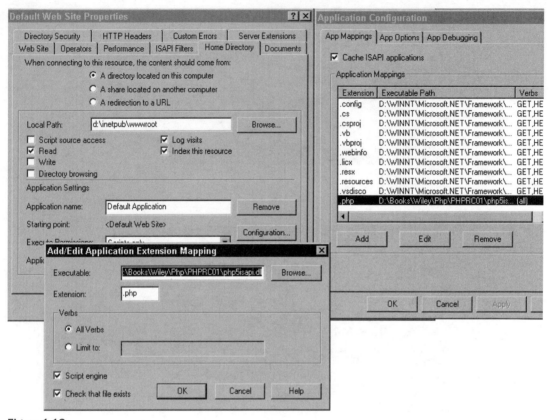

Figure 1-18

Testing and Troubleshooting

Testing your installation of PHP is really as simple as writing a small PHP program and running it. Create a small PHP file to use for tests. Write the following code in it:

```
<?php
echo "Hey, it worked";
?>
```

Save the file as test02.php in any folder within wwwroot (or an appropriate folder if you happen to be running some other OS/Web server combination than Windows 2000/IIS).

Open the file in your browser. You should see the words "Hey, it worked" in your browser. If you see "Page cannot be displayed," there's a problem with your PHP installation or with finding the file, or with the Web server. If you see something that talks about a parse error, you may have made a mistake in entering the code. Coding errors are discussed in more detail in the next few chapters, but in the next section you'll explore some ways you can troubleshoot your basic installation of PHP.

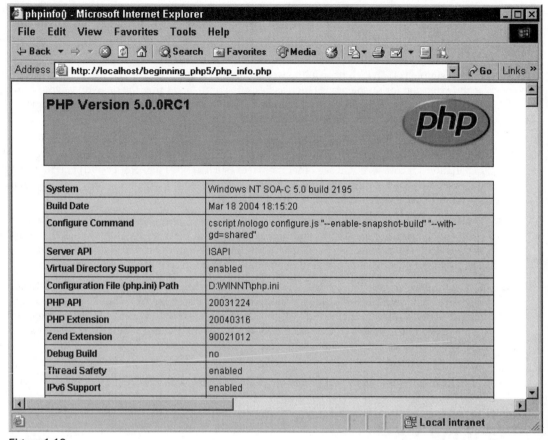

Figure 1-19

Did the file you tested work? Or are you reading this section right now because the file didn't work? Don't worry; it's very common for problems to occur anytime you try something new, especially when it comes to computers and programming. In fact, consider yourself lucky if it didn't work because you'll learn a lot more about PHP and programming from your mistakes than from your successes.

So let's start at the beginning. Troubleshooting and debugging comprise the process of identifying problems, deducing possible causes, logically isolating those causes until you've identified the most likely culprit, and then trying solutions. The end result is that the problem is fixed and if you've done a good job, you'll have fixed the problem (in an elegant, robust way) without causing other problems.

Chapter 5 covers debugging in more detail; for now, though, let's look at the steps for troubleshooting your installation of PHP:

1.   Check that the Web server is on and running properly. In Windows 2000, do this by checking Services (Start ➪ Programs ➪ Administrative Tools ➪ Services), specifically Internet Admin Services and World Wide Web Publishing Service. Just because these are set to `Automatic`

within Services doesn't mean they are on. Stop and restart them if you need to reassure yourself. You can also check to make sure the Web server is running on the default Web site in Internet Services Manager. For Apache on Linux, check the httpd service (you can also test it by entering `http://localhost` in your browser).

2. Place a simple HTML Web page in the wwwroot folder, making sure that it has `.htm` or `.html` as the extension for the filename (such as `test01.htm`), and bring the page up in your browser. Make sure you are using `http://localhost/test01.htm` to bring up the file, not the file location (such as `D:\inetpub\wwwroot\test01.htm`).

3. If the HTML Web page displays properly, you can be sure your Web server is functioning. This implies (assuming your PHP page cannot be displayed) that something is wrong with your PHP installation. Of course, if you see other messages (such as 404 Page Not Found) you may simply not be finding the file properly, so you'd need to take a second look at the file name you chose, the name of your Web folder, and so on.

4. If you think that something is wrong with your PHP installation, reexamine the installation process you used, going carefully through each step, and make sure you placed all the PHP files in the places they belong. Pay particular attention to the names of Windows and System folders because these may differ depending upon your installation of Windows or Linux.

5. Check file permissions. File permissions are very important in Linux systems, and to a lesser degree in Windows 2000 or desktop Windows operating systems. You should be logged in as root or administrator on Linux and Windows systems, and should be able to change permissions as necessary to run scripts from within Web server folders. For external hosting accounts any good FTP utility can modify file permissions on Linux systems.

It's likely that following these steps will isolate the problem so that you can fix it.

Configuring PHP

During installation you modified the `php.ini` file to affect the way PHP runs and what features it includes. Appendix F, *"Configuring PHP5,"* at the end of the book discusses the major settings in the `php.ini` file, as well as some of the extensions currently available for PHP, but in this section we'll go over a few of the most important PHP configurations settings and extensions.

php.ini

The `php.ini` file is parsed when PHP is first loaded and executed, so that PHP behaves (for any script running on that Web server) in a particular way. All lines that are not preceded by a semicolon are working commands; think of everything else in the file as a comment. Following is the text of several sections of the `php.ini-recommended` file. The settings shown are important because they have a direct effect on how PHP behaves (under common operating circumstances), will affect your code, or may affect the security of your applications:

```
;;;;;;;;;;;;;;;;;;;
; Resource Limits ;
;;;;;;;;;;;;;;;;;;;
```

```
max_execution_time = 30    ; Maximum execution time of each script, in seconds
max_input_time = 60      ; Maximum amount of time each script may spend parsing
request data
memory_limit = 8M        ; Maximum amount of memory a script may consume (8MB)

; Whether or not to register the EGPCS variables as global variables. You may
; want to turn this off if you don't want to clutter your scripts' global scope
; with user data. This makes most sense when coupled with track_vars - in which
; case you can access all of the GPC variables through the $HTTP_*_VARS[],
; variables.
;
; You should do your best to write your scripts so that they do not require
; register_globals to be on; Using form variables as globals can easily lead
; to possible security problems, if the code is not very well thought of.
register_globals = Off
```

There's much more information regarding the settings in php.ini in Appendix F.

PHP Extensions

PHP extensions are programmatic capabilities that add to or enhance PHP's built-in capabilities for performing useful work in your PHP programs. Although no special extensions are used in the early chapters of this book, you'll run across some later. Meanwhile, Appendix F covers all of the available extensions.

Caching

Caching is a method by which some results are stored temporarily, so that all processing does not have to be repeated each time a new request is made to the server. One potential disadvantage of running all your code on the server is that if the client (or some machine in between the end user and your site) has a cache going, the user may not get the most recently processed page To work around caching (at least for most browsers and servers), you can place the following code in your programs:

```php
<?php
header("Cache-Control: no-cache, must-revalidate");
header("Pragma: no-cache");
header("Expires: Mon,26 Jul 1997 05:00:00 GMT");
?>
```

The first line works well with HTTP 1.1, the second line with HTTP 1.0, and the third works by specifying a date in the past (more about HTTP in Chapter 2).

Summary

This chapter covered a bit of the history of PHP and several ways to install PHP alongside common Web server software.

You learned how to install PHP on both Windows and Linux platforms, some of the differences about installing PHP as a CGI or as a separate module, the basic meaning of some PHP settings, where PHP files go upon installation, and how to test your installation. The basic definition of troubleshooting and debugging was covered, as well as a series of steps to take if your installation of PHP isn't working.

Exercise

You're not really ready to begin programming exercises at this point, so let's do a different type of exercise that you'll find handy whenever you have to install with or work with PHP on a new platform. To complete this exercise, do the following:

Create a document that summarizes all of the following:

❑   What are the hardware capabilities of the computer on which PHP is running? Describe the CPU, hard drive, RAM, and so on, and any particular limitations you perceive.

❑   What operating system is running on the hardware? List the version, as well as any current patches and known bugs.

❑   What Web server software is running on the machine? List the version, patches, and known bugs. Also, list how the Web server is configured, the root folder, how PHP is set up to work with the Web server, and any file permissions you've set.

❑   What version of PHP was installed? List the version, the files installed, the folders in which they were installed, and any Registry settings that were set or created to support the PHP installation.

❑   What configuration settings were set or changed (from the default) to install PHP? List them.

❑   What extensions were enabled? List them all, and why you enabled them.

Writing Simple Programs

You've installed PHP and the other software components necessary to begin using PHP5, and you know that the majority of your programs will be designed to run from a Web server, using HTML- or XHTML-based Web pages for displaying the user interface and results of data processing in a browser (most likely Internet Explorer for PC users).

What you learn in this chapter is the basis for all your PHP programs that run via a browser-based interface. You'll explore the basic aspects of properly writing a PHP program, interspersing your PHP code within the HTML or XHTML of a Web page, the use of several common PHP functions (such as echo, date(), strlen(), and so on), and creating and using variables. You'll develop several simple programs demonstrating typical PHP5 usage with plain Web pages, and get a short recap of how PHP programs run.

You'll learn about operators and expressions, and briefly examine uniquely useful variables called arrays. Arrays are used for data storage like ordinary variables, but have features that make them quite powerful for many types of data processing.

This chapter provides the foundation for the bulk of the material in later chapters because almost all the data processing you'll do in PHP programs depends directly on your ability to properly name and use variables and PHP's type-related functions, and especially arrays.

Create a Simple PHP Program

Begin by following these steps to write a Web page that will appear in just about any browser you can find.

1. Open Notepad or any handy text editor and enter the following HTML code:

```
<html>
  <head>
    <title>Web Page</title>
  </head>
  <body>
    The text here displays in my browser window
  </body>
</html>
```

2. Save the file with any name you choose and an extension of `.htm` (`simple01.htm`, for example).

3. Open the file in your browser. Figure 2-1 shows the result.

Figure 2-1

4. Based on the installation and setup you did in Chapter 1, you should be able to upload the file to the appropriate server area (if you're working on the machine running the Web server, simply copy the file into a folder served by your Web server software). Bring the file up again from the Web server folder by using the HTTP address for the local host. The result should look exactly the same.

5. Now replace the line beginning with "The text ..." with the following lines:

```
The text here displays the date as a result of PHP5 processing: Today is
<?php
$todaysdate = date("m",time()) . "-" . date("d",time()) . "-" .
date("Y",time());
echo $todaysdate;
?>
```

6. Save the file, upload it if you need to, and refresh it in your browser. Anything happen? Probably not, unless you changed the file extension from `.htm` to `.php`. You see, in order for the Web server to refer the file to the PHP5 processing engine, it first needs to be aware that the file is a PHP file, and it learns this from the file extension. Second, assuming the file has the proper extension, the PHP5 processing engine picks out the sections of PHP code to process by *parsing* the file, looking for the PHP delimiters (`<?php` and `?>`), and then *executing* the PHP code. Parsing means the processing engine reads the individual commands and checks for syntax errors (a very common error you'll find in your PHP code is the parse error). Executing simply means the processing engine actually runs the code and does the processing.

7. Change the file extension to .php and bring up the file from the server.
   This time the code should execute and you should see the date at the end of the line of text.

Explore Some Details

There are many commands, keywords, statements, language constructs, and functions in the PHP programming language, just like any other programming language. The PHP processing engine looks for these during parsing, and if the syntax is correct, it processes them and returns the result of that processing. When you're running a Web application, the results should be compatible with HTML or scripting languages in the Web page in which they appear, so often the results of processing include HTML tags (more about how HTML works in Chapter 3).

The echo function is actually not a function but a language construct, meaning that it doesn't need parentheses to contain arguments, it doesn't return a value (but it does do what it's supposed to do, namely send a string value to the browser), and it has a few other restrictions that functions don't have. echo is not the only language construct in PHP; unset is another example. At this point, the most important thing for you to know is that echo sends a string back to the browser; in later chapters you'll find out more about the distinctions between languages constructs and functions.

So echo sends string data to the user. The data can include HTML code, but if none is present the user will still see the text in his browser (the browser treats it like reading a text file, and "fills in" the HTML to make it appear normally). In this code from the simple example, echo sends the string data you composed for today's date and placed in the $todaysdate variable:

```
echo $todaysdate;
```

The date() function is built in to PHP, meaning that you don't have to write or copy the function into your PHP5 program; it's simply there for you to use at any time. It's written in the same way as functions in most languages. It starts with the name of the function followed by parentheses, and inside the parentheses are arguments—the values, expressions, or more functions that resolve to a value which is then used by the date() function to produce the final answer. Take a look at this line from the example program:

```
$todaysdate = date("m",time()) . "-" . date("d",time()) . "-" .
date("Y",time());
```

The first argument is "m", signifying to the date() function that you want to know the month. The second argument uses the time() function, which gets the current time. The date() function processes the current time and extracts the month as a two-character value. You can use the date() function again to get the day and year from the time() function.

How PHP Code Works

As the preceding example illustrates, the basic requirements for a running PHP program within a Web page are as follows:

❑ Some type of Web page with which the user can interact

❑ A file extension of .php

❑   Recognizable PHP delimiters

❑   PHP code that is syntactically correct

Let's look at each of these in more detail.

Web Pages (User Interface)

It's important to have a firm grasp on how Web pages perform as well as how PHP5 works, because the rendered page is all that the end user ever sees of your PHP programs. By the way, although the rendered output usually is referred to as HTML, HTML is giving way to XHTML, and browsers are becoming capable of processing other, similar output, such as XML with XSLT. Although this book uses HTML to refer to the Web server's output, it also means other languages that browsers can render.

You can write PHP programs such that the PHP5 code is embedded in the HTML directly, or you can write your programs so that the HTML is essentially referenced from your PHP5 code as needed. Either way, all output to the end user should be HTML.

Why? Try opening the .php file as a file instead of as a Web page (in your browser, choose File ➪ Open and locate the file on your hard drive). You won't see the PHP code in your browser (the browser ignores the PHP delimiters and what's between them) but if you choose View ➪ Source, you see the unprocessed PHP code. That's because no Web server or PHP processing engine touched the file before your browser got it.

File Extensions

If you've built Web pages before, you're probably familiar with the .htm and .html filename extensions, and perhaps .shtml as well. These extensions indicate to the browser the file type being opened. The Web server is also aware of these extensions, and if it sees a .php file, it refers that file to the PHP engine for processing. The requirement for a filename extension of .php doesn't come from PHP5, but is the default for most from Web servers for PHP files.

It is possible to configure your Web server to send files with other extensions (such as .htm and .html) to the PHP processing engine. If you make this configuration change, your ordinary HTML Web pages will be processed through the PHP engine (in addition to all your PHP-coded Web pages), although ordinary HTML files won't change as a result (and this adds a bit of overhead). Because the files sent to the users will end with .htm or .html instead of .php, it won't be evident to them that PHP was being used for back-end processing. Whether to add these extensions is your choice, but it's recommended if you want to keep people from knowing that you're using PHP to process your Web application.

PHP Delimiters

Delimiters are used in many types of code to indicate code blocks, data, and so on. They are special characters that tell the parsing program where the data starts and stops. You've probably heard of comma-delimited text, in which case the delimiters are commas. Between one comma and the next, the program or engine parsing the data stream knows it should find data of the appropriate type.

The same concept applies to PHP code embedded in a Web page. The standard delimiters for PHP5 are `<?php` and `?>`. You could use `<?` and `?>`, but `<?php` and `?>` are preferred—and specified by the PHP Extension and Application Repository (PEAR), a very good source of standard PHP code and the subject of discussion in Chapter 14.

Like other settings in PHP5, you can adjust or expand the delimiters that the PHP processing engine will recognize by making changes to the configuration file. For example, you can make PHP5 recognize <% and %> as delimiters. These are called the ASP delimiters, referring to the delimiters commonly used when writing ASP embedded in Web pages. (ASP—Microsoft's Active Server Pages—is similar to PHP.)

You can also delimit PHP code using the HTML script tags, as in this example:

```
<script language="PHP">PHP code goes here</script>
```

"Correct" PHP

Like any programming language, PHP code must be written correctly if it is to run. When you run it from the Web server and it goes through the processing engine, any mistakes in your code generates an error that's displayed to you.

So syntactically correct PHP is required. But writing a program that is syntactically correct (and runs without errors) does not guarantee that your program will produce the "right" answer, because there may be logic errors in your code. This subject is discussed in much greater detail in Chapter 5.

The code in your simple PHP program runs just fine, by the way.

Common Code Markers

PHP uses several characters to mark the end of lines and delimit code blocks. Notice that the two lines of code in the program both end with a semicolon (;), as shown in the echo statement:

```
$todaysdate = date("m",time()) . "-" . date("d",time()) . "-" .
date("Y",time());
echo $todaysdate;
```

In PHP code:

- ❑ Code statements end with a semicolon (;).

- ❑ Code blocks are enclosed in curly braces ({ }).

- ❑ Comments in code begin with // for a single line, or begin with /* and end with */ to comment multiple lines.

Here's how these things look in a block of *pseudo code* (fake code used for outlining processing in PHP or illustrating a point):

```
<?php
//Put an echo statement here
echo "here's a bit of pseudo-code";
if ($var1 == $var2) {
    //do something
    /* here's a multi-line comment
    do something
    do something else
    */
}
?>
```

It's important to remember these requirements, because the processing engine will generate an error and display a parse error when you forget. Folks who have already programmed Visual Basic or ASP are probably the most likely to forget, because semicolons and curly braces are not required in those programs, and the apostrophe (not the //) marks comments.

How Online PHP Programs Run

Unlike desktop applications, which run on your local system when their .exe file is activated, online PHP programs run when a request is made to the Web server. The request tries to get the Web server to retrieve and send the file requested, but before the response is composed, the PHP engine has a chance to process the PHP code in the file.

> *This chapter discusses running online PHP programs. You can run PHP from the command line if you have access to the system on which it is installed, but that was well covered in Chapter 1.*

An important fact that often goes unsaid: Only a single PHP file can run at a given time (because only one file can be requested at a time from the server), and that means that even though you may have many PHP files on the Web server, each must function as its own little program. You can bring in other PHP files by using the include or require constructs (you'll see how to do this later), but doing so is merely like dynamically copying in all the code in those external files and still running a single file as a program. This is not some huge limitation, but it's worth mentioning, because all data and variables are lost each time the single page is processed and the HTTP request is fulfilled. There is a way to preserve data between page requests (using sessions) but the concept of "one file, one program" should be clear.

Any program that interacts with a server can be labeled a client program, and any program that provides services for client programs can be labeled a server. In fact, some programs operate as both client and server. In general use, however, programs such as browsers, FTP programs, and e-mail programs are clients, and make a connection to a server to perform most of their functions. The servers they typically connect to are Web servers, FTP servers, and mail servers.

The client-server relationship is important to PHP because all PHP code runs on the server, whereas the HTML and/or JavaScript code within Web pages is passed untouched back to the client for processing. Technically, you could send PHP code untouched back to the browser for processing there, but because most folks have no means of processing PHP code on their browser, it wouldn't work. One big advantage of the fact that PHP code is processed on the server is that, unlike JavaScript, the end user never has a chance to see your source code.

Web Communications: Internet Protocols and HTTP

Internet protocols define the format for all Internet communications between computers. What this means is that for your computer to talk to another computer across the Internet, both must be speaking the same language. For file transfers, FTP (File Transfer Protocol) is used, and for Web communications, HTTP (HyperText Transfer Protocol) is used.

The next few sections introduce the Internet protocols and discuss how they facilitate communications on the Web. A good understanding of what's going on between the browser and the server is essential for PHP programming, because within the requests and responses flying back and forth from client to server is a wealth of data you can tap into and use.

TCP/IP

The Internet is designed to provide communications between its many interconnected nodes. Every computer or device that has an IP address (that set of four numbers connected by dots, such as 64.71.134.49) is a node on the Internet. The main protocol (actually a suite of networking protocols) used to format data for transit is TCP/IP (Transmission Control Protocol over Internet Protocol.). TCP/IP is simply a method of describing *information packets* (the packages of bits that are individually transmitted across a network) so that they can be sent down your telephone, cable, or T1-line from node to node, until they reach their intended destination.

One advantage of the TCP/IP protocol is that it can reroute information very quickly if a particular node or route is broken or slow. When the user tells the browser to fetch a Web page, the browser parcels up (turns into packets) this instruction using TCP. TCP is a transport protocol, which provides a reliable transmission format for the instruction. It ensures that the entire message is taken apart and packaged up correctly for transmission (and also that it is correctly unpacked and put back together after it reaches its destination).

Before the packets of data are sent out across the network, they need to be addressed (they should include a source address and a destination address in the form of an IP address). So a second protocol called HyperText Transfer Protocol (or HTTP) puts an address label on them, so that TCP/IP knows where to direct the information. HTTP is the protocol used by the World Wide Web in the transfer of data from one machine to another—when you see a URL prefixed with http://, you know that the internet protocol being used is HTTP. You can think of TCP/IP as the postal service that does the routing and transfer, although HTTP is the stamp and address on the letter (data) to ensure it gets there.

The message passed from the browser to the Web server is known as an *HTTP request*. When the Web server receives this request (the request is actually a request for a Web page or file), it checks its stores to find the appropriate page. If it finds the page, it parcels up the HTML contained within (using TCP), addresses these packets to the browser (using HTTP), and sends them back across the network. If the Web server cannot find the requested page, it issues a page containing an error message (in this case, the dreaded Error 404: Page Not Found), it parcels up, and dispatches that page to the browser. The message sent from the Web server to the browser is called the *HTTP response*.

The HTTP Protocol

There's quite a bit more technical detail to all of this, let's look more closely at exactly how HTTP works. When a request for a Web page is sent to the server, it contains more than just the desired URL. There is a lot of extra information that is sent as part of the request. This is also true of the response—the server sends extra information back to the browser. You'll explore these different types of information shortly.

A lot of the information that's passed within the HTTP message is generated automatically, and the user doesn't have to deal with it directly, so you don't need to worry about transmitting such information yourself. Although you don't have to worry about creating this information yourself, you should be aware that this extra information is being passed between machines as part of the HTTP request and HTTP response because the PHP script that you write can enable you to have a direct effect on the exact content of this information.

Whether it's a client request or a server response, every HTTP message has the same format, which breaks down into three sections: the request/response line, the HTTP header, and the HTTP body. The content of these three sections is dependent on whether the message is a request or a response, so you'll examine these two cases separately.

The HTTP Request

The HTTP request that the browser sends to the Web server contains a request line, a header, and a body. Here's an example of the request line and header:

```
GET /testpage.htm HTTP/1.1
Accept: */*
Accept-Language: en-us
Connection: Keep-Alive
Host: www.wrox.com
Referer: http://webdev.wrox.co.uk/books/SampleList.php?bookcode=3730
User-Agent: Mozilla (X11; I; Linux 2.0.32 i586)
```

The Request Line

The first line of every HTTP request is the *request line*, which contains three pieces of information:

❑   An HTTP command known as a method (such as GET and POST)

❑   The path from the server to the resource that the client is requesting

❑   The version number of HTTP (such as HTTP 1.1)

Here's an example:

```
GET /testpage.htm HTTP/1.1
```

The method is used to tell the server how to handle the request. The following table describes three of the most common methods that appear in this field.

Method	Description
GET	A request for information residing at a particular URL. The majority of HTTP requests made on the Internet are GET requests (when you click a link, a GET request is made). The information required by the request can be anything from an HTML or PHP page, to the output of a JavaScript or PerlScript program, or some other executable. You can send some limited data to the browser, in the form of an extension to the URL
HEAD	The same as the GET method, except that it indicates a request for the HTTP header only and no data
POST	Indicates that data will be sent to the server as part of the HTTP body (from form fields, for example). This data is then transferred to a data-handling program on the Web server

HTTP supports a number of other methods, including PUT, DELETE, TRACE, CONNECT, and OPTIONS. As a rule, you'll find that these are less common; they are therefore beyond the scope of this discussion. If you want to know more about these, take a look at RFC 2068, which you can find at www.rfc.net.

The HTTP Request Header

The next bit of information sent is the HTTP header. This contains details of what document types the client will accept back from the server, including the type of browser that has requested the page, the date, and general configuration information. The HTTP request's header contains information that falls into three different categories:

❑   General: Information about either the client or server, but not specific to one or the other

❑   Entity: Information about the data being sent between the client and server

❑   Request: Information about the client configuration and different types of acceptable documents

Here's an example of a request header:

```
Accept: */*
Accept-Language: en-us
Connection: Keep-Alive
Host: www.wrox.com
Referer: http://webdev.wrox.co.uk/books/SampleList.php?bookcode=3730
User-Agent: Mozilla (X11; I; Linux 2.0.32 i586)
```

As you can see, the HTTP header is composed of a number of lines; each line contains the description of a piece of HTTP header information, and its value.

There are many different lines that can comprise a HTTP header, and most of them are optional, so HTTP has to indicate when it has finished transmitting the header information. To do this, a blank line is used.

The HTTP Request Body

If the POST method is used in the HTTP request line, then the HTTP request body contains any data that is being sent to the server—for example, data that the user typed into an HTML form (you'll see examples of this later in the book). Otherwise, the HTTP request body is empty, as it is in the example.

The HTTP Response

The HTTP response is sent by the server back to the client browser, and contains a response line, a header, and a body. Here's an example of the response line and header:

```
HTTP/1.1 200 OK                                         //the status line
Date: Fri, 31st Oct 2003, 18:14:33 GMT                  //the general header
Server: Apache/1.3.12 (Unix) (SUSE/Linux) PHP/4.0.2 //the response header
Last-modified: Fri, 29th Oct 2003, 14:09:03 GMT         //the entity header
                                                        //blank line (header
                                                        complete)
```

The Response Line

The response line contains only two bits of information:

❑   The HTTP version number

❑   An HTTP request code that reports the success or failure of the request

The example response line,

```
HTTP/1.1 200 OK
```

returns HTTP status code 200, which represents the message OK, denoting the success of the request, and that the response contains the required page or data from the server. If the response line contains HTTP status code 404 (mentioned earlier in the chapter), then the Web server failed to find the requested resource. Error code values are three-digit numbers, where the first digit indicates the class of the response. There are five classes of response, as shown in the following table.

Code class	Description
100–199	Informational; indicate that the request is currently being processed
200–299	Denote success (that the Web server received and carried out the request successfully)
300–399	Indicate that the request hasn't been performed because the information required has been moved
400–499	Denote a client error (that the request was incomplete, incorrect, or impossible)
500–599	Denote a server error (that the request appeared to be valid, but that the server failed to carry it out)

The Response Header

The HTTP response header is similar to the preceding request header. In the HTTP response, the header information again falls into three types:

❑   General: contains information about either the client or server, but not specific to one or the other

❑   Entity: contains information about the data being sent between the client and the server

❑   Response: contains information about the server sending the response and how it can deal with the response

Once again, the header consists of a number of lines, and uses a blank line to indicate that the header information is complete. Here's an example header, with the name of each line commented at the end:

```
Date: Fri, 31st Oct 2003, 18:14:33 GMT              //the general header
Server: Apache/1.3.12 (Unix) (SUSE/Linux) PHP/4.0.2 //the response header
Last-modified: Fri, 29th Oct 2003, 14:09:03 GMT     //the entity header
                                                    //blank line (header
                                                    complete)
```

The first line is self-explanatory. On the second line, Server, indicates the type of software the Web server is running. Because this example is requesting a file somewhere on the Web server, the information on the third line refers to the last time the requested page was modified.

The header can contain much more information than this, or different information, depending on what is requested. If you want to know more about the different types of information, you'll find them listed in RFC 2068 (Sections 4.5, 7.1 and 7.2).

The Response Body

If the request was successful, the HTTP response body contains the HTML code (together with any script that is to be executed by the browser), ready for the browser's interpretation. If unsuccessful, a failure code is sent.

Running PHP Scripts via an HTTP Request

Actually, any client application (not just a browser) that can send an HTTP request to a Web Server can activate and run a PHP program. In fact, it's not a requirement that the file display anything to the user (meaning you don't have to embed your code in a Web page). If a properly formatted HTTP request is sent to the Web server, asking for a file containing PHP code, and the file has the appropriate filename extension, the PHP program will run.

The Web Server

If you (or your system administrator) have properly set up the Web server software for the OS it's running on and for PHP, you can expect that HTTP requests for files containing PHP code will be properly handled and that your PHP programs will run.

The PHP Processing Engine

PHP is actually composed of function modules, a language core (named the Zend engine, now out as version 2.0), and a Web server interface. The interface allows PHP to communicate with the Web server machine-to-machine. The function modules give PHP its many valuable capabilities, although the Zend engine (the language core) does the hard work of analyzing, translating, and executing the incoming code (Zend does just a little bit more than that, but you get the idea). It's important to note that PHP is compiled at the moment it runs, on the server, therefore making your life much simpler by avoiding the need to precompile the code specifically for each type of machine you expect it to run on.

Using Variables in PHP

Just about every programming language uses variables; in fact it's hard to imagine having the capability to perform data processing without variables in some form. Variables are one of the most fundamental structures in programming, and they're usually easy to create and use. You can recognize variables in PHP because they begin with a dollar sign ($). So if you write a dollar sign followed by a name, you have a PHP variable.

Variables do not need to be declared and initialized in PHP, and they don't need a data type set because PHP is what's called a loosely typed language (see the *"Strongly Typed and Loosely Typed Languages"* section later in this chapter for more information). You create a variable simply by including it in an expression, and setting it to a value at the same time. For example, the first example in this chapter set the $todaysdate variable to the current date value:

```
$todaysdate = date("m",time()) . "-" . date("d",time()) . "-" .
  date("Y",time());
```

Issues Concerning Creating Variables

As you may already know, there are several issues related to variables that are specific to any language that uses them: The issues are:

❑ Naming

❑ Data Type

❑ Scope

Let's discuss each of these issues in more detail.

Naming Variables

Variables are meant to contain data for the purpose of performing data processing operations on it. They are called variables because their data values can vary depending upon what processing has been done to their values.

So a variable really consists of two parts: the variable's name and the variable's value. Because you'll be using variables in your code frequently, it's best to give your variable names you can understand and remember. Like other programming languages, PHP has certain rules you must follow when naming your variables:

❑ Variable names begin with a dollar sign ($).

❑ The first character after the dollar sign must be a letter or an underscore.

❑ The remaining characters in the name may be letters, numbers, or underscores without a fixed limit.

Variable names are case-sensitive ($Variable and $variable are two distinct variables), and names longer than 30 characters are somewhat impractical. In this book we use a few coding conventions that are practical as well as useful, and you'll find adopting a good set of coding conventions is worthwhile. We discuss them in detail in Chapter 6, but we'll also mention several of our coding conventions as we talk about variable names and so on in the next few chapters.

Here's an example of a variable named in a PHP program:

```
$my_first_variable = 0;
```

You might be wondering why this variable is set to a value of zero. In PHP, there's not much point in naming a variable without giving it a value in some way because the act of naming a variable creates it in your program. So while we're creating it, we're also assigning a value of zero to it. Of course, you can create variables and assign any value you like to them, not just zero.

In some languages, you can be restricted (and in some cases prevented entirely) from using a variable without first explicitly declaring (creating) it. But PHP enables you to use variables at any point just by naming them. This is not always the blessing you might think; if you happen to use the same variable name twice by mistake, no error message is generated, and you may end up with a hard-to-find bug. In most cases, though, it works just fine and is a helpful feature.

Data Types

Another consideration when creating a variable is its type or data type. What is a data type, you ask? Data type describes the type of data that a variable holds. If you've ever done any work with databases, you've probably noticed that fields in a database table are often assigned a data type, and that the data type is what distinguishes between strings, numbers, dates, Boolean values, and so on.

The data type of an item determines what kind of processing can be applied to it, as well as how much memory it requires. For example, if you have a data item with a data type of string and a value of 1995, you cannot add it to another string value of 5 and expect to get the number 2000, unless your programming language is especially designed to automatically interpret data types and modify them according to the context in which they are used (fortunately, PHP does just that, but more on that later).

Instead, you'll get a data type error, or perhaps the two strings will be concatenated (joined together into a single string) and your answer would be 19955, not at all what you were expecting.

Strongly Typed and Loosely Typed Languages

In the preceding example, data type rules for a strongly typed language were violated and an error resulted. But PHP is a loosely typed language, and so it saves you from this kind of error by figuring out what you were trying to do and fixing it for you.

The term *strongly typed* means a language requires explicit declaration of variables types and will generate errors if you try to use operators on them incorrectly, or will give you incorrect answers (not the answer you'd expect) as in the example. *Loosely typed* languages don't require a declaration of variable type, and automatically convert variable type depending upon the context in which they are used and the operations you perform on their values.

PHP is loosely typed, but enables you to check data type whenever you want to. It also enables you to set and use data types if you want to. Although you don't have to explicitly declare variable and assign a data type, you can determine what data type a variable happens to be at during processing, as well as cast (set) variables to a specific data type as needed.

PHP Data Types

Although PHP is loosely typed, it does support many common simple and structured data types. Simple data types are types that contain a range of values that can be ordered in one dimension (strings, numbers, Booleans, and so on), whereas structured data types include arrays and objects. PHP has eight simple types, which are described in the following table:

Data type	Description
Boolean	Scalar; either True or False
Integer	Scalar; a whole number
Float	Scalar; a number which may have a decimal place
String	Scalar; a series of characters
Array	Compound; an ordered map (contains names mapped to values)
Object	Compound; a type that may contain properties and methods
Resource	Special; contains a reference to an external resource, such as a handler to an open file
NULL	Special; may only contain NULL as a value, meaning the variable explicitly does not contain any value

Programmers use terms such as scalar, compound, and special to signify characteristics of data types. Scalar signifies that the values the data type holds may be ordered along a scale. For example, numbers are ordered from lower to higher, and characters are ordered in alphabetically. Compound means the data contains multiple data items; for example, arrays contain both index numbers and values associated with them. And special means a special number or value that has a meaning significant to the application, such as a file handler.

Arrays are discussed later in this chapter, and full coverage is given to objects (and new object-oriented programming features available in PHP5) in later chapters.

Converting Data Types in PHP

Under ordinary circumstances, you might never need to force the value in a variable from one type to another, but sometimes it helps to be able to do that, such as when you need to make sure you are using a particular type, or when you are preparing output for another program. PHP includes built-in functions for *casting* (setting) a type.

The PHP function gettype() can be used to determine the current type of a variable, and settype() forces a variable to a particular type. For example, the following code sets the value of a variable as an integer, and then changes it to a string, each time echoing the type. The actual characters that make up the value stay the same, but the data type is changed.

```
$my_var = 1995; //$my-var is a numeric value
echo "The varaivle is now a ". gettype($my_var) . "<br>";
$my_var = settype($my_var, "string"); //$my_var is now a string
echo "The variable is now a " . gettype($my_var);
```

The PHP gettype() function returns a string value describing the type it found (such as string, integer, and so on). PHP also contains functions that check for specific types, such as is_string, is_int, and so on. These functions should be used whenever you need to check for a specific type, rather than comparing the gettype() string value returned (for example, integer) to the string you were hoping for (again, integer).

Variable Scope

With the code you've seen so far, you're probably comfortable with the notion that if you create a variable by giving it a name in your code, and then set a value for that variable, you can use it as much as you like, whenever you like, to perform whatever data processing functions you want. That's true to a degree, but there are some limitations. These limitations have to do with *scope*.

Scope refers to where a variable (actually, the value contained in the variable) may be reached for manipulation. As mentioned, most variables are available anywhere in your PHP program, but when you formally write a function (Chapter 6 includes a detailed discussion of functions), the variables in it are *local*, meaning they can only be recognized and used within the function. Here's an example of a simple function:

```
$my_data = "Outside data";
function send_data() {
$my_data = "Inside data";
echo $my_data;
}
send_data(); //sends the inside data to the user
echo $my_data; //sends the outside data to the user
```

This function just returns data. If the function is called, as in the second-to-last line of code, the output to the user will be Inside data.

However, if the variable $my_data is echoed from outside the function, as shown in the last line of code, Outside data will be sent to the user because $my_data outside the function is not the same as $my_data inside the function, even though both variable names are the same. The scope of $my_data inside the function is said to be local to the function. And by the way, once the function has completed its work, $my_data inside the function is destroyed and its value is lost.

The Global Keyword

Naturally, there is a way to get at outside variables from inside a function. If a variable is declared with the global keyword, it can be accessed from inside a function, as shown in the following example (Chapter 6 contains much more detail about global):

```
$my_data = "Outside data";
function send_data() {
global $my_data;
echo $my_data;
}
send_data(); //sends the outside data to the user
echo $my_data; //also sends the outside data to the user
```

Static Variables

If you use the keyword static when you create a variable inside a function (meaning the scope of the variable is local to the function, and would ordinarily be lost once the function has run), the variable and its value are preserved between calls to the function. This capability is useful in certain situations in which you'd like to know how many times the function has been called. For example, suppose you wanted to call a function 100 times to return a record from a database, but cause the function to refuse to return records once the value 100 is reached. Specifying a static variable that increments by one each time the function is called would do the trick, as shown here (with a little pseudo code):

```
function get_record() {
    static $counter = 0;
    $counter++;
    //check to see if $counter < 100
    //if < 100, run code that gets the record from the database
    //if $counter = or > 100, echo "No more records"
}
```

This works because each time the function is called, $counter is incremented and the value is still there the next time the function is called.

Defined Constants

You can also define value-containers called *constants* in PHP. Constants, as their name implies, can be defined (using the define() function) only once in a PHP program, and their value can never be changed nor can they be undefined. They differ from variables in that their names do not start with the dollar sign, but other than that they can be named in the same way variables are.

Constants may only contain scalar values such as Boolean, integer, float, and string (not values such as arrays and objects), can be used from anywhere in your PHP program without regard to variable scope, and are case-sensitive. To define a constant, use the `define()` function, and include inside the parentheses the name you've chosen for the constant, followed by the value for the constant, as shown here:

```
define("my_constant", "1995"); //my-constant always has the string value "1995"
echo my_constant; //sends "1995" to the user (note this is not an integer)
```

Operators and Expressions

Processing data is accomplished in PHP, as it is in other programming languages, by way of operators and expressions. Operators are the symbols that tell PHP what operations to perform, and expressions are the individual sets of variables and operators that make a result when processing is complete.

PHP Operators

In PHP, you create a variable and set a value to it by using the equal sign, as in:

```
$my_data = "Hello";
```

The equal sign is an *operator*. Operators are used to perform data processing on variable values. In this case, the equal sign is called the *assignment* operator, because it assigns the string data value to the variable just created.

There are quite a few operators in most programming languages; some of them perform arithmetic, just like you would in a simple equation; some of them operate on string or date data; and some of them perform other functions. They all carry out data processing on variable values.

Operators that need only one operand are called unary operators; for example, the ++ operator can be appended to the end of a variable name (the operand) to increment the variable by one. Because the ++ operator can be placed before the variable or after the variable, it is said to allow both prefix and postfix notation.

Operators that need two operands are called binary operators; the equal sign used in "$my_data = "Hello"" is one example. Because the operator is placed between the operands, it is said to be using infix notation.

And some languages contain tertiary operators requiring three operands. For example, PHP allows use of the ? operator, which is a shorthand If statement. Such a statement would begin with an expression followed by the question mark, then two possible outcomes separated by a colon ("expression ? outcome01 : outcome02", meaning "if expression is true then do outcome01, but if not true then do outcome02"). Because the operator is inside the operands, it is also said to use infix notation.

PHP Expressions

Expressions are any code that evaluates to a value. The assignment of a value to a variable is an expression in itself, although we tend to think of expressions as similar to equations (like $a = $b + $c, where $b + $c is the expression we have in mind).

Therefore, $a = 5 is an expression, because it evaluates to the value 5. If you write $a = $b + $c, you know you're adding $b and $c first, and then setting $a equal to the resulting value. You can make expressions arbitrarily complex (as complex as you'd like) and you can use any of the operators on any appropriate values to get a result. In fact, the main portion of PHP functionality comes from its processing (evaluation) of expressions.

One key part of evaluating an expression, particularly complex expressions, is operator precedence. As in arithmetic or math, it sometimes makes a difference which part of an expression is evaluated first. There is a default precedence of operations, and you can directly control precedence by inserting parentheses. For example, because the multiplication operator (*) has precedence over the addition operator (+), the expression 2 + 2 * 12 results in a value of 26 (2 * 12 is evaluated first, by default, and then added to 2), whereas (2 + 2) * 12 results in a value of 48 (the parentheses force 2 + 2 to be added together first, then the result of that is multiplied by 12).

Operator Types

The following operator types are available in PHP:

Type	Description
Arithmetic	Perform common arithmetical operations, such as addition and subtraction
Assignment	Assign values to variables
Bitwise	Perform operations on individual bits in an integer
Comparison	Compare values in a Boolean fashion (true or false is returned)
Error Control	Affect error handling (several new ones in PHP5)
Execution	Cause execution of commands as though they were shell commands
Incrementing/Decrementing	Increment or decrement a variable
Logical	Boolean operators such as AND, OR, and NOT that can be used to include or exclude (more on this in Chapter 4)
String	Concatenates (joins together) strings
Array	Perform operations (such as append or split) on arrays

An exhaustive list and reference for each operator aren't provided here because that information is easily available online at www.php.net (just go to the site, click documentation, and you'll find operators listed in the table of contents). When an operator is used in this book, though, some of its peculiarities are discussed.

String Operators and Functions

There is only one string operator: the dot (.), but PHP contains plenty of string functions that enable you manipulate strings effectively. The following sections discuss how the concatenation operator and several of the string functions work.

Using the Concatenation Operator

The concatenation operator (.) can be used between string values to join them together. Here's how it's done in a PHP program:

```
<?php
$first_name = "Joe";
$last_name = "Blow";
$whole_name = $first_name . " " . $last_name;
echo "First name plus last name = <b>$whole_name</b>";
?>
```

Notice that a space is added to the $whole_name value by concatenating " " (a space between quotes) into the $first_name and $last_name values. There's also a space before and after the concatenation operator each time it's used. This is not necessary, but makes the code a little easier to read. The following code would work just as well:

```
$whole_name = $first_name." ".$last_name;
```

To make the answer more readable when displayed in the Web page, HTML tags are added to the echoed response (the <b> and </b> tags to make text bold):

```
echo "First name plus last name = <b>$whole_name</b>";
```

Unless you need to include special characters such as quotes in your HTML, you can simply insert the HTML into your text, which will be properly formatted by the browser when the page is displayed. As you can see, the variable $whole_name was simply inserted right into the line of code. In many programming languages it's not possible to do this, but PHP is smart enough to understand that when you use a variable name in a string you want its value—not its name—placed in the string. Of course, if you want the name to be displayed in the string, you must escape the dollar sign (precede the dollar sign with a slash) so PHP knows not to insert the value:

```
echo "First name plus last name = <b>\ $whole_name</b>";
```

Using the strlen() function

The strlen() function finds the length of a string. It counts all characters in the string and returns the total. In the following example, the total number of characters is placed into the variable named $string_length:

```
$string_length = strlen($whole_name);
```

Interestingly, using the concatenation operator to join together a string (such as "The length of the name is") and a numerical value (such as the length of the string contained in $string_length) has the effect of making the entire response a string data type.

The string length function is useful whenever you need a count of the characters in a string, such as when validating data that might go into a database.

Using the strstr() function

The strstr() function gets any part of a string that is after the first instance of a particular character or string within a string. In the next example, the $whole_name variable value (Joe Blow) is searched until the first occurrence of the space character, and then the strstr() function returns everything after that space. Additional occurrences of the search string within the searched string make no difference whatsoever. If the string you seek isn't found within the string being searched, the function returns a value of FALSE.

```
$part_after_space = strstr($whole_name, " ");
echo "The part of the string after the space is <b>" .
$part_after_space . "</b>";
```

Using the strpos() function

The strpos() function is used to determine whether a search string exists within a searched string, and returns a numeric value indicating the location at which the search string begins, if found. In the following example, searching for the string o within the $whole_name value (Joe Blow), returns the position value "1". You might have expected to receive the number 2, because o is the second letter in the name, but like many other programming languages, PHP often uses sets of values starting with 0 rather than 1, so the location is specified as "1".

```
$letter_position = strpos($whole_name, "o");
echo "The position of the letter &quot;a&quot; is <b>" .
$letter_position . "</b>";
```

In this particular case, PHP is examining the string Joe Blow as though it were an array of characters (which, in fact, it is in PHP), and uses array index values (0,1,2,3,4, and so on) for the location of each character. (There's an "Arrays" section coming up in just a few pages.)

Using the chr() function

The chr() function returns a string character value corresponding to the decimal ASCII value entered as the argument. You can find tables of ASCII characters all over the Internet, and it is often convenient to use them, especially for special characters. For example, the ASCII character for a line feed is 10 and for a carriage return is 13. There really aren't keyboard characters you can enter for these characters, so if you need to include them in a string, you just use chr(10) and chr(13) and the alphabetic characters they represent are inserted into your string.

Try It Out   Work With Strings

Time to create some simple PHP programs that demonstrate how you can use operators in expressions with variables. This program demonstrates working with strings. You'll use the string operator, the dot (.), and several of PHP's built-in string functions. Here's what to do:

1. Create a file in any text editor, and save it as working_with_strings.php. Place it in the folder supported by the Web server (if you're working on the machine running the Web server) or upload it to the appropriate folder on the Web server (and upload it again each time you make changes).

2. Enter the following code in your file (the screen highlights the PHP portions of code):

```
<html>
<head>
<title>Beginning PHP5</title>
<meta http-equiv="Content-Type" content="text/html; charset=iso-8859-1">
</head>
<body bgcolor="#FFFFFF">
<table width="100%" border="1">
  <tr>
    <td width="49%"><font face="Arial, Helvetica, sans-serif"><b>Working With
        Strings</b></font></td>
    <td width="51%"> </td>
  </tr>
  <tr>
    <td width="49%"><font face="Arial, Helvetica, sans-serif" size="-1">Using
        Concatenation - the . operator</font></td>
    <td width="51%"><font face="Arial, Helvetica, sans-serif" size="-1">
<?php
$first_name = "Joe";
$last_name = "Blow";
$whole_name = $first_name . " " . $last_name;
echo "First name plus last name = <b>$whole_name</b>";
?>
</font></td>
  </tr>
  <tr>
    <td width="49%"><font face="Arial, Helvetica, sans-serif" size="-1">
Finding
        String Length - using <b>strlen()</b></font></td>
    <td width="51%"><font face="Arial, Helvetica, sans-serif" size="-1">
<?php
$string_length = strlen($whole_name);
echo "The length of the name is <b>" . $string_length . "</b>";
?>
</font></td>
  </tr>
  <tr>
    <td width="49%"><font face="Arial, Helvetica, sans-serif" size="-
1">Getting
        Part of a String - using <b>strstr()</b></font></td>
    <td width="51%"><font face="Arial, Helvetica, sans-serif" size="-1">
<?php
$part_after_space = strstr($whole_name, " ");
echo "The part of the string after the space is <b>" . $part_after_space .
"</b>";
?>
</font></td>
  </tr>
```

```
   <tr>
     <td width="49%"><font face="Arial, Helvetica, sans-serif"
size="-1">Finding
       Position of Part of a String - using <b>strpos()</b></font></td>
     <td width="51%"><font face="Arial, Helvetica, sans-serif" size="-1">
<?php
$letter_position = strpos($whole_name, "o");
echo "The position of the letter &quot;o&quot; is <b>" . $letter_position .
"</b>";
?>
</font></td>
   </tr>
   <tr>
     <td width="49%"><font face="Arial, Helvetica, sans-serif" size="-1">Return
       a character based on an ASCII value - using <b>chr()</b></font></td>
     <td width="51%"><font face="Arial, Helvetica, sans-serif" size="-1">
<?php
$ascii_character_returned = chr(97);
echo "The character corresponding to ASCII decimal value 97 is <b>"
. $ascii_character_returned . "</b>";
?>
</font></td>
   </tr>
 </table>
 </body>
 </html>
```

3. Save the file, upload it if required, and then display it in your browser. You should see a result similar to Figure 2-2.

How It Works

The PHP program you just created is embedded in a complete HTML Web page, and within the HTML <body> element the parts of the program are contained within an HTML <table> purely for readability. When the Web page file is requested from the Web server by a browser, the PHP code is parsed and executed, and the results inserted into the HTML stream returned to the browser.

The concatenation operator (.) is used to join string values (including a blank space) together:

```
<?php
$first_name = "Dave";
$last_name = "Mercer";
$whole_name = $first_name . " " . $last_name;
echo "First name plus last name = <b>$whole_name</b>";
?>
```

The strlen() function finds and returns the length of a string. In this program, it returns a number indicating the count of characters in the string value contained in the $whole_name variable.

The strstr() function finds and returns any part of a string that is after the first instance of a particular character or string within a string. In this program, it searches the $whole_name variable value ("Dave Mercer") until it finds the first occurrence of the space character, and then returns everything after the first space.

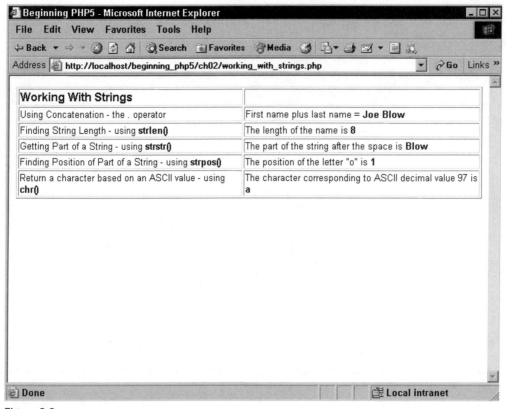

Figure 2-2

The strpos() function finds and returns a number indicating the position within a string or a search string. In this case, searching for the string a within the $whole_name value, returns the position value 1. (Remember that the values start with 0, so the second position is 1.)

The chr() function returns a string character value corresponding to the decimal ASCII value entered as the argument. In this program, the string character for ASCII value 97 is returned.

Arithmetic Operators in PHP

In PHP, the arithmetic operators (plus, minus, and so on) work much as you would expect, enabling you to write expressions as though they were simple equations. For example, $c = $a + $b adds $a and $b and assigns the result to $c. (The = operator is entirely different than the comparison operators == and ===, which are discussed in Chapter 4.)

And just like ordinary equations, operator precedence makes a difference, and you can affect this precedence using parentheses. Here's an example:

```php
<?php
$first_number = 20;
$second_number = 30;
```

```
$third_number = 3;
$fourth_number = 2;
$total = $first_number * $second_number / $third_number + $fourth_number;
$total2 = $first_number * $second_number / ($third_number + $fourth_number);
echo "Twenty times thirty divided by three plus two is <b>$total</b><br>";
echo "Twenty times thirty divided by (three plus two) is <b>$total2</b>";
?>
```

The difference made by the parentheses is clear when you run the program because the first echo statement returns a value of 202, whereas the second echo statement returns a value of 120.

Special Assignment Operators

The equals sign can be combined with other operators to give you a special assignment operator that makes it easier to write certain expressions. The special assignment operators (such as +=, −=, and so on) simply give you a shorthand method for performing typical arithmetic operations, so that you don't have to write out the variable name multiple times. For example, you can write

```
$first_number += $second_number;
```

rather than

```
$first_number = $first_number + $second_number;
```

This also works for other kinds of operators. For example, the concatenation operator can be combined with the equals sign (as .=) so that the current value on the left side is concatenated to the value being assigned on the right, like this:

```
$a = "Start a sentence ";
$b = "and finish it.";
$a .= $b //gives Start a sentence and finish it.
```

The main arithmetic, string, and bitwise operators support combination in this fashion; check the PHP Web site for more information about which operators can be combined like this.

Using the Increment/Decrement Operators

There are often times when it's useful to add or subtract from a number the same amount over and over. This situation occurs so frequently that there are special operators to perform this task: the increment and decrement operators. They are written as two plus signs or two minus signs respectively, preceding or following a variable name, like so:

```
$a = ++$a; //adds one to $a and then returns the result
$a = $a++; //returns $a and then adds one to it
$b = --$b; //subtracts one from $b and then returns the result
$b = $b--; //returns $b and then subtracts one from it
```

The location of the operators does make a difference. Placing the operators before the variable name causes the effect (adding or subtracting one) to happen before the value of the variable is returned; placing the operators after the variable name returns the current value of the variable before causing the effect.

Interestingly, you can use the increment and decrement operators in a limited way with characters as well. For example, you can "add"one to the character B and the returned value is C. However, you cannot subtract from (decrement) character values.

Using PHP Math Functions

PHP incorporates many common mathematical functions, including some that require arguments, some that don't require arguments, and some in which arguments are optional. For example, you can use the `floor()` function to round a number down, no matter what the fractional amount is. But you must provide an argument to the function, otherwise, what would be the point? The argument is the initial value to find the floor for. For example, the find the floor value of 100.01, you'd use a line of code like this:

```
$a = 100.01;
$floor_a = floor($a);
```

On the other hand, functions like `pi()` and `rand()` require no arguments. The `pi()` function returns the value of pi to 14 decimal places (the default is 14, but your actual precision depends on your setting of the `precision` directive in your `php.ini` file). The `rand` function generates a (pseudo) random number from 1 to `RAND_MAX` (the maximum number, that varies by operating system), unless you supply it with arguments limiting the range of numbers from which the function can choose.

Try It Out   Work With Numbers

Here's a little program that demonstrates working with numbers. You'll do some familiar operations, and a few that might not be so familiar, using some of the operators available with PHP, and some of the built-in functions. Once again, you embed your PHP code in HTML so that a Web page can display the results.

1. Open your HTML editor and enter the following code. (Although it's good practice for you to enter all of this code, you may instead choose to download the file—`working_with_numbers.php`—from this book's Web site.)

```
<html>
<head>
<title>Beginning PHP5</title>
<meta http-equiv="Content-Type" content="text/html; charset=iso-8859-1">
</head>

<body bgcolor="#FFFFFF">
<table width="100%" border="1">
  <tr>
    <td width="57%"><font face="Arial, Helvetica, sans-serif"><b>Working With
      Numbers</b></font></td>
    <td width="43%"> </td>
  </tr>
  <tr>
    <td width="57%"><font face="Arial, Helvetica, sans-serif" size="-1">Using
      the Addition Operator (+)</font></td>
    <td width="43%"><font face="Arial, Helvetica, sans-serif" size="-1">
<?php
$first_number = 20;
```

```
$second_number = 30;
$total = $first_number + $second_number;
echo "Twenty plus thirty is <b>$total</b>";
?>
</font></td>
  </tr>
  <tr>
    <td width="57%"><font face="Arial, Helvetica, sans-serif" size="-1">Using
       the Increment Operator (++)</font></td>
    <td width="43%"><font face="Arial, Helvetica, sans-serif" size="-1">
<?php
$first_number = 20;
$first_number = ++$first_number;
echo "Twenty incremented by one is <b>$first_number</b>";
?>
</font></td>
  </tr>
  <tr>
    <td width="57%"><font face="Arial, Helvetica, sans-serif" size="-1">Using
       the Multiplication and Division Operators (* and /)</font></td>
    <td width="43%"><font face="Arial, Helvetica, sans-serif" size="-1">
<?php
$first_number = 20;
$second_number = 30;
$third_number = 3;
$fourth_number = 2;
$total = $first_number * $second_number / $third_number + $fourth_number;
$total2 = $first_number * $second_number / ($third_number + $fourth_number);
echo "Twenty times thirty divided by three plus two is <b>$total</b><br>";
echo "Twenty times thirty divided by (three plus two) is <b>$total2</b>";
?>
</font></td>
  </tr>
  <tr>
    <td width="57%"><font face="Arial, Helvetica, sans-serif" size="-1">Special
       Assignment Operators - Using += and *=</font></td>
    <td width="43%"><font face="Arial, Helvetica, sans-serif" size="-1">
<?php
$first_number = 20;
$second_number = 30;
$total = $first_number += $second_number;
$total2 = $first_number *= $second_number;
echo "Twenty plus_equals thirty is <b>$total</b><br>";
echo "Twenty time_equals thirty is <b>$total2</b>";
?>
</font></td>
  </tr>
  <tr>
    <td width="57%"><font face="Arial, Helvetica, sans-serif" size="-1">
Getting
       the absolute value of a number - Using abs()</font></td>
    <td width="43%"><font face="Arial, Helvetica, sans-serif" size="-1">
<?php
$first_number = -2.7;
```

```
echo "The absolute value of -2.7 is <b>" . abs($first_number) . "</b>";
?>
</font></td>
   </tr>
   <tr>
     <td width="57%"><font face="Arial, Helvetica, sans-serif" size="-1">
Converting
       a binary number to a decimal number - Using bindec()</font></td>
     <td width="43%"><font face="Arial, Helvetica, sans-serif" size="-1">
<?php
$binary_number = 10101111;
$decimal_number = bindec($binary_number);
echo "The decimal equivalent of the binary number 10101111 is
<b>$decimal_number</b>";
?>
</font></td>
   </tr>
   <tr>
     <td width="57%"><font face="Arial, Helvetica, sans-serif" size="-1">Round
       Numbers up or down - Using ceil() and floor()</font></td>
     <td width="43%"><font face="Arial, Helvetica, sans-serif" size="-1">
<?php
$first_number = 2.4;
echo "2.4 rounded up is <b>" . ceil($first_number) . "</b> and rounded down is
<b>"
. floor($first_number) . "</b>";
?>
</font></td>
   </tr>
   <tr>
     <td width="57%"><font face="Arial, Helvetica, sans-serif" size="-1">Finding
       the maximum or minimum value - Using max() and min()</font></td>
     <td width="43%"><font face="Arial, Helvetica, sans-serif" size="-1">
<?php
$max_value = max(2,3,4);
$min_value = min(2,3,4);
echo "The max value of 2,3,4 is <b>" . $max_value . "</b>, and the min value is
<b>" . $min_value . "</b>";
?>
/font></td>
  </tr>
  <tr>
    <td width="57%"><font face="Arial, Helvetica, sans-serif" size="-1">Get the
      value of PI - Using pi()</font></td>
    <td width="43%"><font face="Arial, Helvetica, sans-serif" size="-1">
<?php
echo "The value of PI is <b>" . pi() . "</b>";
?>
</font></td>
   </tr>
   <tr>
     <td width="57%"><font face="Arial, Helvetica, sans-serif" size="-1">Get a
       random vnumber - Using rand()</font></td>
     <td width="43%"><font face="Arial, Helvetica, sans-serif" size="-1">
```

```php
<?php
echo "A random number is <b>" . rand() . "</b>";
?>
/font></td>
 </tr>
 <tr>
   <td width="57%"><font face="Arial, Helvetica, sans-serif" size="-1">Get the
     square root - Using sqrt()</font></td>
   <td width="43%"><font face="Arial, Helvetica, sans-serif" size="-1">
<?php
$first_number = 20;
echo "The square root of twenty is <b>" . sqrt($first_number)
. "</b>";
?>
</font></td>
   </tr>
</table>
</body>
</html>
```

2. Save the file as working_with_numbers.php, upload it if required, and then display it in your browser. Figure 2-3 shows the result.

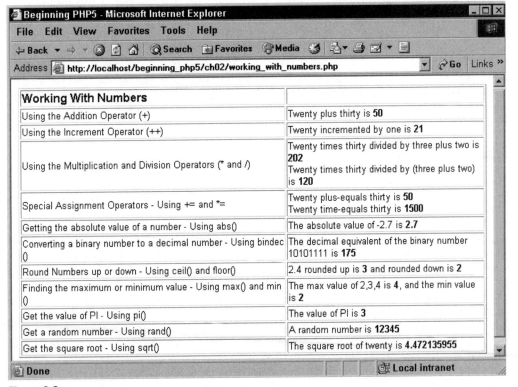

Figure 2-3

How It Works

You use the same format for displaying results in this program as you did with the last. This program demonstrates some simple calculations with operators, some basic use of built-in functions, and the results of several built-in functions that take no arguments (such as pi()).

In the code you set some values and then processed them with different sets of parentheses to illustrate how operator precedence works:

```php
<?php
$first_number = 20;
$second_number = 30;
$third_number = 3;
$fourth_number = 2;
$total = $first_number * $second_number / $third_number + $fourth_number;
$total2 = $first_number * $second_number / ($third_number + $fourth_number);
echo "Twenty times thirty divided by three plus two is <b>$total</b><br>";
echo "Twenty times thirty divided by (three plus two) is <b>$total2</b>";
?>
```

Then increment and decrement operators were used to add or subtract one from the numerical value contained in the variables $a and $b.

```php
$a = ++$a; //adds one to $a and then returns the result
$a = $a++; //returns $a and then adds one to it
$b = --$b; //subtracts one from $b and then returns the result
$b = $b--; //returns $b and then subtracts one from it
```

The use of the pi() and rand() functions demonstrates how to make PHP generate values for pi or that are random. Just write out the function with no arguments in between the parentheses, and that's all there is to it (other than using the equals sign to assign the value to a variable).

Arrays

Arrays are variables of type array (notice array is referred to as a data type), so you might be wondering why there's a whole section of this chapter for them. Yes, arrays are variables, but they are very special and powerful variables, and so deserve their own section.

Technically, arrays are lists made up of *keys* (the indexes) and *values*, which are the values contained in each *element*. Elements are the value containers in an array. You can think of an element as being similar to a separate variable, and being made up of a name/value pair.

Although some books imply that arrays can be very complex and hard to grasp, there's an easy way to think about them comfortably: Arrays are variables with many value containers, and several ways to access any particular value. They are almost like mini relational databases that are dynamic, in that they reside in memory only as long as the current program is executing (unless you store them in the session or in a real database between page requests). Array names are like the names of tables in a database, and an array container that contains another array is like a related table in a database. This analogy is not precise, but it can be very helpful when thinking about how to create or access arrays and their values.

Array Indexes

The `array()` function (actually, it is a language construct, not a function, but is written the same way as a function) is used to create an array, and accepts as arguments the values you want to place in the array. An element in an array can be accessed by its *index number*. An index number is like a little address by which you can access that particular variable spot within an array. Because all the variable spots in an array begin with the name of the array, each particular spot must have its own unique number. Index numbers for arrays begin with zero (0). For example, in the following line of code, the `$my_array` variable is set equal to an array that has four elements numbered 0, 1, 2, and 3:

```
$my_array = array ("cat", "dog", "horse", "goldfish");
```

The variable `$my_array` is set to the result of the `array()` function. If you ran the `is_array()` function on `$my_var`, the result would be true, indicating that, sure enough, `$my_var` is structured as an array.

To access the values in the array just created, you can use code such as the following:

```
$zero_element = $my_array[0];
$one_element = $my_array[1];
$two_element = $my_array[2];
$three_element = $my_array[3];
```

Using Strings as Array Indexes

Because you can use arrays in so many situations, it's often helpful to give elements a name rather than simply let them adopt the next number (starting with 0) in sequence. For example, the following code produces an array in which each element has a string as a name, and then sets a series of variables to the values of each named string:

```
$my_named_array = array("dog" => "rover", "cat" => "pinky", "hamster" =>
"fluffball");
$my_dog = $my_named_array["dog"];
$my_cat = $my_named_array["cat"];
$my_hamster = $my_named_array["hamster"];
echo "My dog is named $my_dog, my cat is named $my_cat,
  and my hamster is named $my_hamster";
```

The capability to access a value by name is important because you don't need to have any idea what the sequence of values or the actual index number is—you only need to know the name you gave to that element. When using strings as array indexes, it's best to use quotes around the array names. Although it's easy and convenient to leave the quotes off, the online documentation warns against this practice, anticipating the time when the quotes become mandatory and not using quotes will break your code.

If you wanted to, you could still use the index number instead of the names you've assigned, because PHP arrays always keep index numbers as well as any assigned names, so the following code would work exactly the same as the last example:

```
$my_named_array = array("dog" => "rover", "cat" => "pinky",
"hamster" => "fluffball");
$my_dog = $my_named_array[0];
$my_cat = $my_named_array[1];
$my_hamster = $my_named_array[2];
echo "My dog is named $my_dog, my cat is named $my_cat,
  and my hamster is named $my_hamster";
```

Initializing Arrays

You can *initialize* (create and set initial values for) arrays in a number of ways. For example, you can use the `array()` function, as you've already done or you can end a variable name with square brackets (`[]`). Writing a variable name and placing empty square brackets at the end causes PHP to decide that you intend to create an array, and to begin to increment the index from zero if it is the first element in the array, as shown here:

```
$my_array[] = "first element";
```

If you want to give the element a name, just put it inside the square brackets, like so:

```
$my_array["first"] = "another_first element";
```

If you used `$my_array["first"]` again, PHP would overwrite the value you just assigned instead of creating a new element. If you use `$my_array[]` again, PHP would assign an index number (the next one in sequence) and create a new element on your array.

An interesting thing about arrays: a single array can hold many different values, each of a different type as required by your program (the indexes for each element can be only strings or integers). This means you really can use an array to hold data much like a record in a database table holds data.

Working with Arrays

Sometimes after creating and initializing an array (especially with values from a record in a database table) it can be a bit difficult to know what those values might be, and therefore hard to debug your code. Fortunately, the `print_r()` function enables you to print out the entire list contained in an array, along with the names of each indexed element. To follow along with this example, create a simple HTML page and embed the following PHP code in it:

```php
<?php
$my_named_array = array("dog" => "rover", "cat" => "pinky",
 "hamster" => "fluffball");
print_r($my_named_array);
?>
```

Run the file in your browser. Figure 2-4 shows the result.

Using `print_r` is very helpful if you want to look at all the contents of an array. In Chapter 4 you'll learn about specialized loops, which also provide very easy access to all the values in an array.

Arrays are real workhorses in PHP, as in many other languages, and PHP comes complete with many built-in functions specifically for working with arrays. You'll explore a couple of the most used functions here, and begin to work with them more in Chapters 3 and 4; you'll notice that many of them are similar to functions you can use on databases.

There are often times when you don't know how many elements are in an array, but you can use the `count()` function to count them (or the elements in any variable for that matter), like this:

```
$number_of_elements = count($my_array);
```

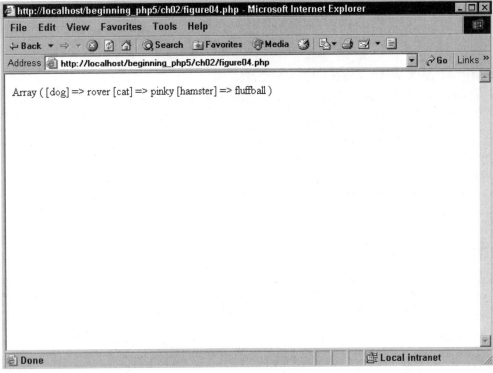

Figure 2-4

The `array_count_values()` function is not quite the same, because it returns (as an array) the frequency of occurrence of matching values in the array used as an argument to it. The element names in `$returned_array` are the values in `$argument_array`, and the values in `$returned_array` are the number of times the value occurred in the `$argument_array`. This may be this easier to understand by reading the following code:

```
$argument_array = array("dog", "dog", "cat", "cat", "hamster");
$returned_array = array_count_values($argument_array);
print_r($returned_array);
```

This prints out:

```
Array
(
    [dog] => 2
    [cat] => 2
    [hamster] => 1
)
```

The `array_flip()` function is useful when you need to swap values for key names and vice versa. For example, if you have a list of people's names as element names in an array, and the value of each is a SSN (Social Security number), you may want to flip the array so you can access each person by his SSN (because the SSN should be unique, although their names may be duplicated in some cases). You could accomplish this using the following code:

```
$my_people_array = array("John" => "555-66-7777", John => "444-55-3333");
$my_ssn_array = array_flip($my_people_array);
```

You could then use $my_ssn_array to look people up uniquely, even though John appears twice.

Sorting Arrays With sort() and asort()

It's often convenient to sort the elements in an array, such as when you want to produce a list of names in alphabetical order, and you can do just that with the sort() function. If you want to maintain the order of the indexes, use asort(). The sort function rebuilds the indexes into the proper order whereas changing the order of the element values, but asort() keeps the indexes stuck to their element values. The code can be written:

```
$my_unsorted_array = array("Jim", "Bob", "Mary");
$my_sorted_array = sort($my_unsorted_array);
$my_sorted_array_with_unchanged_indexes = asort($my_unsorted_array);
```

Summary

In this chapter you learned the basic steps of writing a simple PHP program, how to embed PHP code in HTML (using the correct file extension) and run the program from the Web server, and how to write PHP code correctly (with semicolons, delimiters, backslashes, and so on).

You explored how PHP programs are interpreted by the Zend engine, and how the Web server knows when to send code to it, and you learned that PHP code runs on the server and therefore is not transmitted in source code format to the end user.

Like many programming languages, PHP makes extensive use of variables, but there's no need to declare variables before using them. And although PHP variables are always of some data type, that type need not be explicitly declared, and PHP is always converting data types from one to the other behind the scenes, according to the context in which the data is used.

You examined some of the built-in PHP functions for working with strings and numbers, as well as arrays, and you created a few example pages to see how the code works in practice. But as you might imagine, you've only just begun to build the simplest PHP programs; Chapter 3 sheds a lot of light on how "real" PHP programs are constructed, and gets into HTTP and HTML forms in great detail.

Exercises

1. Create a PHP program that rearranges sentence one into sentence two, and outputs what it is doing (and the result) to the user. The two sentences are:

    a. now is the time for all good men to come to the aid of their country

    b. the time is now to come to the aid of good men in the country

2. Create a PHP program that creates two arrays of numbers and adds the values in each array to their corresponding values by index number. The two arrays should have the following values:

    a. 2,4,6,8,10

    b. 3,5,7,9,11

PHP, HTML, and State

By now you're familiar with HTTP, simple PHP programs, variables, and some of the PHP built-in functions, and although you can do a lot with what you've already learned, there's a key ingredient missing: user interaction! That's what this chapter is all about, at least as far as Web-based applications are concerned.

If you remember back before 1994 (a million years ago in Web time), early Web pages consisted of text, images, and links. The backgrounds were gray; there were no tables (much less DHTML and style sheets) to help structure pages; and there was little user interaction. The introduction of HTML elements for forms and form fields opened the door to direct, form-based interaction between the user and the Web server. HTML forms are today one of the most used (and most useful) means for interacting with online applications.

You'll explore HTML forms, but you'll also learn what kinds of data are available in HTTP requests and responses, and how you can use PHP to capture that data and then use it in your programs.

You'll examine the specifics of talking to the Web server (using the GET and POST methods), the format of requests and responses sent between client and server (and all the great data you can extract from them), and the nature of applications running across the Internet. You'll look at the concept of state, the lack of state in HTTP Web communications, and several methods for working around that deficiency. You'll get a look at PHP sessions as well.

HTML Primer

If you're an HTML wizard and have an in-depth understanding of the structure of HTML, you can probably skip this section, but for those of you who've never dissected HTML code or the HTML specification, read on. You'll recall that PHP's "middle name" is hypertext and that alone tells you that PHP is intertwined with HTML (Hypertext Markup Language). Understanding how HTML—particularly the HTML <form> element—works is very important to proficiency with PHP.

HTML was created by Tim Berners-Lee and Robert Caillau in 1989. It is a subset of Standard Generalized Markup Language (SGML). SGML was defined by International Standards in 1986 as ISO 8879:1986. SGML is designed to provide a common format for markup languages. HTML is called an SGML application because it is a language, whereas XML is simply a subset of the SGML specification used to make your own markup languages (more on XML in Chapter 8).

Like most SGML applications, HTML includes a Document Type Definition (DTD) that specifies the syntax of markup elements. You'll see examples of the HTML DTD throughout this primer.

> *The World Wide Web Consortium (W3C) can be found at www.w3.org. This organization maintains the HTML specification (now the XHTML specification). Visit the site and look for the HTML 4.01 specification to see all the elements and attributes.*

HTML is a markup language, not a programming language. The primary purpose of HTML is to display data or content (such as text and images) along with hypertext links. HTML tags (the "commands" in HTML) help the Web page designer arrange the display of text, graphics, and multimedia. The only elements that give something resembling programmatic functionality are used to make tables, links, forms, and frames.

HTML is written in plain text, and when a page is requested all the code is sent in plain text format. Here's a simple HTML Web page (without a body):

```
<html>
<head>
<title>The Title</title>
</head>
</html>
```

> *Although the convention for many years was to write HTML tags uppercase (as in <HTML>), the HTML specification actually has no preference, and you can write conforming HTML tags either way, or even a mixture of upper and lower case (as in <hTmL>). However, the latest standard for HTML is now XHTML, which adheres to the XML specification, so there is a difference between uppercase and lowercase tags. XHTML specifies lowercase for tag names, which is why nearly every HTML tag in this book is lowercase. Browsers won't care whether the tags are uppercase or lowercase, but using lowercase will make it a lot easier to change your HTML to conform to XHTML.*

An HTML Web page is made up of HTML tags, and most (but not all) of these tags have both beginning (opening) and ending (closing) tags. HTML tags are delimited by the angle brackets (<>). An HTML tag is named for the element it represents. For example, the tags <html> and </html> are the opening and closing tags for the HTML element. These tags signify the beginning and ending of the entire HTML document. Within these tags are the tags for the <head> of the document and for the title of the document. Tags contained within other tags are said to be *nested*.

Some HTML elements have only a beginning tag, such as the IMG element. When writing an IMG element (the IMG element inserts an external image file into a Web page) all you write is <img>, without en ending </img>. However, to tell the browser where to find the external image file, you place what is called an *attribute* in the beginning tag. HTML attributes are like fields in a database, or properties in an object, or variables in a program. They have names (such as SRC), and are containers for values. In fact, you set the value of the SRC attribute in the <img> tag to the URL of the image file name (like this: <img SRC="http://www.example.com/images/example.gif">). When the user's browser receives the HTML of the Web page, the browser reads the HTML, finds the URL of the image file, requests that file as well, and then inserts the file into the rendered Web page at the appropriate spot.

The HTML Document Type Definition

A DTD declares what elements and attributes (and a few other things) that are allowed in an HTML document. Although an HTML document is made up of HTML tags, the HTML DTD uses a special format to specify what elements and attributes you can use. For example, because the HTML DTD specifies an IMG element, you can use the IMG element in a Web page.

But it's still up to the maker of your browser to properly recognize and display elements and attributes specified in the HTML DTD. In fact, deviations from the HTML specification are the primary reason a Web page may look (and work) fine in one browser and not in another.

Technically, HTML documents should start with a line indicating the DTD to be used, contained within the <!DOCTYPE> element. The DOCTYPE declaration indicates to the browser the proper DTD to use, but the inclusion of this line is not enforced by browsers. Many Web pages have no DOCTYPE declaration, but are still rendered correctly in browsers. Here's a DOCTYPE declaration inserted by Dreamweaver (a popular Web page design tool):

```
<!DOCTYPE HTML PUBLIC "-//W3C//DTD HTML 4.01 Transitional//EN">
```

The Form and Input Elements

One of the primary HTML elements you'll be working with is the <form> element. Take a look at how it's specified in the HTML DTD:

```
<!ELEMENT FORM - - (%block;|SCRIPT)+ -(FORM) -- interactive form -->
<!ATTLIST FORM
  %attrs;                           -- %coreattrs, %i18n, %events --
  action       %URI;         #REQUIRED -- server-side form handler --
  method       (GET|POST)       GET    -- HTTP method used to submit the form --
  enctype      %ContentType;  "application/x-www-form-urlencoded"
  accept       %ContentTypes; #IMPLIED  -- list of MIME types for file upload --
  name         CDATA          #IMPLIED  -- name of form for scripting --
  onsubmit     %Script;       #IMPLIED  -- the form was submitted --
  onreset      %Script;       #IMPLIED  -- the form was reset --
  accept-charset %Charsets;   #IMPLIED  -- list of supported charsets --
  >
```

The DTD for <form> begins with a line that names it as an element, and then specifies a list of attributes (ATTLIST). Notice the action attribute, which tells the browser where to send the contents of the form, and the method attribute, which tells the browser how to send the contents of the form.

The <input> element makes text fields, radio buttons, check boxes, and so on in a form. Here's its DTD:

```
<!ENTITY % InputType
  "(TEXT | PASSWORD | CHECKBOX |
    RADIO | SUBMIT | RESET |
    FILE | HIDDEN | IMAGE | BUTTON)"
  >
<!-- attribute name required for all but submit and reset -->
<!ELEMENT INPUT - O EMPTY             -- form control -->
```

```
<!ATTLIST INPUT
   %attrs;                                -- %coreattrs, %i18n, %events --
   type          %InputType; TEXT         -- what kind of widget is needed --
   name          CDATA        #IMPLIED -- submit as part of form --
   value         CDATA        #IMPLIED -- Specify for radio buttons and
checkboxes
   --
   checked       (checked)    #IMPLIED -- for radio buttons and check boxes --
   disabled      (disabled)   #IMPLIED -- unavailable in this context --
   readonly      (readonly)   #IMPLIED -- for text and passwd --
   size          CDATA        #IMPLIED -- specific to each type of field --
   maxlength     NUMBER       #IMPLIED -- max chars for text fields --
   src           %URI;        #IMPLIED -- for fields with images --
   alt           CDATA        #IMPLIED -- short description --
   usemap        %URI;        #IMPLIED -- use client-side image map --
   ismap         (ismap)      #IMPLIED -- use server-side image map --
   tabindex      NUMBER       #IMPLIED -- position in tabbing order --
   accesskey     %Character;  #IMPLIED -- accessibility key character --
   onfocus       %Script;     #IMPLIED -- the element got the focus --
   onblur        %Script;     #IMPLIED -- the element lost the focus --
   onselect      %Script;     #IMPLIED -- some text was selected --
   onchange      %Script;     #IMPLIED -- the element value was changed --
   accept        %ContentTypes; #IMPLIED -- list of MIME types for file upload --
   >
```

The type attribute of the element specifies the type of control that will appear on the screen in your browser (text makes a text field, radio makes a radio button, and so on).

To create a Web page with a form in it, you could write the following HTML code in plain text, upload it to a Web server (or even just open it directly in your browser), and it would display as a nicely formatted Web page:

```
<html>
<head>
<title>
</title>
</head>
<body bgcolor="white">
<form method="post" action="http://www.example.com">
Username:<input type="text" name="username"><br>
Password:<input type="password" name="password"><br>
<input type="submit" value="Login">
</form>
</body>
</html>
```

This code creates a simple form with two fields (username and password) and a submit button. When submitted, the form's contents are sent to www.example.com.

How can you make HTML forms and PHP work together to make Web pages that are dynamically generated (rather than simply copied to your browser by the Web server)? First, you create a Web page using plain text HTML tags, and include an HTML form within that page. Then, you write PHP code within the Web page, making sure the code is properly enclosed by the <?php and ?> delimiters.

When the Web page is requested by a browser, any PHP code in it is resolved or processed by the PHP scripting engine before the results are returned to the user, and the results of PHP processing are placed in exactly the same spot as the original PHP code. You also could write your code so that it is only processed when there is a form submission (you'll see how in the next few sections). It may even use some of the submitted form data in its processing.

The end result of the PHP processing is HTML compatible, but because the PHP scripting engine has a chance to perform some processing before the final version of the Web page is sent, some of the content of the page (any parts generated by the PHP code) may differ each time the page is requested. And if processing takes place in response to a form submission, there are a great variety of interactive features that can be created.

Accessing PHP and HTTP Data

You know how HTTP works and you basically understand clients and servers, so you're very cognizant of the interaction between your browser (a client application) and the Web server (a server application) when running PHP programs online. In this chapter you explore HTML forms and examine how they facilitate user interactions with the Web server (and thereby your PHP programs). These topics deserve a lot of attention because HTTP, HTML, and PHP are tightly intertwined. A good understanding of what's going on between the browser and the server is essential for PHP programming because within the requests and responses flying back and forth from client to server is a wealth of data you can utilize.

Each time you click a link or submit a form, you send a great deal of data about your system and your browser to the Web server, and each time the Web server responds, it sends you a great deal of data about itself. PHP has the capability to capture the data that is submitted by a browser, and also provides a means of getting at data about PHP's installation on the server. For instance, if you go to your favorite PHP-driven Web site and log in, it's likely that a predefined variable named $_POST is filled (on the server) with your username and password, another predefined variable named $_SERVER contains information about the current Web server environment, and that both are available to the PHP application running the site. These aspects of PHP are discussed in depth in the next few sections, but it's really kind of surprising how much data is available (especially considering that most folks aren't even aware of it). Read on to learn how to access all this data.

Predefined Variables

PHP automatically makes quite a few variables (called *predefined variables*) available anywhere in your program. They are array variables, and you can access them by name, like any other variable. By default, PHP is configured not to populate these variables (in the php.ini file, the default register_globals =Off is in place), you must use their entire name to access their data. For example, if a form has a text field named username and this field is filled out and submitted (and assuming the form's submission method is POST), you can access the field's data by code such as this:

```
$my_new_username = $_POST[username];
```

Predefined variables are also called *superglobal* variables because they can be accessed without regard to scope. Predefined variables consist of most of the information contained in HTTP requests and responses, including server variables, query strings, form variables, and so on. You can use predefined variables for any purpose, just like ordinary variables, but some of them may or may not be present for any given installation of PHP because Web servers vary in the data provided via HTTP. In the next section you'll see how to retrieve the data in predefined variables.

In addition to predefined variables, you can use the built-in PHP function `phpinfo()` to get basic PHP installation and operating information. This function not only enables you to test whether PHP is installed and working (as you saw in Chapter 1), but also enables you to find out many details about how PHP is installed on the server. For example, you can find out what version of PHP is running, what OS your server is running on, and so forth.

Perhaps an easier way to demonstrate what you get from the `phpinfo()` function is simply to run the `test01.php` file created in Chapter 1 again. This time you're running it not just to see if the installation of PHP worked (as you did in Chapter 1) but to examine the various kinds of data it provides. When run from your Web server, `phpinfo()` creates a very nicely formatted and detailed page (including all the required HTML tags) describing the PHP version, operating system, version of the ZEND engine, settings in your `php.ini` file, additional modules, and predefined variables, as shown in Figure 3-1.

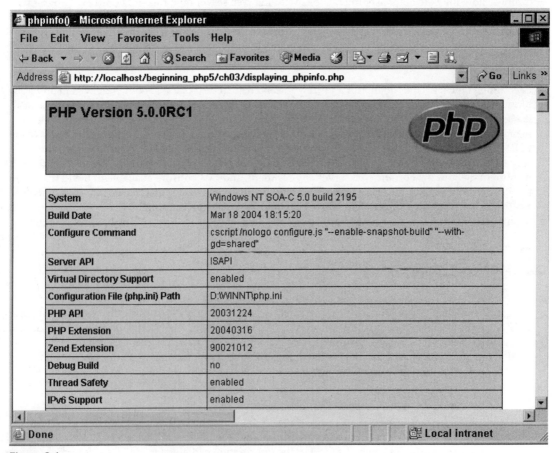

Figure 3-1

Variables in HTTP Request and Response

There's a surprising amount of data passed back and forth between the client and the Web server (and vice versa). For example, not only is the IP address of the client passed to the Web server with each request (not actually very surprising, as how else would the Web server know where to send the response) but also details about what version of browser is making the request, cookies, form data, Web server version, and so on. The data is contained in predefined variables structured as associative arrays, so that you can access them by name, just like you would access any other array. The contents of each and what you might want to use them for are presented after the following "Try It Out."

There is a setting in your configuration file (php.ini) called register_globals. The default is off (since PHP4.2), and it restricts how you can access some predefined variables. From a practical standpoint, this means you should use the full name of the array ($_SERVER['DOCUMENT_ROOT'] is the example given) to access data in predefined variables. There is the function (import_request_variables()) that will import GET, POST, and Cookie variables into the global scope, so you can access them directly by name, but the full array name is recommended and therefore used in this book.

Try It Out   Display $GLOBALS

The following code demonstrates displaying the contents of the $GLOBALS predefined variable. The code goes inside a nicely formatted HTML Web page:

```php
<?php
echo "<pre>";
print_($GLOBALS);
echo "</pre>";
?>
```

Run this code in your browser (name the file displaying_predefined_vars.php) and you'll see what the $GLOBALS array contains. Don't be too surprised if they all turn out to be empty at the moment. However, at the end of this section is a figure showing what the predefined variables look like when displayed.

Don't forget to place the file in the appropriate folder that's published by your Web server. From here on out it's assumed that you've created any Web server-accessible folders you want and are placing your files in them as needed.

How It Works

The print_r() function prints out information about variables in a format that is easy for people to read. It's especially useful with arrays because it prints the keys and values one after the other. Use it with the HTML <pre> tags so it prints nicely on the page, rather than all on one line.

SuperGlobal Arrays

The predefined arrays are described in the following table. They're called superglobals because they can be accessed form anywhere in a PHP program without having to use the global keyword and without regard for scope.

Array	Description
$GLOBALS	Has a reference to every variable that has global scope in a PHP program. Many of the variables in it are also in other superglobal arrays
$_SERVER	Includes everything sent by server in the HTTP response, such as the name of the currently executing script, server name, version of HTTP, remote IP address, and so on. Although most Web server software produces the same server variables, not all do, and not all server variables necessarily have data in them
$_GET	Contains all the querystring variables that were attached to the URL, or produced as a result of using the GET method
$_POST	Contains all the submitted form variables and their data. You use variables from the $_POST or $_REQUEST arrays extensively in most of your PHP programs. For example, to make use of a username or password (or any other data) submitted as part of a form, you'll use PHP variables from the $_REQUEST array
$_COOKIE	Contains all cookies sent to the server by the browser. They are turned into variables you can read from this array, and you can write cookies to the user's browser using the setcookie() function. Cookies provide a means of identifying a user across page requests (or beyond, depending upon when the cookie expires) and are often used automatically in session handling
$_FILES	Contains any items uploaded to the server when the POST method is used. It's different from the $_POST array because it specifically contains items uploaded (such as an uploaded image file), not the contents of submitted form fields
$_ENV	Contains data about the environment the server and PHP are operating in, such as the computer name, operating system, and system drive
$_REQUEST	Contains the contents of the $_GET, $_POST, and $COOKIE arrays, all in one
$_SESSION	Contains all variables that are currently registered as session variables. Because you have programmatic control over the variables registered in the session, the contents of this array at any given moment depend on what your program does and whether you use sessions

The following code makes a page showing the contents of the SuperGlobal variables just discussed. If you look closely at the code, you'll notice that much of it is the same thing over and over; that's because each variable (with a bit of HTML thrown in for formatting) is being displayed. Save the code as displaying_predefined_vars.php before running it from your browser:

```
<html>
<head>
<title>Untitled Document</title>
<meta http-equiv="Content-Type" content="text/html; charset=iso-8859-1">
</head>
<body bgcolor="#FFFFFF">
<table width="100%" border="1">
  <tr><td colspan="2"><font face="Arial, Helvetica, sans-serif" size=
"-1"><b>Displaying Predefined Variables</b></font></td>
  </tr>
```

```
   <tr><td width="40%" valign="top"><font face="Arial, Helvetica, sans-serif"
size="-1">Globals - $GLOBALS</font></td>
     <td width="60%"><font face="Arial, Helvetica, sans-serif" size="-2">
<?php
echo "<pre>";
print_r($GLOBALS);
echo "</pre>";
?>
</font></td>
   </tr>
   <tr><td width="40%" valign="top"><font face="Arial, Helvetica, sans-serif"
size="-1">Server - $_SERVER</font></td>
     <td width="60%"><font face="Arial, Helvetica, sans-serif" size="-1">
<?php
echo "<pre>";
print_r($_SERVER);
echo "</pre>";
?>
</font></td>
   </tr>
   <tr><td width="40%" valign="top"><font face="Arial, Helvetica, sans-serif"
size="-1">Get - $_GET </font></td>
     <td width="60%"><font face="Arial, Helvetica, sans-serif" size="-1">
<?php
echo "<pre>";
print_r($_GET);
echo "</pre>";
?>
</font></td>
   </tr>
   <tr><td width="40%" valign="top"><font face="Arial, Helvetica, sans-serif"
size="-1">Post - $_POST </font></td>
     <td width="60%"><font face="Arial, Helvetica, sans-serif" size="-1">
<?php
echo "<pre>";
print_r($_POST);
echo "</pre>";
?>
</font></td>
   </tr>
   <tr><td width="40%" valign="top"><font face="Arial, Helvetica, sans-serif"
size="-1">Cookie - $_COOKIE</font></td>
     <td width="60%"><font face="Arial, Helvetica, sans-serif" size="-1">
<?php
echo "<pre>";
print_r($_COOKIE);
echo "</pre>";
?>
</font></td>
   </tr>
   <tr><td width="40%" valign="top"><font face="Arial, Helvetica, sans-serif"
size="-1">Files - $_FILES</font></td>
     <td width="60%"><font face="Arial, Helvetica, sans-serif" size="-1">
<?php
echo "<pre>";
```

```
  print_r($_FILES);
  echo "</pre>";
?>
</font></td>
  </tr>
  <tr><td width="40%" valign="top"><font face="Arial, Helvetica, sans-serif"
size="-1">Environment - $_ENV</font></td>
    <td width="60%"><font face="Arial, Helvetica, sans-serif" size="-1">
<?php
echo "<pre>";
print_r($_ENV);
echo "</pre>";
?>
</font></td>
  </tr>
  <tr><td width="40%" valign="top"><font face="Arial, Helvetica, sans-serif"
size="-1">Request - $_REQUEST</font></td>
    <td width="60%"><font face="Arial, Helvetica, sans-serif" size="-1">
<?php
echo "<pre>";
print_r($_REQUEST);
echo "</pre>";
?>
</font></td>
  </tr>
  <tr><td width="40%" valign="top"><font face="Arial, Helvetica, sans-serif"
size="-1">Session - $_SESSION</font></td>
    <td width="60%"><font face="Arial, Helvetica, sans-serif" size="-1">
<?php
echo "<pre>";
print_r($_SESSION);
echo "</pre>";
?>
</font></td>
  </tr>
</table>
</body>
</html>
```

When you run this page on the server, you'll see something like Figure 3-2.

Links

If you've ever done any Web page design or programming, you're undoubtedly familiar with the structure of a link in HTML. In technical terms, an HTML link uses the anchor element (whose starting and ending tags are <a> and </a>), and one of its main attributes, href, which has a URL as its value. Text or images placed inside the beginning and ending <a> tags make a link that, when clicked, goes to the URL in the href attribute, like this:

```
<a href="http://www.myplace.com">Click Here</a>
```

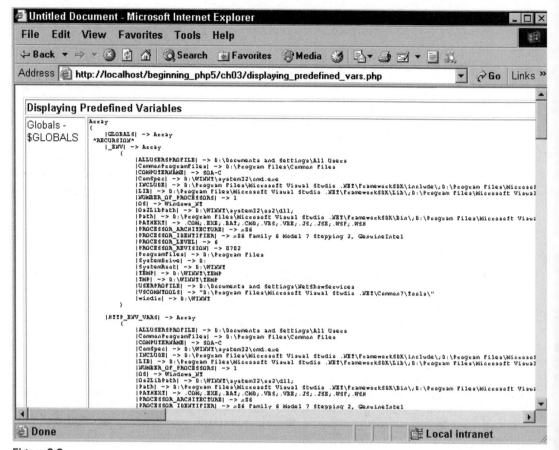

Figure 3-2

So clicking a link is one form of user interaction enabling you to communicate with the server. But it's pretty limited, because all you can do is make a request for the page that's already supplied by the site designer. For example, if I click a link to the About page, the only reason it goes to the right page is because the site designer has already hard-coded the link with the URL for that page.

Query Strings

Somewhat more flexible is the *query string*, which is attached to the end of the URL in a link. A query string can consist of as many *name/value pairs* as you (the developer) want to supply. The big difference is that PHP provides a means by which the user can supply values that can be embedded in the query string. Say, for example, that the user has entered a value of John as his first name, and your PHP program can make use of that value via its variable name ($first_name, for instance).

The term name/value pair is a generic way of referring to any situation in which you have a named container for a value. Name/value pairs include fields in a table in a database, variables, HTML and XML attributes, and so on.

You could write a PHP program that generates a query string attached to a URL using code such as this (assuming you had the $first_name and $last_name variables already set):

```
<a href="http://www.myplace.com?first_name=<?php echo $first_name; ?>">Click
Here</a>
```

When this code runs, it produces the following output:

```
<a href="http://www.myplace.com?first_name=John">Click Here</a>
```

Notice how a query string is constructed: a question mark followed by the name of the first name/value pair, an equals sign, and the value in the first name/value pair. If you had both a first name and a last name, you could have included both name/value pairs in the query string by connecting them with an ampersand (&), like so:

```
<a href="http://www.myplace.com?first_name=<?php echo $first_name;
?>&last_name=<?php echo $last_name; ?>">Click Here</a>
```

Putting both name/value pairs in the query string would result in the following (if you're a dead movie star):

```
<a href="http://www.myplace.com?first_name=John&last_name=Wayne">Click
Here</a>
```

Query strings are often useful (especially in preserving values between page requests, which are discussed that a bit more later in the chapter), but as you can see they are still quite limited. For one thing, to place a user-supplied value in a query string, you have to already have it. You could get it from a database, but if you needed to get it from the user before using it, you'd have to provide the user with some free form method of supplying it. And that brings us to a very powerful method for user interaction, the HTML form.

HTML (Web) Forms

As previously mentioned, there are two main methods by which you can interact with an online application running within your browser: click a link or submit a form. Clicking a link can request a page from the Web server, and if the application developer included data in a query string, clicking the link also sends that data. However, when you fill out a form and submit it, you have a much richer opportunity to send data to the Web server. Although some of the form fields may be preset (such as data in a query string) others (such as text and textarea fields) give you a great deal of control over the data you send. HTML forms are therefore used extensively to create user interaction capability that mimics the kind of interaction displayed in desktop applications.

HTML Form Elements

The HTML specification describes HTML elements related to forms, including the <form> element (begins and ends a form), the <input> element (makes several types of form field, including text fields, radio buttons, submit buttons, and so on), the <textarea> element (makes a text field with multiple columns and line), and the <select> element (makes drop down and static list boxes).

Each of these elements also has attributes. For example, the <form> element includes an attribute named method. The method attribute can be set to post (like this: method="POST") within the beginning form tag, and it makes the HTTP request's method be POST when the form is submitted.

Although it's common to refer to an HTML element as a tag, the term tag refers only to the beginning or ending HTML delimiter. For example, <p> is the beginning tag of the HTML element P (for paragraph) and </p> is the ending tag of this element. Together, the <p> and </p> tags make up the P element. By the way, the text between them (that is displayed in your browser as a paragraph) is their content.

When properly written, HTML form elements combine to create a very powerful means of user interaction for online applications. In the following sections each form field element and its attributes are discussed in detail.

The <form> Element

What happens when you submit a form in HTML? The user fills out the various text boxes and clicks a Submit button when ready; the information that is supplied is then bundled up in one of the two ways and sent to the Web server. The Web server can then pull out this information, and supply it to the PHP script engine. PHP manipulates this information and sends it back as part of the HTTP response to the browser. All you need to do to make a form is create a pure HTML Web page with opening and closing <form> tags. Any controls such as text field, check boxes, and radio buttons that are placed between the <form> tags, automatically become part of the form that is sent to the Web server. For example:

```
<form name="myform" action="myform_processor.php" method="POST">
<input type="text" name="first_name">
<input type="submit" name="button" value="Send Response">
</form>
```

In this example, the form is named myform, and when it's submitted it sends the request (using the POST method) and all the data filled out by the user to the PHP file named myform_processor.php for processing. Of course you can send the request to any page or file you choose, even back to the page the user is currently on, keeping in mind that the page being requested should have code for accepting the data sent and working with it.

The first <input> element uses the type attribute to specify the type of form field to display, in this case a text box. Although the name of the form (myform) is not very important in this example, the name of the first <input> element is extremely important, because PHP automatically makes a variable named $first_name from the name you give the <input> element, and sets that variable equal to the value entered in the field by the user. The variable is part of the $_GET or $_POST array, depending upon the submission method you set for the form.

The second <input> element has a type of submit, so it renders as a Submit button. The value attribute is set to Send Response, so it displays a caption of Send Response on top of the Submit button. Neither its name nor value is very important in this example (so far as PHP processing is concerned), but you should know that both the name and value are available to your PHP program for processing when the form is submitted.

Essentially, when a user fills out the form and submits it, the names and values of the form fields become variables available to the receiving PHP program (specified in the action attribute of the <form>

element). When you understand that, the full range of user interaction with HTML forms becomes apparent.

Here are a few tidbits of useful information about HTML forms:

❑ You can have more than one form in a single Web page, and each one (and its form fields) can be submitted independent of the others.

❑ Names are not generally important for forms, unless you are using JavaScript to decide which one to work with or submit.

❑ Values submitted in forms are always strings, although once they get to your PHP program they may be converted to any data type as you use them.

❑ Not all form field names and values become available to your PHP program when a form is submitted. For example, only the value of the selected radio button (in a group of radio buttons) is submitted.

Attributes of the <form> Element

The <form> element has a whole host of attributes, but you can get by using only two of them, action and method. Other attributes, such as id, class, dir, lang, language, name, style, and title are universal to most or all HTML tags, and shouldn't need further explanation. The more obscure attributes accept-char and enctype, which specify the character sets and the mime-type of the form data are outside the scope of this overview, although you'll learn more about enctype in Chapter 7. There is also a target attribute that, like its namesake in the <a> element, enables you to specify a frame or window in which to display the Web page that is sent back in response to the form's submission.

The action Attribute

The action attribute tells the server which page to go to once the user has clicked a submit button on the form. It doesn't matter whether this page is pure HTML, PHP, or uses any server-side technology, as long as the page exists on the Web server. It can be used as follows to link to an HTML page:

```
<form action="myprogram.php">
...
</form>
```

However, when you supply a PHP page as part of the action attribute, what you're actually doing is sending the information entered into this form to the PHP script engine for processing, thereby allowing your PHP application on the server to work with user-supplied data. The action attribute just tells the server which page to go to next—if you saved the earlier page as myprogram.html instead of myprogram.php, the page wouldn't be sent to the PHP script engine and nothing at all would be displayed unless PHP has been configured to parse .html files. Later you'll see what the PHP script engine does when it receives the form.

The method Attribute

The method attribute controls the way that information is sent to the server. As mentioned previously, it can do this in one of the two ways, using either the GET or the POST methods (they are case-insensitive, but the convention is uppercase). The GET method is the default; you use these methods as shown here:

```
<form action="myprogram.php" method="GET">
```

or

```
<form action="myprogram.php" method="POST">
```

There are actually more than two values you can supply to the `method` attribute: HEAD, PUT, LINK, UNLINK, OPTIONS, DELETE, TRACE, and CONNECT. However, these options are not commonly used, and you rarely need to use them, so there's no further discussion of them here. You will, however, want to take a closer look at GET and POST.

The GET Value

The GET value of the `method` attribute tells the browser to append the values the user placed on the form to the URL. Like the query string attached to a URL in a link, the browser adds a question mark to the end of the URL to denote where the URL finishes and the form information starts. The information entered into the form is then transmitted as name/value pairs. If the GET method is specified in the `method` attribute of the `<form>` element, the browser automatically appends the information to the URL when it sends the page request to the Web server.

And just like a query string in a link, you can add more than one name/value pair to a URL if you separate each pair with an ampersand (&). With two name/value pairs, the end of the URL might look like this after being submitted:

```
http://www.nonexistentserver.com/test.php?furryanimal=cat&spikyanimal=porcupine
```

To conform with the XHTML specification, you would want to replace the ampersand with `&amp;`, which is the appropriate XML entity for an ampersand, so your URL and query string would look like this:

```
http://www.nonexistentserver.com/test.php?furryanimal=cat&amp;spikyanimal=
porcupine
```

As mentioned earlier, the name/value pairs are very similar to variables. In fact, once they have been passed to the Web server for processing, PHP makes them available as variables. So, if you submitted your form to the Web server, and moved to another page, the name/value pairs would be available in the PHP script as variables (as part of the `$_GET` array).

Occasionally, you might want to pass spaces in the values that make up the query string. For instance, if you have a form that includes a `<textarea>` element and someone had typed in the line, "I would like to see a dynamic menu in operation," there are several spaces that need to be represented. In this case the addition operator would replace the spaces, as shown here:

```
http://localgost/beginning_php5/ch03/form.php?TextArea=I+would+like+to+see+a+
dynamic+menu+in+operation
```

Some of you are wondering, "But what happens if you want to put an addition operator in the `<textarea>`? How is that represented within a query string?" The character or operator in question has to be replaced by a code, which signifies the particular character. This is known as URL encoding.

URL Encoding

There is a set of characters that can't appear in a URL, and therefore by association, can't appear in a query string either, so they have to be URL encoded.

The encoding process requires you, the user or developer, to do precisely nothing. It's all done for you. The Web browser takes the offending character, whether a bracket or an addition sign, and replaces it with a code value (when sending to the server), and takes the URL encoded value and replaces it with the appropriate character (when displaying in your screen). The URL encoded value is always the same (for example, a blank space is always be represented by %20). The following table lists the most common characters and their code values.

Character	URL Encoding
Tab	%09
Space	%20
!	%21
"	%22
#	%23
%	%25
&	%26
(	%28
)	%29
+	%2B
,	%2C
.	%2E
/	%2F
:	%3A
;	%3B
<	%3C
>	%3E
=	%3D
?	%3F
@	%40
\	%5C

Some of these characters have to be encoded, or they would adopt another meaning in the query string (as you saw earlier, the addition operator is used to denote a space in the query string, and the question mark denotes the start of a query string).

The previous query string with the URL code value for a space in place of the addition operator would look like this:

```
http://localgost/beginning_php5/ch03/form.php?TextArea=I%20would%20like%20
to%20see%20a%20dynamic%20menu%20in%20operation
```

You'll see an example of GET in action a little later. For now, take a look at POST.

The POST Value

One disadvantage you might have discerned from query strings is the rather public nature of their transmission. If you don't want the information sent to appear in the URL, then you will have to rely on the POST method instead. This works almost identically to the GET method; the difference is that the information in the form is sent in the body of the HTTP request, rather than as part of the URL. This means that it isn't visible to everybody, because it isn't attached to the URL. POST can also allow a greater amount of information to be transmitted. There is a physical limit to the amount you can transmit as part of a URL.

Do You Use GET or POST?

There's a mixture of opinion on this one; some people say you should almost never use the GET method because of its insecurity and limit on size; others maintain that you can use GET to retrieve information, but POST should be used whenever you modify data on the Web server. There are no hard and fast rules, though, and these are just guidelines.

One disadvantage of POST is that pages loaded with it cannot be properly bookmarked, while pages loaded with GET contain all the information needed to reproduce the request right in the URL. In many cases you can bookmark the result of a form submission (a search on Alta Vista, for example) by using the GET method, and that's why most search engines use GET. Another disadvantage of POST is that the method itself isn't secure—while the information is placed in the HTTP body and isn't immediately visible, the information isn't encrypted and is still easily obtained by a hacker. To make sure it is secure, you would need to use a secure connection to a secure server.

Which method you use depends on what you want the form to do. If you do use GET, be aware of its shortcomings and its indiscreet nature. If you use POST, beware that it can't be bookmarked by search engines, and just because it is more discreet doesn't mean it is more secure.

HTML Form Fields (Controls) and PHP

With an understanding of the process under your belt, you're ready to look at the most common HTML form field controls you can use to collect information in a form, and see how you can use PHP to get at this information afterward. By the way, you can use the terms *form field*, *control*, and *form element* interchangeably; they all mean the same thing.

All of the following examples in this section will require two Web pages. The first page retrieves information posted by the user, and the second sends the information from the Web server and scripting engine back to the browser. Note that it is entirely possible to combine a form and it's response into a single file, but this gets cumbersome when your programs become a bit more complex. In fact, PHP programs often contain many files making up an application.

The first Web page doesn't have to contain any PHP script at all. In fact, on many sites, the Web page that contains the form will be pure HTML and will have the suffix .htm or .html. That's the format for all of the following examples (although later on, as your applications become more complex, the format will deviate quite a bit). Obviously there is no need to send any information to the PHP scripting engine, because if it contains no PHP, then this will just add overhead (add to the time it takes to process and generate the Web page to be returned to the browser).

Let's get started by looking at the most common HTML form controls.

Text Fields (Text Boxes)

Text fields or text boxes are probably one of the most familiar controls you will come across on any form. They are created using the `<input>` element and by setting the `type` attribute to text.

```
<input type="Text" name="TextBox1">
```

Their advantage is that they can take whole sentences of text from the user. This makes them ideal for open-ended questions, where there can be a vast and unpredictable range of possible answers.

Back to the practical side of things, the following example is a Web page in which you take the user's favorite author and display it to the screen on the next page.

Try It Out   Use Text Fields

1. Open your text editor and type in the following HTML:

```
<html>
<head><title></title></head>
<body>
<form method="GET" action="text.php">
Who is your favorite author?
<input name="Author" type="text">
<br>
<br>
<input type="submit" value="submit">
</form>
</body>
</html>
```

2. Save it as text.html, and close the file.

3. Start a new file in your editor and type the following code:

```
<html>
<head><title</title></head>
<body>
Your favorite author is:
<?php
echo $_GET['Author'];
?>
</body>
</html>
```

4. Save it as `text.php`, and close the file.

5. Open `text.html` in your browser and type a name in the text box (see Figure 3-3).

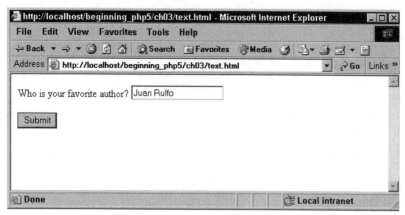

Figure 3-3

6. Click the Submit button, and the author name you supplied is displayed (see Figure 3-4).

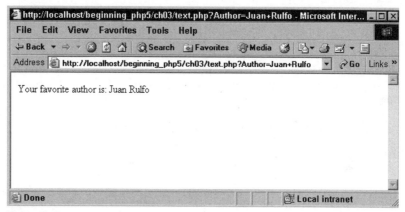

Figure 3-4

How It Works

First of all, note the URL at the top of the screen in Figure 3-4. A query string has been appended to the end of the page named `text.php`. That was added by the Web browser, because you instructed it to do so in the program `text.html` with the following HTML:

```
<html>
<head></head>
<body>
<form method="GET" action="text.php">
Who is your favorite author?
...
```

Setting the method attribute to GET has passed the form information as a query string, rather than hiding it. Take a look at the query string at the top of Figure 3-4. It reads:

```
?Author=Juan+Rulfo
```

You already know that query strings are made up from name/value pairs. In this example, Author is the name and Juan Rulfo is the value in this example. The query string picks up Author as its name from the following highlighted line in your first program, text.html:

```
Who is your favorite author?
<input name="Author" type="text">
<br>
```

The name attribute of the <input> tag has set this control to have the name Author. You added the value when you entered the name of your favorite author in the text field.

The second program, text.php, is actually one line of text, followed by one line of PHP:

```
Your favorite author is:
<?php
echo $_GET['Author'];
?>
```

The line of PHP displays the contents of the variable called $_GET['Author']. Nowhere within the code have you physically created this variable; it's automatically part of the $_GET array. What you've created is an HTML text box and given it the name Author. When the form went to the Web server and the PHP script engine, the PHP engine created the $_GET array with a variable named $Author. If you'd called your text box Name, then your variable would have been called $_GET['Name']. That's all this example program does.

Why This Example Might Not Be Working for You

If the query string is passed, but it fails to return an author name (see Figure 3-5) or returns with a warning, you've most likely confused the cases in your two programs:

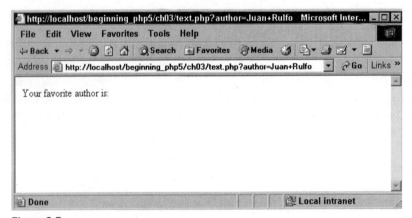

Figure 3-5

If, for example, you had the following line in text.html, with a lowercase a:

```
<input name="author" type="text">
```

whereas in text.php you had $_GET['Author'] with an upper case A:

```
echo $_GET['Author'];
```

the program will break because variable names in PHP are case-sensitive. Although HTML itself isn't case-sensitive, PHP is taking the variable name from the name you assigned to the HTML text field, so it is creating the PHP variable $_GET['author'], not $_GET['Author']. You must make sure that the name of the HTML text field and the name you use in your PHP script are absolutely identical, case and all.

Text Areas

If you want to have a text field that allows multiple lines to be typed, you need a completely different HTML control: the <textarea> element. Use the element's attributes to set the size and number of rows and columns of the control, among other features. For example,

```
<textarea name="WebSites" rows="30" cols="50">
```

creates a text area named WebSites whose size is 30 rows by 50 columns. A text area is designed to take whole sentences from the user. Its advantage is that you can set the size, and it can take many lines of text. <textarea> requires a closing tag, and you can place default text for each line inside the tags.

Ready to try using a text area?

Try It Out   Use Text Area

1.   Start your Web page editor and type the following:

```
<html>
<head><title></title></head>
<body>
<form method="POST" action="textarea.php">
What are your favorite web sites?
<textarea name="WebSites" cols="50" rows="5">
http://
http://
http://
http://
</textarea>
<br>
<br>
<br>
<input type="submit" value="Submit">
</form>
</body>
</html>
```

2.   Save it as textarea.html. Close the file.

3. Create another file and type the following:

```
<html>
<head><title></title></head>
<body>
Your favorite web sites are:
<?php
echo $_POST['WebSites'];
?>
</body>
</html>
```

4. Save this as `textarea.php`.

5. Open `textarea.html` in your browser (see Figure 3-6) and type in the URLs of some of your favorite Web sites.

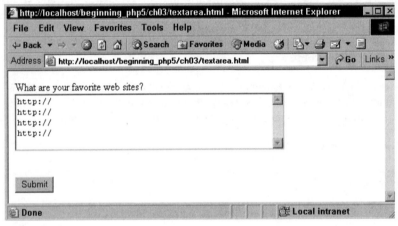

Figure 3-6

6. When you're finished (you don't have to fill in all four sites), click the Submit button. Figure 3-7 shows a result that should be something like yours.

How It Works

Not quite as neat and tidy as the previous example, is it? But don't let that distract you from an important point, which is the URL that reads:

```
http://localgost/beginning_php5/ch03/textarea.php
```

There's no query string attached. And that's because in the first of these two programs you set method to equal POST.

```
<html>
<head><title></title></head>
<body>
```

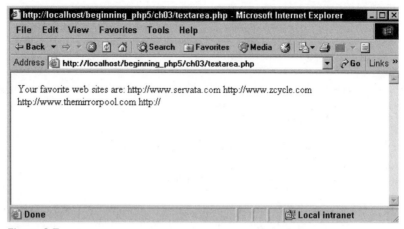

Figure 3-7

```
<form method="POST" action="textarea.php">
What are your favorite web sites?
...
```

You needed to make that change to ensure that your form details aren't freely visible. There's little else of particular interest on the Web page, apart from the `<textarea>` element:

```
<textarea name="WebSites" cols="50" rows="5">
http://
http://
http://
http://
</textarea>
```

It's set to be five rows high, and 50 columns across to get it to the size you need. Unlike in normal HTML, the text inside the `<textarea>` element doesn't require line breaks (the `<br>` tag); it's enough to start it on a new line to get it displayed on a new line. The name of the textarea control is set to `WebSites`, and then in the second program (`textarea.php`), this variable is referenced in PHP as `$WebSites`, once again taking care to ensure the cases are identical:

```
...
Your favorite web sites are:
<?php
echo $_POST['WebSites'];
?>
...
```

The entire contents of the `<textarea>` element are then dumped to the screen, but the carriage returns that separated them in the HTML page are automatically collapsed by the browser, along with any extra white space, to make the details fit in.

Check Boxes

A check box is another control that, like a text field, is created in HTML using the `<input>` element. It provides a single box that can be ticked or not, depending on the option chosen. It doesn't require any data from the user, other than a click in the check box, so any data this control contains is quite different from the text field. In HTML it looks very similar—the only difference is the type:

```
<input name="Choice" type="checkbox">
```

A check box is appropriate when you have a question that requires a strict yes/no answer. Check boxes also have a checked attribute, which takes no value. Supply this attribute in the control and the check box will be checked by default:

```
<input name="Choice" type="checkbox" checked>
```

The control also has a value attribute set to on by default.

Some of the advantages of check boxes over other forms of input control aren't immediately obvious, but they become clear after you've used several of them. The following exercise utilizes just one check box and returns the contents of it to the screen.

Try It Out   Use a Check Box

1.   In you Web page editor type the following code:

```
<html>
<head><title></title></head>
<body>
<form method="POST" action="checkbox.php">
Have you ever eaten haggis before?
<input name="Choice" type="checkbox">
<br>
<br>
<input type="submit" value="Submit">
</form>
</body>
</html>
```

2.   Save it as checkbox.html, and close the file

3.   Start a new file and type in the following:

```
<html>
<head><title></title></head>
<body>
<?php
echo $_POST['Choice'];
?>
</body>
</html>
```

4.   Save it as checkbox.php, and close the file.

5.   Open checkbox.html in your browser and check the check box as shown in Figure 3-8.

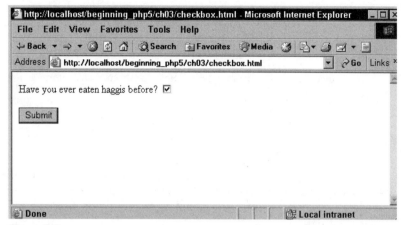

Figure 3-8

6. Click Submit. The choice echoed out is "on," as shown in Figure 3-9.

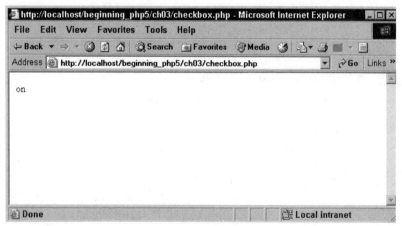

Figure 3-9

7. Click your browser's Back button, uncheck the check box, and click Submit again. Because the box was unchecked this time, nothing shows up in the browser.

How It Works

Again, there's no query string on the end of the URL because you used the POST method to pass your form information to the Web server. You set this in the first of the two programs, checkbox.html:

```
<html>
<head><title></title></head>
<body>
<form method="POST" action="checkbox.php">
```

The check box form control is created with the <input> element:

```
Have you ever eaten haggis before?
<input name="Choice" type="checkbox">
```

In checkbox.php, you call the PHP variable, which has exactly the same name as the control you set in checkbox.html:

```
<?php
echo $_POST['Choice'];
?>
```

The only difference is that the variable is now created with a value that wasn't assigned by you. If the check box was ticked by the user, then it contains the value on. If it wasn't, then it contains nothing at all.

Multiple Check Boxes

What happens if you want to use more than one check box? If you're familiar with radio buttons, you know that selecting one radio button in a group of radio buttons automatically moves the choice from whatever button was selected before to your current selection. Check boxes don't work like that, and their advantage is that each check box is counted as an individual entity—you can have several check boxes ticked, or you can have none checked at all.

Let's modify the previous example to include several check boxes.

Try It Out   **Use Multiple Check Boxes**

1.   Open your Web page editor and save the following as checkboxes.html:

```
<html>
<head><title></title></head>
<body>
<form method="POST" action="checkboxes.php">
Have you ever eaten haggis before?
<input name="Choice1" type="checkbox" value="Haggis">
<br>
Have you ever eaten snails before?
<input name="Choice2" type="checkbox" value="Snails">
<br>
Have you ever eaten locusts before?
<input name="Choice3" type="checkbox" value="Locusts">
<br>
<br>
<input type="submit" value="Submit">
</form>
</body>
</html>
```

2.   Close the file, then create a new file and type in the following:

```
<html>
<head><title></title></head>
```

```
<body>
<?php
echo "$_POST[Choice1]<br>";
echo "$_POST[Choice2]<br>";
echo "$_POST[Choice3]<br>";
?>
</body>
</html>
```

3. Save the file as `checkboxes.php`.

4. Open `checkboxes.html` in your browser (see Figure 3-10).

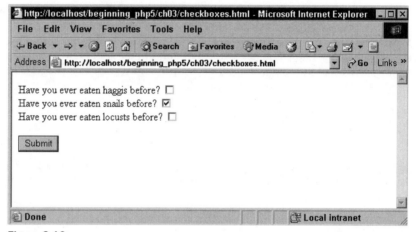

Figure 3-10

5. Select one or more options and click Submit. The program displays your choice(s) (see Figure 3-11).

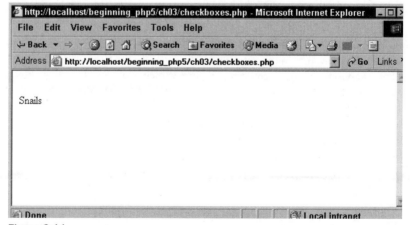

Figure 3-11

How It Works

The `value` attribute for each check box is set in the first program:

```
Have you ever eaten haggis before?
<input name="Choice1" type="checkbox" value="Haggis">
<br>
Have you ever eaten snails before?
<input name="Choice2" type="checkbox" value="Snails">
<br>
Have you ever eaten locusts before?
<input name="Choice3" type="checkbox" value="Locusts">
```

This has the effect of setting a value for each check box after it has been checked. For example, if the Choice1 check box is ticked, it will have the value of Haggis (rather than the default on), and that value is then passed on to the $Choice1 variable in your checkboxes.php page. If the check box isn't ticked, nothing is passed on to the PHP variable of the same name. In the second program, checkboxes.php, you display the contents of the three variables set independently in the first program like so:

```
echo "$_POST[Choice1]<br>";
echo "$_POST[Choice2]<br>";
echo "$_POST[Choice3]<br>";
```

Each of three check box controls was named and set independently. It's possible to set all three inputs to have the same name, but that might not yield the results you expect. For example, change the following code in the program checkboxes.html:

```
Have you ever eaten haggis before?
<input name="Choice" type="checkbox" value="Haggis">
<br>
Have you ever eaten snails before?
<input name="Choice" type="checkbox" value="Locusts">
<br>
Have you ever eaten locusts before?
<input name="Choice" type="checkbox" value="Snails">
```

Run the program again and select more than one option. Surprised at the outcome? You get only one answer, the last selected option in the list. What happens is that PHP stores each occurrence of the variable over whatever the variable contained before. Whichever is the last check box to be set, that's the last value the variable is set to. What you can do, though, is add a pair of square brackets ([]) to the name of each HTML control:

```
Have you ever eaten haggis before?
<input name="Choice[]" type="checkbox" value="Haggis">
<br>
Have you ever eaten snails before?
<input name="Choice[]" type="checkbox" value="Snails">
<br>
Have you ever eaten locusts before?
<input name="Choice[]" type="checkbox" value="Locusts">
```

This creates an array of variables within the $_POST array. To distinguish the different variables, PHP adds a number, which acts as a unique identifier, to the end of each variable name. The first version of the variable has a zero in square brackets ([0]) added to the end, the second has a one in square brackets([1]), and third version has a two in square brackets([2]).

To get PHP to display the contents of these variables, refer to the variable explicitly with its full name, such as $_POST[Choice][0]. In $_POST[Choice][0] you find the value Haggis if Haggis was selected. In variable $_POST[Choice][1] you find the value Snails if Snails was selected, and so on for the rest of the HTML controls that share the same name. Without the square brackets, you can't create an array from an HTML form, although you can still create arrays as much as you like in your PHP program, as discussed in Chapter 2.

Radio Buttons

Radio buttons are the selfish cousins to check boxes. If you have a selection of answers or options but only one of the options can be selected at a time, then you should use radio buttons. Once again, radio buttons are created using the <input> element, setting the type attribute to Radio.

```
<input name="Question1" type="radio" value="Porto">
```

Radio buttons, like check boxes, have a checked attribute in HTML, which again takes no value. If you supply this attribute in the control, the check box is checked by default:

```
<input name="Question1" type="radio" checked>
```

If you supply no value for the value attribute, it is set to "on" by default.

Contrary to check boxes, to connect a set of radio buttons, you must supply each radio button in your group with the same name. For example:

```
<input name="Question1" type="radio" value="Porto">
<input name="Question1" type="radio" value="Lisbon">
<input name="Question1" type="radio" value="Madrid">
```

This method tells the Web server that all of these buttons are connected. If you give each radio button control a different name, the user can select each option independently, just like a check box.

Try It Out   Use Radio Buttons

1.   Open your Web page editor and type in the following code:

```
<html>
<head><title></title></head>
<body>
<form method="GET" action="radio.php">
What is the capital of Portugal?
<br>
<br>
<input name="Question1" type="radio" value="Porto">
Porto
<br>
```

```
<input name="Question1" type="radio" value="Lisbon">
Lisbon
<br>
<input name="Question1" type="radio" value="Madrid">
Madrid
<br>
<br>
<input type="submit" value="Submit">
</form>
</body>
</html>
```

2. Save the file as `radio.html`, and close it.

3. Create a new file and type in the following:

```
<html>
<head><title></title></head>
<body>
<?php
echo "You selected the answer: $_GET[Question1]";
?>
</body>
</html>
```

4. Save the file as `radio.php`.

5. Open `radio.html` in your browser and select an answer (see Figure 3-12).

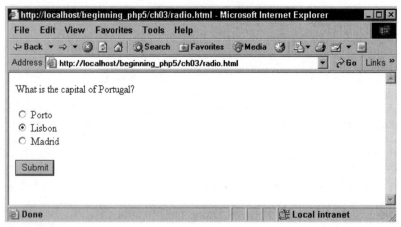

Figure 3-12

6. Click Submit and view the results of the choice you made (see Figure 3-13).

How It Works

The method of transmission is changed to GET, so the query string is visible once more. A questionnaire is actually the one time when this might be useful. It confirms the answer that's selected, which would

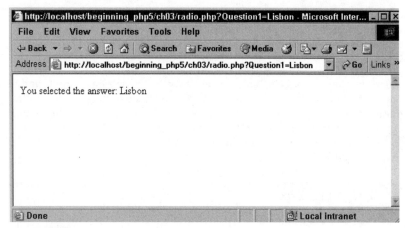

Figure 3-13

admittedly be more useful if the answer wasn't already displayed in the body of the page. That aside, take a quick look at the programs. The first program, radio.html, sets three radio button controls. They all have the same name, Question1, but with three different values to reflect the different answers:

```
<input name="Question1" type="radio" value="Porto">
Porto
<br>
<input name="Question1" type="radio" value="Lisbon">
Lisbon
<br>
<input name="Question1" type="radio" value="Madrid">
Madrid
```

Then in the second program, radio.php, you only need to display the contents of the one variable because there can only ever be one answer to the question:

```
<?php
echo "You selected the answer: $_GET[Question1]";
?>
```

List Boxes

List boxes or drop-down list boxes are controls that typically display several items in a list. Sometimes they have an arrow next to them that enable the user to scroll down to additional items. They work a little different in HTML because they're created with two elements: <select> and <option>. Essentially, they provide the same functionality as the radio buttons, given that usually you can only select one item from a predetermined list of options.

The <select> element that creates the list box encloses a number of <option> elements, each of which contains the text that corresponds to an item on the drop-down list:

```
<select name="Price">
    <option>Under $5,000</option>
```

```
        <option>$5,000-$10,000</option>
        <option>$10,000-$25,000</option>
        <option>Over $25,000</option>
    </select>
```

However, there are times when being able to select several items is appropriate, and you can allow multiple items to be selected by adding the `multiple` attribute to the `<select>` element. This gives PHP two things to think about. You'll deal with both of these options in the following example in which you get information from the user about the price of a car he wants to purchase and its engine size. The first question allows only single answer, and the second allows multiple items, which can be selected by holding down the Shift key.

Use a List Box

1. Open your Web page editor and type in the following:

```
<html>
<head><title></title></head>
<body>
<form method="POST" action="listbox.php">
What price of car are you looking to buy?
<br>
<br>
<select name="Price">
    <option>Under $5,000</option>
    <option>$5,000-$10,000</option>
    <option>$10,000-$25,000</option>
    <option>Over $25,000</option>
</select>
<br>
<br>
What size of engine would you consider?
<br>
<br>
<select name="EngineSize[]" multiple>
    <option>1.0L</option>
    <option>1.4L</option>
    <option>1.6L</option>
    <option>2.0L</option>
</select>
<br>
<br>
<input type="submit" value="Submit">
</form>
</body>
</html>
```

2. Save the file as `listbox.html` and close it.

3. Create another new file and type in the following:

```
<html>
<head><title></title></head>
```

```
<body>
<?php
echo "Price Range: $_POST[Price]";
$Choice0 = $_POST['EngineSize'][0];
$Choice1 = $_POST['EngineSize'][1];
$Choice2 = $_POST['EngineSize'][2];
$Choice3 = $_POST['EngineSize'][3];
echo "<br>Engine Size(s): $Choice0";
echo "$Choice1";
echo "$Choice2";
echo "$Choice3";
?>
</body>
</html>
```

4. Save this file as listbox.php.

5. Open listbox.html in your browser and select one option from the top box, and one or more from the bottom list box (see Figure 3-14).

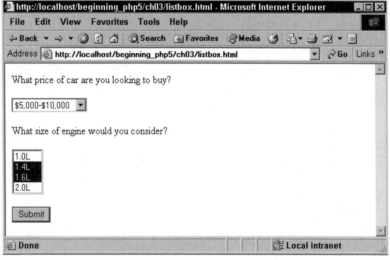

Figure 3-14

6. Click Submit. Figure 3-15 shows an example result.

How It Works

In the first program, listbox.html, a list box is created with four items, and multiple selections are allowed. The <select> element's name attribute is set to Price:

```
<select name="Price">
    <option>Under $5,000</option>
    <option>$5,000-$10,000</option>
    <option>$10,000-$25,000</option>
    <option>Over $25,000</option>
</select>
```

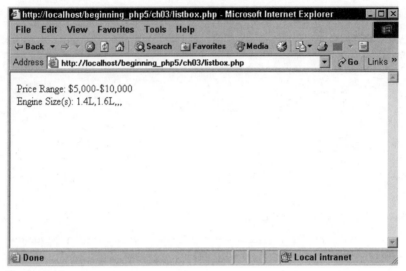

Figure 3-15

In the second program, `listbox.php`, the name attribute is referred to with the PHP variable `$-POST[Price]`:

```php
<?php
echo "Price Range: $_POST[Price]";
...
```

There's absolutely nothing out of the ordinary going on here, and it should look very familiar up to this point. It's on the second list box in `listbox.html` that things depart from the norm:

```html
<select name="EngineSize[]" multiple>
    <option>1.0L</option>
    <option>1.4L</option>
    <option>1.6L</option>
    <option>2.0L</option>
</select>
```

Well, actually everything looks pretty much the same apart from the top line, which sets the name attribute to be `EngineSize[]`. Attaching the brackets (`[]`) to the end of a control name is a cue to PHP to treat it as an array.

```php
$Choice0 = $_POST['EngineSize'][0];
$Choice1 = $_POST['EngineSize'][1];
$Choice2 = $_POST['EngineSize'][2];
$Choice3 = $_POST['EngineSize'][3];
echo "<br>Engine Size(s): $Choice0,";
echo "$Choice1,";
echo "$Choice2,";
echo "$Choice3,";
```

As mentioned earlier, during the creation of an array, PHP creates a new variable of the same name with an index number bolted on. There are four items on the list, so there are four index numbers. The contents of each one must be displayed because each index number refers to an item in the array. Array indexes always start at zero, so $EngineSize[0] refers to the first option in the list, 1.0L. It contains this item only if that option is selected, otherwise it contains the contents of the first <select> option chosen on that page.

In this example, this option is selected, so $EngineSize[0] does indeed contain the value 1.0L. The same goes for $EngineSize[1] which relates to the second option. $EngineSize[2] and $EngineSize[3] don't contain anything because no more values were selected in the list box. If only one option were selected, then only $EngineSize[0] would contain a value. Only if all four options were selected would $EngineSize[2] and $EngineSize[3] contain any values. If only the last two items were selected, then the variables $EngineSize[0] and $EngineSize[1] would contain 1.6L and 2.0L, respectively. $EngineSize[2] and $EngineSize[3] still wouldn't contain any values. To easily display the values with the echo statement, variables for each choice were created and set them to the string values in the array variables.

Please remember that if you have set error reporting to on so that you can view errors from your browser ("display_errors = On" must be set in your php.ini file,) you will display some warnings for the unselected values of the engine size because not all the $_POST['EngineSize'][] variables will be set.

Hidden Form Fields

There are times when you want to take information contained in a Web page, and pass it to another Web page without requiring any input from the user. There's another setting for the <input> control that enables you to pass information in a field just as if it were a text box but keeping the control and its contents hidden. This is known as a hidden form field (or hidden control).

Hidden form fields come into play in a slightly different manner than the controls already demonstrated. They're probably more useful on PHP pages that contain forms because you can use them to send information contained within PHP variables. Here's a typical hidden form field on a form:

```
<input type="hidden" name="Hidden1" value="Secret Message">
```

There's no screenshot of this because the control wouldn't appear on the page. Any form that submitted it though would have a variable called $Hidden1 that contains the text Secret Message. To use the hidden form field in a PHP page, you can write the whole HTML form in echo() statements, transferring the contents of PHP variables via HTML controls as shown here:

```
<?php
$Message1="This message is invisible";
echo "<form>";
echo "<input type='hidden' name='Hidden2' value='$Message1'>";
echo "<input type='submit' value='Submit'>";
echo "</form>";
?>
```

This entire HTML form is written in PHP statements and it enables you to create a variable called $Hidden2 and transfer the contents of $Message1 into it. Of course, this is not the only way to keep data available across form submissions or page requests; cookies, sessions, and so on are discussed later on in this chapter.

Now for an example that takes the contents of a `<select>` list box and displays the user's choice on the next page. The preceding process is used to write the HTML form in PHP echo statements as well.

Try It Out   Use the Hidden Form Field

1. Open your Web page editor and type the following:

```
<html>
<head></head>
<body>
<?php
$Message1="Bugs Bunny";
$Message2="Homer Simpson";
$Message3="Ren & Stimpy";
echo "<form method='GET' action='hidden2.php'>";
echo "Which of the following would win in a shootout?";
echo "<select name='ListBox'>";
echo "<option>$Message1</option>";
echo "<option>$Message2</option>";
echo "<option>$Message3</option>";
echo "</select><br><br>";
echo "<input type='hidden' name='Hidden1' value='$Message1'>";
echo "<input type='hidden' name='Hidden2' value='$Message2'>";
echo "<input type='hidden' name='Hidden3' value='$Message3'>";
echo "<input type='submit' value='Submit'>";
echo "</form>";
?>
</body>
</html>
```

2. Save the file as hidden.php and close it.

3. Start a new file and type in the following:

```
<html>
<head><title></title></head>
<body>
<?php
echo "The three options were:<br>";
echo "$_GET[Hidden1]<br>";
echo "$_GET[Hidden2]<br>";
echo "$_GET[Hidden3]<br>";
echo "<br>You selected:<br>";
echo "$_GET[ListBox]";
?>
</body>
</html>
```

4. Save the file as hidden2.php and close it.

5. Open hidden.php in your browser and make a selection (see Figure 3-16).

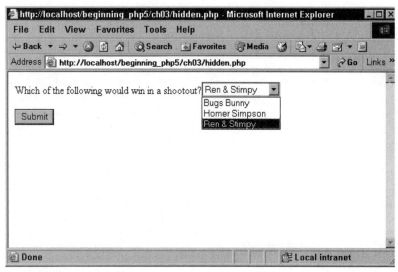

Figure 3-16

6. Click Submit to view the results (see Figure 3-17).

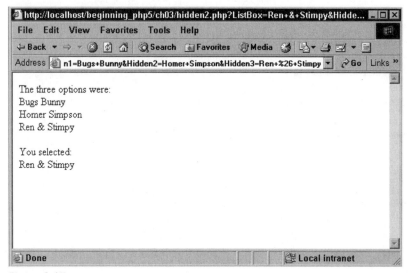

Figure 3-17

How It Works

Once you get over the process of creating the HTML form in echo statements rather than straight HTML code, this is really very straightforward. The main difference is that you can leave out the apostrophes in the variable name in the array. Three variables are created to form the basis of the `<select>` list box:

```
$Message1="Bugs Bunny";
$Message2="Homer Simpson";
$Message3="Ren & Stimpy";
```

They are respectively $Message1, $Message2, and $Message3. Next, the HTML form is created using echo statements. Absolutely nothing differs from a normal HTML form, except that when you want to use quotation marks in the HTML, you have to use single quotation marks and not double ones or you'll break the echo statement. The first line just tells you to send the form contents to hidden2.php via the GET method:

```
echo "<form method='GET' action='hidden2.php'>";
```

Some explanatory text is displayed and then the `<select>` list box is started:

```
echo "Which of the following would win in a shootout?";
echo "<select name='ListBox'>";
```

It gets three options, the contents of the variables $Message1, $Message2, and $Message3, respectively.

```
echo "<option>$Message1</option>";
echo "<option>$Message2</option>";
echo "<option>$Message3</option>";
```

The `<select>` list box is closed and a couple of line breaks are added:

```
echo "</select><br><br>";
```

Then the three variables already used are passed as hidden form fields to the form:

```
echo "<input type='hidden' name='Hidden1' value='$Message1'>";
echo "<input type='hidden' name='Hidden2' value='$Message2'>";
echo "<input type='hidden' name='Hidden3' value='$Message3'>";
```

The three variables will turn up on the form as $Hidden1, $Hidden2, and $Hidden3, respectively. A Submit button is added to the form, and the form is closed:

```
echo "<input type='submit' value='Submit'>";
echo "</form>";
```

The second PHP page just displays the contents of the controls created in the first page. The contents of the three hidden form fields are displayed first:

```
echo "The three options were:<br>";
echo "$_GET[Hidden1]<br>";
echo "$_GET[Hidden2]<br>";
echo "$_GET[Hidden3]<br>";
```

This is useful because normally the contents of the entire list box aren't transferred across. Only the option selected by the user is passed over to the next PHP page. However, sometimes you want to have all of the list box contents available in your PHP page. This is one effective method for transferring this type of information.

The last lines just display the contents of selection made by the user.

```
echo "<br>You selected:<br>";
echo "$_GET[ListBox]";
```

Hidden form fields are used to perform this type of task later in this book.

Password Fields

Passwords are essentially text fields that blank out the input with asterisks when the user types in text. They store and transmit information in the same way as text fields:

```
What is your password?
<input name="Password" type="password">
```

There's no difference in the processing between text and password types of text fields, so no example is provided here. If you want to see one in action, just go back to the previous example text.html and change the type to password. However, if you choose to transmit this information, using GET, then notice that the password is not encrypted in the query string and will be visible to all and sundry. That isn't to say once again that POST is a secure method of sending data, just that the information isn't as immediately visible. If you want security you must use something like SSL (Secure Sockets Layer) to actively encrypt your data.

Submit Buttons and Reset Buttons

Submit buttons have been used copiously throughout this chapter, so there's no need for an example that demonstrates how they work. However, there are a couple of points to note. First, what happens if you need more than one submit button in a form? In this case you will have to set the name and value attributes of the Submit buttons on your page as well. For example:

```
<input value="Button 1 pressed" type="submit" name="Submit1">
<input value="Button 2 pressed" type="submit" name="Submit2">
```

This, as you might expect, creates variables in PHP that PHP can pick up. In fact, this code would create one variable in PHP depending on which button is pressed. If you press Submit1 then a variable called Submit1 is created within the $_GET or $_POST array. If you press Button 2, then Submit2 is created. The contents of Submit1 are Button 1 pressed, while the contents of Submit2 are Button 2 pressed. There's actually nothing useful to be done with this yet, so there's no example now.

Secondly, the Submit button offers no respite if you type in the wrong information. Although you can't actually undo information sent via the Submit button, the Reset button control offers a little help because it can be used to set the state of all controls on the form to their initial state.

```
<input type="reset">
```

Using Values Returned from Forms in Your PHP Scripts

You've seen all manner of controls, and how PHP handles their contents, but you still haven't done anything practical with the contents other than to dump them into another Web page. Admittedly, without any of the features that you'll learn about in the next chapter, manipulating the contents of variables is hard. However, you learned about mathematical and string operators in the last chapter and you can combine that knowledge with concepts presented in this chapter.

In the last example in this chapter, you'll create a loan application form that asks for the amount of money that a user wants to borrow, and calculates the amount of money that a fictional bank called NAMLLU can offer that person based on his age and salary. You give the user a simple yes or no answer at the end of the calculation.

Although the program's loan calculation acceptance formula might seem complex, it's really quite straightforward (and isn't based on any company's formula). The loan amount for a person is calculated using three numbers, as follows:

❑ Salary Allowance variable: The user's annual salary divided by 5.

❑ Age Allowance variable: The user's age divided by 10; round the result down to the nearest whole number; and then subtract one.

❑ Loan Allowance variable: The Salary Allowance variable multiplied by the Age Allowance variable.

The Age Allowance variable automatically excludes anyone who is younger than 20, because the formula always return a zero, and anything multiplied by zero is zero. Here's an example of figuring the Loan Allowance variable for a 19-year-old, where `First figure` is the Salary Allowance variable:

```
First figure * (19/10 - (19 Modulus 10) /10))-1
```

Remember that the `Modulus` operator is used to return the remainder from a division sum. This calculation works out to:

```
First figure * (1.9 - 0.9) -1
```

which works out to:

```
First figure * 0
```

For any age under 20, the Loan Allowance variable always returns zero because no matter what the Salary Allowance variable is, when multiplied by a zero, it returns zero.

Here's another example of how this works: A 57-year-old user whose annual salary is $50,000 applies for a loan through your loan application form.

❑ His Salary Allowance variable is `50,000/5 = 10,000`.

❑ His Age Allowance variable is `(57/10 - (57 Modulus 10)/10)) - 1 = 4`.

❑ His Loan Allowance variable is `10,000* 4 = $40,000` (Salary Allowance variable multiplied by Age Allowance variable).

If the Loan Allowance variable is more than the amount the person wants to borrow, you say yes; otherwise, you say no.

Try It Out   The Loan Application Form

This program needs two pages (and nearly all of the controls introduced in this chapter). The first page takes the loan details from which you get the person's first name, second name, age, address, salary, and the amount he wants to borrow. The second page, the PHP page, does the calculation for you and delivers a verdict.

1.   Open your Web page editor and type in the following:

```
<html>
<head><title></title></head>
<body>
<b>Namllu Credit Bank Loan Application Form</b>
<form method="POST" action="loan.php">
First Name:
<input name="FirstName" type="text">
Last Name:
<input name="LastName" type="text">
Age:
<input name="Age" type="text" size="3">
<br>
<br>
Address:
<textarea name="Address" rows="4" cols="40">
</textarea>
<br>
<br>
What is your current salary?
<select name="Salary">
<option value=0>Under $10000</option>
<option value=10000>$10,000 to $25,000</option>
<option value=25000>$25,000 to $50,000</option>
<option value=50000>Over $50,000</option>
</select>
<br>
<br>
How much do you want to borrow?<br><br>
<input name="Loan" type="radio" value="1000">Our $1,000 package at 8.0% interest
<br>
<input name="Loan" type="radio" value="5000">Our $5,000 package at 11.5% interest
<br>
<input name="Loan" type="radio" value="10000">Our $10,000 package at 15.0% interest
<br>
<br>
<input type="submit" value="Click here to Submit application">
<input type="reset" value="Reset application form">
</form>
</body>
</html>
```

2. Save this file as `loan.html`. Close it.

3. Create a new file and type the following:

```
<html>
<head><title></title></head>
<body>
<b>Namllu Credit Bank Loan Application Form</b>
<br>
<br>

<?php
$SalaryAllowance = $_POST['Salary']/5;
$AgeAllowance = ($_POST['Age']/10 - ($_POST['Age']%10)/10)-1;
$LoanAllowance = $SalaryAllowance * $AgeAllowance;
echo "Loan wanted:$_POST[Loan]<br>";
echo "Loan amount we will allow:$LoanAllowance<br><br>";
if ($_POST['Loan'] <= $LoanAllowance) echo "Yes, $_POST[FirstName]
$_POST[LastName], we are delighted to accept your application";
if ($_POST['Loan'] > $LoanAllowance) echo "Sorry, $_POST[FirstName]
$_POST[LastName], we cannot accept your application at this time";
?>
</body>
</html>
```

4. Save this file as `loan.php`.

5. Open `loan.html` in your browser (see Figure 3-18) and supply some details.

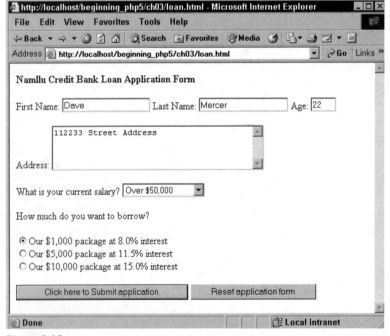

Figure 3-18

6. Click the Submit application button and you should see something like Figure 3-19.

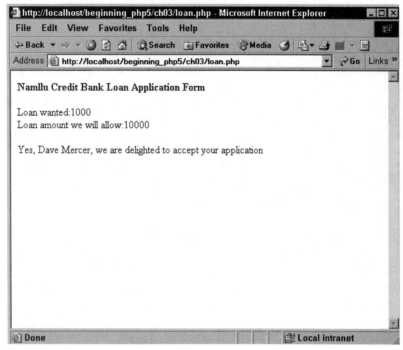

Figure 3-19

How It Works

You'll have earned a break after examining these two programs. Although the first is lengthy, it isn't doing anything out of the ordinary, and certainly nothing you haven't already encountered in this chapter. The loan form (loan.html) contains eight controls. The first three are all text fields, used for accepting the first name, last name, and age of the applicant:

```
<input name="FirstName" type="text">
Last Name:
<input name="LastName" type="text">
Age:
<input name="Age" type="text" size="3">
```

You should be able to see now that they will create the variables $_POST[FirstName], $_POST[LastName], and $_POST[Age] on the PHP page.

The address is entered into a <textarea> control:

```
<textarea name="Address" rows="4" cols="40">
</textarea>
```

This in turn creates a PHP variable $_POST[Address]. You don't make use of all of the PHP variables created in the form, but there are similar examples in later chapters and some of them are used there.

The next control is a drop-down list box, which contains a set of salary ranges:

```
<select name="Salary">
<option value=0>Under $10000</option>
<option value=10000>$10,000 to $25,000</option>
<option value=25000>$25,000 to $50,000</option>
<option value=50000>Over $50,000</option>
</select>
```

You can't actually store a range as a value, so instead, the lowest value in the range is assigned as a particular value to each radio button. This creates just one PHP variable, $_POST[Salary], which holds the value associated with whichever range has been selected by the user. If there has been no range selected, the radio button returns no value. Notice that the first value is set to zero, and as before this zero in the formula ensures that anybody with a salary of less than $10,000 is automatically refused a loan. (I'm a bit mercenary!)

The next control is a group of three related radio buttons:

```
How much do you want to borrow?<br><br>
<input name="Loan" type="radio" value="1000">Our $1,000 package
at 8.0% interest
<br>
<input name="Loan" type="radio" value="5000">Our $5,000 package
at 11.5% interest
<br>
<input name="Loan" type="radio" value="10000">Our $10,000 package
at 15.0% interest
<br>
```

These all have the same name, because the variable only ever needs to contain one value depending on what the user has selected. This group of three buttons creates just one PHP variable, $Loan.

The last two controls are a submit button and a reset button:

```
<input type="submit" value="Click here to Submit application">
<input type="reset" value="Reset application form">
```

The submit button utilizes the action attribute that was set at the top of the form, so it knows where to send the form:

```
<form method="POST" action="loan.php">
```

As you see, the first program stores and transmits the information in the form, but it's the second program, loan.php, that takes these values and performs some simple operations on them to approve or reject the loan claim. The first line creates a new variable, the Salary Allowance, which is the user's salary divided by five:

```
$SalaryAllowance = $_POST['Salary']/5;
```

The second line calculates the more complex Age Allowance formula, which you want to return a whole number, based on the user's age divided by 10. If there is any remainder left over from the division, you remove it by rounding the answer downward to the nearest whole number. Use the modulus operator on the user's age to calculate the remainder on the user's age. Subtract one from the result to get the variable, as explained earlier. The final line returns a 0 if the user enters his age as a value between 0 and 19, a 1 if the age supplied is a value between 20 and 29, a 2 if the age supplied is a value between and 30 and 39, and so on. The result of this calculation is stored in the new $AgeAllowance variable:

```
$AgeAllowance = ($_POST['Age']/10 - ($_POST['Age']%10)/10)-1;
```

Fortunately, the next line is much simpler. It takes the two figures just calculated, multiplies them together, and stores them in a new variable $LoanAllowance, which is the final figure for how large a loan the user is allowed to take out.

```
$LoanAllowance = $SalaryAllowance * $AgeAllowance;
```

The next two lines just echo() a confirmation on the Web page of the amount supplied by the user for the loan he wants, and the amount of loan that you will allow:

```
echo "Loan wanted:$_POST[Loan]<br>";
echo "Loan amount we will allow:$LoanAllowance<br><br>";
```

The next two lines use the <= (less than or equals) operator, which enables you to make a decision based on the information you've been given. The operator determines whether the loan amount requested by the user is less than or equal to the amount that you (the bank) will allow. If it is, you display a message on the Web page saying that you're delighted to accept the application. This structure is discussed in detail in the next chapter; so don't worry it's covered briefly here.

The display message is also personalized with the names the user provided on the form:

```
if ($_POST['Loan'] <= $LoanAllowance) echo "Yes, $_POST[FirstName]
$_POST[LastName], we are delighted to accept your application";
```

The final line of PHP script handles the rejection situation—if the amount the user wants to borrow exceeds the amount the bank will authorize. It displays a message saying that the application is rejected.

```
if ($_POST['Loan'] > $LoanAllowance) echo "Sorry, $_POST[FirstName]
$_POST[LastName], we cannot accept your application at this time";
```

That's all there is to these programs. Oh, one tiny little detail: the nature of the information in a real-life application is sensitive, so use the POST method to transmit it. Remember, POST is only more discreet; hackers can just as easily hijack information sent via this method. For real security, use an SSL certificate to encrypt communications between the user and the Web server.

Possible Improvements to the Form

Of course, the form isn't perfect; indeed if you try hard enough, you can break it, or cause it to display illogical values. That's because there's no kind of *validation* performed on the values received from the user. What's to stop a user supplying a totally erroneous value for his age such as 965? You know it can't be true, but you can't stop it. In the next few chapters you'll examine ways of tightening this up, by checking the values and only allowing values within a certain range, or even that the user has actually supplied a value, but that's enough for now.

The Concept of State

You're familiar with how desktop applications such as Excel, Word, Dreamweaver, and so on work. You start them up, they appear on your screen, and you do your work via documents, menu choices, dialog boxes, controls, and form fields. It can easily appear that there is no separation between the application's data processing logic and the user interface, but in fact every time you choose something from a menu, click a button, or enter something in a form field, you are actually using the user interface, and the user interface is communicating what you just did to the programming logic inside the application. The application then responds by performing its processing and providing a response to the user interface. For some actions you take there may be no visible response, whereas for others it is plain that a great deal of processing has taken place behind the scenes.

The point of this discussion is that as you provide input to the application via the user interface, you change the overall *state* of the application. You can think of state as the exact condition, moment to moment, of all the data and variables in the application. And the application has an obligation to take note of state changes, because it might have to respond to these changes with an action of its own (which then further changes the state of the application).

There are many things besides user interaction that can change the state of an application. For example, suppose you're playing a game and you have 15 seconds to make your move. The application will monitor the system clock and may make an action entirely independent of anything you do (except make your move) based on how many seconds have elapsed (another case of state change). What does this have to do with you? Well....

As a programmer, you may not think much about state when programming desktop applications, because you're used to seamless communications between your user interface and your programming logic. But programming for the Web forces you to address the issue, because HTTP communications are stateless. HTTP is a stateless protocol because there is no built-in mechanism that tracks the state of every object in the user interface and informs the programming logic of it, or vice versa.

Instead, communications between browser and server take the form of clicks on links or form submissions. Not only is this driven by the user (instead of being automatic), but for folks with slower connections or intermittent connections it can be slow and time-consuming. So building an online application with PHP requires you to use other mechanisms for maintaining state, and you need to take measures to cope with the fact that the user interface is disconnected and may not respond at all in the way you would ordinarily expect.

State Maintenance

The most direct way in which you'll be involved with state in PHP programs is when trying to preserve variable values between page requests because each page is its own program, and once the program is done processing, all variables and values are lost—the program's done, and everything is erased out of memory. Unlike desktop applications, which maintain data in memory until you shut them down, a PHP program runs only when a page request activates it, and then only until processing is completed and/or HTML or text content is returned to the user.

PHP is able to bridge the gap between each request-response and the next, providing persistence of data—and, yes, prolonged interactivity. This process of continually updating the server with information, a major ingredient in most interactive sites, is necessary to maintain a session. Session maintenance is how you refer to a series of interactions, beginning with the user accessing or logging on to a site, and ending with the user logging out or being timed out for inactivity.

The key to this process is usually a *cookie* (a small piece of data stored on the client's computer) or some sort of a variable that the client and server pass back and forth, often called a *session key*. These cookies and keys are used to help the server know which client it is interacting with for any given request. Just as a username identifies a user to a system, a session key (or an appropriate cookie) identifies a client to a Web site.

Sessions also maintain state across page requests and you'll examine them in detail a little later. First, take a look at some other methods available to you, including the use of hidden form fields, query strings, databases, and cookies.

Hidden Form Fields

You've seen how hidden form fields work to send data (coded by the designer) back to the server when the form is submitted. If you want to maintain state using hidden form fields (for example, a unique value representing a product the user is working with, such as the product ID), you can simply place the current product ID value into a hidden form field. Of course, the idea is that you would have the user select the product from a drop-down box (the select element) and then submit the form, using something like this code:

```
<form action="myform.php" method="post">
<select name="selected_product_id">
<option value="121">Product 121</option>
<option value="122">Product 122</option>
</select>
<input type="submit" name="button" value="Select Product">
</form>
```

You could return a page to him using the following code:

```
<input type="hidden" name="chosen_product_id" value="<?php echo
$selected_product_id; ?>">
```

Before the page is returned, the user's input would be processed as follows (assuming he chose product 122):

```
<form action="myform.php" method="post">
<input type="hidden" name="chosen_product_id" value="122">
```

So the next time he submits this form, part of the data submitted would be chosen_product_id, which PHP would turn into $chosen_product_id, and which you could then use anytime you wanted to perform processing on the product he chose, no matter how many page requests ago he chose that product. Don't forget, though, you'll need to populate that same hidden form field value each time the user requests another page or you'll lose that value.

Query Strings

Query strings can be used in exactly the same way as hidden form fields to maintain state values across page requests. However, as previously discussed, their name/value pairs are displayed for all to see in the address bar of the browser, along with the URL. This is a very insecure method of transmitting data, and as you've probably guessed, easy for malicious users to break, disable, or otherwise mess with.

Databases

The mechanics of databases and database access haven't been discussed yet (you'll get to it in Chapters 9, 10, and 11) but you're certainly aware that databases are useful for storing structured information persistently (meaning that the data is retained even if the server is turned off), so you can understand why databases are useful for storing data across page requests. Basically, if you don't mind the extra overhead of making a query on the database each time a page request occurs, you can use a table in the database to store all pertinent data that must be preserved across page requests. The downside, of course, is the overhead involved in those database connections, and the extra effort building the database in the first place.

Cookies

So what are cookies? They're a quick (and some would say messy) method of storing, on the client's computer, small snippets of data that you want to persist between separate visits to a Web site. They aren't very powerful or reliable—you certainly wouldn't want to use them for permanent data storage, because the mere act of switching browsers completely obliterates all your old cookies. But they can be very handy for a wide variety of things. Some of the most common examples of cookie use include the following:

❑ Storing a user's aesthetic preferences for a specific site.

❑ Storing a user key (or keys) that can be used to link users with their personal data—as used in countless shopping basket features, for example.

❑ Providing a semi-permanent session key, enabling a user to remain logged on to a site until he explicitly asks to leave it or the browser closes.

Cookies are best used for small, helpful but non-critical things. One of the best examples of cookie use is to store preferences describing how a user wants your site to appear. Although the capability to customize a site's color scheme is a nice perk for users, those who can't (or won't) use cookies won't be missing much.

Intended as innocuous "helpers" for Web developers, cookies have built up a bad reputation in recent years. They are often overused (for example, to store large quantities of data which is really best kept on the server end) and sometimes even abused (to gather information on consumers without their knowledge, for instance). If used sparingly and responsibly, though, cookies can be useful in a number of situations. They tend to be most useful:

❑ In situations where you know for a fact that all the visitors to your site will have cookie support enabled—on corporate and educational intranets, for example.

❑ To add bells and whistles to a site—features that add to a site's appeal but aren't required to make use of it.

Messing Around with Cookies

Exact details of how cookies are implemented vary from browser to browser, but certain important points apply across the board, and these are as follows:

❑ A cookie is a short piece of data that can be used to store a variable's name and value, along with information on the site from which it came and an expiry time.

❑ Cookies provide client-side storage, usually held in files on the client machine's hard drive.

❑ Web sites can usually only modify their own cookies.

❑ They can be accessed and (if the appropriate security criteria are met) altered at will by the Web server from which they were originally sent.

When a client accesses a Web site that uses cookies, the Web server tells the client (usually a Web browser) to store away a given piece of data for later use. The client is then responsible for storing that data away. Cookie-supporting browsers accomplish this by storing the data in a file named after the site the cookie belongs to, in a directory they keep reserved for this purpose. On subsequent requests to that site, the client sends back a copy of that data—the data persists on the client side until a specified period expires, causing it to be removed from the system. This specified period is set by the server when it tells the client to create the cookie, and is basically a number of seconds for which the client should keep the cookie. If the server tells the client to set an expiry period of zero seconds, the browser should keep the cookie only until the user quits the browser application.

Because cookies are kept on the client side, they're not under the control of the server once they've been created. Users can elect to delete cookies themselves, often simply by clicking a button in their browser, or by deleting the browser's cookie files. They could also edit the contents of the files if the urge took them. Just because you wrote what's in the cookie, doesn't mean you should always expect the right data to come back!

Essentially, cookies are the server telling the client "here's something to remember; remind me of it when you come back next time." Next time could be anything from when you click that link two seconds from now to when you come back next week. That's some serious persistence! It's a little like being at a conference where delegates can be identified by their name badges for as long as they care to wear them.

Web servers send clients cookies in HTTP headers, which are sent before any HTML text. Likewise, clients send back those cookies using HTTP headers. A client knows which cookies to share with a Web site, based on the server and path the client is currently accessing. So, if you're accessing www.php.net, the browser doesn't send any cookies it received from www.wrox.com.

When a cookie is set, a server name and path name can optionally be set—this limits access to the cookie to the specified server and/or path on that server. Clients use this information to determine whether they should send any given cookie. A cookie-enabled browser generally sends any and all cookies that it thinks applicable to a given site in the headers of any given access.

Set and Retrieve Cookies

PHP, as a modern Web scripting language, comes with full support, and setting cookie variables is as simple as making a call to `setcookie()`. As with `header()`, `setcookie()` must be called before any HTML is printed to the client's browser because cookies are set in the HTTP headers, which must be sent before any HTML.

The `setcookie()` function takes six parameters, of which the first three are by far the most important: These are, in order:

1. A string to be used as the name of the variable.

2. A string to be used as the value of the variable.

3. A UNIX timestamp denoting the time at which the cookie will expire.

A UNIX timestamp is simply a long integer that represents a time and date by counting seconds since midnight on 01/01/1970. You can get the current time in this form by using the function `time()`. If you want to set a cookie to expire an hour from now, simply specify `time()+3600` for the third parameter.

The last three parameters to `setcookie()` are less frequently used:

❑ The path to whose files the cookie is relevant; the browser doesn't return cookies that are from inappropriate paths. For example, if you set this parameter to /my/path/number/one and accessed a page in /my/path/number/two, your browser wouldn't send the cookie. If you went back to a page in /my/path/number/one, the browser would send the cookie.

❑ The domain to which the cookie applies; same rules apply as to the preceding parameter. This parameter may be useful if your Web server hosts multiple domains.

❑ An integer called `secure`. Set it to 1 if you only want your cookie to be sent when requesting an SSL-encrypted page. (The cookie won't be stored in an encrypted form on the client's hard drive; this setting merely ensures that the cookie will be encrypted for transmission across the Internet.)

In the simplest possible situation, you could leave off these last three, so that a typical call to `setcookie()` might look like this:

```
setcookie("fontprefs", "", time()+3600);
```

Accessing cookies is even simpler—there's nothing to call at all! Just as it does with POST variables, PHP automatically puts cookie information in the global domain, so it's as simple to use cookie values as it is to use any other variables. For example, the value of a received cookie called `fontprefs` is automatically be available throughout the script as the global variable `$_COOKIES['fontprefs']`.

There are several ways to delete a cookie. Of course, if the client knows where to look on his machine, he can always edit or delete the files in which cookies are stored. However, it's sometimes useful to be able to get the server to delete (or "eat") a cookie, and if this is the case, there are two main options:

❑ Reset the cookie's expiry time to a time in the past: `setcookie("num", "0", time()-9999);`, for example.

❑ Reset the cookie, specifying only its name: `setcookie("fontprefs");`, for example.

Try It Out   Use Cookies To Store User Preferences

Here's a script that stores user-selected choices for font size and typeface in a cookie. On subsequent visits to the page, the cookie is examined, and the preferences stored in it remain in effect. Save the code as `cookies.php`:

```php
<?php
//cookies.php
if ($_POST[type_sel]) {
    setcookie("font[type]", $_POST[type_sel], time()+3600);
}

if ($_POST[size_sel]) {
    setcookie("font[size]", $_POST[size_sel], time()+3600);
}
```

```php
//We define some options for font size and typeface, and as it's now safe to
add an HTML header, we do so:
$type = array("arial", "helvetica", "sans-serif", "courier");
$size = array("1","2","3","4","5","6","7");
echo "<html><head><title>Cookie Test</title></head><body><div align='center'>";

//The following form contains a pair of listboxes, which can be used to
specify the user's preferences:
echo "<form method='POST'>";
echo "What font type would you like to use? ";
echo "<select name='type_sel'>";
echo "<option selected value=''>default</option>";
foreach ($type as $var) {
    echo "<option>$var</option>";
}
echo "</select><br><br>";
echo "What font size would you like to use? ";
echo "<select name='size_sel'>";
echo "<option selected value=''>default</option>";

foreach ($size as $var) {
    echo "<option>$var</option>";
}
echo "</select><br><br>";
echo "<input type='submit' value='Get Cookies'>";
echo "</form>";

//Finally, we echo out some useful information, and format it using
appropriate settings:
echo "<b>Your cookies say:</b><br>";
echo "<font ";
if ($_COOKIE[font][type]) {
    $cookie_font_type = $_COOKIE[font][type];
    echo "face='$cookie_font_type' ";
}

if ($_COOKIE[font][size]) {
    $cookie_font_size = $_COOKIE[font][size];
    echo "size='$cookie_font_size' ";
}
echo ">";
echo "\$font[type] = $cookie_font_type<br>";
echo "\$font[size] = $cookie_font_size<br>";
echo "</font><br>";
echo "<b>Your form variables say:</b><br>";
echo "<font ";

if ($-POST[type_sel]) {
    $post_type_sel = $_POST[type_sel];
    echo "face='$post_type_sel' ";
}

if ($_POST[size-sel]) {
    $post_size_sel = $_POST[size_sel];
```

```
        echo "size='$post_size_sel' ";
    }
    echo ">";
    echo "\$type_sel = $post_type_sel<br>";
    echo "\$size_sel = $post_size_sel<br>";
    echo "</font>";

        echo "</div></body></html>";
    ?>
```

Open cookies.php in your browser and play around with the selections (see Figure 3-20).

Figure 3-20

How It Works

The lines of most interest happen to be the first two functional lines in the script. Remember that cookies are set in the HTTP headers, so you have to place these calls before outputting any HTML:

```
<?php
//cookies.php
if ($_POST[type_sel]) {
    setcookie("font[type]", $_POST[type_sel], time()+3600);
}
```

```
        if ($_POST[size_sel]) {
            setcookie("font[size]", $_POST[size_sel], time()+3600);
        }
```

An expiry time of one hour from the current system time is specified for each cookie.

A pair of arrays containing available font sizes and typefaces are defined, and list boxes subsequently put into the form use these arrays to specify all the possible options. When the form is submitted, the values chosen are posted back to your script to use:

```
        $type = array("arial", "helvetica", "sans-serif", "courier");
        $size = array("1","2","3","4","5","6","7");
        echo "<html><head><title>Cookie Test</title></head><body><div align='center'>";

        //The following form contains a pair of list boxes, which can be used to
        specify the //user's preferences:
        echo "<form method='POST'>";
        echo "What font type would you like to use? ";
        echo "<select name='type_sel'>";
        echo "<option selected value=''>default</option>";
        foreach ($type as $var) {
            echo "<option>$var</option>";
        }
        echo "</select><br><br>";
        echo "What font size would you like to use? ";
        echo "<select name='size_sel'>";
        echo "<option selected value=''>default</option>";

        foreach ($size as $var) {
            echo "<option>$var</option>";
        }
        echo "</select><br><br>";
        echo "<input type='submit'>";
        echo "</form>";
```

Finally, the cookies and the posted form variables are echoed out to show how their values change as selections are made. The variables displayed are formatted with their respective values:

```
        //Finally, we echo out some useful information, and format it using
        appropriate settings:
        echo "<b>Your cookies say:</b><br>";
        echo "<font ";
        if ($_COOKIE[font][type]) {
            $cookie_font_type = $_COOKIE[font][type];
            echo "face='$cookie_font_type' ";
        }

        if ($_COOKIE[font][size]) {
            $cookie_font_size = $_COOKIE[font][size];
            echo "size='$cookie_font_size' ";
        }
        echo ">";
        echo "\$font[type] = $cookie_font_type<br>";
```

```
echo "\$font[size] = $cookie_font_size<br>";
echo "</font><br>";
echo "<b>Your form variables say:</b><br>";
echo "<font ";

if ($_POST[type_sel]) {
    $post_type_sel = $_POST[type_sel];
    echo "face='$post_type_sel' ";
}

if ($_POST[size_sel]) {
    $post_size_sel = $_POST[size_sel];
    echo "size='$post_size_sel' ";
}
echo ">";
echo "\$type_sel = $post_type_sel<br>";
echo "\$size_sel = $post_size_sel<br>";
echo "</font>";

    echo "</div></body></html>";
?>
```

Nothing too tricky there. When you run `cookies.php` for the first time, both your form variables and your cookie variables are empty. If you make a selection from each of the list boxes and click the Submit Query button, you'll fill the form variables with values, and these are echoed to the screen.

So what does this tell you? The form variables `type_sel` and `size_sel` have now been updated with the inputs selected in the preceding form. Note that the cookies are both still empty—don't worry, they're present all right; all you need to do now is refresh the page.

Native Sessions in PHP

A *session* can be defined as a series of related interactions between a single client and the Web server, which take place over an extended period of time. This could be a series of transactions that a user makes while updating his stock portfolio, or the set of requests that are made to check an e-mail account through a browser-based e-mail service. The session may consist of multiple requests to the same script, or of requests to a variety of different resources on the same Web site.

Particularly when you want to work with sensitive (or bulky) information, it makes a lot of sense to submit it once and have it stored on the server. Rather than storing the actual data on the client machine, and have to pass it back and forth between the server and client each time, it's far more practical to keep the data on the server, but give the client a "key" to allow it to uniquely identify itself, and consequently any server-side data associated with it. This key is called a *session identifier*; it uniquely associates a client with a session, and therefore with its data. In PHP, the session identifier is known as the SID (Session ID). SID is a special variable that's specified as a reference number for any particular session.

You saw how to establish a session of sorts when you used cookies to make data persist on the client machine. As noted at the time, though, that isn't a terribly secure way to manage sessions. Fortunately, PHP comes with its own session management system built in, so you don't need to worry too much about the precise implementation details. PHP creates its SID whenever you use the `session_start()`

function, and also by default if you use certain other session-related functions, such as `session_register()`. The value of the SID is kept in a global variable named `PHPSESSID`.

You can think of the SID as being like the reference number on an electric bill: you're given the number, the electric company files your details under that number, and presto! You no longer have to give the company all your details every time you call up to complain about its outrageous charges. The SID is automatically created and passed back and forth for you, each time the user clicks a link or submits form.

When you start a PHP session, the server assigns it a session ID, or SID. Any variables that you register as session variables (you'll see how to do this in a moment) are then stored on the server in a cookie-like file. The name of this file is generally the same as the value of the SID. All the client has to do to access this data is to include the SID in its request to the server. It can use a hidden form field, a query string, a cookie, anything at all, as long as the SID makes it into the HTTP request. The server looks up the appropriate session data and makes it available for use in whatever script it then executes.

If you have cookie support enabled, even this is taken care of, because the session manager automatically sends the client a cookie for the SID value. If you can't (or don't want to) use cookies, the simplest thing to do is to add the SID as a term in all query strings that point back to your Web site.

PHP sessions handle this all very neatly; they're an excellent way to learn how to build interactive sites quickly because they completely free you up from worrying about the nitty-gritty details of implementing persistence, and let you get on with the business of building your site. One particularly nice aspect is the knowledge that you have literally thousands of coders scrutinizing your persistence mechanism (because it's a part of PHP itself!) and ensuring that the underlying code works as well as possible. What's more, sessions are very well documented in the core PHP documentation, available at the official PHP Web site (`www.php.net/`). So, sessions are easy, reliable, and almost universally available; but how exactly do you use them?

In most cases, using PHP sessions is as simple as telling PHP, "I want variables X, Y, and Z to remain persistent," and letting PHP do the work. All that you, the coder, need to worry about is how to tell PHP to register a session variable—that is, make a given variable persistent—and then how to access those variables.

The function for registering a persistent variable for use with PHP sessions is `session_register()`. Given the name (without the dollar sign) of a variable, it makes that variable and its contents persist for the duration of the current session. If there isn't currently a session defined, a new one is created automatically. The length of the session (how long the session remains intact without the user having to use the site) is determined by the session timeout setting in the `php.ini` file. The default is 1,440 seconds (24 minutes).

If you wanted to maintain persistent variables called `myvar1` and `myvar2`, for example, here's how you'd begin your PHP script:

```
<?php
session-register("myvar1");
session-register("myvar2");
?>
```

You must put this code at the top of the script. Behind the scenes, you're using cookies. Again, to not mess with HTTP headers, you must be sure to register all the session variables before any HTML headers are sent out. It's good practice to do so at the very top of a script, in a self-contained snippet of PHP, as shown.

Once you've registered a variable, retrieving its contents is ridiculously simple—just access the session variable as if it were any other global variable! If you used the preceding code to register variables $myvar1 and $myvar2, you can use them just like any other variables. The only difference is that they persist for as long as the session lasts, so that the next time the page is called within the session, by the same user, the variables will contain the same values they had when the page finished executing the last time.

To use PHP sessions with Windows, you may need to modify the variable session.save_path in your php.ini file so that it refers to a valid Windows directory (D:\WinNT\Temp, for example, where D is the letter for your hard drive).

Try It Out   Count Page Accesses

Ready for some more code? This time you'll count the number of times a user has accessed pages on a Web site since the start of the current session. This task is easily accomplished using PHP sessions, with various counters (one for each page on the site) made persistent by registering them with session_register(). Here's the code

```php
<?php
session_register('view1count');
session_register('view2count');
session_register('view3count');
session_register('view4count');
?>
<?php

//The rest of the script illustrates how to make hyperlinks that hand PHP
what it needs to access your session data – namely, SID.
echo "<html><head><title>Web Page Hit Counter</title></head><body>";
if (isset($_GET['whichpage'])) {
    echo "<b>You are currently on page $_GET[whichpage].</b><br><br>\n";
    $_SESSION["view".$_GET['whichpage']."count"]++;
}

for ($i = 1; $i <= 4; $i++) {
    if (isset($_GET['whichpage']) == $i) {
        echo "<b><a href=\"sessions.php?".session_id()."&whichpage=$i\">Page
$i</a></b>";
    } else {
        echo "<a href=\"sessions.php?".session_id()."&whichpage=$i\">Page $i</a>";
    }
    echo ", which you have chosen ".$_SESSION["view".$i."count"]." times.<BR>\n";
}
echo "\n\n<br><br>\n\n";
echo "</body></html>";
?>
```

Save this file as sessions.php. Run it and change pages a few times. Figure 3-21 shows an example result.

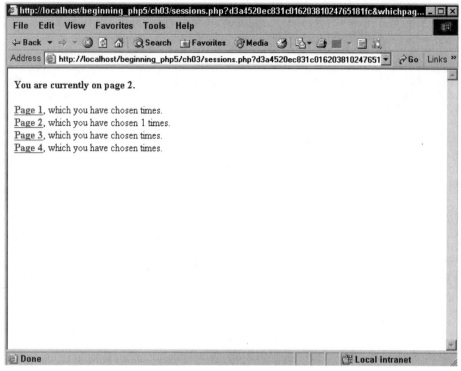

Figure 3-21

Now visit a bunch of other pages and then run the script again. You'll find that these numbers have persisted. Only when you shut down the browser will the session end.

How It Works

This simple program starts by using `session_register()` to register four session variables. They are placed in a separate block of PHP code (starting with `<?php` and ending with `?>`) to make it clear that they sit before anything else, and don't fall foul of any HTML headers:

```php
<?php
session_register('view1count');
session_register('view2count');
session_register('view3count');
session_register('view4count');
?>
```

An HTML header is echoed out, and `$_GET['whichpage']` (denoting which page you're currently on) is tested to see if it's defined. If it is, its value is used to display an appropriate message and determine which page's view count variable you need to increment:

```php
if (isset($_GET['whichpage'])) {
    echo "<b>You are currently on page $_GET[whichpage].</b><br><br>\n";
    $_SESSION["view".$_GET['whichpage']."count"]++;
}
```

A `for` loop begins cycling through each of the four pages you want to use. You display a link for each, along with a message that tells the user how many times that page has been visited during the current session. The link to the current page is displayed in bold type:

```
for ($i = 1; $i <= 4; $i++) {
    if (isset($_GET['whichpage']) == $i) {
        echo "<b><a href=\"sessions.php?".session_id()."&whichpage=$i\">Page
$i</a></b>";
    } else {
        echo "<a href=\"sessions.php?".session_id()."&whichpage=$i\">Page $i</a>";
    }
    echo ", which you have chosen ".$_SESSION["view".$i."count"]." times.<BR>\n";
}
echo "\n\n<br><br>\n\n";
echo "</body></html>";
?>
```

Each of the links specifies three things: the current script (specified by `sessions.php`), the current session (identified by `session_id()`), and the page to which you want to link (that's what `$_GET['whichpage']` is for). And that's it. All the session handling code you had to worry about was there in the first four lines. It could hardly be simpler!

Summary

This chapter covered the many predefined variables available to your PHP program anytime a request and response occurs between the client and the Web server. The display and use of individual predefined variables such as $_SERVER, $_REQUEST, and so on also were discussed.

You learned the basics for making your PHP programs interactive: query strings in links (using the <a> element) and HTML forms (using the <input>, <textarea>, and <select> elements). You also learned the differences between the GET and POST methods, and examined the circumstances under which you might want to use one over the other.

Finally, you explored the concept of state, what it means that HTTP is stateless, and how to overcome HTTP's stateless limitations using hidden form fields, query strings, cookies, sessions, and even databases to store and transmit state information across page requests.

Exercise

PHP contains a very useful function named `isset()`, which tells your PHP program whether a particular variable has been set. For example, suppose you have a page with a form containing a Submit button named `login` and another one named `logout`. When your user submits the form, you can tell which button he clicked by using the `isset()` function, like this:

```
if (isset($login)) {
//do this
} elseif (isset($logout)) {
//do this
}
```

For this exercise, create a Web page containing a form that submits to itself, and make your PHP program use the isset() function to tell when a form submission has occurred. If a form submission has not occurred, make your program display a form asking for the user's first and last name (but not the answer), and if a form submission has occurred, make your program not display the form but instead display the answer (a short statement such as: "Your first name is XX and your last name is XX.").

Hints: Use a hidden form field to determine if the form has been submitted, and use the $PHP_SELF variable to make the form submit back to itself.

Decisions, Loops, and Arrays

PHP5, like any good programming language, contains structures that allow for decision-making based on current data while the application is running. This is the essence of programming and application design, because the capability of an application to respond to changing inputs is what makes computers so powerful. Interestingly, these structures are quite simple and straightforward, yet yield an immense variety of capabilities when coupled with the blinding processing speed computers are capable of.

Decision-making code blocks in programming are called control-flow structures, or branching structures. They perform sets of basic instructions conditionally, based on values or expressions that may be constant or may be updated with each new go-round through the loop. They are all relatively simple in form, such as the if statement structure, but can be written in combination to create elaborate decision-making logic within your application.

In this chapter you'll practice stating the problem in plain language and write pseudo code reflecting the problem statement. You'll learn how Boolean logic works and use several PHP structures. The break statement and work with arrays and multidimensional arrays are also included.

Designing PHP Program Logic

There are many ways to set about building an application, but a step-by-step approach can save time and reduce frustration. One good method is to start by defining the problem (problem statement), then write pseudo code (computer instructions similar to actual programming language code but in plain English) based on the problem statement, and finally write the actual PHP code based on the pseudo code. The pseudo code often serves as the basis for comments, something that will be discussed much more in Chapter 5.

Problem Statement

For example, if you intend to build an application for clients of a mortgage company, and one of the features is a mortgage calculator, it's very likely that one of the expected outcomes is mortgage payment amounts. The calculation for mortgage payments amounts is dependent upon the interest rate, term, and initial balance of the loan, so you'd also expect that your application would have to gather these data from some source (possibly the user, or perhaps an online source of current interest rates).

Unless you happen to be using a canned application or Web Service to generate payment amounts and due dates, your application will be generating these answers. The processing methodology of this feature could be expressed in logical terms completely unrelated to any programming language: "Accept as input values the loan balance, interest rate, and loan term. Assume equal monthly payments starting on the first of the month and recurring for the life of the loan. Calculate each payment amount and due date and generate HTML code to display the data to the user. Repeat calculation until all payments are accounted for, and then return the HTML to the user in the form of a Web page."

This statement of the problem, although not quite pseudo code, is a good start at defining the inputs, processing, and outputs required of the feature you are about to program. Once you've done this step, you could easily write pseudo code from the problem statement, and then actual code from the pseudo code.

Writing Pseudo Code

What is pseudo code? There's really not a hard and fast definition, here's a general definition that works well and makes the term easier to understand: Pseudo code is a series of statements in plain language that are logically structured much like the code in the program will be.

Of course, to write pseudo code effectively you must have some knowledge of the way the language you intend to use works, because pseudo code is meant to be similar enough to the actual programming code statements required that you can very quickly convert it directly to programming code.

Pseudo code for the preceding problem statement, written to be converted to PHP5, could be something like the following:

```
//Validate incoming values for loan balance, interest rate, and loan term
using validation functions
//Set a variable for payment amount to the result of the calculation for
payment amounts based on incoming values
//Set a variable for payment dates as an array, and iterate through the
payment date calculation the number of times equivalent to the number of
payments required
//Set a variable equal to a string containing HTML to display payment
amounts and dates, and insert payment dates and amount each time through the
loop above. Add the next HTML, payment date, and amount to the string each
time through
//Calculate total number of payments and total payment amount by setting
variables equal to these values each time through the loop and incrementing
them
//Set a variable equal to a string containing HTML for displaying totals
//Send back to the user the HMTL and values generated.
```

In addition to demonstrating some basic pseudo code writing techniques, you'll notice that the technique of repeating calculations (or other data processing) is common. In fact, this technique of looping through the same calculations over and over is very common. The point of this discussion is that many of the programming language structures you'll use are simply control-flow structures in which decisions are made based on values found or created dynamically (while the application is running), and often the decision-making structures are coupled with loops so the calculations are repeated over and over until the final answer has been found. Just about every kind of data processing relies on the same control-flow structures and loops, no matter what the language.

Boolean Logic

Boolean logic is very important to control-flow structures because Boolean values are often used to express the "condition" that determines which set of processing instructions is followed (essentially, what decision is made). Boolean logic gets its name from George Boole, who devised Boolean algebra. Extraordinary work, overall, but for the purposes of this chapter, only the simplest knowledge of his work will serve.

Boolean Terms

You've probably used Boolean logic while looking up something on a search engine. For example, putting the word "and" in search terms means "retrieve documents containing this A *and* that". And is a Boolean term, and so are *or* and *not*. These are terms used in everyday life all the time, and everyone implicitly understand what they mean. There is also a special term—*xor*—that means "if either are true, but not both." There are also special operators that mimic or and and (|| and &&) but have a higher level of precedence (Chapter 2 contains more background on this subject).

If you think of them in terms of the results of a search, you can see that including or in a search gives the broadest possible result, although xor, not, and and each successively narrow the search more. Try it on your favorite search engine (if it supports Boolean logic).

When constructing a piece of data processing logic, you can use Boolean terms to set the conditions under which processing takes place. For example, in an if..then...else..end if control-flow structure, the if is followed by an expression that is either true or false (true and false are called Boolean values). If true, the code immediately after the if part of the block is processed. If false, processing bypasses these statements and goes directly to the else, and if there is no else processing bypasses the rest of the control-flow structure entirely.

Boolean Values

The Boolean values true and false are represented by TRUE and FALSE. Although you can convert to Boolean values, in most cases you don't need to for your expression to trigger the appropriate action within a control-flow structure. The following values are taken as Boolean FALSE:

- ❏ The integer zero (0)
- ❏ The float zero.zero (0.0)
- ❏ An empty string ("")
- ❏ The string zero ("0")
- ❏ An array with zero elements
- ❏ An object with zero member variables
- ❏ The special type NULL (including any unset variables)

All other values are considered TRUE. Keep in mind that whether an expression is true or false depends on the outcome of the evaluation, not on the values being compared. For example, if value A is 20 and value B is 30, and the comparison asks whether value A is less than value B, the outcome would be TRUE. For decision-making purposes there can be only two possible outcomes: true or false. There is no *maybe* allowed in these structures.

Previously your variables could hold numbers or text, but Boolean values are held in a third type of variable, which can hold one of two absolute values: true or false. You can set any variable to one of these two values:

```
$Variable = true;
```

However, if you then display the value on the screen, you see a numeric value:

```
1
```

So you can see that Boolean values have both numeric and literal values. On its own, this isn't particularly interesting, but once you start needing to make decisions based on the outcome of situations, and having to say either a given condition is true or false (or, equivalently, evaluates to 1 or 0), you'll find that you use Boolean values a lot.

Using Boolean Terms and Values

An expression can simply evaluate to a value that is then compared to some other value to determine whether the expression is true or false. It can also evaluate to a set of values (in the form: this *and* that, this *or* that, or this *not* that), each of which is tested, and these statements can be connected by the Boolean operators named and, or, and xor. *Not* is represented by the ! operator in PHP.

When using sets of values as a condition, if the first expression is true and the second is false, and the two are connected by and, the entire condition is false, and processing bypasses the first set of processing statements. Conversely, if both expressions are true and connected by and, the entire condition is true and statements in the first block of code are processed. The other sets of statements also cause a decision to be made based on the Boolean value returned after processing all statements.

A table of outcomes for a simple control-flow block using if..then..else/elseif..end if can illustrate how these conditions work. (Note that then and end if are represented by curly braces in PHP; the if statement is covered in much more detail later in this chapter.) Here's the code (the ANDs and OR are uppercase to highlight them; these terms are case-insensitive):

```
$my_var = 27;
$my_var02 = 30;
if ($my_var == $my_var02) {
   //do these lines of code
} elseif ($my_var + 3 == $my_var02) {
   //do these lines of code
} elseif ($my_var + 3 == $my_var02 AND $my_var == $my_var02) {
   //do these lines of code
} elseif ($my_var == $my_var02 OR $my_var == $my_var02-3) {
   //do these lines of code
} elseif ($my_var == $my_var02 AND !$my_var == $my_var02-3) {
   //do these lines of code
}
```

The following table shows the possible outcomes:

Condition	Outcome(s)
$my_var == $my_var02	The only true outcome here is if both variables contain an exactly equivalent value. All other cases are false
$my_var + 3 == $my_var02	The result of the expression $my_var + 3 is evaluated first, and then the comparison takes place
$my_var + 3 == $my_var02 AND $my_var == $my_var02	The outcome is determined after both expressions are evaluated, and is only true if both expressions are true
$my_var == $my_var02 OR $my_var == $my_var02 - 3	Both expressions must be evaluated, but now if either of them are true the outcome is true, obviously a broader condition than if both are required to be true
$my_var == $my_var02 - 3 AND !($my_var == $my_var02)	The first expression must be true and the second must be false in order for the entire set of conditions to be met, in which case the whole thing is true. Remember, the second expression must be false because that is the only case where the ! operator would return true

As you can see, you can choose conditions that fit just about any circumstances. For example, you might write a control-flow structure that looks for a particular value being submitted by the user. If you write the condition so that one and only one value turns the code in the structure "on", there are many, many possibilities to miss that one value and never execute the code. Sometimes that's what you want. Other times, you want to make sure the code almost always executes, except in a very specific case. You might write a condition such that the code executes unless a particular value is submitted, like this:

```
if ($submitted_value !== $my_internal value) {
//do this code
}
```

Using control-flow structures by themselves, in combination, and together with loops offers many means to make your program do the things you want it to do. Instead of simply executing all lines of the program one after the other, a control-flow structure gives you the ability to choose whether you want to execute a particular line of code, and it enables you to make comparisons between different variables and values to make those decisions.

Conditional or Branching Statements

In its simplest form, a conditional piece of code means either "execute one line of code" or "don't execute it at all," depending on whether a specified criterion is met. A more complex variation is to either "execute this line of code" or "execute that line of code" depending on which condition is met. You can extend this to execute one complete section of code, or execute another complete section of code. Finally, it's possible to list a whole heap of possible outcomes to a certain condition. If the result of the condition is outcome number 1, then execute section 1 of code; if the result is outcome number 2, then execute section 2; if the result is outcome number 3 then execute section number 3, and so on.

An Example of Branching

So far this is a rather abstract discussion, so perhaps an example from day-to-day life would be helpful. Shopping is a fairly mundane activity but it works rather well in illustrating the type of decision-making your program might have to perform.

Imagine that you have to compile a list of items that you will need to make a cheese sandwich for your lunch. You'll have to check to see if there are any items you need to make the sandwich and go with your lunch, and buy them at the store if necessary. Here's the process:

- ❑ Check the fridge to see if you have milk, cheese, and butter.
- ❑ If you don't, add what's missing to your grocery list and proceed; if you have everything, proceed.
- ❑ Check the bread bin to see if you have any bread.
- ❑ If you haven't, add bread to your list and proceed; if you have, proceed.
- ❑ If you already have all of the items needed, make a cheese sandwich; if not, proceed.
- ❑ Go to the supermarket.
- ❑ Buy the items you need.
- ❑ Make a cheese sandwich.

This example represents just a small portion of the logical decision-making process that you use as you make your way through each day. You often check for certain conditions (do you have the necessary food items) before taking certain steps (such as making a sandwich), and depending on the conditions (you're out of cheese), you may take more steps (such as going to the store and buying food) to accomplish your objective (such as making a cheese sandwich).

The example is typical of decision-making statements in PHP. When you write PHP programs, parts of the code are written to deal with specific situations and if a particular situation doesn't arise, then there is no need to run the PHP code that relates to it.

You could actually represent this example's entire process quite easily with a PHP program. In fact, the statements in the example are close enough to what you need that you could use them as pseudo code (they would actually fit most programming languages pretty well because this kind of decision-making process can be represented in most programming languages with if statements).

For example, you could write the following code in PHP, assuming you have variables named $fridge and $bread_bin that hold string values consisting of the items in them:

```php
if ($fridge == "milk and cheese and butter") {
    if ($bread_bin == "bread") {
        make_sandwich();
    } else {
        go_to_store();
        make_sandwich();
    }
} else {
    go_to_store();
    make_sandwich();
}
```

In other words, if the fridge has milk and cheese and butter, then check to see if the bread bin has bread. If both these conditions are true, stay home and make your sandwich. If the bread bin has no bread, however, you must go to the store and get some before you can make your sandwich.

And if the fridge has no milk and cheese and butter, then you must still go to the store and purchase the missing items before making a sandwich, regardless of whether you have bread or not (it's implied that you will also check the bread bin and if there is no bread you'll pick some up while you're getting the other things on your list, so you don't need to check again).

if Statements

You learned a little about the if statement in Chapter 2, and having touched upon it again here, you probably have a good idea of how it works. Abstractly it works like this:

```
if (a condition is true) { execute a line of code; }
```

The if statement only executes any code (within the curly braces) if the condition is true. If the condition isn't met, then the code is completely ignored, and isn't executed by PHP at all.

Here's another example:

```
if (weather is rainy) { put up umbrella; }
go outside;
```

The second line executes no matter what, but you only put up your umbrella if it is raining.

If you need to execute a whole section of code, you need to put the code on separate lines after the condition and between braces:

```
if (a condition is true){
    execute the contents of these braces;
}
```

So to expand on the umbrella example, you could say:

```
if (weather is rainy){
    put up umbrella;
    put on raincoat;
}
go outside;
```

Once again the "go outside" clause is always executed, but you only put up the umbrella and put on the raincoat if the condition "weather is rainy" is true.

Using Boolean Operators in Control-Flow Structures

Some of the most common (you may have noticed these already) uses for Boolean terms and values are in control-flow structures such as the if..then..else statement and switch..case statement. These structures depend upon evaluation of expressions that result in a Boolean value (true or false). If the result is true, one set of statements is run; if not, another set of statements is run.

Operators that result in a Boolean value are called Boolean operators, and include comparison operators (such as greater-than and less-than), equals and not equals, and so on. Some of these were introduced in Chapter 3 so that you could make a decision in the loan application form. In fact, any time you need to create a condition to make any kind of decision, you have to use one of these operators. There are four broad categories, and you should examine examples of each one in action.

The > and < Operators

You're probably already familiar with the greater than and less than operators—they're fairly fundamental in basic math and are equally important in programming. In PHP you can use them to compare two constants, a constant with a variable, or two variables. Depending on what the outcome of the comparison is, a certain course of action can be pursued. With constants, the result is self-evident, as this example shows:

```
if (5 < 6) { echo "Five is smaller than six"; }
```

You still need to dig below the surface to examine what's going on. The conditional part of the if statement is the part contained within parentheses. It can evaluate to one of the two Boolean values, true or false. In fact, that's all it can ever evaluate to because either a condition is met or it isn't met. So the example line returns true. The if statement only executes if the condition inside evaluates to true.

The preceding example isn't all that useful because you already know that five is smaller than six. However, if you compare the contents of a variable to a number, such as a lucky number, then the answer depends upon the value of the variable $lucky_number:

```
If ($lucky_number < 6) { echo "Our lucky number is smaller than six"; }
```

Or, you can compare two variables for an outcome:

```
If ($lucky_number < $lottery_number) { echo "Our lucky number is too small"; }
```

And of course, you can use the results of this condition to not just display a message but to determine a particular course of action:

```
If ($lucky_number < $lottery_number){
    echo "Our lucky number is too small";
     $lucky_number = $lucky_number + 1;
}
```

Here's a simple example in which the PHP program "thinks" of a number between one and ten and you have to guess the number. To get PHP to "think" of a number, you use the PHP random number generating function named rand(). How it works is discussed after the example.

Try It Out   Use Comparison Operators

1. Open up your Web page editor and type in the following:

```
<html>
<head><title></title></head>
```

```
<body>
<?php
if (isset($_POST['posted'])) {
    $number = rand(1,10);
    if ($_POST['guess'] > $number) {
        echo "<h3>Your guess is
          too high</h3>";
        echo "<br>The number is
          $number, you don't win, please play again<hr>";
    } else if ($_POST['guess'] < $number) {
        echo "<h3>Your guess is too low</h3>";
        echo "<br>The number is
          $number, you don't win, please play again<hr>";
    } else {
        echo "<br>The number is
          $number, you win, please play again<hr>";
    }
}
?>
<form method="POST" action="guessgame.php">
<input type="hidden" name="posted" value="true">
What number between 1 and 10 am I thinking of?
<input name="guess" type="text">
<br>
<br>
<input type="submit" value="Submit">
</form>
</body>
</html>
```

2. Save the file as guessgame.php, and open it in your browser. Enter a guess in the text field and click the Submit button. Figure 4-1 shows an example result.

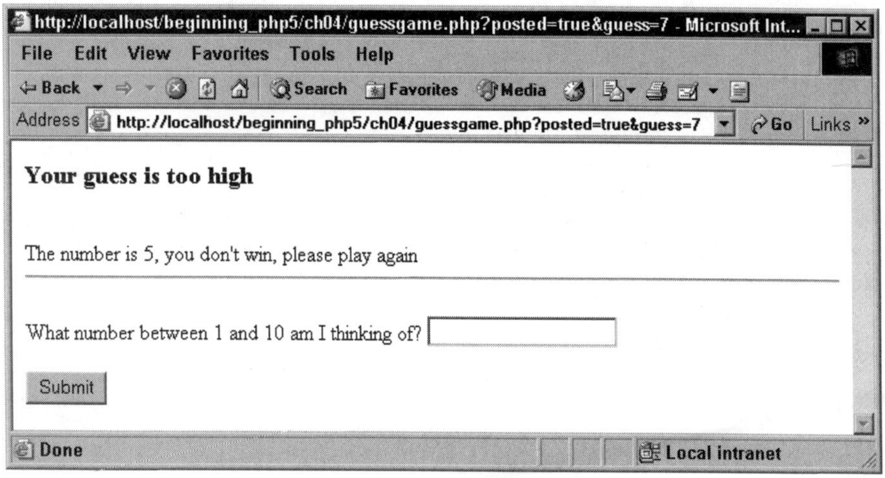

Figure 4-1

How It Works

This example cheats a little bit in that it doesn't get PHP to generate a random number until after the user submits his guess. This has no effect on the outcome, because the random number generated is totally uninfluenced by the guess the user has supplied. Here's the code that creates the random number:

```
$number = rand(1,10);
```

The rand() function is extremely simple to use—you just supply it with a minimum value and a maximum value separated by a comma and it generates a random number between and including these two values. The result is stored in the $number variable.

When it first opens, the form asks the user for a number and stores the answer in a text box with the name attribute set to guess.

```
What number between 1 and 10 am I thinking of?
<input name="guess" type="text">
```

The data in the guess input field is passed back to script when the form is submitted; the $_POST[posted] variable is set, so you can use the isset() function to tell whether to perform the rest of the processing (the first if statement).

Then comparison operators are used to determine if the number submitted is higher, lower, or the same as the random number chosen. The number that the user supplied, which is stored in $_POST[guess], is compared to the number that PHP is "thinking" of. If the value stored in $guess is higher than the value stored in $Number, the code between the next set of braces is executed:

```
if ($_POST['guess'] > $number) {
    echo "<h3>Your guess is
     too high</h3>";
    echo "<br>The number is
     $number, you don't win, please play again<hr>";
```

The code after the first curly brace informs the user that the guess was too high, tells him what the number the program was "thinking" of, and invites him to play again.

Next, there is an else if statement. To get it started, end the first block of code with a closing curly brace, write in the else if statement, and begin another code block with an opening curly brace. This statement acts as another if statement, and checks to see if the guess is too low. If so, the code in its block is executed:

```
} else if ($_POST['guess'] < $number) {
    echo "<h3>Your guess is too low</h3>";
    echo "<br>The number is
     $number, you don't win, please play again<hr>";
```

This time the user is informed that his guess was too low, told what the number was, and invited to play again.

The final code block completes the PHP script. If the script gets this far, the user's number is already determined to be neither too high nor too low and must match the program's random number, so the else block of code executes. It tells the user that he's won and asks him to play again:

```
} else {
    echo "<br>The number is
    $number, you win, please play again<hr>";
    }
}
?>
```

The main effect of using the hidden form field and the isset() function is to cause the programming to run only if the form has been submitted.

The == and === Operators

You might already have noted that the equals sign has two different distinct usages in PHP. The single equal sign is the assignment operator; the double equal sign is the equality operator. This is an important difference, if you consider the following:

```
$lucky_number = 5;
$lucky_number = 7;
```

These lines set the value of $lucky_number as 5 and then, whatever was previously the value (5, in this case) in the variable is assigned a new value (7). In other words, the second line here overrides the first line.

What's different is that the equality operator doesn't affect the contents of the variable in any way in the following line:

```
if ($lucky_number == 7) echo ("Your lucky number is seven");
```

Other programming languages, such as Visual Basic, use the equals sign (=) not strictly as an assignment operator, but also as a comparison operator, depending upon context. It's very easy to make the mistake of assigning a value when you mean to compare values in PHP, if you are used to the way other languages do comparisons. For example:

```
$lucky_number = 5;
If ($lucky_number = 7) {
    echo "Your number is $lucky_number";
} else {
    echo "Your number is $lucky_number";
}
```

In this example, the output will be "Your number is 7" (the first case), rather than "Your number is 5" (the second case), because rather than comparing the two values, the equals sign within the if statement actually resets the value (assigns the value) of 7 to $lucky_number. Remember, in PHP you must be sure that you use single for assignment and double for equality. If you don't you might get unexpected results.

There is a second version of the equality operator, one that was introduced in PHP4.01. This operator uses three equals signs and evaluates to true only if the values are equal and the data types of the values/

variables are also equal:

```
if ($lucky_number === $random_number) {
    echo "Your lucky number is $random_number";
}
```

The triple equals sign is very useful in situations where you need to know not just whether the values are equal, but are also the exact same type, such as when you want to know if you have a Boolean true or false value, and not a value that resolves to one of them without actually being a Boolean type (as discussed in the *"Boolean Values"* section earlier in the chapter).

The != and <> Operators

The reverse of the equality operator == is the inequality operator !=. If you happen to be reading someone else's PHP code, it's easy to miss the ! sign (exclamation point), but it makes a world of difference to the meaning of the expression, so keep your eyes peeled for it.

```
if ($lucky_number != 7) {
    echo ("Your lucky number most definitely isn't seven");
}
```

The symbols != literally stand for not equal to!

There is a second notation for not equal to, using the less than and greater than operators. It's used in the following way in an if statement:

```
if ($lucky_number <> 7) {
    echo ("Your lucky number most definitely isn't seven");
}
```

The only time that either of these operators (!= or <>) causes the expression to evaluate to false is if the value in $lucky_number is 7. Just think of the <> operator as "not."

Let's reuse the simple question/radio-button answer script from Chapter 3. This time you'll not only ask the question, but also tell the user whether he got the answer correct.

Try It Out   **Use the Equality and Inequality Operators**

    1.   Open your Web page editor, and type in all of the following code:

```
<html>
<head><title></title></head>
<body>
<?php
if (isset($_POST['posted'])) {
    if ($_POST['question1'] == "Lisbon") {
        echo "You are correct, $_POST[question1] is the right answer<hr>";
    }

    if ($_POST['question1'] != "Lisbon") {
        echo "You are incorrect, $_POST[question1] is not the right answer<hr>";
```

```
        }
    }
    ?>
    <form method="POST" action="quiz.php">
    <input type="hidden" name="posted" value="true">
    What is the capital of Portugal?
    <br>
    <br>
    <input name="question1" type="radio" value="Porto">
    Porto
    <br>
    <input name="question1" type="radio" value="Lisbon">
    Lisbon
    <br>
    <input name="question1" type="radio" value="Madrid">
    Madrid
    <br>
    <br>
    <input type="submit">
    </form>
    </body>
    </html>
```

2. Save the as `quiz.php`, and close it.

3. Open the file in your browser, choose Madrid as the answer, and click Submit Query. Figure 4-2 shows the result.

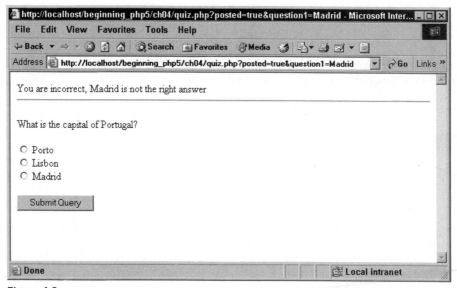

Figure 4-2

4. Try a different answer by selecting a different city on this screen, to see what the response is.

How It Works

The `if` statements simply check for the value `Lisbon` attached to the variable named `$_POST[question1]`. If the value is `Lisbon`, you give a positive response; if the value is not `Lisbon`, you provide a negative response.

Logical Operators (AND, OR, !)

The logical operators are a little less fearsome than they sound, and although they were discussed earlier in the Boolean sections of the chapter, it's time for you to put them to work. One good way to understand how to incorporate them into your programs to simply say what they do in plain language, because their English usage alerts you to the way they are used in PHP. For example, if the day is Sunday and the weather is sunny, then you will go to the beach. The same goes for PHP:

```php
if ($day == "Sunday" AND $weather === "Sunshine") {
    echo ("Off to the beach then");
}
```

AND can also be written using the ampersand operator twice (`&&`):

```php
if ($day == "Sunday" && $weather == "Sunshine") {
    echo ("Off to the beach then");
}
```

The OR and ! operators are similarly straightforward. You could rephrase the example code by using the OR operator to say the opposite thing:

```php
if ($day == "Monday" OR $weather == "rainy") {
    echo ("Not going to the beach today then");
}
```

If it is Monday or the weather is raining then you can't got to the beach. The OR operator is also represented by the double bar (double pipe) sign ||, so the preceding code can also be written like this:

```php
if ($day == "Monday" ||$weather == "rainy") {
    echo ("Not going to the beach today then");
}
```

An interesting note that probably won't affect your code, but one that you should be aware of, is that the `&&` and AND operators have slightly different precedence. The same goes for the || and OR operators. The `&&` and || operators take precedence over their textual alternatives.

Although there is a NOT operator, you can't use the word "not." The NOT operator is actually an exclamation mark. If it goes outside the parentheses, it reverses the result inside them, so that if the condition is originally returns true, then it becomes false, and vice versa. For example, if the day isn't Sunday then you can't go to the beach:

```php
if !($day == "Sunday") {
    echo ("Not going to the beach today then");
}
```

You might surmise that this has exactly the same effect as the inequality operator != introduced earlier, but it doesn't. The inequality operator applies only to the expression it is part of, although the exclamation point outside of the parentheses in an if statement applies to the entire condition (the part inside the parentheses). In fact, you can reverse the result of a condition that doesn't even have any operators in it. Just place a variable inside a condition part of an if statement, and if the variable has no value, the following code shows how the condition will then be false, but will be activated if the condition is preceded by the exclamation point. If you read it to yourself, it sounds like, "If the $answer variable does not contain anything, then echo a statement."

```
if !($answer) {
    echo ("There's no answer");
}
```

This statement only prints a message if there is no value in the $answer variable or the value is zero (which in PHP is equivalent to being empty). Can you work out why? It's because the ! operator negates the truth-value of $answer, so if $answer returns false, !($answer) returns true, and the if statement executes. This is an important point because oftentimes the condition you'll use in an if statement is simply the result of evaluating an expression or the result of a function, and if true, the if statement proceeds with processing, and if false, it does not. There may be no operators whatsoever in the condition.

There's still quite a bit more detail to go into about logical operators, but to break it up, try out this little program that uses a couple of these operators.

Try It Out   Use the Logical Operators

Here's a program that a car hire company might use to verify whether somebody can drive one of its cars. A prospective driver must hold a driving license, and be aged 21 or older. This program checks for these details and more.

1. Open your Web page editor and type in the following code:

```
<html>
<head><title></title></head>
<body>
<b>Namllu car hire company</b>
<?php
if (isset($_POST['posted'])) {
    if ($_POST['age'] > 20 and $_POST['license'] == "on") {
        echo ("Your car hire has been accepted.<hr>");
    }

    if ($_POST['age'] < 21 or $_POST['license'] == "") {
        echo ("Unfortunately we cannot hire a car to you.<hr>");
    }
} else {
?>
<form method="post" action="car.php">
<input type="hidden" name="posted" value="true">
```

```
First name:
<input name="first_name" type="text">
Last name:
<input name="last_name" type="text">
age:
<input name="age" type="text"size="3">
<br>
<br>
Address:
<textarea name="address" rows=4 cols=40>
</textarea>
<br>
<br>
Do you hold a current driving license?
<input name="license" type="checkbox">
<br>
<br>
<input type="submit" value="Submit application">
</form>
</body>
</html>
<?php
}
?>
```

2. Save this file as car.php and close it.

3. Open the file in your browser and type in some details, as shown in Figure 4-3.

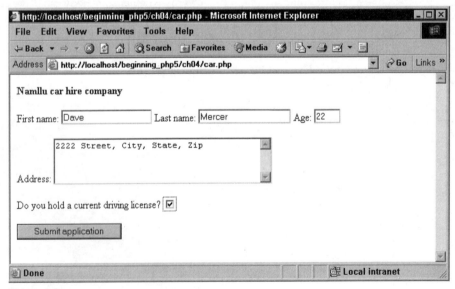

Figure 4-3

4. Click Submit application. Figure 4-4 shows example results.

Figure 4-4

How It Works

To pick up additional information, this HTML form is a bit longer than other forms you've made (the artists among you may want to lay out the form better, but simple works best for now). There's also an else statement to cause the form to be displayed only if it has not been posted, because once a person has an acceptable application there's no need to redisplay the form (don't forget to put the <?}?> after the end of the HTML form).

Proper processing of the PHP code depends on picking up data from two HTML input fields (a text box named age and a check box named license). These variables are received as $_POST[age] and $_POST[license] after the form's submitted. The following HTML does the work of providing the form and Submit button.

```
<input name="age" type="text"size="3">
<br>
<br>
Address:
<textarea name="address" rows=4 cols=40>
</textarea>
<br>
<br>
Do you hold a current driving license?
<input name="license" type="checkbox">
```

The text box has the name attribute age, so a variable named $_POST[age] is created to hold the user's age. The check box control (license) is either set to on or off. The $_POST[license] variable can either hold the value on or it can hold no value at all.

The value on is actually browser dependent, but given that Internet Explorer, Netscape Navigator, and Opera all use it, you shouldn't encounter any problems using it. If your browser is different and the example doesn't work, then use the echo () *statement to interrogate the* $license *variable, and amend the code accordingly (more about using the* echo () *statement for debugging purposes in Chapter 5).*

The PHP script makes use of both these variables. The first if statement in car.php says that if the age is greater than 20, and the user is a license holder, then you can accept the car hire:

```
if ($_POST['age'] > 20 and $_POST['license'] == "on") {
      echo ("Your car hire has been accepted.<hr>");
   }
```

The second block says the reverse: if either the user's age is less than 21, or the user isn't a license holder, the car rental is refused:

```
if ($_POST['age'] < 21 or $_POST['license'] == "") {
      echo ("Unfortunately we cannot hire a car to you.<hr>");
}
```

That's all there is to the script.

One last contingency: what happens if the user puts in an age between 20 and 21, say 20.5? Unlikely, but something the script should be able to handle. The script actually pushes the boundaries a little, because either age condition will accept it and you will get two answers. In situations like this, perhaps it would be best to use the >= or <= operators (greater-than or equal-to and less-than or equal-to). Makes sense, doesn't it? You could use the following code to produce a better result:

```
if ($_POST['age'] >= 21 and $_POST['license'] == "on") {
      echo ("Your car hire has been accepted.<hr>");
} else {
      echo ("Unfortunately we cannot hire a car to you.<hr>");
}
```

switch Statements

In using the if statement, you've probably noticed that sometimes there are multiple conditions to check for. You could write large if statements with else if blocks, but frequently it's just easier to write a switch statement. The switch statement works exactly like it sounds; it switches control from one block to another based on a particular input value.

Here's an example of the switch statement in use:

```
switch ($grade) {
    case $grade>90:
          echo ("You got an A.");
          break;
    case $grade>80:
        echo ("You got a B.");
        break;
```

```
    case $grade>70:
        echo ("You got a C.");
        break;
    case $grade>50:
        echo ("You got a D.");
        break;
    case $grade<50:
        echo ("You got an F. ");
        break;
    default:
        echo ("You failed");
}
```

Instead of `if` and `else if`, there's now just `case` (represented by the variable named `$grade`), followed by code blocks that each test for the value of `$grade`, and then a set of actions. In each case the PHP program has something different to execute. It's good practice to have a default case because default is a catch-all that makes sure something happens (leave default out, and you'll realize it when all you get is a blank screen with no output and also no error messages).

You will have noticed the `break` command in the `switch` statement. When PHP encounters `break`, it stops what it's doing, drops out of the whole switch structure, and picks up the programming thread after the closing brace. It doesn't continue checking for further compliance with other criteria, even though a grade of 80 percent would have met all of these criteria. This is useful because you don't have to write countless little catch-alls for every conceivable situation. If you want all criteria checked, then just omit the keyword `break`, although you should note that `break` only works in conjunction with the `switch` statement, and not the `if` statement (but note that you can confuse yourself if you put a break within an `if` statement that happens to be inside a `switch` statement or `for` loop, and so on, because although the `if` statement won't break, the `switch` statement or `for` loop will).

If you omit the word break, all statements evaluate to true, and you get A, B, C, D, and F with a score of 80.

```
switch ($State) {
    case "IL":
        echo ("Illinois");
        break;
    case "GA":
        echo ("Georgia");
        break;
    default:
        echo ("California");
        break;
}
```

If you just supply a value (IL, in this example) next to the `case` keyword, PHP automatically checks the variable you supplied in the `switch` parentheses for equality with the value next to case, whether numerical or textual.

There's a colon, not a semicolon, after the `case` keyword. Actually, either colon or semicolon works fine (the colon is used in the online documentation), so use whichever you please.

You should only provide cases for values you expect to occur and intend to work with (even if you simply want the `switch` statement to break off processing). For example, you can leave case occurrences within switch empty except for a `break` statement. Then, if that `case` is encountered, the `switch` statement will break and no more processing within it will occur. That happens in the following code if someone enters HH for the `$State` variable. The case for HH is activated and processing ends, unlike what happens for values that are unknown, which activates the default case and echoes out California):

```
switch ($State) {
    case "HH":
       break;
    case "IL":
        echo ("Illinois");
        break;
    case "GA":
        echo ("Georgia");
        break;
    default:
        echo ("California");
        break;
    }
```

Try It Out   Use switch Statements

This example creates a form that enables the user to select destination and grade values for booking a holiday. These values are then used to (very simply) calculate a price for the type of vacation selected.

1.   Open your text editor and type in the following:

```
<html>
<head><title></title></head>
<body>
<b>Namllu holiday booking form</b>
<br>
<br>
<?php
if (isset($_POST['posted'])) {
    $price = 500;
       $starmodifier = 1;
    $citymodifier = 1;
    $destination = $_POST['destination'];
    $destgrade = $_POST['destination'] . $_POST['grade'];
      switch($destgrade) {
       case "Barcelonathree":
           $citymodifier = 2;
           $price = $price * $citymodifier;
           echo "The cost for a week in $destination is $price";
           break;
       case "Barcelonafour":
           $citymodifier = 2;
           $starmodifier = 2;
           $price = $price * $citymodifier * $starmodifier;
           echo "The cost for a week in $destination is $price";
           break;
       case "Viennathree":
```

```
                $citymodifier = 3.5;
                $price = $price * $citymodifier;
                echo "The cost for a week in $destination is $price";
                break;
        case "Viennafour":
                $citymodifier = 3.5;
                $starmodifier = 2;
                $price = $price * $citymodifier * $starmodifier;
                echo "The cost for a week in $destination is $price";
                break;
        case "Praguethree":
                $price = $price * $citymodifier;
                echo "The cost for a week in $destination is $price";
                break;
        case "Praguefour":
                $starmodifier = 2;
                $price = $price * $citymodifier * $starmodifier;
                echo "The cost for a week in $destination is $price";
                break;
        default:
                echo ("Go back and do it again");
                break;
    }
}
?>
<form method="POST" action="holiday.php">
<input type="hidden" name="posted" value="true">
Where do you want to go on holiday?
<br>
<br>
<input name="destination" type="radio" value="Prague">
Prague
<br>
<input name="destination" type="radio" value="Barcelona">
Barcelona
<br>
<input name="destination" type="radio" value="Vienna">
Vienna
<br>
<br>
What grade of hotel do you want to stay at?
<br>
<br>
<input name="grade" type="radio" value="three">
Three star
<br>
<input name="grade" type="radio" value="four">
Four star
<br>
<br>
<input type="submit" value="Book Now">
</form>
</body>
</html>
```

2. Save the file as `holiday.php` and close it.

3. Now open the file in your browser, enter some details in the form, and click the Book Now button. Figure 4-5 shows an example result.

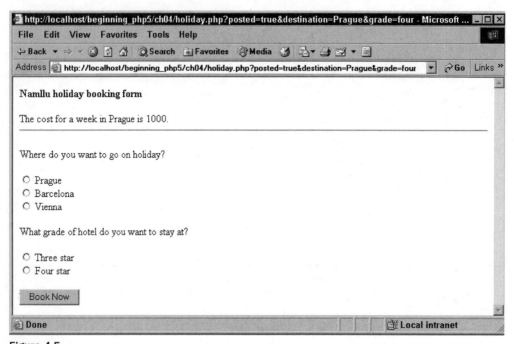

Figure 4-5

How It Works

There were two claims about `switch`: that it's easier to read and that it uses few lines of code. The first is subjective. Consider the second: this program could have been written as a series of `if` statements, and it would have used a huge number lines of PHP script in between the `<?php?>` markers, as you can imagine, but `holiday.php` has used just 41 lines.

Take a look at how this comes together. When the page is opened, you see the HTML form and understand that you need to make some choices. Once the form is submitted, the PHP code is activated because the `$_POST[posted]` variable is set, and this is detected within the first (and only) `if` statement by the `isset()` function. Next, the code inside the `if` statement begins to run, starting by setting a few variables, as shown here:

```
    $price = 500;
    $starmodifier = 1;
    $citymodifier = 1;

$destination = $_POST['destination'];
```

The next line introduces a new variable, $destgrade, which is a concatenation of the contents of the $_POST['destination'] and $_POST['grade'] variables.

```
$destgrade = $_POST['destination'] . $_POST['grade'];
```

So, if you chose Barcelona and four star, $destgrade would contain Barcelonafour. The number of lines is reduced (over multiple if statements) in part by feeding the condition variable to the switch statement only once:

```
switch($destgrade) {
```

All seven possible outcomes need to be captured. (The three hotel choices multiplied by two star grades is six, plus anything that isn't one of these choices.) The six possible correct outcomes are Barcelona and three star, Barcelona and four star, Prague and three star, Prague and four star, Vienna and three star, Vienna and four star. So the possible variables in $destgrade can only be Barcelonathree, Barcelonafour, Praguethree, Praguefour, Viennathree, and Viennafour, and a case is tailor-made for each.

Because all of the cases perform a similar action, just examine this one example:

```
case "Barcelonathree":
    $citymodifier = 2;
    $price = $price * $citymodifier;
    echo "The cost for a week in $destination is $price";
    break;
```

For the Barcelonathree case, the $citymodifier is set to two and multiplied by the price. Then the price and destination are displayed and you break to the end of the program. If the value in $destgrade doesn't match any correct case, then something must be wrong and you tell the user to go back and do it again.

It's good practice to add a break at the end even though it does nothing:

```
default:
    echo ("Go back and do it again");
    break;
}
```

It means that your code is less likely to generate errors if you ever add another case after the else.

Loops and Arrays

There are three kinds of loops in PHP—while, do while, and for—that you'll explore here, and then you'll examine a related feature, the array, which you saw briefly earlier in the book. An array is a set of indexed variables that, especially when coupled with the loop, can prove very useful. Loops coupled with arrays enable you to create hundreds or even thousands of variables using only three or four lines of code.

Loops

You explored the branching (conditional) statement earlier in the chapter. It enables you to introduce decision-making into your PHP code. Loops are similar to branching statements in that the next line of code to be executed depends upon whether a condition is true or false.

However, loops differ from conditional statements because the contents of the loop may be executed over and over again. The condition is tested, and the code in the loop is executed if the condition holds. Then the condition is tested again; if it still is correct, the code in the loop is executed again, and maybe again, and again and again. . . . You get the picture. Each passage through the loop is known as an *iteration*.

As you read on you'll see that each type of loop is suited to a different situation.

while Loops

The `while` loop is the simplest of the loops, and it bears some similarity to the `if` statement because it checks the result of a condition. Depending on whether the condition is true or false, the section of code (placed within braces) after the conditional statement is executed:

```
while (a condition is true){
    execute the contents of these braces;
}
```

After the contents of the loop are executed, the condition at the top is tested again, and the code might be executed again, and so on. If the condition is tested and found to be false, the code in braces is ignored, and PHP proceeds to the first line beyond the end of the braces. Here's a pseudo code example:

```
while (the moon is full){
    the coyotes will howl;
}
```

So if the moon isn't full, the coyotes won't be howling, but for the duration of the moon being full, they will howl. Here's another example. Say you want to inform a user shopping on an e-commerce site that his credit limit has been exceeded. You might use something like the following PHP code snippet to display a message when the user's shopping bill exceeds the credit limit:

```
while ($shopping_total > $credit_limit){
    echo ("You have exceeded your credit limit,
        so the last item from your basket will be removed");
    $last_purchase_but_one = $shopping_total - $last_purchase;
    $last_purchase = $last_purchase_but_one;
}
```

So, if the user exceeds his credit limit `$credit_limit`, his last purchase is cancelled, removing its value (`$last_purchase`) from the total bill (`$shopping_total`). Then you'd change the value of `$last_purchase` to be the value of the last purchase but one, `$last_purchase_but_one`, so you can iterate through the loop, removing one item at a time from the shopping list, until `$shopping_total` is below `$credit_limit`.

You may have noticed that if `$credit_limit` has a negative value, this loop could continue to iterate indefinitely. If you use a condition that might always be true, an infinite loop may occur, meaning that there's no way for your program to end because the condition never becomes false. It won't generate an error; it just continues to execute the contents of the loop over and over again. When you write code that uses loops, you should bear this in mind. More on infinite loops later in the chapter.

To try out the `while` loop, you're going to extend the loan application example you wrote in Chapter 3. You'll remember that you asked the user to choose a loan package, and then your PHP program approved or rejected the loan. Now imagine that you've approved several possible loan packages from which the user can choose. There are three different loans packages, each offering a different amount at a different interest rate per month. The new program is going to tell you how long it's going to take to pay the loan back.

Of course, to do this you need another piece of information from the user: the amount of money the user is willing to pay each month. The loan also requires the user to pay interest on the loan each month. In other words, if I borrowed $1000 at 5% interest per month, and I was repaying $100 a month, I'd also have to pay $50 interest for the first month. So really I'm only actually pay $50 of my outstanding loan in the first month. In the second month, I'd owe $950, so if I was repaying another $100 this month, 5% loan interest on $950 would be $47.50. Obviously the calculations can get complex rather quickly, although the formula to do the calculation will remain the same each month:

```
Payment = Monthly Payment - Interest
Debt = Debt - Payment
```

All you need to do is perform these two calculations over and over until the debt is zero, and then count up how many payments were required to do that. You don't know how many months this will take unless you're a mathematical whiz, but then you don't need to be—you can get PHP to use a while loop to do the job for you.

Try It Out   Use a while Loop

1. Open your Web page editor and type in the following:

```
<html>
<head><title></title></head>
<body>
<b>Namllu credit bank loan form</b>
<?php
if (isset($_POST['posted'])) {
    $duration = 0;
    switch ($_POST['loan']) {
    case "1000";
        $interest = 5;
        break;
    case "5000";
        $interest = 6.5;
        break;
    case "10000";
        $interest = 8;
        break;
    default:
        echo "You didn't enter a loan package!<hr>";
        exit;
    }
    while ($_POST['loan'] > 0)
    {
        $duration = $duration + 1;
        $monthly = $_POST[month] - ($_POST['loan']*$interest/100);
        if ($monthly <= 0)
```

```
        {
            echo "You need larger repayments to pay off your loan!<hr>";
            exit;
        }
    $_POST['loan'] = $_POST['loan'] - $monthly;
    }
    echo "This would take you $duration months to pay this off at the
interest rate of $interest percent.<hr>";


}
?>
<form method="POST" action="loan.php">
<input type="hidden" name="posted" value="true">
<br>
How much do you want to borrow?<br><br>
<input name="loan" type="radio" value="1000">our $1,000 package at
5.0% interest
<br>
<input name="loan" type="radio" value="5000">our $5,000 package at
6.5% interest
<br>
<input name="loan" type="radio" value="10000">our $10,000 package at
8.0% interest
<br>
<br>
How much do you want to pay a month?
<input name="month" type="text" size="5">
<br>
<br>
<input type="submit" value="Calculate">
</form>
</body>
</html>
```

2. Save the file as `loan.php` and close it.

3. Open the file in your browser. Select the $1,000 package, enter 100 as the payment, and click Calculate button. Figure 4-6 shows the result.

How It Works

The form asks the user to make two choices: the amount of the loan, which is then stored in the variable `$_POST['loan']`, and the amount he wants to pay each month, which is stored in the variable `$_POST['month']`. These two variables are then used in the script in `loan.php`. There are only two structures being used in the script. The first is a `switch` structure, which was introduced in the last section. First initialize the `$duration` variable, which will hold a count of the number of monthly repayments that will be needed for the user to repay the loan. Then the `switch` statement is used to choose the interest rate because the rate depends on the loan the user selected in the HTML form:

```
$duration = 0;
switch ($_POST['loan']) {
case "1000";
   $interest = 5;
   break;
```

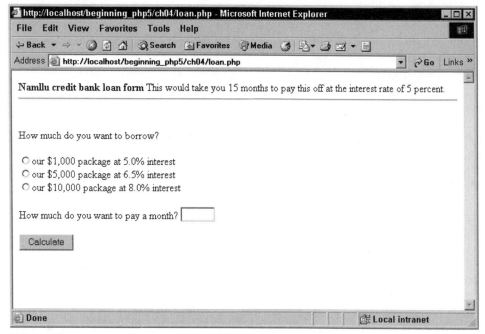

Figure 4-6

```
case "5000";
    $interest = 6.5;
    break;
case "10000";
    $interest = 8;
    break;
default:
    echo "You didn't enter a loan package!<hr>";
    exit;
}
```

There are only three possible values $_POST[loan] could evaluate to: 1000, 5000, and 10000. The value of $loan is used to set the variable $interest to the corresponding interest rate, using the switch statement. If none of the three loan values is picked, you tell the user so, and stop the program right there because the user didn't enter a value.

Before you can enter the while loop, the conditional statement must to be validated. The condition is that you can iterate as long as $_POST[loan] hasn't reached zero; in other words, as long as the debt hasn't been paid off:

```
while ($_POST[loan] > 0){
```

The $_POST[loan] value is the condition that starts the loop, because the $loan must be 1000, 5000 or 10000, not zero. Next, the month counter, $duration, was initially set to zero, so it's incremented by one, to indicate that this is the first time around the loop:

```
$duration = $duration + 1;
```

The next line calculates how much money will be paid toward the loan this month, including interest:

```
$monthly = $_POST['month'] - ($_POST['loan'] * $interest / 100);
```

To get this month's interest payment, the percentage interest is divided by 100 percent, and the result is multiplied by the loan amount. Then, to calculate how much of the loan will be repaid this month, subtract this month's interest payment from the fixed monthly payment. This provides the answer to the first part of the calculation mentioned at beginning of the example:

```
Payment = Monthly Payment - Interest
```

However, you might be wondering why you're creating a new variable called $monthly at this point in the program. Why not just use the following line instead?

```
$month = $month - ((($_POST['loan'] / 100) * $interest);
```

The reason is that you want the value of $_POST['month'] to remain constant over all of the loops, representing the fixed $100 monthly repayment. If you use this line of code, $_POST['month'] would change value over each loop because you'd be subtracting the monthly interest from it with each iteration. So you use a different variable, $monthly, to represent the total amount repaid this month. Each time you go around the loop, it holds a different value.

Ignore the next if statement for the moment; it doesn't alter the values of the variables. Now that you've got a value for how much to subtract from the loan this month, you can adjust the figure in the overall $_POST['loan']:

```
$_POST['loan'] = $_POST['loan'] - $monthly;
```

To see what's really happening, step through the loop now. The first time around the loop, the variables contain their initial values:

```
$_POST['loan'] = 1000
$interest = 5
$duration= 0
$_POST['month']= 100
```

So the first line effectively reads:

```
while (1000 > 0)
```

Yes, 1000 is bigger than 0, and you safely proceed inside the loop to the first line of code, which now reads:

```
$duration = 0 + 1;
```

$duration now equals one. The next line is:

```
$monthly = 100 - (1000 * 5 / 100);
```

Calculating the contents of the parentheses you get:

```
$monthly = 100 - (50);
```

And $monthly is equal to 50. You reach the final line:

```
$_POST['loan'] = 1000 - 50;
```

So $loan is now $950. Next is the closing brace, meaning the end of the iteration. You jump back to the condition part of the loop, and when you test it this time it reads:

```
while (950 > 0)
```

The condition still hasn't been met, and you venture into the loop once more. $duration changed to 1 during the previous loop, so this time it reads:

```
$duration = 1 + 1;
```

Now $duration has the value 2. The next line is changed slightly from the last loop, because the value of $loan is different. It now reads:

```
$monthly = 100 - (950 * 5 / 100);
```

That leaves $monthly with a value of 52.5. This has an effect on the remaining loan calculation:

```
$_POST[loan] = 950 - 52.5;
```

After this, $_POST['loan'] holds the value 897.5. So the actual interest payments decrease over time because the loan amount decreases. However, the monthly loan payment remains fixed, so effectively the amount of the loan being repaid each month increases. The first month the user pays off $50, the second, $52.50, and so on.

You jump back to the condition at the beginning of the loop and test it again:

```
while (897.5>0)
```

It still hasn't been met, so you're back around the loop a third time. In fact, you have to go around the loop 15 times before the loan is paid off, but you now have an idea of what is going on.

Infinite Loops

You probably know that paying back loans at a very slow rate is a bad idea because the interest to be paid outstrips your payments, and the loan gradually increases so that it can never be paid off. This rather frightening prospect could also have lethal implications for the example program. If the user enters a value that is too low, then the program loop continues indefinitely—an infinite loop—because the condition of $Loan>0 will never be false. By default a PHP script should only execute for 30 seconds, infinite loop or not. However, on Windows 2000 and IIS 5, your browser may eventually freeze, and if you're not careful your Web server will freeze up, too.

This means that you must make sure that infinite loops don't occur. In the loan example, you can do this by checking for repayment values that are too low; however, this value is entirely dependent on which loan package is selected. Therefore you have to use a little more brainpower and construct a search in the loop itself. Now, the only time an infinite loop will occur is if you're actually adding to the $loan value each month. Take another look at the relevant line of code in the program:

```
$_POST['loan'] = $_POST['loan'] - $monthly;
```

But you are *subtracting* $monthly from $_POST['loan']. The only way you can increase the loan value is if you have a negative value in $monthly (subtracting a negative value is equivalent to adding a positive value). So you perform a check to see if $monthly is smaller than or equal to zero. As long as it isn't, you can be sure that the loan amount is going to decrease with each iteration of the loop, and it can only do this a finite amount of times. It doesn't really matter how many times it takes: PHP can iterate many thousands of times in just one second.

If you encounter an infinite loop condition, break out of the loop using the exit command, first displaying a message to the user:

```
if ($monthly <= 0){
    echo "You need larger repayments to pay off your loan!";
    exit;
}
```

You don't want to display anything afterward, so you use the exit command to prevent further output to the Web page.

On the other hand, if you finish iterating correctly, you display the final contents of the $duration variable:

```
echo "This would take you $duration months to pay this off at the Interest
rate of $interest percent.";
```

This lets the user know how long it would take him to pay off the loan. Despite the loop being only 5 lines long, it's taken some time to explain it in detail. If you're still not happy with the workings, go back and put some different figures in, work out what should happen on paper, writing out the results of the loop each time, and then check that your results concur with what PHP returns. They should be identical.

do while Loops

The do while loop is similar in operation to the while loop, except for one small point: the conditional statement is tested at the end of the loop, not the beginning. This has a subtle but important difference: the contents of the braces are executed at least once, even if the condition turns out to be false:

```
do{
    execute the contents of these parentheses;
}
while(a condition is true); // go back and do it again
```

Go back to the shopping example and change it to do while. You can see that it alters the whole working of the code:

```
do{
    echo ("You have exceeded your credit limit,
                        so the last item from your basket will be removed");
    $last_purchase_but_one = $shopping_total - $last_purchase;
    $last_purchase = $last_purchase_but_one;
} while ($shopping_total > $credit_limit);
```

You'd print the warning message before you'd even checked to see if the user had exceeded his credit limit! That's not what you want to do at all.

Here's a different situation, one in which a do while loop would be useful. If you had to travel on an interstate highway from Exit 14 to Exit 103, it could be represented as:

```
do{
    drive until next exit;
} while ($exit != 103);
```

It stands to follow that, if you wanted to get off the highway, you'd have to drive at least until the next exit, so it would be necessary to iterate at least once. And if the next exit isn't Exit 103, you'd want to iterate again, and so on until you reach the right exit. Another good example of using do while in PHP would be if you definitely need to perform a calculation at least once, but might also need to perform the calculation over and over again until you get a certain answer. Say for example, that you had a prime number checker. To check if a number is a prime, you need to divide it by every number from two up to the value of the number itself minus one. You could let the do while loop do it for you:

```
do{
    $remainder = $possible_prime_number % $number;
    $number=$number + 1;
} while ($remainder != 0 AND $number < $possible_prime_number);
```

The prime number candidate $possible_prime_number is divided by each number from 2 up to one less than $possible_prime_number itself, using the modulus operator (%) to determine if there is a remainder from each division. During each iteration you perform one division and test for a remainder. When no remainder is found, you drop out of the loop, because you know then the number can't be a prime.

You have to do at least one division to find whether the candidate number is divisible by another number, and that's why the do while is suitable here. If you reach the value of the candidate number without dropping out of the loop, you know that the candidate number is only divisible by itself or 1, so it must be a prime number. Simple!

Another common situation where do while proves useful is when you need to wait for user input. Do you remember the number guessing game program, where you get PHP to produce a random number from 1 to 10? What if you wanted to modify it so that the user has to keep guessing until the right number is picked? One simple option is to place the code in a do while loop, which iterates until the right number is guessed.

Give your understanding of do while loops a try here by fleshing out the prime number checker code snippet into a proper example in PHP.

Use do while Loop

1.   Start your Web page editor and type in the following:

```html
<html>
<head><title></title></head>
<body>
<?php
if (isset($_POST['posted'])) {
    $count=2;
    do
    {
        $remainder = $_POST['guess'] % $count;
        $count = $count + 1;
    } while ($remainder != 0 and $count < $_POST['guess']);
    if (($count < $_POST['guess']) || ($_POST['guess'] == 0)) {
        echo ("Your number is not prime<hr>");
    } else {
        echo ("Your number is prime<hr>");
    }
}
?>
<form method="POST" action="check.php">
<input type="hidden" name="posted" value="true">
What is your number:
<input name="guess" type="text">
<br>
<br>
<input type="submit" value="Check if number is prime">
<br>
</form>
</body>
</html>
```

2.   Save the file as check.php and close it.

3.   Open it in your browser, enter a number, and click the Check If Number Is Prime button.

Figure 4-7 shows an example result.

How It Works

The purpose of the HTML form is solely to extract a number from the user:

```
What is your number:
<input name="guess" type="text">
```

The number is passed to the $_POST['guess'] variable, which then sets up a count variable:

```
$count=2;
```

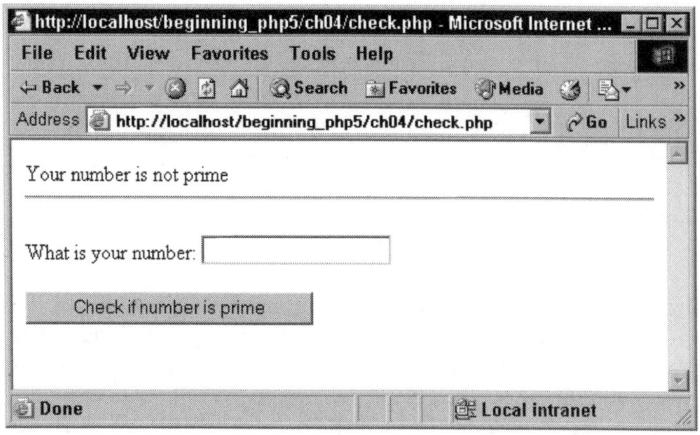

Figure 4-7

It's set to 2 because you don't want to start dividing by 1; after all, every whole number is exactly divisible by 1! Next you start the do loop:

```
do {
```

Inside the loop you start by checking for a remainder when you divide our $_POST['guess'] number by the value of the $count variable. Then increment the $count variable:

```
$remainder = $_POST['guess'] % $count;
$count = $count + 1;
```

These two lines form the whole body of the loop. Not bad considering that the user had entered the number 25634, this loop would have been dividing 25634 by 2, 3, 4, 5, 6, 7, 8, and so on, all the way up to 25633. That's a lot of iterations. At the end of every iteration you test to see if two things have happened: there is no remainder from the division, and the value of $count has reached the candidate prime number $_POST['guess'] yet:

```
} while ($remainder != 0 AND $count < $_POST['guess']);
```

When you drop out of the loop, it must be because one of these two conditions has occurred. If you drop out of the loop but the value of $count doesn't match $_POST[guess], it must be because the candidate prime number has been divided exactly by the number in $count, so $_POST[guess] isn't prime. You must also take into account a guess of zero, which gives a remainder of zero when divided by any number, but is not prime. Otherwise, if the two variables have matching values, then you must have a prime number:

```
if (($count < $_POST['guess']) || ($_POST['guess'] == 0)) {
    echo ("Your number is not prime<hr>");
} else {
    echo ("Your number is prime<hr>");
}
```

The last step is to display the results to the user.

for Loops

The `for` loop is best used when you want to repeat a section of code a specified amount of times. In other words, it gives you the ability to specify the number of times you iterate around the loop. The condition part of the loop is more complex than in the `while` loop because it is composed of three parts:

```
for (set loop counter; test loop counter; add or subtract from the counter){
    execute the contents of these braces;
}
```

The `for` loop introduces the concept of a loop counter, a variable that is used to count the number of times you've been around the loop (number of iterations), and to terminate the loop when the set number of iterations has been exceeded. The first two parts of the `for` loop's condition are to set the loop counter, that is to set the number of iterations you want the loop to make, and to test the loop counter—to check whether the set number of iterations has been surpassed. The third part of the condition ensures that you change the value of the counter with each iteration. The three parts to the condition enable you to construct some complex conditions and loops. None of the parts of the condition is actually compulsory, but to begin with you'll be using all three.

How the `for` loop can be used? Well, what's the best way to print out your name 10 times in a row? You could use the `echo` command 10 times, but that would get quite tiresome. You could also use the `while` loop that you just learned, and create a variable inside it to count the number of iterations, as follows:

```
$counter=0;
while ($counter<10){
    echo "My name is Chris!";
    $counter=$counter+1;
}
```

But how many times does this go around the loop? Is it 9 because when you reach 10, you stop? Is it 11 because you start the loop counter at 0? It is actually 10, but you have to go back, think about it logically, and work it out in your head. The number of iterations is much easier to keep track of with a `for` loop:

```
for ($counter = 1; $counter <= 10; $counter ++){
    echo "My name is Chris!";
}
```

You don't have to keep track of the loop counter, either; that's done for you.

You can get some experience with the `for` loop in the following "Try It Out."

Try It Out   Use a for Loop

This example creates a dynamic form that takes a value from the user, uses it to set the number of HTML controls displayed on a second page, and then displays the contents of these controls on a third page (note that the HTML contents of all three pages exist inside their respective `if` statements within this single page of code, and are displayed only when the right conditions are met, namely, the existence of the `$_POST[posted]` and `$_POST[posted01]` variables). Give it a try.

1. Nudge your Web page editor to make sure it's still awake, and type in the following:

```
<html>
<head><title></title></head>
<body>
<?php
if (isset($_POST['posted'])) {
    echo "<form method='POST' action='dynamic.php'>";
    for ($counter = 0; $counter < $_POST['number']; $counter ++)
    {
        $offset = $counter + 1;
        echo "<br>Please enter the name of child number $offset<br>";
        echo "<input name='child[]' type='text'>";
    }
    echo"<br>Press the button to move on<br>";
    echo "<input type='submit' value='Next'>";
    echo "<input type='hidden' name='posted01' value='true'></form>";

} else {

    if (isset($_POST['posted01'])) {
        $count=0;
        echo "Your children's names are:";
        do
        {
            $childs_name = $_POST['child'][$count];
            echo"<br><b>$childs_name</b>";
            $checkempty = $childs_name;
            $count = $count + 1;
        } while ($checkempty != "");
        if ($count == 1) {
            echo "Not applicable";
        }
    }

?>
<hr>
<form method="POST" action="dynamic.php">
<input type="hidden" name="posted" value="true">
How many children do you have?
<input name="number" type="text">
<br>
<br>
<input type="submit" value="Send Number">
<br>
</form>
<?
}
?>
</body>
</html>
```

2. Save this file as `dynamic.php` and close it.

3. Open the file in your browser (Figure 4-8 shows the interface) and enter a number (play along and enter a number greater than zero, even if you have no children).

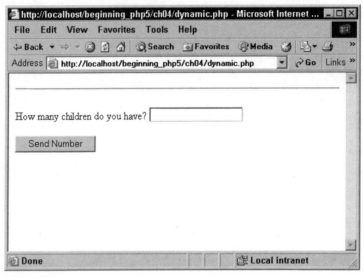

Figure 4-8

4. Click Send Number and the next page displays the same number of text boxes as you entered for the number of children. Figure 4-9 shows an example result for a user who entered 3 in the How Many Children Do You Have box.

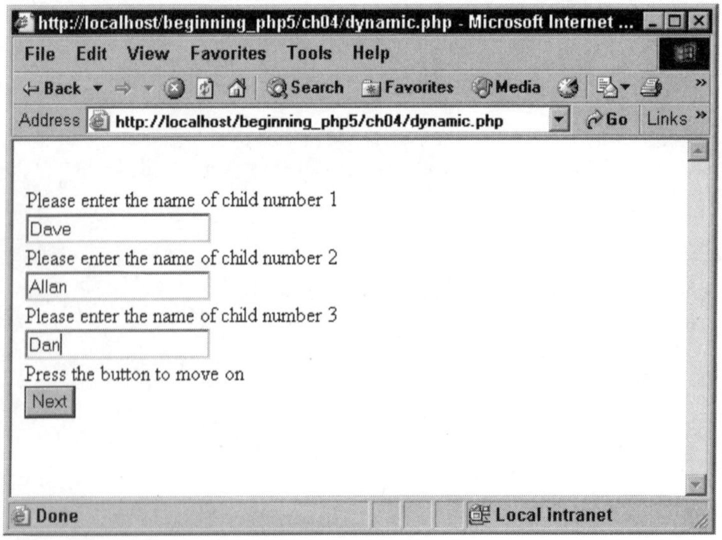

Figure 4-9

5. Enter some names into the text boxes, click Next, and the names are displayed, as Figure 4-10 shows.

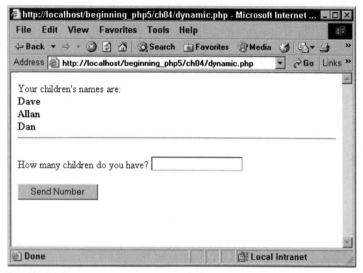

Figure 4-10

How It Works

This task isn't as easy as it first might have seemed. You start with a simple form asking for a number. That number is passed as the variable $number to the script.

```
How many children do you have?
<input name="number" type="text">
```

Then in the PHP script, a little trickery is introduced. After you've detected that the form has been submitted (by checking the isset() quality of the hidden form field named $_POST[posted]), you send a <form> tag as part of an echo statement, essentially telling the browser that you want to create a form:

```
<?php
if (isset($_POST['posted'])) {
    echo "<form method='POST' action='dynamic.php'>";
```

Inside the <form> tag you need to create a number of text boxes. You know how many are needed because the user supplied the number on the previous page, and it is contained in the variable $_POST[number]. This is a perfect time to introduce a for loop. You want to display the number of text boxes to match $_POST[number], but if the user doesn't have any children, then you don't want to display any text boxes at all. This means you have to start the $counter at zero, and if the value in $_POST[number] is zero, you want to jump over the loop entirely. So the counter starts at zero, and is incremented by one at the end of each loop. The loops continue while the counter is lower than the number of children $_POST[number]:

```
for ($counter = 0; $counter < $_POST['number']; $counter ++){
```

Inside the loop is a problem. You need to personalize each text box with a number, yet if you display the current count of the loop, the text box number will be one less than what it should be. So you create an offset variable to get around this, which is just $counter plus one:

```
$offset = $counter + 1;
```

Then you start getting to the meat of the script. You display a message instructing the user to enter the name of a child:

```
echo "<br>Please enter the name of child number $offset<br>";
```

You add the text box next. The interesting bit here is that when you set the text box's name attribute, you add brackets after it to denote that it's an array, then each time a name is passed to $_POST['child'], it's stored in a new element of child: $_POST['child'][0], $_POST['child'][1], $_POST['child'][2] and so on:

```
        echo "<input name='child[]' type='text'>";
    }
```

The loop actually ends there. Each time you iterate through a loop you just display a bit of text and a text box, for as many times as the value of the variable $number. After that you drop out of the loop, display a Submit button, insert another hidden form field named posted01 so you can detect the second time the form is submitted, and close the form.

```
    echo"<br>Press the button to move on<br>";
    echo "<input type='submit' value='Next'>";
    echo "<input type='hidden' name='posted01' value='true'></form>";
```

The second code block, activated by checking the isset() quality of the _POST[posted01] variable, prints out the names you've just supplied to the array. Sounds easy enough, but first you must take into account that the variable $number has not been passed to the new script. It only existed the last time the page was rendered. So, you're left with a situation where you know names might have been supplied to the array $_POST[[child][], but you don't know how many, if any. So you resort to your old friend the do while loop. You have to set the child counter $count manually, starting it at zero, because it might be zero.

```
    } else {

        if (isset($_POST['posted01'])) {
            $count=0;
            echo "Your children's names are:";
```

Then start a do while loop because you want the contents of the loop to run at least once:

```
            do {
```

On entering the loop, you display the first item in the array, $_POST[child][0]. If there's nothing in the array, then nothing apart from the line breaks is displayed. Otherwise it displays the first child's name:

```
                echo"<br><b>$_POST['child'][$count]</b>";
```

Alter the contents of the $checkempty variable to be the contents of $child[0]. If it's empty, $checkempty will trigger the end of the loop later on. If it's not empty you'll iterate again.

```
$checkempty = "$_POST['child'][$count]";
```

Increment the count:

```
$count = $count + 1;
```

Check to see if $checkempty is an empty variable. If it is, drop out of the loop; if not, continue:

```
} while ($checkempty != "");
```

Then there's a check to see whether the number of children entered was zero. If it was, you display an appropriate message:

```
    if ($count == 1) {
        echo "Not applicable";
    }
}
```

Loops are powerful tools for your programming. What if you'd put in 20 children in this example? Without using loops, your code would have needed 20 lines to read in their names, and 20 more to echo them out. You also lose flexibility without loops because you'd have to fix the number of name fields to read in; loops enable you to be more dynamic.

Arrays

You've already encountered arrays in this book, but now it's time to explore them in depth. An array is a set of variables that all have the same name but a different index. Each member of the array is called an *element*. You create arrays in the same way you create variables, except that each element's name must be followed by its index in square brackets:

```
$states_of_the_USA[1] = "Washington";
$states_of_the_USA[2] = "California";
```

Because the index numbers are numeric values, no quotes are required to specify them in the array name.

You don't have to assign values to the elements in order numerically; you can enter values in any order, and with or without any particular index number associated with them:

```
$ states_of_the_USA [49]="Alaska";
$ states_of_the_USA [13]="Alabama";
```

In fact, you don't have to use numeric indexing at all—you can use characters instead. The characters are inside quotes inside the brackets. Arrays having names for elements rather than index numbers are often known as associative arrays:

```
$state_capital["CA"] = "Sacramento";
$state_capital["IL"] = "Springfield";
```

If you want to access the contents of an associative array, using quotation marks around the element name is optional. For example, to echo out Sacramento, you can type either:

```
echo $state_capital["CA"];
```

or

```
echo $state_capital[CA];
```

Both get it displayed on the Web page. The online documentation says that eventually the ability to access array elements by name without using quotes may change, but for now it works fine.

One last feature of arrays in PHP is that you can actually assign different data types and variables to the values within the array. Here are some examples:

```
$number[1]=24;
$number[2]="twenty three";
$number[2]=$variable;
$number["CA"]=$variable;
```

However, this poses a couple of questions. How does PHP know how big an array should be? And how much memory should it assign to an array? The answers to these questions are in the following sections.

Initialization of Arrays

Setting the initial values of array variables is, not surprisingly, a process known as *initialization*. You've seen the two ways to initialize arrays (create an array variable by naming it and setting its value) in this book already: you don't worry about the indexing and let PHP do it for you automatically. You create one item in the array, and then you create another with the same name:

```
$author[]="William Shakespeare";
$author[]="Franz Kafka";
```

Without the square brackets, PHP wouldn't know that you're dealing with array variables, and would replace the first value with the second one. The brackets indicate that you want to store the values in an array. The lack of an index value lets PHP decide where to put them. You'll find that if the $author[] array hasn't been used before, then the values in this example would be stored in $author[0] and $author[1]. PHP will carry on assigning new values to the next element in the array.

And of course the second way to initialize an array is to use explicit index values:

```
$author[0]="William Shakespeare";
$author[1]="Franz Kafka";
```

Here you don't have to abide by the constraints of auto-numbering that PHP otherwise imposes on you; and you can assign index values out of sequence, as described earlier. Where arrays are concerned, PHP is different from many programming languages on two counts. First, you don't have to predefine the data type of the array, stating whether it will contain numbers or text. This is consistent with PHP's policy on variables: you don't have to choose a data type; PHP does it for you. Second, you also don't have to specify how large the array is before it is created because PHP determines how large the maximum index number in the array needs to be.

There are two more ways of populating arrays in PHP and both make use of the `array ()` construct. The first assigns values directly, without specifying anything about the index numbers or array elements. For example, the authors code snippet can be redefined as follows:

```
$author = array ("William Shakespeare", "Franz Kafka");
```

Again, this asks PHP to automatically generate the index values.

There are no size limits on arrays like these, so you could also write the following line:

```
$states_of_the_USA = array ("Alabama", "Alaska", "Arizona", "Arkansas",
"California", "Colorado", "Connecticut", "Delaware", "Florida", "Georgia",
"Hawaii", "Idaho", "Illinois", "Indiana", "Iowa", "Kansas", "Kentucky",
"Louisiana", "Maine", "Maryland", "Massachusetts", "Michigan", "Minnesota",
"Mississippi", "Missouri", "Montana", "Nebraska", "Nevada", "New Hampshire",
"New Jersey", "New Mexico", "New York", "North Carolina", "North Dakota",
"Ohio", "Oklahoma", "Oregon", "Pennsylvania", "Rhode Island", "South
Carolina", "South Dakota", "Tennessee", "Texas", "Utah", "Vermont",
"Virginia", "Washington", "West Virginia", "Wisconsin", "Wyoming");
```

PHP will automatically generate the index values, with the first state receiving an index value of zero, and Wyoming having the value 49.

However, this can be a little counter-intuitive; you know there are 50 states in the USA, and if you finish with 49, you get that niggling feeling that one has been left out. The second way to create an array variable using the `array()` function gets you around this. It makes use of the `=>` operator to enable you to pick the index you want the array to start at:

```
$states_of_the_USA = array (1 => "Alabama", "Alaska", "Arizona", "Arkansas",
"California", "Colorado", "Connecticut", "Delaware", "Florida", "Georgia",
"Hawaii", "Idaho", "Illinois", "Indiana", "Iowa", "Kansas", "Kentucky",
"Louisiana", "Maine", "Maryland", "Massachusetts", "Michigan", "Minnesota",
"Mississippi", "Missouri", "Montana", "Nebraska", "Nevada", "New Hampshire",
"New Jersey", "New Mexico", "New York", "North Carolina", "North Dakota",
"Ohio", "Oklahoma", "Oregon", "Pennsylvania", "Rhode Island", "South Carolina",
"South Dakota", "Tennessee", "Texas", "Utah", "Vermont", "Virginia",
"Washington", "West Virginia", "Wisconsin", "Wyoming");
```

In other words, you place the number you want the index to start at, followed by the `=>` operator, and then your list of values as normal. Now if you echo the contents of `$states_of_the_USA[50]`, it would be Wyoming. It doesn't have to be 1, it equally be 101, and then Wyoming would have the index of 150.

If you want to index a large associative array, then you have to set each value individually. Again, the code makes use of the `=>` operator. For example, with the states, it might be as follows:

```
$states_of_the_USA = array ("al" => "Alabama", "ak" => "Alaska",
"az" => "Arizona", "ar" => "Arkansas", "ca" => "California", "co" =>
"Colorado", "ct" => "Connecticut", "de" => "Delaware", "fl" => "Florida",
"ga" => "Georgia", "hi" => "Hawaii", "id" => "Idaho", "il" => "Illinois",
"in" => "Indiana", "ia" => "Iowa", "ks" => "Kansas", "ky" => "Kentucky",
"la" => "Louisiana", "me" => "Maine", "md" => "Maryland", "ma" =>
"Massachusetts", "mi" => "Michigan", "mn" => "Minnesota", "ms" =>
"Mississippi", "mo" => "Missouri", "mt" => "Montana", "ne" => "Nebraska",
"nv" => "Nevada", "nh" => "New Hampshire", "nj" => "New Jersey", "nm" =>
```

```
"New Mexico", "ny" => "New York", "nc" => "North Carolina", "nd" => "North
Dakota", "oh" => "Ohio", "ok" => "Oklahoma", "or" => "Oregon", "pa" =>
"Pennsylvania", "ri" => "Rhode Island", "sc" => "South Carolina", "sd" =>
"South Dakota", "tn" => "Tennessee", "tx" => "Texas", "ut" => "Utah", "vt" =>
"Vermont", "va" => "Virginia", "wa" => "Washington", "wv" => "West
Virginia", "wi" => "Wisconsin", "wy" => "Wyoming");
```

Slow, but it does the job.

Iterating Through an Array

If you've created an array with lots of entries, you don't want to have to go back and individually retrieve each item in the array. It makes for a lot of extra work. This is where loops work hand-in-hand with arrays. If you want to print out the name of each of the 50 states on your Web page, you can just use the for loop to do it for you. To display all 50 states in the 1 to 50 indexed $states_of_the_USA array would take a grand total of three lines, excluding the line that creates the array:

```
for ($counter=1; $counter<51; $counter++) {
    echo"<BR>$states_of_the_USA[$counter]";
}
```

The line between the braces selects an element from the $states_of_the_USA array, by placing the variable $counter between the brackets to use as the index. Because $counter is a variable, the index can then be changed by changing the value of $counter. The for loop says, "Start the counter at one, and go up to the value 50, in increments of one." So the $counter variable is substituted for 1, 2, 3, and so on, for each iteration (that <br> is used to display each state on a new line):

```
echo"<br>$states_of_the_USA[1];
echo"<br>$ states_of_the_USA[2];
echo"<br>$ states_of_the_USA[3];
etc...
```

There's nothing to preclude you from using while or do while loops, although you'd have to create a loop counter and set it yourself. The following while loop would do the same as the for loop:

```
$counter = 1;
while ($counter < 51) {
    echo"<br> $states_of_the_USA[$counter]";
    $counter = $counter + 1;
}
```

It just takes an extra couple of lines to do it, that's all.

Ready to try your hand at iterating through an array?

Try It Out   Iterate Through an Array

Sticking with the states, you're going to create two arrays in this example, one that holds all of the states' names, and one that holds the names of all of the states' capitals. You'll be able to select the name of a state from a drop-down list box, and the program will search through the corresponding array to find the state capital. You'll employ loops and arrays several times to ensure that you don't have to create 50 lines of HTML to display any of the answers.

1. Open your favorite Web page editor and type in the following:

```
<html>
<head><title></title></head>
<body>
<?php
if (isset($_POST['posted'])) {
    $state_capital = array (0 => "Montgomery", "Juneau", "Phoenix", "Little
Rock", "Sacramento", "Denver", "Hartford", "Dover", "Tallahasse", "Atlanta",
"Honolulu", "Boise", "Springfield","Indianapolis", "Des Moines", "Topeka",
"Frankfort", "Baton Rouge", "Augusta", "Annapolis", "Boston", "Lansing",
"Saint Paul", "Jackson", "Jefferson City", "Helena", "Lincoln",
"Carson City", "Concord", "Trenton", "Santa Fe", "Albany", "Raleigh",
"Bismarck", "Columbus", "Oklahoma City", "Salem", "Harrisburg",
"Providence", "Columbia", "Pierre", "Nashville", "Austin", "Salt Lake City",
"Montpelier", "Richmond", "Olympia", "Charleston", "Madison", "Cheyenne");
    for ($counter=0; $counter<50; $counter++)
    {
        if($_POST['hiddenstate'][$counter]==$_POST['state'])
        {
            echo"The state capital of $_POST['state'] is
<b>$state_capital[$counter]</b><hr>";
        }
    }
}
?>
<form action="capitals.php" method="POST">
<input type="hidden" name="posted" value="true">
What state do you want to know the capital of?
<select name="state">
<?php
$states_of_the_USA = array (1 => "Alabama", "Alaska", "Arizona", "Arkansas",
"California", "Colorado", "Connecticut", "Delaware", "Florida", "Georgia",
"Hawaii", "Idaho", "Illinois", "Indiana", "Iowa", "Kansas", "Kentucky",
"Louisiana", "Maine", "Maryland", "Massachusetts", "Michigan", "Minnesota",
"Mississippi", "Missouri", "Montana", "Nebraska", "Nevada", "New Hampshire",
"New Jersey", "New Mexico", "New York", "North Carolina", "North Dakota", "Ohio",
"Oklahoma", "Oregon", "Pennsylvania", "Rhode Island", "South Carolina", "South
Dakota", "Tennessee", "Texas", "Utah", "Vermont", "Virginia", "Washington",
"West Virginia", "Wisconsin", "Wyoming");
for ($counter = 1; $counter < 51; $counter ++) {
    echo"<option>$states_of_the_USA[$counter]</option>";
}
echo "</select><br><br>";
for ($counter = 1; $counter < 51; $counter++) {
    echo"<input type='hidden' name='hiddenstate[]'
value='$states_of_the_USA[$counter]'>";
}
?>
<input type="submit" value="Find Capital">
</form>
</body>
</html>
```

2. Save the file as `capitals.php.` and close it.

3. Open the file in your browser and select a state.

4. Click the Find Capital button to get an answer: Figure 4-11 shows the answer for a user who selected the state of Hawaii.

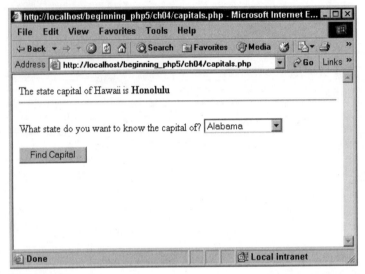

Figure 4-11

How It Works

This example demonstrates exactly how much code you can save by using loops and arrays. If only it could have saved you from typing the data in as well!

For this example, the first page was changed into a PHP one so that you could use PHP's `array()` function to avoid typing in 50 lines of HTML in the `<select>` list box. It starts by creating an HTML form:

```
<form action="capitals.php" method=post>
What state do you want to know the capital of?
```

Next you create a drop-down list box:

```
<select name="state">
```

Moving into the PHP script, the names of the states are fed into an array called `$states_of_the_USA`, beginning at index 1:

```
<?php
$states_of_the_USA = array (1 => "Alabama", "Alaska", "Arizona", "Arkansas",
"California", "Colorado", "Connecticut", "Delaware", "Florida", "Georgia",
"Hawaii", "Idaho", "Illinois", "Indiana", "Iowa", "Kansas", "Kentucky",
"Louisiana", "Maine", "Maryland", "Massachusetts", "Michigan", "Minnesota",
```

"Mississippi", "Missouri", "Montana", "Nebraska", "Nevada", "New Hampshire",
"New Jersey", "New Mexico", "New York", "North Carolina", "North Dakota", "Ohio",
"Oklahoma", "Oregon", "Pennsylvania", "Rhode Island", "South Carolina", "South
Dakota", "Tennessee", "Texas", "Utah", "Vermont", "Virginia", "Washington",
"West Virginia", "Wisconsin", "Wyoming");

A loop is created to iterate 50 times, placing the name of each state in the list box.

```
for ($counter = 1; $counter < 51; $counter ++) {
    echo"<option>$ states_of_the_USA[$counter]</option>";
}
echo "</select><br><br>";
```

When the loop is finished, the list box is closed. You might have expected the next line to supply a Submit button and to close the form. However, a problem arises here if you think ahead to the next page: you need all of the states to be available on the next page, not just this page. Why? Well, consider how you find the state capital of a particular state. You locate the index of the state in the $states_of_the_USA array, and then look up the state capital that's present at the same index of the $state_capital array. For example, the contents of $states_of_the_USA [1] is Alabama, so the contents of $state_capital[1] is Montgomery. You can do this because you made sure that the capital at any particular index in $state_capital is the capital of the state located at the same index in $states_of_the_USA. In other words, the data in the two arrays correspond by index.

Now, if you passed only the state selected from the list box to the next script, then you wouldn't be passing along the index of this state within $states_of_the_USA. Without that information, you can't look up the corresponding index of $state_capital and find the capital of the selected state.

What can you do? Obviously, you need to pass some information about the index of the state to the next script, so you simply pass the full array of states to the next script.

Create a second loop, and use it to create an array containing 50 hidden controls, $_POST ['hiddenstate']. Then fill that array with the states present in $states_of_the_USA.

```
for ($counter = 1; $counter < 51; $counter++) {
    echo"<input type='hidden' name='hiddenstate[]' value='$
states_of_the_USA[$counter]'>";
}
```

After you've read across the names of 50 states, add a submit query button and close the form:

```
<input type="submit" value="Find Capital">
</form>
```

The PHP program now has two sets of data. The first is obtained from the drop-down list box, and contains the name of the single state that the user selected. It's stored in the variable $state. The second is a list of the 50 states, in alphabetical order, stored in the array $hiddenstate. (Because PHP populated this array, the index numbers run from 0 to 49. This isn't a problem; you just need to be aware of it. The first line deals with it.) Now create an array with the names of the 50 state capitals. To match the indexes of the $hiddenstate array, you need to make the array indexes run from 0 to 49:

```
$state_capital = array (0 => "Montgomery", "Juneau", "Phoenix", "Little Rock",
"Sacramento", "Denver", "Hartford", "Dover", "Tallahasse", "Atlanta",
```

```
"Honolulu", "Boise", "Springfield", "Indianapolis", "Des Moines", "Topeka",
"Frankfort", "Baton Rouge", "Augusta", "Annapolis", "Boston", "Lansing",
"Saint Paul", "Jackson", "Jefferson City", "Helena", "Lincoln", "Carson City",
"Concord", "Trenton", "Santa Fe", "Albany", "Raleigh", "Bismarck", "Columbus",
"Oklahoma City", "Salem", "Harrisburg", "Providence", "Columbia", "Pierre",
"Nashville", "Austin", "Salt Lake City", "Montpelier", "Richmond", "Olympia",
"Charleston", "Madison", "Cheyenne");
```

The $hiddenstate and $state_capital now arrays now correspond by index, which makes the rest of the program very straightforward. In fact you just need one loop, which runs from 0 to 49:

```
for ($counter=0; $counter<50; $counter++)
{
```

Inside you nest a conditional statement that checks to see if the current state is equal to the state that the user selected. If it is, you display the contents of the corresponding element of $state_capital, making use of the correspondence between the arrays:

```
if($_POST['hiddenstate'][$counter]==$_POST['state])
{
    echo"The state capital of $_POST['state'] is
<b>$state_capital[$counter]</b><hr>";
}
}
```

If there isn't a match, continue iterating through the for loop until there is one. Using the list box, there is only a finite set of choices, so you know there will always be a match. That's all this program needs to do.

Improvements to the Program

The preceding program was not as easy as it could have been so that you could see how two separate arrays can be linked by an index number. If you actually wanted to run an example like it, it'd be much simpler to use an associative array, where you link the array items within one array statement like this:

```
$state_capital = array ("Alabama" => "Montgomery", "Alaska" => "Juneau",
"Phoenix" =>"Arizona", "Arkansas" => "Little Rock", "California" =>
"Sacramento", "Colorado" => "Denver", "Connecticut" => "Hartford",
"Delaware" => "Dover", "Florida" => "Tallahasse", "Georgia" => "Atlanta",
"Hawaii" => "Honolulu", "Idaho" => "Boise", "Illinois" => "Springfield",
"Indiana" => "Indianapolis", "Iowa" => "Des Moines", "Kansas" => "Topeka",
"Kentucky" => "Frankfort", "Louisiana" => "Baton Rouge","Maine" => "Augusta",
"Maryland" => "Annapolis", "Massachusetts" => "Boston", "Michigan" =>
"Lansing", "Minnesota" => "Saint Paul", "Mississippi" => "Jackson",
"Missouri" => "Jefferson City", "Montana" => "Helena", "Nebraska" =>
"Lincoln", "Nevada" => "Carson City", "New Hampshire" => "Concord",
"New Jersey" => "Trenton", "New Mexico" => "Santa Fe", "New York" => "Albany",
"North Carolina" => "Raleigh", "North Dakota" => "Bismarck", "Ohio" =>
"Columbus", "Oklahoma" => "Oklahoma City", "Oregon" => "Salem",
"Pennsylvania" => "Harrisburg", "Rhode Island" => "Providence", "South
Carolina" => "Columbia", "South Dakota" =>"Pierre", "Tennessee" =>
"Nashville", "Texas" => "Austin", "Utah" => "Salt Lake City", Vermont" =>
"Montpelier", "Virginia" => "Richmond", "Washington" => "Olympia", "West
Virginia" => "Charleston", "Wisconsin" => "Madison", "Wyoming" => "Cheyenne");
```

Then you could output the capital using the state name variable, $state, as the index.

Iterating Through Non-Sequential Arrays

It's pretty simple to iterate through arrays whose elements have been populated sequentially (first element populated first, second element second, third element third, and so on). But is it that simple if the elements weren't populated sequentially? For example:

```
$array[56993]="absolutely huge";
$array[1]="quite small";
$array[499]="quite big";
```

Actually, non-sequential arrays aren't that much of a problem, and your old methods still work. It doesn't matter to PHP if you store the values out of order because it considers them to be in the straightforward numerical order of the index values. The only problem is that when you check through all of the elements sequentially, you might find yourself checking a lot of empty space in a large array like this example, which contains only three values!

current() and key() Functions

PHP uses a pointer to keep track of which element it's at when it moves through an array. The pointer indicates the element that is currently being used by the script. You can use the current() function to view the value of that element, and you can use the key() function to find out its index value. (Key is another name for index.)

Here's a little code snippet to illustrate how current() and key() work. When you first open a PHP script with this code in it, you might wonder which index PHP first looks at first.

```
$director[4]="Orson Welles";
$director[1]="Carol Reed";
$director[93]="Fritz Lang";
$director[24]="Jacques Tourneur";
```

You can find out by adding the next couple of lines, which return the current index of $Director[], and echo it:

```
$current_index_value = key($director);
echo ($current_index_value);
```

The key() function returns the value 4. Why? Because it returns the index value of the first item you placed into the array (when your script first runs, the first element you entered is the current element), which was Orson Welles at index 4 (the key produced by the key() function). If you use the current() function, it returns the value Orson Welles (the value of the current element produced by the current() function):

```
$current_contents = current($director);
echo ($current_contents);
```

Now, if you then added the following line to the array:

```
$director[]="Alfred Hitchcock";
```

`Alfred Hitchcock` would be placed in the array at the index value 94, not zero, because to PHP, the lowest value in the set of index numbers being used is 93, and the next unfilled element is numbered 94. How can you test to find out what the index value of the new element is, given that the `key()` and `current()` functions return information on the first item to be placed in the array? Read on.

next() and prev() Functions

To find out the index value of a new element added to an array, you use the `next()` and `prev()` functions. These functions enable you to navigate through arrays by moving the pointer to the next or previous element in the array. They both take the name of the array to navigate through as an argument. For example, in the preceding array creation list:

```
$director[4]="Orson Welles";
$director[1]="Carol Reed";
$director[93]="Fritz Lang";
$director[24]="Jacques Tourneur";
$director[]="Alfred Hitchcock";
```

You call the `next()` function before checking the current index, and the contents of the current element:

```
next($director);
$current_index_value = key($director);
echo ($current_index_value);
```

The value displayed is 1, and the `current()` function returns the name `Carol Reed`.

If you call `next()` three more times:

```
next($director);
next($director);
next($director);
next($director);
$current_index_value = key($director);
echo ($current_index_value);
```

The value 94 is displayed. If you now call the `current()` function:

```
$current_contents = current($director);
echo ($current_contents);
```

The browser displays Alfred Hitchcock.

The `prev()` function is used in a similar way. Take the preceding example and add one occurrence of `prev()` after the four of `next()`:

```
next($director);
next($director);
next($director);
next($director);
prev($director);
$current_index_value = key($director);
echo ($current_index_value);
```

You'll see 24, which is the index value associated with Jacques Tourneur, because you've moved forward through four items of the array and back through one. This is fairly straightforward, although one question that springs to mind is: what happens when you move next() beyond the last item in the array, or prev() before the first?

```
prev($director);
$current_index_value = key($director);
echo ($current_index_value);
```

The answer is: nothing at all. The code snippet would return no value. It won't generate an error (as it would in some programming languages); the pointer just moves beyond the end of the array. However, you wouldn't be able to move it back again:

```
prev($director);
next($director);
next($director);
$current_index_value = key($director);
echo ($current_index_value);
```

This would still return nothing at all.

So, you can see that the order in which you choose to populate the array makes no difference to the order in which they'll be navigated. Any new value placed in the array is placed in the element immediately above the filled element with the highest index. So if the highest filled element had index 34, the next value would be placed in index 35.

Just remember: to navigate through the arrays, use the next() and prev() functions, and to display the current position (the element the pointer is currently pointing to), use the current() and key() functions.

list() and each() Functions

If you're iterating through a non-sequential array, you can make life easier for yourself. Rather than looping through loads of empty values, you can use the list() and each() functions to return only the elements in the array that contain data. This enables you to display the entire contents of an array with the minimum amount of fuss. You use the while loop to perform this task for you, like this:

```
while (list(IndexValue,ElementContents) = each(ArrayName))
```

This says: for each element of the array Arrayname, set IndexValue equal to the element's index, and ElementContents equal to the contents of the element. If you only want to return either the index or the contents, then you can just omit the appropriate attribute:

```
while (list(IndexValue) = each(ArrayName))
```

Or:

```
while (list(,ElementContents) = each(ArrayName))
```

For the Directors code snippet you could write the following code to display the name of each director in the array:

```
while (list($element_index_value, $element_contents) = each($director)){
    echo "<br>$element_index_value - $element_contents";
}
```

You don't have to call the variables $element_index_value and $element_contents; that's just been done here for clarity's sake. You could just as easily have called them:

```
while (list($MickeyMouse, $DonaldDuck) = each ($Director)){
    echo "<BR>$MickeyMouse - $DonaldDuck";
}
```

Either way, the result would be as follows:

```
4 - Orson Welles
1 - Carol Reed
93 - Fritz Lang
24 - Jacques Tourneur
94 - Alfred Hitchcock
```

All you've got to remember is that list() returns the index value first and the element contents second. That provides you with some useful tools, which are applicable even if the array doesn't happen to have numerical index.

Iterating Through String-Indexed Arrays

The rules for navigating through associative arrays are similar to those for numerically indexed ones, but there are some slight differences. The first difference is that the following lines, which would have worked fine if the array were numerically indexed, will now create a numerically indexed array:

```
$state_capital["GA"]="Atlanta";
$state_capital["IL"]="Springfield";
$state_capital["CA"]="Sacramento";
$state_capital[] = "Cheyenne";
```

The value Cheyenne will be stored in the array item $state_capital[0]. It's not too surprising, given that PHP has no idea what you want to create as an index value, which might be WY, but it might just have easily been AB or 4563, so instead it just tries to find the biggest numerical index. Because you haven't added a numerical index, PHP starts at the beginning with zero.

The current() and key() functions will still work in the way you expect on associative arrays. If you try the following code:

```
$what_state = current($state_capital);
$what_abbreviation = key($state_capital);
echo "$what_abbreviation - $what_state";
```

You'll find that it returns the first element to be filled in the array, which was index GA containing Atlanta. And you can also iterate through each list as before:

```
$state_capital["GA"]="Atlanta";
$state_capital["IL"]="Springfield";
$state_capital["CA"]="Sacramento";
$state_capital[] = "Cheyenne";
next($$state_capital);
$what_state = current($state_capital);
$what_abbreviation = key($state_capital);
echo "$what_abbreviation - $what_state";
```

This time you display the result IL - Springfield. The functions list() and each() also function the same way. You can set up the following array:

```
$state_capital = array ("GA" => "Atlanta", "IL" => "Springfield",
"CA" => "Sacramento", "WY" => "Cheyenne");
```

Then you can feed the array to the each function, and use list() to display the contents as before:

```
while (list($state_abbreviation, $state_name) = each ($state_capital)){
    echo "<br>$state_abbreviation - $state_name";
}
```

This produces the list of abbreviations and state names as expected, and displays them in the order you created them:

```
GA - Atlanta
IL - Springfield
CA - Sacramento
WY - Cheyenne
```

What happens, though, if you want PHP to create or preserve a different order? Keep reading.

Sorting Arrays

There are several functions that PHP provides for sorting arrays, and you'll explore the five most commonly used: sort(), asort(), rsort(), arsort(), and ksort(). They all work in conjunction with the list() and each() functions that you just examined.

The sort() Function

sort() is the most basic of the sorting functions. It takes the contents of the array and sorts them into alphabetical order. The function requires only an array name to sort the array:

```
sort(ArrayName)
```

If you create an array of directors using the array structure:

```
$director = array ("Orson Welles","Carol Reed","Fritz Lang","Jacques Tourneur");
```

You can sort the elements by supplying the array name to the sort() function as follows:

```
sort($director);
```

To view the effect this function has had on the array, you can use the list() and each() functions again. As previously stated, the order in which items are stored in the array is the order in which they were created in the array. With this directors array you'd expect the following order:

```
$Director[0]= "Orson Welles"
$Director[1]= "Carol Reed"
$Director[2]= "Fritz Lang"
$Director[3]= "Jacques Tourneur"
```

After using sort(), though, a different pattern emerges, as the sort() function resorts in alphabetic order, and then rebuilds the index numbers to match the new alphabetic order, as shown here:

```
$Director[0]= "Carol Reed"
$Director[1]= "Fritz Lang"
$Director[2]= "Jacques Tourneur"
$Director[3]= "Orson Welles"
```

You can check this, using the earlier code snippet to display the contents of the list on the screen:

```
while (list($IndexValue, $DirectorName) = each ($Director)){
    echo "<BR>$IndexValue - $DirectorName";
}
```

The asort() Function

The function asort() takes arrays created with a string index and sorts them according to their contents. You are probably asking, "Isn't this just what sort did?" Not quite. The assort() function leaves the index numbers or element names intact, instead of rebuilding them like the sort() function did. Recall the state capitals code snippet:

```
$state_capital = array ("GA" => "Atlanta", "IL" => "Springfield",
"CA" => "Sacramento", "WY" => "Cheyenne");
```

You'd expect the array to be created as follows:

```
$state_capital["GA"]= "Atlanta"
$state_capital["IL"]= "Springfield"
$state_capital["CA"]= "Sacramento"
$state_capital["WY"]= "Cheyenne"
```

If you perform a sort on it:

```
sort($state_capital);
```

You get the following order:

```
$state_capital[0]= "Atlanta"
$state_capital[1]= "Cheyenne"
```

```
$state_capital[2]= "Sacramento"
$state_capital[3]= "Springfield"
```

In other words, the string index values are replaced by numerical indexes—not particularly useful. However, if you call the `asort()` function:

```
asort($state_capital);
```

The order would be:

```
$state_capital["GA"]= "Atlanta"
$state_capital["WY"]= "Cheyenne"
$state_capital["IL"]= "Sacramento"
$state_capital["CA"]= "Springfield"
```

This time, the elements have been sorted alphabetically, and the string indexes have been retained. Again, you can use `list()` and `each()` to show that this has been the case:

```
while (list($state_abbreviation, $state_name) = each ($state_capital)){
    echo "<br>$state_abbreviation - $state_name";
}
```

The rsort() and arsort() Functions

The functions `rsort()` and `arsort()` work in a similar way to their close relations `sort()` and `asort()`. The only difference is that they return the array elements in reverse alphabetical order. You can use `rsort()` to reverse the list of directors:

```
$director = array ("Orson Welles","Carol Reed","Fritz Lang","Jacques Tourneur");
rsort($director);
```

You can call `arsort()` to reverse the list of state capitals:

```
$state_capital = array ("ga" => "Atlanta", "il" => "Springfield",
"ca" => "Sacramento", "wy" => "Cheyenne");
arsort($state_capital);
```

You should be able to work out what the results are. If you want to check, adapt the code from the preceding sections to display the answers. These functions are useful if you need to sort in descending order rather than ascending order.

The ksort() Function

The `ksort()` function sorts the contents of an associative array according to the index. It's applied in exactly the same way as the other sort functions, but it arranges an associative array in alphabetical order of string indexes. It's useful to be able to sort by the index numbers or element names when you are manipulating data by them instead of by the actual values. In the state capitals example, for instance:

```
$state_capital = array ("ga" => "Atlanta", "il" => "Springfield",
"ca" => "Sacramento", "wy" => "Cheyenne");
ksort($state_capital);
```

`ksort()` would yield the following order:

```
$state_capital["ca"]= "Sacramento"
$state_capital["ga"]= "Atlanta"
$state_capital["il"]= "Springfield"
$state_capital["wy"]= "Cheyenne"
```

So if you happen to be using the state abbreviations instead of the state names for some purpose, you can still perform a sort.

Multidimensional Arrays

It is possible to create an array of arrays. Such beasts are known as multidimensional arrays. They are useful when representing data that needs two sets of indexes, such as coordinates on a map or graph. You can carry on nesting arrays in a multidimensional array until PHP runs out of memory, which would probably be in under 100 nested arrays. (If you can think of a sensible practical use of any more than 10 nested arrays, then you deserve a medal.) Multidimensional arrays are set up in the same way as normal arrays, except that you call the array structure as an argument to itself, like this:

```
ArrayName = array (index => array (Array contents))
```

An example might be an array in which each element represents one member from a group of people, and each element is also an array, used to store the details for each person:

```
$phone_directory = array ("John Doe" => array ("1 Long Firs Drive",
"777-000-000"), "Jane Doe" => array ("4 8th and East","777-111-111"));
```

This array now has entries for John Doe and Jane Doe; and each element represents an array with two entries, one for an address and one for a phone number. To actually get hold of this information, you have to use a nested loop to get it:

```
$phone_directory = array ("John Doe" => array("1 Long Firs Drive",
"777-000-000"),
                            "Jane Doe" => array("4 8th and East","777-111-111"));
while (list($person) = each($phone_directory)){
   echo("<br>$person");
   while (list(,$personal_details) = each ($phone_directory[$person])) {
      echo (" $personal_details");
   }
}
```

The `<br>` tag and the space before `$personal_details` in the `echo` statement are simply used to make the displayed details more presentable. Multidimensional arrays aren't encountered very often, so they won't be discussed any more here, although you're now aware of them.

Practical Demonstration of Arrays

This chapter's covered a lot of material, so instead of an extensive example at the end, you'll just deal with a short one—but it includes many of the features you just learned about. So take a deep breath and charge right in.

Try It Out   **Combine Array Features in a Practical Example**

This example takes a set of mythical students and asks for the grades they got on their Math exam. Among other things, you'll sort them into grade order (A is highest, F is lowest) on the Web page. Some <table> tags are included to make everything more presentable.

1. Prod your Web page editor into life, and type in the following:

```
<html>
<head><title></title></head>
<body>
<form method="POST" action="exam.php">
<input type="hidden" name="posted" value="true">
<table border="1">
<?php
$student = array("Albert Einstein","Ivan the Terrible","Napoleon","Simon
Bolivar","Isaac Newton");
while (list(,$name) = each($student))
{
    echo "<tr><td>What grade did <b>$name</b> get in math?</td>";
    echo"<td><select name='math[]'>
        <option>grade A</option>
        <option>grade B</option>
        <option>grade C</option>
        <option>grade D</option>
        <option>grade F</option>
    </select>";
    echo"<input type='hidden' name='student[]' value='$name'></td>";
}
?>
</tr>
<tr><td> </td><td>
<input type="submit" value="Get Grades">
</td></tr>
</form>
</table>

<?php
if (isset($_POST['posted'])) {
?>
<hr>
<table border="1">
<tr><td colspan="2">
In math the grades were in order:
</td></tr>
<?php

    while (list($index,$value)=each($_POST['math']))
    {
        $gradestudent[]=$_POST['math'][$index].$_POST['student'][$index];
    }
    asort($gradestudent);
    while (list($index,$value)=each($gradestudent))
```

```
    {
        $student_index = $_POST['student'][$index];
        $math_index = $_POST['math'][$index];
        echo "<tr><td><b>$student_index</b></td><td>$math_index</td></tr>";
    }
}
?>
</table>
</body>
</html>
```

2. Save file as exam.php and close it.

3. Open the file in your browser, and type in some grades. Figure 4-12 shows an example.

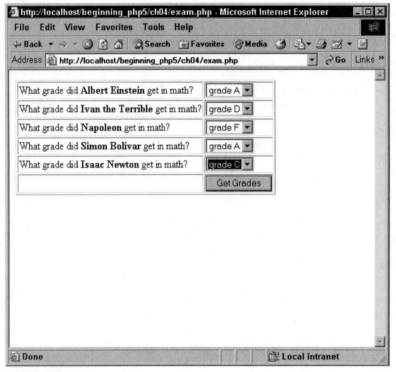

Figure 4-12

4. Click the Get Grades button and the grades are sorted, not only in order of grade, but also in alphabetical order of students' names where two or more students have the same grade (see Figure 4-13).

How It Works

This little program had a difficult conundrum to sort out that you may have spotted. You need to sort the grades array, which corresponds by index to the student array. But how can you relate the sorted array of

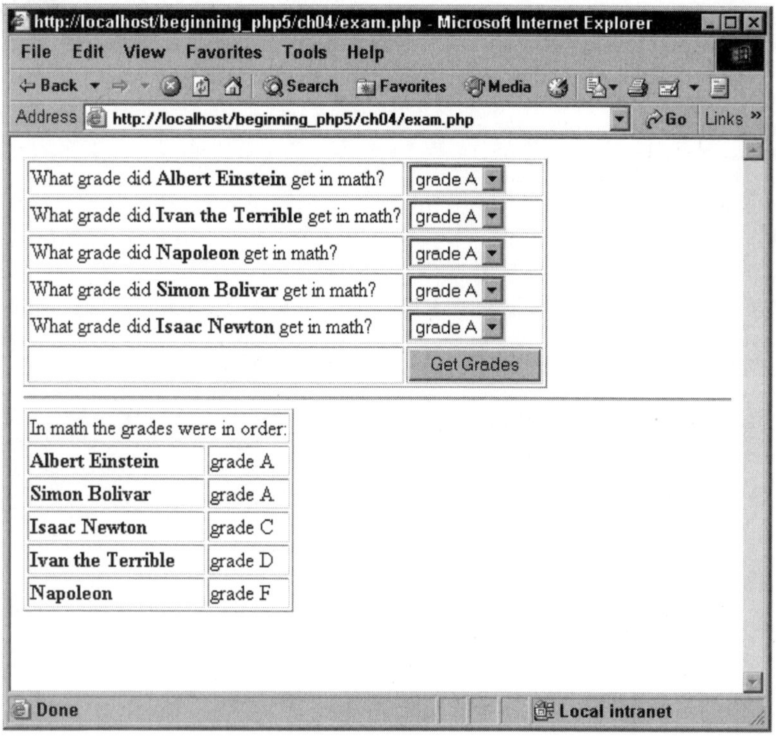

Figure 4-13

grades back to the array of students? Without too much difficulty, as it turns out, although it calls for a bit of sleight of hand.

The program creates a dynamically created form that supplies the names of the students from an array called $student:

```
<form method="POST" action="exam.php">
<input type="hidden" name="posted" value="true">
<table border="1">
<?php
$student = array("Albert Einstein","Ivan the Terrible","Napoleon","Simon
Bolivar","Isaac Newton");
```

A while loop is constructed to iterate through the contents of the student array. Because you only want the names and not the indexes in the student array, you ask list() to return only the names:

```
while (list(,$name) = each($student))
{
```

For each student in the list, you display a question asking for that student's grade:

```
echo "<tr><td>What grade did <b>$name</b> get in math?</td>";
```

Then you create a drop-down list box that contains five options, each corresponding to a grade from A to F. To store the grades, you create an array $math that PHP can pass to the next script:

```
echo"<td><select name='math[]'>
    <option>grade A</option>
    <option>grade B</option>
    <option>grade C</option>
    <option>grade D</option>
    <option>grade F</option>
</select>";
```

You pass the values across to the second part of the script via a hidden HTML control that has the same name as the array which holds the students' names. Indicate that the control needs to be an array by adding brackets. Pass the control names for each student, and then end the loop:

```
    echo"<input type='hidden' name='student[]' value='$name'></td>";
}
```

At the end of the loop add a Submit button and close the form:

```
?>
</tr>
<tr><td> </td><td>
<input type="submit" value="Get Grades">
</td></tr>
</form>
</table>
```

The second part of the program receives the form data. It's composed of a loop, a sort, and another loop.

The first loop is used to associate the two arrays received from the form. You do this by concatenating the grade to the student's name, and storing the result in a new array called $gradestudent:

```
<hr>
<table border="1">
<tr><td colspan="2">
In math the grades were in order:
</td></tr>
<?php
    while (list($index,$value)=each($_POST['math']))
    {
        $gradestudent[]=$_POST['math'][$index].$_POST['student'][$index];
    }
```

You know from examining the first script that the contents of an index in the $math array relate to the contents of the same index in the $student array. So this concatenation is a valid way of combining the related values from each array. The resulting $gradestudent array contains this:

```
Grade CAlbert Einstein
Grade FIvan The Terrible
Grade BNapoleon
Grade DSimon Bolivar
Grade AIsaac Newton
```

Now sort $gradestudent and you should get the order you want:

```
asort($gradestudent);
```

You are still left with the problem of how to display the results, which look a little unsightly in the format displayed before the sort. You can print out a sorted list of grades side-by-side with the students' names using the following snippet of code:

```
    while (list($index,$value)=each($gradestudent))
    {
        echo
"<tr><td><b>$_POST['student'][$index]</b></td><td>$_POST[math][$index]</td>
</tr>";
    }
}
?>
</table>
```

Can you see how this works? Remember that the $gradestudent array is sorted on grade. During the sort, the order of the elements was rearranged, but each index still contains the same content as before the sort. Each element in the $gradestudent array is simply a concatenation of the corresponding elements in the $math and $student arrays. So, what happens if you echo out elements from the $_POST['math'] and $_POST['student'] arrays, but in the order that the indexes occur in sorted $gradestudent? Because the indexes of all of these arrays correspond, you find that the $math and $student arrays are echoed out in grade order, too, as the table shows:

$Index	$Student	$Math	Sorted $GradeStudent
4	Isaac Newton	Grade A	"Grade AIsaac Newton"
2	Napoleon	Grade B	"Grade BNapoleon"
0	Albert Einstein	Grade C	"Grade CAlbert Einstein"
3	Simon Bolivar	Grade D	"Grade DSimon Bolivar"
1	Ivan The Terrible	Grade F	"Grade FIvan The Terrible"

You know that using list() and each() provides index values from the sorted $gradestudent array in the order that they occur in the array, so the code snippet echoes out elements from the $_POST['math'] and $_POST['student'] arrays in grade order, too. And that's it.

The array_multisort() Function

The array_multisort() function sorts multiple arrays or a multidimensional arrays. It takes arrays as arguments. When sorting multiple arrays, the function sorts the first array and notes the indexes of any repeated entries in the array. It then sorts the repeated entries according to the contents of the corresponding indexes in the second array. Finally, the function sorts the second array into the same order as the sorted first array. Take a look at the preceding example. You could change the code in exam.php to use `array_multisort()`:

```php
<?php
array_multisort($math,$student);
while (list($index,$value)=each($student))
{
    echo "<br>$student[$index] - $math[$index]";
}
?>
```

Now consider what would happen if this function was asked to sort the following year's math grades (stored in the $math array) for these students (whose names are stored in the $student array):

```
Albert Einstein - Grade A
Ivan The Terrible Grade F
Napoleon Grade D
Simon Bolivar Grade D
Isaac Newton Grade A
```

The `array_multisort()` function first sorts the $math[] array, giving A, A, D, D, F. Because there are two entries for each of A and D, the function notes the indexes of the two A entries (0 and 4), turns to the second array $student[] and sub-sorts elements 0 (Albert Einstein) and 4 (Isaac Newton) alphabetically by name. The same is done for the two D entries. When the function is finished sub-sorting, it notes the final index order of the $math array (0, 4, 2, 3, 1), and sorts $student[] into the same order. Both arrays are now sorted primarily by grade and secondly by name.

foreach Loops

There's an extension to the `for` loop known as the `foreach` loop, that you use when you have an array with an unknown number of elements. It iterates until the end of the array. The loop has two formats. The first is as follows:

```php
foreach ($ArrayName As $ArrayItem){
    execute the contents of these braces;
}
```

This means that for each item in the array, you'll iterate around the loop. An example of this would be the crowd attendance at a baseball game. You might want to store the name of each fan in the baseball stadium in a database. But until the day of the game, you don't know how many fans will actually turn up. In pseudo code the example would look like this:

```php
foreach ($crowd As $fan){
    Add $fan to database...
}
```

It would go through the crowd adding a fan at a time. PHP doesn't need to be told how many fans attended the game because it can work this out from the number of items in the array $crowd.

The second format is:

```php
foreach ($ArrayName As $ArrayIndexValue => $ArrayItem){
    execute the contents of these braces
}
```

This is the same as the first format, but it makes the array index value available as well. Take a quick look at how `foreach` works in the context of an example.

Use foreach

This example uses the list of states and displays each state in the array, along with the index value that PHP has assigned to the state.

1. Start your Web page editor and type in the following code:

```
<html>
<head><title></title></head>
<body>
<?
$states_of_the_USA = array ("Alabama", "Alaska", "Arizona", "Arkansas",
"California", "Colorado", "Connecticut", "Delaware", "Florida", "Georgia",
"Hawaii", "Idaho", "Illinois", "Indiana", "Iowa", "Kansas", "Kentucky",
"Louisiana", "Maine", "Maryland", "Massachusetts", "Michigan", "Minnesota",
"Mississippi", "Missouri", "Montana", "Nebraska", "Nevada", "New Hampshire",
"New Jersey", "New Mexico", "New York", "North Carolina", "North Dakota",
"Ohio", "Oklahoma", "Oregon", "Pennsylvania", "Rhode Island", "South
Carolina", "South Dakota", "Tennessee", "Texas", "Utah", "Vermont",
"Virginia", "Washington", "West Virginia", "Wisconsin", "Wyoming");
foreach($states_of_the_USA as $state_index => $state){
    echo "<br>$state_index - $state";
}
?>
</body>
</html>
```

2. Save this file as `foreach.php`. and close it.

3. Open the file in your browser, and scroll down just to check that all 50 states are there, with values running from 0 to 49. See Figure 4-14.

How It Works

This couldn't be simpler. You first create the array with the names of all 50 states, which is called `$states_of_the_USA`:

```
$states_of_the_USA = array ("Alabama", "Alaska", "Arizona", "Arkansas",
"California", "Colorado", "Connecticut", "Delaware", "Florida", "Georgia",
"Hawaii", "Idaho", "Illinois", "Indiana", "Iowa", "Kansas", "Kentucky",
"Louisiana", "Maine", "Maryland", "Massachusetts", "Michigan", "Minnesota",
"Mississippi", "Missouri", "Montana", "Nebraska", "Nevada", "New Hampshire",
"New Jersey", "New Mexico", "New York", "North Carolina", "North Dakota",
"Ohio", "Oklahoma", "Oregon", "Pennsylvania", "Rhode Island", "South
Carolina", "South Dakota", "Tennessee", "Texas", "Utah", "Vermont",
"Virginia", "Washington", "West Virginia", "Wisconsin", "Wyoming");
```

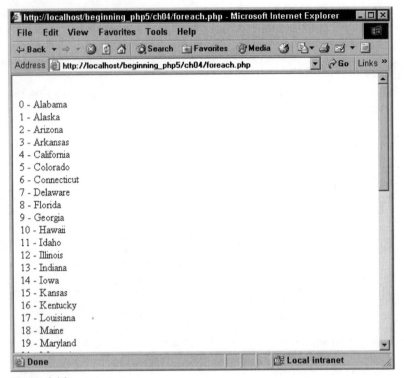

Figure 4-14

Then supply the array name as the first argument to the foreach loop:

```
foreach ($states_of_the_USA As $state_index => $state){
```

The second and third arguments are variable names that you create yourself that hold the index value and the corresponding element in the array, respectively. You execute the contents of the braces for each of the 50 members in the array:

```
    echo "<br>$state_index - $state";
}
```

This has the effect of displaying each index value and each state in the array on a separate line.

There are two points to note here. First, the current array element and array index are available as separate variables. Because each iteration processes a new array element, each time you go around the loop the variables are effectively assigned a new value.

And second, you haven't supplied a count of how many elements there are in the array anywhere in the program. PHP has worked this out for itself, and that's the main advantage of using a foreach loop. This factor enables you to iterate through an array that might not be in any numerical or alphabetical order. There might also be missing entries in the array, but it doesn't have to check every index value, only the elements that contain values. You could include the following code, which adds a new element to the array of states:

```
$states_of_the_USA[100]="Atlantis";
```

Then if you reperformed the `foreach` loop, it would be able to add this value to the end of the Web page without needing to check through elements 50–99.

Summary

This chapter introduced a major part of the PHP language: decision making. Its foundation is the `if` statement, which has quite a few different formats and is fairly flexible in that it can be nested, or extended using `else if`. The `switch` statement offered you a better method of handling multiple conditions, and while there are guidelines for when you should use `if`, `else if`, and `switch`, ultimately it's the choice of you, the programmer.

The examples were growing in size as you worked through the chapter, and the code contained within them was quite repetitive. At the end of the chapter, you saw how PHP deals with repetition using loops. One of the main reasons for using loops is that they can cut down on the amount of code written. They can also be used to write code to variables in arrays much more quickly and efficiently than linear code.

While being conceptually different, loops and arrays are actually closely linked in PHP, as you've seen. You need loops to perform repetitious operations, and one such useful operation is to fill large related sets of indexed variables known as arrays. You examined the three types of loop—`while`, `do while` and `for`—and observed that each was suited to different types of task, so the choice of which one to use depended upon the situation. You explored arrays in more depth, and demonstrated the methods you can use to populate them.

You looked at PHP features for iterating through arrays, including arrays that don't have sequential or numerical indexes. You also learned how arrays can be sorted, and did some practical work that made use of arrays.

Exercise

"We have a Web site, and it's outdated. It doesn't look very nice, but we're having a graphic artist redo the logo, so we'll probably be getting a lot more traffic once it's done. We'll be hiring more people to keep up with demand, and we want to have a way to gather resumes online.

"It should be easy for people to find the job listings, but the link shouldn't be the biggest thing on the page. We'll want to have their contact information, of course, and a search for jobs. If they don't have a college degree, they might as well not apply unless they're looking for entry-level jobs in the sales department or the shipping department. None of the jobs pays more than $20,000 to start, but management positions do offer incentive bonuses. They should send their salary requirements and at least 2 years of work experience, except for management positions (management positions must have at least 5 years experience, unless they have a Ph.D.). We'd like people to be able to search for jobs and apply for the ones they think would be a good fit for them, and also to be able to submit their resume and find out what jobs they qualify for."

Whew! Well, that's often exactly how the requirements for an application are first presented: someone who probably doesn't know much about what programmers do asks you to devise a program to do a particular function.

This exercise will definitely give you some practice in how to go from the statement of the problem all the way to the finished product. Your job is to decipher what's been said, use the capabilities of PHP to perform the processing, and collect the data and respond to the user with Web pages. To complete this exercise, you should include the following in addition to your finished program:

❑ A list of all required information, in addition to what has been presented.

❑ A description of the screens that you'll make, why you'll make them (why they are needed), and how the user will interact with them.

❑ A short description of how you'll integrate the screens with the existing Web site.

There's no one single PHP programming solution for this exercise, although all solutions will perform similar processing and use similar steps. Because databases or file system haven't been discussed yet, there's no way for you to store the resumes long-term, and the resume information will be lost once processing is complete.

You've got your assignment. Go on, get started!

Hint: To build a solution, try to lay out the problem as a series of screens first, and ask yourself what you'd expect to see. The, review the PHP capabilities that have been discussed so far to see which ones might be able to provide the data, and exactly what data must be present to complete the next step. It's much easier to arrive at a workable solution by breaking down the execution of the solution into small steps.

Robust and Healthy Code

It's easy (and sometimes necessary) to slap applications together quickly, without taking the time to make sure they'll be robust and healthy over the long term. For applications that are large, complex, or critical, it's worthwhile to use a formal software development process. That process examines, documents, and provides metrics for the development lifecycle, including design, development, change orders, maintenance, updates, and termination.

This chapter is all about writing robust and healthy code, and whenever possible you should spend the extra effort to make sure your code has these qualities. Plus, learning how to create good code gives you an edge because if you adopt good coding habits and practices, you're more likely to create high-quality code the first time around.

What are these qualities? A robust program doesn't fail easily, and can cope with a wide variety of input. If it can't proceed or reach the desired outcome for some reason, it *fails gracefully*, meaning it allows the user to proceed to the next logical option with a meaningful message (and certainly doesn't display PHP or SQL error messages). In addition, healthy code is written with plenty of internal documentation, so it's easy to understand what was intended when you or someone else has to go back in and do more work later, and it's written not just so it works, but so the structures make sense and are abstracted from each other to a degree that it's unlikely a small change in one spot will cause bugs in other spots. Together, these qualities make your programs better, and easier to maintain.

In this chapter you learn the basics of testing, troubleshooting, and debugging, and how to use PHP5 error handling functions. You'll also create a string handling function to validate form submissions, use regular expressions for validation, and experiment with the new try/catch functions.

Testing and Debugging

Debugging was actually introduced in Chapter 1, when you learned to troubleshoot your installation of PHP. This chapter continues that discussion, and then takes a more detailed look at a formal debugging process.

After you've decided what your application or program should do, the process of building the program begins. You may be working with graphic artists building the pages that are rendered to the user (and this might be done in parallel with or before writing much code), and you also may be drawing diagrams or making outlines of the logical flow of your program. But at some point you'll write some code.

Typically, you'll write code and insert it into Web pages, as you've already done, or perhaps generate the HTML code for the Web pages via the `echo` statement or from with objects. Most likely, you'll write enough code to perform an understandable set of functions, and then bring up the pages in your browser to test it.

Testing is the first step in debugging. Obviously, if you haven't tested your code and found an error, there's nothing to debug yet. Quick little jobs whipping out a simple dynamic feature such as displaying the current date for a single page don't require a formal testing protocol; either the correct date appears or it doesn't. But more complex, full-featured applications require a higher level of testing, and a formal process for identifying and tracking the errors found. In this chapter we concentrate on just the testing required for debugging your code, but in a real production environment you'll encounter much more formal testing systems.

Values That Break Your Code

The first time you write the code for an application, it's tempting to assume the values you'll work with will fall neatly into the range of those you expected. But because PHP applications are designed to work with data submitted by users on the Internet, your application could instead receive values deliberately intended to break it (when your application fails or is hacked, it's broken).

Consequently, testing your code with unexpected values is a good part of any testing protocol. Before you examine the kinds of unexpected values your application might encounter in real use, consider data in Web applications.

All data submitted by a browser to your Web server is formatted as strings. For example, the number 1995 might be a year, or a price, but when it passes to the Web server via an HTTP request, it comes into the PHP processing engine as a string. Strings can be empty or contain any number of characters. If your program is expecting a number, that's okay, because PHP is very forgiving about data types. But if your program is expecting a string of a certain length and gets none, that could be a problem.

Even if the value received is numeric in nature (composed of all valid digit characters) so that it is properly turned into a number by PHP, the number could be too high or too low (outside the range of acceptable values), and that could also be a problem.

One of the first steps to take to protect your application is to define the ranges of values (whether string, number, date, or what-have-you) and then to test your application with values that fall outside these ranges (and don't forget to use empty or nil values as well as large and other strange values).

There can be other problems such as submitted values that fall into the appropriate range or data type, but are still bad in some way. For example, an e-mail address might be limited to 100 characters in your database, so what happens if a person submits an e-mail address that contains 101 characters? And what happens if someone forgets to include the @ in his e-mail address? The data submitted is still a string, and may look superficially like an e-mail address, but these kinds of errors can still cause problems.

So you may end up testing to make sure that the submitted string is actually formatted as a string, number, date, or whatever, and then proceeding to test whether it falls into the right range of values, and then performing more tests to make sure it is actually the right length and perhaps even that it contains some special characters pertinent to the kind of data it's supposed to be. Sounds like a lot of trouble, to be sure, but users are notorious for entering bad data and data that looks good but cannot be processed properly (such as "three" for "3"), so the extra time you spend testing now is definitely worthwhile.

Basic Error Types

As you write code, you test frequently at small milestones in your project, not after weeks of writing an entire application. It's very common for the first test to result in errors that PHP can catch programmatically. Syntax (or parse) errors, for example, occur when you leave out a semicolon or forget to close off a control-flow block with a curly brace. PHP provides some very descriptive error messages to help you find and fix these types of errors, and once you're familiar with the error messages, it's pretty easy to take care of the syntax errors.

An application's inability to find or open a file or connect to a database is another type of error that PHP catches. These errors are called *runtime errors* because they occur while the program is running. PHP still detects them programmatically and generates error messages for them.

Errors that PHP can catch and generate an error message for are often easy to find and fix, but sometimes error messages can be a little frustrating because they're, well, cryptic (like any programming language) until you get used to them. (PHP error messages are discussed in more depth later in the chapter.)

There's another significant type of error called a *logic* error, which occurs when your program has no syntax errors, runs fine, and produces an incorrect response or answer. Sometimes these are easy to find and debug; and other times they just drive you crazy because they may occur infrequently, or only under special conditions.

The most common syntax, runtime, and logic errors—and ways to debug them—are discussed throughout the rest of this chapter.

Debugging PHP Script

You've done your best to make your code watertight, and yes, some errors still manage to seep through. How do you go about removing the little blighters? That process is called *troubleshooting*. Troubleshooting gradually eliminates potential causes of problems until you've found the right one and then change the code to eliminate it. Troubleshooting works for both syntax and logic errors. Of course, each time you change something, you must test again, to see if the correction worked, if the change you made provided more clues as to the nature of the problem, or if it may have caused a new problem elsewhere.

Understanding PHP Error Messages

Whenever PHP encounters an error condition that affects its capability to complete data processing, it generates an error message. Serious errors cause PHP to simply stop whatever it's doing and quit processing , displaying a "Fatal Error" error message on the screen (if you've enabled the display of error messages in your configuration file). Errors that are not quite as serious may interrupt only a small part of the overall processing PHP is attempting to do, and in that case perhaps only a "Warning" error message is displayed. Errors that don't affect processing may still occur, and those you have to figure out for yourself.

Configuring PHP for Error Handling

You can set a number of options in the php.ini file to help you control PHP's behavior when errors are encountered. Some of the more important of these configuration settings are:

❑   display_errors: Sets the display of error messages to the screen on or off. Note that if you set error messages off, a serious error may leave the user with a blank screen.

❑   error_reporting: Can be set using a value representing the level of error reporting to perform. For example, setting this option to the value 3 means the first two error types of error messages listed in the documentation will be generated.

❑   log_errors: Tells PHP whether to log errors to the error log. As with any other logging system, you may need to decide how many error messages you want to accumulate in the log file.

❑   track_errors: Enable this option and the most recent error message, whatever it be, is always available in the built-in $php_errmsg variable. This variable is not a superglobal variable; it's available only within the scope in which the error occurred.

PHP Error Types

In the broad scheme of things there are basically only two types of errors: errors that break your program through bad syntax or a runtime problem, and errors that simply produce the wrong answer. PHP makes several error levels available within that first category:

❑   Fatal Error: Completely shuts down processing. There are fatal runtime errors, compile-time errors, and parse errors.

❑   Warning: Indicates that an error condition may have occurred, but the script will go on processing beyond the point at which the error occurred.

❑   Notice: Indicates that something of interest may have happened. These errors include runtime notices and user-generated notices.

If you've enabled the display_errors option in php.ini, error messages will be displayed to the screen, and that's often the fastest way to find and debug errors while you're building an application. For production applications, you may want to disable the display_errors option, and have errors logged instead.

Syntax Errors

Syntax errors are simply errors in writing your code, such as typos, missing symbols or marks, and incorrect use of operators. They can't be parsed properly, and generate error messages. There are several common causes of syntax errors that you can learn to avoid:

❑   Simple typos: It's easy to type a semicolon or a curly brace instead of a colon or square bracket. Learn to check your spelling and syntax as you type.

❑   Not properly closing statements: Put all the braces in your statements even when they aren't technically required for the code to run. It's a little more work, but once you get used to it, you'll be more apt to code them correctly, without missing braces. Look out for improperly closed code like this:

```
        for ($myloop01 = 0; $myloop01<10; $myloop01++)
        {
        for ($myloop02 = 2; $myloop02<20; $myloop02++)
        {
        for ($myloop03 = 3; $myloop03<30; $myloop03++)
        {
        for ($myloop04 = 4; $myloop04<40; $myloop04++)
        {
... More code goes here...
        }
        }
```

❑ Code not indented properly: It's not always obvious if the loops are closed 10 pages of code later, but indenting the code certainly helps, as well as make it easier to understand afterward. Try formatting your loops this way:

```
for ($myloop01 = 0; $myloop01<10; $myloop01++)
{
    for ($myloop02 = 2; $myloop02<20;$myloop02++)
    {
        for ($myloop03 = 3; $myloop03<30; $myloop03++)
        {
            for ($myloop04 = 4; $myloop04<40; $myloop04++)
            {
                ... More code goes here...
            }
        }
    }
}
```

From the indentation, it's pretty easy to see the missing brace.

❑ Forgetting to end a statement with a semicolon: It's true that there are a few instances in which it is acceptable to leave the semicolon off at the end of a line, but not having a semicolon when you should is a big problem. Always insert the semicolon, even when you don't have to, to enforce the habit.

❑ Misspelling the name of a function: Even a small typo in the name of a function will cause an error. Transposing, omitting, or adding letters to a function name are all errors to avoid. Be careful with your typing, and check your spelling often (don't count on any spell-checking program to catch function name errors.

❑ Forgetting the closing quotes for a string, or incorrectly mixing single and double quotes: It's easy to forget to close quotes on a string, or how many single quotes you've used, especially when you're constructing long strings with lots of variables interspersed, like this:

```
echo "This is the beginning of a string with " . $number " quotes, both
single, like this \' and double, like this \" and quotes in HTML, like this
<img src="image.gif">;
```

The first two quotes (the single and the double) are properly escaped, but the last two double quotes in the HTML are not. Additionally, the finishing double quote is left off. PHP would generate parse errors (incorrect syntax) on this statement.

As mentioned, you'll see syntax errors frequently the first time you test your code. Although PHP provides some very good error messages, one difficulty you might encounter when debugging is finding out exactly where the error is occurring. For example, suppose you have the following code and try to run it:

```php
<?php
//generate a parse error
$line of code = "error: no semicolon"
?>
```

This code produces a syntax or parse error. The PHP processing engine can't completely parse the code because of the error (missing semicolon), so the code doesn't run. Instead it generates the following error message:

```
Parse error: parse error in /home/servata/www/error_test_file.php on line 3
```

The error message contains a description of the error and the line number that generated it. Sometimes, though, the line number can be misleading, such as when you forget a curly brace, as shown in this example:

```php
<?php
//generate a parse error
if ($my_test == 0) {

    //do something
} else {
?>
<html>
<head>
<title></title>
</head>
<body>
lots of html here<br>
lots of html here<br>
lots of html here<br>
lots of html here<br>
lots of html here<br>
lots of html here<br>
lots of html here<br>
lots of html here<br>
lots of html here<br>
lots of html here<br>
lots of html here<br>
lots of html here<br>
lots of html here<br>
lots of html here<br>
lots of html here<br>
</body>
</html>
```

And the error message:

```
Parse error: parse error in /home/servata/www/error_test_file02.php on line 31
```

As good as this information is, in this particular case, the line number is misleading because there are only 29 lines in the code, and even if you look at the bottom of the file it may not be apparent that the problem is a missing curly brace, because you've closed off your PHP properly before beginning your HTML.

Most PHP errors are on or very close to the line number noted in the error message—but not always. It really pays to be attentive to writing good code in the first place, and with some practice you can avoid most syntax errors altogether. To eliminate them, just rewrite your code and test again.

Logic Errors

Logic errors occur when your code runs but doesn't produce the right answer. For example, if you were supposed to add two numbers but have subtracted them instead, the code runs just fine, but hopefully you notice right away that the answer is wrong.

Logic errors can be difficult to detect, particularly when an incorrect answer only occurs under a special set of circumstances. If getting the right answer is critical (such as when performing bank transactions), it pays to have a more elaborate and comprehensive testing program specifically designed to test all possible inputs. And when reporting errors, the reports must specify in detail the circumstances under which each error occurred.

You'll have logical errors in odd ways. For example, you run the program and it either starts returning data that can't possibly be correct, or it doesn't return any data at all. In some cases it may not even return any output to the screen. At times your program works fine, but then you give it to the user and it suddenly breaks. All of these are usually the result of mistakes in the logic of program.

There is further distinction to make here between the types of logical error. Some logical errors occur at runtime, and only under certain conditions. For example, the PHP code seems fine, and is even accepted and executed by the PHP engine, but errors occur when you run the program, stopping your program from completing. These are known as runtime errors. Runtime errors that stop your program from completing execution are termed *fatal*. Syntax errors are invariably fatal, but runtime errors that stop your program's execution only under certain circumstances, aren't always fatal.

The second type of logical error doesn't actually cause your program to break but runs to completion and then returns incorrect information or no information at all. These are, for want of a better description, unexpected output errors. Let's take a deeper look at runtime errors first.

Runtime Errors

Runtime errors differ from parse errors in that they occur after the PHP engine has successfully parsed and is executing your code. Runtime errors are often caused by a bad connection to an outside resource such as a file or a database, but sometimes the errors are more mundane (although still hard to find). For example, PHP will throw an error if you try to divide by zero. In the next few sections you'll explore these error types, but the file and database connections are covered in later chapters.

Dividing By Zero

Mathematically, there's no acceptable way to divide by zero (no correct answer can be represented) so inadvertently dividing by zero causes PHP to emit an error. No one would deliberately create an application that tries to divide by zero (except perhaps as an example of a program that won't work), so this type of error is usually caused unintentionally. Because variables are used to contain and process values and often depend on user input, and because users sometimes enter erroneous values, you can easily see how division by zero might occur in practice.

For example, suppose you have a form in which you ask a user to enter several values (quantities for an order, or the number of children he has, or the like) and then use these numbers to calculate a discount, total price, rooms required, or that kind of thing.

If the user happens to make a mistake or simply forgets to enter a value, or just doesn't properly understand what he's supposed to do, you could easily end up with a situation in which the program tries to divide by the non-existent number. Depending on the calculations, then, an attempt to divide by zero could be made, and an error will be thrown.

Here's a very simple form that demonstrates what happens when a divide-by-zero error is encountered. Fire up your trusty HTML editor and enter the following code, naming it `divide_by_zero.php`:

```
<html>
<head><title></title></head>
<body>
<b>Divide Any Number (except zero)</b>
<br>
<br>
<?php
if (isset($_POST['posted'])) {

    $first_number = $_POST['first_number'];
    $second_number = $_POST['second_number'];
    $answer = $first_number / $second_number;
    echo "Your answer is " . $answer . "<br>";

}
?>

<form method="POST" action="divide_by_zero.php">
<input type="hidden" name="posted" value="true">
Please enter the first number:
<br>
<br>
<input name="first_number" type="text" value="0"><br>
Please enter the second number:
<br>
<br>
<input name="second_number" type="text" value="0"><br>
Divide when ready!
<br>
<br>
<input type="submit" value="Divide">
```

```
    </form>
  </body>
</html>
```

Run the code. Figure 5-1 shows the form displayed.

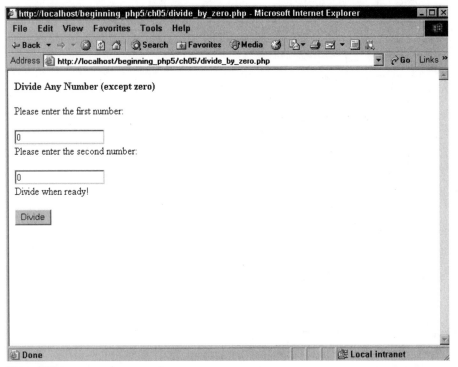

Figure 5-1

Try it out both with and without numbers inserted. Figure 5-2 shows the result of an attempt to divide by zero.

This is a very simple example, but notice that it doesn't show any kind of a parse error if the user enters appropriate values. As you develop, remember that most of the time you'll be inclined to use appropriate values, and it's easy to miss this type of error as you test and check your application.

In this example notice that if you happen to enter (or leave) the first number as 0, no error is generated (the answer is zero; try it to see for yourself!). And even if the second number is erased from the screen entirely, PHP still interprets the empty string as 0, and produces the error message. One thing you can do to at least reduce the possibility of error is to set the default values of the first_number and second_number form fields to 1 instead of 0 in your HTML code. You also could validate incoming values to make sure they are not equal to zero. (Validation of form submission values is covered later in this chapter.)

So in your applications, watch out for the possibility of division by zero, as well as other mathematical functions that may cause problems, such as calculating the square root of a negative number.

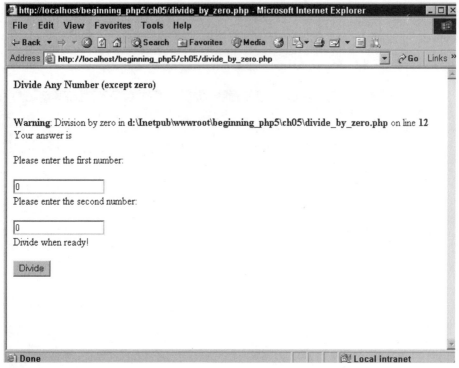

Figure 5-2

Infinite (Never-Ending) Loops

Looping structures are some of the most basic programming constructs in any language, and they are also the foundation for one of the most common errors in programming, the infinite or never-ending loop. Their power inherently makes them susceptible to this error because they are designed to keep running until a particular condition is met. If that condition is never met, they never end.

In PHP, one of the problems with using looping structures such as while and do while is that if the condition that you set is never matched, PHP executes the loop a potentially infinite number of times within the limits of the max_execution_time setting (in the php.ini file). If the max_execution_time setting is exceeded, PHP emits a warning error and ends processing. Like any error message, you can display it and see what happened, but you cannot recover from this particular error condition. Consider the following, but do not attempt to run it:

```
$cntr=1;
$test = True;
while ($test)
{
    $cntr++;
}
```

While the counter variable ($cntr) is incremented each time through the loop, $test has no possibility of becoming False, so the loop never ends. If you happen to be running this on a Windows server, you could well crash the server (Linux machines running Apache seem to behave in a much better fashion, but you'll still get the warning when you exceed `max_execution_time`).

To fix this type or error (or make sure it never happens in the first place) make certain that whatever condition is used to run the loop has some way to force it to become `False` (or whatever value it needs to be to end the loop).

Logical Output Errors

If your application has no parse errors, and never emits a warning for a runtime error, it can still give you a logical output error. Basically, this means that your program has been executed correctly, but you just didn't set up your processing properly, or you didn't anticipate that a particular value might be used during processing. You get output correctly, just not the value you expected.

A very good example of this is when you use percentages. For example, suppose you are expecting the user to enter a percentage number of 0.0775 (the sales tax rate in California), but the user instead enters 7.75. Imagine what that would do to the total sales tax charged on his order! But nothing in this scenario would automatically cause a warning or error; PHP would simply perform the calculations and give the answer. It's really up to you to anticipate and avoid these errors, and only plenty of thorough testing will give you confidence in your application.

Functions Without a Return Value

When you create your own functions (covered in Chapter 6), you may include the `return` statement, instructing the function what value to `return` when the function is called. Not all functions need a `return` statement, so it's relatively easy to forget to include one. And if you leave the return statement out when it's required, your function will return nothing.

If you use that function and expect a result from it that you use elsewhere, it might be a while before you realize that your function is returning nothing. Uncovering this mistake can be very frustrating, so always give your functions at least one test run to make sure they are returning a result if you expect them to.

Function Arguments Order Incorrect

Functions frequently need to be sent arguments to perform their processing. Functions expect arguments in a particular order, and if you happen to mix that order up, the function has no way to know that. So if your function happens to require two numerical values which it then performs a calculation on, and you mix up the order of these arguments, watch out! You'll get a value back, alright, but it won't be correct.

Setting Values vs. Comparing Values

One common mistake in PHP is to use the equals sign (=) to try to compare values, when in fact it sets a value instead. No warning is given; if you screw this one up, PHP simply sets the value and proceeds on that basis. It's very common to find this mistake in `if...then...else` structures, like this:

```
If ($my_value = $your_value) {
    //Do this
} else {
    //Do that
}
```

Unfortunately, it doesn't look obviously wrong, and because it sounds right in your head (after all, you're probably reading either usage of = or == in your head as "equals"), especially if you're familiar with another language that allows the single = sign for comparison, it's not always easy to avoid. There's no magic bullet for this one; just be careful: use = to set values, and use == to compare values.

Debugging and Handling Errors in PHP5

PHP5 has new try/catch functions, and they provide valuable new ways of handling errors in PHP (you'll examine these functions—and try them out for yourself—at the end of the chapter), but PHP also provides more traditional ways for you to debug and find errors, and to handle them gracefully if they occur as your application is running. In this section you'll explore these traditional means.

Preventing the Display of Private Information

Consider that some error messages not only display the exact path and name of the file in which the error occurred, they also point out the line number. This could be all that an experienced programmer or hacker needs to subvert your application to his own ends. It is nobody else's business how your paths and filenames are set up, especially the ones containing scripts, include files, and so on. PHP error messages can be quite verbose, and it is this wealth of information that becomes harmful when it tells users not only that a file handle cannot be opened, but also gives the exact path that the script was trying to open! Turn off error reporting after you're done programming an application and before you copy it over to the production site.

And be aware that other applications PHP makes use of may reveal even more of this type of error information; PostgreSQL and other databases can be very specific about SQL statements that contain errors

Roll-Your-Own Debugging Tools

You can write HTML and PHP code with the very simplest text editors available, but if you do, you won't have any fancy tools available to precompile your code, detect parse errors before the code runs, or capture variable values as the code runs. All is not lost, however, because there are some effective ways to do these things for yourself, and they work very well.

Using echo()

Just about anytime you set a variable value, you can also echo out that value so it displays on the screen. You can do it within functions, you can do it inside loops, you can do it during normal processing—basically you can put an echo statement just about anywhere in your code. And if you identify the location of the echo statement (perhaps by putting text in it such as "Inside the For loop" or "Inside the 2nd If statement"), you can use multiple echo statements within your code and still know what happens at each moment during processing. For example, if you have a form that accepts a name and e-mail address from the user and then processes them in some way, you can find out what happens during processing with the following code:

```php
<?php
echo "Name is :" . $name . "<br>";
echo "Email is :" . $email . "<br>";
// do processing
echo "Name after processing is:" . $name . "<br>";
echo "Email after processing is:" . $email . "<br>";
```

```
    // do more processing
    echo "Name after more processing is:" . $name . "<br>";
    echo "Email after more processing is:" . $email . "<br>";
    ?>
```

The name and e-mail values can change each time processing occurs, but you see that because the text that goes along with the values is slightly different as well.

Errors Inside the HTML Source Code

If PHP generates an error and sends a warning or fatal error message back with whatever HTML code it was able to complete processing on, the error doesn't always automatically display on the screen. If the error occurs in the middle of an HTML tag, or in the middle of generating an HTML form control, browsers are so forgiving of HTML coding mistakes that the page might appear to display normally, even though the data you're expecting is not present. One of the first things to do anytime you're having trouble is check the HTML source code your browser got back and make sure there are no hidden PHP errors. While you're doing that, take the time to make sure that values you're expecting (but that may be hidden inside the HTML source code) are present as well.

For example, suppose you use PHP code to connect to a database, retrieve some records, and then use those records within a `for` loop to construct an HTML `<select>` element. If you're familiar with HTML, you know that the tags for the `<select>` element not only begin and end with `<select>` and `</select>`, but that between these tags there are also `<option>` elements. If one of your `<option>` elements is incorrect (with a PHP error message, for instance), the browser simply ignores it. On the screen you'll see the drop-down list rendered from the `<select>` element and all the "good" `<option>` elements, but in the HTML source code you'll see something like the following:

```
<select name="select_customer_id">
   <option value="1">John Doe</option>
   PHP error message
   <option value="3">Jane Doe</option>
</select>
```

So you'd be completely missing customer number 2, but would never see the problem displayed as an error message on the screen, even though it's plainly visible in the HTML source code.

Form Validation

Here's a maxim for you: Users can, and will, enter anything and/or nothing in your HTML forms, no matter how easy you make it to use the forms or what you expect the users to enter. Likewise, malicious users will deliberately enter oddball data to try to break your applications. Form validation on both the client and the server is your main defense.

One way to deal with this is to limit the values permitted in a certain text box. In `loan.php`, for example, you'll recall that the program passed the person's age into a variable called `$age`, and the PHP page then validated that value against a more realistic range of age values:

```
if ($age < 1 or $age > 130)
{
    echo "Incorrect age value entered. Please enter an age between 1 and 130.";
    break;
}
```

Of course, you're not limited to simply informing the user he's entered an inappropriate age value. You can take any other steps you want at this point, now that you've identified an inappropriate value.

Using the exit Statement

Performing validation is great, but if you encounter incorrect data, what can you do? Sometimes you just need to quit processing, and that's what the exit statement is for. Although the break statement exits the current structure, the exit statement ends all processing. You can use either method to end processing, but exit is much more abrupt, so be careful where you use it. No further HTML, PHP code, or text is executed after an exit is encountered, and unless you're very careful, the user may get back an unexpected result, such as a partially completed page. So why don't you rebuild the loan application example and tighten it up a bit more against possible user errors by incorporating some form validation logic.

Try It Out   Form Validation

1. Open loan.php (from Chapter 4), save it as loan_fv.php, and insert the following changes:

```
<html
  <head><title></title></head>
  <body>
<b>Namllu credit bank loan form</b>
<?php
if (isset($_POST['posted'])) {

    $age = $_POST['age'];
    $first_name = $_POST['first_name'];
    $last_name = $_POST['last_name'];
    $address = $_POST['address'];
    $loan = $_POST['loan'];
    $month = $_POST['month'];

    //validation
    if ($age < 10 OR $age > 130)
    {
      echo "Incorrect Age entered - Press back button to try again";
      exit;
    }
    if ($first_name == "" or $last_name == "")
    {
      echo "You must enter your name - Press back button to try again";
      exit;
    }
    if ($address == "")
    {
      echo "You must enter your address - Press back button to try again";
      exit;
    }
    if ($loan != 1000 and $loan != 5000 and $loan != 10000)
    {
        echo "You must enter a loan value - Press back button to try again";
        exit;
    }
```

```php
$duration = 0;
switch ($loan) {
case "1000";
   $interest = 5;
   break;
case "5000";
   $interest = 6.5;
   break;
case "10000";
   $interest = 8;
   break;
default:
   echo "You didn't enter a loan package!<hr>";
   exit;
}
while ($loan > 0)
 {
   $duration = $duration + 1;
   $monthly = $month - ($loan * $interest / 100);
   if ($monthly <= 0)
     {
       echo "You need larger repayments to pay off your loan!<hr>";
       exit;
     }
 $loan = $loan - $monthly;
 }
   echo "This would take you $duration months to pay this off
at the interest rate of $interest percent.<hr>";

}
?>
<form method="POST" action="loan_fv.php">
<input type="hidden" name="posted" value="true">
<br>
```

```html
First Name:
<input name="first_name" type="text">
Last Name:
<input name="last_name" type="text">
Age:
<input name="age" type="text" size="3">
<br>
<br>
address:
<textarea name="address" rows="4" cols="40">
</textarea>
<br>
<br>
what is your current salary?
<select name="salary">
<option value=0>under $10000</option>
<option value=10000>$10,000 to $25,000</option>
<option value=25000>$25,000 to $50,000</option>
<option value=50000>over $50,000</option>
```

```
    </select>
    <br>
    <br>
    How much do you want to borrow?<br><br>
    <input name="loan" type="radio" value="1000">Our $1,000 package at 5.0%
interest
    <br>
    <input name="loan" type="radio" value="5000">Our $5,000 package at 6.5%
interest
    <br>
    <input name="loan" type="radio" value="10000">Our $10,000 package at 8.0%
interest
    <br>
    <br>
    How much do you want to pay a month?
    <input name="month" type="text" size="5">
    <br>
    <br>
    <input type="submit" value="calculate">
    </form>
    </body>
    </html>
```

2. Save this file as `loan_fv.php` and then close it.

3. Open the file in your browser and enter some values that are out of bounds or otherwise
    incorrect. Figure 5-3 shows one of the error messages a user could receive.

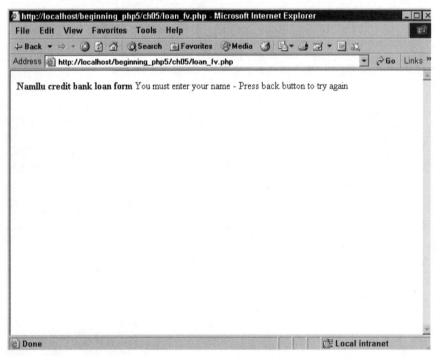

Figure 5-3

How It Works

You could enter someone else's address, or an age other than your own, and there's no way PHP can check for incorrect entries of this type. But what we can do with our new code is make sure that the user hasn't simply forgotten to add a detail, or maliciously supplied obviously wrong information about their age. We use four `if..then..else` statements to do this. The first checks to see whether the age entered is between 10 and 130, otherwise we can be pretty sure that the person is lying:

```
if ($age < 10 OR $age > 130)
{
    echo "Incorrect Age entered - Press back button to try again";
    exit;
}
```

If the condition is not met, you display the "error" message and exit there. If the condition is met, you don't need to do anything further.

The second `if` statement checks for first and last names being present. The `""` denotes an empty string (a string with no characters in it), and this is how you check for one:

```
if ($first_name == "" or $last_name == "")
{
    echo "You must enter your name - Press back button to try again";
    exit;
}
```

Do the same check for the `$address` variable:

```
if ($address == "")
{
    echo "You must enter your address - Press back button to try again";
    exit;
}
```

And then check the values of the radio buttons to validate that one was selected.

```
if ($loan != 1000 and $loan != 5000 and $loan != 10000)
{
    echo "You must enter a loan value - Press back button to try again";
    exit;
}
```

If the `$load` variable is not equal to any of these values, you know that the user didn't select a value.

Preventing User-Inserted HTML: HTMLSpecialChars()

Another way users can abuse your applications is by entering HTML code directly in as part of their data entry into your form fields. This works because HTML is plain text, and when it comes back out, it's processed by the browser just like any other plain text characters that form HTML code. For example, if you have created an application that accepts user input for directory listings, a slick user might insert <b> before his name, and </b> after his name, so that his listing would have his name in bold. Nice trick, but unfair to the other users.

While this exact situation might not be a serious problem, under other circumstances it could be used to break your HTML or otherwise thwart your intent. Fortunately, PHP provides the HTMLSpecialChars() function, which changes HTML tags into special characters (more on this shortly). It just requires a string argument to work, like this:

```
$String = HTMLSpecialChars("<b>The bold tags won't appear after processing </b>");
```

A variable name will also do the trick:

```
$String ="<B> The bold tags won't appear after processing </B>";
$String = HTMLSpecialChars($String);
```

The HTMLSpecialChars() function converts any HTML tags into the what are called *special characters*. Special characters in HTML are simply entities that represent the HTML characters they have been translated from. For example, <b> is translated into < (for the less-than sign), the letter b, and > (for the greater-than sign). When the browser receives these special characters, it displays them on the screen as the HTML characters they represent, instead of processing and rendering them as ordinary HTML tags.

This feature is often used when you want to make a Web page that discusses HTML tags (when you need to display the tags in plain text rather than letting the browser process them), but it certainly comes in handy for preventing users from entering their own HTML into your PHP application.

Ultimately, there is no limit to the degree of error checking you can perform. In fact, you could preset all variable values in advance, but then what would be the point of providing a form? You could just automatically do everything in advance. Seriously, it really helps to try to think like a user. The ratio of users to hackers is pretty small, meaning that most users who break your application do so unintentionally. They'll either not understand what you meant, or simply make a mistake. So attempt to think like your users, try your applications out on family members and friends, and try to anticipate all the possible responses, accounting for them as comprehensively as possible. The extra work you put in will be well worth it.

String Validation and Regular Expressions

All the data your application receives from the user's browser is formatted as strings, as you know. So PHP's wealth of string manipulation functions come in very handy for validating data entered by the user, or reformatting string data into sequences acceptable as other data types. But PHP contains other functions, called *regular expression* functions, that are a quantum leap more powerful when it comes to manipulating data. You'll explore both of these subjects in the next few sections.

String Validation

You can use PHP's string manipulation functions in a variety of clever ways to perform basic validation of data being entered by users. In this section you'll see a few common ones, but remember, you can easily devise your own, using the functions covered here, other PHP functions, or combinations of all of them. You've already had a go at a few of these (like strlen() and substr()) in Chapter 2 and in some of our other example scripts, but it doesn't hurt to use them again in a validation context.

Using strlen()

Some data is always a certain length, such as U.S. ZIP codes, which are always 5 digits or, in the case of ZIP+4, 5 digits, a hyphen, and 4 more digits. So one way to validate data entered as postal codes is to use the strlen() function like this:

```
If (strlen($postal_code) == 5 or strlen($postal_code) == 10) {
    //check to make sure if 10 the dash is in spot 6
       //do something
} else {
    //send error message
}
```

Using strstr()

In the preceding example you needed to find out if the character in the sixth spot of the incoming string was actually a hyphen. The strstr() function is useful for determining this because as its name implies, it looks for a string within a string. In this example, you want it to look for a one-character string consisting of a hyphen. This code would work:

```
if (strlen($postal_code) == 5
  or strlen($postal_code) == 10) {
     if (strlen($postal_code) == 10) {
         if (strstr($postal_code, "-")) {
             //do something
         }
     }
} else {
    //send error message
    }
```

You also want to use the strstr() function to check for a space at the sixth position, just in case the user omitted the hyphen but entered a space.

Using substr()

Continuing with the same example, suppose you want to separate out the +4 portion of the ZIP+4. You know that this portion begins at spot 7, and should be four characters long. You could employ the substr() function for this purpose. As arguments, the substr() function takes the string in question, an integer representing the position to start looking at, and an optional integer specifying the number of characters to return. Code like this would work:

```
If (strlen($postal_code) == 5
  or strlen($postal_code) == 10) {
     If (strlen($postal_code) == 10) {
         $plus4_portion = substr($postal_code,7,4)
     }
} else {
   //send error message
}
```

Using addslashes() and stripslashes()

For applications in which you allow the user to enter data that may be going into a database, it's a great idea to use the `addslashes()` function. This function adds slashes wherever it finds string characters that might cause a problem for database entries (the `'`, `"`, `\`, and NULL characters). Later, when you output the data to the user again, you must use the `stripslashes()` function to—you guessed it—remove those slashes that `addslashes()` inserted.

Why is there a function dedicated to protecting your database entries? If you've ever composed a SQL string for inserting a record (or for just about any database function, for that matter), you're aware that SQL tends to be very intolerant of misplaced apostrophes (if you've not used SQL yet, you'll get that experience in Chapters 9–11).

So perhaps you're SQL string is supposed to look like this:

```
$query = "INSERT INTO clients (username) values('$username')";
mysql_query($query);
```

Now, if the user enters joeblow for his username, the query should run without a hitch. But if the user enters joe'blow, your query blows up because your database sees:

```
$query = "INSERT INTO clients (username) values('joe'blow')";
```

It might be a little hard to see, but if you look carefully you can see that the apostrophe in the user's username looks to the database like a broken set of delimiters. How can you ensure this doesn't happen? Apply the `addslashes()` function to the value entered by the user, and the username stored in the database will be correct. For example, using this would work:

```
$username = addslashes($username);
$query = "INSERT INTO clients (username) values('$username')";
mysql_query($query);
```

When this code runs, if the user enters joe'blow, `addslashes` converts that value to joe\'blow. The slash escapes the apostrophe, thereby causing your database to accept both characters (the slash and the apostrophe in combination) without blowing up your query.

But you must take care to use `stripslashes()` when outputting the username to the user again. Otherwise the user sees joe\'blow as his username, and if he doesn't remove the slash, the next time he edits his username he'll end up with joe\\\'blow entered because `addslashes` will try to escape both characters, and this could cause problems.

And you also must make sure to use `addslashes` anywhere that the user's username is used, because although it is properly seen on the screen as joe'blow, it is stored as joe\'blow, and only by using the `addslashes()` function again (like when he logs in) can you be sure the database will match up the values correctly.

Regular Expressions

Finding a specific string within another one is quite helpful in some situations, and of course if you know what the string you're looking for, the substr() function can handle the situation for you. But suppose you don't know exactly what string you'll be looking for. If you even know a little about the string, you can use regular expressions and PHP's regular expression functions to help you find it.

Suppose, for example, that you know you'll be looking for a string made up of all alphabetic characters and no numerical characters. In that case, you at least know the *pattern* you're looking for, and that's enough to start with. The simplest pattern is a word or a single character, as in the earlier strstr() example, which is looking for the hyphen:

```
if (strstr($postal_code, "-")) {
```

And to separate out data values in a string (a string of comma-separated values, for instance), you can use the explode() function, which separates characters in a string by a characters and puts the results into an array. The function takes two arguments, first the string to separate on and then the name of the array into which to put the results. You can use explode() with a simple if statement to test for the existence of a particular word within a string, as shown in the following code:

```php
<?php
$words = "you, should, vote, happily";
$wordarray = explode(",", $words);
foreach ($wordarray as $word) {
    if ($word == "vote") {
        echo "Found string 'vote'";
    }
}
?>
```

But although you can use a simple PHP function like strstr() to find a matching character within a larger string of characters, or the explode() function for slightly more complex matching operations, you'll often find the need for much more complex patterns to match. That's where regular expressions come in handy.

Regular expressions, called regexps, are like a mini-programming language for creating very powerful patterns. They use a special notation to form the patterns that are used to match the values (or parts of values) that you provide. Certain characters take on special meanings in the context of a regexp, enabling you to broaden or narrow matches against sub-strings in the data. Some regexps will find characters belonging to a specified group; others find characters repeated a certain number of times. Regular expressions necessarily follow certain rules of syntax, which will be outlined as you read on.

> *Regular expressions are not limited to PHP. Languages such as Perl and Python, along with UNIX utilities like sed and egrep use the same notation for finding patterns in text. PHP's regular expression functions that follow Perl notation are called PCRE functions and begin with preg (for Perl Regular Expression), whereas ordinary PHP regular expression function are termed Posix-Extended regular expression functions. Don't use the ordinary (posix-extended) PHP regexp functions on binary data (they're not binary-safe); use the PCRE regexp functions instead.*

So let's take a look at how to pattern match with some of the PHP regular expression functions, starting with the ereg() function.

Using ereg()

It works (after a fashion), but it's clunky, complicated, hard coded (the word "vote" is actually part of the code, instead of coming as input; indeed, the entire array is hard-coded), and worse still, the explode() function actually keeps all the punctuation—the string "you" won't be found but "you," (with the comma) would. This looks like a difficult problem, but it should be easy. Here's how it looks using a regular expression:

```php
<?php
$words = "you, should, vote, happily";
if (ereg("vote", $words)) {
    echo "Found string 'vote'";
}
?>
```

Use the PHP function ereg() and just specify the pattern (the word you want to match that constitutes the actual regexp) and the string you want to match it against. It returns True if the pattern match was successful (in this case, on finding the character sequence "vote" in the string held by $words) and False if it wasn't.

You can also specify a third argument in ereg(): the name of an array, which is used to store successfully, matched expressions. Here's the preceding example modified to make use of it like this:

```php
<?php
$words = "you, should, vote, happily";
if (ereg("vote", $words, $reg)) echo "Found string '$reg[0]'";
?>
```

Literal text written as a string is the simplest regular expression of all to look for, but you don't have to search for just the one word—you could look for any particular phrase. However, all the characters you're searching for must match exactly—words (with correct capitalization), numbers, punctuation, and even whitespace:

```php
<?php
$words = "Vote twice or more if you can.";
if (ereg("twice if", $words, $reg)) echo "Found string '$reg[0]'";
?>
```

This string won't match, because it's not an exact match. Similarly, spaces inside the pattern are significant:

```php
<?php
$words1 = "The bigdog is in the pound...";
$words2 = "...but the dog is in the cornfield";
$regexp = " dog";
if (ereg($regexp, $words1, $reg)) echo "Found string '$reg[0]'";
if (ereg($regexp, $words2, $reg)) echo "Found string '$reg[0]'";
?>
```

This finds only the second dog because both `ereg()` calls are specifically looking for a space followed by the three letters "d", "o", and "g".

Special Characters

Regular expression notation includes the use of special characters (not to be confused with HTML special characters). Special characters in regular expressions enable you to specify more advanced matches in which portions of the match may be one of a number of characters, or where the match must occur at a certain position in the string.

As you've already seen, you can use a backslash to escape certain characters' special meanings. For example, to echo a double-quote character ", you have to use the escape sequence \" (just like the `addslashes()` function does for the database entry strings).

The characters that are given special meaning within a regular expression, which you will need to backslash if you want to use literally, are:

```
. * ? + [ ] ( ) { } ^ $ | \
```

Any other characters automatically assume their literal meanings. For example, if you want to specifically match "..." in the preceding text samples, you'd have to say:

```php
<?php
$words1 = "The bigdog is in the pound...";
$regexp = "pound\.\.\.";
if (ereg($regexp, $words1, $reg)) echo "Found string '$reg[0]'";
?>
```

If you used the regexp "pound...", you'd find it still matched the test string, but would also match in the following case, because the dot is not considered just a dot in a regex; it is considered a special character that makes anything:

```php
<?php
$words1 = "The bigdog is in the pound but the dog is in the cornfield.";
$regexp = "pound...";
if (ereg($regexp, $words1, $reg)) echo "Found string '$reg[0]'";
?>
```

This returns the following:

```
Found string 'pound bu'
```

As mentioned, this happens because the dot (.) is a special character. It matches against any single character except the new line. So it matches any single characters after "pound", not just three dots in a row.

A Few Shortcuts And Options

There are several options available to you for formulating patterns to match against. Go ahead and check them out.

Character Classes: [xyz]

Square brackets surrounding a pattern of characters is called a character class, and signifies that any of that set of characters is acceptable. For example, the regexp "w[ao]nder" matches against both the words "wander" and "wonder".

To make a set of characters unacceptable, the character class is started with a carat (^). For example, the regexp "^1234567890" will match against any character that isn't a number.

And you can use the hyphen to specify a range of characters. For instance, the preceding example can be rewritten as [^0-9], and a lowercase letter can be matched with [a-z].

You can use one or more of these ranges alongside each other, so if you wanted to match a single hexadecimal digit, you could write [0-9A-F]. The brackets contain the whole expression, and represent just a single character to be matched against any of the characters specified by either of the ranges in the class. If you used [0-9][A-F], you'd match a digit followed by a letter from A to F.

Some character classes such as digits, letters, and various types of whitespace are going to come up again and again. There are some neat shortcuts for these. Here are the most common ones, and what they represent:

Shortcut	Expansion	Description
\d	[0-9]	Digits 0 to 9
\w	[0-9A-Za-z_]	A "word" character
\s	[\t\n\r]	A whitespace character (space, tab, newline or return)

And here are the shortcuts' negative forms:

Shortcut	Expansion	Description
\D	[^0-9]	Any non-digit
\W	[^0-9A-Za-z_]	A non-"word" character
\S	[^\t\n\r]	A non-blank character

Anchors

Character classes match characters anywhere in a string, but there are certain symbols that can be used is a way to indicate the location on the string where the match must occur. These symbols are called *anchors*.

The two anchors are ^ , which appears at the beginning of the pattern, anchoring a match to the beginning of the string, and $, which appears at the end of the pattern, anchoring it to the end of the string. To see if a string ends with a full stop (remember, the full stop is a special character) you could use a regexp like this: "\.$". Likewise, you can use "^B" to see if there's a capital "B" at the beginning of the string.

Word Boundaries

To help you properly search for words when the words may be preceded or followed by a variety of punctuation marks, there are special symbols called *word boundaries*. Word boundary symbols enable you to designate a pattern as having to match the beginning or ending of a word. They are required because words aren't always separated by spaces, but are sometimes separated by commas, periods, and other punctuation marks.

For example, you can use the special \b word boundary symbol to find one-letter words using the regexp "\b\w\b". Like the anchor symbols, \b doesn't actually match any character in particular, but matches the point between something that isn't a word character (\W or one end of the string) and something that is (hence \b for boundary).

Alternatives

In some cases, you may want to use a symbol that causes an either/or condition. The "either-or" operator in a regular expression is the same as the bitwise "or" operator: |. For example, to match either "yes" or "maybe" you'd use the regexp "yes|maybe".

Qualifiers

Qualifier symbols—?, +, and *—enable you to create regexps that match against a set of characters that may occur once, may occur more than once, or may even not occur at all. The simplest is ?, which matches the immediately preceding character(s) or metacharacter(s) if they either appear once or not at all. For instance, to match the word "he" or "she", you can use "s?he". Notice how the "s" and the "h" are separated by the question mark (?). That's what tells the regexp to look for either character. If the "s" doesn't appear (as in the word "he"), a match is still found.

To make a series of characters (or metacharacters) optional, group them in parentheses: you can match either "man" or "woman" with the regexp "(wo)?man".

You can match something one or more times by using the plus sign. To match an entire word without specifying how long it should be, use "\w+".

You also may have something that could occur any number of times but might not be there at all (that is, zero or one or many). For that you need what's called "Kleene's star" (the * quantifier, which is simply called the star from here on out). So, for example, to find a capital letter after any (but possibly no) spaces at the start of the string, you'd use "^\s*[A-Z]".

The three qualifiers available are demonstrated by the following examples:

- ❑   hea?t   Matches either "heat" or "het"
- ❑   hea+t   Matches "heat", "heaat", "heaaat"...
- ❑   hea*t   Matches "het", "heat", "heaat"...

Novice programmers tend to overuse combinations of dots (representing anything) and stars (representing anything or nothing), often with unexpected, and unwanted, results. Some rules of thumb:

❑ A regular expression should almost never start or finish with a starred character.

❑ Using .* or .+ in the middle of a regular expression will match as much of your string as they possibly can.

Quantifiers

Quantifiers are used to set limits and ranges on the number (quantity) of characters to be matched. For example, \s{2,3} matches against 2 or 3 spaces (or the other characters mentioned previously in the shortcut table). \s informs the regexp to look for spaces, and the curly braces surrounding the 2,3 tell the regexp to use these figures as a range: from 2 to 3 characters. Think of the 2 as the minimum number and the 3 as the maximum number. Quantifier ranges work in a similar way as the ranges specified in character classes, but the syntax is a bit different: you use the symbol for the character to match first, then within curly braces (instead of brackets) you put the quantities you want separated by a comma.

Leaving out either the maximum or the minimum (but leaving in the comma) signifies "or more" and "or fewer", respectively. For example, {2,} denotes "2 or more", while {,3} is "3 or fewer". In these cases, the same warnings apply as for the star operator.

You can put a few of these special characters together, and do some cool things. For example, you can specify exactly how many things are to be in a row by putting just that number inside the curly brackets: "\b\w{5}\b" (matches a five-letter word).

Summary of Metacharacters

Here's a summary of the metacharacters you've just seen:

Metacharacter	Meaning
[abc]	any one of the characters a, b, or c
[^abc]	any one character other than a, b or c
[a-z]	any one ASCII character between a and z
\d \D	a digit; a non-digit
\w \W	a "word" character; a "non-word" character
\s \S	a whitespace character; a non-whitespace character
\b	the boundary between a \w character and a \W character
.	any character (apart from a new line)
(abc)	the phrase "abc" as a group
?	preceding character or group may be present 0 or 1 times

Metacharacter	Meaning
+	preceding character or group is present 1 or more times
*	preceding character or group may be present 0 or more times
{x,y}	preceding character or group is present between x and y times
{,y}	preceding character or group is present at most y times.
{x,}	preceding character or group is present at least x times.
{x}	preceding character or group is present x times.
^	the beginning of the string
$	the end of the string

Validating Data Entry

One of the most common items entered by users in Web applications is the e-mail address, which just happens to provide an excellent subject for validation because of its unique format. First, it's not easy to define a length, because you never know what could be allowed as the "name" portion of the address. Second, it contains the @ sign, which is not typically found in other common data entry items. And third, there is a requirement for a .com, .net, .org, or some other acceptable ending after the domain name.

An e-mail address is requested on Web forms so frequently because it may be the only contact information you can get from a person, and if for any reason the e-mail address isn't valid, that's the end of it; you're not going to be able to contact that person.

So there's plenty of incentive to validate e-mail addresses. And there are plenty of e-mail address validation routines around. Some are highly complex and can validate e-mail addresses with a high degree of precision; others are very simple and have a lower percentage of success. One of the simplest routines just checks to make sure the @ sign is present once; obviously, if there's no @ sign, the e-mail address cannot be valid, and if the @ sign is present more than once the address is also invalid. But users could provide an @ sign and still not give a valid address.

Regexps come in handy for creating an e-mail address validation routine because they can do quite a bit of conditional checking. For example, there should be some characters before and after the @ sign in any e-mail address. And there should be a dot (.) preceded by and followed by more characters on the right side of the @ sign. And there are some characters that aren't permitted on either side of the @ sign (such as a blank space). Regexp patterns can be constructed to detect anomalies in e-mail address structure very precisely, such as this one:

```
^[^@ ]+@[^@ ]+\.[^@ \.]+$
```

This pattern may not make much sense right off the bat; let's spread it out so you can see what's really there. The following table identifies each symbol in order and describes what it's doing:

Symbols	Matches
^	The beginning of the string...
[^@]	...there is one character, which can be anything other than an ampersand or a space
+	...which is repeated one or more times
@	There is then an ampersand
[^@]	Next, there is one character that can be anything other than an ampersand or a space
+	...which is repeated one or more times
\.	There is then a period (which must be escaped)
[^@ \.]	There is one character that can be anything other than an ampersand, a space, or a period
+	...which is repeated one or more times. The last one must be followed immediately by...
$	...the end of the string

As complicated as this pattern appears to be, it's really a simple one and by no means foolproof. There are much more complex e-mail address/URL parsing procedures out there, and they can be very longwinded.

Next, you can use this regexp with ereg() to validate incoming e-mail addresses.

Try It Out   Validate E-mail Addresses

1. Enter the following code into your Web editor:

```
<html>
<head><title></title></head>
<body>
<?php
//email_validation.php
if (isset($_POST['posted'])) {

    $email = $_POST['email'];
    $theresults = ereg("^[^@ ]+@[^@ ]+\.[^@ \.]+$", $email, $trashed);
    if ($theresults) {
        $isamatch = "Valid";
    } else {
        $isamatch = "Invalid";
    }

    echo "Email address validation says $email is " . $isamatch;
}
```

```
?>
<form action="email_validation.php" method="POST">
<input type="hidden" name="posted" value="true">
Enter your email address for validation:
<input type="text" name="email" value="name@example.com">
<input type="submit" value="Validate">
</form>
</body>
</html>
```

2. Save the file as email_validation.php and close it.

3. Run the script, and try out the validation process with "good" and "bad" e-mail addresses.
    Figure 5-4 shows an example result after a bad e-mail address was submitted; notice the
    incorrectly entered address displayed at the top.

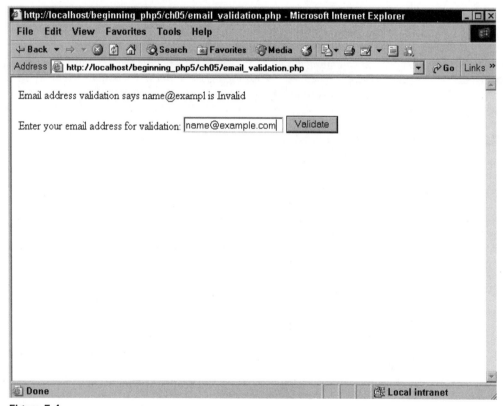

Figure 5-4

How It Works

The regexp pattern does the pattern matching via the ereg() function. When the form is submitted,
the string supplied is captured in the $email variable (from the $_POST[email] variable). Then,
ereg() is used to check whether it is valid. If it is, the word "Valid" is placed inside the $isamatch

variable. If not, the word "Invalid" is placed inside the $isamatch variable. The results are then echoed out to the user:

```php
<?php
//email_validation.php
if (isset($_POST['posted'])) {
    $email = $_POST['email'];
    $theresults = ereg("^[^@ ]+@[^@ ]+\.[^@ \.]+$", $email, $trashed);
    if ($theresults) {
        $isamatch = "Valid";
    } else {
        $isamatch = "Invalid";
    }
    echo "Email address validation says $email is " . $isamatch;
}
?>
```

A default e-mail address is provided within the email form field to show the user what format his data entry must have (hopefully he'll understand that he needs to replace this value with a real one).

This script is a good start on validating e-mail addresses, but it's not perfect. It allows characters after the @ sign that aren't legal in a domain name (*, for example), and it doesn't actually verify that the domain entered exists. The best way to verify e-mail addresses is to see if the server you're sending to accepts them; even a properly formatted e-mail address is invalid if the server you're sending to doesn't accept it.

Using Regexps to Validate URLS

Domain names and full URLs (Uniform Resource Locators) provide great subjects for the pattern-matching abilities of regexps. The structure of a domain name is simply a name followed by a dot followed by a domain name extension (such as .com, .net, .org, and so on), but there are limitations of the characters that can be present in the name, and there's no need to prefix the domain name with www (or anything else for that matter). URLs include domain names, but are prefixed with http://, and a complete URL may include the path (the folder names separated by slashes), the filename, and even a query string attached to the end. There are quite a few variations, and like e-mail addresses it's important to get it right.

Here's the format of a Uniform Resource Locator (URL):

Protocol (such as ftp or http)
Domain or server name (such as wrox.com; the www is not required)
Folder and file path (optional in some cases, includes folder and filename separated by slashes, such as images/myimage.gif)
Querystring (optional, starts with ? and then one or more name/value pairs).

Again, regexps to the rescue! This time, try this helpful (and highly aesthetically pleasing) snippet:

```
^[a-zA-Z0-9]+://[^ ]+$
```

Similar to the key line in the last sample script, this expression can be used in a line like this:

```
$theresults = ereg("^[a-zA-Z0-9]+://[^ ]+$", $intext, $trashed);
```

In the following example, you'll check out URLs for correct formatting.

Check for Correctly Formatted URLs

1. Start your Web page editor and type in the following:

```
<html>
<head></head>
<body>
<?php
//url_validate.php
if (isset($_POST['posted'])) {
   $url = $_POST['url'];
   $theresults = ereg("^[a-zA-Z0-9]+://[^]+$", $url, $trashed);
   if ($theresults) {
      $isamatch = "Valid";
   } else {
      $isamatch = "Invalid";
   }
   echo "URL validation says $url is " . $isamatch;
}
?>
<form action="url_validate.php" method="POST">
<input type="hidden" name="posted" value="true">
Enter your URL for validation:
<input type="text" name="url" value="http://www.example.com" size="30">
<input type="submit" value="Validate">
</form>
</body>
</html>
```

2. Save this file as `url_validate.php` and close it.

3. Run the script and test the script by trying to validate several URLs, some valid and some not.

Figure 5-5 shows an example result of the URL validation script after an incorrect URL was submitted.

How It Works

Similar to `email_validation.php`, this script is mostly powered by a single regular expression via the `ereg()` function:

```
$theresults = ereg("^[a-zA-Z0-9]+://[^]+$", $url, $trashed);
```

The regexp pattern matches valid URLs, but unfortunately it also matches quite a few other things that are not valid URLs. Like many regexp patterns, you'll find that it is very difficult to get perfect matching without spending a lot of time working on it (some URL patterns are hundreds of characters in length, and still aren't perfect). The main idea is to try to eliminate the most common errors that people make, and be satisfied with that. After all, any slight change in what constitutes a valid URL (or e-mail address) may throw your regexp off, so what's perfect one day may be flawed the next, through no fault of your own.

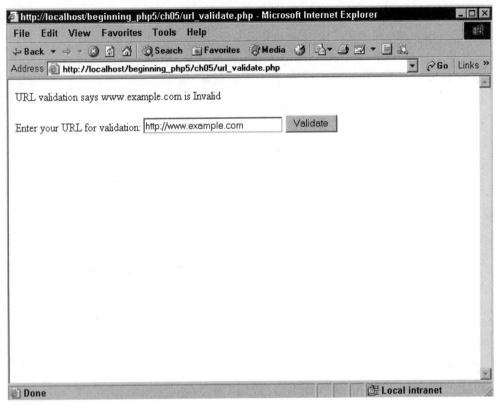

Figure 5-5

Using Regexps to Check File Path Parameters

The file system and the functions PHP provides to work with files and folders are discussed in Chapter 7; but let's take a quick look at some regexp functions that you'll find helpful in protecting data you store in files (yes, files—databases aren't the only means of persistent data storage; common text files are often used to store application data for extended periods).

> *In persistent data storage the term persistent is used to signify data that lives on even after your application quits or the system is turned off.*

These functions (and the example code you'll create) can be very useful for limiting access to certain folders and files because they make it easy to match things that are file or folder names. Although you may want to allow access to certain files and folders, there may be others that no one but the system administrator should have access to.

In the following example, you'll stop users from traversing the directory tree, by removing potentially sensitive information from the file path. A variation of the ereg() function named ereg_replace() does the heavy lifting.

To get the job done, you write a pattern that, when run with the `ereg_replace()` functions, replaces any "../", "/", or "\" from the path. In UNIX systems the trailing slashes are used, whereas in windows systems backslashes are used, and colons are used on Mac OS systems. Also, the code will remove any absolute paths, that is, starting with "/" or [A-Z].

Try It Out   Prevent Users from Accessing Sensitive Files

1. Open your Web page editor and type in the following:

```
<html>
<head><title></title></head>
<body>
<?php
//clean_path.php
if (isset($_POST['posted'])) {
    $path = $_POST['path'];
    $outpath = ereg_replace("\.[\.]+", "", $path);
    $outpath = ereg_replace("^[\/]+", "", $outpath);
    $outpath = ereg_replace("^[A-Za-z][:\ |][\/]?", "", $outpath);
    echo "The old path is " . $path . " and the new path is " . $outpath;
}
?>
<form action="clean_path.php" method="POST">
<input type="hidden" name="posted" value="true">
Enter your file path for cleaning:
<input type="text" name="path" size="30">
<input type="submit" value="Clean">
</form>
</body>
</html>
```

2. Save the file as `clean_path.php` and close it.

3. Run the program. The program output should look like Figure 5-6.

As you can see, PHP can be used to filter out user input that is potentially dangerous as well as that which is simply incorrect.

How It Works

The first line of the program gets rid of ".." patterns (used to move up a level in the directory tree):

```
$path = ereg_replace("\.[\.]+", "", $inpath);
```

The second line eliminates trailing slashes or backslashes:

```
$outpath = ereg_replace("^[\/]+", "", $outpath);
```

The third line gets rid of DOS/Windows-style prefixes (for example "C:\"):

```
$outpath = ereg_replace("^[A-Za-z][:\|][\/]?", "", $outpath);
```

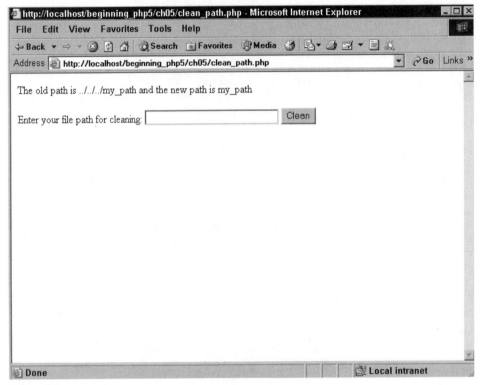

The old path is ../../../my_path and the new path is my_path

Enter your file path for cleaning: [   ] [Clean]

Figure 5-6

Handling Errors Gracefully

The primary difference between an error handled gracefully and one handled sloppily is what the user sees. Of course, inside your program you might want to do all sorts of things to handle errors properly, but to the user seeing a nicely written statement within a page he just tried to view is much cleaner than simply letting PHP's built-in errors appear randomly.

Like many languages PHP is gradually becoming more mature, and in PHP5 new error-handling capabilities have been built in (we'll get to these in a moment). Let's discuss how error work, and then we'll follow through from the point at which PHP starts up all the way through running your programs in real-time.

Configuring PHP for Error Handling

The main configuration settings you'll want to use for non-production (construction) system settings are the error_reporting level, the display errors setting, and the log_errors setting. There is more configuration-setting data in the *"Configuring PHP"* appendix, but these three are the ones you'll probably be most interested in. The first one sets the level of errors you'll see, the second sets whether errors will even be displayed in your browser (something you don't want for production sites), and the third sets whether errors are recorded in a log file.

Suppressing Error Messages

Not strictly a debugging tip, but sometimes you know about errors in your PHP script and you don't want to remove them at all, but ignore them or handle them separately. In that case there's a special notation that PHP uses: the @ notation. When it's used with a function, it suppresses any mention of errors within that function. For example, the following function runs with the @ symbol in front:

```
function ProcessFormDetails ($Name, $Email)
{
    // do some processing here
}
@ProcessFormDetails($Name, $Email);
```

Because of the @ symbol, any errors within that function are not be returned. Of course, if the function has an error within it, it still returns a value zero. If the error is one that is fatal and would normally cause execution to halt, it still stops the script, but it won't return any output. Although this suppression could cause some confusion, it can still be a useful tool. And you can then handle the error separately within your function, returning a customized message to the user.

Checking the Error Log

By default, PHP doesn't send error messages to the Web server's error log. However, PHP can log errors if you want it to. PHP can log to a file if you add the following directives to the php.ini file:

```
log_errors = On
error_log = /var/log/php.log
```

PHP also has an error_log function, which makes it possible to have unexpected situations logged in the event that you haven't anticipated every possible situation and programmed a way to handle it. If you suppressed errors using the method mentioned previously, then you might also want to check any errors that occur.

The error_log function can take up to four arguments, but only the first two of them are compulsory. It has the following format:

```
error_log("Error Message", MessageType, "Destination", "Extra Headers");
```

The first argument, Error Message, is the actual error message received. The second, MessageType, is the code signifying where you want this error message sent; there are four possible values:

❑   0: Send to PHP error log

❑   1: Send to the e-mail address supplied in the third argument

❑   2: Send to a PHP debugging connection, only when debugging has been enabled

❑   3: Send to a destination log file, with the path specified in the third argument

The third argument, Destination, takes either an e-mail address or file path, and the fourth, Extra Headers, can be used to send extra information in the form of e-mail headers, when used with an e-mail address.

If you want further information about an error, such as when it actually occurred, then you can enable the error log or error log functions and then check the information contained in the log.

Try/Catch—New in PHP5

PHP5 has several new capabilities to help you respond to errors gracefully. They are centered around the new try/catch exception-handling capabilities. Basically, you set up a `try` block around all the code you want to run that may generate errors. Then, depending upon the error generated, you use a `catch` block to decide what to do with the error. One big advantage is that it's easy to capture errors inside function blocks.

The try/catch functionality generates exceptions, and exceptions are objects. You "throw" exceptions using the `new Exception` statement within a `try` block, and the `catch` block then deals with them. After you've thrown an exception, it is an object and can be used in the same way any other object can be used (more on objects later in the book). The `getMessage` method of the `Exception` object lets you get the message associated with whatever error was encountered. In the following example we demonstrate using try/catch.

Try It Out   Use Try/Catch with Form Validation

1. Fire up your trusty HTML editor and create the following file:

```
<html>
<head><title>Beginning PHP5</title></HEAD>
<body bgcolor="#FFFFFF">
<?php
if (isset($_POST[posted])) {

    //put the submitted values into regular variables

    $first_name = $_POST[first_name];
    $last_name = $_POST[last_name];
    $birth_date = $_POST[birth_date];
    $phone = $_POST[phone];
    $age = $_POST[age];
    $address = $_POST[address];
    $city = $_POST[city];
    $state = $_POST[state];
    $postal_code = $_POST[postal_code];

    //make an array of field names and data types

    $field_names = array("first_name" => "string",
            "last_name" => "string",
            "birth_date" => "date",
            "phone" => "string",
            "age" => "integer",
            "address" => "string",
            "city" => "string",
```

```php
                "state" => "string",
                "postal_code" => "string");
   //try checking the data type of each submitted value based on the name of the
field

    function form_validate($fns) {
        foreach ($fns as $key => $value) {
            $field_value = $key;
            global $$field_value;
            //echo "actual field value is " . $$field_value . "<br>";
            switch ($value) {
                Case "string";
                    if ((strlen($$field_value) < 1) or (strlen($$field_value) > 99))
                        { throw new Exception("Please enter a string value between
                        1 and 100 characters in the <b>$key</b> field");
                        }
                    break;
                Case "date";
                    if (!ereg("^ [0-9]{4}\-([1-9]|(0[1-9])|(1[0-2]))\-([1-9]|(0[1-
                    9])|([1-2][0-9])|3[0-1])$",$$field_value)) {
                        throw new Exception("Please enter a valid date formatted
                        as YYYY-MM-DD in the <b>$key</b> field");
                        }
                    break;
                Case "integer";
                    if (!is_numeric($$field_value)) {
                        throw new Exception("Please enter a number without decimal
                        places or alphabetical characters in the <b>$key</b>
                        field.");
                        }
                    break;
                default;
                    break;
            }
        }
    }
    //catch the exception and produce an error message
    try
    {
        form_validate($field_names);
    }
    catch (Exception $e)
    {
        echo $e -> getMessage();
        echo "<br>";
    }
}
//if no errors thank the user
if (!is_object($e) and isset($posted)) {
    echo "Thanks for your entry. We'll be in touch.";
} else {
//return the filled out form to the user and ask them to try again
?>
<form action="try_catch.php" method=post>
```

```
<input type="hidden" name="posted" value="true">
  <table width="50%" border="1">
    <tr>
      <td colspan="2"><font face="Arial, Helvetica, sans-serif" size="-1">Please
        enter contact info:</font></td>
    </tr>
    <tr>
      <td width="26%"><font face="Arial, Helvetica, sans-serif" size="-1">First
        Name</font></td>
      <td width="74%">
        <input type="text" name="first_name" value="<?php echo $first_name; ?>">
      </td>
    </tr>
   <tr>
     <td width="26%"><font face="Arial, Helvetica, sans-serif" size="-1">Last
       Name</font></td>
     <td width="74%">
       <input type="text" name="last_name" value="<?php echo $last_name; ?>">
     </td>
   </tr>
  <tr>
    <td width="26%"><font face="Arial, Helvetica, sans-serif" size="-
1">BirthDate</font></td>
      <td width="74%">
        <input type="text" name="birth_date" value="<?php echo $birth_date; ?>">
      </td>
    </tr>
    <tr>
      <td width="26%"><font face="Arial, Helvetica, sans-serif" size="-1">Phone
        Number</font></td>
      <td width="74%">
        <input type="text" name="phone" value="<?php echo $phone; ?>">
      </td>
</tr>
<tr>
  <td width="26%"><font face="Arial, Helvetica, sans-serif" size="-1">Age
</font></td>
      <td width="74%">
        <input type="text" name="age" value="<?php echo $age; ?>">
      </td>
    </tr>
    <tr>
      <td width="26%"><font face="Arial, Helvetica, sans-serif" size="-1">Address
</font></td>
      <td width="74%">
        <input type="text" name="address" value="<?php echo $address; ?>">
      </td>
    </tr>
    <tr>
      <td width="26%"><font face="Arial, Helvetica, sans-serif" size="-1">City
</font></td>
      <td width="74%">
        <input type="text" name="city" value="<?php echo $city; ?>">
      </td>
    </tr>
```

```
        <tr>
          <td width="26%"><font face="Arial, Helvetica, sans-serif" size="-1">State
</font></td>
          <td width="74%">
            <input type="text" name="state" value="<?php echo $state; ?>">
          </td>
        </tr>
        <tr>
          <td width="26%"><font face="Arial, Helvetica, sans-serif" size="-1">Postal
            Code</font></td>
          <td width="74%">
            <input type="text" name="postal_code" value="<?php echo $postal_code; ?>">
            <input type="submit" value="send info" name="submit">
          </td>
        </tr>
    </table>
    </form>
<?php
}
?>

</body>
</html>
```

2.   Save the file as try_catch.php and close it.

3.   Open it in your browser (see Figure 5-7), enter values for each field, and see what error messages you get. Figures 5-8 and 5-9 show some example error messages.

And when you enter all the data correctly, you get a happy message! Try it!

How It Works

You start with a form to collect data from the user, knowing that you'd like to make sure the data is of particular types. The form could easily be extended to many other types of data. Then, as in all of the other examples, you use the isset() function to determine whether the form has been submitted (in several places this time). The submitted data is put into ordinary variables, and you make an array of field names and data types to be used later to key the validation routines. The array looks like this:

```
//make an array of field names and data types

$field_names = array("first_name" => "string",
        "last_name" => "string",
        "birth_date" => "date",
        "phone" => "string",
        "age" => "integer",
        "address" => "string",
        "city" => "string",
        "state" => "string",
        "postal_code" => "string");
```

You haven't gotten into building databases yet (you will later in the book), but you could easily load the field names and data types (as well as other validation information) from a database. In fact, if you think about it for a minute, you could store quite a bit of information about the form and validation processing

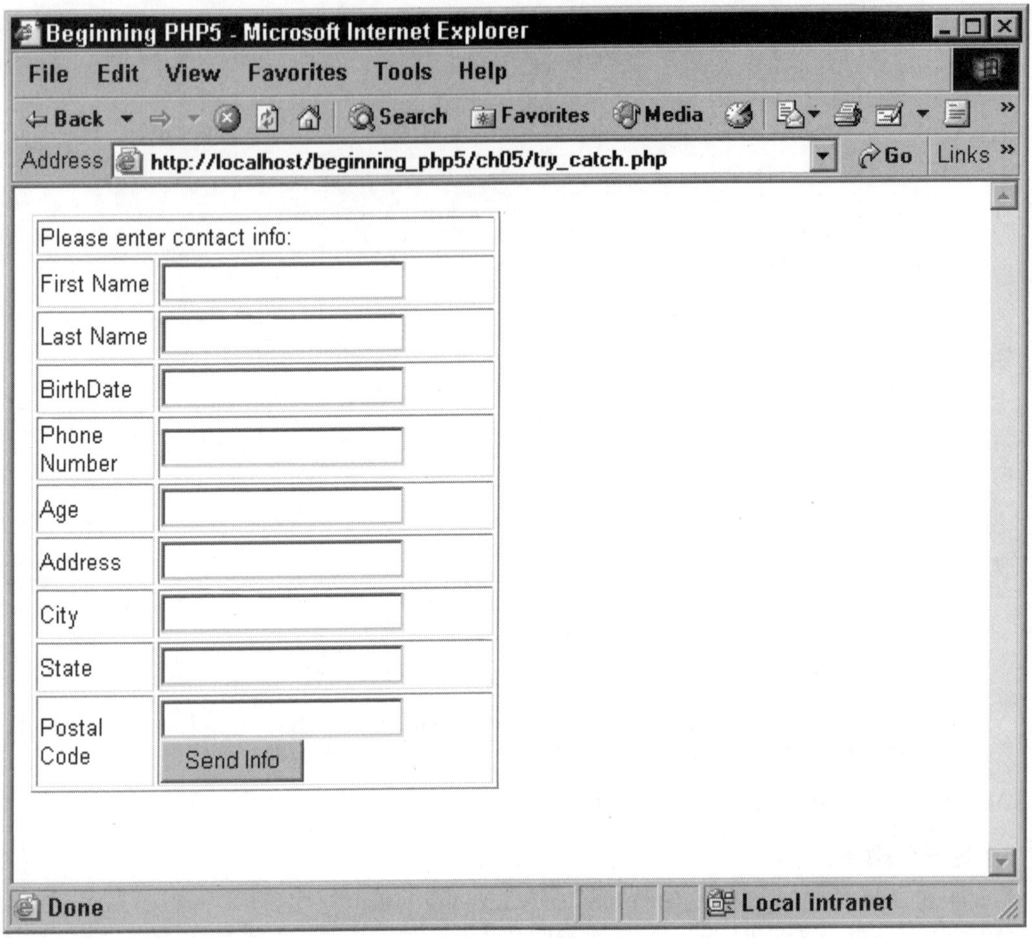

Figure 5-7

in a database. Although it requires a bit more work up front, the client could then easily modify the number and type of fields displayed in the form, and rest assured that the form would still be processed properly.

Next, you write a function that does the validation. Inside the function a `foreach` loop is used to iterate through the field names and values and perform the appropriate processing on them. You didn't necessarily need to create a function, but it helps when you have several arrays of field values to check. The function starts like this:

```
function form_validate($fns) {

    foreach ($fns as $key => $value) {
```

Then, you get the name of the field into a variable, and then use PHP's variable capability to address the submitted HTML form field's value, like so (we have to use the global keyword because we're inside a

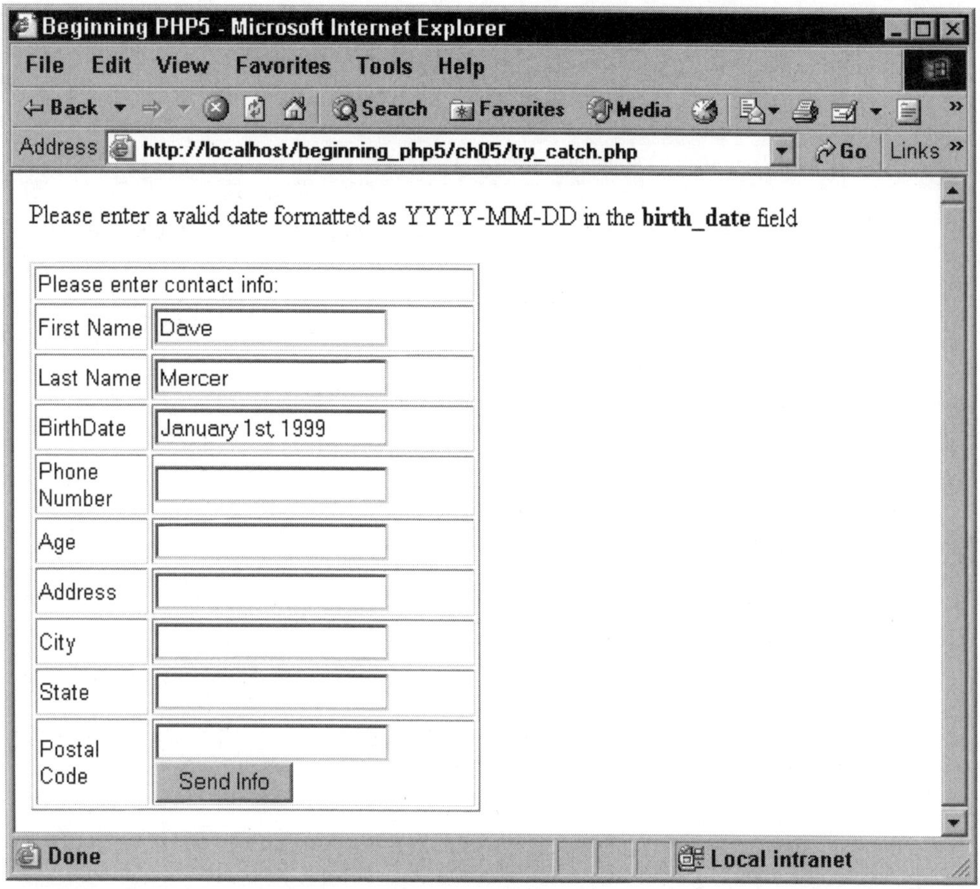

Figure 5-8

function block, but much more detail on functions and this particular aspect of them can be found in Chapter 6):

```
$field_value = $key;

global $$field_value;
```

Next, you use a switch Case block to separate out the types of validation you perform. Inside each case you run a few tests on the submitted value to see what you've got:

```
switch ($value) {
   Case "string";
     if ((strlen($$field_value) < 1) or (strlen($$field_value) > 99)) {
        throw new Exception("Please enter a string value between 1 and 100
        characters in the <b>$key</b> field");
   }
     break;
```

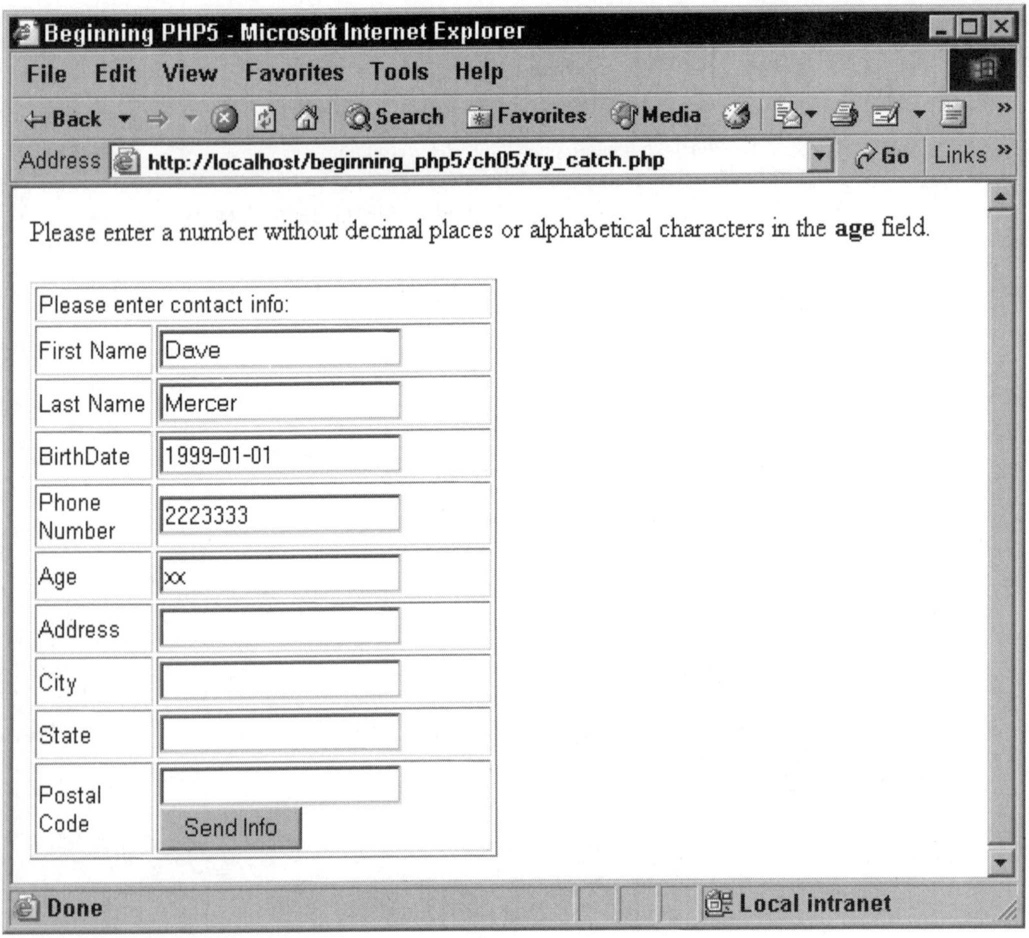

Please enter a number without decimal places or alphabetical characters in the **age** field.

Please enter contact info:	
First Name	Dave
Last Name	Mercer
BirthDate	1999-01-01
Phone Number	2223333
Age	xx
Address	
City	
State	
Postal Code	Send Info

Figure 5-9

```
Case "date";
    if (!ereg("^[0-9]{4}\-([1-9]|(0[1-9])|(1[0-2]))\-([1-9]|(0[1-9])|
    ([1-2][0-9])|3[0-1])$",$$field_value)) {
        throw new Exception("Please enter a valid date formatted as YYYY-MM-DD
in the <b>$key</b> field");
    }
    break;
Case "integer";
    if (!is_numeric($$field_value)) {
    throw new Exception("Please enter a number without decimal places or
    alphabetical characters in the <b>$key</b> field.");
    }
    break;
    default;
    break;
}
```

Notice the `throw new Exception` statement that occurs if any of the tests fail. For example, if a string value does not have between 1 and 99 characters, an exception is thrown. When you throw an exception, you assign it a message, shown in the string value placed in parentheses after the exception.

You use try/catch to run the function on the submitted values. Inside the `try` block, the function is run, and inside the `catch` block any exceptions are caught and the message is displayed. (You can perform any kind of error handling you want in the `catch` block.) Also, if an exception occurs, processing of the function is terminated and the `Exception` object is created, with its message, like this:

```
try
{
   form_validate($field_names);
}

catch (Exception $e)
{
    echo $e -> getMessage();
    echo "<br>";
}
```

The last bit of functionality is that if there are errors, the values entered by the user and an error message are displayed so that the user can fix the problem without having to reenter all that data. If there are no errors, you simply display a "Thank You" message. The form fields are filled with existing data because their `value` attributes are set to `echo` the submitted data (and `value` includes nothing the first time the form is displayed). The following `if` block controls whether the user sees a "Thank You" message by checking to see if Exception (`$e`) is an object, and also whether the form has been submitted:

```
//if no errors thank the user
if (!is_object($e) and isset($posted)) {
    echo "Thanks for your entry. We'll be in touch.";
} else {
//return the filled out form to the user and ask them to try again
?>
```

Summary

In this chapter you've explored the basic testing, troubleshooting, and debugging, error-handling functions, string validation (to capture erroneous data before it messes with your programs), regular expressions (for advanced validation), and the new try/catch functions in PHP5.

Bugs occur in every program. Some bugs are the result of bad syntax, and some are logical errors (the result of processing that works but doesn't produce the right answer, or processing that is correct but produces the wrong answer given bad input). Each type of bug can be found and corrected with a step-by-step process of testing, troubleshooting, and debugging, over and over again until it's right.

When it comes to error checking, the sky's the limit. You are constrained only by your available time and your coding skills. As demonstrated in this chapter, error checking is not only a way of avoiding unsightly and potentially security-damaging error messages, it is a way of ensuring that users give appropriate input whenever they are asked for it. The way in which you process that input is solely up to you. The "smarter" you make your script at recognizing and handling bad input, the better the source of data it is. You can use many of the string validation and regular expression functions you've seen to do exactly this.

With a little planning (and, optionally, judicious use of regular expressions), error handling can make your site better in many ways. Just remember Murphy's Law: If something can go wrong, it will. With that in mind, try to one-up Murphy: Look for the places where things are most likely to go wrong, and modify your scripts accordingly. A little foresight now can save a tremendous amount of hassle later.

Exercise

Create at least three regular expressions and insert them into the appropriate spots in the most recent form validation example. Suggested regular expressions are:

❑ 7–and 10-digit U.S. phone numbers

❑ Social Security numbers

❑ Gender using M and F for male and female

Writing High-Quality Code

High-quality code is code that works well, works efficiently, is well documented, is easy to debug and maintain, and is also easy for others to work with. But because there are many different ways to code applications and produce the same functionality, you may end up working with code that does the job, but is poorly written and therefore hard to maintain.

Establishing and following a formal development process can be a pain (especially if you're used to seat-of-the-pants programming), but it helps produce high-quality code and is essential for the success of larger projects. And although some differences in coding style are to be expected, and perhaps even encouraged, using a consistent approach (as defined by a coding standard) brings great benefits, especially when building larger projects within an organization. Using a coding standard, such as the ones discussed in this chapter, is a vital part of high-quality code.

Another gauge of high-quality code is how well it is structured. Functions and include files should be used whenever you are performing the same processing, or nearly the same, in multiple locations in your program, simply because using them means only having to modify the code in one place, rather than many. These indicators are among those discussed in this chapter that can guide you in writing first-rate code.

In Chapter 5 you discovered how to make your code more graceful handling errors, more secure, and more efficient. In this chapter you continue along the path to quality code by learning about coding standards and the use of functions, objects, and `include`/`require` statements. You'll also review development processes and learn how to optimize your code. As you can tell, there's a lot of work involved in creating high-quality code, but you won't be sorry—it'll be well worth your effort.

Development Planning

The importance of planning is stressed throughout this book. Although not every job allows for a good deal of planning up front, it's always best to fight for the time to properly plan your applications. Once you've invested the effort to plan your application, coding it almost becomes a breeze.

Formal Software Development Processes

There are any number of formal software development processes you might use; all have certain features in common, such as writing a specification, developing testing protocols, and so forth. If you work for a company that builds software for the government, you may be required to adhere to a software development process defined by a standard, such as ISO 12207 (ISO stands for International Standards Organization). Or, perhaps your company uses a less formal approach such as Rapid Application Development, in which several developers share responsibility for rapidly creating and modifying the workings of an application.

Whichever development process is used, following formal procedures in a standard way increases the odds of successfully completing the project on time and within budget. As you can imagine, a scattershot approach is very inefficient, especially if there are multiple developers at work.

That said, it isn't unusual for even the most well-managed projects to have delays, changing specifications, mistakes, hard-to-find bugs, and so on. That just means that deciding upon and following a formal procedure is more important than ever.

The next few sections discuss some of the basic features that formal software development processes share.

Writing a Specification

Writing a specification is a great first step, but one that's often ignored or slighted because it is often difficult to accurately and completely define what the final product should be. If you've ever read about how movies are made, for example, you know that the finished product may bear little resemblance to the original book or screenplay. A movie may not follow the script exactly, but there is always a script—it'd be very hard to convince anyone to put up money to make a movie without a script.

How much specification writing should be used for various applications? Let me give you some analogies to photography or movie-making:

❑ **Snapshot:** Some applications are like amateur photography—an abrupt snapshot and that's it. Of course, the result you get is much like that quick photograph, but sometimes that's all you need. A minimal application, such as displaying the current date on a Web site, doesn't really require any written specification. Little thought is used in deciding its location, and certainly no heavy thinking is involved in writing the code.

❑ **Portrait:** Even small applications, if done competently, are more like professional photography. The lighting is good, the subject is framed properly, and the quality of the image is excellent. They cost a bit more in both money and time, but some thought is put into how the result looks onscreen, and the color, font, weight, and size of the text. The programming is commented correctly, with proper use of conventions (even for a very small application). One or two paragraphs of specification may be all that is needed to completely define what's required.

❑ **Commercials:** Commercials are much more expensive, professionally done, and scripted. They are akin to small but professionally designed applications for a specific use. Likely there is little improvisation in them, and it's pretty easy to predefine (and ensure during production) all aspects of the process so that the final product is very closely aligned with the original script and goals of the production. Applications such as an e-mail newsletter manager are similar in that they are fairly simple in design and architecture. A good specification can be created in advance of production, and can be followed to completion without much deviation.

❑ **Movie:** A movie is like a very complex application in that it even though it may be scripted from end to end, the final cut may be very different from what was originally specified. That's because many of the final decisions are made once filming is finished, and depend upon the reaction of the filmmakers to what they have on film. A complex application is similar because you often won't know what is good or bad (or unnecessary) about the application you've created until beta testers or users use it a bit. And as an expensive project, once you're committed to it, it deserves as much modification as needed to make it right (from the user's standpoint, making it right can be summed up as "it works").

The point of these analogies is that some projects don't require much (if any) specification, and others require lots, but even when a good specification is created prior to any coding, there's still likely to be much change and retooling as the application takes shape. And that leads directly into the next subject, the coding process.

The Coding Process

There's a school of thought that says, "If you program all the little functions independently, then put them together, you'll have a finished application." The idea is that, if you can define what each part is supposed to do, and program that, then you should be able to put all of the parts together and have a working application. This is true to a degree, but often what distinguishes a (technically) working application from a great application is how well integrated the parts are (how efficiently and elegantly they work together).

The ease with which other people grasp how to use the application is also very important. Because many applications are intended for use by people, and people have varying perceptions and understandings of words, images, forms, and so on, the design of user interfaces is actually more art than science.

Given that there are so many tools that make it easy to develop a working model of an application fast, it's no surprise that Rapid Application Design (RAD) and Extreme Programming are popular. There are several definitions of RAD, but basically it means quickly developing a user interface that does the required tasks, and exposing it to users early in the development cycle. This is a relatively inexpensive process, and because you repeat the process several times quickly, you can hone in on a user-friendly design in a very short time. Once you have a good feel for all the aspects that are needed to satisfy the basic goals of the application, you can then spend the effort to properly organize, document, and optimize your application.

Extreme Programming is similar to RAD, but generally means you use two programmers to write the code so that they can assist each other, fill in for each other if one must take a break (or leaves the company), and otherwise arrive at the solution much quicker. Extreme Programming puts into practice the notion that "two heads are better than one," with real results in many cases.

Testing, Debugging, and Maintenance

Ever hear of a program or application that stopped at version 1.0? A program that was designed so well that it's never needed a revision, change, update, bug fix, etc.? Of course, not. There aren't any! And for good reason. Not only do most applications have bugs even after they're released, there's really no end to bugs, only the prospect of getting them to be insignificant enough so that for most people, under most circumstances, the application works well.

In addition, the environment in which applications operate (including protocols, operating systems, and other applications) changes constantly. And sharp hackers continually find new and interesting ways to defeat security and crack applications. Finally, good users will provide comments about other features they'd like in the application.

The bottom line is that the cycle of testing, debugging, and improving applications doesn't really end, but the rate of fixes and changes drops to a manageable level and becomes maintenance. This portion of the development process can't be avoided, but there's always the capability to manage the process well.

Optimizing Your Code

Imagine for a moment that you have 1,000 Web pages, and that each needs to display the current date and today's welcome message. Knowing PHP, you immediately see that it would be less work to have the pages dynamically generate the date and a message via a line or two of PHP code than to manually update 1,000 pages every day.

But you also want some way to write the code once and insert it into all the pages dynamically, so that if you ever changed the message it would change across all the pages at once. And of course, this common problem is solved easily in a number of ways with PHP functions such as `include` and `require`.

Using PHP and other functions to save yourself work is one way to optimize your code. Optimization isn't limited to just reusing code; the word also describes many techniques you can use to make your code run faster and more efficiently (using less computational resources such as CPU cycles, RAM, or hard drive space), to avoid rewriting code, or to make your programs easier to debug or maintain.

The rest of this chapter focuses in detail on practices that can save you lots of time and make your code more robust as well. These practices include formal coding standards, writing program logic as functions, and using the `require()` and `require_once()` functions.

Using Coding Standards

Just about any programmer you ask will tell you that properly indenting code for branching (control-flow) code blocks makes the code much easier to read, and therefore easier to debug and maintain. But there are actually several ways to indent code, such as using the tab or using multiple spaces. Either technique results in indented code that is easier to read, but for the sake of consistency it's pretty clear that you should use the same technique throughout a project, especially when collaborating with other programmers. Like most folks, you'll probably pick up some habits that you stick with when writing code. There's nothing wrong with that, but you may find yourself required to change your habits if you move from a company that codes one way to a company that uses another way.

Any conventions about what techniques to use when writing your programs (that don't actually affect whether the code runs properly) can be classified as *coding standards*. These include documentation and comments, indenting, naming conventions, the format of function calls, how to include code residing in other files, and so on.

We discuss (and try to follow) the PHP Extension and Add-on Repository (PEAR) coding conventions in this book. Writing to these standards makes your code ready for the repository. By the way, several of the conventions refer to class files, and there is more detail about objects and classes in the last section of this chapter as well as in Chapters 12 and 13. PEAR is the topic of Chapter 14. Here are the basic PEAR coding standard conventions:

- **Indenting:** Use four spaces, no tabs. Some text editors allow you to set the Tab key so that it produces four spaces instead of a tab, and this setting may make your life easier if you're used to using the Tab key for indenting. The PEAR coding standard also recommends that you break lines at 75–85 characters, but there is no hard and fast rule on this.

- **Naming conventions:** The PEAR coding standard has conventions for naming everything from classes to functions to variables.

  - Classes: Use descriptive names, start the name with an uppercase letter, and divide your classes into categories, with each category and subcategory name separated by an underscore (such as `Cart_orderitem` for an item ordered within the context of a shopping cart).

  - Functions and methods: Use lowercase letters to start a function name, and studly caps for subsequent words in the name. For example, `getData()` is a good name for a method that retrieves data, and `calcTax()` is a good name for a function that calculates tax. (Although it's not the PEAR standard, you may use underscores between words in your function and method names as well: `array_combine()`, for example.)

    You haven't encountered methods yet; they are like functions but exclusive to objects. You'll learn more about them later in the book, in the chapters that discuss objects.

  - Constants: Use all uppercase characters, with underscores separating the words in the name.

  - Global variables: Use an underscore to precede the name of the global variable.

  - Predefined values: Use lowercase letters for `true`, `false`, `null`.

- **Formatting function calls:** There's no space between the name of the function, the opening parenthesis, and the beginning of the arguments. Use one space after the comma separating each argument, like this:

```
$somevariable = myFunction($arg1, $arg2, $arg3);
```

  The PEAR coding standard also indicates that there should be spaces before and after the equals sign when a variable is set equal to the result of a function call. Putting spaces between operators at all times makes your code much easier to read and understand.

- **Formatting control-flow structures:** Use one space between the beginning of the statement and the condition, like so:

```
if (this equals that) {
    //do something;
}
```

  Always use curly braces, even if they are technically optional.

- **Comments:** Use a double slash (//) to comment lines of code, like this:

```
//here is a comment
```

Use /* and */ to comment blocks of code, like this:

```
/*
here are several lines of code
here are several lines of code
here are several lines of code
here are several lines of code
*/
```

Use PHPDoc standards (www.phpdoc.de) for writing inline comments about object classes.

❏ **Including code:** You'll learn the details about including (or requiring) files containing code (or content) later in this chapter. The PEAR coding standard indicates you should use require_once() to unconditionally include class files, and include_once to conditionally include class files.

❏ **Delimiters:** Use <?php to start and ?> to end PHP code blocks.

❏ **Defining functions:** When writing functions, place the name of the function and the definition of its arguments on one line, follow with a beginning brace, and after all other lines of code, end with a closing brace. This is called the "one true brace" convention. Also, place any arguments with default values at the end of the argument list in the function definition, and always make your functions return a meaningful value if they are supposed to return anything. Here is an example:

```
function myFunction($arg1, $arg2 = '')
{
    if (this equals that) {
        do something;
    }
    return true;
}
```

❏ **Example URLs:** Whenever you need to specify a fake URL (such as http://www.fake_url.com) use example.com, example.net, and so on, like this: http://www.example.com).

Writing User-Defined Functions in PHP

PHP contains quite a number of built-in functions, such as isset(), strlen(), and so on. And although built-in functions always accomplish very useful tasks, you can be sure that not every possible function can exist in any version of PHP, even in future versions. So suppose you need a function that doesn't exist in PHP. That's where user-defined functions come into the picture—essentially you have the capability to author your own functions, and make them do whatever you want!

Any functions that you create are called user-defined functions. You use the function keyword to define a function and, once defined, that function may be used anyplace in your code, simply by calling its name. When combined with the capability to include files, functions become a very powerful tool in your programming arsenal.

Functions enable you to encapsulate sections of code as though they were independent stand-alone programs. You can pass values into them, and get values out of them. You can call functions at any time during your PHP script, and redirect the flow of execution in this way.

Functions also introduce the idea of scope (fully discussed later in this chapter) into your programs. The normal process in your PHP programs is that once a variable is created, the name you have assigned to it, and the value, persist until you alter it or until the script ends. However, in functions you have to learn to deal with the idea that variables might only exist inside a function, whereas outside it they have no value.

In this chapter you'll build some functions that will work on the same principle as the readymade ones you've already used: when you supply them with information, they will perform an operation and return an answer.

The Structure of Functions

Functions are sections of code that are defined by the user to perform a specific task, and given a name by which to call them. You already know that functions can take values called arguments as input, perform some operations, and then may return another value. The function transfers any argument values into new variables called *parameters*, which can then be used within the function. You've used PHP's built-in functions extensively in this book so far; to do things like get the data type of a variable (`gettype()`) right through to sorting arrays (`sort()`). Writing your own function means you get to give it your own made-up name, but you call it the same way as calling the built-in functions.

Take a look at how functions work, step-by-step:

1. The function is written with a name followed by parentheses. Inside the parentheses are the names of any values the function accepts (these values, called arguments, are optional), written as variable names (preceded by a dollar sign like any normal variable) and separated by commas.

2. The function is called by writing its name and parentheses. If the function requires any arguments, they are included within the parentheses and are separated by commas. Arguments may be variables or hard-coded values, and do not have to be the same as the variable names in the argument list in the defined function.

3. When the function is called, arguments passed to it are turned into *parameters*, and the parameters are used inside the function to perform the data processing specified by the function. Think of parameters as placeholders for values being passed into the function.

4. The `return` keyword may be used to pass values back out to the calling code after data processing is complete inside the function. Returning values is optional; some functions just do their work and then end without any further notification required. However, it is a good idea to at least return a `true` or `false` value to indicate to the rest of your code whether the function successfully completed its work.

5. If a value is passed back out of the function, it can be expressed using the `echo` statement, or it can be assigned to a variable outside the function.

Defining and Calling Functions

You begin creating a function by writing the `function` keyword followed by a space and then the name you want the function to be addressed by. If you want your function to accept arguments (it doesn't have to), list them in parentheses after the name of the function. Then the code that runs when the function is called is placed within curly braces, the same way you delimit blocks of code in conditional structures. Here's the syntax:

```
function functionname (parameters)
{
    //put your function code here
}
```

For example, if you want to write a function that calculates a bonus, code such as this would do:

```
function bonus($sales)
{
    $bonus = $sales * 0.15;
    return $bonus;
}
```

Notice the `return` statement in this example. If your function simply records something in a database, there may not be any return value. If you want the function to send data back out, you must use the `return` statement, in the manner shown. For example, this is what it would look like if you had some code calling your newly defined function:

```
$my_total_sales = 120499;
//find out my bonus, based on my total sales
$my_bonus = bonus($my_total_sales);
```

Because the example returns the result of the calculation on the incoming value (in this case, $120,499), as set in the variable $my_total_sales), the variable $my_bonus will end up being set equal to the outgoing value returned by the function.

You can put as many lines of code as you want in a function, and a line of code can do anything within the bounds of what PHP can ordinarily do: connect to a database, open a file, match a regexp pattern, and so on. You can also make the function `echo` text out, or `print` something to the screen.

The `return` statement, by itself, doesn't display a value; it just passes the result (if any) to the function. The process of executing the contents of a function within a PHP script is known as *calling* the function.

You can supply a function directly with a number:

```
echo (bonus(120499));
```

or you can furnish the function with the name of an already created variable:

```
$total_sales=120499;
echo (bonus($total_sales));
```

You can supply more than one parameter to the function, but you must separate each parameter with a comma as illustrated here:

```
function bonus($total_sales, $bonus_factor)
{
    $bonus = $total_sales * $bonus_factor;
    return $bonus;
}
```

To call the modified bonus function, you'd supply two values: `total_sales` and `bonus_ factor`, like this:

```
$total_sales = 120000;
$bonus_factor = 0.15;
echo (bonus($total_sales, $bonus_factor));
```

Functions can be defined anywhere within your PHP program. It's common to define functions in a separate file and simply `include` (or `require`) that file at the beginning of the main processing file you're creating. You don't need to define or initialize your variables before you define your function; you do, however, need to make sure they are defined or initialized before you *call* the function.

For example, the following code works:

```
<?php
$total_sales = 190999;             // Execution will start here
$bonus_factor = 0.15;
echo (bonus($total_sales, $bonus_factor)); // Function called here
function bonus($total_sales, $bonus_factor) // Function defined here
{
    $bonus = $total_sales * $bonus_factor;
    return $bonus;
}
?>
```

But the following also works just fine:

```
<?php
function bonus($total_sales, $bonus_factor) // Function defined here
{
    $bonus = $total_sales * $bonus_factor;
    return $bonus;
}
$total_sales = 190999;             // Execution will start here
$bonus_factor = 0.15;
echo (bonus($total_sales, $bonus_factor)); // Function called here
?>
```

And here's an important note about the way functions work. You can use any variable names outside the function to pass values inside the function. For example, suppose instead of using exactly the same names (`$total_sales` and `$bonus_factor`) both outside and inside the bonus function, you used `$out_total_sales` and `$out_bonus_factor` for the variables that exist outside the function, and `$in_total_sales` and `$in_bonus_factor` for the variable inside the function. It would work just fine, and would simply look like this:

```
<?php
function bonus($in_total_sales, $in_bonus_factor) // Function defined here
{
    $bonus = $in_total_sales * $in_bonus_factor;
    return $bonus;
}
$out_total_sales = 190999;             // Execution will start here
$out_bonus_factor = 0.15;
echo (bonus($out_total_sales, $out_bonus_factor)); // Function called here
?>
```

Now take another look at parameters and how they work. When you write a function and define it with one or more variables within the parentheses following the function name, the variables are said to be arguments. When you actually call a function and send data into it (as arguments to the function), the values in the arguments (whether they come in as variables or as hard-coded values) are turned into parameters. Parameters are like temporary variables inside a function, and whereas they are being processed within the function (and perhaps take on new values during processing) they remain parameters.

After the resulting values of processed parameters are passed back out of the function, the parameters vanish. What parameters do (appear when the function is called and then disappear when the function completes processing) is completely unrelated to any variables you might create inside the function.

Before you write another user-defined function as a working example, here's a recap:

❑ User-defined functions are named by the developer.

❑ Functions may take parameters, which are values or variables defined in parentheses after the function name.

❑ Multiple parameters are separated by commas.

❑ The code of the function body is provided in braces after the function name and parameters.

❑ You must use the `return` keyword inside the function to return a value that you can use outside the function.

❑ If there is no value to return, the `return` keyword just denotes the end of the function code.

❑ Functions aren't actually executed until called from a line of code within your PHP script.

❑ You may call a function either before or after it appears in the code—it doesn't matter where you put a function in your code.

❑ You can call a function as few or as many times as you need, and you can send any values you like into the function, sending them as hard-coded values or as values inside their own variables.

That last item in the recap list should clue you in about code reuse; not having to rewrite the lines of code processed by a function every time you need those lines of code to run is a major savings in coding and debugging effort.

Now take the `holiday.php` example code from earlier chapters and write a function to calculate the expenses for the holiday break week. You'll see that you end up saving quite a few lines of code.

Try It Out   Using a Simple Function

1. Enter the following code and save it as `holiday3.php` (you can use sections of your previously written code to save time if you like):

```
<html>
<head><title></title></head>
<body>
<b>Namllu Holiday Booking Form</b>
<?php
function calculator($price, $city_modifier, $star_modifier)
```

```
{
   return $price = $price * $city_modifier * $star_modifier;
}
if (isset($_POST['posted'])) {
   $price = 500;
   $star_modifier = 1;
   $city_modifier = 1;
   $destgrade = $_POST['destination'].$_POST['grade'];
   switch($destgrade) {
      case "Barcelonathree";
         $city_modifier = 2;
         break;
      case "Barcelonafour";
         $city_modifier = 2;
         $star_modifier = 2;
         break;
      case "Viennathree";
         $city_modifier = 3.5;
         break;
      case "Viennafour";
         $city_modifier = 3.5;
         $star_modifier = 2;
         break;
      case "Praguethree";
         break;
      case "Ppraguefour";
         $star_modifier = 2;
         break;
      default;
         $city_modifier = 0;
         echo ("Please go back and try it again");
         break;
   }
   if ($city_modifier <> 0)
   {
      echo "The cost for a week in $_POST[destination] is " . "$" .
calculator($price, $city_modifier, $star_modifier);
   }
}
?>
<form method="POST" action="holiday3.php">
<input type="hidden" name="posted" value="true">
Where do you want to go on holiday?
<br>
<br>
<input name="destination" type="radio" value="Prague">
Prague
<br>
<input name="destination" type="radio" value="Barcelona">
Barcelona
<br>
<input name="destination" type="radio" value="Vienna">
Vienna
<br>
```

```
<br>
What grade of hotel do you want to stay at?
<br>
<br>
<input name="grade" type="radio" value="three">
Three star
<br>
<input name="grade" type="radio" value="four">
Four star
<br>
<br>
<input type="submit" calue="Check Prices">
</form>
</body>
</html>
```

2. Save and close the file

3. Open holiday3.php (see Figure 6-1) in your browser, enter some choices, and submit the form. The holiday3.php example should work just fine:

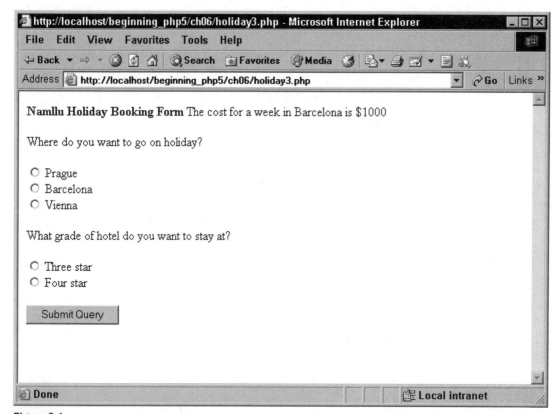

Figure 6-1

How It Works

The holiday form should be very familiar by now, it's simply capturing two variables from the user via the $_POST variable ($_POST[destination] and $_POST[grade]) and passing them along to the PHP script. The PHP code starts with the function (named calculator) to calculate the cost of our holiday:

```
function calculator($price, $city_modifier, $star_modifier)
{
    return $price = $price * $city_modifier * $star_modifier;
}
```

The user-defined calculator() function takes three parameters: the basic price of the holiday, the adjustment to the price for the chosen city, and the final adjustment for the star rating of the hotel. It multiplies these three variables together and returns one value ($price), the total price of the hotel.

The rest of the program works the same as before, concatenating destination and grade into a single value that is used to switch through the various options. There is one small change within the default option, though: the content of the $city_modifier variable is changed to zero if none of the cases are executed. Before executing the calculator() function, you check to see whether the $city_modifier variable has been set to 0; if it hasn't, you can call the function within the echo() statement, using the concatenate operator (the period) to add text to your function result:

```
if ($city_modifier <> 0)
{
    echo "The cost for a week in $_POST[destination] is " . "$" .
    calculator($price, $city_modifier, $star_modifier);
}
```

Switching Functions

In the same way that you can use the switch structure to switch among various processing options within a PHP program, you can write your own functions that accept incoming values and, based on those values, switch among various other functions for processing. This is a very powerful feature of user-defined functions in PHP.

Here's a quick example. Suppose you want to create an application that pulls records from various tables in a database. You might send an input value in a variable called $table_name to the switching function, and within that function decide which query function to run, as shown in this code:

```
function query_switch($table_name)
{
    switch ($table_name){
        case "clients":
            $query = query__clients_gen());
                break;
        case "orders":
            $query = query_orders_gen());
                break;
        case "employees":
```

```
                $query = query_employees_gen());
                break;
        default:
            echo "Please select a table name";
    }
}
function query_client_gen()
{
    //composes a database query to select records from the clients table
}
function query_orders_gen()
{
    //composes a database query to select records from the orders table
}
function query_employees_gen()
{
    //composes a database query to select records from the employees table
}
```

The beauty of using this type of structure is that you can place the functions you've written into an include file, and then `include` the functions in any page, making it easy to add the composition of database queries to any page you like. In addition, you only need to change the code once if you're making an improvement to it, and the code is easier to read through. In fact, once you're confident that the functions do what you intend, you don't really have to read through them as you're coding, you can just call them whenever you need them.

Because you can assign the result of a function (one that has a return value) directly to a variable, you can simply use the result of a function in a `switch..case` statement. For example, suppose you create a small management function that tells you how many hits occurred on a page. You can take the number of hits returned by the function and use it to `echo` out an easy-to-understand message to the user, as this code shows:

```
switch ($hit_counter = get_hits($current_page)){
    case $hit_counter <100:
        echo "Few hits today";
        break;
    case $hit_counter <1000:
        echo "Lots of hits today";
        break;
    case $hit_counter <10000:
        echo "Too many hits today";
        break;
}
```

The variable `$hit_counter` would then be able to store whatever the function `get_hits($current_page)` returned (where `$current_page` is set to the filename of the current page, and gets the total number of hits today from your hit tracking program). You can place and set the value of the `$hit_counter` variable right inside the brackets of the `switch()` statement.

As a utility, you could set this function within each page and have it run once each time the page is displayed. The user would immediately see an indication of the number of hits for that page (although some users might be tempted to keep refreshing the page to up the number of hits).

How Values Get Inside Functions

As discussed earlier, parameters are placeholders representing values passed into a function. But there is more than one way to get a value into a parameter so that the function can work on it. You can pass a value into a function *by value* or *by reference*. The difference is subtle, but sometimes very important.

When you pass a value into a function by value, you assign the value directly to a parameter. But when you pass a value into a function by reference, you connect the parameter directly to a variable outside the function, forcing the outside variable to adopt whatever value the parameter gets.

Passing Values By Value

All the functions you've seen so far passed values by value. A value is passed into the function by entering the value (literally, or by naming the variable containing the value) into the spot reserved for that value (the place within the parentheses following the function call).

For instance, in the first bonus example, you can pass in the total sales value by entering a number directly into the spot reserved for the argument, or you can simply set a variable equal to total sales and then enter the variable name into that spot. The following code shows both methods of passing by value:

```
function bonus($total_sales)
{
    $bonus = $total_sales * 0.15;
    return $bonus;
}
$total_sales = 120499;
echo "Your bonus is " . bonus($total_sales);
echo "Your total sales were " . $total_sales;
echo "Your total sales were $120,499 and your bonus is " . bonus(120499);
```

Notice that even after the value of `$total_sales` is set outside the function and then passed inside the function for processing, the external value of `$total_sales` is not changed. No surprises here.

Passing Values By Reference

Passing values into a function by reference has a completely different effect. The external variable used to contain the value being passed into the function is actually changed while the value is being processed. It changes because, in fact, you're not passing a value into the function, you're passing a reference that points directly to the external function. It's as though all processing operations taking place inside the function are actually affecting the external variable directly.

How is it done? Put the ampersand (&) before the name of the argument to be passed by reference. Our next example shows this for the `$salary` argument.

So suppose you were adding a bonus to a variable called `$salary`. Obviously you could do that outside the function, but perhaps it would be a little easier and cleaner to do it inside the function. The following code shows how this could work:

```
function bonus($total_sales,&$salary)
{
    $bonus = $total_sales * 0.15;
```

```
    $salary = $salary + $bonus;
    return $salary;
}
$total_sales = 120499;
$salary = 40000;
bonus($total_sales,$salary);
echo "Your salary, including your bonus is " . $salary;
echo "Your total sales were " . $total_sales;
```

In this case, you don't need to set any variable to the value resulting from calling the bonus() function; you set $salary to 40,000, then pass it by reference into the bonus() function, and when the function is done, it passes the value directly back into the $salary variable by reference. Neat, eh!

Setting Default Parameter Values

Like many other programming and computer related things, you can write your functions to have default values. For example, you can define an argument as having a default value, which the parameter for that argument will adopt when the function is called, provided you don't pass a value in for that argument.

But there is one catch: you must define any arguments with default values to the right of any arguments without default values. This is a little odd, but if you don't write your functions that way, they won't work as you'd expect. The following example writes the bonus function with a default value of $40,000 for salary to the right of the argument for total_sales:

```
function bonus($total_sales,&$salary = 40000)
{
    $bonus = $total_sales * 0.15;
    $salary = $salary + $bonus;
    return $salary;
}
$total_sales = 120499;
bonus($total_sales);
echo "Your salary, including your bonus is " . $salary;
echo "Your total sales were " . $total_sales;
```

This means that if you supplied no $salary value to the function, it would automatically use 40000 to calculate with. But if you do pass a value (higher, lower, the same—it doesn't matter) to the function for salary, the function would use the passed value to calculate with.

Parameter Order Matters

When you call a PHP function, whether you wrote it or it's built-in, the order in which you pass argument values does matter. If you leave an argument(s) out at the end of the list of arguments, you can leave off the last comma separating arguments. Also, if you leave out an argument, the function will automatically assume a zero value for a numerical argument, or an empty string for a string argument (unless the function defines a default parameter value itself), and continue processing. You'll only get a warning or error message when a required argument (one without any default value set) is missing, but of course, the level of warning or error message you receive will depend on the version of PHP you're using and also possibly on the way you're set error reporting.

Scope of Variables

Scope was discussed a bit in Chapter 2, and now that discussion expands. You can create variables in a PHP script both external to a function (outside the function) and internal to the function (inside the function). If you create a variable named $total_sales outside a function, for example, and then pass its value inside a function that performs processing on an internally created variable named $total_sales, you have two distinct variables named $total_sales in existence in your script. Obviously, this situation is not going to work unless the two variables stay separate. So PHP uses the concept of scope (like so many other languages), and differentiates between the two variables so it doesn't get mixed up.

If you think about it, there are many situations where it would be convenient to use variables with the same name in one script or program. Scope allows PHP to work with two variables of the same name, so long as they remain in their appropriate places. (In much the same way, namespaces provide a means for XML elements of the same name to work within the same XML document and still stay separate. XML namespaces are discussed in Chapter 8.)

Variables created in a PHP script have a lifetime as well as scope. A variable created inside a function stays in existence only as long as the function is processing. When the function finishes, the variable is lost, unless you define it as a *static* variable (more on static variables a little later in the chapter). So you say the scope of the variable is inside the function, and the lifetime of the variable is as long as the function is performing its work (a new inside variable is created each time the function is called, and it has a new life). All variables in a PHP script reach the end of their lives when the script is done.

Global and Local Variables

Variables that are created outside a function remain alive until the script ends, and are therefore said to have global scope, meaning they can be accessed from anywhere in the script. However, to access them within a function, you must use the global keyword. Placing the keyword global before the name of a variable means that you can use it within the function (but you can't then create another variable of the same name because that name is now taken within the function as well). Variables that are created inside a function are described as having local scope.

Here's an example of how local and global variables work:

```php
<?php
$global_message = "Global Message";
function addto_message($global_message)
{
    global $global_message;
    $global_message .= " And More";
    return $global_message;
}
addto_message($global_message);
echo "The global message is " . $global_message;
?>
```

This example produces a statement with the value "The global message is Global Message And More" because running the function changes the value of $global_message. It only changes because the global keyword is used; it's almost like passing the argument into the function by reference.

In fact, putting the `global` keyword in front of a variable name inside the function does reference a superglobal array variable named $_GLOBALS. In this case, creating the variable $global_message (or any variable, for that matter) in the PHP script outside the function (and thereby with global scope) automatically sets it as part of the $_GLOBALS variable. So there are really two ways to access global variables from inside a function: by preceding their names with the `global` keyword (like this: `global $global_message`), or by using $_GLOBALS superglobal array variable (like this: $_GLOBALS[global_message]).

Creating Static Function Variables

You'll recall from Chapter 2 that creating a variable inside a function with the keyword `static` in front of it allows that variable to persist beyond the time the function runs. And because the static variable exists only in the local scope of the function, both the variable and its most recently accumulated value will be available next time the function runs. This can be useful anytime you want to count something that happens or is measured within the function.

For example, suppose you want to count the records returned each time records are retrieved from a database. You could write something like this:

```php
<?php
function get_records($table)
{
    //make database connection
    //retrieve records
    //get_record_count
    static $record_count;
    //set $record_count equal to number of records returned, plus any current
    //value it holds
    echo "current total records retrieved is " . $record_count;
    //return something
}
```

Although the example is mostly pseudo code, it shows how to set the $record_count variable so that it is static. And it should be clear that each time the function runs (at least, as long as the PHP script is running), the $record_count variable will be incremented by the number of records returned. For example, if you retrieved 20 records the first time, 30 records the second time, and 40 records the last time the function was called within a PHP script, then $record_count would be set to 90 by the end of the script. Of course, you could echo out the current record count each time, as this example did.

Here's a quick recap of global, local, and static variables:

❑   Global variables have values that persist throughout the whole program, but to use them inside a function you have to prefix them with the keyword `global` or address them using the $_GLOBALS superglobal array.

❑   Local variables have values that exist only inside of a function and only for the duration of one function call.

❑   Static variables are local variables that persist in value inside the function every time the function is called.

Next, create a small application that demonstrates how these work.

Try It Out   **Demonstrating Scope**

1.   Open your Web page editor and enter in the following:

```
<html>
<head><title></title></head>
<body>

<font size=-1>
<?php
$global_message = "Global Message";
function my_function()
{
    $local_message = "Local Message";
    static $static_number = 0;
    echo "<br>the contents of global message are " . $GLOBALS["global_message"];
    echo "<br>the contents of local message are " . $local_message;
    echo "<br>the contents of static number are " . $static_number;
    return $static_number = $static_number+1;
}
echo "<b>Calling the function for the first time:</b>";
my_function();

echo "<br><br><b>Outside the function:</b>";
echo "<br>the contents of global message are " . $global_message;
echo "<br>the contents of local message are " . $local_message;
echo "<br>the contents of static number are " . $static_number;
echo "<br><br><b>Calling the function for the second time:</b>";

my_function();
echo "<br><br><b>Outside the function:</b>";
echo "<br>the contents of global message are " . $global_message;
echo "<br>the contents of local message are " . $local_message;
echo "<br>the contents of static number are " . $static_number;
echo "<br><br><b>Calling the function for the third time:</b>";

my_function();
echo "<br><br><b>Outside the function:</b>";
echo "<br>the contents of global message are " . $global_message;
echo "<br>the contents of local message are " . $local_message;
echo "<br>the contents of static number are " . $static_number;
?>
</font>
</body>
</html>
```

2.   Save this as `scope.php`. and close the file.

3.   Open up your browser and render `scope.php`.(see Figure 6-2).

How It Works

This program has no practical application, but given that variable scope is a difficult subject to grasp, the program emphasizes how the different types of variables work in PHP. The first line creates and assigns

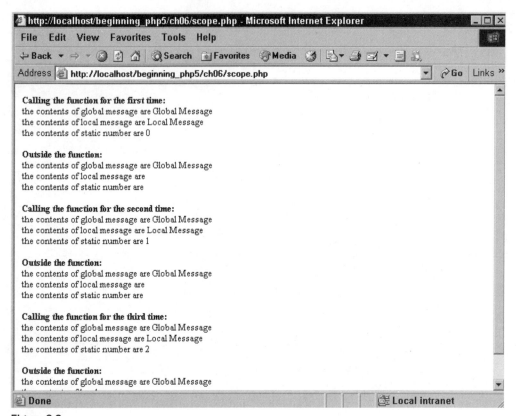

Figure 6-2

$global_message:

```
$global_message = "Global Message";
```

The function (named my_function) is defined:

```
function my_function()
{
```

Inside it, a local variable, called $local_message, and a static variable called $static_number, are created:

```
$local_message="Local Message";
static $static_number = 0;
```

The next three lines display the contents of the global, local, and static variables within the function:

```
echo "<br>the contents of global message are " . $GLOBALS["global_message"];
echo "<br>the contents of local message are " . $local_message;
echo "<br>the contents of static number are " . $static_number;
```

The `return` statement alters the contents of the `$static_number` variable, incrementing it by 1:

```
    return $static_number = $static_number+1;
}
```

The program starts by calling `my_function()`:

```
echo "<b>Calling the function for the first time:</b>";
my_function();
```

You see the contents of the global, local, and static variables, which are "Global Message", "Local Message", and 0 inside the function. Once the function is finished running, the contents of these variables are shown outside the function. You may get undefined variable warnings, depending on what level of error reporting you have set—this is normal if you think about it. `$local_message` and `$static_number` are only defined within the function body, and so do not exist outside of it:

```
echo "<br><br><b>Outside the function:</b>";
echo "<br>the contents of global message are " . $global_message;
echo "<br>the contents of local message are " . $local_message;
echo "<br>the contents of static number are " . $static_number;
```

The function is called several more times, and each time shows what the variables inside the function are set to, as well as what they are outside the function. The `$static_number` variable inside the function is the only one that changes.

Nesting

It's possible to create and call functions within functions. This is called *nesting*, but under most circumstances this capability isn't very useful. You've already looked at calling functions from within functions, and by itself this is helpful. But to define and call a function inside a function can lead to problems.

For example, you could write a `parent` function that would, within itself, define another function (call it the `child` function). The problem is that if you call the `parent` function twice, you're in effect trying to define the `child` function twice, and you can't redefine existing functions, so the script would fail. Most of the time you're better off just defining functions separately.

But there is another situation (besides using functions for switching, as discussed a few sections ago) when it would be useful to call a function from inside a function: recursion (a function calling itself).

Recursion

Calling a function from within itself is known as *recursion*. Calling a function recursively creates a looping structure, in that the function will continue to call itself until a condition is met. However, you have to create the condition explicitly within the lines of code in the function, and if you don't ensure that there is some kind of "stop" value that will be reached no matter what, your function may recurse (and you may curse a few times yourself) infinitely. Here's a quick example.

Calling a Function Recursively

1. Start up your Web page editor and type the following:

```
<html>
<head></head>
<body>
<?php

if ($_POST[posted]) {

    $num = $_POST[num];
    function recursion($num) {
        if ($num <= 1) {
            return 1;
        } else {
            return $num * recursion($num-1);
        }
    }
    echo "The factorial of " . $num . " is " . (recursion($num));
}
?>
<form method="POST" action="recursion.php">
<input type="hidden" name="posted" value="true">
I would like to know the factorial of
<input name="num" type="text">
<br>
<br>
<input type="submit" value="Get Factorial">
</form>
</body>
</html>
```

2. Save this as `recursion.php` and close the file.

3. Open `recursion.php` in your browser. Figure 6-3 shows the page.

Of course, once you have chosen your value and pressed the Get Factorial button, the faithful recursive example tells you the answer. Figure 6-4 shows an example:

How It Works

First declare the recursion function, and give it $num_value as an argument:

```
<?php

if ($_POST[posted]) {

    $num = $_POST[num];
    function recursion($num) {
        if ($num <= 1) {
            return 1;
        } else {
```

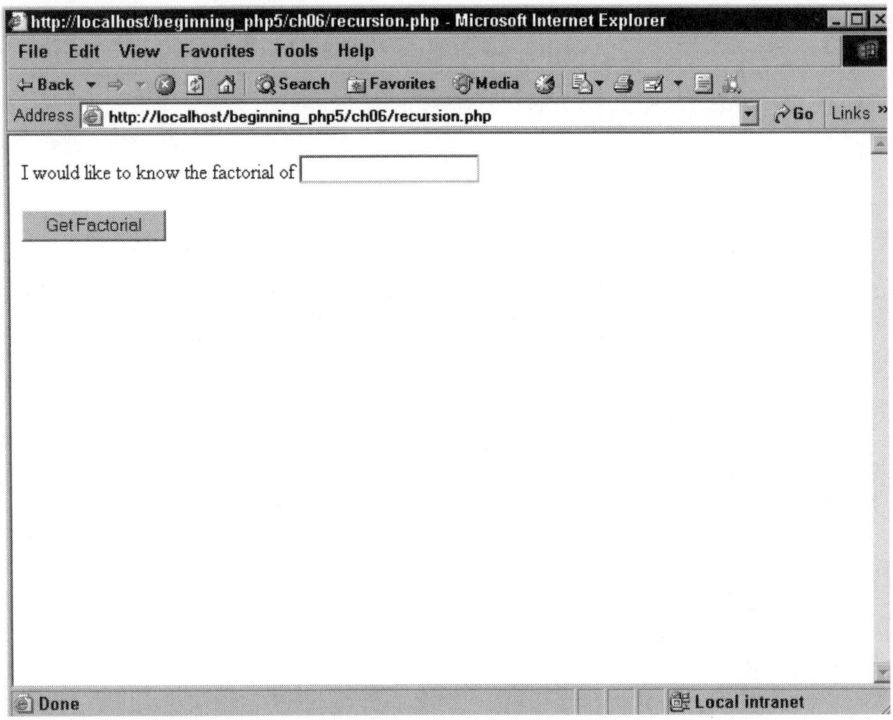

Figure 6-3

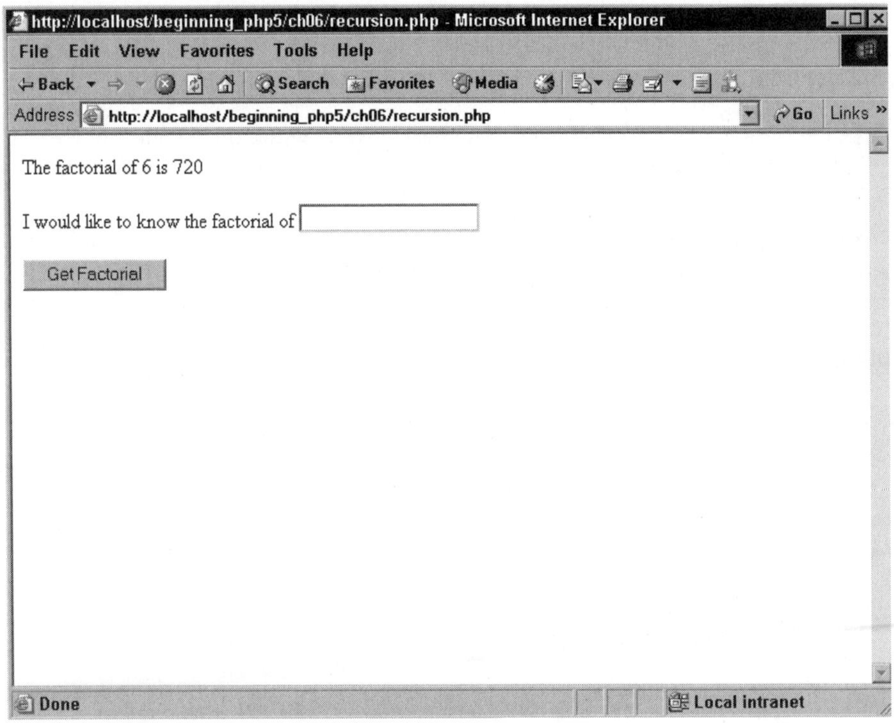

Figure 6-4

```
            return $num * recursion($num-1);
        }
    }
    echo "The factorial of " . $num . " is " . (recursion($num));
}
?>
```

Next, make sure that $num has not been given as zero or one; if it has, you return 1 (you already know that the factorial of one is one). If you have a number greater than one, execute the recursive part of the function. Finally, you echo the result.

Each time through the loop you not only multiply by the most recent number (that's the recursive part), but you also use the steadily dwindling value to make sure the loop eventually ends. (It's easy to break the script with larger numbers, and that it doesn't work with negative numbers, but for this example, it works well enough.)

The Include and Require Statements

Another way to make your code easier to use and maintain is to use include files. Actually, you've used them several times already and have seen how easy it is to bring external files into the current script and run them. All you have to do is use either the include or require constructs (remember, they're language constructs, not functions, even though they are called in a similar fashion) with the name of the file you want to bring in, and that's that. The only difference between the two is how they handle failure to bring in the external file. A failure of include results in a warning; a failure of require results in a fatal error.

There are a few fine points about how they work:

❑ You include or require a file by inserting the construct within PHP code, but parsing drops out of PHP mode and into HTML mode at that point, so you still have to put the code in the included file inside proper PHP delimiters to make it run.

❑ You may include or require a file from within a function, but if so, any variables created in the code in the included file have local scope within the function.

❑ The PHP script within the include file is evaluated (run) when it is included. Any PHP variables that have values are available in the main file, just as though the entire block of code had been directly written inside the file.

Here are a few examples of how to write these constructs in your code (you can include full absolute or relative paths if you like):

```
include("filename")
require ("filename");
```

For example, to include the file test.txt, you would type:

```
include("test.txt");
```

If the file test.txt contained the text "Hello", then this text would be included on the Web page, just as though it had been coded directly into it.

Interestingly, within the include or require functions you can also add variable names or concatenate them to the name of the filename, inside the brackets, as long as it creates a legal file name:

```
$Name ="1";
include ("test" . $Name . ".txt");
```

The result of this concatenation is test1.txt, and if there is a file of that name, it will be included—otherwise an error is generated.

So when are include files handy? Use them to:

- ❑ Include text files in the page.
- ❑ Define variables and/or constants and details of certain error messages.
- ❑ Insert the values of HTTP variables in the page.
- ❑ Execute a separate PHP script (even when it may return nothing).
- ❑ Place commonly used functions that you need but don't want to define in every page.

Include files are useful in that they can be added directly to a file, but you can create code that decides whether that file should be included or not. That's exactly what you're going to do in the next example.

Try It Out   Conditional Includes

1. Start up your Web page editor and type in the following words:

   ```
   File One included
   ```

2. Save this as a text file and call it file1.txt.
3. Close it and create a new text file and type in the following:

   ```
   File Two included
   ```

4. Save this as a text file and call it file2.txt.
5. Now close that file, start another new file, and type in the following:

```
<html>
<head><title></title></head>
<body>
<?php
if (isset($_POST['posted'])) {
    $choice = $_POST['choice'];
```

```
        if ($choice <> "") {
            include("file" . $choice . ".txt");
            echo "<hr>";
        }
    }
    ?>
    <form method="POST" action="include.php">
    <input type="hidden" name="posted" value="true">
    What file do you wish to include?
    <select name="choice">
    <option value="1">file one</option>
    <option value="2">file two</option>
    </select>
    <br>
    <br>
    <input type="submit" value="Get Text">
    </form>
    </body>
    </html>
```

6. Save this as include.php in the same place as the two text files.

7. Open include.php in your browser and make a choice. Figure 6-5 shows an example result.

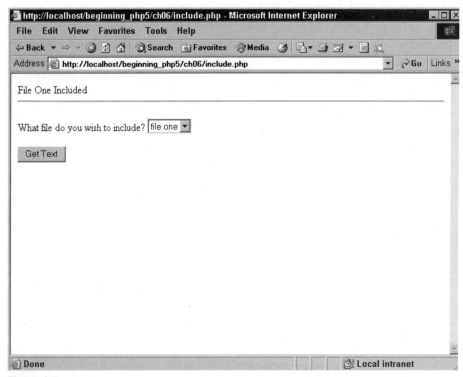

Figure 6-5

How It Works

First a little form is created to offer the user two choices in a drop-down box named "choice". Then, when the following code runs, it simply checks to see which value was chosen (if you chose file one, for example, the value provided was 1) and uses that value to construct the filename to include.

```php
<?php
if (isset($_POST['posted'])) {
    $choice = $_POST['choice'];
    if ($choice <> "") {
        include("file" . $choice . ".txt");
        echo "<hr>";
    }
}
?>
```

Of course, you'd already made the text files `file1.txt` and `file2.txt` and entered a little bit of text in them (otherwise you'd have gotten an error message. Did you?).

Things To Be Careful About with Include and Require

Many Web servers are not set up to parse `.inc` files, so it's better to put includes in `.php` files. That way their (potentially sensitive) contents are never visible unintentionally to the everyone out there. For example, if someone knows (or just suspects) that you have `.inc` files on your site (perhaps containing sensitive information such as database passwords), they can simply enter the complete URL in their browser, and they can see the unevaluated source code. Always put a `.php` extension on your include files to make sure they get evaluated.

And if you want to include another include file via a `common.inc.php` file that goes at the top of every page (it's a common practice to do this) but worry that some function might accidentally be defined twice, use `include_once` or `require_once`. These work the same way as `include` and `require`, but will only include the same file once, no matter how many times they are actually included.

Summary

Functions are blocks of code that can be called up within your program. They're either defined automatically in PHP, such as the array functions `sort()` and `ksort()` that you saw in previous chapters, or created by the users themselves (user-defined functions), as demonstrated in this chapter. They can be thought of as little black boxes that return a value if you feed them the appropriate variables. Variables are passed to them via arguments defined at the beginning of the function. Unless you pass them by reference, the value a function returns doesn't have any effect on the variables outside it. You can use the value the function returns to switch to different cases, and follow different courses of actions.

You saw that variables act differently inside functions because of something called scope. Variables with local scope lasted only while the function was in action, and were then terminated, unless you added the `static` keyword. Variables defined outside functions had to be used with the `global` keyword, or the GLOBALS array, inside functions to differentiate them. You also looked at include files and the `include()`, `require()`, `include_once()`, and `require_once()` functions, and learned how to use them to modularize your code.

Exercise

Write a function that enables the user to construct his/her own Web form, with the capability to choose field names and field types, and then allows the users to submit the form to the page and see what they submitted echoed back to them. Use a `switch..case` statement to select various functions within your main function.

Files and Directories

Would you like to visit a Web site in which code in the pages could take control of your hard drive and do anything its designer specified, such as write or erase files and directories? Of course not, and that's why the makers of JavaScript left those capabilities out of the language. PHP does not have the capability to write or erase files from the user's hard drive, but it can write or erase files and directories on the server. This is a good thing because often the easiest and most effective way to accomplish a particular functionality within an application is to use the server's file system.

Files are stored in folders on your hard drive (or someone else's hard drive), and because they retain their data after the machine is shut down, they are a *persistent* storage mechanism, instead of temporary storage such as RAM. Both directories and files are files, but directories are a special kind of file made for storing other files. Directories are created hierarchically inside other directories, starting with the root directory and proceeding down from there.

Files can contain any kind of data, and also can contain quite a bit of information about themselves, such as who owns them and when they were created. PHP makes working with the file system easy by including functions that enable you to obtain information about files, as well as open, read from, and write to them. This chapter is all about the PHP functions for working with the file system. You'll learn to read and write files with PHP, open and close files with fopen() and fclose(), rename and delete files, navigate within files, and read directory entries. You'll also see how to check file permissions and users, and accept file uploads. It's a big chapter, so let's just get started.

There are many different types of file systems; although if you're used to Windows you may not be very familiar with the others. Most Windows systems simply allow unfettered access to files and folders, whereas Linux systems typically restrict file and folder access by way of various permissions for users on the system. The NTFS file system that may be used with Windows NT/2000 and above works more like the file system on Linux machines, in that it also enables you to establish permissions.

Whether the file system uses permissions to control access to particular files and how those permissions are set are important to you as a PHP developer because some functions require specific permissions to be set before they can do their work. Fortunately, PHP also provides functions for checking and setting permissions, and for checking the access level of the current user (PHP typically runs under the authority of the same user as Apache (on Linux/Apache servers) or is provided a guest Internet account on IIS systems.

File and Directory Handling

Everything on your hard drive is stored as a file of one kind of another, although most folks think in terms of files and directories. There are ordinary program files, data files, files that are folders, and special files that help the hard drive keep track of the contents of folders and files. PHP has functions built in that can work with any file that can be found, but typically we'll be working with text files that contain data.

The terms directory and folder are used interchangeably in this book, and sometimes that's confusing if you aren't used to it. When you think about it, though, folders and directories hold files in an organized manner, so they both have the same function and it's not surprising that the terms are equivalent.

A file is nothing more than an ordered sequence of bytes stored on hard disk, floppy disk, CD-ROM, or other storage media. A directory is a special type of file that holds the names of other files and directories (sometimes denoted as subdirectories) and pointers to their storage area on the media. All you need to know to manipulate files and directories is how to connect your scripts to them.

There are many differences between the Linux and Windows operating systems, one of them being the way directory paths are specified. UNIX-based systems such as Linux use forward slashes to delimit elements in a path, like this:

```
/home/dan/data/data.txt
```

Windows uses backslashes:

```
C:\MyDocs\data\data.txt
```

Fortunately, PHP on Windows automatically converts the former to the latter in most situations, so something like:

```
$fp = fopen("/data/data.txt", "r");
```

shouldn't cause you any problems even if you are running the script on a Windows platform. There are some cases in which the path will be used directly (when you copy an uploaded file from the temporary directory to an archive directory, for example), in which case the backslashes are necessary. Because PHP interprets – as escaping the following character, the string will need to be specified like this:

```
"C:\\MyDocs\\data\\data.txt"
```

You'll learn an easy way to automatically convert forward slashes to backslashes in PHP later on.

Working with Files

PHP provides two sets of file-related functions, distinguished by the ways in which they handle files: some use a *file handle*, or a *file pointer* as it is commonly called; others use *filename strings* directly. The same is true of PHP's directory-related functions, for that matter.

A file handle is simply an integer value that is used to identify the file you want to work with until it is closed. If more than one file is opened, each file is identified by its own uniquely assigned handle.

A file handle is contained in a variable (named like any other PHP variable, and in examples typically $fp, for file handle). The integer value the file handle variable contains identifies the connection to the file you are working with. For example, once you open a file with fopen() you can use the fwrite() function to write data out to a file. The fwrite() function needs a file handle (named $fp in this case) that points to the file it is to work with:

```
Fopen($fp, "myfile.txt", "w+");
fwrite($fp, 'Hello world!');
```

In this example, $fp is the variable representing the file handle (the integer value it contains is set when you use fopen() to open the file specified in the first line). The fwrite() function writes the text contained in the second argument (second line) into the file represented by the file handle.

On the other hand, the file() function, which used to read data from a file, takes a string argument that holds the path to the file:

```
$lines = file('./data.txt');
```

These new functions are introduced shortly.

Unless otherwise specified, all the functions mentioned in this chapter return True when a given operation is successful and False upon error.

Are you ready to work with a file?

Opening and Closing Files

There are typically three steps involved in working with a file:

1. Open the file you want to work with by associating a file handle with it.
2. Read from or write to the file using the file handle.
3. Close the file using the file handle.

The fopen() Function

The fopen() is used to open a file, returning a file handle associated with the opened file. It can take two or three arguments: filename, mode, and the optional use_include_path.

The file handle also can be used it to detect whether the file opened okay—if it did, the file handle is a positive integer; if not, the file handle is zero. Operations on files and directories are prone to errors, so you should always allow for things to go wrong when using them. It's good practice to use some form of error-checking procedure so that if an error occurs (perhaps you don't have necessary privileges to access the file, or the file doesn't even exist), your script will exit tidily, preferably with an appropriate error message. For example, because of the way PHP interprets integers in the context of Boolean operations, you can make use of the fact that the value of the file pointer resolves to True if the operation succeeds and False if it fails. This enables you to test to see if the file opened by using a script like this:

```
$fp = fopen("./data.txt", "r");
if(!$fp) die ("Cannot open the file");
```

Alternatively, you can write it like this:

```
if(!($fp = fopen("./data.txt", "r"))) die ("Cannot open the file");
```

This doesn't test to see if $fp is equal to the result of the fopen() function call (that would use the == equality operator), but simply tests whether the operation succeeded in opening the file. This is a shorthand trick to run the test and, if the operation succeeds, store the file handle in $fp for later use. Use the form with which you're most comfortable.

The first argument of the fopen() function specifies the name of the file you want to open, which can be just a filename, or a relative ("./data.inc", for example) or absolute ("/myfiles/data.inc") path to a file. (You'll see what happens if you simply specify the filename as data.txt when you look at the use_include_path argument a little later.) You can even specify a file on a remote host, opening it with an HTTP URL or via FTP, as these examples show:

```
if(!($fp = fopen("http://www.whatyoumaycallit.com/index.html", "r")))
        die ("Cannot open the file.");

if(!($fp = fopen("ftp://ftp.whatyoumaycallit.com/pub/index.txt", "r")))
        die ("Cannot open the file.");
```

A remote file can only be opened for reading—you can't modify or write to the file.

> If you're not familiar with command-line file operations on either UNIX or Windows, you might be a little confused by the relative path notation. From the perspective of a file, a dot (.) refers to the directory the file is in, and two dots (..) refers to the immediate parent directory. For example, ./data.txt points to a file called data.txt in the same directory as the script, and ../data.txt points to a file called data.txt in the directory above the one containing the script. ../../../data.txt backs up the directory tree three levels before looking for the data.txt file. An absolute path is distinguished by the fact that it begins with a /, indicating that the path is specified relative to the root of the file system, not to the location of the script. For example, C:/Inetpub/wwwroot/index.php is an absolute path.

The second argument of the fopen() function (named mode) specifies how the open file is to be used. You can open a file for reading, writing, or appending to, by giving mode one of the following values:

Value	Description
r	Open file for reading only. The file position indicator is placed at the beginning of the file
r+	Open file for reading and writing. The file position indicator is placed at the beginning of the file
w	Open file for writing only. Any existing content will be lost. If the file does not exist, PHP attempts to create it

Value	Description
w+	Open file for reading and writing. Any existing file content will be lost. If the file does not exist, PHP attempts to create it
a	Open file for appending only. Data is written to the end of an existing file. If the file does not exist, PHP attempts to create it
a+	Open file for reading and appending. Data is written to the end of an existing file. If the file does not exist, PHP attempts to create it

The file position indicator is PHP's internal pointer that specifies the exact position in a file where the next operation should be performed.

The mode argument of the fopen() function can also take the value b to indicate that the opened file should be treated as a binary file. Although this is irrelevant for platforms such as Linux, which treats text and binary files identically, you may find it useful if you're running on Windows because Windows (and the Mac) have different ways of setting the end-of-line characters for text files (Windows uses CRLF, Mac uses CR, and Linux uses LF). The default mode of the fopen() function (since PHP 4.3.2) has been set to binary for all platforms that distinguish between text and binary files, meaning that no end-of-line character translation takes place. Using b as part of the mode argument is recommended, so your code should be written to apply or use the appropriate end-of-line characters for the platform on which you are running.

The third (optional) argument of the fopen() function is named use_include_path. If use_include_path is set to 1, and the filename isn't specified as a relative or absolute path, the function searches for the file specified by filename first in the script's own directory, and then in the directories defined by the variable include_path (set in the php.ini file).

The include path is especially useful if you want to specify a directory in which you put include files that are commonly accessed by your scripts. Here, for example, include_path has been given the value /home/apache/inc in the php.ini file, and the following function call is executed:

```
fopen("data.txt", "r", 1);
```

If this call now fails to find the file data.txt in the current directory, it will search in the directory /home/apache/inc.

The fclose() Function

Once you've finished working with a file, it needs to be closed. You can do this using fclose(), specifying the open file by using its associated file handle as a single argument, like this:

```
fclose ($fp)
```

Although PHP should close all open files automatically when your script terminates, it's good practice to close files from within your script as soon as you're finished with them because it frees them up quicker for use by other processes and scripts—or even by other requests to the same script.

Getting Information About a File

Files contain much information about themselves, such as their size, when they were modified, who owns them, and so forth. PHP includes the stat() function to enable you to capture information about a file by providing the filename as an argument to the function.

The stat() function returns an indexed array that contains file statistic and information within each spot in the array. There are 13 array spots:

Index Number	Associative Name	Information Contained
0	Dev	Device number
1	Ino	Inode number
2	Mode	Inode protection mode
3	nlink	Number of links
4	uid	Userid of owner
5	gid	Group id of owner
6	rdev	Device type, if inode device
7	size	Size in bytes
8	atime	Time of last access
9	mtime	Time of last modification
10	ctime	Time of last change
11	blksize	Blocksize of file system IO
12	blocks	Number of blocks allocated

The following code snippet shows how to use the stat() function to retrieve the size of a file in bytes, assuming the file myfile.txt exists:

```
$my_file_stats = stat("myfile.txt");
$my_file_size = $my_file_stats[7];
```

Not every piece of information that can be retrieved with the stat() function is available on all operating systems. For example, if you're running your Web server and PHP on Windows 98 with the Personal Web server, there will be no group or user id available because those systems don't provide for such things. This subject is covered in more detail in the *Ownership and Permissions* section later in this chapter.

Reading and Writing to Files

Now take a look at a couple of the PHP functions you can use to read and write the data in file. Although they're quite simple, you can use together to implement a basic working script.

The fread() Function

The `fread()` function can be used to extract a character string from a file. It takes two arguments: a file handle `fp` and an integer length. The function reads up to length bytes from the file referenced by `fp` and return them as string. For example, you open a file with:

```
$fp = fopen("data.txt", "r")
```

And then say:

```
$data = fread($fp, 10);
```

`fread()` will read the first 10 bytes from `data.txt` and assign them to `$data` as characters in a string.

The function leaves the file position indicator 10 bytes lower down the file, so that if you repeat the call to `fread()`, you'll get the same data, but rather the next 10 bytes in the file. If there are less than 10 bytes left to read in the file, `fread()` simply reads and returns as many as there are.

The fwrite() Function

You can use the `fwrite()` function to write data to a file. It requires two arguments: a file handle (`$fp`) and a string (string of text to write to the file), and writes the contents of string to the file referenced by `fp`, returning the number of bytes written (or –1 on error). For example, after opening a file with `$fp = fopen("data.txt", "w")`, you could say:

```
fwrite($fp, "ABCxyz");
```

This writes the character string `"ABCxyz"` to the beginning of the file `data.txt`. Having used write-only mode to open the file, you'll lose any prior contents (and even create the file if it didn't already exist); however, repeating this call appends the same six bytes to what you just written, so that the file contains the characters `"ABCxyzABCxyz"`. Once again, it's the file position indicator in action.

If you specify an integer length as a third argument, it stops writing after length bytes (assuming this is reached before the end of string). For example:

```
fwrite($fp, "abcdefghij", 4);
```

writes the first 4 bytes of `"abcdefghij"` (that is, `"abcd"`) to the file referenced by `$fp`. If string contained fewer than length bytes, it would be written to the file in full.

Ready to try it out?

Try It Out   A Simple Hit Counter

One very popular use for Web scripts is the hit counter, which is used to show how many times a Web page has been visited and therefore how popular the Web site is. Hit counters come in different forms, the simplest of which is a text counter. Here's a simple script for such a counter:

```php
<?php
//hit_counter01.php
$counter_file = "./count.dat";
```

```
if(!($fp = fopen($counter_file, "r"))) die ("Cannot open $counter_file.");
$counter = (int) fread($fp, 20);
fclose($fp);

$counter++;

echo "You're visitor No. $counter.";

$fp = fopen($counter_file, "w");
fwrite($fp, $counter);
fclose($fp);
?>
```

Save this script as `hit_counter01.php` and give it a try. Figure 7-1 shows a sample run.

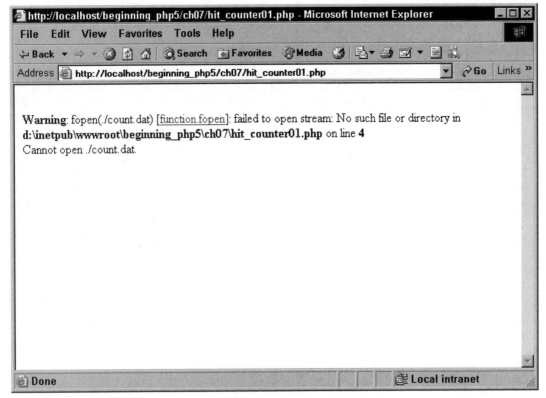

Figure 7-1

An error! Not surprising. Note that the script assumes you already have a data file named `count.dat` in the current directory, that is, the directory from which you ran the script. If this file doesn't exist, an error occurs and the script aborts with an error message to that effect.

You can make the file by saving a blank text file using a text editor (such as Notepad in Windows; don't forget to save as type All Files, or `.txt` will be appended to the end of the filename), or by using the

UNIX touch command if you're running Linux:

```
> touch count.dat
```

Try it again. Figure 7-2 shows the result.

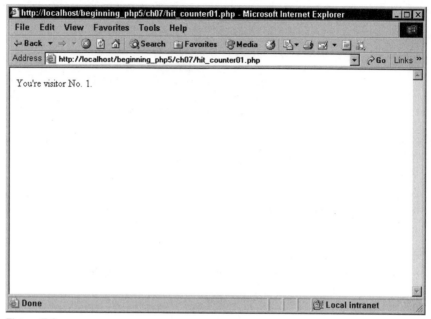

Figure 7-2

If you want to, you can specify a count number to start with inside the data file. If you're running the script on the Linux platform, make sure your Web server has read and write permissions to this data file.

How It Works

First of all, the file count.dat (in the current directory) is called by fopen() in read-only mode:

```
$counter_file = "./count.dat";
if(!($fp = fopen($counter_file, "r"))) die ("Cannot open $counter_file.");
```

The file handle returned by fopen() is assigned to the variable $fp, which can be used from now on to refer to the open file. The function returns False upon error, so in the event that the specified file doesn't exist or that an error occurs while opening it, the script will die with an appropriate error message.

Next, the script uses the file handle to read the hit count value from the open file. As you can see, the script calls fread() to read 20 bytes from the data file (enough to store at least half a million hits):

```
$counter = (int) fread($fp, 20);
```

Because fread() returns a string value, the last number of accesses read from the data file needs to be converted to an integer value, so it's typecast accordingly.

The `fclose()` function closes the file referenced by the file handle `$fp`, writing any unwritten data out to the file:

```
fclose($fp);
```

After closing the data file, the script increments the counter and tells the visitor how many times the page has been accessed:

```
$counter++;
echo "You're visitor No. $counter.";
```

If you stopped here, the counter would never change because the data file remains the same—you have yet to store the incremented counter in the data file. To do that, open the file again by calling `fopen()`, but this time in write-only mode, a mode that overwrites the existing contents of the file.

```
$fp = fopen($counter_file, "w");
fwrite($fp, $counter);
fclose($fp);
```

By calling `fwrite()` with the `$counter` variable as the second argument, you ensure that the exact length of the string is written to the data file, so the length argument is not required. Close the file with `fclose()` when you're finished with it.

You may decide to get creative and make a graphical counter. Used in conjunction with a set of images, the simple text counter script you've produced here can be modified to display graphics. For instance, if you have an image for each counter digit (`1.gif`, `2.gif`, `3.gif`, and so on), you could use each digit value to specify the image associated with the digit:

```
<?php
//hit_counter02.php
$counter_file = "./count.dat";
$image_dir = "./images";
if(!($fp = fopen($counter_file, "r"))) die ("Cannot open $counter_file.");
$counter = (int) fread($fp, 20);
fclose($fp);

$counter++;

for ($i=0; $i < strlen($counter); $i++) {
    $image_src = $image_dir . "/" . substr($counter, $i, 1) . ".gif";
    $image_tag_str .= "<img src= \"$image_src\" border=\"0\">";
}

echo "You're visitor No. $image_tag_str.";

$fp = fopen($counter_file, "w");
fwrite($fp, $counter);
fclose($fp);
?>
```

This script (call it `hit_counter02.php`) simply adds a `for` loop to step through possible values for the `$counter` variable, associating each digit value with a corresponding digit image. The loop tests to see if every digit has been processed by testing the length of the string held in the $counter variable. Figure 7-3 shows what it looks like when the script is run.

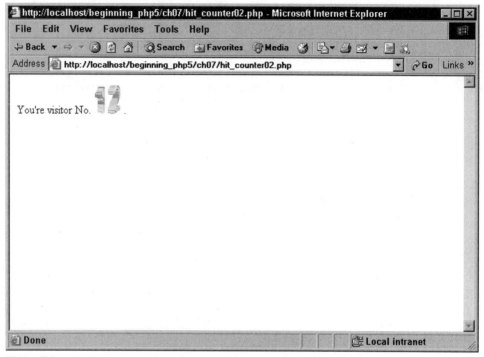

Figure 7-3

Reading and Writing Characters in Files

What if you wanted to read the entire contents of a file, or perhaps analyze it one character at a time. You could do both of these using fread() without too much trouble; for example:

```
do {$one_char = fread($fp, 1); $counter .= $one_char; } while ($one_char);
```

However, PHP provides a set of functions that make this sort of thing much more straightforward:

❑   fgetc()

❑   feoff()

❑   fgets()

❑   fgetcsv()

❑   fputs()

The fgetc() function can be used to read from files one character at a time. fgetc() takes a single argument, a file handle fp, and returns just one character from the file it points to; it returns False when it reaches the end of the file. This is basically the same as the `fread()`:

```php
$one_char = fgetc($fp)
```

is equivalent to saying:

```php
$one_char = fread($fp,1)
```

What if you modify the original hit counter example to use `fgetc()`? You could have:

```php
<?php
//hit_counter03.php
$counter_file = "./count.dat";
if(!($fp = fopen($counter_file, "r"))) die ("Cannot open $counter_file.");

do {
    $one_char = fgetc($fp);
    $counter .= $one_char;
} while($one_char);
$counter = (int) $counter;
fclose($fp);
...
```

You use a `while` loop to read the entire contents of the data file because `fgetc()` reads from the file one character at a time. And you need to know when to stop reading, so you assign the last-read character to a dummy variable, and when that's `False`, you can stop looping. But there's a flaw. As soon as you read either `"0"` or `" "` from the file, the loop condition fails and you won't read any more data. If you plan to attract more than nine hits, this is going to be a big problem.

Fortunately, there's another way to do this, using the `feof()` function.

The `feof()` function serves a single, simple purpose: it returns `True` on reaching the end of a specified file (or if an error occurs) and returns `False` otherwise. It takes just one argument—the relevant file handle:

```php
feof($fp)
```

So you can use its logical negative as the condition in the loop, to test whether the file position indicator has reached the end of the file:

```php
<?php
//hit_counter04.php
$counter_file = "./count.dat";
if(!($fp = fopen($counter_file, "r"))) die ("Cannot open $counter_file.");
while(!feof($fp)) $counter .= fgetc($fp);
$counter = (int) $counter;
fclose($fp);

$counter++;

echo "You're visitor No. $counter.";
```

```
$fp = fopen($counter_file, "w");
fwrite($fp, $counter);
fclose($fp);
?>
```

The `feof()` function tells the `while` statement when to quit (when the end of the file is reached after reading through it character by character with the `fgetc()` function), and the counter is forced to an integer data type using the `(int)` statement.

If you use `fgetc()` to try to read a large file, though, the script's going to take ages to run because it reads only one character at a time. Fortunately, PHP provides `fgets()` to help you read sets of characters. This function takes two arguments, `fp` and `length`, and returns a string of maximum length (length - 1) in bytes, as read from the file pointed to by `fp`. It stops reading for any one of three reasons:

- ❑ The specified number of bytes has been read.

- ❑ A new line is encountered.

- ❑ The end of the file is reached.

The difference between `fgets()` and `fread()` is that `fgets()` stops reading when it reaches end-of-line and reads up to length - 1 bytes, while `fread()` reads past end-of-line and reads up to length bytes. You can apply `fgets()` to the hit counter like this:

```
<?php
//hit_counter05.php
$counter_file = "./count.dat";
if(!($fp = fopen($counter_file, "r"))) die ("Cannot open $counter_file.");
$counter = (int) fgets($fp, 20);
fclose($fp);

...
```

Because the counter needs only one line from the data file, the call to `fgets()` returns the last counter value, as you want it to.

If you've ever done any work with importing and exporting data, you know about the comma-separated-value (CSV) format for data. (CSV even has its own file extension: `.csv`.) In CSV files, data values are separated or delimited by commas, and string values are often contained or enclosed within double quotes in between the commas. The `fgetcsv()` function reads the data in files with the assumption that it is properly formatted in CSV and puts the data it finds in a line into an array. Naturally, once you have an array of data you can easily manipulate it.

The `fgetcsv()` function must be given a valid file handle, a numerical value higher than the length of each line (including the end-of-line characters), and you can optionally specify data delimiters (the default is comma) and data enclosures (the default is double-quotes). The following code snippet shows how you might retrieve a line of data values from a file in CSV format:

```
$file_handle = fopen("my_csv_text_file.csv", "r");
$my_data_values_array = fgetcsv($file_handle, 1000, ",");
```

The result would be an array named $my_data_values_array, and if the first data value in the line of text was someone's first name (Bob, for example) then $my_data_values_array[0] would equal "Bob". Note that a blank line within the text file is treated as a single NULL field, not an error.

The fputs() function is simply an alias for fwrite(); the two are functionally identical.

Reading Entire Files

There are also some functions that provide access to the complete contents of files in one go. These include:

- ❏ file()
- ❏ fpassthru()
- ❏ readfile()

The file() function takes just one argument: a string containing the name of a file. For example:

```
file("/home/chris/myfile.txt")
```

returns the entire contents of myfile.txt (in the directory /home/chris/) as an array, using the newline character (CR LF on the Windows platform) to delimit elements. The newline character remains attached at the end of each line stored in the array. This function doesn't require you to specify a file handle because you can refer to the filename explicitly; it automatically opens, reads, and, once it's done, closes the file.

Here's the file() version of the original hit counter:

```php
<?php
//hit_counter06.php
$counter_file = "./count.dat";
$lines = file($counter_file);
$counter = (int) $lines[0];

$counter++;

echo "You're visitor No. $counter.";

if(!($fp = fopen($counter_file, "w"))) die ("Cannot open $counter_file.");
fwrite($fp, $counter);
fclose($fp);
?>
```

The entire contents of the data file are read into the array $lines and only the first element of the array (the first line of the file) is extracted. You could actually do just the same using a mixture of feof() and fgets() like this:

```php
$fp = fopen ("./count.dat", "r");
while (!feof($fp)) $lines[] = fgets($fp, 1024);
fclose ($fp);
```

But you don't need to because the `file()` function does it all for you. As with `fopen()`, it can also fetch files on a remote host:

```php
$file_lines = file( "http://www.whatyoumaycallit.com/index.html" );
foreach($file_lines as $line) echo $line;
```

Although this function can be very useful for reading the entire contents of a file, you should exercise caution when using it—if it tries to read a very large file, it may end up consuming all the memory allocated to PHP. That wouldn't be a good move.

The `fpassthru()` function is the one to use if all you want to do is read and print the entire file to the Web browser. It takes a single argument, a file handle, which it uses to read the remaining data from a file (that is, from the current position until end-of-file). It then writes results to standard output. Here's the corresponding version of the hit counter:

```php
<?php
//hit_counter07.php
$counter_file = "./count.dat";
if(!($fp = fopen($counter_file, "r"))) die ("Cannot open $counter_file.");
$counter = (int) fread($fp, 20);
fclose($fp);

$counter++;

if(!($fp = fopen($counter_file, "w"))) die ("Cannot open $counter_file.");
fwrite($fp, $counter);
fclose($fp);

if(!($fp = fopen($counter_file, "r"))) die ("Cannot open $counter_file.");
echo "You're visitor No. ";
fpassthru($fp);
?>
```

Only data from the current file position onward is written. If you read a couple of lines from a file before calling `fpassthru()`, for example, only the subsequent contents of the file will be printed. The file is closed when the function finishes reading, so there's no need to call `fclose()`—in fact, if you do, you get a warning that the file pointer is not valid.

The `readfile()` function enables you to print the contents of a file without even having to call `fopen()`. It takes a filename as its single argument, reads the whole file, and then writes it to standard output, returning the number of bytes read (or `False` upon error). Apply it like this:

```php
<?php
//hit_counter08.php
$counter_file = "./count.dat";
if(!($fp = fopen($counter_file, "r"))) die ("Cannot open $counter_file.");
$counter = (int) fread($fp, 20);
fclose($fp);

$counter++;

if(!($fp = fopen($counter_file, "w"))) die ("Cannot open $counter_file.");
```

```
fwrite($fp, $counter);
fclose($fp);

echo "You're visitor No. ";
readfile($counter_file);
?>
```

As in the previous script, all read and write operations on the data file take place before the incremented counter is echoed out.

Random Access to File Data

As you may have realized, it'd be more efficient if you opened the file for both read and write operations with a single fopen() call. However, using the functions you've met so far, you can only manipulate data sequentially, that is, in the same order that it is (or will be) arranged in the file. This puts a major limitation on what you can usefully achieve by doing it this way; once the file position indicator passes a certain point in a file, you need to close and reopen the file before you can access data at that point. Unless your data access is terribly well organized in advance (not likely in real-life situations, where it's often impossible to predict what you might need to do), you'd end up opening your data file as many (if not more) times as before.

What you really need is some way to move the file position indicator around in the file without having to close and reopen the file. There are a couple of functions that do just that:

❑   fseek()

❑   ftell()

PHP provides a number of functions that are designed to let you read from or write to specific positions within a file. Specifying a file handle (such as $fp) and an integer offset (5 in the following example) as arguments, fseek() will move the file position indicator associated with fp to a position determined by offset. By default, the offset is measured in bytes from the beginning of the file. Here's an example:

```
fseek($fp, 5);
$one_char = fgetc($fp);
```

This code places the file's file position indicator associated with handle $fp just after the fifth byte in that file. The call to fgetc() therefore returns the contents of the sixth byte. A third optional argument (called *whence* in the documentation) can be specified with any of the following values to calculate the relative offset:

❑   SEEK_SET: The beginning of the file + offset.

❑   SEEK_CUR: Current position + offset (default).

❑   SEEK_END: End of the file + offset.

fseek() is rather unusual because it's an integer PHP function that returns 0, not 1, upon success (it also returns –1 upon failure). You can't use this function with files on remote hosts opened through either an HTTP, URL, or FTP.

The `ftell()` function takes a file handle and returns the current offset (in bytes) of the corresponding file position indicator. For example:

```
$fpi_offset = ftell($fp);
rewind()
```

This is similar to the rewind button on your cassette player—it takes a file handle and resets the corresponding file position indicator to the beginning of the file. You can say:

```
rewind($fp);
```

which is functionally equivalent to:

```
fseek($fp, 0);
```

As you saw earlier, the `fpassthru()` function outputs file data from the current file position onward. If you have already read data from a file but want to echo the file's entire contents, you need to call `rewind()` first.

You can use `rewind()` to revise the counter script so that it only has to open the data file once, for both reading and writing:

```php
<?php
//hit_counter09.php
$counter_file = "./count.dat";
if(!($fp = fopen($counter_file, "r+"))) die ("Cannot open $counter_file.");
$counter = (int) fread($fp, 20);
$counter++;

echo "You're visitor No. $counter.";
rewind($fp);
fwrite($fp, $counter);
fclose($fp);
?>
```

As you see, the data file is only opened once, in read and write mode. After reading the last access number from the file and displaying it, you rewind the file to reset the file position indicator.

Try It Out   Navigate Within a File

Here's another example that uses these three navigating functions (`fseek()`, `ftell()`, and `rewind()`):

```php
<?php
//nav_file.php
$name_field_len = 15;
$country_code_field_len = 2;
$country_field_len = 20;
$email_field_len = 30;

if(!($fp = fopen("./address.dat", "r")))
        die ("Cannot open the address data file.");
```

```
do {
    $address = '';
    $field = fread($fp, $name_field_len);
    $address .= $field;

    $field = fread($fp, $country_code_field_len);
    $address .= $field;
    $field = fread($fp, $country_field_len);
    $address .= $field;
    $field = fread($fp, $email_field_len);
    $address .= $field;
    echo "$address<BR>";
} while ($field);

rewind($fp);

echo "<BR>";

fseek($fp, $name_field_len);

do {
    $country_code = fread($fp, $country_code_field_len);
    fseek($fp, ftell($fp) + $country_field_len +
                        $email_field_len +
                        $name_field_len + 1);
    //NB: change '+1' to '+2' on Win32 platforms
    echo "$country_code<BR>";
} while($country_code);

fclose($fp);
?>
```

This script assumes you have an address book data file called address.dat in the current directory that looks like this (note that you must be very careful about the number of characters—even blank characters—in each field):

```
Wankyu Choi      KRRepublic of Korea    wankyu@whatyoumaycallit.com
James Hetfield   USUnited States        james@headbangers.com
Nomura Sensei    JPJapan                nomura@nosuchsite.com
```

Here's the output from a test run:

```
Wankyu Choi KRRepublic of Korea wankyu@whatyoumaycallit.com
James Hetfield USUnited States james@headbangers.com
Nomura Sensei JPJapan nomura@nosuchsite.com

KR
US
JP
```

Records in this data file are separated by a newline character. (As mentioned earlier, a newline character is CR LF for Windows platforms, CR for Mac, and LF for Linux.) Each field has a set length: 15 characters for the name field, two characters for the country code field, and so on.

How It Works

The example starts by opening address.dat for reading in the current directory. First, it displays all the records as they are. When fread() reaches end-of-file, $field is set to False and the first loop terminates:

```
if(!($fp = fopen("./address.dat", "r")))
                    die ("Cannot open the address data file.");
do {
    $address = '';
    $field = fread($fp, $name_field_len);
    $address .= $field;
    $field = fread($fp, $country_code_field_len);
    $address .= $field;
    $field = fread($fp, $country_field_len);
    $address .= $field;
    $field = fread($fp, $email_field_len);
    $address .= $field;
    echo "$address<BR>";
} while ($field);
```

Then the data file rewinds, and the file position indicator moves to the end of the first name field entry, so that you're ready to read and display the country code field values:

```
rewind($fp);
fseek($fp, $name_field_len);
```

A do...while loop is initiated. Within it, you assign the country code data to a variable with fread(), move the file position indicator to the start of the next country code field, and finally output the country code that was just read. You start by assigning a value to $country_code:

```
do {
    $country_code = fread($fp, $country_code_field_len);
```

Determine the exact position of the next country code field as follows:

❑   Get the current position of the file position indicator, as returned by ftell($fp).

❑   Add to this the total length of the remaining fields and a trailing newline character.

By using this as the second argument in a call to fseek(), you set the file position indicator to the appropriate point in the file:

```
fseek($fp, ftell($fp) + $country_field_len + $email_field_len +
                                    $name_field_len + 1);
```

For Windows platforms, the length of a CR LF combination should be given as 2 instead of 1 (1 is fine for Linux and Mac). You echo the recorded value and close the loop, which cycles as long as $country_code is True:

```
        echo "$country_code<BR>";
    } while($country_code);
```

Finally, the file is closed:

```
fclose($fp);
```

Getting Information on Files

Earlier in this chapter, you saw how you could run into problems if you ran the counter script and the file count.dat didn't exist, and you made sure you performed some basic error checking when you opened the file. That's a very simple approach—if something does go wrong, the user won't necessarily know what the problem is.

PHP provides some functions that enable you to access useful file information. For example, rather than just spewing out a standard error message when you fail to open a file, you can use file_exists() to discover whether the file exists. If it doesn't, you can infer that the current user is the first visitor to the site and create the data file. You can say:

```
file_exists("/home/chris/count.dat")
```

This returns True if count.dat exists in /home/chris/, and False otherwise. The error checking for your hit counter might now take this form:

```
<?php
//hit_counter_10.php
$counter_file = "./count.dat";
if(file_exists($counter_file)) {
    if(!($fp = fopen($counter_file, "r+")))
                die("Cannot open $counter_file");
    $counter = (int) fread($fp, filesize($counter_file));
    $counter++;
    rewind($fp);
}
else {
    if(!($fp = fopen($counter_file, "w")))
                die("Cannot open $counter_file");
    $counter = 1;
}

echo "You're visitor No. $counter.";

fwrite($fp, $counter);
fclose($fp);
?>
```

This is just one of a number of functions that return helpful information on a given file. In a similar fashion, you can use the filesize() function to determine exactly how many bytes should be read from the counter data file. Just as with file_exists(), this function takes a filename string argument directly instead of a file handle:

```
filesize("/home/chris/count.dat")
```

This returns the size of the specified file in bytes, or `False` upon error. You could use `filesize()` to determine how many bytes should be read from the data file to get the number of hits:

```php
<?php
//hit_counter11.php
$counter_file = "./count.dat";
if(file_exists($counter_file)) {
    if(!($fp = fopen($counter_file, "r+")))
                    die("Cannot open $counter_file");
    $counter = (int) fread($fp, filesize($counter_file));
    $counter++;
    rewind($fp);
}
...
```

Time-Related Properties

Besides their contents, files have other properties that can provide useful information. These will principally depend on the operating system in which they are created and modified. On UNIX platforms such as Linux, for example, properties include creation date, modification date, last access date, and user permissions. With just a little extra code, you can make the hit counter show when the last access was made. The function `fileatime()` returns the last access time for a file in a UNIX timestamp format, and returns the last date on which the file was modified in a Windows format.

A UNIX timestamp is a long integer whose value can be interpreted as the number of seconds between the UNIX Epoch (January 1, 1970) and a specified time and date.

PHP provides two other time-related file functions:

❑   `filectime()` returns the time at which the file was last changed as a UNIX timestamp. A file is considered changed if it is created or written, or when its permissions have been changed.

❑   `filemtime()` returns the time at which the file was last modified as a UNIX timestamp. The file is considered modified if it is created or has its contents changed.

The `getdate()` function is also very useful when working with timestamps. It returns an associative array containing the date information present in a timestamp. The array includes such values as the year, the month, the day of the month, and so on. You can set a variable ($my_date) equal to the value returned by `getdate()`, and then access the month, for example, with `$my_date['month']`.

Try It Out	Display the Last Access Time to the Counter Data File

This example uses the `getdate()` function to read the date values from the `fileatime()` function for the file named in the variable `$counter_file`.

```php
<?php
//last_counter_access.php
$counter_file = "./count.dat";
if(file_exists($counter_file)) {
    $date_str = getdate(fileatime($counter_file));
    $year = $date_str["year"];
```

```
$mon = $date_str["mon"];
$mday = $date_str["mday"];
$hours = $date_str["hours"];
$minutes = $date_str["minutes"];
$seconds = $date_str["seconds"];

$date_str = "$hours:$minutes:$seconds $mday/$mon/$year";

if(!($fp = fopen($counter_file, "r+")))
                 die("Cannot open $counter_file");

$counter = (int) fread($fp, filesize($counter_file));
$counter++;

echo "You're visitor No. $counter.";
echo "The last access was made at $date_str";
rewind($fp);
}
else {
    if(!($fp = fopen($counter_file, "w")))
                 die("Cannot open $counter_file");
    $counter = 1;
    echo "You're visitor No. $counter.";
}

fwrite($fp, $counter);
fclose($fp);

?>
```

Figure 7-4 shows what it should look like (note that on Windows systems, the file creation time may be displayed, instead of the last access time).

How It Works

If the specified count.dat file exists, the script gets the last access time for the data file as a UNIX timestamp. This is converted to an associative array containing date information with the getdate() function, values are extracted from the appropriate elements, arranged, and stored in a string variable:

```
$counter_file = "./count.dat";
if(file_exists($counter_file)) {
    $date_str = getdate(fileatime($counter_file));
    $year = $date_str["year"];
    $mon = $date_str["mon"];
    $mday = $date_str["mday"];
    $hours = $date_str["hours"];
    $minutes = $date_str["minutes"];
    $seconds = $date_str["seconds"];

    $date_str = "$hours:$minutes:$seconds $mday/$mon/$year";
```

When you create, write to, or read from a file, UNIX considers the file to have been accessed (Windows is a bit different, and may consider the file changed only under other circumstances, and as we mentioned

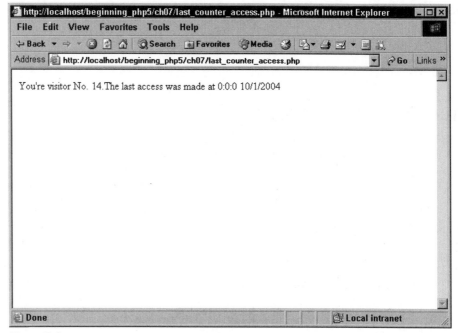

Figure 7-4

previously, may show the file creation time instead of the last access time). For this reason, you call
filetime() before reading from the data file. Still conditional on the actual existence of the
count.dat file, you open it and read its entire contents into the variable $counter, increment that
variable, and print it out along with the formatted date information. Then, rewind() the file position
indicator (so that you're ready to write the new count) and close the body of the if statement:

```
    if(!($fp = fopen($counter_file, "r+")))
                    die("Cannot open $counter_file");

    $counter = (int) fread($fp, filesize($counter_file));
    $counter++;

    echo "You're visitor No. $counter. "
    echo "The last access was made at $date_str";
    rewind($fp);
}
```

Now look at the else clause; if the file count.dat didn't already exist, you create it with fopen(),
specifying write-only. Initialize the counter at 1 and incorporate it in a displayed message:

```
else {
    if(!($fp = fopen($counter_file, "w")))
                    die("Cannot open $counter_file");
    $counter = 1;
    echo "You're visitor No. $counter.";
}
```

Finally, write the new counter value to the count.dat file, and close it with fclose():

```
fwrite($fp, $counter);
fclose($fp);
```

Ownership and Permissions

You also can get information on file ownership and permissions. On a UNIX system like Linux, all files are associated with a specific user and a specific group of users, and assigned flags that determine who has permission to read, write, or execute their contents. Some Windows file systems and operating systems work this way, and some don't. For example, the Windows NT File System (NTFS) enables you to assign owners and permissions, while Windows 98 doesn't.

User groups are defined in UNIX so that permissions can be easily extended to a certain set of users without extending them to everyone on the system. For example, several users who are working on the same project might want to share files with each other, but with no one else.

Each of these three permissions (read, write, and execute) can be granted to (or withheld from):

❑   The file owner: By default, the user whose account was used to create the file.

❑   A group of users: By default, the group to which the owner belongs.

❑   All users: Everyone with an account on the system

Users and groups in UNIX are identified by ID numbers as well as names. If you want to get information on a user by his ID number, you can use the posix_getpwuid() function, which returns an associative array with the following references:

Name	Description
name	The shell account username of the user
passwd	The encrypted user password
uid	The ID number of the user
gid	The group ID of the user
gecos	A comma-separated list containing the user's full name, office phone, office number, and home phone number. On most systems, only the user's full name is available
Dir	The absolute path to the home directory of the user
shell	Absolute path to the user's default shell

Another PHP function, posix_getgrgid(), returns an associative array on a group identified by a group ID. It contains the following elements of the group structure:

Name	Description
Name	The name of the group
Gid	The ID number of the group
members	The number of members belonging to the group

You can use the following three functions to get at this information from your PHP scripts. Each takes a single argument, a filename string.

- ❏ `fileowner()`: Returns the user ID of the owner of the specified file.

- ❏ `filegroup()`: Returns the group ID of the owner of the specified file.

- ❏ `filetype()`: Returns the type (`fifo`, `char`, `dir`, `block`, `link`, `file`, or `unknown`) of the specified file.

For example, you can use `filetype()` to check whether a given filename is a file or a directory (make sure you have a file named `counter.php` in the folder; create it if you need to):

```php
<?php
//file_type.php
$filename = "./counter.php";
$filegroup = filegroup($filename);
$fileowner = fileowner($filename);
$filetype = filetype($filename);

if ($filetype == 'dir') {
   echo "$filename is a directory.";
} else if ($filetype == 'file') {
   echo "$filename is a file.<br>";
} else {
   echo "$filename is neither a directory nor a file.<br>";
}

echo "It belongs to user no.$fileowner and group no.$filegroup.<br>";
echo "<br>The user $fileowner info<br>";
$user_info_array = posix_getpwuid($fileowner);

foreach ($user_info_array as $key => $val) {
   echo "$key => $val<br>";
}

echo "<br>The group $filegroup info<br>";
$group_info_array = posix_getgrgid($filegroup);

foreach ($group_info_array as $key => $val) {
   echo "$key => $val<br>";
}
?>
```

Figure 7-5 shows a sample run on a Windows machine. Notice the error that results from attempting to use on Windows a function that only works on Linux machines. You can either find a Linux machine to run this on, or move on to the next example to get similar information about Windows files.

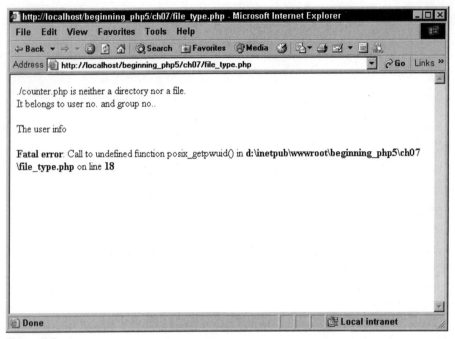

Figure 7-5

The is_dir() and is_file() Functions

Often you must know whether a file is a directory (remember, directories and files are all files, but directories are a special kind of file). For example, suppose you want to create a system that travels through the hierarchy of folders, you'd need to detect when a file was actually a folder, so you could attempt to enter the folder and continue traveling the hierarchy. By the same token, if you want to view only the files in a folder, you'd need to detect when a file is a file. PHP has two functions to help you out:

❑   is_dir() is designed specifically to work with directories. It returns True if the given filename refers to a directory.

❑   is_file() returns True if the given filename refers to a regular file.

It's very simple to rewrite the previous script so that it produces the same results using these functions:

```php
<?php
$filename = "./counter.php";
if(is_dir($filename)) {
 echo "$filename is a directory.";
} else if (is_file($filename)) {
 echo "$filename is a file.";
} else {
 echo "$filename is neither a directory nor a file.";
}
?>
```

As noted earlier, if you use `filetime()` in Windows, it returns the last modified date; and because Windows doesn't support file ownership, `filegroup()` and `fileowner()` both return zero.

Get Information on a Windows File

Here's a sample script that displays some properties on a given file:

```php
<?php
//file_win_info.php
function date_str($timestamp) {
    $date_str = getdate($timestamp);
    $year = $date_str["year"];
    $mon = $date_str["mon"];
    $mday = $date_str["mday"];
    $hours = $date_str["hours"];
    $minutes = $date_str["minutes"];
    $seconds = $date_str["seconds"];
    return "$hours:$minutes:$seconds $mday/$mon/$year";
}
function file_info($file) {

    $file_info_array["filesize"] =
                    number_format(filesize($file)) . " bytes.";
    $file_info_array["filectime"] = date_str(filectime($file));
    $file_info_array["filemtime"] = date_str(filemtime($file));
    if(!isset($_ENV[WINDIR])) {
        $file_info_array["fileatime"] = date_str(fileatime($file));
        $file_info_array["filegroup"] = filegroup($file);
        $file_info_array["fileowner"] = fileowner($file);
    }
    $file_info_array["filetype"] = filetype($file);

    return $file_info_array;
    }

    $filename = "./count.dat";
    $file_info_array = file_info($filename);

    echo "<center>Stats for $filename</center>";
    foreach($file_info_array as $key=>$val) {
        echo ucfirst($key) . "=>". $val . "<br>";
    }
    ?>
```

Figure 7-6 shows how it looks on a Windows system.

How It Works

Taking some lines of code from the last version of the hit counter, you can put them in a complete function named `date_str()`, which returns a formatted date string:

```php
function date_str($timestamp) {
    $date_str = getdate($timestamp);
```

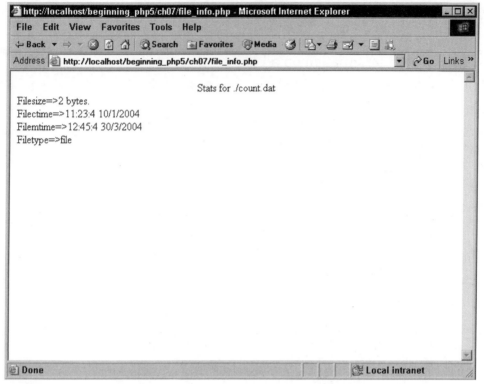

Figure 7-6

```
$year = $date_str["year"];
$mon = $date_str["mon"];
$mday = $date_str["mday"];
$hours = $date_str["hours"];
$minutes = $date_str["minutes"];
$seconds = $date_str["seconds"];

return "$hours:$minutes:$seconds $mday/$mon/$year";
}
```

The next file_info() function introduces a set of new file-related functions that return useful information on a given file:

```
function file_info($file) {
    $file_info_array["filesize"] =
                number_format(filesize($file)) . " bytes.";
    $file_info_array["filectime"] = date_str(filectime($file));
    $file_info_array["filemtime"] = date_str(filemtime($file));

if(!isset($_ENV[WINDIR""])) {
    $file_info_array["fileatime"] = date_str(fileatime($file));
```

```
        $file_info_array["filegroup"] = filegroup($file);
        $file_info_array["fileowner"] = fileowner($file);
    }

    $file_info_array["filetype"] = filetype($file);
    return $file_info_array;
    }
```

The environment variable $_ENV[WINDIR] is only set on the Windows platform; you access it via $_ENV and use it as a flag to denote whether the script is being run on a Windows platform. If it is set in the preceding code, you don't read the three fields that Windows doesn't support. Please note that the old $HTTP_ENV_VARS could be used as well, so long as you used the global keyword on it to make it visible inside your function. Although that still works, it's deprecated in favor of the $_ENV superglobal. An advantage of using the superglobal $_ENV is that you don't have to declare it as global to access from inside functions.

Finally, you specify a file, call the file_info() function, and print out the contents of each element in the array it returns:

```
$filename = "./count.dat";
$file_info_array = file_info($filename);

echo "<center>Stats for $filename</center>";
foreach($file_info_array as $key=>$val) {
    echo ucfirst($key) . "=>". $val . "<br>";
}
```

Working with Files You Own

Now that you've seen how you can check who owns a file, you're in a position to do some basic things such as copy, rename, and delete files. To do so, it's sometimes necessary to discover the exact path of a file, for which PHP includes some very useful functions, such as basename().

Splitting the Name and Path from a File

It's often very useful to be able to separate a filename from its directory path, and the basename() function does exactly that, taking a complete file path and returning just the filename. For example, the following call assigns index.html to $filename:

```
$filename = basename("home/james/docs/index.html");
```

You can specify a directory path, in which case the rightmost directory name is returned. Here's an example that assigns the value docs to $dirname:

```
$dirname = basename("home/james/docs");
```

Basically, basename() is a means of getting the last whole string after the rightmost slash.

Copying, Renaming, and Deleting Files

PHP also enables you to copy, rename, and delete files. The functions to perform these operations are `copy()`, `rename()`, and `unlink()`, respectively.

The `copy()` function takes two string arguments referring to the source and destination files, respectively. The following function call copies the source file `copyme.txt` to the destination file `copied.txt`:

```
if(!copy("./copyme.txt", "copied.txt")) die("Can't copy the file copyme.txt
to copied.txt!");
```

The `rename()` function is used to rename a file as follows:

```
if(!rename ("./address.dat", "address.backup"))
die("Can't rename the file address.dat to address.backup!");
```

You can use these functions to upgrade the hit counter, so that it backs up its counter data after a given interval (once an hour, once a day, once a week, and so on):

```php
<?php
//hit_counter12.php
$counter_file = "./count.dat";
$counterbackup_file = "./count.backup";
$backup_interval = 24*60*60;

if(file_exists($counter_file)) {
    $date_str = getdate(fileatime($counter_file));
    $year = $date_str["year"];
    $mon = $date_str["mon"];
    $mday = $date_str["mday"];
    $hours = $date_str["hours"];

$minutes = $date_str["minutes"];
    $seconds = $date_str["seconds"];
$date_str = "$hours:$minutes:$seconds $mday/$mon/$year";

    if((time() - fileatime($counterbackup_file)) >= $backup_interval) {
        @copy($counter_file, $counterbackup_file . time());
    }

    if(!($fp = fopen($counter_file, "r+")))
                    die("Cannot open $counter_file");
    $counter = (int) fread($fp, filesize($counter_file));
    $counter++;
    echo "You're visitor No. $counter. The
                    last access was made at $date_str";
    rewind($fp);
}
else {
    if(!($fp = fopen($counter_file, "w")))
                    die("Cannot open $counter_file");
    $counter = 1;
    echo "You're visitor No. $counter.";
```

```
}

fwrite($fp, $counter);
fclose($fp);

?>
```

Figure 7-7 shows the result (again, Windows systems may not display the correct last access time).

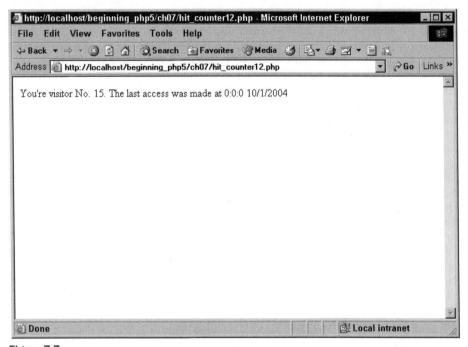

You're visitor No. 15. The last access was made at 0:0:0 10/1/2004

Figure 7-7

The $backup_interval variable is set in hours and subsequently multiplied by 3600 (one hour is 3,600 seconds). Whenever the script is run, it checks the last access time for the counter data file. It also checks the current time by calling the time() function, which returns the current UNIX timestamp—that is, the current time in seconds since January 1, 1970, at 00:00:00.

If the last access time precedes the current time by more than $backup_interval seconds, the existing data file is backed up by using unlink() and copy() functions. Appending the current time to the name of each file prevents old counter backup data from being deleted:

```
@copy($counter_file, $counterbackup_file . time());
```

You can suppress any error messages the copy() function might churn out by putting the error suppressing operator @ before the function name. Suppressing error messages is convenient because sometimes you know in advance that you may get them but that they're not serious, and you just don't want them appearing.

The `unlink()` function takes a single string argument referring to the name of a file you want to delete. For example, if you wanted to say adios to the file `trash.txt` in the current directory, you'd say:

```
if(!unlink("./trash.txt")) die ("Can't delete the file trash.txt!");
```

Where did `unlink()` come from? Using the name unlink for the delete file function may seem odd, particularly if you don't have any experience with UNIX-like systems. Why not just call it delete? Well, in a UNIX file system, there's a difference between the physical arrangement of files on a storage medium and the corresponding directory structure. It's perfectly possible, indeed common on UNIX, for different parts of a directory system to be stored on physically separate devices. Files are stored in a specific location in the directory system by linking that point in the directory tree (called an *inode*) to the physical location where the file's data is stored. In UNIX, a file path is actually just a unique identifier for one of these inodes.

Interestingly, in a UNIX system it's possible to link more than one point in the file system (more than one inode) to the same physical data, using what's called a hard link (see the Unix mainpage for the `ln` command for details). The data can be retrieved as long as there's at least one link to it. However, when all of the links have been destroyed, the data itself is deleted. So what you're actually doing when you use the command `unlink()` is destroying one of these links.

Because there's normally only one link to a file's data, unlinking it effectively deletes the file. If there's another link floating around the file system somewhere, the file isn't actually deleted. On Windows, it's not possible to link more than one point in the file system to the same data, so unlinking the file is equivalent to deleting it in all cases.

Many versions of PHP for Windows do not support the `unlink()` function at all. Workarounds exist, but vary greatly according to which Web server is being used. With Apache, for example, it's possible to pass a command like `del filename` direct to Windows, using a `system()` or `exec()` function call. If you've a combination such as this, you can mimic `unlink()` with the following code:

```
if(!isset($_ENV[WINDIR])) {
    $userfile = str_replace("/", "\\", $file);
    exec("del $file");
    if(file_exists("$file")) die("Can't delete the file $file.");
}
else if(!@unlink($file)) {
    die("Can't delete the file $file.");
}
```

Because `del` expects backslashes in the given path, use `str_replace()` to replace all the forward slashes in the path.

Working with Directories

PHP enables you manipulate to directories in much the same way as files, providing a number of equivalent functions. Some directory functions use a directory handle, whereas others use a string containing the name of the directory with which you want to work. A directory handle is similar to a file handle; it's an integer value pointing to a directory, which can be obtained by specifying the directory in a call to the `opendir()` function:

```
$dp = opendir ("/home/james/")
```

Upon error, this returns False. As you may have guessed, you can close a directory by specifying the appropriate handle to the function closedir():

```
closedir($dp);
```

The readdir() function returns the next entry listed in the open directory. This list includes entries for . (used to specify the current directory) and .. (likewise, specifying the parent of the current directory). PHP maintains an internal pointer referring to the next entry in the list just as the file position indicator points to the position where the next file operation should occur.

Try It Out   **List Directory Entries**

Here's how to set up a loop to get all the entries from a specified directory:

```php
<?php
//dir_list.php
$default_dir = "/Inetpub/wwwroot/beginning_php5/ch07";
if(!($dp = opendir($default_dir))) die("Cannot open $default_dir.");
while($file = readdir($dp))
  if($file != '.' && $file != '..') echo "$file<br>";
closedir($dp);
?>
```

Figure 7-8 shows an example result.

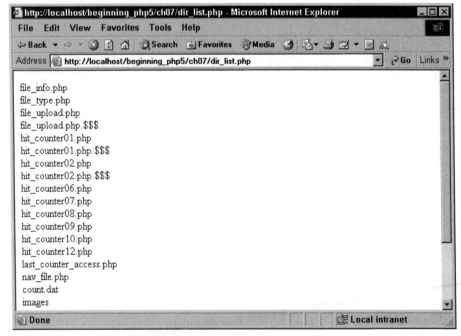

Figure 7-8

291

How It Works

You first get a handle on the directory given (Inetpub/wwwroot/beginning_php5/ch07 for this example), and then set up a loop that reads entries from that directory, and (as long as they're not "." or "..") prints them out. The loop is conditional on the return value of readdir(), which will be False when the list of entries is exhausted:

```
while($file = readdir($dp))
    if($file != '.' && $file != '..') echo "$file<br>";
```

Finally, closedir(). closes the directory.

The returned filenames are not sorted in any way. To sort them, you need to set up two loops. First though, you read the entries into an array:

```
<?php
$default_dir = "/Inetpub/wwwroot/beginning_php5/ch07";
if(!($dp = opendir($default_dir))) die("Cannot open $default_dir.");
while($file = readdir($dp)) $filenames[] = $file;
closedir($dp);
```

The $filenames array now contains every entry in the directory. You didn't use any indexing number in the array, so PHP automatically takes care of the indexing.

Finally, sort() is called to arrange the array entries in ascending order, and display all except the current and parent directories:

```
sort($filenames);
for($i=0; $i < count($filenames); $i++)
    if($filenames[$i] != '.' && $filenames[$i] != '..')
        echo $filenames[$i] . "<br>";
?>
```

Other Directory Functions

Just as with files, PHP provides a range of ways to manipulate directories, including the following functions:

❑   rewinddir()

❑   chdir()

❑   rmdir()

❑   mkdir()

❑   dirname()

❑   (dir)

The rewinddir() function resets PHP's internal pointer when you want to move back to the first entry in a given directory while working with it. This function is the directory counterpart to the rewind()

function for files, specifying the relevant directory handle. The rest of the directory handling functions take a path string directly instead of using a directory handle.

The chdir() function call changes PHP's current directory to the given directory:

```
if(chdir("/Inetpub/wwwroot/beginning_php5/ch07"))
echo "The current directory is / Inetpub/wwwroot/beginning_php5/ch07.";
else
echo "Cannot change the current directory to /home
Inetpub/wwwroot/beginning_php5/ch07.";
```

The rmdir() function removes a given directory. The directory must be empty, and you need appropriate permissions to remove it. For example:

```
rmdir("/tmp/rubbish/");
```

The mkdir() function creates a directory as specified in its first argument. You can also specify a directory mode argument as a three-digit octal number. The following code snippet first tests whether / Inetpub/wwwroot/beginning_php5/ch07/test exists. If it does, it's removed, and the same directory is then recreated, with all permissions granted to all users (permissions are applied only on Linux systems):

```
$default_dir = "/ Inetpub/wwwroot/beginning_php5/ch07";
if(file_exists($default_dir)) rmdir($default_dir);
mkdir($default_dir, 0777);
```

The dirname() function returns the directory part of a given filename. For example:

```
$filepath = "/ Inetpub/wwwroot/beginning_php5/ch07/index.html";
$dirname = dirname($filepath);
$filename = basename($filepath);
```

The string $dirname will now contain "/Inetpub/wwwroot/beginning_php5/ch07", and $filename will hold index.html.

PHP offers an alternative object-oriented mechanism for working with directories: the dir object. To use this method, you need to instantiate the object first by calling the dir() constructor with the name of the directory you want to work with as follows:

```
$dir = dir("/Inetpub/wwwroot/beginning_php5/ch07");
```

The dir object provides two properties: handle and path. These refer to the directory handle and the path, respectively:

```
echo $dir->handle; # echoes the directory handle
echo $dir->path; # echoes "/Inetpub/wwwroot/beginning_php5/ch07"
```

You can use the handle property with other directory functions such as readdir(), rewinddir() and closedir().

The `dir` object supports three methods: `read()`, `rewind()`, and `close()`, which are functionally equivalent to `readdir()`, `rewinddir()`, and `closedir()`, respectively. You can use the object to rewrite the directory listing script:

```php
<?php
$default_dir = "/Inetpub/wwwroot/beginning_php5/ch07";
$dir = dir($default_dir);
while($file = $dir->read()) if($file != '.' && $file != '..')
    echo $file . "<br>";
$dir->close();
?>
```

Traversing a Directory Hierarchy

As you learned in Chapter 6, recursion is particularly useful when a script has to perform repetitive operations and iterate over a given set of data, and traversing a directory hierarchy is a very good example. A directory may hold subdirectories as well as files. If you want to create a script that lists all the files and subdirectories under a given directory, you'd make one that reads the entries in the current directory, and if the next entry is a file, display its name. If the next entry is a subdirectory, display its name and go into it and return to reading the entries in the current directory.

As you can see, the second step repeats the whole process by itself, when necessary. The recursion continues until there are no more subdirectories left to traverse. Here's an example script:

```php
<?php
//nav_dir.php
$default_dir = "/home/james";
function traverse_dir($dir) {
    echo "Traversing $dir....<br>";
    chdir($dir);
    if(!($dp = opendir($dir))) die("Can't open $dir.");
    while($file = readdir($dp)) {
        if(is_dir($file)) {
            if($file != '.' && $file != '..') {
                echo "/$file<br>";
                traverse_dir("$dir/$file");
                chdir($dir);
            }
        }
        else echo "$file<BR>";
    }
    closedir($dp);
}
traverse_dir($default_dir);
?>
```

The `traverse_dir()` function is based on the concept of recursion and traverses the whole directory hierarchy under a specified directory. First, the function echoes out which directory it is currently going through. Then, a call to `chdir()` ensures that the `$dir` directory string argument is equal to PHP's current working directory:

```php
function traverse_dir($dir) {
    echo "Traversing $dir....<br>";
```

```
    chdir($dir);
    if(!($dp = opendir($dir))) die("Can't open $dir.");
    while($file = readdir($dp)) {
```

Recursion occurs when the next entry is a subdirectory. You exclude both the single dot (.) file and the double dot (..) file from the returned entries—this is absolutely crucial for this example; otherwise the script would be thrown into an infinite loop.

```
if(is_dir($file)) {
    if($file != '.' && $file != '..') {
        echo "/$file<br>";
```

The `traverse_dir()` function calls itself to go further down the directory hierarchy, and the function changes the current working directory back to its original state:

```
            traverse_dir("$dir/$file");
        chdir($dir);
    }
  }
    else echo "$file<BR>";
  }
 closedir($dp);
}
traverse_dir($default_dir);
?>
```

With the power of recursion as demonstrated in this sample script, you can create your own version of the Linux shell command `find`.

Creating a Directory Navigator

Now you're ready to build a fairly powerful directory navigator that you can use to scan the contents of existing directories and to make new ones. You'll create a file named `common_php5.inc.php` file, with a number of sections that help the application perform its job.

First you set the default directory, filename, and size of the textbox:

```
<?php
//specify the default directory
$default_dir = "./docs";

//specify the default name for new files
$default_filename = "new.txt";

//specify the size of the text area box
$edit_form_cols = 80;
$edit_form_rows = 25;
```

Set the file extensions you can handle:

```
//specify the file extensions to handle
$text_file_array = array( "txt", "htm", "html", "php", "inc", "dat" );
$image_file_array = array("gif", "jpeg", "jpg", "png");
```

These three functions create the header, the footer, and any error messages you need:

```php
function html_header() {
    ?>
    <html>
    <head><title>Welcome to Web Text Editor</title></head>
    <body>
    <?php
}

function html_footer() {
    ?>
    </body>
    </html>
    <?php
}

function error_message($msg) {
    html_header();
    echo "<script>alert(\"$msg\"); history.go(-1)</script>";
    html_footer();
    exit;
}
```

Process the date information:

```php
function date_str($timestamp) {
    $date_str = getdate($timestamp);
    $year = $date_str["year"];
    $mon = $date_str["mon"];
    $mday = $date_str["mday"];
    $hours = $date_str["hours"];
    $minutes = $date_str["minutes"];
    $seconds = $date_str["seconds"];

    return "$hours:$minutes:$seconds $mday/$mon/$year";
}
```

Then you return information about the file, and also check the filename extension:

```php
function file_info($file) {
    global $text_file_array;
    $file_info_array["filesize"] =
                    number_format(filesize($file)) . " bytes.";
        $file_info_array["filectime"] = date_str(filectime($file));
    $file_info_array["filemtime"] = date_str(filemtime($file));
    if(!isset($_ENV[WINDIR])) {
        $file_info_array["fileatime"] = date_str(fileatime($file));
        $file_info_array["filegroup"] = filegroup($file);
        $file_info_array["fileowner"] = fileowner($file);
    } else {
        $file_info_array["fileatime"] = "not available";
        $file_info_array["filegroup"] = "not available";
```

```
            $file_info_array["fileowner"] = "not available";
    }

    $extension = array_pop(explode(".", $file));

    if (in_array($extension, $text_file_array)) {
     $file_info_array["filetype"] = "text";
    } else {
     $file_info_array["filetype"] = "binary";
    }

    return $file_info_array;
}
```

Save your file as common_php5.inc.php.

Start your navigator script by including the file you just saved:

```php
<?php
//navigator.php
include "common_php5.inc.php";
```

Then define some functions. First is the mkdir_form() function, which displays a form to create a new directory:

```php
function mkdir_form() {
    global $dir;
?>
<center>
<form method="POST"
    action="<?php echo "$_SERVER[PHP_SELF]?action=make_dir&dir=$dir"; ?>">
<input type="hidden" name="action" value="make_dir">
<input type="hidden" name="dir" value="<? echo $dir ?>">

<?php
echo "<strong>$dir</strong>"
?>

<br>
<input type="text" name="new_dir" size="10">
<input type="submit" value="Make Dir" name="Submit">

</form>
</center>
<?php
}
```

The make_dir() function creates a given directory:

```php
function make_dir() {
    global $dir;
    if(!@mkdir("$dir/$_POST[new_dir]", 0700)) {
        error_message("Can't create the directory $dir/$_POST[new_dir].");
```

```
        }
        html_header();
        dir_page();
        html_footer();
    }
```

And then the display() function prints out the contents of a given file in a new window. By comparing the file extension with elements in $text_file_array and $image_file_array, it determines the file type—text, image, or binary:

```
function display() {
    global $text_file_array, $image_file_array;
    $extension = array_pop(explode(".", $_GET[filename]));
```

Next, the extension is checked against the types included in the text file array and the image file array. It will refuse to display a binary file:

```
if(in_array($extension, $text_file_array)) {
    readfile("$_GET[dir]/$_GET[filename]");
    }
    else if(in_array($extension, $image_file_array)) {
            echo "<img src=\"$_GET[dir]/$_GET[filename]\">";
    }
    else echo "Cannot be displayed. $_GET[dir]/$_GET[filename] has not been
            recognized as a text file, nor as a valid image file. ";
    }
```

The dir_page() is the main function, the one that scans the directory hierarchy and lists directory entries, displaying them with a trailing slash. This is where the meat of the script lies:

```
function dir_page() {
    global $dir, $default_dir, $default_filename;

    if($dir == '') {
        $dir = $default_dir;
    }
    if (isset($_GET['dir'])) {
     $dir = $_GET['dir'];
    }

    $dp = opendir($dir);

?>
<table border="0" width="100%" cellspacing="0" cellpadding="0">
<?php
```

Two loops are set up to sort the entries in a given directory: a while loop to read all the entries in the current working directory, and a for loop to display the entries after they're sorted:

```
while($file = readdir($dp)) $filenames[] = $file;
sort($filenames);
```

```
for($i = 0; $i < count($filenames); $i++)
{
    $file = $filenames[$i];
```

If the next entry is " . " (indicating the current directory), the function ignores it and continues the next loop cycle. However, if the current working directory is the default directory, both " . " and " . . " are ignored:

```
if($dir == $default_dir && ($file == "." || $file == ".."))
        continue;
    if(is_dir("$dir/$file") && $file == ".")
        continue;
    if(is_dir("$dir/$file")) {
```

If the entry is " . . " (indicating the parent directory), the function trims the name of the current directory from the $dir variable, to create a hyperlink pointing to the parent directory.

```
if($file == ".."){
```

The $current_dir holds the rightmost directory name with the following basename() function call:

```
$current_dir = basename($dir);
```

If the $dir variable contains "/home/apache/htdocs/images", for example, $current_dir is assigned the value "images".

When creating a link, the dir_page() function uses the ereg_replace() function to remove occurrences of the value in the $dir variable:

```
$parent_dir = ereg_replace("/$current_dir$","",$dir);
```

Following this line, the $parent_dir holds the value "/home/apache/htdocs" because the pattern /$current_dir$ matches the trailing string "/images".

```
    echo "<tr><td width=\"100%\ " nowrap>
        <a href=\"$_SERVER[PHP_SELF]?dir=$parent_dir\">$file/
        </a></td></tr>\n";
}
```

If the next entry is a subdirectory, the function creates a link pointing to it:

```
    else echo "<tr><td width=\"100%\" nowrap>
            <a href=\"$_SERVER[PHP_SELF]?dir=$dir/$file\">
            $file/</a></td></tr>\n";
}
```

If the next entry is a file, it creates a link to open a new browser that displays its contents:

```
    else echo "<tr><td width=\"100%\" nowrap>
            <a href=\"$_SERVER[PHP_SELF]?action=display&dir=$dir&filename=$file\"
                target=\"_blank\">$file</a></td></tr>\n";
```

```
      }
  ?>
  </table>
  <?php
      mkdir_form();
  }
```

When you run the script, it first tests to see if the directory specified is above the default directory (for security reasons, the user should never be able to access files that aren't directly under the default directory). The ereg() pattern matching function returns False if the $dir variable doesn't contain the value in $default_dir, in which case the $dir variable is assigned that value:

```
if(empty($dir) || !ereg($default_dir, $dir)) {
    $dir = $default_dir;
}
```

Finally, you call functions that correspond to the value in $action, defaulting to dir_page():

```
if (!empty($_POST['action'])) {
    $action = $_POST['action'];
}
if (!empty($_GET['action'])) {
    $action = $_GET['action'];
}
switch ($action) {
    case "make_dir":
        make_dir();
        break;
    case "display":
        display();
        break;
    default:
        html_header();
        dir_page();
        html_footer();
        break;
}
?>
```

After a sample run, Figure 7-9 shows the two files and one new folder in the current folder.

Figure 7-10 shows the contents of the file new01.txt.

Building a Text Editor

With the basics of PHP's file and directory handling capabilities under your belt, let's build a simple text file editor. It will take a filename as an argument, edit the file, and then save it. If it's not given an existing filename, the editor will create a new file.

First, think what the script will look like when finished. The picture in your mind eventually translates to the end user interface. Because it's an editor, it needs a place where it stores text and lets the user

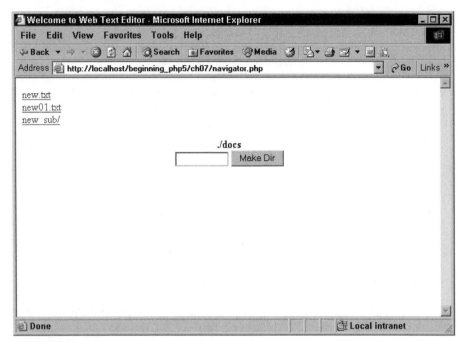

Figure 7-9

Figure 7-10

manipulate it. You won't have to worry about implementing specific editing features such as typing in characters, deleting them, moving the cursor, and so on, because the HTML tag <textarea> can handle all the editing features you'll need. All you have to do is throw in a form that displays a scrolling text box, an edit field for typing in a file name, and a button to save the text.

Next to consider are how to alert the user upon errors and how to get his confirmation about possibly disastrous actions such as overwriting an existing file. Some simple JavaScript tricks can achieve the goal. You can put a snippet of JavaScript into an HTML page by enclosing the code within the following tag combination:

```
<script> JavaScript code goes here </script>
```

For example, if you want to alert the user about an error, you can use the JavaScript's alert() method:

```
<script> alert("Warning! An error occurred!"); </script>
```

That opens a small window displaying the specified error message. You can use the history.go(-1) method to tell the browser to return to the previous page upon error:

```
<script>
alert("Warning! An error occurred! Let's get back to the previous page!");
history.go(-1);
</script>
```

Getting confirmation from the user is just as easy. The confirm() method does the trick:

```
<script>
result = confirm("Warning! Are you sure?");
if(!result) history.go(-1);
</script>
```

The confirm() method returns the user's decision. If he presses the YES button, True is returned and the specified action is executed. If he presses CANCEL, False is assigned to the variable result, causing the browser to fall back to the previous page. You'll use some of these tricks in the sample script.

You start by putting global variables and commonly used functions in the common.inc include file. As previously shown, it's good practice to put common elements that are shared and reusable by related scripts into a common include file. Name the revised include file common_php5_02.inc.php. First, the script presents a function to process error messages. This function provides a message to the user, and also sends him back to the previous page:

```
<?php
function error_message($msg) {
    echo "<script>alert(\"$msg\"); history.go(-1)</script>";
    exit;
}
```

The next function is just a copy of the date_str() function that you created earlier:

```
function date_str($timestamp) {
  $date_str = getdate($timestamp);
```

```
        $year = $date_str["year"];
        $mon = $date_str["mon"];
        $mday = $date_str["mday"];
        $hours = $date_str["hours"];
        $minutes = $date_str["minutes"];
        $seconds = $date_str["seconds"];

        return "$hours:$minutes:$seconds $mday/$mon/$year";
    }
```

The last function for the common_php5_02.inc.php file is file_info():

```
function file_info($file) {
    global $text_file_array;
    $file_info_array["filesize"] = number_format(filesize($file)) . " bytes.";
    $file_info_array["filectime"] = date_str(filectime($file));
    $file_info_array["filemtime"] = date_str(filemtime($file));
    if(!isset($_ENV['WINDIR'])) {
    $file_info_array["fileatime"] = date_str(fileatime($file));
    $file_info_array["filegroup"] = filegroup($file);
    $file_info_array["fileowner"] = fileowner($file);
    } else {
    $file_info_array["fileatime"] = "not available";
    $file_info_array["filegroup"] = "not available";
    $file_info_array["fileowner"] = "not available";
    }

    $extension = array_pop(explode(".", $file));

    if (in_array($extension, $text_file_array)) {
     $file_info_array["filetype"] = "text";
    } else {
     $file_info_array["filetype"] = "binary";
    }
    return $file_info_array;
}
```

Note how you extract the extension from a given file with explode(".", $file). This breaks up the filename using the dot (.) as a delimiter, and returns the resulting pieces as an array. The last element of the array is extracted using the array_pop() function, and is stored in $extension. For this example, the extension is not the second element.

One final section in common_php5_02.inc.php creates an array of filename extensions to look for:

```
//specify the file extensions to handle
$text_file_array = array( "txt", "htm", "html", "php", "inc", "dat" );
```

Now you're ready to create the structure of the main processing file, editor_php5.php. Start by creating the header for an ordinary HTML Web page:

```
<html>
<head><title>Welcome to Web Text Editor</title></head>
<body>
```

```
<form method="POST" action="<?php echo $_SERVER['PHP_SELF']; ?>">
<input type="hidden" name="posted" value="true">
```

Next, begin the PHP code and pull in (using the `require()` function) the `common_php5.inc.php` file. Then set the directory to use:

```
require("common_php5_02.inc.php");
//specify the default directory
$dir = "/Inetpub/wwwroot/beginning_php5/ch07/docs";
```

Check whether the user has clicked a button, and if so, set the proper value for the eventual `select..case` statement:

```
if (isset($_POST['save_edited_file'])) {
    $action_chosen = "save_file";
} elseif (isset($_POST['create_new_file'])) {
    $action_chosen = "save_file";
} elseif (isset($_POST['edit_existing_file'])) {
    $action_chosen = "edit_existing_file";
}
```

Begin the `select..case` statement and lay out the `save_file` case. This code checks to see if the file exists, and if so, uses JavaScript to ask the user if he wants to overwrite the file:

```
switch ($action_chosen) {
 case "save_file";

        if (file_exists("$dir/$_POST[filename]")) {
            echo "<script>result = confirm(\"Overwrite
                '$dir/$_POST[filename]'?\"); if(!result) history.go
(-1);</script>";
        }
```

Try to open (or create) the file, and if it fails, use the `error_message()` function to send the user an error message:

```
        if ($file = fopen("$dir/$_POST[filename]", "w")) {
          fputs($file, $_POST[filebody]);
          fclose($file);
        } else {
          error_message("Can't save file $dir/$_POST[filename].");
        }
```

The last chunk of code in the `save_file` case uses HTML to display the primary buttons that allow the user to perform the available tasks in the application. Notice the variation of the directory listing code to fill the drop-down box. The same code is also used in the default case. Don't forget the `break` at the end of the case:

```
        //display the main buttons
        ?>
        <table border="1" align="center"><tr><td>
```

```
              <strong>Create (or Overwrite) New File or Edit Existing File</strong>
              </td></tr>
              <tr><td>
              <input type="submit" name="create_new_file" value="Create New File">
              <input type="text" name="filename" value="new.txt">
              </td></tr>
              <tr><td>
              <input type="submit" name="edit_existing_file" value="Edit Existing
      File">
              <select name="existing_file">
              <?php

              if($dp = opendir($dir)) {
                  while($file = readdir($dp)) {
                      if($file !== '.' && $file !== '..' &&
                              is_file($dir."/".$file)) {
                      ?>
                      <option value="<?php echo $file; ?>">
                              <?php echo $file; ?></option>
                      <?php
                  }
              }
              } else {
                      error_msg("Can't open directory $dir.");
                  }

              closedir($dp);

              ?>
              </select>
              </td></tr></table>
              <?php

          break;
```

Now lay out the edit_existing_file case. Set the file particulars, including the filebody, and put the results of the file_info() function into $file_info_array:

```
  case "edit_existing_file";

          $filepath = "$dir/$_POST[existing_file]";
          $filebody = implode("",file($filepath));
          $file_info_array = file_info("$filepath");
```

Check to see if the file is a text file, and if so, reset the filebody so you'll know not to edit it:

```
          if ($file_info_array["filetype"] != "text") {
              $filebody = $filepath . " is not a text file. Can't edit.";
              $editable = 0;
          } else {
              $editable = 1;
          }
```

Display the file stats:

```
        ?>
        <table border="1" width="70%" align="center">
        <tr><th width="100%" colspan="2">
        <center><strong>Stats for Existing File named <?php echo
"$dir/$_POST[existing_file]"; ?>
        </td></tr>
        <?php
        $file_info_array = file_info("$dir/$_POST[existing_file]");

        foreach ($file_info_array as $key=>$val) {
            echo "<tr><th width=\"30%\">". ucfirst($key)
            . "</td><td width=\"70%\">" . $val
            . "</td></tr>\n";
        }
        ?>
    </table>
```

The final chunk of code in the `edit_existing_file` case allows the user to edit the code and save the result:

```
        <br>
        <table border="1" align="center"><tr><td>
        <strong>Editing Existing File named <?php echo $_POST['existing_file'];
?></strong>
        </td></tr>
        <tr><td>
        <?php

        if ($editable == 0) {
            echo $filebody;
        } else {
            ?>
            <input type="hidden" name="filename" value="<?php echo
$_POST['existing_file]; ?>">
                <textarea rows="4" name="filebody" cols="40" wrap="soft">
                <?php
                echo "$filebody";
                ?>
                </textarea><br>
                <input type="submit" name="save_edited_file" value="Save Edited
File">
                <?php
        }
        ?>
        </td></tr></table>
        <?php

    break;
```

The `default` case is a copy of the last portion of the `save_file` case:

```
    default;
            //display the main buttons
```

```
                    ?>
                    <table border="1" align="center"><tr><td>
                    <strong>Create (or Overwrite) New File or Edit Exist-
ing File</strong>
                    </td></tr>
                    <tr><td>
                    <input type="submit" name="create_new_file" value="Create
New File">
                    <input type="text" name="filename" value="new.txt">
                    </td></tr>
                    <tr><td>
                    <input type="submit" name="edit_existing_file" value="Edit
Existing File">
                    <select name="existing_file">
                    <?php

                    if($dp = opendir($dir)) {
                        while($file = readdir($dp)) {
                            if($file !== '.' && $file !== '..' && is_file
($dir."/".$file)) {
                        ?>
                    <option value="<?php echo $file; ?>"><?php echo $file; ?></option>
                    <?php
                            }
                        }
                    } else {
                        error_msg("Can't open directory $dir.");
                    }
                    closedir($dp);

                    ?>
                    </select>
                    </td></tr></table>
                    <?php
                break;
```

The final code in the file ends the `select..case` statement and finishes off the HTML for the page, including the closing `</form>` tag.

```
    }
    ?>
        </form>
        </body>
    </html>
```

And that pretty well covers how to deal with the members of the server file system family.

Uploading Files

Wouldn't it be nice if you could upload files from a local machine to the server using the directory navigator you just created? PHP offers an easy way to put this sort of functionality into your applications. You can let users upload files with their browsers using an `<input>` form tag of the type `file`. The `<form>` tag's `enctype` attribute, which is usually omitted when creating a normal form, also needs to be set to `multipart/form-data`.

Here's a sample upload form:

```
<form method="POST" enctype="multipart/form-data"
        action="<?php echo "$_SERVER[PHP_SELF]?action=upload_file&dir=$dir"; ?>">
    Local Filename <input type="file" name="userfile">
    <input type="submit" name="submit" value="Upload">
</form>
```

The `action` attribute of the form should point to a PHP script that will handle the uploaded file. You don't have to provide the second text input tag unless you want to let users choose a different filename with which the uploaded file will be stored on the server.

Once a file is uploaded, the following variable values become available for use via the superglobal `$_FILES` array:

Variable	Description
$_FILES[userfile]	The array in $_FILES that contains the other array values
$_FILES[userfile][name]	The original path and the filename of the uploaded file
$_FILES[userfile][size]	The size of the uploaded file in bytes
$_FILE[userfile][type]	The type of the file (if the browser provides the information)

Suppose a user has just uploaded a 20,000-byte ZIP file, `C:\docs\projects.zip`, using this form. These variables now contain the following:

❑ `$_FILES[userfile][tmp_name]`: The path to the file in the temporary directory (as set in `php.ini`) plus the temporary filename in the format `"php-###"` format (where `"###"` is a number which is automatically generated by PHP), for example, `"/tmp/php-512"`.

❑ `$_FILES[userfile][name]`: `"C:\docs\projects.zip"`

❑ `$_FILES[userfile][size]`: `20000`

❑ `$_FILES[userfile][type]`: `"application/x-zip-compressed"`

You can set these values to normal variables if you like, as shown here:

```
//get the userfile particulars
    $userfile_name = $_FILES['userfile']['name'];
    $userfile_tmp_name = $_FILES['userfile']['tmp_name'];
    $userfile_size = $_FILES['userfile']['size'];
    $userfile_type = $_FILES['userfile']['type'];
    if(isset($_ENV['WINDIR'])) {
        $userfile = str_replace("\\\\","\\", $_FILES['userfile']['name']);
    }
```

The uploaded file is saved in the temporary directory set in `php.ini` and destroyed at the end of the request, so you need to copy it to somewhere else. For security reasons, it's recommended that you use the `move_uploaded_file()` function instead of the `copy()` function:

```php
$archive_dir = "/Inetpub/wwwroot/beginning_php5/ch07/docs";
$filename = basename($userfile_name);
if(!@move_uploaded_file($userfile, "$archive_dir/$filename"))
        echo "Error: $filename cannot be copied.";
else echo "Successfully uploaded $filename.";
```

You may want to set a limit on the size of an uploaded file and check whether the uploaded file is larger than the limit by using the `$userfile_size` variable:

```php
$archive_dir = "./docs";
$max_filesize = 200000;
$filename = basename($userfile_name);
if($userfile_size > $max_filesize)
    echo "Error: $filename is too big. " .
    number_format($max_filesize) . " bytes is the limit.";
else if(!copy($userfile, "$archive_dir/$filename"))
        echo "Error: $filename cannot be copied.";
else echo "Successfully uploaded $filename.";
```

Another way to limit the size of the uploaded file is to use a hidden field in the upload form:

```php
<input type="hidden" name="max_file_size" value="200000">
...
if($userfile_size > $max_file_size)
    echo "Error: $filename is too big. " .
    number_format($max_file_size) . " bytes is the limit.";
```

Setting the limit within the script is a much more secure method because anyone can edit the Web page containing the upload form and increase the limit all he wants.

Try It Out   File Uploading

Here's a complete example of how to implement the file-uploading feature:

```php
<?php
//file_upload.php
function upload_form() {
    ?>
    <table border="1" align="center">
    <tr><td>
    <form method="POST" enctype="multipart/form-data"
        action="<? echo $_SERVER['PHP_SELF'] ?>">
        Upload file!
        <input type="file" name="userfile">
        <input type="submit" name="action" value="upload">
    </form>
    </td></tr>
    </table>
    <?
}
function upload_file() {
   //set the archive directory
```

```
        $archive_dir = "/Inetpub/wwwroot/beginning_php5/ch07/docs";
        //get the userfile particulars
        $userfile_name = $_FILES['userfile']['name'];
        $userfile_tmp_name = $_FILES['userfile']['tmp_name'];
        $userfile_size = $_FILES['userfile']['size'];
        $userfile_type = $_FILES['userfile']['type'];
        if(isset($_ENV['WINDIR'])) {
            $userfile = str_replace("\\\\","\\", $_FILES['userfile']['name']);
        }
        $filename = basename($userfile_name);
        if($userfile_size <= 0) die ("$filename is empty.");
        if(!@move_uploaded_file($userfile_tmp_name, "$archive_dir/$filename"))
            die("Can't copy $userfile_name to $filename.");
        if(isset($_ENV['WINDIR']) && !@unlink($userfile))
            die ("Can't delete the file $userfile_name.");
        echo "$filename has been successfully uploaded.<BR>";
        echo "Filesize: " . number_format($userfile_size) . "<BR>";
        echo "Filetype: $userfile_type<BR>";
    }
?>
<html>
<head><title>File Upload</title></head>
<body>
<?php
if($_POST[action] == 'upload') {
    upload_file();
} else {
    upload_form();
}
?>
</body>
</html>
```

Figure 7-11 shows the upload form once a file to upload (0.gif in this example) has been found.

A user uploading this file sees the output shown in Figure 7-12.

How It Works

When a user uploads a file from his local machine, the script first retrieves the $_FILES values and then tests the platform on which it is run. If it's the Windows platform, all occurrences of double forward slashes need to be reduced to single slashes:

```
//set the archive directory
    $archive_dir = "/Inetpub/wwwroot/beginning_php5/ch07/docs";

    //get the userfile particulars
    $userfile_name = $_FILES[userfile][name];
    $userfile_tmp_name = $_FILES[userfile][tmp_name];
    $userfile_size = $_FILES[userfile][size];
    $userfile_type = $_FILES[userfile][type];
if(isset($_ENV[WINDIR])) $userfile =
str_replace("\\\\","\\$",$_FILES[userfile][name]));
```

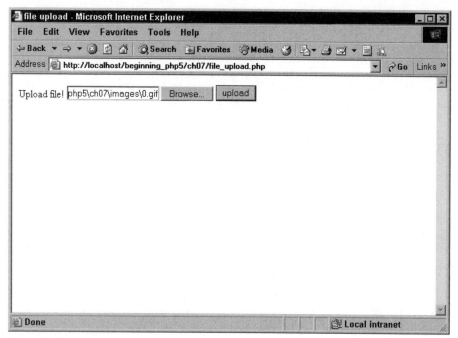

Figure 7-11

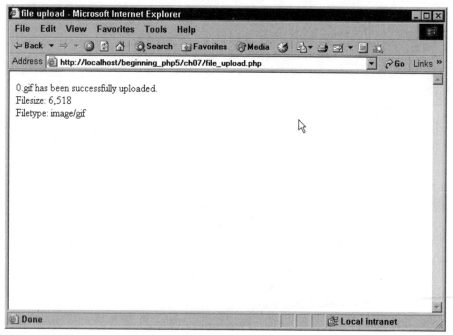

Figure 7-12

If the size of the file is less then 0, the user submitted the form without designating a file to be uploaded:

```
if($userfile_size <= 0) die ("$filename is empty.");
```

If everything looks fine, the script copies the uploaded file to an archive directory and tests to see whether it's running on Windows. If not, it's okay to use `unlink()` to delete the temporary file. Then echo back to the user that the file has been uploaded, as well as the file's size and type.

Summary

In this chapter you learned how to work with files as well as how to read and write to them. We created a simple Web text editor, learned how to work with directories, and created a directory navigator.

During the course of this chapter you explored most of the essential file/directory manipulating functions that PHP provides. Some used a file or directory handle—a pointer referring to an open file or directory—although others used string variables containing the name of a file or directory. To use functions requiring a handle, you went through this process:

1. Opened a file or directory to be used using `fopen()` or `opendir()`.

2. Worked with the open file or directory using the file manipulation functions `fread()`, `fgets()`, `fpassthru()`, and `readdir()` among others.

3. Closed it using `fclose()` or `closedir()`.

Finally, you created a text editor that can scan through the directory hierarchy and manipulate entries in it.

Some functions rarely used in Web applications weren't discussed. For a full list of the file/directory functions, refer to the online PHP function list: `http:// php.net/manual/ref.filesystem.php`.

Exercise

Create a PHP application that can be used to find a particular directory when given a valid parent directory to search. Make the application look through the given directory, as well as all directories under the given directory.

8

XML

XML—eXtensible Markup Language—is a relatively recent innovation. It was originally designed to be a human-readable means of exchanging structured data, and yet it has gained ground very quickly as a means of storing structured data as well. Although XML is different from databases in many ways, both are methods of formatting/storing structured data persistently, and both have advantages and drawbacks.

XML isn't really a language but instead is a specification for creating your own markup languages. It is a subset of Standard Generalized Markup Language (SGML, the parent of HTML). XML is intended to allow easy exchange of data between disparate applications. If you read an XML document (and are familiar with HTML) you'll notice similarities in the way HTML and XML documents are formatted. Although HTML has a fixed set of elements and attributes defined in the HTML specification, XML enables you to write your own elements and attributes, thereby providing the capability to define your own language in XML or to use someone else's definition. Essentially, you can format any data you wish using XML.

In addition, XML provides facilities for making the data definition available, in a readable format, to any other application online. So an application that knows nothing about your application can still exchange data as long as both applications have XML parsing capability.

For these reasons XML is rapidly becoming the data exchange standard, and PHP5 has many new features and functions that make working with XML data fast and efficient, as well as more intuitive. PHP5 includes all the XML functions found in PHP4, as well as new functions based on simpleXML (a built-in PHP extension that supports common XML operations).

In this chapter you learn XML basics as well as how to read and write XML documents with an xml parser and with simpleXML functions. You also examine the Document Object Model (DOM) and learn how XML is utilized in Web services. Finally, you manipulate XML documents with simpleXML functions.

What Is XML?

XML is a specification for creating your own markup languages. A document created according to the rules of the XML specification looks similar to HTML in that it contains elements and attributes coded as tags. Nevertheless, browsers do not attempt to directly format and display XML documents unless formatting information is provided in some way.

XML documents are human readable, and yet there are many applications designed to parse XML documents and work efficiently with their content. PHP5 has new XML-related functions that can easily be used to work with XML documents, or transform non-XML data into XML documents.

You can make your own XML document as easily as this:

```
<?xml version="1.0" ?>
<php_programs>
    <program name="cart">
        <price>100</price>
    </program>
    <program name="survey">
        <price>500</price>
    </program>
</php_programs>
```

The first line of this document specifies the version of XML that's being used (notice the delimiters `<?xml` and `?>`—awfully close to PHP's delimiters, so make sure to use the full `<?php` to start your PHP code). The second line defines the root element of the document (named `programs`). There can only be one root element for an XML document. The third line defines a child element of the root element, named `program`, and it contains an attribute named `name` that is set equal to `cart`.

From these lines, it should be obvious that this XML document is about PHP programs, and that there are two programs available (cart and survey), and that the price of cart is $100, whereas the price of survey is $500. The root element may contain multiple elements (in the example there are two `program` elements in the root element), and like HTML, XML documents are composed primarily of elements and attributes.

Another feature of XML documents is that their elements may contain other elements and plain text as content, whereas their attributes may be set directly equal to values. Oh and, it's pretty easy to read, but there are also many parser programs that make it easy to process with programs as well.

Anyone can write XML documents, and many folks also program their applications and programming languages to handle XML documents, both reading existing documents and composing their own new ones. The XML specification is free for anyone to use; the World Wide Web Consortium (at www.w3.org, the same place as the HTML and XHTML specs are maintained) authored and maintains the latest versions of the spec.

Although you can write XML documents just by laying out a few elements and attributes, often you want predefined elements and attributes, so that when you exchange data with another person or application, both parties to the transaction know exactly what the element and attribute names mean. Predefined elements and attributes are specified in a document type definition (DTD) or by an XML Schema, both of which are discussed a little later in this chapter. Frequently you'll find that before you write an XML document, you'll need to either find or write your own DTD or XML Schema. Once you write a DTD, you can publish it on the Web, and anyone who needs to write an XML document compatible with yours (or receive one from you and validate it) has the capability to check the published DTD as he reads your document.

XML Document Structure

There are two terms you hear over and over when discussing XML: *well-formed* and *valid*. A well-formed XML document follows the basic syntax rules (to be discussed in a minute), and a valid document also follows the rules imposed by a DTD or an XML Schema.

Being well-formed is the most basic requirement for XML documents; one that is not well-formed is not really an XML document. It's kind of like a script that someone tried to write in PHP but which contains fatal syntax errors; yes, it looks like PHP, but it really isn't until all the syntax errors are removed. A well-formed XML document may contain any elements, attributes, or other constructs allowed by the XML specification, but there are no rules about what the names of those elements and attributes can be (other than the basic naming rules, which are really not much of a restriction) or about what their content can be. It is in this extensibility that XML really derives a lot of its power and usefulness; so long as you follow the basic rules of the XML spec, there's no limit to what you can add or change.

A well-formed document does not need to be valid, but a valid document must be well formed, otherwise it couldn't be read in the first place. If a document is well formed, and it contains a reference to a DTD or XML Schema, your XML parser has the opportunity to reference the DTD or Schema and determine whether the document is valid. An XML document is valid if the elements, attributes, and so on that it contains follow the rules in the DTD or Schema. By definition then, the DTD or Schema contains rules about what elements or attributes may be contained in the document, what data those elements and attributes are allowed to have, and so on. In fact, the whole purpose of having a DTD or Schema is to define exactly what elements and attributes are allowed, and exactly what data they can contain.

Although referencing a DTD or Schema limits the name/value pairs (elements, attributes, and many of the other XML constructs) you may have in your XML document, the big advantage is that applications that know nothing about each other can still communicate effectively when they share the capability to parse XML because they can both read a well-formed document, and understand its contents if it is valid. Being readable by either humans or machines, and, by virtue of a DTD or XML Schema, knowing specifically what the elements and attributes mean, is another feature that makes XML so powerful.

Major Parts of an XML Document

An XML document may contain an optional prolog, and then the mandatory root element (including any content and other elements, attributes, and so on), with an optional section at the end for other data. The following list identifies the requirements within these major sections.

- ❑ XML documents should contain an `xml version` line, possibly including a character encoding declaration.

- ❑ Valid XML documents contain a DTD or an XML Schema, or a reference to one of these if they are stored externally.

- ❑ XML documents usually contain one or more elements, each of which may have one or more attributes. Elements can contain other elements or data between their beginning and ending tags, or they may be empty.

- ❑ XML documents may contain additional components such as processing instructions (PIs) that provide machine instructions for particular applications; CDATA sections, which may contain special characters, such as those found in scripts that are not allowed in ordinary XML data; notations, comments, entity references (aliases for entities such as special characters), text, and entities.

Here's an example of an XML document that is both well formed and valid:

```
<?xml version="1.0" standalone="no"?>
<!DOCTYPE Client SYSTEM "http://www.example.com/dtds/client.dtd">
<clients>
    <client>Joe</client>
    <client>Jim</client>
</clients>
```

Notice the reference to an external DTD located at the URL specified. This means that the document can be validated by reading the DTD and then checking the document to make sure that it conforms to the DTD. Of course, you could manually read through the document and compare it with the elements, attributes, and other document components specified in the DTD, but there are many applications available that can automatically validate an XML document against a DTD or an XML schema. And because the DTD or Schema is available either directly in the document or online, it's easy for these applications to perform the validation function for you automatically as they parse the document.

Well-Formed XML Documents

A well-formed XML document follows the XML specification syntax. The syntax, of course, follows some basic rules, the most common of which are listed here:

❑   There is only one parent element containing all the rest of the elements in the document.

❑   XML documents should (but are not strictly required to) begin with an XML declaration that gives the XML version number being used. For example:

```
<xml version="1.0">
```

❑   Character encoding declarations may be included with the XML version line, and must be included for encodings other than UTF-8 or UTF-16. The code might look like this:

```
<xml version="1.0" encoding="UTF-8">
```

❑   If an XML document contains a DTD or a reference to an XML Schema that must appear before the first element in the document.

❑   XML elements can be made from start and end tags (written much like HTML tags) or can be a single tag with a terminator (like the <br /> tag in XHTML). Unlike HTML, there is no allowance for elements that have only a starting tag and are not self-terminated. Elements with start and end tags are considered non-empty (meaning they can contain content) whereas empty tags do not contain content (empty elements sometimes signify something on their own, like the <br /> tag in XHTML), like this:

```
<client>John Doe</client>
<break />
```

❑ XML attributes can be written inside non-empty XML elements, and must have a name and a value; the value must be enclosed in delimiters, such as double quotes. No attribute name may appear more than once inside a single element.

❑ XML elements must be properly nested, meaning any given element's start and end tags must be outside the start and end tags of elements inside it, and inside the start and end tags of elements outside it. Here's an example:

```
//not good
<parent><child></parent></child>
//good
<parent>child></child></parent>
```

❑ CDATA sections (sections of data that make up scripts, for example) must be delimited by [CDATA and]].

❑ XML elements may not be named using "xml," "XML," or any upper- or lower-case combination of these characters in this sequence. Names must start with a letter, an underscore, or the colon, but in practice, you should never use colons. Names are case-sensitive. Numbers, the hyphen, and the period are valid characters to use after the first character.

❑ Comments are delimited like HTML comments (<!-- and -->).

Using XML Elements and Attributes

XML elements and their attributes form the hierarchical structure of an XML document, and contain its content (the content of an XML document is its data). Although there can be only one root element, the root element may contain multiple elements of the same name (often referred to as child elements), and child elements can also contain multiple elements of the same name. So you might have a document like this:

```
<clients>
  <client ID="1">Joe</client>
  <orders>
    <order ID="1">ProductA</order>
    <order ID="2">ProductB</order>
  </orders>
  <client ID="2">Jim</client>
  <orders>
    <order ID="1">ProductA</order>
    <order ID="2">ProductB</order>
  </orders>
<client>
</clients>
```

As you can see, part of the content of this document is put into elements (the name of each client is between the beginning and ending `client` elements) and part of the content is the value of attributes (the ID numbers of the clients and their orders are specified in the ID attributes of the `client` and `order` elements).

There is some controversy about when to use an attribute and when to use an element for containing data. Although there is no hard and fast rule, a good rule of thumb is to use an element when there is the possibility that you might need to specify the same thing more than once (for example, although you may only have one order at present, you can expect there will be more orders for a single client), and when you're sure the data will only occur once (for example, each client may have one, and only one, ID number), use an attribute.

Valid XML Documents: DTDs and XML Schemas

DTDs are special documents written in Extended Backus Naur Format (EBNF), which is not an XML language and therefore isn't so easy to parse. DTDs specify constraints on XML elements, attributes, content, and more. XML Schemas serve the same purpose, but are written in the XML Schema language, and can easily be parsed and processed using the same application that was used to read the XML document. XML Schemas are also much more capable than DTDs for defining detail in your elements and attributes (such as data type, range of values, and so forth) and are therefore preferred over DTDs by many XML authors. Both can be referenced in the XML document before the first element, and both have other means of being included within an XML document (you'll see how in just a bit).

If a DTD or schema is present or is referenced in an XML document, some or all of the elements and content of the document may be validated against the DTD or schema. The primary added value of a validated XML document is that the processing application "knows" something about the content of the document, such as how many times a given element may appear within another element, what values an attribute may assume, and so on.

As mentioned previously, anyone can author an XML document, and anyone can define a DTD or XML Schema against which to validate an XML document. This being the case, the World Wide Web Consortium has made the next version of HTML into XHTML, using the existing DTD for HTML (yes, HTML has always been based on a formal DTD), with very small modifications, as the definition of all the elements, attributes, and other components allowed in an XHTML document. The main difference between HTML and XHTML is the fact that an XHTML document must conform to the XML specification, whereas HTML documents are not required to do so.

Complicating things further, browsers will display HTML documents even if they are not well-formed HTML, let alone well-formed XHTML. But browsers will display XHTML documents as XML if the file extension is `.xml`, and as regular Web pages if the file extension is `.htm` or `.html`. Of course, to display an XHTML document as a regular Web page, the reference to the XHTML DTD must be valid, and the document must be well formed. In the next few sections you'll examine a portion of the DTD for XHTML, show how the DTD can be referenced in an XHTML document, and see how it displays in the browser when the file extension is `.xml` and when it is `.htm`.

The DTD for XHTML

There are three DTDs for XHTMl,. They're located at:

❑   `www.w3.org/TR/xhtml1/DTD/xhtml1-strict.dtd`

❑   `www.w3.org/TR/xhtml1/DTD/xhtml1-transitional.dtd`

❑   `www.w3.org/TR/xhtml1/DTD/xhtml1-frameset.dtd`

These three DTDs complement their HTML counterparts, and are, in fact, quite similar. If you enter these links in your browser, you'll actually see the DTD in plain text.

Here is some code showing how a DTD (the strict version) is written for the XHTML language, but just for the image (IMG) element. The DTD for HTML is shared with XHTML (with very small differences to ensure that XHTML documents conform to the XML spec), although only XHTML actually conforms to the XML specification. What this means is that you'll find all the HTML elements and attributes present in XHTML, but if you use them in an XHTML document you must conform strictly to the rules imposed by XML (such as proper nesting and termination of elements).

```
<!--
    To avoid accessibility problems for people who aren't
    able to see the image, you should provide a text
    description using the alt and longdesc attributes.
    In addition, avoid the use of server-side image maps.
    Note that in this DTD there is no name attribute. That
    is only available in the transitional and frameset DTD.
-->

<!ELEMENT img EMPTY>
<!ATTLIST img
  %attrs;
  src           %URI;           #REQUIRED
  alt           %Text;          #REQUIRED
  longdesc      %URI;           #IMPLIED
  height        %Length;        #IMPLIED
  width         %Length;        #IMPLIED
  usemap        %URI;           #IMPLIED
  ismap         (ismap)         #IMPLIED
  >
<!-- usemap points to a map element which may be in this document
    or an external document, although the latter is not widely supported -->
```

In this example (keeping in mind that it is written in EBNF) you can see that on the first line following the comment, there is a callout for ELEMENT, and the name of the element is img, and it is EMPTY (contains no content between the non-existent beginning and ending tags). However, even though it is formally empty, its src attributes *does* contain data in the form of a URI (for our purposes the same as a URL) that specifies where the image file can be found.

Following the ELEMENT callout is a list of attributes that may be included with the img tag in an XHTML document. Those of you familiar with HTML and XHTML no doubt recognize the src attribute as the URL (or URI) that specifies the location of the image file and is REQUIRED.

So this portion of the DTD for XHTML documents specifies that it is permissible to include the IMG element in such documents. If this DTD is referenced in an XHTML document (the entire DTD, not just this portion), and the document includes the img element with an appropriate src attribute, then the document could be said to be valid (at least as far as the img element is concerned). However, if you tried to include an element name *imge* or *image* or *images*, a validating XML parser would produce an error, because according to the DTD such elements are not defined, and therefore the document is not valid. And note that although the img element does not need to be terminated in an HTML document, it must be properly terminated in an XHTML document.

Referencing DTDs and XML Schemas

To validate an XML document, there needs to be a either a reference to an external file containing the DTD or XML Schema, or the DTD or schema must be included with the XML document. Referencing XML Schemas is slightly more complex, so first take a look at how DTDs are referenced.

To reference an external DTD, a DOCTYPE declaration is used. The DOCTYPE declaration provides some information regarding how to locate the DTD and what its name is. For example, this line shows how a DTD is referenced using a URL:

```
<!DOCTYPE html
      PUBLIC "-//W3C//DTD XHTML 1.0 Strict//EN"
      "http://www.w3.org/TR/xhtml1/DTD/xhtml1-strict.dtd">
```

The html after the <!DOCTYPE in the first line signifies that the root element is named html, and is required. If the DTD is an external document, it can be located anywhere, and identified by any URI (Uniform Resource Locator) that the application reading it understands and has access to, not just a URL over the Internet.

A big limitation of DTDs is that only one external DTD can be referenced in a document, and there is no DTD support for adding prefixes to element or attribute names anyway, although you can call out a namespace for a document that references a DTD.

A namespace is a definition of the source of names for elements and attributes (so far as XML is concerned). Designating the source of an element or attribute name means that you can use the same name to represent different things within a single document. A namespace can be identified within an XML document by referencing it via a special reserved XML keyword, the xmlns (XML Namespace) attribute, like this:

```
xmlns = "http://www.w3.org/1999/xhtml"
```

This URL is the official namespace of XHTML. The element and attributes names for this namespace are defined within the XHTML DTD, and the xmlns attribute serves only to define the namespace for the root element of the XHTML document (the root element is html). Defining the namespace for the root element in this manner also serves to define the namespace for all the rest of the elements and attributes in the document.

External XML Schemas

You can reference an XML Schema by referencing the location of the XML Schema document with a URI. Typically, this is written into the XML document by putting the xmlns attribute as part of the root element and setting it to the location of the schema so that the namespace is defined and the parser also knows where to look for the XML Schema.

To reference an XML Schema, an xmlns attribute may be added to the root element of the document, as shown here:

```
<?xml version="1.0" encoding="UTF-8"?>
<customer xmlns="http://www.example.com/customer.xsd" cust_id="1">
   <cust_name>John Doe</cust_name>
</customer>
```

Of course, this implies that you have already written the XML Schema document that defines the `customer` (and its `cust_id` attribute) and `cust_name` elements, named this document `customer.xsd`, and placed the document in the root folder of the `http://www.example.com` Web site. Although this book won't get into the details of writing an XML Schema, suffice it to say that XML Schema is a much richer language for specifying elements, attributes, and other components of an XML conforming language, and because it is written according to the guidelines of the XML specification, it is easier to process as well.

For documents that can be validated against an XML Schema, any number of namespaces can be declared using the `xmlns` attribute, each associated with an external XML Schema. For example, you might have one XML Schema for which the element `farm` means an area used for agricultural purposes, and another for which the element `farm` means a number of server computers all performing the same task. If you want to create an XML document that uses both elements (for example, describing how the farm manages its IT) you need some way to distinguish between the two.

Because both XML Schemas can be referenced in a single document, you can use the `xmlns` attribute to identify them by URL, and you can create prefixes that can precede any element names from either one. For example, you might use code such as the following to do this:

```
xmlns:agri = "http://www.example.com/agricultural.xml"
xmlns:serv = "http://www.example.com/server.xml"
```

Thereafter, any element preceded by `agri:` would be defined by the agricultural schema, and any element preceded by `serv:` would be defined by the server schema. This prevents confusion about the meaning of these elements.

Writing an XML Document with XHTML

For an XHTML document, there is also a requirement to specify a namespace. Although DTDs don't lend themselves to multiple references, you can still specify one namespace, and the XHTML spec makes this a requirement.

To write an XHTML document, start by indicating the version of XML you're using, provide a DOCTYPE declaration referencing the XHTML DTD, and then insert the `xmlns` attribute indicating the namespace of the document (inserting the `xmlns` attribute into the root element makes the root element defined by the DTD, and by default all of its child elements as well). Here's an example:

```
<?xml version="1.0" encoding="UTF-8"?>
<!DOCTYPE html
     PUBLIC "-//W3C//DTD XHTML 1.0 Strict//EN"
     "http://www.w3.org/TR/xhtml1/DTD/xhtml1-strict.dtd">
<html xmlns="http://www.w3.org/1999/xhtml" xml:lang="en" lang="en">
  <HEAD>
    <title>An xhtml example</title>
  </head>
  <body>
    <p>This document is an example of an xhtml document.
       It can contain images <img src="http://www.example.com/images/image.gif
" /> as well as links <a href="http://example.com/">example.com</a> and any
other html elements.
    </p>
  </body>
</html>
```

Of course, this document looks very much like an ordinary HTML document, and will be displayed just like any Web page written in HTML in most browsers if you save it with the extension .htm or .html, but it conforms to the XML specification, and is not only well formed but also valid. (If you save it with the extension .xml, it will be displayed in XML format by Internet Explorer.)

Web Services

Another example of the power of XML is found in the design of Web services. Web Service is the name given to a unit of programmed logic that is available across the Internet, and the name XML Web Service is applied when the Web Service is accessible via XML languages for accessing such services.

So how do Web services work, and why are they valuable? Consider how you define and then call a function in a PHP program. First you write the function, giving it a name and parameter list, and adding all the processing logic required for it to do its job. Then, you can call it and expect it to perform just by naming its name and passing the appropriate parameters.

That's great, but suppose you could do the same thing across the Internet, accessing predefined functions (and thereby other data stores, including databases) by simply identifying them by their URL and name, and passing the appropriate parameters. This would mean you could build an application that theoretically is distributed (meaning it doesn't matter where the programming logic is coded or the data is stored) anywhere across the Internet.

And that is exactly what you can do with Web services. Calling a function that someone else coded, using someone else's database, or even multiple functions and multiple databases, anywhere across the Internet is what Web services are for. But you need a little bit of specialized help to access Web services, because they may run from any platform, using any language and any database, and there are some translation issues. That's where SOAP and WSDL come in:

❑ Simple Object Access Protocol (SOAP) is an XML language that provides for defining an envelope, body, and other parts to send and receive Web Service calls. You insert your Web services calls in a SOAP envelope.

❑ Web Service Description Language (WSDL) is another XML language that is used to define the name, type, and arguments associated with a call to a Web Service.

Although Web services are one of the most important uses for XML, and there are quite a few Web services-related applications available that make it easy to develop both PHP Web services and the client code that calls them, the subject is beyond the scope of this book. Please see Wrox's *Professional PHP Development* for a great deal of interesting information on this topic.

PHP and XML

There have been PHP functions available for connecting to, retrieving data from, and manipulating data in databases almost since PHP was first written. More recently, as the XML specification gained prominence as a means of exchanging and storing data, PHP has added functions that make it easier to work with XML documents.

Because of the nature and format of XML documents, much of the work on adding XML functions to PHP has centered on properly parsing XML documents, and manipulating them while remaining in conformance with the XML specification. To effectively parse and manipulate XML documents, these functions need to be able to get at and work with the names and the values of elements and attributes, as well as the many other types of XML document components.

Next, you'll explore XML functions that have been built into PHP over the years, including the most recent additions such as the simpleXML extension. XML functions that were available in PHP4 are discussed first, followed by the simpleXML extension and the Document Object Model (DOM) extension, and finally the PHP5 extensions.

PHP4 XML Functions

PHP5 maintains backward compatibility with many PHP4 features, so we'll start off this section discussing some of the PHP4 XML functions before moving on to the new XML functions available in PHP5. The XML parser functions found in PHP4 implement James Clark's expat (a parser for XML 1.0 written in the C language). Expat parsers can tell you if an XML document is well-formed, but do not validate XML documents, so parsers created using these functions must receive well-formed XML documents or an error will be generated (but fortunately you can find out where the error occurred).

Here are a few of the most common functions:

❑   xml_parser_create: This is the basic function to create an xml parser, which can then be used with the other XML functions for reading and writing data, getting errors, and a variety of other useful tasks. Use xml_parser_free to free up the resource when done.

❑   xml_parse_into_struct: Parse XML data into an array structure. You can use this function to take the contents of a well-formed XML file, turn it into a PHP array, and then work with the contents of the array.

❑   xml_get_error_code: Gets XML parser error code (defined as constants, such as XML_ERROR_NONE and XML_ERROR_SYNTAX). Use xml_error_string to get the textual description of the error based on the error code.

❑   xml_set_option: There are several options that can be set for an xml parser: XML_OPTION_CASE_FOLDING and XML_OPTION_TARGET_ENCODING. The case folding option is enabled by default, and means that element names will be made uppercase unless it is disabled. Target encoding enables you to specify which encoding is used for the target; the default is the encoding used by xml_parser_create, which in turn is ISO-8859-1. Use xml_parser_get_option to find out what options are currently set for an xml parser.

There are also a number of other xml parser-related functions for setting up handlers of various types (for common xml components, such as processing instructions, character data, and so on).

Try It Out   **Create an XML Document**

In this example, you use ordinary strings and PHP string-handling functions to create an XML document. Interestingly, this works (in a very crude way) without any PHP XML functions at all. You'll capture input for names and values of several elements and attributes, and then use the data to create an XML document, then store it as a file. The drawback, of course, is that you have very little capability to create or work with a document of arbitrary complexity; we can only have two elements with two attributes each, and no validation. But, sometimes, all you need to do is output a little bit of XML, and as we demonstrate here you can do it without any XML functions.

To make this example work, you need to create a subfolder (under your Web folder containing this file) named xml_files. You'll store the XML files you create and read from in there (be sure to properly specify your default directory, $default_dir, if it differs from the example's). Start your HTML editor and enter the following code, saving it as php_xml.php:

```
<html>
<head>
<title>PHP XML Functions</title>
<meta http-equiv="Content-Type" content="text/html; charset=iso-8859-1">
</head>
<body bgcolor="#FFFFFF">
<form method="POST" action="php_xml.php">
<input type="hidden" name="posted" value="true">
<table width="100%" border="1" cellpadding="10">
  <tr><td><h2>Using PHP XML Capabilities</h2>
<?php
if (isset($_POST['posted'])) {
    $cmdButton = $_POST['cmdButton'];
    $root_element_name = $_POST['root_element_name'];
    $element01_name = $_POST['element01_name'];
    $att0101_name = $_POST['att0101_name'];
    $att0101_value = $_POST['att0101_value'];
    $att0102_name = $_POST['att0102_name'];
    $att0102_value = $_POST['att0102_value'];
    $element0101_name = $_POST['element0101_name'];
    $att010101_name = $_POST['att010101_name'];
    $att010101_value = $_POST[att010101_value];
    $att010102_name = $_POST['att010102_name'];
    $att010102_value = $_POST['att010102_value'];
    switch ($cmdButton) {
        case "Create XML Document";
            //format an xml document
            $xml_dec = "<?xml version=\"1.0\" encoding=\"UTF-8\"?>";
            $doc_type_dec = "";
            $root_element_start = "<" . $root_element_name . ">";
            $root_element_end = "</" . $root_element_name . ">";
            $xml_doc = $xml_dec;
            $xml_doc .= $doc_type_dec;
            $xml_doc .= $root_element_start;
            $xml_doc .= "<" . $element01_name . " "
              . $att0101_name . "=" . "'" . $att0101_value . "'" . " "
              . $att0102_name . "=" . "'" . $att0102_value . "'" . ">";
            $xml_doc .= "<" . $element0101_name . " "
              . $att010101_name . "=" . "'" . $att010101_value . "'" . " "
              . $att010102_name . "=" . "'". $att010102_value . "'" . ">";
            $xml_doc .= "</" . $element0101_name . ">";
            $xml_doc .= "</" . $element01_name . ">";
            $xml_doc .= $root_element_end;
            //open a file and copy the xml text into it, then close it
            $default_dir = "/Inetpub/wwwroot/beginning_php5/ch08/xml_files";
            $fp = fopen($default_dir . "/" . $_POST['xml_file_name'] . ".xml", w);
```

```
                $write = fwrite($fp, $xml_doc);
                $response_message = "XML document created";
                break;
            default;
                break;
        }
    }
?>

<table width="100%" border="1"><tr>
    <td><font face="Arial, Helvetica, sans-serif" size="-1">
    <b>Create a Well-formed XML Document</b></font></td>
    </tr><tr><td><table width="100%" border="1"><tr>
    <td colspan="3"><font size="-1"><b><font face="Arial, Helvetica,
    sans-serif">Response =
    <?php echo $response_message; ?></font></b></font></td>
    </tr><tr>
    <td><font size="-1"><b><font face="Arial, Helvetica,
    sans-serif">Element or Attribute</font></b></font></td>
    <td><font size="-1"><b><font face="Arial, Helvetica,
    sans-serif">Name</font></b></font></td>
    <td><font size="-1"><b><font face="Arial, Helvetica,
    sans-serif">Value</font></b></font></td>
    </tr><tr>
    <td><font size="-1"><b><font face="Arial, Helvetica,
    sans-serif">Root Element:</font></b></font></td>
    <td><input type="text" name="root_element_name">
    </td><td> </td></tr><tr>
    <td><font size="-1"><b><font face="Arial, Helvetica,
    sans-serif">Element01:</font></b></font></td>
    <td><input type="text" name="element01_name">
    </td><td> </td></tr><tr>
    <td><font size="-1"><b><font face="Arial, Helvetica,
    sans-serif">Attribute0101:</font></b></font></td>
    <td><input type="text" name="att0101_name">
    </td><td><input type="text" name="att0101_value">
    </td></tr><tr>
    <td><font size="-1"><b><font face="Arial, Helvetica,
    sans-serif">Attribute0102:</font></b></font></td>
    <td><input type="text" name="att0102_name">
    </td><td><input type="text" name="att0102_value">
    </td></tr><tr><td>
    <font size="-1"><b><font face="Arial, Helvetica, sans-serif">Element0101:
    </font></b></font></td>
    <td><input type="text" name="element0101_name">
    </td><td> </td></tr><tr>
    <td><font size="-1"><b><font face="Arial, Helvetica,
    sans-serif">Attribute010101:</font></b></font></td>
    <td><input type="text" name="att010101_name">
    </td><td><input type="text" name="att010101_value">
    </td></tr><tr>
    <td><font size="-1"><b><font face="Arial, Helvetica,
    sans-serif">Attribute010102:</font></b></font></td>
    <td><input type="text" name="att010102_name">
```

```
    </td><td><input type="text" name="att010102_value">
    </td></tr><tr>
    <td><b><font face="arial, Helvetica, sans-serif">
    Current XML Files</font></b><hr>

    <?php
        $default_dir = "/Inetpub/wwwroot/beginning_php5/ch08/xml_files";
        if (!($dp = opendir($default_dir))) {
            die("Cannot open $default_dir.");
        }
        while ($file = readdir($dp)) {
            if ($file != '.' && $file != '..') {
                echo "$file<HR>";
            }
        }
        closedir($dp);
    ?>
    <font size="-1"><b><font face="Arial, Helvetica, sans-serif">Name
    of new XML Document File:</font></b></font>
    </td><td colspan="2" valign="bottom">
    <input type="text" name="xml_file_name" size="30">
    </td></tr><tr><td> </td>
    <td colspan="2">
    <input type="submit" name="cmdButton" value="Create XML Document">
    </td></tr></table></td></tr>  </table>
    </td></tr></table>
</form>
</body>
</html>
```

Once you've saved the file as php_xml.php, run it, and use the form (see Figure 8-1) to create a well-formed XML document.

first_xml.xml is the name of the first XML document created with this form. If you use the same element names and values, first_xml.xml will have the following contents once it is created:

```
<?xml version="1.0" encoding="UTF-8"?><root_element><element01 att0101="att one
val" att0102="att two val"><element0101 att010101="att one one val" att010102=
"att one two val"></element0101></element01></root_element>
```

Open the .xml file (first_xml.xml or whatever you named it). Your result should be something like Figure 8-2 if your browser can parse XML.

How It Works

This is a standard Web page made from HTML. It displays a table with a form that enables the user to enter names and values for a fixed set of XML elements and attributes. When the form is submitted, the isset() function allows us to determine that fact, and the code runs. After capturing the values from

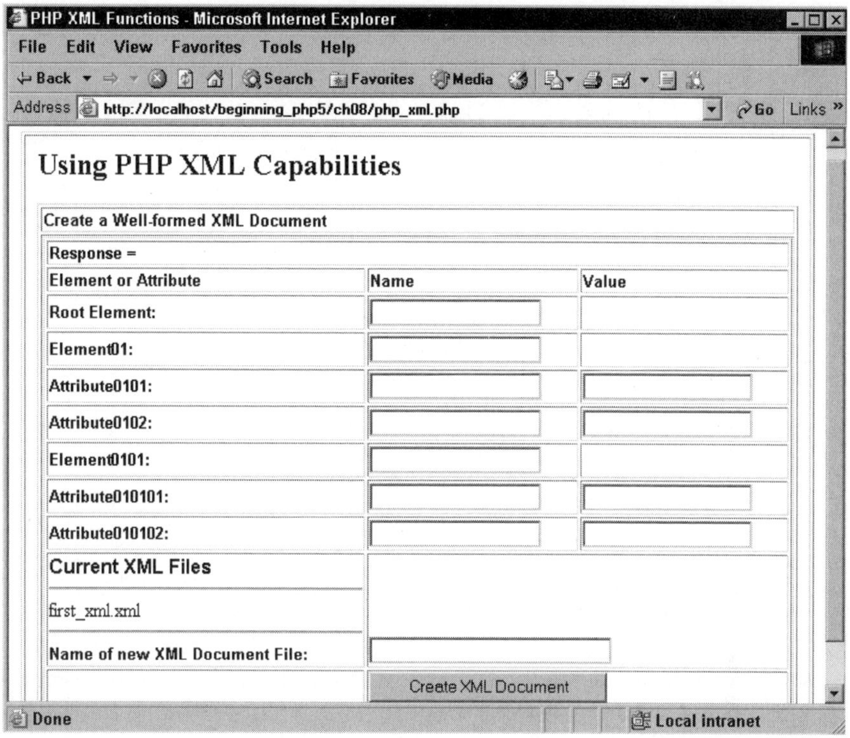

Figure 8-1

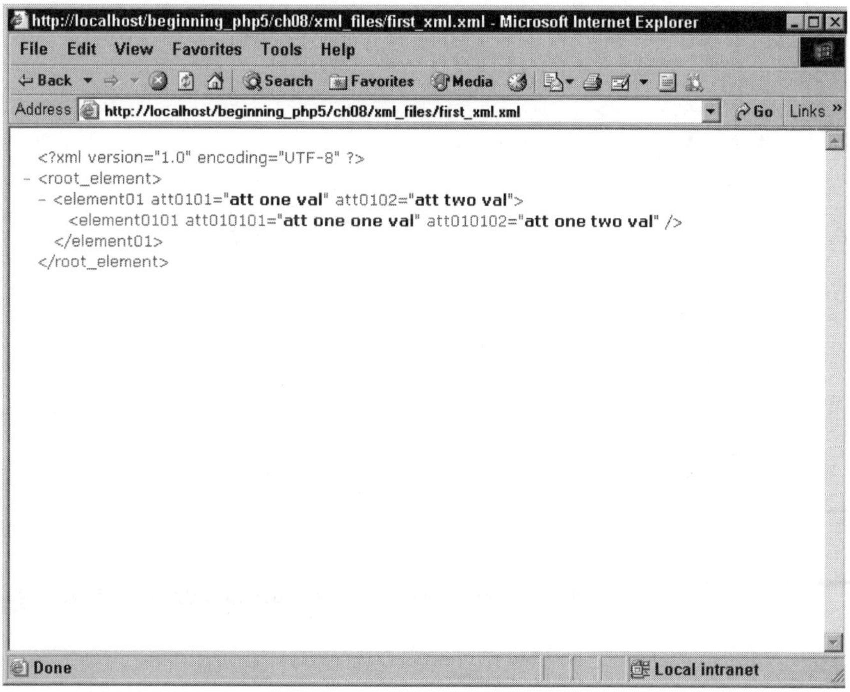

Figure 8-2

the $_POST variable, a `switch case` block is then used to decide which block of code to run. Although there's only one choice in the `switch case` block now, it's there so you can add more choices to it later if you want:

```php
<?php
if (isset($_POST['posted'])) {
    $cmdButton = $_POST['cmdButton'];
    $root_element_name = $_POST['root_element_name'];
    $element01_name = $_POST['element01_name'];
    $att0101_name = $_POST['att0101_name'];
    $att0101_value = $_POST['att0101_value'];
    $att0102_name = $_POST['att0102_name'];
    $att0102_value = $_POST['att0102_value'];
    $element0101_name = $_POST['element0101_name'];
    $att010101_name = $_POST['att010101_name'];
    $att010101_value = $_POST['att010101_value'];
    $att010102_name = $_POST['att010102_name'];
    $att010102_value = $_POST['att010102_value'];
    switch ($cmdButton) {
        case "Create XML Document";
```

For this example the code block formats the data provided by the user into a string containing all the proper components of a well-formed XML document:

```php
//format an xml document
            $xml_dec = "<?xml version=\"1.0\" encoding=\"UTF-8\"?>\n";
            $doc_type_dec = " ";
            $root_element_start = "<" . $root_element_name . ">";
            $root_element_end = "</" . $root_element_name . ">";

            $xml_doc = $xml_dec . "\n";
            $xml_doc .= $doc_type_dec . "\n";
            $xml_doc .= $root_element_start . "\n";
            $xml_doc .= "<" . $element01_name . " "
              . $att0101_name . "=" . "'" . $att0101_value . "'" . " "
              . $att0102_name . "=" . "'" . $att0102_value . "'" . ">" . "\n";
            $xml_doc .= "<" . $element0101_name . " "
              . $att010101_name . "=" . "'" . $att010101_value . "'" . " "
              . $att010102_name . "=" . "'" . $att010102_value . "'" . ">" . "\n";
            $xml_doc .= "</" . $element0101_name . ">\n";
            $xml_doc .= "</" . $element01_name . ">\n";
            $xml_doc .= $root_element_end;
```

Next, a file is opened and the XML document is written to the file (you need to properly specify the default directory, and yours may differ from this example's):

```php
                //open a file and copy the xml text into it, then close it
                $default_dir = "/Inetpub/wwwroot/beginning_php5/ch08/xml_files";
                $fp = fopen($default_dir . "/" . $_POST['xml_file_name'] . ".xml", w);
                $write = fwrite($fp, $xml_doc);
```

Finally, a response is created and the code block ends with a break:

```
$response_message = "XML document created";
break;
```

XML Parsers

Now you've seen how to create an XML document using nothing more than ordinary PHP string functions, but it should be clear that these functions provide no easy way to manipulate your XML document. You could write some regular expressions and special functions of your own to make the job easier, but of course, the authors of PHP realized that and came up with some for you.

The next example demonstrates the use of the xml_parser_create() and xml_parse_into_struct() functions. It also uses the file_get_contents() function to retrieve the contents of a file and turn it into a string.

Try It Out   **Read an XML Document**

For this example, we'll make a copy of the php_xml.php file and name it php_xml02.php. Then we'll copy a new Switch Case block in, and a new table for displaying the results.

1.   Make a copy of php_xml.php, save the copy as php_xml02.php, and open it in your HTML editor.

2.   Enter the following code:

```
if (isset($_POST[posted])) {

    $xml_file_chosen = $_POST[xml_file_chosen];
    $cmdButton = $_POST[cmdButton];

    switch ($cmdButton) {
```

3.   Cut this code and paste it in place of the old section beginning with if (isset and ending with switch ($cmdButton).

4.   Now enter the following code and cut and paste it over the old case section:

```
case "Parse an XML Document";

    //find the file specified
    $default_dir = "/Inetpub/wwwroot/beginning_php5/ch08/xml_files";
    $xml_string = file_get_contents
    ($default_dir . "/" . $xml_file_chosen,"rb");

    // Read our existing data and turn it into arrays
    $xp = xml_parser_create();
    xml_parse_into_struct($xp, $xml_string, $values, $keys);
    xml_parser_free($xp);

    break;
```

5. Create the following HTML table and then cut and paste it over the old table:

```
<table width="100%" border="1">
    <tr><td><font face="Arial, Helvetica, sans-serif" size="-1">
<b>Parse an XML Document</b></font></td></tr><tr><td>
    <table width="100%" border="1"><tr><td>
    <font face="Arial, Helvetica, sans-serif" size="-1">
<b>Choose XML File</b></font></td></td>
    <td><select name="xml_file_chosen">

        <?php
        $default_dir = "/Inetpub/wwwroot/beginning_php5/ch08/xml_files";
        if (!($dp = opendir($default_dir))) {
            die("Cannot open $default_dir.");
        }
        while ($file = readdir($dp)) {
            if ($file != '.' && $file != '..') {
                echo "<option value='$file'>$file</option>\n";
            }
        }
        closedir($dp);
        ?>

    </select></td></tr><tr>
    <td><font face="Arial, Helvetica, sans-serif" size="-1">
    <b>XML File Contents</b></font><hr>

    <?php
    if ($cmdButton == "Parse an XML Document") {
        echo "Keys array<BR><BR><PRE>";
        print_r($keys);
        echo "</PRE><BR><BR>Values array<BR><BR><PRE>";
        print_r($values);
        echo "</PRE>";
    }
    ?>

</td><td>
<input type="submit" name="cmdButton" value="Parse an XML Document">
</td></tr></table>
</td></tr></table>
```

6. Save the file, and then give it a try. Remember to change the form's action attribute to the new filename, php_xml02.php. You should see the XML file you created using the original php_xml.php script listed in the drop-down box (and others, if you created several). Select it and click the Submit button. Figure 8-3 shows the Keys and Values arrays that should print to your screen.

How It Works

The code starts the `case` block by finding the file you've selected, and then opens the file and reads it as a string into the variable $xml_string. Next, it uses the xml_parser_create function to make a new parser object (named $xp), and the xml_parse_into_struct() function to turn the XML document into a set of arrays, one for the keys and one for the values.

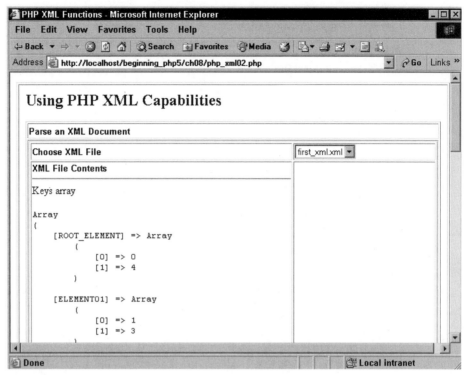

Figure 8-3

As you can see, the arguments the xml_parse_into_struct() function takes the xml parser (stored in a variable named $xp), the string variable (containing the XML document as a string), and the names of the two arrays you want to create:

```
//find the file specified
$default_dir = "/Inetpub/wwwroot/beginning_php5/ch08/xml_files";
$xml_string = file_get_contents($default_dir . "/" . $xml_file_chosen,"rb");

// Read our existing data and turn it into arrays
$xp = xml_parser_create();
xml_parse_into_struct($xp, $xml_string, $values, $keys);
xml_parser_free($xp);
break;
```

The code for the HTML table simply provides a means of choosing the .xml file to parse. Then, if the button has been clicked, it uses the print_r() function to print the two array structures to the screen. It's the HTML <PRE> tags that make the data display nicely:

```
<table width="100%" border="1">
   <tr><td><font face="Arial, Helvetica, sans-serif" size="-1">
<b>Parse an XML Document</b></font></td></tr><tr><td>
   <table width="100%" border="1"><tr><td>
     <font face="Arial, Helvetica, sans-serif" size="-1">
```

```
   <b>Choose XML File</B></font></td></td>
     <td><select name="xml_file_chosen">

         <?php
         $default_dir = "/Inetpub/wwwroot/beginning_php5/ch08/xml_files";
         if (!($dp = opendir($default_dir))) {
             die("Cannot open $default_dir.");
         }
         while ($file = readdir($dp)) {
             if ($file != '.' && $file != '..') {
                 echo "<option value='$file'>$file</option>\n";
             }
         }
         closedir($dp);
         ?>

     </select></td></tr><tr>
     <td><font face="Arial, Helvetica, sans-serif" size="-1">
     <b>XML File Contents</b></font><hr>

         <?php
         if ($cmdButton == "Parse an XML Document") {
             echo "Keys array<BR><BR><PRE>";
             print_r($keys);
             echo "</PRE><BR><BR>Values array<BR><BR><PRE>";
             print_r($values);
             echo "</PRE>";
         }
         ?>

   </td><td>
   <input type="submit" name="cmdButton" value="Parse an XML Document">
   </td></tr></table>
   </td></tr></table>
```

The Document Object Model

The Document Object Model (DOM) is simply a hierarchical model for interacting with documents. It enables access to the parts of a document by addressing them directly via their lineage in the document.

You can model XML documents with the DOM because there is a specific relationship among the parts of any XML document. As you've seen, there can be only one root element, and it is the parent of all the rest of the elements in an XML document. This means that the root element is at the bottom (hence the name) of the hierarchy or tree from which the rest of the elements spring. Therefore, the relationship between the components of an XML document can be inferred programmatically (and that's just what the PHP DOM extension functions do; we'll talk about this more in just a bit).

For any given element, elements inside it are its children (or child elements), whereas the element it is inside of is its parent (or parent element). So you can think of elements as parents and children, or you can think of elements as being like a tree, with root, branches, and leaves. Within the DOM, both ways of thinking about XML document components are valid. Elements and other components of an XML document are considered to be *nodes* within the DOM.

The DOM Extension

The DOM extension follows the Worldwide Web Consortium's DOM Level 2 recommendation closely. This recommendation states, "the DOM is an application programming interface (API) for valid HTML and well-formed XML documents." With the DOM, any well-formed XML document can be programmatically built, navigated, and nodes added, edited, and deleted.

Configuring PHP with `with-dom=dom_dir` makes this extension available. For PHP on Windows, copy `libxml2.dll` or `iconv.dll` to the System32 folder. So please see the documentation for further instructions.

Support for any DOM extension functions is still experimental (which is why there are no examples in this book), but you can refer to *Professional PHP Programming* (Wrox) for a more in-depth explanation of the PHP DOM extension.

Using the PHP DOM Extension Functions

PHP's DOM functions include `domxml_new_doc()` to create new XML documents, `domxml_open_file()` to open an XML document file as a DOM object, and `domxml_open_mem()` to create a DOM object from an XML document already in memory. These functions return a DOM object, not a string or other common data type. When you use the PHP DOM extension functions, you typically first create a `DOMDocument` object and then manipulate it using functions that are part of the class of that object. There are a number of object classes available, and by starting with a `DOMDocument` object, you can then examine it and retrieve new objects reflecting XML document components such as elements, attributes, and so on.

For example, to open the XML file created earlier, you might use code like this to create a DOM object named $my_dom_obj:

```
$my_dom_obj = domxml_open_file("first_xml.xml");
```

Then, to create a variable representing the root element found within the document, you might use code like this:

```
$the_root_element = $dom->document_element();
```

You can also manipulate the DOM object you've created with quite a few other PHP DOM functions, including `create_element()`, which creates a new element, and `append_child()`, which appends an element as a child of an existing element.

If you want to find a particular element in an XML document that has been arranged by the DOM, for example, you could use the `get_element_by_tagname` function of the `DOMElement` object to find that element as a node in the DOM, and it would be found as a child node within the hierarchy of root, branch, leaf in the DOM.

There are many other classes of objects available in the PHP DOM extension, as well as quite a few functions for using them to create and manipulate XML documents. Their object-oriented nature makes them more suitable for a book such as *Professional PHP Programming*, to which you can refer for further information about the DOM and PHP.

PHP5 XML Functions

PHP4 included some basic XML parsing features, but PHP5 contains many new features and functions based on libxml2. Support for simpleXML in PHP5 is automatically turned on; there is no need to include any additional extensions. PHP5 also supports XML document validation when referencing a DTD or an XML Schema.

The SimpleXML Extension

The simpleXML extension is also experimental, but has been completely overhauled in PHP5. This extension is installed by default, with –enable–simplexml. It includes functions for working with XML documents that make common operations fairly easy, such as the ability to take a string and convert it to an XMLformatted document and display it. The primary advantage is that the XML document becomes an object that can be processed like other objects in PHP, with elements, attributes, and their data accessible using normal object operations (don't worry if you don't understand much about objects yet; they're discussed in greater detail in later chapters).

The functions include:

❑ simplexml_load_file: takes a file path as an argument, and if the contents of the file are well-formed XML will load the contents as an object.

❑ simplexml_load_string: takes a string as an argument, and the string should be well-formed XML. Converts the string to an object.

❑ simplexml_import_dom: takes a node from a DOM document and turns it into a simplexml node.

❑ simplexml_element->asXML: returns a well-formed XML string from a simpleXML object.

❑ simplexml_element->attributes: provides the attributes and values defines within a well-formed string of XML.

❑ simplexml_element->children: method provides the child elements of an element.

❑ simplexml_element->xpath: method runs an XPath query on a simpleXML node.

Using simplexml_load_string()

You can write out (or get as a result from an expression or function) a string that is formatted as well-formed XML within a PHP program. Once you have the string, you can turn it into a simpleXML object using the simplexml_load_string() function. To turn a string named $string into a simpleXML object based on a string of XML inside your PHP program, just do something like this:

```
<?php
$string = <<<XML
<?xml version='1.0'?>
<root_element>
  <child01>My first element</child01>
  <child02>My second element</child02>
</root_element>
XML;
$xml_string = simplexml_load_string($string);
?>
```

Try reading an XML string with the `simplexml_load_string` function first. All you need to do is supply a string to the function. And once you have your simpleXML object, you can use the object's `asXML()` function to display it as properly formatted XML.

Here's an example of using the `simplexml_load_string` and `simplexml_element`'s `asXML` method. Open your text editor and create a `.php` document containing the following code:

```php
<?php
//The asXML method formats the parent object's data in XML version 1.0.
//create an XML formatted string
$my_xml_string = <<<XML
<a>
  <b>
    <c>text content</c>
    <c>more text content</c>
  </b>
  <d>
    <c>even more text content</c>
  </d>
</a>
XML;

//load the string into an object
$xml_object = simplexml_load_string($my_xml_string);
//display the contents of the xml object
echo $xml_object->asXML();
?>
```

Save this document as `create_xml_doc.php`, and then open it in your browser. Figure 8-4 shows the result.

Using simplxml_load_file()

Alternatively, if your XML happens to be in a file, you can turn the contents of the file into a simpleXML object using the `simplexml_load_file()` function. Whichever way you come up with your simpleXML object, it can be manipulated in the same way with the other simpleXML functions.

To simplify things, an external file is used to contain the XML strings, and read them with the `simplexml_load_file()` function. For example, if you want to read an XML file such as the one you created in the very beginning of the chapter, you can use the `simplexml_load_file()` function. Here's the XML file again (save it as `php_programs.xml`):

```xml
<?xml version="1.0" ?>
<php_programs>
    <program name="cart">
       <price>100</price>
    </program>
    <program name="survey">
       <price>500</price>
    </program>
</php_programs>
```

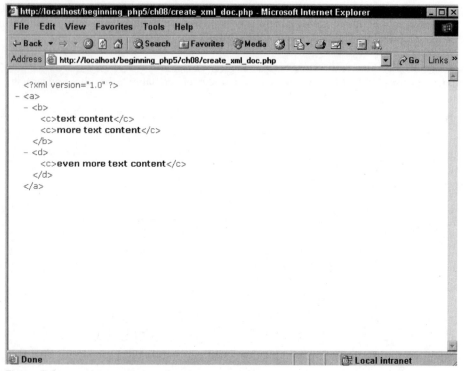

Figure 8-4

To read the names and values of the elements and attributes in this XML document, use the simpleXML function for loading a file: `simplexml_load_file()`. Just begin a PHP document (name this one `simplexml_01.php`), and then set a variable to the result of the `simplexml_load_file()` function, like this:

```php
<?php
$php_programs = simplexml_load_file('php_programs.xml');
```

The variable contains an object that can be used much like an ordinary array. To get the names and values from the variable, use the `foreach` statement to return keys and values, just like with an ordinary array:

```php
foreach ($php_programs->program as $program_key => $program_val) {
echo "The root element <B>php_programs</B> contains an element named
<B>$program_key</B><BR>";
```

But we can't directly echo out the contents of the `$program_val` variable; it contains an array-like object as well, and we must therefore use a `foreach` statement on it as well, both for its child elements and its attributes, like this:

```php
foreach($program_val->children() as $child_of_program_key =>
$child_of_program_val)
```

```
{
    if ($child_of_program_key == "price") {
        foreach($program_val->attributes() as $att => $val) {
            if ($att == "name") {
                foreach($program_val->price as $the_price) {
                    echo "This <B>$program_key</B>
                    element has an attribute named <B>$att</B> and is named
                    <B>$val</B>.<BR>";
                    echo "This <B>$program_key</B>
                    element has a child element named <B>$child_of_program_key</B>
                    and the value of <B>$child_of_program_key</B> is
                    <B>$the_price</B>.<BR>";
                    echo "Therefore, we can say that the <B>$child_of_program_key</B>
                    of the <B>$val</B> <B>$program_key</B> is
                    <B>\$$the_price</B>.<BR><BR>";
                }
            }
        }
    }
}
?>
```

The result in your browser should look like Figure 8-5.

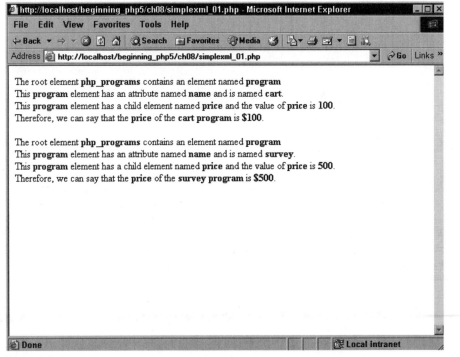

Figure 8-5

Changing a Value with simpleXML

Not only can you read the parts of an XML document into a simpleXML object, you can also change data in the in-memory document. All you need to do is properly address the data you want to change, and then set it equal to the value you want it to have, as you'll see in the following example.

Try It Out   **Change the Value of a Node**

Create a new file, save it as `simplexml_change_value.php`, and enter the following code into it:

```php
<?php
$xmlstr = <<<XML
<php_programs>
    <program name="cart">
        <price>100</price>
    </program>
    <program name="survey">
        <price>500</price>
    </program>
</php_programs>
XML;

$first_xml_string = simplexml_load_string($xmlstr);
$first_xml_string->program[0]->price = '250';

echo "<PRE>";
var_dump($first_xml_string);
echo "</PRE>";
?>
```

Save the file and then run the script. Figure 8-6 shows the result.

How It Works

After you read in the XML string to the variable named `$xmlstr`, you can address the parts of the document in almost the same way as if it were an array, using array-style names and index numbers for each level. You know from the string you read in that `program` and `price` are elements, and that the first price encountered should be 100, but in the second line of code shown here, that value is reset to 250, and then the contents are dumped to the screen using the `var_dump` function (`var_dump` is a utility function in PHP for displaying the structure and data in PHP variables, no matter what kind they are). Notice we use the HTML `<PRE>` tags to maintain formatting of the dumped data.

```php
$first_xml_string = simplexml_load_string($xmlstr);
$first_xml_string->program[0]->price = '250';
echo "<PRE>";
var_dump($first_xml_string);
echo "</PRE>";
```

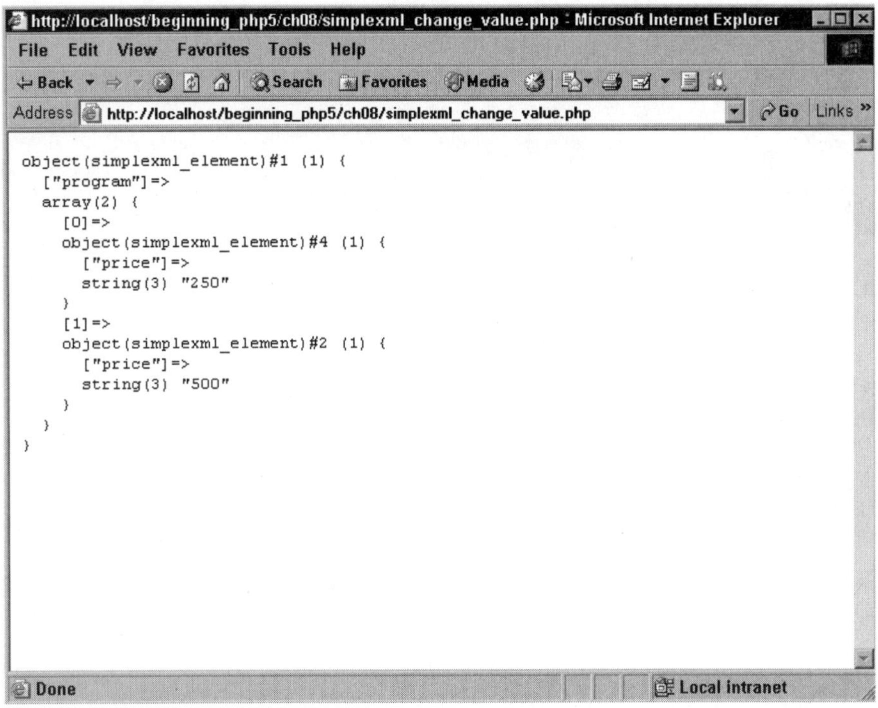

Figure 8-6

Try It Out   Import a DOM with simpleXML

One of the nice things about simpleXML is how easy it is to get DOM objects into it, and vice versa. Create a new file and save it as simplexml_dom.php, with the following code:

```php
<?php
$xmlstr = <<<XML
<php_programs>
    <program name="cart">
        <price>100</price>
    </program>
    <program name="survey">
        <price>500</price>
    </program>
</php_programs>
XML;

$dom = new domDocument;
$dom->loadXML($xmlstr);
$s_dom = simplexml_import_dom($dom);

echo "The price of the first program is <B>$"
. $s_dom->program[0]->price . "</B>";
?>
```

Save the file and then run it. Figure 8-7 shows the result.

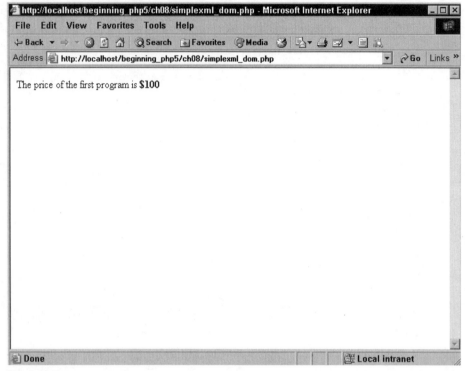

Figure 8-7

How It Works

In this example you first create a new XML document from the domDocument class by using the new keyword (more on creating object with the new keyword in the chapters about objects), and then you pull your XML string into the DOMDocument object using the loadXML function of the object. Finally, you echo out the contents of interest to you.

```
$dom = new domDocument;
$dom->loadXML($xmlstr);
$s_dom = simplexml_import_dom($dom);
echo "The price of the first program is <B>$"
. $s_dom->program[0]->price . "</B>";
```

Summary

In this chapter you explored the basics of XML, including the rules by which an XML document is determined to be well formed and valid. You examined Document Type Definitions (DTDs) written in Extended Backus Naur Format (EBNF) and how they can be referenced to validate an XML document. Namespace support in XML, and how multiple XML Schema documents can be referenced within an XML document were also topics of this chapter,

You checked out the Document Object Model, the hierarchical model of XML document structure, and reviewed some PHP functions related to the DOM. You also looked at some of the older XML Parser functions in PHP4, and the newer simpleXML extension as it appears in PHP5.

You created examples to make and read XML documents, work with XML documents using the simpleXML functions, and go from simpleXML to DOM functions. Although you haven't explored all of the object-oriented functions found in simpleXML and the DOM extension, you've found ways to effectively create and manipulate XML documents and many of their components.

Exercise

Create an application that reads an XML file with multiple elements and attributes into a simpleXML object, changes the values of some or all of its elements or attributes, and then returns the modified document back into the file.

An Introduction to Databases and SQL

You've spent the last couple of chapters seeing how your PHP scripts can use external files to store and retrieve data. Although direct file access does a great job in many circumstances, it's pretty limited as data storage solutions go—what you see is what you get, no more, no less. Any sifting, sorting, or other work that has to be done on the data ultimately falls to you and your scripts, and the more data there is to handle, the longer it takes the script to deal with it. This might not present much of a problem when you're dealing with a few kilobytes of data, but who's to say when those kilobytes will grow into megabytes (or even gigabytes) of data. If you're actively setting out to build a successful, popular, data-driven Web site, you really have to allow for that volume possibility.

Just think—if a large commercial site such as Amazon accessed all its data directly from plain text files, it could take you months just to track down a single book, let alone place an order!

Databases are specifically designed to get around this problem. With their own special capabilities of organization and immaculate record keeping, you can almost imagine them as the super-hero staffed lending libraries of the IT world. No more searching for hours through shelves of musty tomes; just a word at the front desk, a blur of blue and red, and the last remaining copy of *Love in the Time of Cholera* appears—as if by magic—on the desk in front of you.

This is the first in a series of three chapters in which you'll explore databases and learn how you can use them to start creating powerful, efficient (and potentially very large) PHP applications. You'll examine the general advantages of using databases rather than files to store your data. You'll also learn about some of the popular databases that you're likely to come across, and how they differ.

Relational databases will be explained, and you'll explore related concepts such as normalization and indexing. You'll see how to set up MySQL, a database system that's freely available and widely used with PHP, and learn some PHP functions for connecting to a database in MySQL as well as how to use MySQL to retrieve and modify the contents of a database.

There's a lot of ground to cover in this chapter, so you may find it's a little heavier on theory than most. It won't all be brain strain, but the practical element involves getting a database up and running on your test machine, and that will be a lot easier if you already understand what's needed. For that reason, PHP itself takes something of a back seat until the last few sections, when you hook

PHP up to your working database in preparation for the next two chapters. If you're someone who's already familiar with databases and how they work, you may want to skip straight on to that—otherwise, it all starts right here!

Storing Data

Whenever you start work on a data-driven application, one of the first design decisions you have to make is this: what's the best data store to use? In other words, how and where is the application going to store and access its data. The correct choice is always going to depend on the application's requirements. At the simplest level, you should be asking questions like:

- ❑ How much data will the application use?
- ❑ How often will it need access to the data?
- ❑ How often will it need to modify the data?
- ❑ How many users are likely to want access to the data at once?
- ❑ How will the data grow over time?
- ❑ How much do I stand to lose if the data is broken, stolen, or lost?

If the answer to any of these questions is "a lot," then you probably want to steer clear of using plain text files to store your data.

> *That's not to say that text files are useless—for instance, when visitors attempt to enter a password-protected area, an Apache Web server (unless configured otherwise) authenticates them against a plain text file containing a complete list of user IDs and passwords. This isn't a problem as long as it's dealing with a small group of users, but if it has to validate hundreds at the same time, it must scan the text file one line at a time until it finds a match. One unlucky user would have to wait for Apache to find his details on the last line of the file before it let him enter the password-protected area, and that could cost quite some time.*

Often, the most efficient alternative is to use a database engine—or to use its more technical name, a Database Management System (DBMS)—to store, retrieve, and modify the data for you. A good database engine really just serves as a very, very smart go-between for you and your data. It organizes, catalogs, backs up, and a whole lot more besides, all with a view toward making that data quicker and easier to work with.

So where does all the data go? Well, it depends to some extent on the database engine you're using. Chances are, though, it'll end up being stored as streams of bits and bytes in a number of files—yes, files! Truth is you can't really get away from using files at some point. The trick is in finding ways to use them as efficiently as possible, and a good database engine has many, many such tricks up its metaphorical sleeves.

Databases and Databases

At this point it's worth taking a moment to look at exactly what the word database refers to. Strictly speaking, a database is just an efficiently organized collection of data, just as a library is really no more than an ordered collection of books. However, everyone tends to use the word library to refer to the institution as a whole—not just the books, but the staff, its working practices, and the building, too—and the same is true of databases. So, when you hear someone talk about a database, he's more than likely referring to the whole caboodle: the database engine *and* the data.

This isn't so surprising because under normal circumstances the only contact you ever have with the raw data is through the DBMS, or database engine to be slightly less formal. Most of the time you never see the join, so there's no real practical distinction. Later we discuss installing the database, connecting to the database, talking to the database, and so on—just remember that we're using the word in its more common, all-encompassing sense.

Database Architectures

Before we get going here, you need to settle on a particular database with which to experiment, and that means first deciding on the type of database architecture you're going to use. There are two main options: embedded and client/server. Let's take a quick look at both.

Embedded Databases

An embedded database runs—and stores its data—on the same machine as the program that wants to use it (PHP in this case). The database is not networked, and only one program can connect to it at any given time. Moreover, the database can't be shared between different machines because each one would simply end up storing and manipulating its own separate version of the data. It's analogous to having your own personal library, staff and all, to which you have exclusive access. For smaller applications there can often be advantages to using an embedded database. For larger systems, the advantages provided by the larger Relational Database Management Systems (RDBMS) tip the scales in their favor and as a result, most commercial enterprises use client/server database architectures.

Long-standing, popular examples of embedded database engines include dBase and DBM, and PHP provides connectivity to both. A more recent addition to the fold is SQLite, which is not just available as a PHP5 extension, but is actually bundled as part of the PHP5 download. For that reason alone it's well worth a look, and some impressive performance stats certainly help back up its placement as the rising star of PHP database technologies. You can learn more about SQLite in Appendix C, *Using SQLite*.

Client/Server Databases

Client/server databases are designed for use over networks, enabling multiple users (who may be scattered across a whole host of different locations) to work simultaneously with the same data. The database (the term database is also often used as shorthand for Database Management System, or DBMS) itself acts as a server, not unlike the Web servers discussed in the opening chapters. In principle it can field requests from just about anywhere with a network connection and a suitable client program. That said, there's no reason why you can't run both on the same machine.

Client/server databases are more closely analogous to the earlier metaphor of the public lending library. It's open to anyone who has a membership card (is registered with the library) and, with several staff members on the reception desk, can deal with requests from a number of visitors at once. The visitors may be there in person, or may call in on the telephone.

The actual job of finding or returning a book to the shelf might then be delegated to an assistant, but visitors don't need to worry about that. Each receptionist may have to deal with several visitors at once, but if he's good at his job, he'll spend a reasonable amount of time on each, and all visitors feel that they're getting good service. Likewise, when several users access a client/server database engine at the same time, the engine regularly switches its attention among them, giving each one the sense that she's being attended to all the while.

This is the kind of database you're more likely to find being used in a large company, where large quantities of data need to be shared among large numbers of people, where access may be needed from all sorts of different locations, and where having a single centralized data store makes important jobs like administration and backup relatively straightforward. Any applications that need to access the database use specialized, lightweight client programs to communicate with the server.

RDBMSs (Relational Database Management Systems) are often expensive and complex to set up and administer. The widely acknowledged big three in this field are Oracle, DB/2 (from IBM), and SQL Server (from Microsoft). All three are massive, feature-rich systems, seemingly capable of just about any kind of data storage and processing that a modern business could need. The flip side of the coin is that these systems are big and expensive, and may contain more functionality than you will ever need.

Fortunately there are alternatives such as PostgreSQL and MySQL, which are both Open Source client/server database systems that have proven very popular with PHP developers for many years. They're fast, stable, easily meet the needs of most small-to-medium sized projects, and, to top it all, they're free!

Choosing a Database

In principle, you can use any of these database systems in your PHP applications. There's even no reason why you can't hook one application up to several different database engines. To keep these chapters to a reasonable length, however, the focus will be on just one—MySQL.

Compared to the other choices, it offers several advantages:

❑   It's one of the most popular databases being used on the Web today.

❑   It's freely available as a download to install and run on your own machine.

❑   It's easy to install on a wide range of operating systems (including Windows and UNIX).

❑   It's available as a relatively cheap feature in many Web-hosting packages.

❑   It's simple to use and includes some handy administration tools.

❑   It's a fast, powerful client/server system that copes well with very large, complex databases, and should stand you in good stead when it comes to larger projects.

If you're not too fussed about the last criterion (and particularly if you don't want to pay out extra for database functionality on your Web account!) you might well find that an embedded database such as SQLite does a perfectly good job.

MySQL is a freely available RDBMS, which fully joined the Open Source Community only recently, when it was released under the GNU Public License (GPL). Even before it went free, you didn't need a license unless you wanted to make money out of it, or run the server on the Windows platform (the Windows version of MySQL was shareware). Because you now don't have to pay a dime to use it, this alone makes

MySQL a solid candidate for developing database applications. If the GPL worries you for any reason, or you need to incorporate MySQL into a commercial application, you can still buy a commercially licensed version from the developers at www.mysql.com.

That said, a lot of the concepts to be introduced here and in the following chapters extend well beyond one specific database engine, so I still recommend following along with MySQL for the time being.

Setting Up MySQL

You'll use MySQL for the database examples in this book, so you need to get it up and running.

At time of writing, the latest production release is MySQL 4.0, and you can find the server files (both as source code and as precompiled binaries for a wide range of platforms) on the MySQL site at www.mysql.com/downloads/mysql-4.0.html.

Details of installation (such as how you install it, and where the crucial files end up) can vary quite a lot, depending on factors such as the operating system you use and the particular type (source code or precompiled) of MySQL package you've downloaded, so let's look at several different versions of the installation process.

Installing on Windows

The Windows binary is provided as a ZIP file (for example, mysql-4.0.16-win.zip) containing a number of files including an executable called setup.exe. Run this file, and an installation wizard prompts you with a few settings options. These just determine which files are to be installed and where they are to be stored. The defaults (a Typical install in C:\MySQL) should be fine.

All of the core MySQL programs are stored in the bin directory of your installation. Assuming you've gone with the default settings, you'll find them in C:\mysql\bin. Most of these programs (such as mysql.exe, mysqladmin.exe, and mysqld.exe) are command-line tools, so do not try to run them by double-clicking their icons. You'll see them in action a little later on.

One very useful tool that comes with the standard Windows release of MySQL is the snappily titled winmysqladmin.exe, which provides you with a useful interface for controlling the MySQL server program. It's a graphical program, so you can run it by double-clicking as normal.

The first time you run it, you're prompted to enter a username and password, which generate a database user account for the administration tool to use. The administration tool then starts the MySQL server program, which, if installed properly, should come up first time.

Once it's running, winmysqladmin hides itself in your system tray (at the right-hand end of your Start bar), where it's represented by a traffic light. A green (go) light shows when the server's running, and a red (stop) light when it's not.

Right-clicking the icon brings up a menu that enables you to start and stop the server, and shows the winmysqladmin window (see Figure 9-1) from which you can view and edit various parameters on the server.

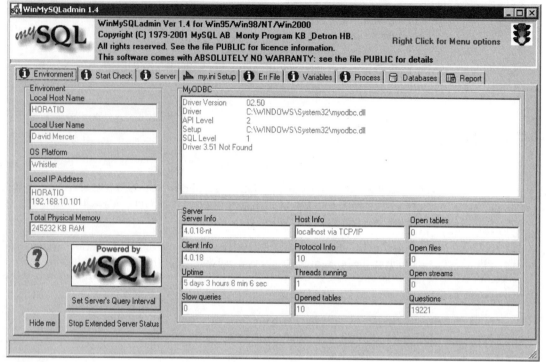

Figure 9-1

Installing on Linux

Linux users can install MySQL from a package or by compiling from source code. If you're after RPMs, then make sure you download the server, the client, the include files and libraries, and the client shared libraries for the correct platform. You should end up with the following four files (although the exact names may vary according to the MySQL version and OS you're working with):

- ❑ MySQL-4.0.16.i386.rpm
- ❑ MySQL-client-4.0.16.i386.rpm
- ❑ MySQL-devel-4.0.16.i386.rpm
- ❑ MySQL-shared-4.0.16.i386.rpm

If you're after the source code, you just need the tarball, mysql-4.0.18.tar.gz.

Installing MySQL Using RPMs

Install RPMs using the following command:

```
> rpm -Uvh filename.rpm
```

Install them in the order listed in the preceding section.

When you install the first package, which contains the MySQL server, the following documentation appears on the screen:

```
PLEASE REMEMBER TO SET A PASSWORD FOR THE MySQL root USER !
This is done with:
/usr/bin/mysqladmin -u root password 'new-password'
See the manual for more instructions.

Please report any problems with the /usr/bin/mysqlbug script!

The latest information about MySQL is available on the web at http://www.
mysql.com
Support MySQL by buying support/licenses at http://www.tcx.se/license.htmy.
Starting mysqld daemon with databases from /var/lib/mysql
```

The mysqladmin program is one of the client tools, so you have to wait to set your password until after you install the client package, which you'll do a little later in this chapter. However, the RPM immediately starts up the MySQL server program mysqld (for MySQL daemon). It also creates the startup and shutdown script /etc/rc.d/init.d/mysql, that ensures that MySQL starts whenever your computer is booted, and shuts down conveniently whenever it is halted. You can use this script to start and stop mysqld, with the commands:

```
> /etc/init.d/mysql start
```

```
> /etc/init.d/mysql stop
```

Now install the MySQL-client, MySQL-devel, and MySQL-shared packages, and you are ready to move on to *Configuring MySQL* section of this chapter.

Installing MySQL from Source

It's fairly simple to install MySQL source code. Downloaded the mysql tarball from the MySQL Web site and install it like this:

```
> tar -zxvf mysql-4.0.18.tar.gz
> cd mysql-4.0.18
> ./configure --prefix=/usr
> make
```

If make fails, it is often because of a lack of memory, even on fairly high-spec machines. In that case, try:

```
> rm -f config.cache
> make clean
> ./configure --prefix=/usr --with-low-memory
> make
```

If that doesn't work, you may find some help at www.mysql.com/doc/en/Compilation_problems .html.

Assuming configure and make have run without a hitch, simply run the following statements to complete the installation:

```
> make install
> mysql_install_db
```

You need some scripts to start and stop the MySQL server, mysqld. Here's one typical startup script:

```
#!/bin/bash
/usr/bin/mysqld_safe &
```

And one typical script to shut the server down:

```
#!/bin/bash
kill 'cat /usr/var/$HOSTNAME.pid'
```

These scripts are in the source code download for this book (www.wrox.com). If you choose to create startup and stop scripts yourself, produce the files using your favorite text editor, and then use the chmod command to tell the system that they are executable scripts. If you saved the startup script as startmysqld, for example, you would need to type:

```
> chmod ugo+rx startmysqld
```

Configuring MySQL

With the MySQL database engine installed and running on your local test machine, take a few moments to configure the system.

MySQL, like most networked systems (including other client-server databases, operating systems, and many more besides), requires you to log in with a specific user account before doing anything else. This is a fairly obvious security measure, and it limits access to the data by specifying permissions for each account. For example, one user may only have permission to view existing data; another may have permission to add new data, and perhaps even change other users' permissions.

root is the name traditionally given to a system's most senior user, who automatically has permission to view and modify *all* data and settings: a powerful position to be in. When MySQL installs, it creates the root account automatically, but doesn't set a password for it! Right now, your pristine installation could be wide open to use and abuse by anyone with a MySQL client and a network connection to the server, and you need to do something about that.

To set up a root account from the command line, follow these steps:

1. Call up a command prompt and navigate to the directory containing the MySQL program files (typically C:\mysql\bin\ on Windows or /usr/bin/ on Linux).

2. Type in the following command, substituting a suitably obscure password of your own in place of elephant:

```
> mysqladmin -uroot password elephant
```

With the command line still in place, try out a few commands. For example, executing the command mysqlshow gives you a list of the databases currently available through your server:

```
> mysqlshow
+-----------+
| Databases |
+-----------+
| mysql     |
| test      |
+-----------+
```

Right now it shows that the server has already created two databases for itself. The first, called mysql, is where it stores all the information it uses to authenticate users. The second is an empty test database. mysqlshow can also show you what's inside a database, as long as you have the correct password:

```
> mysqlshow -uroot -p mysql
Enter password: ********
Database: mysql
+--------------+
|    Tables    |
+--------------+
| columns_priv |
| db           |
| func         |
| host         |
| tables_priv  |
| user         |
+--------------+
```

So here's another clue about what's lurking inside that mysql database—all the system data is arranged into six named tables. This is your first direct glimpse of the data storage model that MySQL uses to organize its data. Before you dig any deeper, let's take a quick look at some more theory, and see how collections of tables such as these help you store data efficiently.

Relational Databases

One key characteristic of databases that you haven't looked at so far is how a database organizes data for users to interact with. Whenever you use the database engine to retrieve, modify, or add new data, you need to know what to ask for—moreover, when you come to design a database for yourself, you need to tell the database engine what sort of data to expect where, and how it's all meant to hang together.

Most of the databases you considered earlier use what's known as a relational data model. As such, they're known as relational databases (or Relational Database Management Systems—RDBMS). They arrange data into tables, each of which is divided into rows and columns.

In database parlance, each row in a table (apart from the heading) represents a data *record*: a set of intrinsically connected pieces of data. Likewise, each column represents a *field*: a specific type of data that has the same significance for each record in the table.

> For all practical purposes, the term row is synonymous with record, whereas column is synonymous with field. This is useful to bear in mind when visualizing tables.

Suppose that the manager of a touch-rugby team (don't worry if you aren't familiar with touch rugby —the sport is incidental to the topic and won't affect your understanding of databases in any way) sets up a database so that he can track the matches in which his players compete. Naively, he asks each player to enter his details into the database after each match. After the second round of matches, the manager's table looks like this:

Player_Number	Name	Phone_number	Date_Played	Nickname
42	David	555–1234	03/03/04	Dodge
6	Nic	555–3456	03/03/04	Obi-d
2	David	555–6543	03/03/04	Witblitz
14	Mark	555–1213	03/03/04	Greeny
2	David	555–6543	02/25/04	Witblitz
25	Pads	555–9101	02/25/04	Pads
6	Nic	555–3456	02/25/04	Obi-d
7	Nic	555–5678	02/25/04	Nicrot

He soon realizes that this is going to make for a huge table after everyone on the team has played an entire season's worth of games. As you can see, the structure of the table is inefficient because each player's details—number, name, phone number, and so on—are entered every time he plays a match.

Such redundancy is undesirable in a database. For example, say that the player with the number 6 keeps dropping the ball, and his teammates decide to give him a new nickname (which won't be mentioned here). To update the table, every one of this player's records would have to be modified to reflect his new nickname.

In addition, every time a player enters his details after a match, all of that information is consuming valuable space on the hard drive. Redundancy is terribly inefficient, wasting a great deal of time and space.

Fortunately, in the early 1970s, Dr. E. F. Codd came up with a unique and powerful way to alleviate this type of problem. He stipulated a set of rules that, when applied to data, ensure that your database is well designed. In truth, he stipulated no small number of rules, but for most purposes you need only concern yourself with the first few. These requirements can be divided up into what are called *normal forms*, and making sure your data complies with these normal forms goes a long way to ensuring good relational database design. Let's take a look at what normalization is all about.

Normalization

Normalization is defined as "the process of breaking up the data into several tables, so as to minimize the number of times you have to repeat the same data." The normal forms are degrees of normalization, and they are governed by an elegant set of rules that can be summarized as follows:

First Normal Form (1NF)

❑ Create a new table for each new set of related data you want to store.

❑ Eliminate repeating information in an individual table.

❑ Uniquely identify each record with a primary key.

For example, in 1NF you could split the preceding table into a player information table:

Player_Id	Name	Phone_number	Nickname
42	David	555–1234	Dodge
6	Nic	555–3456	Obi-d
14	Mark	555–1213	Greeny
2	David	555–6543	Witblitz
25	Pads	555–9101	Pads
6	Nic	555–3456	Obi-d
7	Nic	555–5678	Nicrot

And match log table:

Player_Id	Date_Played
42	03/03/04
6	03/03/04
2	03/03/04
14	03/03/04
2	25/02/04
25	25/02/04
6	25/02/04
7	25/02/04

Notice how the original table splits naturally into these two new tables. This is because the original table provided data about two distinct things (or *entities*): players and matches. Each new table contains data concerning just one entity. The split into entity tables is an important part of the normalization process.

Now you can take another step toward conforming to the first normal form: eliminating repeating information in an individual table. There's some redundant information in the player information table that can be removed to give you the following:

Player_Id	Name	Phone_number	Nickname
42	David	555–1234	Dodge
6	Nic	555–3456	Obi-d
2	David	555—6543	Witblitz

Continues

Player_Id	Name	Phone_number	Nickname
14	Mark	555–1213	Greeny
25	Pads	555–9101	Pads
7	Nic	555–5678	Nicrot

Are you done with this table yet? There's no longer any duplicated information, and the table represents only related information (information about the player entities). But what about a unique identifier? Each entity must have (at least) one unique field—in other words, a field in which no entries are repeated. Because of the exclusive nature of this field, each entry in it uniquely identifies (IDs) each record in the table. The field used to ID records is often known as the *primary key*. Only one primary key is permitted per table.

> Remember, by moving the player information to one table and the match log entries to another, you simplify the process of modifying a player's details—you only have to modify one record in the player table.

You could add a unique key, which would assign a unique number to each record, but let's look at the information closely. In any given sport, a player's number must be unique, so you know that all the values in the Player_Id field are unique. But the Nickname field is also unique because each player can only have one nickname at a time. Which one should you choose? You've already seen that nicknames can change, based on performance, so the Player_Id field is the sensible choice for a primary key.

What about the match log table? Unfortunately, the Player_Id field is no longer unique because each player plays on many dates. Obviously, the date field can't be unique either, so you can't make a unique identifier out of either field. In this case, you need to add one yourself (you'll learn how later in the book). Once that's done, both tables are in first normal form. Adding an ID field could have hidden uses, especially if you wanted to join the information in the two fields of the match log table to create a unique key that you could relate to some other data (the number of tries scored per player per match, for example).

The second normal form has two goals, which are applicable only after you've achieved 1NF.

Second Normal Form (2NF)

❑   Create new tables for each new group of values that apply to many records.

❑   Relate new tables to existing tables with a *foreign key* (a key that identifies records in a different table).

Because both example tables contain a common field (Player_Id), whose values correspond between tables, you have a way to *join* them together—you don't actually *need* a foreign key to accomplish this, but there are definitely advantages to using foreign keys (For a more in-depth discussion on them, please go to www.mysql.com/doc/en/ANSI_diff_Foreign_Keys.html for a discussion on MySQL foreign keys.) This means that records in one table have a well-defined relationship to records in the other. The database now has all the information it needs to answer complex queries involving both tables, which it couldn't answer by looking at either table in isolation. With tables related like this, the database can truly be termed *relational*. The specific relationship described here is also called a one-to-many relationship. For each record in the player information table, you may have many records in the match log table. The ability to construct meaningful one-to-many relationships is a good indicator that your database meets the requirements of the second normal form.

Third Normal Form (3NF)

The third normal form's goal is to eliminate fields that do not depend on the primary key.

This is where the real world and the elegance of theory can collide. To some extent, it reverses the premise of a master table relationship by suggesting that anytime you may have data repeat in a record such as ZIP codes in a list of addresses, that data should be stored in a separate table and linked back to the individual records that use them with a new keyed relationship. Make no mistake; the purists will chastise you roundly for not doing it this way. But the truth is, database design is often a series of trade-offs; and you do sometimes have to weigh design idealism against a novel but useful concept—simplicity. The requirements of the third normal form simply may not satisfy your needs; and it's all right for you to decide on a case-by-case basis what will work best for any given situation.

Other Normal Forms

Believe it or not, there are more normal forms, the fourth and fifth among them. The fourth normal form states that you should isolate independent multiple relationships. This rule primarily seeks to deal with the problems of many-to-many relationships, where many records may have relationships to intersecting records in another table that may in turn link back to multiple records in the first table. Confused? Don't feel bad. This is where things get pretty hairy and you don't need to hold yourself accountable to this standard. The concept is placed here because you may very well encounter this situation down the road and it's useful as a strong suggestion for dealing with these issues.

Talking to Databases with SQL

At this point, you probably aren't at all surprised to learn that MySQL itself is a relational database. In fact, you're about to start applying the principles we've just been discussing with your very own database engine. First, though, you need to learn a little about the language used to interact with relational databases—a language called SQL.

SQL, the Structured Query Language, is a standard command set used to communicate with a relational database management system on any given platform. Every task such as creating databases or tables, as well as saving, retrieving, deleting, and updating data from databases, is done via SQL statements. Implementation of SQL features vary among RDBMS vendors, but because the basic concepts are identical, applying skills learned on one platform to another should be no more difficult than porting a computer program written for one platform to another using the same language. In this section you'll examine some basic features of SQL: data types, indexes, keys, and queries.

> *There are some differences in the way MySQL implements certain things and the ANSI SQL standard. You can check out a list of these differences at www.mysql.com/doc/en/Differences_from_ANSI.html.*

SQL Data Types

When you create a database table, the type and size of each field must be defined. A field is similar to a PHP variable except that you can store only the specified type and size of data in a given field. Therefore, unlike PHP variables, you can't insert characters into an integer field, for example. The three usual sets of data types are supported in MySQL: numeric, date/time, and characters, which are described in the following tables:

Numeric Data Types	Description	Range/Format
`INT`	Normal-sized integer	(–231 to 231 –1), or (0 to 232 –1) if `UNSIGNED`
`TINYINT`	Very small integer	(–27 to 27 –1), or (0 to 28 –1) if `UNSIGNED`
`SMALLINT`	Small integer	(–215 to 215 –1), or (0 to 28 –1) if `UNSIGNED`
`MEDIUMINT`	Medium-sized integer	(–223 to 223 –1), or (0 to 224 –1) if `UNSIGNED`
`BIGINT`	Large integer	(–263 to 263 –1), or (0 to 264 –1) if `UNSIGNED`
`FLOAT`	Single-precision floating-point number	Minimum non-zero ±1.176 × 10 – 38; maximum non-zero ±3.403 × 10 + 38
`DOUBLE/REAL`	Double-precision floating-point number	Minimum non-zero ±2.225 × 10 – 308; maximum non-zero ±1.798 × 10 + 308
`DECIMAL`	Float stored as string	Maximum range same as `DOUBLE`

Date/Time Data Types	Description	Range/Format
`DATE`	Date	YYYY–MM–DD format. Range 1000–01–01 to 9999–12–31
`DATETIME`	Date and time	YYYY–MM–DD hh:mm:ss format. Range 1000–01–01 00:00:00 to 9999–12–31 23:59:59
`TIMESTAMP`	Timestamp	YYYYMMDDhhmmss format. Range 19700101000000 to sometime in 2037
`TIME`	Time	hh:mm:ss format. Range –838:59:59 to 838:59:59
`YEAR`	Year	YYYY format. Range 1900 to 2155

Character Data Types	Description	Range/Format
CHAR	Fixed-length string	0–255 characters
VARCHAR	Variable-length string	0–255 characters
BLOB	Binary Large Object	Binary data 0–65535 bytes long
TINYBLOB	Small BLOB value	Binary data 0–255 bytes long
MEDIUMBLOB	Medium-sized BLOB	Binary data 0–16777215 bytes long
LONGBLOB	Large BLOB value	Binary data 0–4294967295 bytes long
TEXT	Normal-sized text field	0–65535 bytes
TINYTEXT	Small text field	0–255 bytes
MEDIUMTEXT	Medium-sized text	0–16777215 bytes
LONGTEXT	Large text field	0–4294967295 bytes
ENUM	Enumeration	Column values are assigned one value from a set list
SET	Set value(s)	Column values are assigned zero or more values from a set list

The difference between a CHAR and VARCHAR type field is that the former stores a fixed-length value no matter how short it may be, whereas the latter stores exactly as many bytes as necessary to keep a given value. Suppose you insert the string dodge into the fields defined as char_field CHAR(10) and varchar_field(10), for example. They will store the same string slightly differently:

```
char_field: 'dodge      '// five blank spaces are right padded
varchar_field: 'dodge' // no space
```

It follows that declaring character fields as VARCHAR type will save you some disk space. Don't be tempted to use VARCHAR type fields for storing every string, though, because that has drawbacks, too. The MySQL server processes CHAR type fields much faster than VARCHAR type, for one thing, because their length is predetermined. If your strings don't vary in length much, you're better off using CHAR type fields. Moreover, when your strings are all the same length, VARCHAR takes up more disk space, because it has to store the length of each string in one additional byte.

A final note on VARCHAR/CHAR type fields: if your table has at least one VARCHAR field, all character fields are converted to VARCHAR type even if you define them otherwise.

Indexes and Keys

Inexperienced database designers sometimes complain about their database engines being slow, a problem that's often explained by the lack of an *index*. An index is a separate sorted list of a selected field (or fields) in a table. To explain why indexing a table has a dramatic effect on database performance, first consider a table without indexes. Such a table is basically the same as a plain text file because the database engine must search it sequentially. Rows in a relational database are not inserted in any particular order—the server inserts them in an arbitrary manner. To make sure it finds all entries matching the information you want, the engine must perform a full table scan, which is slow and inefficient, particularly if there are only a few matches.

Now consider an indexed table. Instead of moving straight to the table, the engine can scan the index for items that match your requirements. Because the index is a sorted list, this scan can be performed very quickly. The index guides the engine to the relevant matches on the database table, and a full table scan is not necessary.

So why not just sort the table itself? This might be practical if you knew that there was only one field on which you might want to search. However, this is rarely the case. Because it's not possible to sort a database by several fields at once, the best option is to use an index, which is separate from the table.

What about the case of searching multiple tables at once? This is where you *really* benefit from an index. Searching for a possible match across joined databases without indexes is a terrible idea—the engine would have to check all possible combinations of rows in one table with those in another. For two tables each with 500 rows, this would be 500 times 500, or 250,000 combinations! Indexing speeds searches up dramatically. The engine checks the index of the first table to find the position of matches to the first part of the query, and then it uses the index to the second table to find matches to the second part of the query. In other words, you pull out the relevant records directly.

A *primary key* is a special index that, as you saw at the beginning of the chapter, is used to ID records and to relate tables to one another, providing the relational database model. Each related table must have one (and only one) primary key.

Indexes and primary keys can be derived from combinations of fields. For a key to be formed in this way, the combination of items from each field must still be unique.

Because an index brings about a significant boost in performance, you could create as many indexes as possible for maximum performance gain, right? Not always. An index is a sure-fire way to increase the speed of searching and retrieving data from a database, but sacrifices performance when saving or updating records, and also increases the size of a table. Why? When you insert a record into an indexed table, the database engine has to record its position in the corresponding index table. Do the math!

What's more, if you have more than one index on a table, multiple write operations have to be performed on the index table, too. So when creating indexes on a table, don't create more than you need. Limit indexed columns to those that will be searched or sorted frequently. If required, you can create additional indexes on a table as you need them to increase performance.

Queries

SQL statements or *commands* are used to construct queries. Queries are the questions your application asks a database engine, which then returns the records that meet the criteria specified in the query. Queries return an array of records that meet the specified conditions, and contain information from selected fields. PHP, and other languages that support database connectivity for that matter, can treat the returned array as a normal array variable. We'll return to this topic later; for now, just bear it in mind. The returned array of records, called the result set, is the database engine's answer to your query. If you ask the engine to retrieve the records containing John as the first name, for example, it returns all of the records conforming to the query. If none are found, NULL (discussed in the next section) is returned.

Some SQL commands are literally commands that tell the database engine to do something instead of asking for an answer: "Delete those rows of information that contain John as the first name!" SQL commands of this type don't return a result set.

NULL

Consider the following scenarios:

A class takes a spelling test at school, but the teacher has yet to mark the test sheets and insert the results into a database table. It would be unfair of the teacher to insert default values into the results column before the sheets have been marked because a default score is irrelevant in this context. What could you place in the column to signify that you are awaiting data?

You want to construct a database table containing information about endangered bird species. One of the fields provides the fastest recorded flight speed for each bird in the table. You begin to create records for endangered penguins, and then you remember—penguins can't fly! What do you place in the flight speed column to indicate that the field is not applicable to penguins?

In both of these cases data is missing from a table. The only difference is that, in the first case, the situation is temporary because the teacher will soon add the missing test results to the table, but in the second case the values for the flight speed of penguins is impossible to obtain. You need a way to represent missing data in fields.

In a MySQL table, a NULL entry represents a missing value. NULL doesn't belong to any particular data type, but it can replace any value. Because it is not a data type or value, but it can be a field entry, the concept of a NULL is often difficult to grasp for beginners and experienced programmers alike. Programmers often have a mistaken idea of NULL. For example, a common mistake is to think of NULL as zero, which is wrong because zero is a value; NULL is not. Strings filled with one or more blank spaces, and strings of zero length, may also be mistaken for NULL because string is a data type, but NULL isn't. NULL is nothing, no data type, no value.

So what happens if the result set from one of your queries contains a NULL, and that result set is then used in your program in subsequent calculations? The rule of thumb for math with NULL is that it propagates. Any arithmetic operation involving a NULL returns NULL. This makes sense because how could you provide results when all the data needed to perform the calculation is not present? This also applies to dividing a NULL value by zero; NULL is returned.

Query Commands

MySQL queries issued to manipulate data in a table can be constructed using the following main commands:

- ❏   SELECT: Retrieves data from a database.

- ❏   DELETE: Deletes data from a database.

- ❏   INSERT—Inserts data into a database.

- ❏   REPLACE: Replaces data in a database. If the same record exists in a table, the command overwrites the record with the new data.

- ❏   UPDATE: Updates data in a table.

The rest of the command set involves creating or modifying the database structures, rather than the data stored in the database:

❑   CREATE: Creates a database, table or index.

❑   ALTER: Modifies the structure of a table.

❑   DROP: Wipes out a database or table.

You'll see more of these commands as you work through the next few chapters. Just to give you a taste though, let's take a look at the typical form of a MySQL SELECT query, which retrieves records from a table:

```
mysql> SELECT field1, field2, ... , fieldn FROM table WHERE condition;
```

The first thing to note is that each query is terminated with a semicolon, just as a PHP statement is. A query statement may expand to multiple lines. The following, slightly more specific query, is essentially the same as this generic case:

```
mysql> SELECT last_name, first_name
    -> FROM user
    -> WHERE first_name = 'John'
```

Take a closer look at the FROM, WHERE, and ORDER BY clauses in the query. The query returns any record *from* the user table *where* the value of the first_name field is John. Assuming you have a table called user, here's a sample of the query's output:

```
Simpleton John
Smith John
Thomas John
```

Now let's put this into practice and have some fun with MySQL!

A Quick Play with MySQL

You'll start working with the MySQL server using the client program mysql and a few simple database queries. Along the way, you'll play with some database settings, create some new users (without quite as much access to everything as the root user has), and get a taste of how queries work in practice.

Starting the mysql Client Program

Fire up the mysql client by issuing the following command at your command prompt:

```
> mysql -uUSER -pPASSWORD -hHOST
```

Replace the USER, PASSWORD, and HOST arguments to reflect your personal settings. For example, if your database username and password are phpuser and phppass and you're connecting to the host db.whatever.com, the command would look like this:

```
> mysql -uphpuser -pphppass -hdb.whatever.com
```

All the arguments are optional. If missing, the following values are assumed for them:

Argument	Value
-u	Your shell account username
-p	No password
-h	localhost

The mysql client now connects to the database server running on the specified HOST with the given user ID/password combination. You may also specify a database to use by providing its name at the end of the command, like this:

```
> mysql -uUSER -pPASSWORD test
```

You should see a response similar to the following:

```
Welcome to the MySQL monitor.  Commands end with ; or \ g.
Your MySQL connection id is 4 to server version: 4.0.18-nt

Type 'help;' or '\ h' for help. Type '\ c' to clear the buffer.

mysql>
```

If the mysql client complains that it can't connect to the specified server, check to see if the provided arguments are correct.

Selecting a Database to Use

To see the list of databases available, use the SHOW DATABASES command:

```
mysql> SHOW DATABASES;
+---------------+
| Database      |
+---------------+
| mysql         |
| test          |
+---------------+
2 rows in set (0.00 sec)
```

This is mostly the same information you got from mysqlshow earlier: there are still two databases, mysql and test, available in the system. This time, though, you're also told how many rows were returned (2) and how long it took the server to execute the query (0.00 seconds to two decimal places).

In fact, you can use the mysql client to do just about anything that the other, more specialized client programs can, as long as you know the correct syntax. Let's dig a little deeper.

To select a particular database, you can utilize the USE databasename syntax. Let's have a poke around inside one of the databases:

```
mysql> USE mysql;
Database changed
```

Your MySQL server is now ready to work with the database mysql. A word to the wise: be careful how you use the user table; it contains important information that you probably don't want to delete.

For the sake of readability, it is recommended that SQL keywords are written in uppercase characters, and user-defined names such as table and field names are lowercase. Remember that on the Linux/UNIX platforms, arguments are case-sensitive: Mysql, MYSQL, and mysql are all different database names.

Looking at Tables Inside a Database

You can use the SHOW TABLES command to list the existing tables in the currently selected database:

```
mysql> SHOW TABLES;
+-----------------+
| Tables in mysql |
+-----------------+
| columns_priv    |
| db              |
| func            |
| host            |
| tables_priv     |
| user            |
+-----------------+
6 rows in set (0.00 sec)
```

Once again, a slight elaboration on the results you previously got from mysqlshow. This time you can have a look at what's going on inside the tables. For example, let's see how the user table is structured. Use the DESCRIBE command, or DESC for short:

```
mysql> DESC user;
+-----------------+--------------------+------+-----+---------+-------+
| Field           | Type               | Null | Key | Default | Extra |
+-----------------+--------------------+------+-----+---------+-------+
| Host            | varchar(60) binary |      | PRI |         |       |
| User            | varchar(16) binary |      | PRI |         |       |
| password        | varchar(16)        |      |     |         |       |
| Select_priv     | enum('N','Y')      |      |     | N       |       |
| Insert_priv     | enum('N','Y')      |      |     | N       |       |
| Update_priv     | enum('N','Y')      |      |     | N       |       |
| Delete_priv     | enum('N','Y')      |      |     | N       |       |
| Create_priv     | enum('N','Y')      |      |     | N       |       |
| Drop_priv       | enum('N','Y')      |      |     | N       |       |
| Reload_priv     | enum('N','Y')      |      |     | N       |       |
| Shutdown_priv   | enum('N','Y')      |      |     | N       |       |
| Process_priv    | enum('N','Y')      |      |     | N       |       |
 . . .

 . . .
| File_priv       | enum('N','Y')      |      |     | N       |       |
| Grant_priv      | enum('N','Y')      |      |     | N       |       |
| References_priv | enum('N','Y')      |      |     | N       |       |
| max_connections | int(11) unsigned   |      |     | 0       |       |
+-----------------+--------------------+------+-----+---------+-------+
31 rows in set (0.00 sec)
```

This command describes the user table's structure—what fields are defined and how they've been configured. For example, you can see the Host field can hold up to 60 characters and is defined as a primary key. The User field also is defined as a primary key. That doesn't mean that the Host and User fields are both primary keys (you should remember that this is forbidden). Instead, the combination of the Host and User fields works as a sole primary key in Host-User format.

For example, if user john at localhost has been given the server access privileges, `localhost-john` becomes the primary key value for his record. Another user at localhost whose name is also john cannot be inserted as a record in this table. However, john at whatever.com can.

All the fields in the user table except the Host, User, Password, are declared as `ENUM('N', 'Y')`. This means that only one from the specified set of values (either N or Y in this case) can be used in each field. Note that N is the default value when no value is provided.

Using SQL to Look at Data

All the queries you've given to the mysql client so far have been specific to the MySQL database engine, and won't necessarily work with another system, whether or not it supports SQL. Now that you're working down at the level of actual data, though, it's time to use some bona fide SQL statements to find out what's there.

Let's say you want to find out if there are any users registered with access privileges from the local machine `localhost`. You might do this by issuing the following SELECT query:

```
mysql> SELECT User,Host FROM user;
+-----------+-----------+
| User      | Host      +
+-----------+-----------+
| root      |localhost  +
| dodge     |doggiesr   +
| james     |digistrawb +
+-----------+-----------+
3 rows in set (0.00 sec)
```

Because there are only three rows, it's not hard to see that only `root` is currently registered as a local user. Of course, it might be somewhat harder to spot this if you had a few hundred more users registered in the database, so here's another way to get the same result:

```
mysql> SELECT User FROM user WHERE Host='localhost';
+-----------+
| User      |
+-----------+
| root      |
+-----------+
1 row in set (0.00 sec)
```

Using a WHERE clause narrows the scope of the retrieved records. This works much the same as PHP's if statement, except that the former uses a single equal sign (=) whereas the latter uses two (==) to test for equality.

If you wanted the server to retrieve all fields available instead of a few specified ones, you could use the * wildcard. For example:

```
mysql> SELECT * FROM tablename;
```

This command would retrieve all of the records from tablename.

Manipulating Data in a Database

Now let's create a new database user, by *inserting* a new record into the user table using the INSERT command:

```
mysql> INSERT INTO user VALUES(
    -> 'localhost',
    -> 'phpuser',
    -> Password('phppass'),
    -> 'N', 'N', 'N', 'N', 'N', 'N', 'N',
    -> 'N', 'N', 'N', 'N', 'N', 'N', 'N',
    -> 'N', 'N', 'N', 'N', 'N', 'N', 'N',
    -> 'N', 'N', 'N', 'N', 'N', 'N', 'N');
Query OK, 1 row affected (0.00 sec)
```

This INSERT query creates a record for the user phpuser, using the password phppass, in the user table, and specifies no access privileges. Each string value is placed within single quotes—this issue is discussed in greater detail later on. As you can see, the mysql client reports that the query was successfully executed, and that one row of data has been inserted as requested.

MySQL saves database user passwords after encrypting them. It uses its own password encryption scheme (which is different than Linux's), so use MySQL's built-in password() function to encrypt your password.

What if you change your mind and want to give user phpuser (who presently has no access privileges at all) the server administration privileges Reload_priv and Shutdown_priv? You could update the user table to reflect your whimsical decision using an UPDATE query, like this:

```
mysql> UPDATE user SET Reload_priv='Y', Shutdown_priv='Y'
    -> WHERE User='phpuser';
Query OK, 1 row affected (0.00 sec)
Rows matched: 1 Changed: 1 Warnings: 0
```

The mysql client reports that only one row matched the condition set in the query and that it has been successfully updated. User phpuser now has server administration privileges only: phpuser is only allowed to reload or shut down the server.

The WHERE clause is optional, and when omitted, the UPDATE query changes all the records in a given table with the new values provided. Warning: Make sure you don't change records by accident. A nightmare can sometimes turn into reality if you're not careful because a careless UPDATE query could, for example, change 10,000 user records to have the same password. Even worse, all the records in a table could unwittingly be deleted with a DELETE query such as:

```
mysql> DELETE FROM test;
Query OK, 0 rows affected (0.00 sec)
```

Here all of the records in the table test have been deleted. Don't be fooled by the mysql client reporting that no row is affected by this query. Following the query, the server has no way of knowing how many rows are affected (deleted) because they're gone forever after the query. Note that the syntax of this example DELETE command contains no clauses. Thankfully, you may specify which records are to be deleted with a WHERE clause:

```
DELETE FROM tablename WHERE condition(s);
```

Now you change you mind again and want to give user phpuser all of the server administration privileges. What do you do? You can make either another UPDATE query or you can REPLACE the whole record. The syntax is pretty simple:

```
mysql> REPLACE INTO user VALUES(
    -> 'localhost', 'phpuser', Password('phppass'),
    -> 'Y', 'Y', 'Y', 'Y', 'Y', 'Y', 'Y',
    -> 'Y', 'Y', 'Y', 'Y', 'Y', 'Y', 'Y',
    -> 'Y', 'Y', 'Y', 'Y', 'Y', 'Y', 'Y',
    -> 'Y', 'Y', 'Y', 'Y', 'Y', 'Y', 'Y');
Query OK, 1 row affected (0.00 sec)
```

So REPLACE overwrites an old record with a new one. Note that the new record and the old record must have the same value in a field designated as a key (or the combined key formed by the Host and User fields in this case). The difference between the UPDATE and REPLACE commands is that UPDATE replaces only the selected set of fields in a record, whereas REPLACE replaces the whole record with the given values.

Finally, to activate the newly created account phpuser, you need to flush privileges, reloading the privilege information from the table. (The server normally reads the access privilege information only once, when it's loaded.) First, exit mysql client, by typing quit, (otherwise you'll get an error saying that your SQL syntax is incorrect). Then:

```
> mysqladmin -uUSER -pPASSWORD -hHOST flush-privileges
```

Alternately you can issue the FLUSH PRIVILEGES command to reflect the change in the mysql client program:

```
mysql> FLUSH PRIVILEGES;
```

Using GRANT and REVOKE Commands

GRANT and REVOKE commands enable you to allocate and remove database privileges as you choose. They can be used at various levels of your database permissions structure, going from global to database to table to column level—depending on how fine grain you want your control to be. Of course, for whatever permissions you can grant a user, you can use a corresponding REVOKE statement to remove them.

In the following sections you'll see how to use these commands to control permissions on your tables. For example, earlier you created a new user by manipulating the user table directly. You can achieve the same goal more simply using the GRANT command. Let's see how.

GRANT

Here's the simplest form of the GRANT command:

```
mysql> GRANT ALL PRIVILEGES ON *.* TO
    -> phpuser@localhost IDENTIFIED BY 'phppass';
```

It gives every access privilege on every database in the system to the user phpuser at localhost if he logs on to the server using the password phppass. Note that the user and host arguments are *not* given in quotes.

If you want to let this user access the tables in the test database only, you'd use the following command:

```
mysql> GRANT ALL PRIVILEGES ON test.*
    -> TO phpuser@localhost IDENTIFIED BY 'phppass';
```

Here, test.* denotes all tables in the test database. Similarly you can grant access to only the sample table in test:

```
mysql> GRANT ALL PRIVILEGES ON test.sample
    -> TO phpuser@localhost IDENTIFIED BY 'phppass';
```

By replacing the ALL PRIVILEGES keyword with a selection of query types, a set of access privileges can be granted:

```
mysql> GRANT SELECT,INSERT,UPDATE ON test.*
    -> TO phpuser@% IDENTIFIED BY 'phppass';
```

With this command, the user phpuser can issue only SELECT, INSERT, and UPDATE queries to any of the tables in the test database. Any other query, such as DELETE, won't be allowed. Wildcards like * are extremely useful. For example, by replacing localhost with the % wild card, you can allow the user phpuser to access the specified tables from any server.

You can also specify the host with a partial domain name: if you used phpuser@%.whatever.com for instance, only users with the user ID phpuser connecting from the domain whatever.com would be granted access to the server.

You can split hairs even further, by specifying the fields that the user can access:

```
mysql> GRANT SELECT (User, Host) ON mysql.user
    -> TO phpuser@localhost IDENTIFIED BY 'phppass';
```

Here the user phpuser can issue only SELECT queries on the User and Host fields in the user table.

You can use the WITH GRANT OPTION clause to give the specified user the capability to grant other users any privileges he has at the specified privilege level:

```
mysql> GRANT ALL PRIVILEGES ON test.*
    -> TO phpuser@localhost IDENTIFIED BY 'phppass' WITH GRANT OPTION;
```

This command is equivalent to creating another superuser, called phpuser. Be careful with the WITH GRANT OPTION clause: two users with different privileges can easily team up and extend their privileges by exchanging them!

REVOKE

The REVOKE command removes access privileges from a user. If you want to revoke *all* privileges given to user phpuser, for example, issue the following command:

```
mysql> REVOKE ALL PRIVILEGES ON *.* FROM phpuser;
```

You can specify multiple usernames by separating them with commas:

```
mysql> REVOKE ALL PRIVILEGES ON *.*
    -> FROM phpuser@localhost, phpuser2, phpuser3;
```

All specified users must exist, and possess the specified privileges, in order for this command to work.

The following command revokes only the SELECT privilege from the user phpuser:

```
mysql> REVOKE SELECT ON *.* FROM phpuser@localhost;
```

Again, you can split hairs by specifying field names:

```
mysql> REVOKE SELECT (User, Host) ON mysql.user FROM phpuser@localhost;
```

If you modify the grant tables using GRANT or REVOKE commands, the changes take effect immediately. You don't have to flush privileges or reload the server.

Connecting to MySQL from PHP

Okay, let's get back to PHP, and look at how you can tap into all this database power from your dynamic Web pages.

If you're feeling a little overwhelmed after going through all those SQL statements, don't worry! It's not essential that you understand every last detail at this stage. You just want to get an overall feel for how you go about interacting with a relational database such as MySQL. You'll become a lot more familiar with the specifics as you move on and start building applications for yourself.

Just as you used client programs to access the MySQL database server from the command line, PHP needs some client code of its own to talk to MySQL.

In the days of PHP4, this was a no-brainer because the necessary code was integrated right into the depths of PHP itself. Unfortunately that's no longer the case, and PHP5 expects the MySQL client libraries to be present on your system before compiling with PHP support. This is quite easy for Linux users: just ensure that you compile PHP5 using the –with-mysql option.

For Windows users, it's a little more complex. You need to:

1. Ensure that the libmysql.dll library is in your system root path (libmysqli for versions of MySQL 4.1 and later).

2. Uncomment the mysql extension in the extensions section of your php.ini file.

3. Ensure that your php_mysql.dll extension is in a folder where PHP can find it. (This is set in the extension directory setting in the php.ini file.)

4. Restart your Web server after you've implemented these changes.

That's it! Nothing too complicated—it's just like using any other extension in PHP. With everything set up, let's look at what you need to do to get PHP5 and MySQL talking to each other.

PHP MySQL Connectivity

To work with a MySQL server (or any other RDBMS) in PHP, you must follow these steps:

1. Open a connection to the server.

2. Work with databases in the server.

3. Close the connection.

Does this list sound familiar? You followed similar steps when working with files and directories in the preceding chapter. No big deal!

Basic Connection Functions

Let's begin this section by exploring some basic PHP functions you can use to work with MySQL:

❑ mysql_connect(): Creates a connection to a MySQL server. It takes three string arguments: the hostname; the database username, and the database user password. The function returns a link identifier when it successfully connects to the specified MySQL server (or NULL upon error):

```
$link_id = mysql_connect("localhost", "phpuser", "phppass");
```

The link identifier works much the same as a file or directory handle. You'll use it later to issue queries. All of the arguments are optional, and when none are provided, "localhost", the Web server owner's username, and an empty password are all assumed.

❑ mysql_close(): The link to the MySQL server is closed when the script is terminated. If you want to close the connection earlier, use this function, with the link identifier as its argument:

```
mysql_close($link_id);
```

The function returns true on success and false upon error. If the link identifier is omitted, the previously opened link is used (if not specified otherwise, all mysql_* functions which take an optional link ID argument assume the previously opened link in its absence).

❑ mysql_list_dbs(): PHP's equivalent to MySQL's SHOW DATABASES command. Its only argument is the (optional) link identifier. It returns a pointer ($result below) to the array containing the names of available databases:

```
$result = mysql_list_dbs($link_id);
```

❏ `mysql_select_db()`: Used to select a database, returning `True` on success and `False` upon error. It takes the name of the database as an argument, although a link identifier argument is optional. Here's an example:

```
mysql_select_db("mysql", $link_id);
```

If no connection has been made before calling this function, it attempts to establish a link before selecting the specified database. Let's take a moment to illustrate how you can connect to the local MySQL server with the account you created earlier, using PHP:

```
$link_id = mysql_connect("localhost", "phpuser", "phppass");
if(mysql_select_db("mysql", $link_id)) echo "Connected to the localhost.";
else die ("Connection failed.");
```

This code establishes a connection to the local MySQL server, and selects the `mysql` access privilege database. If the connection fails, an error message is displayed.

❏ `mysql_list_tables()`: Equivalent to MySQL's SHOW TABLES command. The database name and the optional link identifier are taken as arguments. A pointer is returned to the array containing the names of available tables associated with the database:

```
$result = mysql_list_tables("mysql", $link_id);
```

❏ `mysql_num_rows()`: Use to find the number of rows in a result set returned by a given query. It takes the result set pointer as an argument:

```
$num_rows = mysql_num_rows($result);
```

Use it on result sets returned by SELECT queries, and other functions that retrieve rows.

❏ `mysql_affected_rows()`: Use instead of `mysql_num_rows()` to get the number of rows affected by INSERT, UPDATE, or DELETE commands. It takes an optional link ID argument:

```
$num_rows = mysql_affected_rows($link_id);
```

A DELETE query with no WHERE clause wipes out all the records in a given table and causes the `mysql_affected_rows()` function call to return zero.

The return value of `mysql_num_rows()` and `mysql_affected_rows()` is the actual count of rows selected/affected. The return value from `mysql_list_dbs()` and `mysq_list_tables()` is a pointer to a result set.

`mysql_fetch_row()`: Use to retrieve the rows of records returned from the server. It takes a result set pointer returned from a previous query, and returns an array corresponding to the fetched row (or `False` if there are no more rows left):

```
$fetched_row = mysql_fetch_row($result_set);
```

PHP maintains an internal pointer to the row returned from a previous query. Each subsequent call to this function moves the pointer to the next row available. When the pointer moves past the result set array boundary, `mysql_fetch_row()` returns `False`.

For a comprehensive list of MySQL functions, please see Appendix B.

Try It Out   Connect to a MySQL Server in PHP

Here's a sample script, `db_connect.php`, which uses the functions already introduced to list the databases and tables available to the MySQL user `phpuser`:

```php
<?php
$link_id = mysql_connect("localhost", "phpuser", "phppass");
$result = mysql_list_dbs($link_id);

while($db_data = mysql_fetch_row($result)) {
        echo $db_data[0]. "<BR>";
        $result2 = mysql_list_tables($db_data[0]);
        $num_rows = mysql_num_rows($result2);
        while($table_data = mysql_fetch_row($result2)) {
           echo "--" . $table_data[0]. "<BR>";
        }
        echo "==> $num_rows table(s) in " . $db_data[0] . "<P>";
}
?>
```

This script lists all databases available and tables in each of them. Here's a sample run:

```
mysql
--columns_priv
--db
--func
--host
--tables_priv
--user
==> 6 table(s) in mysql
test_db
--sample_table1
--sample_table2
==> 2 table(s) in test_db
```

Hang on, though! If you've been following along with the SQL commands, you probably got an error. If you did, go back to the section on GRANT and REVOKE, and grant phpuser enough privileges to be able to look at the tables in the databases, and then run the script again. Alternatively, you can follow along and view the error-handling section after this example.

How It Works

The script first makes a connection to the server with the given set of values: `localhost`, `phpuser`, and `phppass`. Replace the values here with the appropriate ones for you, if you want to use your own username and password instead of those you gave to the user you created earlier.

The link identifier returned by the mysql_connect() function is used by the mysql_list_dbs() function call. In fact, you don't need to pass the link identifier to the latter function because mysql_list_dbs() would assume the last opened link in the absence of a link argument, like so:

```
$result = mysql_list_dbs();
```

A common mistake is overwriting the result pointer when you issue another query while stepping through the result set returned from a previous query. Just as you can open multiple files with different file handles, you should maintain multiple result sets by assigning unique pointers to each set.

In this example, a while loop in the script cycles through the result set returned by the mysql_list_dbs() function call. Another while loop is set up to look into every element in the result set returned by the mysql_list_tables() function call. Both loops are terminated when there are no more rows left in the result sets because $db_data and $table_data are False when the mysql_fetch_row() function is done fetching the returned rows.

```
while($db_data = mysql_fetch_row($result)) {
        echo $db_data[0]. "<BR>";
        $result2 = mysql_list_tables($db_data[0]);
        $num_rows = mysql_num_rows($result2);
        while($table_data = mysql_fetch_row($result2)) {
          echo "--" . $table_data[0]. "<BR>";
        }
        echo "==> $num_rows table(s) in " . $db_data[0] . "<P>";
}
```

Each of the arrays returned by mysql_list_dbs() and mysql_list_tables() contains only one element; the name of a database $db_data[0] and the name of a table $table_data[0], respectively. If you want to retrieve more than one field from a table, you can refer to each one by a corresponding array index:

```
$result_set = mysql_fetch_row($result);
$first_column = $result_set[0];
$second_column = $result_set[1];
$third_column = $result_set[2];
```

You haven't used the mysql_close() function, but it's seldom used in real-life applications unless you need to close the connection for some reason before your applications end. PHP automatically closes the open connection before your script ends.

You learn more about how MySQL and PHP can work in tandem in the following chapters.

Handling Server Errors

Now let's try something rather dumb: take the last script, change the database username to no_such_user, and see what happens. Unless you've set the error reporting level in the php.ini configuration file to suppress them, a bunch of warnings are thrown out:

```
Warning: MySQL Connection Failed: Access denied for user: 'no_such_user@local
host' (Using password: YES) in /home/apache/htdocs/db_connect.php on line 3
```

```
Warning: Supplied argument is not a valid MySQL-Link resource in /home/apache/
htdocs/db_connect.php on line 5

Warning: Supplied argument is not a valid MySQL result resource in /home/
apache/htdocs/db_connect.php on line 6

Warning: Supplied argument is not a valid MySQL result resource in /home/
apache/htdocs/db_connect.php on line 8
```

Why do you get such uninformative warnings? It's simple—the script you just created isn't smart enough to say what went wrong upon error; it just knows that it tried to access some MySQL resources but failed. PHP is generating the warnings, but the errors are on the database server.

PHP provides a couple of functions that catch server errors and determine what went wrong, returning values from the server's own error-handler. If a MySQL server encounters an error while executing a specified task, it returns the text and number of the error message. You can get at these values using the PHP functions mysql_errno() and mysql_error().

The mysql_errno() function returns the error number and mysql_error() returns the error text from the previous MySQL operation. They both take an optional link identifier argument (defaulting to the previously-opened link):

```
$MYSQL_ERRNO = mysql_errno($link_id);
$MYSQL_ERROR = mysql_error($link_id);
```

These functions assume the connection to the server has already been made, so if you call them to see why a connection has failed, no error is reported because no opened link is available. As you've seen, though, you can still use the die() function to exit with a message that the connection attempt has failed:

```
if(!mysql_connect("localhost", "no_such_user", "phppass"))
                                        die("Connection failed!");
```

The only problem with this approach is that PHP still churns out its own warning messages when the connection attempt fails. To prevent warnings and/or error messages, either precede the function call with the error message suppressing operator @, or use the error_reporting() function.

You can use the error_reporting() function call to set the level of error reporting that PHP applies while executing subsequent code. By specifying error_reporting(0), you can ensure that no PHP error/warning messages will be invoked. This is what you do in the following example.

It's not a good idea to set the level to produce warnings in production environment because they might scare away your users. Set it to a higher level only when you are debugging your applications.

Try It Out   Handle Server Errors

We're going to define a couple of functions that you'll find very useful in later sections. Create a new file called common_db.inc and enter the following code:

```php
<?php
$dbhost = 'localhost';
$dbusername = 'phpuser';
$dbuserpassword = 'phppass';
$default_dbname = 'mysql';

$MYSQL_ERRNO = '';
$MYSQL_ERROR = '';

function db_connect(){
    global $dbhost, $dbusername, $dbuserpassword, $default_dbname;
    global $MYSQL_ERRNO, $MYSQL_ERROR;

    $link_id = mysql_connect($dbhost, $dbusername, $dbuserpassword);
    if(!$link_id) {
        $MYSQL_ERRNO = 0;
        $MYSQL_ERROR = "Connection failed to the host $dbhost.";
        return 0;
    }
    else if(empty($dbname) && !mysql_select_db($default_dbname)) {
        $MYSQL_ERRNO = mysql_errno();
        $MYSQL_ERROR = mysql_error();
        return 0;
    }
    else return $link_id;
}

function sql_error() {
    global $MYSQL_ERRNO, $MYSQL_ERROR;

    if(empty($MYSQL_ERROR)) {
        $MYSQL_ERRNO = mysql_errno();
        $MYSQL_ERROR = mysql_error();
    }
    return "$MYSQL_ERRNO: $MYSQL_ERROR";
}
?>
```

You can include this file in later examples, and expand it as necessary. Note the function db_connect(), which is dedicated to making connections to the MySQL server. You'll use it a lot!

You should be aware that this file contains some pretty important information that you don't want to fall into the hands of unethical users. It's generally suggested that files containing plain-text passwords be stored outside of your Web tree for security purposes. PHP can still access them there, and this prevents a user from getting at the file in a nonprogrammatic way, such as tricking the server into offering up the page as plain text. The file has to be executed, which would prevent the password from being displayed.

Now try the following script, db_connect.php, with an incorrect username/password combination or nonexistent database names:

```php
<?php
include "common_db.inc";
error_reporting(0);
```

```
$link_id = db_connect();
if(!$link_id) die(sql_error());
else echo "Successfully made a connection to $dbhost.<BR>";
?>
```

Try the script using an invalid username or password, and you should see the following error message:

```
0: Connection failed to the host localhost.
```

If $default_dbname is empty, you get:

```
1046: No Database Selected
```

If it's set to a nonexistent database name (no_such_db for example), you see:

```
1049: Unknown database 'no_such_db'
```

How It Works

Once you've included these variable and function definitions, you specify error_reporting(0) to prevent PHP from displaying any error/warning messages.

You also could have suppressed error messages by prefixing the following mysql_connect() and mysql_select_db() function calls with an @ symbol.

If the database connection is made successfully, db_connect() returns a link identifier. Otherwise, it sets global variables $MYSQL_ERRNO and $MYSQL_ERROR accordingly, and returns zero to indicate an error. Consequently, the script dies:

```
if(!$link_id) die(sql_error());
```

Rather than directly specifying an error message, you've called sql_error() to produce one for you:

```
function sql_error() {
   global $MYSQL_ERRNO, $MYSQL_ERROR;

   if(empty($MYSQL_ERROR)) {
      $MYSQL_ERRNO = mysql_errno();
      $MYSQL_ERROR = mysql_error();
   }
   return "$MYSQL_ERRNO: $MYSQL_ERROR";
}
```

Basically all this function does is return a character string containing the error number and error message, separated by a colon, but it will be quite useful to you in situations where you can't assume that the returned variables have been defined. For example, you might want to call sql_error() following a database query error; the trouble is that $MYSQL_ERRNO and $MYSQL_ERROR would not have been defined. To make this function useful in such an event (as well as the failed connection you're anticipating), check the $MYSQL_ERROR global variable's value. If it's empty, call mysql_errno() and mysql_error() again and assign values to both.

After a successful connection, db_connect() attempts to select the default database, which you've set in the $default_dbname global variable. You can improve db_connect() by having it take an optional argument $dbname, so that it selects whichever database is specified in the argument:

```
function db_connect($dbname='') {
    global $dbhost, $dbusername, $dbuserpassword, $default_dbname;
    global $MYSQL_ERRNO, $MYSQL_ERROR;

    $link_id = mysql_connect($dbhost, $dbusername, $dbuserpassword);
    if(!$link_id) {
        $MYSQL_ERRNO = 0;
        $MYSQL_ERROR = "Connection failed to the host $dbhost.";
        return 0;
    }
    else if(empty($dbname) && !mysql_select_db($default_dbname)) {
        $MYSQL_ERRNO = mysql_errno();
        $MYSQL_ERROR = mysql_error();
        return 0;
    }
    else if(!empty($dbname) && !mysql_select_db($dbname)) {
        $MYSQL_ERRNO = mysql_errno();
        $MYSQL_ERROR = mysql_error();
        return 0;
    }
    else return $link_id;
}
```

You can now call it like this:

```
$link_id = db_connect("sample_db");
```

The connection held by $link_id will automatically use the database sample_db. If you don't specify an argument, db_connect() defaults to the database specified by $default_dbname.

Creating Databases and Tables from MySQL

Let's go back to the command line to construct a database from the mysql client. To create a database called sample_db, you just have to say:

```
mysql> CREATE DATABASE sample_db;
Query OK, 1 row affected (0.05sec)
mysql>
```

Removing it is just as simple:

```
mysql> DROP DATABASE sample_db;
Query OK, 0 rows affected (0.00sec)
mysql>
```

The number of rows mysql counts as having been affected doesn't include the ones it has removed. You could have just deleted thousands of data entries, but from the information presented here, you'd have no way of knowing! This is all the more reason to use extreme caution—this small, harmless-looking command will totally wipe out the specified database and all the tables in it, and won't even hint at what it's done, let alone ask you for confirmation. You have been warned!

Assuming you just got rid of your sample_db database, CREATE it again. You'll use it rather a lot in the next couple of chapters, and the rest of the examples in this chapter take you through the steps to set it up with a structure and records.

Creating a database table is a little more complicated. Let's say you want to create a table called user. Start off with the obvious syntax:

```
mysql> CREATE TABLE user;
ERROR 1113: A table must have at least 1 column
mysql>
```

Okay, you're going to need a little more than that. Although a database can quite happily exist without any tables living under its roof, tables are rather more fussy. Give it some structure by putting a list of the field descriptors within parentheses following the table name. The field descriptors each follow the form:

```
fieldname TYPE(length)
```

For example, you could create a very simple two-field table with:

```
mysql> CREATE TABLE test_table (name CHAR(40), number INT);
Query OK, 0 rows affected (0.06sec)
mysql>
```

You already had a look at the various types of variables supported by MySQL. You also have the option of specifying attributes for each of the fields—to do so, simply append them to the descriptor. You can use any combination of the attributes described in the following table.

Attributes	Description
BINARY	Makes the field's value case-sensitive. Works only with CHAR and VARCHAR type fields
NULL or NOT NULL	NOT NULL fields cannot take a NULL value. Fields that are declared NULL will store a specified default value whenever a NULL value is given. If there is no default value provided, they simply store NULL. If unspecified, NULL is assumed
DEFAULT default_value	Specifies the default value to store when NULL is given
AUTO_INCREMENT	When a NULL value is placed in an AUTO_INCREMENT field, the field value is set to one greater than its current maximum value in that table. AUTO_INCREMENT only works with unique, integer type fields There can be only one AUTO_INCREMENT field per table

After you've listed all those that you need, you can specify selected fields as holding indexes, primary keys, and unique values. Here's a quick recap of what each of these entails:

❑ KEY/INDEX: These are synonymous keywords that specify fields to be used as indexes. The specified field entries are copied to a separate index table, where they're listed against pointers to the corresponding entries in the original table. They're then sorted, producing an index much the same as you'd find in the back of a book. If you specify multiple fields (`"field1"`, `"field2"`, `...`) for your index, the index sorts first on `"field1"`, and then any duplicate values in `"field1"` are sorted on `"field2"`, and so on.

❑ PRIMARY KEY: You can specify exactly one field in any given table as a primary key; it is then be used as an index of unique values. Consequently, each entry can be used in other tables as a unique reference to the record to which it belongs—it's essentially the glue that holds a relational database together. To use a field as a primary key, it must be declared NOT NULL. Once again, if you pass more than one field name when defining a primary key, the specified field names are combined to create a primary key.

❑ UNIQUE: The value of each entry in a unique field must be unique among all other entries in the same field. That is, if one record's entry in the field contains the value 10, it's guaranteed that no other entry in that field will have the same value. As mentioned, uniqueness is a requirement for AUTO_INCREMENT fields.

In the course of the next couple of chapters, you'll see a lot of examples based around a homemade relational database comprising two tables. The first is called user, and it serves as a record of all users registered on an imaginary Web server. The other, access_log, contains relative paths to the Web pages each user accesses, plus counters measuring how many times she visits each page. Both tables are housed in the sample_db database.

The first table, user, is structured as follows:

Field	Type	Null	Attributes
Usernumber	MEDIUMINT(10)	no	AUTO_INCREMENT
Userid	VARCHAR(8)	no	BINARY
Userpassword	VARCHAR(20)	no	BINARY
Username	VARCHAR(30)	no	none
Userposition	VARCHAR(40)	no	none
Useremail	VARCHAR(50)	no	none
Userprofile	VARCHAR (250)	no	none

The usernumber field has an AUTO_INCREMENT attribute, so the field is automatically incremented (that is, its value increased by 1) whenever a new record is inserted with a NULL value in the first field. For example, when a new user registers and his record is added to the user table, the user number assigned will be one more than the largest number that's already in the table. You also declare this field UNIQUE, ensuring that no two rows can have the same value.

The fields userid and userpassword are both variable-length strings (lengths specified as 8 and 20 characters, respectively). They are declared BINARY, and are therefore case-sensitive. By default, character fields are case-insensitive.

The userid field will be defined as a primary key and used to establish a relationship with the access_log table, which also has a userid field.

The userposition field describes the position that a player on the team holds—in the example there are values such as Mid and Link, but you could easily modify this to football positions such as quarterback or wide receiver if your database was used to store information about an American football team.

The second table, access_log, is defined as follows:

Field	Type	Null	Attributes
page	VARCHAR(250)	no	None
userid	VARCHAR(8)	no	BINARY
visitcount	MEDIUMINT(5)	no	None
accessdate	TIMESTAMP(14)	yes	None

A TIMESTAMP type field can always take a NULL value because it stores the current system time in YYYMMDDhhmmss format when a new record is inserted, or an existing record is updated, unless it is explicitly given a date and time to store.

The access_log table has the same userid field as the user table. The userid field serves as the key to define a relationship between the two tables.

Now that you've defined the structures of the tables, let's create them and their home, the sample_db database.

If you're dreading the prospect of typing in the following 12-line SQL statement (because you don't want to have to retype the whole thing when it doesn't work the first time), here are a couple of suggestions.

If you're running PHP from UNIX, use the edit *command from the mysql command line, which calls the text editor of your choice (this command doesn't work on Windows). This is held in the* $EDITOR *environment variable, and is typically the vi editor:* mysql> edit. *If you make a typo, just reissue the edit command again. Your editor still has what you previously typed in.*

The previous command is remembered by the mysql client program. You can go back a single line by pressing the up arrow key.

You can save your lines of SQL in a text file and feed it to the mysql client: > mysql uphpuser pphppass hlocalhost < query.sql

The following CREATE TABLE command creates the user table in the sample_db database:

```
mysql> CREATE TABLE user (
    ->      usernumber MEDIUMINT(10) DEFAULT '0' NOT NULL AUTO_INCREMENT,
    ->      userid VARCHAR(8) BINARY NOT NULL,
    ->      userpassword VARCHAR(20) BINARY NOT NULL,
```

```
    ->      username VARCHAR(30) NOT NULL,
    ->      userposition VARCHAR(50) NOT NULL,
    ->      useremail VARCHAR(50) NOT NULL,
    ->      userprofile TEXT NOT NULL,
    ->      PRIMARY KEY (userid),
    ->      UNIQUE usernumber (usernumber)
    ->  );
Query OK, 0 rows affected (0.69 sec)
mysql>
```

The following CREATE TABLE command creates the access_log table:

```
mysql> CREATE TABLE access_log (
    ->      page VARCHAR(250) NOT NULL,
    ->      userid VARCHAR(8) BINARY NOT NULL,
    ->      visitcount MEDIUMINT(5) DEFAULT '0' NOT NULL,
    ->      accessdate TIMESTAMP(14),
    ->      PRIMARY KEY (userid, page));
Query OK, 0 rows affected (0.00 sec)
mysql>
```

The userid in the access_log table isn't declared as a primary key or a unique value because a user can access multiple Web pages, and each visited Web page constitutes a record in the table. Instead, the combination of userid and page is defined as the primary key.

Creating the Sample Database and Tables with PHP

If all has gone according to plan, you are now the proud owner of a couple of tables, user and access_log. All well and good, but is the main topic slipping away? The fact is that it's just as easy to generate these tables from PHP scripts. Let's see how you might create the same database and tables using PHP instead of the mysql client.

First, you need a way to issue queries to the MySQL server from within PHP. The mysql_query() function is for precisely that purpose. It takes a query string as its first argument, and makes that query on the currently selected database, using the link identifier specified as the second argument. (As usual, you can omit the identifier, in which case the last opened link is assumed.) If no link is currently open, it attempts to establish a connection first.

Do not use semicolons to terminate query strings when using them as arguments to PHP functions because they may cause your script to kick up errors.

If the given query is successfully executed, mysql_query() returns a non-zero value pointing to the returned result set, or False upon error. The following call is equivalent to having made the query SHOW DATABASES in the mysql client:

```
$link_id = db_connect();
$result = mysql_query("SHOW DATABASES", $link_id);
while($query_data = mysql_fetch_row($result)) {
  echo $query_data[0],"<P>";
}
```

This passes the expected list of databases to a table, returning a pointer to that table. You then just fetch each row and echo it out. It should look like this:

```
mysql
sample_db
test
```

`$link_id` could have been omitted from the previous code snippet because the `mysql_query()` function would have defaulted to the last opened connection.

If you want to specify the name of the database to issue a query on, you can use the PHP function `mysql_db_query()` like this:

```
$result = mysql_db_query("sample_db", "SHOW TABLES");
```

This call returns the list of tables available in the sample_db database—even if you haven't used `mysql_select_db()` to select it explicitly.

You can also use `mysql_query()` to create and drop databases:

```
$result = mysql_query("CREATE DATABASE dummy_db");
$result = mysql_query("DROP DATABASE dummy_db");
```

PHP provides you with another alternative—a pair of functions specifically designed for creating and dropping databases: `mysql_create_db()` and `mysql_drop_db()`. Both take the name of a database to be created or dropped as the first argument, followed by an optional link identifier, and return `True` if a database is successfully created/dropped and `False` upon error. For example:

```
$link_id = db_connect();
if(!mysql_create_db("dummy_db", $link_id)) die(sql_error());
                    echo "Successfully created the database dummy_db.";
if(!mysql_drop_db("dummy_db", $link_id)) die(sql_error());
                    echo "Successfully dropped the database dummy_db.";
```

Try It Out — Create a Database and Tables

The following script is an alternative to your earlier exploits at the command line. First, it creates the sample_db database, and then it defines the tables user and access_log as specified previously.

```
<?php
include "./common_db.inc";

$dbname = "sample_db";
$user_tablename = 'user';
$user_table_def = "usernumber MEDIUMINT(10) DEFAULT '0' NOT NULL
AUTO_INCREMENT,";
$user_table_def .= "userid VARCHAR(8) BINARY NOT NULL,";
$user_table_def .= "userpassword VARCHAR(20) BINARY NOT NULL,";
$user_table_def .= "username VARCHAR(30) NOT NULL,";
$user_table_def .= "userposition VARCHAR(50) NOT NULL,";
```

```
$user_table_def .= "useremail VARCHAR(50) NOT NULL,";
$user_table_def .= "userprofile TEXT NOT NULL,";
$user_table_def .= "PRIMARY KEY (userid),";
$user_table_def .= "UNIQUE usernumber (usernumber)";

$access_log_tablename = "access_log";
$access_log_table_def = "page VARCHAR(250) NOT NULL,";
$access_log_table_def .= "userid VARCHAR(8) BINARY NOT NULL,";
$access_log_table_def .= "visitcount MEDIUMINT(5) DEFAULT '0' NOT NULL,";
$access_log_table_def .= "accessdate TIMESTAMP(14),KEY page (page),";
$access_log_table_def .= "PRIMARY KEY (userid, page)";

$link_id = db_connect();
if(!$link_id) die(sql_error());

if(!mysql_query("CREATE DATABASE $dbname")) die(sql_error());

echo "Successfully created the $dbname database.<BR>";

if(!mysql_select_db($dbname)) die(sql_error());

if(!mysql_query("CREATE TABLE $user_tablename ($user_table_def)"))
                                            die(sql_error());

if(!mysql_query("CREATE TABLE $access_log_tablename ($access_log_table_def)"))
  die(sql_error());

echo "Successfully created the $user_tablename and $access_log_tablename
tables.";

?>
```

Assuming that you followed along with the command line example, running this script would generate a nice friendly error:

```
1007: Can't create database 'sample_db'. Database exists
```

To overcome this, simply go back to the command, and use the mysql client to DROP the sample_db database, and then run the script again. You should see the following output:

```
Successfully created the sample_db database.
Successfully created the user and access_log tables.
```

How It Works

The script is very straightforward. It begins by including common_db.inc, giving you use of the functions db_connect() and sql_error(), which you defined earlier:

```
<?php
include "./common_db.inc";
```

You then define the variables that describe the two tables. This is where all the hard work pays off—you just have to specify the same field descriptors that you did at the command line:

```
$dbname = "sample_db";
$user_tablename = "user";
$user_table_def = "usernumber MEDIUMINT(10) DEFAULT '0' NOT NULL
AUTO_INCREMENT,";
$user_table_def .= "userid VARCHAR(8) BINARY NOT NULL,";
$user_table_def .= "userpassword VARCHAR(20) BINARY NOT NULL,";
$user_table_def .= "username VARCHAR(30) NOT NULL,";
$user_table_def .= "userposition VARCHAR(50) NOT NULL,";
$user_table_def .= "useremail VARCHAR(50) NOT NULL,";
$user_table_def .= "userprofile TEXT NOT NULL,";
$user_table_def .= "PRIMARY KEY (userid),";
$user_table_def .= "UNIQUE usernumber (usernumber)";

$access_log_tablename = "access_log";
$access_log_table_def = "page VARCHAR(250) NOT NULL,";
$access_log_table_def .= "userid VARCHAR(8) BINARY NOT NULL,";
$access_log_table_def .= "visitcount MEDIUMINT(5) DEFAULT '0' NOT NULL,";
$access_log_table_def .= "accessdate TIMESTAMP(14),KEY page (page),";
$access_log_table_def .= "PRIMARY KEY (userid, page)";
```

Connect to the server with the following:

```
$link_id = db_connect();
if(!$link_id) die(sql_error());
```

Create the sample_db database:

```
if(!mysql_query("CREATE DATABASE $dbname")) die(sql_error());
echo "Successfully created the $dbname database.<BR>";
```

And then select it with `mysql_select_db()`:

```
if(!mysql_select_db($dbname)) die(sql_error());
```

Subsequent calls to `mysql_query()` create the user and access_log tables. If an error occurs during a query, the error number and text are displayed by calling the `sql_error()` function.

```
if(!mysql_query("CREATE TABLE $user_tablename ($user_table_def)"))
                                                die(sql_error());

if(!mysql_query("CREATE TABLE $access_log_tablename ($access_log_table_def)"))
                                                die(sql_error());
```

If you make it through to the end of the script, you confirm a successful run:

```
echo "Successfully created tables $user_tablename and $access_log_tablename.";
?>
```

Recall that the `sql_error()` function calls the `mysql_errno()` and `mysql_error()` functions if the `$MYSQL_ERRNO` variable is empty:

```
if(empty($MYSQL_ERRNO)) {
    $MYSQL_ERRNO = mysql_errno();
    $MYSQL_ERROR = mysql_error();
}
```

This ensures that the function returns the error number and text even when a database connection is successful but a subsequent query fails.

Altering Tables

So you've created a database, and populated it with carefully constructed tables. You've used it for a while and not had too much trouble—it's not perfect, but it does the job. Then out of the blue, you realize one day that your little database isn't all it's cracked up to be. You've caught on to the fact that your tables are badly designed. You've found some new data that doesn't quite fit the format you expected. Any number of things can make you sit up and realize that you need to modify the tables in your database.

MySQL provides the `ALTER TABLE` command to do just that. With this command you can:

❑   Add and delete fields or indexes (`ADD` and `DROP`).

❑   Change the definition of existing fields (`ALTER`, `CHANGE`, and `MODIFY`).

❑   Rename fields (`CHANGE`) or even the table itself (`RENAME AS`).

For example, if you wanted to change the name of the table test to tested, you could issue the following command:

```
mysql> ALTER TABLE test RENAME AS tested;
Query OK, 0 rows affected (0.02 sec)
```

The `AS` keyword is optional—this works just as well:

```
mysql> ALTER TABLE test RENAME tested;
Query OK, 0 rows affected (0.02 sec)
```

Let's add a new `ENUM` field to the user table. Call it sex; it can be used to indicate whether a user is male or female:

```
mysql> ALTER TABLE user ADD sex ENUM('M', 'F') DEFAULT 'M';
Query OK, 0 rows affected (0.24 sec)
Records: 0  Duplicates: 0 Warnings: 0

mysql> DESC user;
```

Field	Type	Null	Key	Default	Extra
...					
sex	enum('M','F')	YES		M	

```
10 rows in set (0.00 sec)
```

The new field is added as the last field in the table. You can insert a new field in the middle of a table by means of the keyword AFTER. Now drop the field so that you can insert it again:

```
mysql> ALTER TABLE user DROP sex;
Query OK, 0 rows affected (0.08 sec)
Records: 0 Duplicates: 0 Warnings: 0
```

To place the new sex field right after the username field, you could say:

```
mysql> ALTER TABLE user ADD sex ENUM('M', 'F') DEFAULT 'M' AFTER username;
Query OK, 0 rows affected (0.09 sec)
Records: 0  Duplicates: 0 Warnings: 0
```

```
mysql> desc user;
+-----------------+-------------------+------+-----+------------+----------+
| Field           | Type              | Null | Key | Default    | Extra    |
+-----------------+-------------------+------+-----+------------+----------+
| ...             |                   |      |     |            |          |
| sex             | enum('M','F')     | YES  |     | M          |          |
+-----------------+-------------------+------+-----+------------+----------+
10 rows in set (0.00 sec)
```

To place a new field at the start of the field list, you'd use the FIRST keyword instead, because there would be no preceding field.

If you're running a site aimed at female visitors, you'd probably want the default value of the sex field changed from M to F:

```
mysql> ALTER TABLE user ALTER sex SET DEFAULT 'F';
Query OK, 0 rows affected (0.01 sec)
Records: 0  Duplicates: 0 Warnings: 0
```

To change the whole definition of a field, use the MODIFY keyword:

```
mysql> ALTER TABLE user MODIFY userprofile VARCHAR(250) NOT NULL
    -> DEFAULT 'No Comment';
Query OK, 0 rows affected (0.01 sec)
Records: 0  Duplicates: 0 Warnings: 0
```

To change the field's name and its definition, you can use the CHANGE keyword:

```
mysql> ALTER TABLE user CHANGE userposition playerposition
VARCHAR(50) NOT NULL;
Query OK, 0 rows affected (0.01 sec)
Records: 0  Duplicates: 0 Warnings: 0
```

Adding or dropping indexes or primary keys is just as easy:

```
mysql> ALTER TABLE user ADD INDEX (username);
Query OK, 0 rows affected (0.08 sec)
Records: 0  Duplicates: 0 Warnings: 0
mysql> ALTER TABLE user DROP INDEX username;
Query OK, 0 rows affected (0.09 sec)
Records: 0  Duplicates: 0 Warnings: 0
```

Experiment a little with the ALTER TABLE command, and you'll soon master it. As an exercise, change back the structure of the user table.

Altering table structures in PHP is as simple as issuing any other query using the mysql_query() function. Assuming you're connected to the sample_db database, the following line is all it takes to drop the index registerdate:

```
mysql_query("ALTER TABLE user DROP INDEX registerdate");
```

Inserting Data into a Table

It's time to insert some data into the tables you created. (You'll see how to insert data using PHP in the next chapter, where it's dealt with in great detail.)

Unsurprisingly, you use the SQL command INSERT to insert new records into a table. Try this:

```
mysql> INSERT INTO access_log VALUES('/score.html', 'Pads', 2, NULL);
Query OK, 1 row affected (0.00 sec)

mysql> SELECT * FROM access_log WHERE userid = 'Pads';
+-------------+--------+------------+----------------+
| page        | userid | visitcount | accessdate     |
+-------------+--------+------------+----------------+
|/score.html  | Pads   |          2 | 20040804153559 |
+-------------+--------+------------+----------------+
1 row in set (0.00 sec)
```

If you're inserting a string value, you have to specify it in quotes.

If you wanted to carry on using this syntax, you'd need to specify all the values to be inserted into every corresponding field in a table. You give NULL as a value for the accessdate field, which is of type TIMESTAMP so that it saves the current system time in the format YYYYMMDDhhmmss. You provide a NULL or 0 value to an integer type field with an AUTO_INCREMENT attribute.

If you want to insert values into only a subset of the fields in a table, you use a slightly different syntax:

```
mysql> INSERT INTO access_log (page, userid, visitcount)
    -> VALUES('/stats.html', 'Pads', 1);
Query OK, 1 row affected (0.00 sec)
```

Assuming this query is successful, the specified fields are given the values listed, whereas the rest are assigned default values. For example, accessdate is a timestamp field, so its default is the current system time—just what you want:

```
mysql> SELECT * FROM access_log WHERE userid = 'Pads';
+-------------+--------+------------+----------------+
| page        | userid | visitcount | accessdate     |
+-------------+--------+------------+----------------+
|/score.html  | Pads   |          2 | 20040804153559 |
|/stats.html  | Pads   |          1 | 20040804152382 |
+-------------+--------+------------+----------------+
1 row in set (0.00 sec)
```

Escaping Quotes

When you insert a string value into a character or text type fields, make sure no unescaped single quotes are inserted, otherwise you're bound to see an error:

```
mysql> INSERT INTO user (userprofile)
    -> VALUES('I'm a rugby player.');
    '>
    '>
    '> ';
ERROR 1064: You have an error in your SQL syntax near 'm a PHP developer.');
  at line 1
```

Even if you issue the query terminating it with a semicolon, the mysql client insists on getting more of it because the MySQL server expects another single quote to pair off the last one. That's why there's a quote mark before the prompt. When you supply one more single quote to satisfy the server's expectation, it generates an error. The solution? You can either escape the inside single quote:

```
mysql> INSERT INTO user (userprofile) VALUES('I\'m a rugby player.');
```

Or use double quotes to surround the string value:

```
mysql> INSERT INTO user (userprofile) VALUES("I'm a rugby player.");
```

Remember that a backslash (which is used to denote a directory in a path on the DOS/Windows platform, for example) also needs to be escaped. In this case, use a double backslash:

```
mysql> INSERT INTO user (userprofile) VALUES("C:\\Program Files\\PHP");
```

If you try to insert a new record that contains the same value for a primary or unique key of an existing record, an error occurs:

```
mysql> INSERT INTO user (userid, userprofile)
    -> VALUES('Pads', 'I\'m a rugby player.');
ERROR 1062: Duplicate entry 'Pads' for key 1
```

The MySQL server complains that you are trying to insert a duplicate record that contains the same value for a primary key, userid. User Pads already exists in the table. Because the userid field is defined as a primary key, no duplicate entries are allowed.

However, you might want to insert a new record overwriting the existing one. Say, for example, that you inserted wrong values for a user record and rather than deleting the record and inserting it again, you want to replace it with a new correct one. In this case, you'd use the REPLACE command. The only difference between the INSERT and REPLACE is this: if the primary key for the new record duplicates an existing one, REPLACE overwrites the existing record, although INSERT won't, as you've seen.

```
mysql> REPLACE INTO user (userid, userprofile)
    -> VALUES('Pads', 'I\'m a rugby player.');
Query OK, 1 row affected (0.00 sec)
```

Populating the Database Tables

Now you're all set to put some records into your tables. For example, you can use the following INSERT command to insert the record for the user Pads:

```
mysql> INSERT INTO user VALUES(
    -> NULL,
    -> 'Pads',
    -> password('12345'),
    -> 'Brian Reid',
    -> 'Winger',
    -> 'Stickypads@doggiesrugby.co.za',
    -> 'A top class ball-handler.');
```

Use the function password() to encrypt the password 12345. This is a MySQL server function that you'll learn more about these in the next chapter.

Give a NULL value to the usernumber field—you'll remember that because it's an AUTO_INCREMENT field, this automatically adds one to the number assigned to each new user.

Here's how I've populated the user table. Please note that a password field isn't included because the values saved by mysql will be encrypted anyway. You should insert whatever values you want for the password field for each user:

user number	User	User name	User position	User email	User profile
1	Pads	Brian Reid	Winger	Stickypads@ doggiesrugby .co.za	A top class ball-handler
2	Nicrot	Nic Malan	Mid	therot@myw ebsiteaddres s.com	Can't stop the rot
3	Spargy	Andrew Sparg	Mid	Spargy@wha tyoumaycallit. com	Never gets the ball from Dodge
4	Dodge	Dave Mercer	Link	davidm@con techst.com	The admirals!
5	Mac	Murray McCcallum	Winger	murray@dog giesrugby. co.za	That is not my number
6	Greeny	Mark Greenfield	Utility back	greeny@green yweb.co.za	Would never drop the ball over the line

The following command inserts an access log record for user Greeny in the access_log table:

```
mysql> INSERT INTO access_log VALUES(
    -> '/penalties/index.html',
    -> 'Greeny',
    -> 9,
    -> '20040321123155');
```

Again, the accessdate field would normally be assigned a NULL value. The access_log table need only contain a few dummy records for use in the upcoming examples. It will be populated automatically toward the end of the database chapters by the application you build, which uses your table to log the number of accesses made on your fictional Web site.

Congratulations! You now have a database, populated and ready for use!

Summary

In this chapter you tackled the issue of data storage models, examined why databases are the most viable option for mass data storage, and got a brief overview of the benefits of Relational Database Management Systems (RDMBS), encompassing issues such as performance, availability, and security. You learned why MySQL, a freely available RDMBS, is a solid candidate for many of your database needs.

Here's a brief recap of the benefits of a relational database with client/server architecture (remember that not all RDBMS support it):

❑　Performance: Database normalization increases performance dramatically.

❑　Multiuser environment: The only limit on the number of concurrent users is imposed either by the type of license you purchase and/or your hardware performance.

❑　Availability: Based on a network, an RDBMS can fulfill requests "live," making up-to-date data available whenever required. In other words, you can access the database wherever and whenever you like.

❑　Security: Controlling access to data through a well-organized security scheme is essential. MySQL, for example, does not allow direct access to any of its stored data, making it very secure from the operating system level up. A user without correct permissions is not allowed to perform unauthorized operations on the data.

❑　Reliability: When it comes to software, the degree of reliability is generally measured by how often a product "dies" during service, requiring a restart. MySQL, for example, spawns child processes to handle concurrent requests. When a child process goes haywire and eventually dies, it seldom takes with it the database server as a whole, minimizing the impact on the integrity of the data stored in the database.

All in all, if you plan to develop mission-critical multiuser Web applications, you should consider a networked RDBMS for your data storage backend.

You also installed MySQL, and walked through the basics of SQL, the Structured Query Language on which MySQL is based. You familiarized yourself with some of the core SQL queries—SELECT, INSERT, REPLACE, DELETE, and UPDATE—and explored MySQL access privileges.

A script that used PHP functions to connect you to a MySQL server lets you take a peek at the data in its databases. You explored a number of ways to handle errors that occur on the MySQL server. You also looked at creating and modifying tables using SQL statements, and you populated your sample database tables with data, ready for use in the following chapters.

Retrieving Data from MySQL Using PHP

Up to now, we've concentrated mainly on ensuring that you can connect to MySQL, either through the client or through PHP's mysql functions, and create and fill tables with data. One of the first SQL statements you came across in Chapter 9 was a basic SELECT statement. There's quite a lot more you can do to precisely define the kind of data you want to retrieve, and this chapter focuses on the different ways you can use PHP scripts to get at the data stored in a MySQL database.

We start off by looking at PHP's data retrieval functions, and then take a close look at how to construct SQL SELECT statements so that they access the data you want, arranged in the way you want.

You'll learn how to limit the number of results returned, and how to order and group them, and you'll build a "user record" viewer script that'll enable you to navigate around the database tables you developed in the last chapter.

Retrieving Data Using PHP

If you use SELECT statements with mysql_query(), the result set (as you expect to see displayed on the mysql command line) is passed into result memory, and a result identifier is returned. You normally store this in a variable called $result, and use it to specify your result set in subsequent function calls.

You've already seen how mysql_fetch_row() returns a single row of data from a result set. The simple example in the last chapter used a while loop to step through each row of a result set for the SHOW DATABASES statement. Here's a slightly more advanced version entitled show_db.php.

You've already seen how mysql_fetch_row() returns a single row of data from a result set. The simple example in the last chapter used a while loop to step through each row of a result set for the SHOW DATABASES statement. Here's a slightly more advanced version entitled show_db.php, which prints out information from the user table in the sample_db database:

```
<?php
include "./common_db.inc";

$link_id = db_connect('sample_db');
$result = mysql_query("SELECT * FROM user", $link_id);

while($query_data = mysql_fetch_row($result)) {
    echo "'",$query_data[1],"' is a ",$query_data[3],"<br>";
}
?>
```

It returns the following:

```
'Nicrot' is a Mid
'Spargy' is a Mid
'Pads' is a Winger
'Dodge' is a Link
'Mac' is a Winger
'Greeny' is a Utility back
```

You begin by connecting to the server with db_connect (which is included in common_db.inc), specifying that you want to use the sample_db database. You query the database with the SQL statement "SELECT * FROM user", whose result set is the entire contents of the user table.

The variable $result stores the returned result identifier, with which you specify the result set when calling mysql_fetch_row(). This in turn fetches the first row of results, from which you echo the second and fourth fields (userid and userposition, respectively). The internal pointer then moves to the next row, and the while loop cycles until all the rows in the table have been fetched.

You can achieve the same result more efficiently by saying:

```
$result = mysql_query("SELECT userid, userposition FROM user", $link_id);

while($query_data = mysql_fetch_row($result)) {
    echo "'",$query_data[0],"' is a ",$query_data[1],"<br>";
}
```

By extracting only the fields in which you're interested, you save both time and memory.

PHP has two more functions that you can use to fetch data: mysql_fetch_array() and mysql_fetch_object(). Both basically work the same as mysql_fetch_row(), the only difference being their return types. This is best illustrated by showing how the preceding example would look if you'd used either of these other functions to fetch values from the result set.

mysql_fetch_array() returns a single associative array from a result set, storing each entry in the record against the respective field name. You'd therefore say:

```
while($query_data = mysql_fetch_array($result)) {
    echo "'",$query_data["userid"],"' is also known as ",
    $query_data["userposition"],"<br>";
}
```

`mysql_fetch_object()` returns a single object from a result set, storing each entry as a property of that object. The properties are named according to the field name, so you might say:

```
while($query_data = mysql_fetch_object($result)) {
    echo "'",$query_data->userid,"' is a ",
    $query_data->userposition,"<br>";
}
```

These two functions are particularly useful in situations where you might need to alter the structure of the database tables. Unless you change the names of the fields, you don't have to worry about the order in which they appear in the table because you can fetch the field value by specifying its name and not its index number. Although both functions are slightly slower than `mysql_fetch_row()`, they do have the added benefit of making your scripts more readable (later in a long stretch of code, for example, you might get confused about to which field is being referred to if you were just specifying indices).

There's one more function that deserves a mention at this point: `mysql_result()`, which returns the value of a specified field in a specified row. It takes the usual result indicator, plus a row number and field name as its arguments. You could rewrite the example like this:

```
$result = mysql_query("SELECT * FROM user", $link_id);
for($i =0; $i < mysql_num_rows($result); $i++){
    echo "'", mysql_result($result, $i, "userid"),"' is a ",
    mysql_result($result, $i, "userposition"),"<br>";
}
```

You also have the option of doing it backward!

```
$result = mysql_query("SELECT * FROM user", $link_id);

for($i = mysql_num_rows($result)-1; $i >=0; $i--){
    echo "'", mysql_result($result, $i, "userid"),"' is a ",
    mysql_result($result, $i, "userposition"),"<br>";
}
```

And your result set will be:

```
'Greeny' is a Utility back
'Mac' is a Winger
'Dodge' is a Link
'Pads' is a Winger
'Spargy' is a Mid
'Nicrot' is a Mid
```

The field name argument can also be written as an integer indicating the field's offset:

```
echo "'", mysql_result($result, $i, 1),"' is a ",
mysql_result($result, $i, 3),"<br>";
```

Another way to jump straight to a specific row of data is to use the `mysql_data_seek()` function. It works in a similar way to the `fseek()` function, which you used in Chapter 7 to navigate within a file stream. It takes as arguments a result indicator and an integer that indicates the position in the result set to move to. As you might expect, the function returns True on success and False if you move past the array boundary. Save this file as show_seek.php and view it in your browser:

```php
<?php
include "./common_db.inc";

$link_id = db_connect('sample_db');
$result = mysql_query("SELECT * FROM user", $link_id);

for($i = mysql_num_rows($result)-1; $i >=0; $i--){
    mysql_data_seek($result, $i);
    $query_data = mysql_fetch_array($result);
    echo "'", $query_data["userid"], "' is also known as ",
    $query_data["username"], "<P>";
}
?>
```

You've now seen a number of different ways to access result sets from your PHP scripts. With these techniques under your belt, you should be able to deal with quite a broad range of situations, and show the data you want, presented the way you want it. However, this is only half the story.

You already know that you can improve the efficiency of your scripts by keeping the result sets small. You did this by specifying the fields you wanted to view in the original SELECT statement:

```php
$result = mysql_query("SELECT userid, username FROM user", $link_id);
```

What's more, you had to go to some trouble to show the results in reverse order. What if you want them displayed alphabetically? The mind boggles! You're going to save yourself a whole lot of bother if you can arrange the data that gets put into the result set. In fact, there is a huge variety of data manipulation that is almost certainly going to be more efficiently performed by a well-constructed SQL query than by PHP itself, in terms of both execution time and complexity. For that reason, let's get back to some pure MySQL and take a look at what's possible with the SELECT command.

SQL Statements for Retrieving Data

Fire up the mysql client again, and let's take a closer look at the SELECT command. Remember that everything covered here is totally applicable to the preceding PHP examples—the table you see at the command line is simply a representation of the result set with which your PHP script ultimately has to deal.

Server Functions

Let's begin by going back to basics, issuing SELECT queries that don't require a database table at all. MySQL has a lot of very useful built-in server functions. Want to know what time it is? Don't have a watch? Ask the server:

```
mysql> SELECT now();
+---------------------+
| now()               |
+---------------------+
| 2000-08-03  16:56:03 |
+---------------------+
1 row in set   (0.00 sec)
```

The now() function returns the current time of the system on which the server is running. You can retrieve the current date and time separately using the curdate() and curtime() functions:

```
mysql> SELECT curdate(), curtime();
+------------+-----------+
| curdate()  | curtime() |
+------------+-----------+
| 2004-03-08 |  16:57:19 |
+------------+-----------+
1 row in set  (0.00 sec)
```

Many of MySQL's built-in functions are very similar to PHP's in both appearance and functionality. However, there are certain subtle differences. For example, MySQL's substring() function works much the same as PHP's substr(), but the former returns a substring counting from 1 whereas the latter counts from 0:

```
mysql> SELECT substring('test',1,1);
+-----------------------+
| substring('test',1,1) |
+-----------------------+
| t                     |
+-----------------------+
1 row in set (0.54 sec)
```

The equivalent call to PHP's substr() function would be:

```
$substring = substr('test', 0, 1);
```

Retrieving Fields

You've already seen how to retrieve data from a database table. If you want to look at the contents of the field userid in table user, you just say:

```
mysql> SELECT userid FROM user;
+--------+
| userid |
+--------+
| Dodge  |
| Greeny |
| Mac    |
| Nicrot |
| Pads   |
| Spargy |
+--------+
6 rows in set (0.05 sec)
```

You can see that six user records exist in the user table. (Note that neither field names nor table names contain any spaces; they must be typed as one word, just as variables in PHP are.)

You can retrieve multiple fields by separating them with commas:

```
mysql> SELECT userid, username FROM user;
+---------+-----------------+
| userid  | username        |
+---------+-----------------+
| Nicrot  | Nic Malan       |
| Spargy  | Andrew Sparg    |
| Pads    | Brian Reid      |
| Dodge   | Dave Mercer     |
| Mac     | Murray McCallum |
| Greeny  | Mark Greenfield |
+---------+-----------------+
6 rows in set (0.00 sec)
```

And you can look at all the fields in the table by specifying *, as in:

```
mysql> SELECT * FROM user;
```

This is equivalent to specifying every field in the table. However, when writing applications, it's worth avoiding this notation, even when you want to get all the fields from a table. If you later alter the structure of the table by adding new fields, or changing the order in which they are arranged, your applications might find that the result sets they retrieve are not the ones they were expecting, with unpredictable results. Let's look at how you can use SQL to specify your result set more clearly.

Limiting the Number of Results Returned

You can narrow the scope of retrieved data by using LIMIT and WHERE clauses. Perhaps you want the MySQL server to retrieve just a few rows of records rather than spewing them all out. You can use a LIMIT clause to tell it to do this. For example, if you want to fetch the first two rows of data matched, counting from record 0, you could say:

```
mysql> SELECT userid, username FROM user LIMIT 0, 2;
+---------+--------------+
| userid  | username     |
+---------+--------------+
| Nicrot  | Nic Malan    |
| Spargy  | Andrew Sparg |
+---------+--------------+
2 rows in set (0.00 sec)
```

If the starting point is not specified, zero is assumed, so the following query achieves the same goal:

```
mysql> SELECT userid, username FROM user LIMIT 2;
```

The LIMIT clause always comes at the end of the query.

A WHERE clause is used to selectively retrieve rows of data according to specified conditions. If you only want to consider players in the Mid position, for example, you could say:

```
mysql> SELECT userid, username FROM user
    -> WHERE userposition = 'Mid';
+--------+--------------+
| userid | username     |
+--------+--------------+
| Nicrot | Nic Malan    |
| Spargy | Andrew Sparg |
+--------+--------------+
2 rows in set (0.00 sec)
```

An equals sign is used to specify the condition (the mid position, in this example). Apart from the equality operator, which is equivalent to PHP's == operator, comparison operators in WHERE clauses look much the same as those in PHP. The following table shows the MySQL comparison operators:

Comparison Operator	Description
=	equal to
!= or <>	not equal to
<	less than
>	greater than
<=	less than or equal to
>=	greater than or equal to

There is also a null-safe comparison operator (<=>) that enables you to use values that may or may not be NULL. For example:

```
mysql> Select 1 <=> NULL;
+------------+
| 1  = NULL  |
+------------+
|       NULL |
+------------+
```

Multiple conditions can be specified using the logical operators AND and OR:

```
mysql> SELECT usernumber, userid, userposition FROM user
    -> WHERE userposition = 'Utility Back'
    -> OR userposition = 'Mid'
    -> AND usernumber < 5;

+------------+--------+--------------+
| usernumber | userid | userposition |
+------------+--------+--------------+
|          2 | Nicrot | Mid          |
|          3 | Spargy | Mid          |
|          6 | Greeny | Utility back |
+------------+--------+--------------+
3 rows in set (0.01 sec)
```

Wait a minute; something's wrong here. You only wanted to list rows of data whose usernumber field values are less than 5, but the last usernumber is 6. Why is this? It's very simple—the AND operator has only been applied to the `userposition='Mid'` condition. When the server retrieves users who are utility backs, it doesn't get as far as the last condition, so the trailing AND operator is useless. To group conditions and force the precedence of these comparisons, simply use parentheses as you would in PHP:

```
mysql> SELECT usernumber, userid, userposition FROM user
    -> WHERE (userposition = 'Utility Back'
    -> OR userposition = 'Mid')
    -> AND usernumber < 5;
+------------+--------+--------------+
| usernumber | userid | userposition |
+------------+--------+--------------+
|          2 | Nicrot | Mid          |
|          3 | Spargy | Mid          |
+------------+--------+--------------+
2 rows in set (0.47 sec)
```

For more information on MySQL operators, please visit www.mysql.com/doc/en/Functions.html.

Ordering the Results

If you need the retrieved rows of data to be sorted on a particular field, you can add an ORDER BY clause:

```
mysql> SELECT usernumber, userid, userposition FROM user
    ->     WHERE usernumber < 5 ORDER BY userid;
+------------+--------+--------------+
| usernumber | userid | userposition |
+------------+--------+--------------+
|          4 | Dodge  | Link         |
|          2 | Nicrot | Mid          |
|          1 | Pads   | Winger       |
|          3 | Spargy | Mid          |
+------------+--------+--------------+
4 rows in set (0.05 sec)
```

When sorting character fields, MySQL orders them according to ASCII value, so that uppercase letters are all placed before any lowercase letters.

An ORDER BY clause sorts retrieved values in ascending order by default, so the preceding ORDER BY clause sorts the values in ascending order by userid.

To sort the values in descending order, use the DESC keyword:

```
mysql> SELECT userid FROM user ORDER BY userid DESC;
+--------+
| userid |
+--------+
| Spargy |
| Pads   |
| Nicrot |
| Mac    |
| Greeny |
| Dodge  |
+--------+
6 rows in set (0.03 sec)
```

You can sort the retrieved rows on multiple fields by separating the field names with commas. The following example sorts userposition (in ascending order) and userid (in descending order):

```
mysql> SELECT userid, username, userposition FROM user
    ->     WHERE userposition = 'Winger'
    ->     OR userposition = 'Mid'
    ->     ORDER BY userposition, userid DESC;
+--------+-----------------+--------------+
| userid | username        | userposition |
+--------+-----------------+--------------+
| Spargy | Andrew Sparg    | Mid          |
| Nicrot | Nic Malan       | Mid          |
| Pads   | Brian Reid      | Winger       |
| Mac    | Murray McCallum | Winger       |
+--------+-----------------+--------------+
4 rows in set (0.00 sec)
```

Bear in mind that ORDER BY works much better on an indexed field because indexed fields are already sorted.

Pattern Matching

With the LIKE or NOT LIKE operators, you can specify patterns to match against, using the following special characters:

❑   % matches any possible string, including empty ones (like * in shell or DOS commands)

❑   _ matches any single character (like ? in shell or DOS commands)

To match all useremail fields ending with doggies_rugby.com, you could say:

```
mysql> SELECT userid, username, userposition, useremail FROM user
    -> WHERE useremail LIKE '%doggiesrugby.co.za'
    -> ORDER BY username;
+--------+-----------------+--------------+-----------------------------------+
| userid | username        | userposition | useremail                         |
+--------+-----------------+--------------+-----------------------------------+
| Pads   | Brian Reid      | Winger       | StickyPads@doggiesrugby.co.za     |
| Mac    | Murray McCallum | Winger       | murray@doggiesrugby.co.za         |
+--------+-----------------+--------------+-----------------------------------+
2 rows in set (0.49 sec)
```

Values in TEXT type fields are case-insensitive. If you want them to be compared case-sensitively, you need to use a BLOB type instead.

The pattern__c matches the userid Mac as two_wild cards will only match against exactly two characters. No matter how many_wildcards you add, mysql tries to find entries with the exact number of characters specified:

```
mysql> SELECT userid FROM user WHERE userid LIKE '__c';
+--------+
| userid |
+--------+
| Mac    |
+--------+
1 row in set (0.00 sec)
```

The NOT LIKE operator does precisely the opposite. Here any userids that don't end in the letter y are selected:

```
mysql> SELECT userid FROM user
    ->      WHERE userid NOT LIKE '%y';
+--------+
| userid |
+--------+
| Dodge  |
| Mac    |
| Nicrot |
| Pads   |
+--------+
4 rows in set (0.00 sec)
```

It is also possible to use regular expressions in MySQL, but that is beyond the scope of this chapter. If you want to look into them in more detail, please see the documentation at: www.mysql.com/doc/en/Pattern_matching.html.

Getting Summaries

Now let's look at how a MySQL server reports summaries on data in a table. MySQL has a number of aggregate functions that summarize the results of a query instead of retrieving rows:

❑ sum() reports the total of a given field.

❑ max() reports the largest number in the given field.

❑ min() reports the smallest number in the given field.

❑ avg() reports the average of the given field.

❑ count() reports the number of rows returned.

For instance, you can retrieve both the minimum and maximum values on integer fields by using the min() and max() functions:

```
mysql> SELECT min(usernumber), max(usernumber) FROM user;
+-----------------+-----------------+
| min(usernumber) | max(usernumber) |
+-----------------+-----------------+
|               1 |               6 |
+-----------------+-----------------+
1 row in set (0.00 sec)
```

The number of rows returned can be obtained by using count(). You can apply it in two ways:

❑ count(*fieldname*) counts only rows where the value of the specified field isn't NULL.

❑ count(*) counts every row in the result set.

The following query uses count(*) to show the number of users with usernmuber less than 3:

```
mysql> SELECT count(*) FROM user WHERE usernumber < 3;
+----------+
| count(*) |
+----------+
|        2 |
+----------+
1 row in set (0.00 sec)
```

More Complex Retrievals

Of course, what we have seen so far is not the end of the story. There are a host of keywords and queries that you can run against MySQL to meet every need. Let's say, for example, that you want a list of the players who have accessed pages ending in `.html` in an access_log table A simple list of the pages visited would give you this information but would probably contain a lot of duplicate entries—especially in a larger database. What you really want is a list of *distinct* values—in other words, no duplicate values. It'll come as no surprise to find that SQL offers the keyword `DISTINCT` to specify such a list. You can use it like this:

```
mysql> SELECT DISTINCT userid FROM access_log WHERE page LIKE '%.html'
    -> ORDER BY userid;
+--------+
| userid |
+--------+
| Brian  |
| Greeny |
| Nicrot |
| Pads   |
+--------+
4 rows in set (0.00 sec)
```

You may want to apply aggregate functions (`min()`, `max()`, `count()` and so on) to specific groups of records rather than to the database as a whole. For example, you might want to count how many of your users play in a specific position. To do so, you can group the rows returned by means of a GROUP BY clause:

```
mysql> SELECT userposition, count(*) FROM user GROUP BY userposition
    -> ORDER BY userposition DESC;
+--------------+----------+
| userposition | count(*) |
+--------------+----------+
| Winger       |        2 |
| Utility back |        1 |
| Mid          |        2 |
| Link         |        1 |
+--------------+----------+
4 rows in set (0.00 sec)
```

If you mix field names and aggregate functions in a single query without using a GROUP BY clause, you're bound to see an error:

```
mysql> SELECT userposition, count(*) FROM user ORDER BY userposition;
ERROR 1140: Mixing of GROUP columns (MIN(),MAX(),COUNT()...) with no GROUP
columns is illegal if there is no GROUP BY clause
```

Remember that an ORDER BY clause goes at the end of a query (unless you LIMIT the query, which must go at the end) and a GROUP BY clause should immediately precede it.

Now let's say that you want to sort your last table by the values in the second column—that is, sort its rows by the user counts returned against each position. You can't refer to count (*) in an ORDER BY clause, so what do you do? MySQL provides a solution: aliases. An *alias* is effectively just a new name for an expression, a field, or even a table. When you specify a field (or expression) in the SELECT statement, you can append a term like AS alias_name to it.

The result of count (*) now shows up in the result set as a field called num_users. What's more, you can treat the alias name as a normal field and use it in an ORDER BY clause:

```
mysql> SELECT userposition, count(*) AS num_users FROM user
    -> GROUP BY userposition ORDER BY num_users;
+--------------+-----------+
| userposition | num_users |
+--------------+-----------+
| Link         |         1 |
| Utility back |         1 |
| Mid          |         2 |
| Winger       |         2 |
+--------------+-----------+
4 rows in set (0.00 sec)
```

What about listing the positions for which you have more than one player? You might say this:

```
mysql> SELECT userposition, count(*) AS num_users FROM user
    -> WHERE num_users > 1 GROUP BY userposition;
ERROR 1054: Unknown column 'num_users' in 'where clause'
```

But there's a problem-num_users can't be defined until you've specified how to group the records, but you need to specify the WHERE clause before the GROUP BY clause or you'll just see a syntax error. The solution is to use a HAVING clause, which enables you to specify a condition on a column or alias at the end of the SELECT statement. Use it in just the same way as WHERE, except that you place it immediately *after* the GROUP BY clause. The server executes the query as it did before, but before returning the result set, it filters out the results that don't meet the specified condition:

```
mysql> SELECT userposition, count(*) AS num_users FROM user
    -> GROUP BY userposition HAVING num_users > 1;
+--------------+-----------+
| userposition | num_users |
+--------------+-----------+
| Mid          |         2 |
| Winger       |         2 |
+--------------+-----------+
2 rows in set (0.00 sec)
```

How would you pull data from both of your tables? Just specify them both in the FROM clause, like this:

```
mysql> SELECT username, page FROM user, access_l
+------------------+--------------+
| username         | page         |
+------------------+--------------+
| Nic Malan        | /score.html  |
| Andrew Sparg     | /score.html  |
| Brian Reid       | /score.html  |
```

```
| Dave Mercer      | /score.html     |
| Murray McCallum  | /score.html     |
| Mark Greenfield  | /score.html     |
| Nic Malan        | /stats.html     |
| Andrew Sparg     | /stats.html     |
| Brian Reid       | /stats.html     |
| Dave Mercer      | /stats.html     |
 . . .

 . . .
| Mark Greenfield  | /log.html       |
| Nic Malan        | /penalties.html |
| Andrew Sparg     | /penalties.html |
| Brian Reid       | /penalties.html |
| Dave Mercer      | /penalties.html |
| Murray McCallum  | /penalties.html |
| Mark Greenfield  | /penalties.html |
+------------------+-----------------+
60 rows in set (0.00 sec)
```

You haven't defined a relationship between the two fields, so this query returns every possible combination of values. However, the MySQL server is smart enough to know which field belongs to which table. What if you use a field name that's in both tables?

```
mysql> SELECT userid, page from user, access_log;
ERROR 1052: Column: 'userid' in field list is ambiguous
```

Well, the error message says it all. In this example, the use of the userid field is ambiguous because you could be specifying either of two separate fields. You know that they refer to the same data, but as far as the server is concerned, the fields are completely independent of one another. You can resolve the ambiguity by explicitly specifying which table from which you want to take the field values, using the following notation:

```
mysql> SELECT user.userid, page FROM user, access_log;
+--------+-----------------+
| userid | page            |
+--------+-----------------+
| Dodge  | /score.html     |
| Greeny | /score.html     |
| Mac    | /score.html     |
| Nicrot | /score.html     |
| Pads   | /score.html     |
| Spargy | /score.html     |
 . . .

 . . .
| Spargy | /log.html       |
| Dodge  | /penalties.html |
| Greeny | /penalties.html |
| Mac    | /penalties.html |
| Nicrot | /penalties.html |
| Pads   | /penalties.html |
| Spargy | /penalties.html |
+--------+-----------------+
60 rows in set (0.01 sec)
```

Every entry in the access log table should correspond to one in the user table—that's the way the database is designed to work. It makes sense really: You're only logging page accesses for registered users, so anyone showing up in the access log must be a registered user. In this case, the userid field is common to both tables. Say, for example, that you want to look at who's been viewing which pages. Now that you can make a distinction between the two fields called userid, you can equate them in a WHERE clause, and narrow the result set as required:

```
mysql> SELECT user.userid, page FROM user, access_log
    -> WHERE user.userid = access_log.userid;
+--------+------------------+
| userid | page             |
+--------+------------------+
| Dodge  | /score.html      |
| Dodge  | /stats.html      |
| Greeny | /log.html        |
| Greeny | /penalties.html  |
| Mac    | /score.html      |
| Nicrot | /log.html        |
| Nicrot | /refs.html       |
| Pads   | /score.html      |
+--------+------------------+
8 rows in set (0.00 sec)
```

You've just witnessed the power of relational databases. The connection you just made to relate data records in multiple tables is called a *join*—you're producing a result set by joining the records from one table to those in another. In your last query, the userid field served as a key to join the user and access_log tables; that is, you used userid to establish explicit relationships between the records in the two tables. Keys are essential in join operations because they are related across tables, removing the need for database designers having to repeat that data in every table.

There are many more advanced join operations than the one you've seen here, but this one is more than adequate for most situations. You may want to read some more advanced MySQL references for further information on additional complex queries and join operations. However, one rule of thumb applies no matter what level you're aiming for in building your SQL muscle: practice makes perfect. Use your mysql client to experiment with queries with a variety of field types—ultimately, that's the only way to really appreciate the possibilities and intricacies of the SQL syntax.

Putting It All Together

Now let's build a user record viewer, entitled userviewer.php, that's going to use the tables from the sample_db database and perform the following functions:

❑ Connect to the database sample_db that holds the user and access_log tables.

❑ Display a list of registered users and navigation links, giving the administrator the option to move back and forth.

❑ Display field name links that can be toggled to sort the list of users either in ascending or descending order on the specified field.

❑ For each user display a link to a new window that presents more detailed information on that user and his access log records.

Figure 10-1 shows what the interface looks like so you'll know what you're working toward.

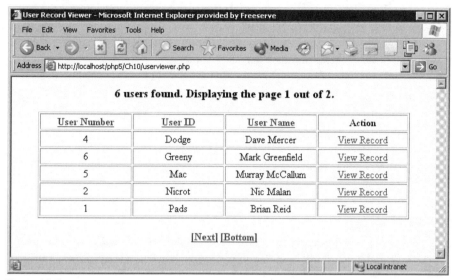

Figure 10-1

It'll take two separate files to create the database browser. The global variables and commonly used functions go into the include file, common_db.inc, and the business end of the browser will be placed in a file calleduserviewer.php. You can assume the existence of database sample_db and tables user and access_log, and that data is present in both these tables.

The common_db.inc File Contents

The following sections explain piece by piece what you should have in the file common_db.inc.

For the sake of brevity, the code for functions db_connect() *and* sql_error() *isn't shown here. These should be exactly as specified in the last chapter.*

Global Variables

There are a few variables that you must use in the script. You can place all of them in common_db.inc, and access them as global variables from within the userviewer script:(changing the variables to reflect your settings):

```php
<?php
$dbhost = 'localhost';
$dbusername = 'phpuser';
$dbuserpassword = 'phppass';
$default_dbname = 'sample_db';
```

Of course you'll change the variables to reflect your settings.

Stipulate the default for number of records to be displayed per page (5):

```php
$records_per_page = 5;
```

Indicate the names of the user and access log tables:

```
$user_tablename = 'user';
$access_log_tablename = 'access_log';
```

Denote holders for MySQL error numbers and error text:

```
$MYSQL_ERRNO = '';
$MYSQL_ERROR = '';
```

And state the size of the new browser window:

```
$new_win_width = 600;
$new_win_height = 400;
```

html_header()

The html_header() function starts an HTML page and defines the JavaScript function open_window() that you can call to open a new window when displaying a user's record:

```
function html_header()
{
    global $new_win_width, $new_win_height;
    ?>
    <HTML>
    <HEAD>
    <SCRIPT LANGUAGE="JavaScript" TYPE="text/javascript">
    <!--
    function open_window(url)
    {
        var NEW_WIN = null;
        NEW_WIN = window.open ("", "RecordViewer",
                               "toolbar=no,width="+
                               <?php echo $new_win_width ?>+
                               ",height="+<?php echo $new_win_height?>+
                               ",directories=no,status=no"+
                               ",scrollbars=yes,resize=no,menubar=no");
        NEW_WIN.location.href = url;
    }
    //-->
    </SCRIPT>
    <TITLE>User Record Viewer</TITLE>
    </HEAD>
    <BODY>
    <?php
}
```

html_footer()

The html_footer() function ends an HTML page (you've already seen the db_connect() and sql_error() functions in action):

```
function html_footer()
{
    ?>
    </BODY>
    </HTML>
    <?php
}

function db_connect($dbname='')
{
    ...
}

function sql_error()
{
    ...
}
```

error_message()

The `error_message()` function reports errors using the JavaScript `alert()` method:

```
function error_message($msg)
{
    html_header();
    echo "<SCRIPT>alert(\"Error: $msg\ ");;history.go(-1)</SCRIPT>";
    html_footer();
    exit;
}
?>
```

With the `.inc` file sorted out, let's go to the business end of the application.

The userviewer.php File Contents

The `userviewer.php` script makes use of the include file `common_db.inc`. It's included from the current directory for the sake of simplicity:

```
<?php
include "./common_db.inc";
```

Remember, though, that in practice it's never a good idea to include your database username and password in Web scripts. Put them in a separate file and place it beyond the Web document root.

Most of the actual code you use to implement the browser is contained in a couple of functions, which gather and display your database information. Let's take a look at those functions now.

list_records()

The `list_records()` function displays a list of registered users, along with navigation links and a record viewer link that calls the `view_record()` function. Start by connecting to the default database,

407

and fetching the total number of registered users. If there aren't any, display an error message to that effect.

```
function list_records()
{
    global $default_dbname, $user_tablename;
    global $records_per_page;
    $PHP_SELF = "userviewer.php";

    $link_id = db_connect($default_dbname);
    if(!$link_id) error_message(sql_error());

    $query = "SELECT count(*) FROM $user_tablename";

    $result = mysql_query($query);
    if(!$result) error_message(sql_error());

    $query_data = mysql_fetch_row($result);
    $total_num_user = $query_data[0];
    if(!$total_num_user) error_message('No User Found!');
```

The $cur_page global variable—denoting the current page number—holds the key to the list navigation. If more than one page of data is returned in the list, you chop it up into multiple pages. The page length is determined by the global variable $records_per_page. The total number of pages is obtained by dividing the total number of users ($total_num_user) by the length of a page ($records_per_page) and rounding up the resulting value with the ceil() function.

You increment the page number before it's echoed out because the $cur_page global variable counts from zero, and the page numbering that you display should start at 1. The variable $record is defined as the upper bound for the LIMIT statement, which you use in a SQL query in a moment. $cur_page is initilized with a value sent once the user has clicked a navigation link. If there is no value, set it to 0:

```
if(empty($_GET['next_page'])) {
    $_GET['next_page'] = 0;
}
$cur_page = $_GET['next_page'];
$page_num = $cur_page + 1;
$record = $cur_page * $records_per_page + 5;
$total_num_page = $last_page_num = ceil($total_num_user/$records_per_page);

html_header();

echo "<CENTER><H3>$total_num_user users found. Displaying the page
                $page_num out of $last_page_num.</H3></CENTER>\n";
```

It's time to begin constructing the SQL query that will pull the data from your database and organize it in the manner you want. The way in which this query is constructed really depends on which link the user clicks. How do you dynamically build a SQL query?

Well, the answer lies in using PHP's special $_GET array. If you send the information for the query in the URL, you can pull the information you need from it, and use it in the query. Remember that on the first visit to the page, there are no values in $_GET, so the first thing to do is initialize all of your values to defaults that you can choose. Set your default order by to be the userid field, the default sort order to be ascending, and the default page number to be 1 (Recall that this entails setting $cur_page to 0).

The sort order can be toggled by clicking field names in the header cell of the list table. This feature is implemented by giving the opposite sort order value to the $sort_order variable before echoing it out in HTML anchors. Take another look at Figure 10-1 presented earlier in the chapter and notice that there are links below the table: Next and Bottom (as well as Top and Prev, which are not visible on the opening screen). These links don't want to change the sort order of the list, they merely enable you to navigate the table, so give them their own sort order variable called $org_sort_order:

```
if (empty($_GET['order_by'])){
    $_GET['order_by'] = 'userid';
}
$order_by = $_GET['order_by'];

if (empty($_GET['sort_order']))
{
    $_GET['sort_order'] = 'ASC';
    $sort_order = 'ASC';
}

if ($_GET['sort_order'] == 'ASC') {
    $sort_order = 'DESC';
    $org_sort_order = 'ASC';
}
else {
    $sort_order = 'ASC';
    $org_sort_order = 'DESC';
}
```

Build a LIMIT clause in $limit_str using variables $cur_page, $records_per_page, and $record to calculate start and end pointers.

```
$limit_str = "LIMIT ". $cur_page * $records_per_page . ", $record";
```

The finalized query is constructed by passing the values you've captured from the $_GET array, and the $limit_str variable that you just created:

```
$query = "SELECT usernumber, userid, username FROM $user_tablename ORDER BY
                $_GET[order_by] $_GET[sort_order]
                $limit_str ";

$result = mysql_query($query);
if(!$result){
error_message(sql_error());
}
?>
```

Now create a table to hold the list:

```
<DIV ALIGN="CENTER">
<TABLE BORDER="1" WIDTH="90%" CELLPADDING="2">
```

```
     <TR>
         <TH WIDTH="25%" NOWRAP>
             <A HREF="<?php echo "$PHP_SELF?action=list_records&
                                    sort_order=$sort_order&
                                    order_by=usernumber"; ?>">
             User Number
             </A>
         </TH>
         <TH WIDTH="25%" NOWRAP>
             <A HREF="<?php echo "$PHP_SELF?action=list_records&
                                    sort_order=$sort_order&
                                    order_by=userid"; ?>">
             User ID
             </A>
         </TH>
         <TH WIDTH="25%" NOWRAP>
             <A HREF="<?php echo "$PHP_SELF?action=list_records&
                                    sort_order=$sort_order&
                                    order_by=username"; ?>">
                 User Name
             </A>
         </TH>
         <TH WIDTH="25%" NOWRAP>Action</TH>
     </TR>
<?php
```

The links you supply in the table headers are an integral part of this program. Each link refers to the userviewer page ($PHP`SELF), and supplies values that will populate the $`GET array, which will then be used in your script once it is run again. Notice that you specify the action as list`records; this is important because you'll use a switch statement at the end of the program to determine which function in the userviewer file you will use.

Next, a while loop steps through the result set, constructing each row in the table. Notice, that the last row contains a JavaScript call to the open_window function that's defined in common_db.inc. You've also specified that action be set to view_record, which means that you'll call the view_record() function instead of list_records()—we'll discuss view_record() in a moment. Here's the code:

```
     while($query_data = mysql_fetch_array($result)) {
         $usernumber = $query_data["usernumber"];
         $userid = $query_data["userid"];
         $username = $query_data["username"];
         echo "<TR>\n";
         echo "<TD WIDTH=\"25%\" ALIGN=\"CENTER\">$usernumber</TD>\n";
         echo "<TD WIDTH=\"25%\" ALIGN=\"CENTER\">$userid</TD>\n";
         echo "<TD WIDTH=\"25%\" ALIGN=\"CENTER\">$username</TD>\n";
         echo "<TD WIDTH=\"25%\" ALIGN=\"CENTER\">
             <A HREF=\"javascript:open_window('$PHP_SELF?action=view_record&
             userid=$userid');\">View Record</A></TD>\n";
         echo "</TR>\n";
     }
?>
</TABLE>
</DIV>
```

```php
<?php
    echo "<BR>\n";
    echo "<STRONG><CENTER>";
```

Finally, you need to build navigation links based on the current page number and the total number of pages. Because the $cur_page variable starts counting from zero, you use another variable, $page_num, to maintain the current page number. If the current page number is greater than 1, you need the Top and Prev links to enable the user to jump to the first page and previous page, respectively:

```php
if($page_num > 1) {
    $prev_page = $cur_page - 1;

    echo "<A HREF=\"$PHP_SELF?action=list_records&
        sort_order=$org_sort_order&order_by=$order_by&next_page=0\">[Top]</A>";

    echo "<A HREF=\"$PHP_SELF?action=list_records&sort_order=$org_sort_order
        &order_by=$order_by&next_page=$prev_page\">[Prev]</A> ";
}
```

Likewise, the Next and Bottom links are displayed if the current page number is smaller than the total number of pages:

```php
if($page_num < $total_num_page) {
    $next_page = $cur_page + 1;
    $last_page = $total_num_page - 1;

    echo "<A HREF=\"$PHP_SELF?action=list_records&sort_order=$org_sort_order
        &order_by=$order_by&next_page=$next_page\">[Next]</A> ";

    echo "<A HREF=\"$PHP_SELF?action=list_records&sort_order=$org_sort_order&
        order_by=$order_by&next_page=$last_page\">[Bottom]</A>";
}

echo "</STRONG></CENTER>";
```

Finish off the list_records() function with a call to the html_footer() function defined in common_db.inc:

```php
html_footer();
}
```

You can run the example now without the use of the View Record links on the right side of the table. In order for those to work, you need to create the view_record() function.

view_record()

The view_record() function displays detailed information about a given user and his or her access log data.

When clicked, a View Record link opens up a new browser window to display the specified user's information by calling the JavaScript function open_window(), which in turn calls the script with the $action variable set to invoke the view_record() function.

You start by fetching the entire record of the specified user (from the user table), along with the access log records (from the access log table). If no access has been made to any of the Web pages currently set up to be logged, a message to that effect is displayed and the script terminates. You don't have to worry about whether $_GET is set in this function because view_record() is called only from the userviewer page itself—in other words, you can't go straight to the view records page without first clicking a link that will set the $_GET variables for you:

```php
function view_record()
{
    global $default_dbname, $user_tablename, $access_log_tablename;
    $PHP_SELF = $_SERVER['PHP_SELF'];
    $userid = $_GET['userid'];

    if(empty($userid)){
        error_message('Empty User ID!');
    }

    $link_id = db_connect($default_dbname);

    if(!$link_id){
        error_message(sql_error());
    }

    $query = "SELECT * FROM $user_tablename WHERE userid = '$userid'";
    $result = mysql_query($query);

    if(!$result){
        error_message(sql_error());
    }

    $query_data = mysql_fetch_array($result);
    $usernumber = $query_data["usernumber"];
    $userid = $query_data["userid"];
    $username = $query_data["username"];
    $userposition = $query_data["userposition"];
    $useremail = $query_data["useremail"];
    $userprofile = $query_data["userprofile"];
```

You display a table of information pertaining to the selected user:

```php
    html_header();
    echo "<CENTER><H3>
        Record for User No.$usernumber - $userid($username)
        </H3></CENTER>";

?>
<DIV ALIGN="CENTER">
<TABLE BORDER="1" WIDTH="90%" CELLPADDING="2">
    <TR>
        <TH WIDTH="40%">position</TH>
        <TD WIDTH="60%"><?php echo $userposition ?></TD>
    </TR>
```

```
    <TR>
        <TH WIDTH="40%">Email</TH>
        <TD WIDTH="60%"><?php echo "<A HREF=\"mailto:$useremail\">$useremail</A>"
        ; ?></TD>
    </TR>
    <TR>
        <TH WIDTH="40%">Profile</TH>
        <TD WIDTH="60%"><?php echo $userprofile ?></TD>
    </TR>

</TABLE>
</DIV>
<?php
    echo "<HR SIZE=\"2\" WIDTH=\"90%\">\n";
```

Then, display a second table, listing the user's access log records:

```
$query = "SELECT page, visitcount, accessdate FROM $access_log_tablename
        WHERE userid = '$userid'";

$result = mysql_query($query);
if(!$result){

    error_message(sql_error());

}
```

The `mysql_num_rows()` function returns 0 when no record is found in the access_log table containing the specified user's access data:

```
    if(!mysql_num_rows($result)){
        echo "<CENTER>No access log record for $userid ($username).</CENTER>";
    } else {
        echo "<CENTER>Access log record(s) for $userid ($username).</CENTER>";
?>
<DIV ALIGN="CENTER">
<TABLE BORDER="1" WIDTH="90%" CELLPADDING="2">
    <TR>
        <TH WIDTH="40%" NOWRAP>Web Page</TH>
        <TH WIDTH="20%" NOWRAP>Visit Counts</TH>
        <TH WIDTH="40%" NOWRAP>Last Access Time</TH>
    </TR>
<?php
        while($query_data = mysql_fetch_array($result)) {
            $page = $query_data["page"];
            $visitcount = $query_data["visitcount"];
```

To get a formatted date string, use PHP's `substr()` function (you'll meet a MySQL server function in the next chapter that does the trick in one go):

```
        $accessdate = substr($query_data["accessdate"], 0, 4) . '-' .
            substr($query_data["accessdate"], 4, 2) . '-' .
            substr($query_data["accessdate"], 6, 2) . ' ' .
```

```
                 substr($query_data["accessdate"], 8, 2) . ':' .
                 substr($query_data["accessdate"], 10, 2) . ':' .
                 substr($query_data["accessdate"], 12, 2);

            echo "<TR>\n";
            echo "<TD WIDTH=\"40%\">$page</TD>\n";
            echo "<TD WIDTH=\"20%\" ALIGN=\"CENTER\">$visitcount</TD>\n";
            echo "<TD WIDTH=\"40%\" ALIGN=\"CENTER\">$accessdate</TD>\n";
            echo "</TR>\n";
        }
    ?>
        </TR>
    </TABLE>
    </DIV>
    <?php
        }
        html_footer();
    }
```

Choosing an Action to Take

The last section of userview.php is the one that's initially run when you execute the script. Depending on the value of the variable $action, it calls one or another of the main functions defined previously. You therefore build dual functionality into one script. Of course, you need a default to be run in the event that it is the first visit to the page, so you check to see whether action has been set, and if it hasn't, you assign it a default value of list_records:

```
if (empty($_GET['action'])){
    $_GET['action'] = 'list_records';
}
switch($_GET['action']) {
    case "view_record":
        view_record();
    break;
    default:
        list_records();
    break;
}
```

All done! Fire up your browser and navigate to the userviewer.php page.

Using the User Viewer

Just to give you an example of how the program runs, let's say you want to list the records by the user name and view the user details for Brian Reid. Depending on the data in your sample_db, your result should look much like Figure 10-2.

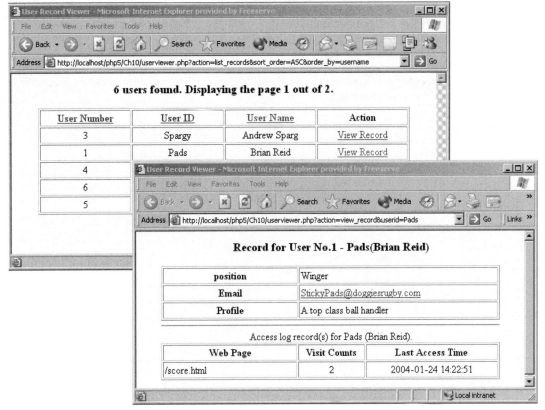

Figure 10-2

Notice the URL in both the windows—the top one tells you that the data has been ordered by the username, and the new window shows you the user details for Brian Reid, accessed by the userid `Pads`.

Summary

In this chapter, you looked at ways of retrieving data from a database, and you used the core MySQL command `SELECT` to retrieve data from a table.

You learned that a number of clauses are often utilized to construct a query to narrow the scope of the retrieved results, order them or group them:

❑   `LIMIT` clause to limit the number of results returned

❑   `WHERE` clause to specify conditions of retrieval

❑   `ORDER BY` clause to order the returned results

❑   `GROUP BY` clause to group the returned results

Also introduced were aliases and simple join operations to retrieve data from multiple tables. You explored built-in MySQL server functions and MySQL-related PHP functions to work with data in a database.

Additionally, you created a user record viewer that can divide the list of user records into a number of pages and gives an option to navigate through them. The script also enabled you to view a specific user's personal data and access log information.

The discussion of database management in the following chapter: inserting, deleting, and updating database records using PHP.

Using PHP to Manipulate Data in MySQL

In this chapter you learn how to manipulate MySQL database records within PHP. Specifically, you'll see how to insert new records into a database table using PHP, and how to delete and update existing records in a database table.

To understand these functionalities using PHP, you'll create user registration and access logger scripts. You'll also upgrade the user record viewer you built in Chapter 10 to enable you to manipulate user records. This chapter concludes the three-chapter series of adventures into the world of MySQL and PHP MySQL connectivity.

Inserting Records Using PHP

You saw how to insert data into a table using the `mysql` client in the preceding chapter. For example, the following query inserts a record for the user Pads:

```
mysql> INSERT INTO user VALUES(
    -> NULL,
    -> 'Pads',
    -> Password(12345),
    -> 'Brian Reid',
    -> 'Winger',
    -> 'Stickypads@doggies_rugby.com',
    -> 'A top class ball-handler.');
```

And you know you can achieve the same goal using PHP:

```
$result = mysql_query("INSERT INTO user VALUES( ... )");
```

Normally, you use PHP variables to insert values into a table instead of specifying them directly in a query:

```
$query = "INSERT INTO user VALUES(NULL, '$userid',
                        password('$userpassword'),
                        '$username', '$userposition', '$useremail',
                        '$userprofile')";
$result = mysql_query($query);
```

Recall that the usernumber field is of AUTO_INCREMENT type—you specify it as NULL so that each new record you add has a usernumber value that's one greater than the last.

It's sometimes quite useful to get at the resulting value; for example, you might want to show a new user his user number on registration. The auto-incremented number generated by the last INSERT query can be obtained using the mysql_insert_id() function. Here's an example:

```
$link_id = db_connect('sample_db');
$result = mysql_query("INSERT INTO user (userid)
                        VALUES('sphinx')");
$usernumber = mysql_insert_id($link_id);
echo "Thank you. Your usernumber is $usernumber.";
```

Special Characters

As you learned in Chapter 10, it's essential to escape every single quote contained in a string value before inserting it into a database table, or it causes an error. In that chapter, you wanted to enter the string "I'm a rugby player." into the TEXT type userprofile field. That particular string works nicely in MySQL as well as PHP because it's surrounded by double quotes. If you were to use single quotes to surround the string, you'd need to escape the quote mark contained within it. Here are some examples:

```
"I'm a PHP developer."
```
works.

```
'I\m a PHP developer.'
```
also works.

```
'I'm a PHP developer.'
```
doesn't work.

But why bother to make the distinction? Surely the best thing to do is to escape all instances of both sorts of quote marks—after all, in PHP, escaped quotes work in both single- and double-quoted string values. The problem is this: it depends upon the program in which you're using it. If you backslashed the single quote in the first example, you'd have this: `"I\'m a PHP developer."`

If you used PHP to echo this out, you'd get the whole string, backslash and all, which is not what you want. With this problem in mind, PHP provides you with a pair of very useful functions: addslashes() and stripslashes().

These two functions are closely related. addslashes() takes a string argument, prefixes every character that should be escaped in database queries with a backslash, and then returns the modified string. stripslashes() complements it by stripping out these backslashes.

The following lines of code show how you might use these functions to insert a record into the user table, having escaped the values as required:

```
$link_id = db_connect('sample_db');
$userprofile = addslashes($userprofile);
$query = "INSERT INTO user (userprofile) VALUES ('$userprofile')";
mysql_query($query, $link_id);
$userprofile = stripslashes($userprofile);
```

Assuming that $userprofile initially contains the following:

```
I'm a PHP developer.
```

you pass it through addslashes(), after which it contains this:

```
I\'m a PHP developer.
```

And now it's safe to pass it to the SQL statement. When you read the value out of the database again, it'll be just as you want it—the server will return the quote character, and not the escape sequence. If you want to use the variable $userprofile in subsequent code, however, you don't want extraneous backslashes messing up your beautifully formatted text, and that's where stripslashes() comes in—you use it to tidy up the string.

htmlspecialchars()

Escaped quotes are by no means the end of the story as far as special characters are concerned. As you know, certain characters have special significance in HTML—<, for example, denotes the start of a tag. If it were contained in a user-entered string that was then presented in an HTML page, it would inevitably throw the browser (or at least the HTML parser program) into a hundred kinds of bother. The parser would assume that everything following it (until a > character was reached) referred to a tag. Suffice to say, it's very unlikely that it would!

To avoid this character looking like the start of a tag, you can represent it in the form of an HTML entity, which looks like this:

```
&lt;
```

The PHP function htmlspecialchars()—which you may remember seeing very briefly in Chapter 5—takes care of translating HTML special characters like this into their entity form, so you've no need to worry about translating them yourself. Just as with the slash adding/stripping functions you just saw, htmlspecialchars() takes a string argument, changes all instances of special characters to corresponding safe forms (entity form in this case) and returns the modified string:

```
$userprofile = htmlspecialchars($userprofile);
```

The following characters are translated:

Special Character	HTML Entity
& (ampersand)	&amp;
" (double quote)	&quot;
< (less than)	&lt;
> (greater than)	&gt;

Now that you've seen some of the subtleties involved in PHP data insertion, let's move on to look at how you can update or delete existing data.

Updating and Deleting Records in Tables

Let's say that one of your registered users asks you to change his name, complaining that it contains a typo. Instead of replacing a whole record for that user with a new value for the username field, you'd probably just want to change his name in the existing record. As you've seen, this is where the UPDATE command comes into play. You'd use a statement like this:

```
UPDATE user SET username = 'Darren Ebbs'
          WHERE username = 'Daren Ebbs'
```

This changes all instances of the value Daren Ebs in the username field to Darren Ebbs.

If you want to throw away an existing record from a table, use the DELETE command:

```
DELETE FROM access_log WHERE page = 'who.html'
```

This deletes any record with page = 'who.html'.

The following UPDATE query is an example of what you should *not* do. It updates every record in the user table in such a way that any user can log on to your site using the password comeonin:

```
UPDATE user SET userpassword = password('comeonin')
```

Worse still, the following query empties the user table:

```
DELETE FROM user
```

Even an experienced database manager can make this kind of blunder—it just takes a bit of carelessness or the accidental dropping of a pen onto the Enter key while typing in a query, so do be careful when using these commands.

Suppose you want to delete all access log records from the year 1999 because they're no longer needed. You'd use a query that looks like this:

```
mysql> DELETE FROM access_log WHERE accessdate LIKE '1999%';
```

A user might want to change his password from time to time. The following query changes his password to guessit:

```
mysql> UPDATE user SET userpassword = password('guessit')
    -> WHERE userid = 'Greeny';
Query OK, 1 row affected (0.00 sec)
Rows matched: 1 Changed: 1 Warnings: 0
```

The server reports that one record matched the specified condition and has therefore been changed. If the server finds no matching record, no update operation is performed:

```
mysql> UPDATE user SET userpassword = password('guessit')
    -> WHERE userid = 'Ginger';
Query OK, 0 rows affected (0.00 sec)
Rows matched: 0 Changed: 0 Warnings: 0
```

You can utilize existing values to update a record. For example, the visitcount field keeps track of how many times a specific user has visited a certain Web page. If the user visits that page again, you need some way to increment its value. You might do this by fetching the current value from the access_log table, incrementing it, and putting it back again. However, you can make the job a lot simpler by using the existing value in your UPDATE query. The following query does exactly what you want—it increments the visitcount field for user Dodge on the /score.html page:

```
mysql> UPDATE access_log SET visitcount = visitcount + 1
    -> WHERE user_id = 'Dodge' AND page = '/score.html';
Query OK, 1 row affected (0.00 sec)
Rows matched: 1 Changed: 1 Warnings: 0
```

You'll need to update the lastaccesstime field separately. We'll discuss this later on in the chapter.

String values can be modified in a similar way:

```
mysql> UPDATE user SET userid = concat(userid, '_1');
Query OK, 1 row affected (0.00 sec)
Rows matched: 6 Changed: 6 Warnings: 0
```

This query uses the MySQL server function to join strings, appending the string _1 to every userid field value. The user ID Dodge, for example, becomes Dodge_1. This method comes in handy when a new user requests a user ID that is already in use, and you want to suggest an alternative.

If you were to use SET userid = userid + '_1', it would set the userid to 0, rather than bundy_1.

Multiple assignments involving the same field are also possible:

```
mysql> UPDATE access_log
    -> SET visitcount = visitcount + 1, visitcount = visitcount * 2;
Query OK, 6 rows affected (0.00 sec)
Rows matched: 6 Changed: 6 Warnings: 0
```

Assignments are evaluated from left to right, so the second assignment will use the incremented visitcount value from the first assignment. That is, it increments and then doubles every value in the visitcount field.

By now you're probably used to seeing a query report at the MySQL command line. If you use a DELETE or UPDATE query, the server automatically tells you how many rows were affected, how long it took to execute the query, counts for rows matched and changed, and any warnings produced.

You can get at the first of these from your PHP scripts by using the function mysql_affected_rows(). This takes a link identifier and returns the number of rows affected by the previous SQL query—a DELETE query in the following example:

```
$link_id = db_connect("sample_db");
mysql_query("DELETE FROM access_log
            WHERE page = '/penalties.html'");
$num_rows = mysql_affected_rows($link_id);
echo "$num_rows user(s) have been deleted.";
```

If just one user had visited the penalties page, this code would echo:

```
1 user(s) have been deleted.
```

If you were to delete all the records in a table, mysql_affected_rows() would return 0.

Working with Date and Time Type Fields

Arguably, of all the MySQL data types, the trickiest to handle properly are date and time types. You need a lot of practice to work with them comfortably. Fields with these types store date and time values in the following formats:

Data Type	Data Format
DATE	2004-01-01
TIME	12:00:00
DATETIME	2004-01-01 12:00:00
TIMESTAMP	20000101120000
YEAR	2004

If you attempt to insert illegally formatted date and/or time values into fields with these data types, the relevant entry is filled with 0s. For example, inserting the string Pads into a TIME type field results in the value "00000000000000" being saved in the field:

```
mysql> select accessdate from access_log where userid = 'Pads' AND page ='';
+----------------+
| accessdate     |
+----------------+
| 00000000000000 |
+----------------+
1 row in set (0.00 sec)
```

The MySQL server provides a set of built-in date- and time-related functions that can help you to ensure that you insert correct values. You've already seen the now() function, which returns the current date and time in DATETIME format:

```
mysql> select now();
+------------------------+
| now()                  |
+------------------------+
| 2004-03-04  19:30:15   |
+------------------------+
1 row in set (0.00 sec)
```

And the curdate() and curtime() functions, which return the same as separate DATE and TIME type values:

```
mysql> select curdate(), curtime();
+------------+-----------+
| curdate()  | curtime() |
+------------+-----------+
| 2004-03-04 | 19:31:33  |
+------------+-----------+
1 row in set (0.00 sec)
```

To work with a TIMESTAMP field, you can specify either the date and time to insert in a string of 14 digits, or NULL to store the current system date and time in the same format. To properly update the access log (completing the example begun earlier), you'd say:

```
mysql> UPDATE access_log
    -> SET visitcount = visitcount + 1, accessdate = NULL
    -> WHERE userid = 'Dodge' AND page = '/score.html';
Query OK, 1 row affected (0.00 sec)
Rows matched: 1 Changed: 1 Warnings: 0
```

The date_format() server function returns a formatted date and time value. It takes a DATE or DATETIME type argument, followed by a formatting string argument. Assuming that lastaccesstime is of the DATE or DATETIME type, you could say:

```
mysql> SELECT date_format('2004-03-04 22:23:00', '%M %e, %Y');
+-------------------------------------------------+
| date_format('2004-03-04 22:23:00', '%M %e, %Y') |
+-------------------------------------------------+
| March 4, 2004                                   |
+-------------------------------------------------+
1 row in set (0.03 sec)
```

There are more than 30 specifiers you can use to construct the formatting string. Here are some of the more common ones:

Specifier	Description
%s	Second in 2-digit numeric form (00,01···)
%i	Minute in 2-digit numeric form (00,01···)
%H	Hour in 2-digit 24-hour numeric form (00,01···)
%h	Hour in 2-digit 12-hour numeric form (00,01···)
%T	Time in 24-hour form (hh:mm:ss)
%r	Time in 12-hour form (hh:mm:ss AM|PM)
%W	Weekday name (Monday, Tuesday, Wednesday···)
%a	Abridged weekday name (Mon, Tue, Wed···)
%d	Day of the month in 2-digit numeric form (01,02,03···)
%e	Day of the month in numeric form (1,2,3···)
%D	Day of the month with an ordinal suffix (1st, 2nd, 3rd···)
%M	Name of the month (January, February···)
%b	Abridged name of the month (Jan, Feb···)
%Y	Year in 4-digit numeric form
%y	Year in 2-digit numeric form

For a complete list, please see the MySQL documentation at www.mysql.com/doc/en/Date_and_time_functions.html#IDX1335.

In the view_record() function of the user record viewer script in the last chapter, you formatted the accessdate field value with the following lines of code:

```
$accessdate = substr($query_data["accessdate"], 0, 4) . '-' .
   substr($query_data["accessdate"], 4, 2) . '-' .
   substr($query_data["accessdate"], 6, 2) . ' ' .
   substr($query_data["accessdate"], 8, 2) . ':' .
   substr($query_data["accessdate"], 10, 2) . ':' .
   substr($query_data["accessdate"], 12, 2);
```

which produced the date and time in this format:

```
2004-01-22 10:31:35
```

Now you can achieve the same goal with a single query:

```
mysql> SELECT date_format(accessdate, '%Y-%m-%d %H:%i:%s')
    -> FROM access_log WHERE userid='Dodge';
+------------------------------------------+
| date_format(accessdate, `%Y-%m-%d %H:%i:%s') |
```

```
+-----------------------------------------------+
| 2004-03-11  12:22:49                          |
| 2004-01-25  16:41:33                          |
+-----------------------------------------------+
2 rows in set (0.00 sec)
```

If you want to know the weekday name of the last access date for a given user, make the following query using the `dayname()` server function that returns the weekday name of a given date value:

```
mysql> SELECT accessdate, dayname(accessdate) FROM access_log
    -> WHERE userid='Dodge';
+----------------+---------------------+
| accessdate     | dayname(accessdate) |
+----------------+---------------------+
| 20040311122249 |Thursday             |
| 20040125164133 |Sunday               |
+----------------+---------------------+
2 rows in set (0.01 sec)
```

The `to_days()` server function calculates the total number of days from the year 0 A.D.:

```
mysql> SELECT to_days(accessdate) FROM access_log
    -> WHERE userid='Dodge';
+---------------------+
| to_days(accessdate) |
+---------------------+
|              732016 |
|              731970 |
+---------------------+
2 rows in set (0.00 sec)
```

Suppose you want to know how many days have passed since a user's last visit to your site:

```
mysql> SELECT userid, to_days(now()) - to_days(accessdate)
    -> FROM access_log GROUP BY userid LIMIT 5;
+--------+-------------------------------------+
| userid | to_days(now()) - to_days(accessdate) |
+--------+-------------------------------------+
| Brian  |                                   7 |
| Dodge  |                                   0 |
| Greeny |                                  47 |
| Mac    |                                  49 |
| Nicrot |                                  47 |
+--------+-------------------------------------+
5 rows in set (0.01 sec)
```

You can see that the user Mac has not been to the site for 49 days. If you were upset about this, you could delete users who haven't visited your site for more than 48 days by issuing the following query:

```
mysql> DELETE FROM access_log WHERE to_days(now()) - to_days(accessdate) > 48;
Query OK, 1 row affected (0.01 sec)
```

This is just a sample of the many date- and time-related server functions MySQL provides. Please refer to the MySQL online reference manual for more information.

425

Getting Information on Database Tables

Finding out information about the database you are working is often as important as the actual data contained within it. For example, it is quite common to need to know something *about* the table in order to decide what action to perform next. Luckily, retrieving database table information from PHP is just as easy as retrieving data from the tables themselves.

There are several functions you can use to look at the structure of a database table:

❑ `mysql_list_fields()`: Call this function first to get information on table fields. It takes three arguments (a database name, a table name, and an optional link identifier) and returns a result pointer that refers to a list of all the fields in the specified table of the specified database. For example, if you want a pointer to list of all the fields in the user table in the sample_db database, you could use:

```
$result = mysql_list_fields("sample_db", "user");
```

The `$result` variable now holds a pointer to a list of fields in the user table. You'll see an example of this shortly.

❑ `mysql_num_fields()`: This takes a result pointer (as returned by the preceding function) and returns the total number of fields from the result set to which it points. If you want to get the number of fields in the user table, just pop the pointer `$result` that you obtained from `mysql_list_fields()` into the `mysql_num_fields()` function:

```
$number_of_fields = mysql_num_fields($result);
```

The variable `$number_of_fields` contains (surprise!) the number of fields in the user table.

❑ `msyql_field_name()`, `mysql_field_len()`, and `mysql_field_type()`: These functions return the field's field name, field length, and field type properties, respectively. Each of them takes both a result pointer and a field index as arguments, which specify the table and field (counting fields from zero) in that order. For example, to get the length of the username field in the user table, first note that username is the fourth field in the table and therefore has a field index of 3 (indexes start at zero), and then you could use:

```
$username_length = mysql_field_len($result, 3);
```

Because you defined username as having a length of 30 characters, `$username_length` should contain 30. The other two functions work much the same way.

❑ `mysql_field_flags()`: This function takes a result set pointer and a field index, and returns a string containing the attribute for the given field. Attributes of a field include NULL or NOT NULL, PRIMARY KEY, UNIQUE, and so on. You can place the attributes of the username field (from the user table) into the variable `$attributes` using the following code:

```
$attributes = mysql_field_flags($result, 3);
```

The only attribute of the username field is NOT NULL, so that is the value of `$attributes`.

Try It Out   Get Information on Fields

Let's take a look at these functions in action. The following script, metadata.php, returns the name, length, and type of each field defined in the user table:

```php
<?php
include_once "./common_db.inc";
$link_id = db_connect();
$result = mysql_list_fields("sample_db", "user", $link_id);

for($i=0; $i < mysql_num_fields($result); $i++ ) {
    echo mysql_fieldname($result,$i );
    echo "(" . mysql_field_len($result, $i) . ")";
    echo " - " . mysql_field_type($result, $i) . "<BR>";
}
?>
```

Figure 11-2 shows the output.

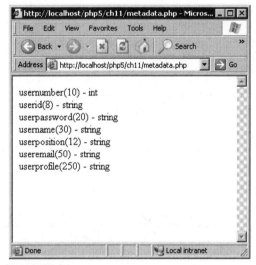

Figure 11-1

How It Works

As usual, start by including the database functions in common_db.inc, and then connect to the server using db_connect():

```php
include_once "./common_db.inc";
$link_id = db_connect();
```

Then call the mysql_list_fields() function, specifying the database, table, and connection that you want to use (sample_db, user, and $link_id, respectively for this example):

```php
$result = mysql_list_fields("sample_db", "user", $link_id);
```

The function returns a pointer to a result set that lists all fields in the user table. Store it in the variable $result, and use it with mysql_num_fields() to find out how many fields the table contains. This sets the upper limit of a for...next loop:

```
for($i=0; $i < mysql_num_fields($result); $i++ ) {
```

Using the loop index to specify which field to work with, call the functions mysql_field_name(), mysql_field_len(), and mysql_field_type(), which return the name, length, and type of the fields available:

```
echo mysql_field_name($result,$i );
echo "(" . mysql_field_len($result, $i) . ")";
echo " - " . mysql_field_type($result, $i) . "<BR>";
```

Some of the field types returned are ambiguous—for example, CHAR and VARCHAR are both returned as string, whereas TEXT is returned as BLOB. To get exact field types (as they are defined in a MySQL table) involves a bit more work. That's where the mysql_field_flags() function comes in, and you can easily modify the code to show the field attributes. Here's the revised code:

```
$link_id = db_connect();
$result = mysql_list_fields("sample_db", "user", $link_id);

for($i=0; $i < mysql_num_fields($result); $i++ ) {
    echo mysql_field_name($result,$i );
    echo "(" . mysql_field_len($result, $i) . ")";
    echo " - " . mysql_field_type($result, $i);
    echo " " . mysql_field_flags($result, $i) . "<BR>";
}
```

Figure 11-2 shows a sample run.

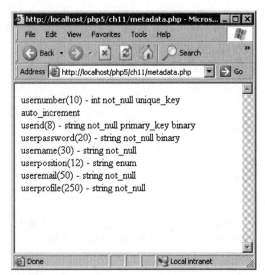

Figure 11-2

Finally, there's a single function that can be used to get all the information on a table's fields in one go: mysql_fetch_field(). If you pass this function a result set pointer and a field index (again, counting fields from zero), it returns an object whose properties include the name of the field and the name of the table to which it belongs, along with its length, attributes, and other details. The following table describes the properties of the returned object.

Property	Description
blob	True if the field is a BLOB
max_length	The maximum length of the field
multiple_key	True if the field is a key but not unique
name	The field name
not_null	True if the field cannot be NULL
numeric	True if the field is numeric
primary_key	True if the field is a primary key
table	The name of the table to which the field belongs
type	The field type
unique_key	True if the field is a unique key
unsigned	True if the field is unsigned
def	Gives the default value if specified
zerofill	True if the field is zero-filled. A zerofill attribute is used to force a number to be a certain width by padding it with leading zeros

Try It Out   Use mysql_fetch_field()

You can use this function to produce a result similar to the previous example. Place the following code in a file called `fetch_field.php`:

```php
<?php
include_once "./common_db.inc";
$link_id = db_connect();
$result = mysql_list_fields("sample_db", "user", $link_id);

for($i=0; $i < mysql_num_fields($result); $i++ ) {
    $field_info_object = mysql_fetch_field($result, $i);

    echo $field_info_object->name . "(" .
    $field_info_object->max_length . ")";

    echo " - " . $field_info_object->type;

    if($field_info_object->not_null){
        echo " not_null ";
    }else{
```

```
        " null ";
   }

   if($field_info_object->primary_key){
      echo " primary_key ";
   }else if($field_info_object->multiple_key){
      echo " key ";
   }else if($field_info_object->unique_key){
      echo " unique ";
   }

   if($field_info_object->unsigned){
      echo " unsigned ";
   }

   if($field_info_object->zerofill){
      echo " zero-filled ";
   }

   echo "<BR>";
}
?>
```

Figure 11-3 shows a sample run.

Figure 11-3

How It Works

This works much the same as the last script, but something looks amiss—the length of each field is reported as 0 bytes. Unfortunately, although it's very versatile, the `mysql_fetch_field()` function contains a small bug that causes its `max_length` property to always contain 0—no matter what size the specified field is defined with. At time of writing, the latest version of PHP is the RC1 version of PHP5—we can but hope this bug is crushed in the next release. Until then, just revert to using `mysql_field_len()` for this particular information:

```
$field_info_object = mysql_fetch_field($result, $i);

    echo $field_info_object->name . "(" .
    mysql_field_len($result, $i) . ")";

    echo " - " . $field_info_object->type;
```

Now the script reports the correct size of each field, as shown in Figure 11-4.

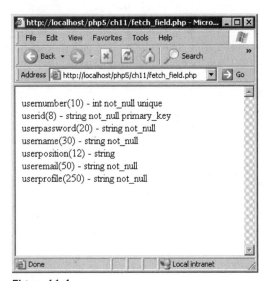

Figure 11-4

The capability to access metadata on database tables is essential to any general-purpose database management application, which won't know anything beforehand about the table structures with which it has to work. To handle tables correctly every time, it has to rely heavily on functions such as those you've just seen.

ENUM Options and Field Defaults

You already encountered ENUM type fields in the preceding chapter, when you included the sex field in the users table. That field could take either one of two values: M or F. For the sake of a nice substantial example, you're now going to modify the userposition field so that it also limits entries to specific, preset values.

The field type for userposition was originally defined as VARCHAR(50) NOT NULL. Assuming that all future users will come from one of the four countries already entered in the field, redefine the field like this:

```
mysql> ALTER TABLE user MODIFY userposition
    -> ENUM('Mid','Link', 'Winger','Utility Back') DEFAULT 'Utility Back';
Query OK, 6 rows affected (0.01 sec)
Records: 0 Duplicates: 0 Warnings: 0
```

If you've added your own records to the table, you'll probably want to modify these values to match your own. All being well, the values previously contained in this field remain intact.

Pop quiz! Which of the PHP functions gives you the default value of a table field? The answer to this lies in the table presented earlier. The `def` property of the object returned by the `mysql_fetch_field` function gives you the default value of any field if one is specified. You can add the following lines to the last example:

```
if($field_info_object->def) echo "<br><b>Default Value:
$field_info_object->def</b> ";
```

Run your example again, the output should look like Figure 11-5.

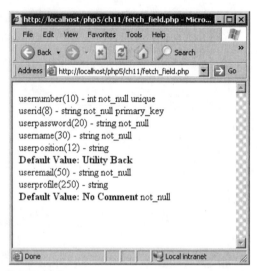

Figure 11-5

Getting a list of options available in an ENUM type field is a little more complicated. Issue the following query:

```
mysql> SHOW COLUMNS FROM user LIKE 'userposition';
```

And here's what you get:

```
+--------------+-----------------------+------+-----+--------------+-------+
| Field        | Type                  | Null | Key | Default      | Extra|
+--------------+-----------------------+------+-----+--------------+-------+
| userposition | enum('Mid','Link',    |      |     |              |      |
|              | 'Winger','Utility Back') | YES |    | Utility Back|      |
+--------------+-----------------------+------+-----+--------------+-------+
1 row in set (0.02 sec)
```

This shows that the Type information actually contains the values you want. Extracting them is a little tricky, but not too hard once you know how.

Try It Out   Get ENUM Options

The following script produces an array whose elements contain each option. The last element of the array holds the default value from the set. Enter this code into a file called enum_options.php:

```php
<?php
include_once "./common_db.inc";
$link_id = db_connect();
mysql_select_db("sample_db");

$query = "SHOW COLUMNS FROM user LIKE 'userposition'";
$result = mysql_query($query);
$query_data = mysql_fetch_array($result);

if(eregi("('.*')", $query_data["Type"], $match)) {
    $enum_str = ereg_replace("'", "", $match[1]);
    $enum_options = explode(',', $enum_str);
}
echo "ENUM options with the default value:<BR>";
foreach($enum_options as $value){
    echo "-$value<BR>";
}
echo "<BR>Default Value: <b>$query_data[Default]</b>";
echo "<P>";

?>
```

Figure 11-6 shows the result.

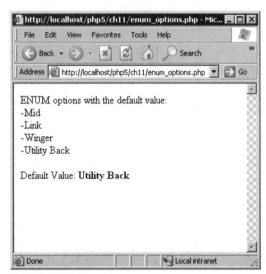

Figure 11-6

How It Works

You start by issuing a SQL query that finds the record containing the definition of the field userposition. This data is fetched in the form of an associative array called $query_data:

```php
$query = "SHOW COLUMNS FROM user LIKE 'userposition'";
$result = mysql_query($query);
$query_data = mysql_fetch_array($result);
```

Field definition entries for Type and Default can now be accessed as array entries $query_data['Type'] and $query_data['Default'], respectively. The former should now contain a string that looks like this:

```
enum('Mid','Link','Winger','Utility Back')
```

To extract the option strings, you must eliminate the preceding string enum, braces and enclosing single quotes. First, use eregi() with the regular expression ('.*') to match everything inside the brackets:

```
eregi("('.*')", $query_data["Type"], $match)
```

The third argument is an array that holds matches for the given pattern—its second element, $match[1], contains the string you want:

```
'Mid','Link','Winger','Utility Back'
```

Assuming this goes to plan, strip off single quotes by calling the eregi_replace() function, and place the modified string in $enum_str:

```
$enum_str = eregi_replace("'", "", $match[1]);
```

which should look like this:

```
Mid, Link, Winger, Utility Back
```

Then explode() the $enum_str variable so that its comma-separated values can be put into the array $enum_options:

```
$enum_options = explode(',', $enum_str);
```

This array now contains each option from the ENUM field as a separate element.

The rest of the script simply steps through the elements in $enum_options and echoes them out. Once you've gone through all the enum values, you echo out the default value in bold font:

```
echo "ENUM options with the default value:<BR>";
foreach($enum_options as $value){
  echo "-$value<BR>";
}
echo "<BR>Default Value: <b>$query_data[Default]</b>";
echo "<P>";
```

You can put this example into a function that returns an array containing each option from a specified ENUM field. Add the following code to the end of the common include file common_db.inc:

```
function enum_options($field, $link_id)
{
    $query = "SHOW COLUMNS FROM user LIKE '$field'";
    $result = mysql_query($query, $link_id);
    $query_data = mysql_fetch_array($result);
```

```
    if(eregi("('.*')", $query_data["Type"], $match)) {
        $enum_str = ereg_replace("'", "", $match[1]);
        $enum_options = explode(',', $enum_str);
        return $enum_options;
    }else{
        return 0;
    }
}
```

You can test it with the following script called `test_enum.php`:

```php
<?php
include_once "./common_db.inc";
$link_id = db_connect();
mysql_select_db("sample_db");

$array = enum_options('userposition', $link_id);
foreach($array as $var){
    echo $var,"<BR>";
}
?>
```

Creating a User Registration Script

Ready to welcome users to your system? If you plan to build a Web site that requires user membership, you'll want to provide some means for new users to register. Here's a garden variety registration script that will step you through the following procedures:

1. Display a "Terms Of Use" page: a user is obliged to agree with these terms if he wants to register as a member.

2. Present one or more registration forms requesting necessary information.

3. Create the user's account: create a new record in the user table and insert relevant information.

4. Let the user know that his membership account has been created.

5. Send a confirmation e-mail to the user's address (part of the information the new user provided when he registered).

To keep the focus on the data aspect of this application, we won't implement the first step (which is just a matter of how you grant access to the actual registration form) or the last step here. Of course, you can always add to the basic application later.

register.php

Creating a new user account involves creating a new entry in the primary key in the user table, which must then be used across all the tables recording the user's activities at your site. The account is also used for authenticating the user when he attempts to enter a password-protected area of your site. So an account comprises both a user ID and a password.

Nothing stops you from saving user passwords as plain text for all to see, but encrypted passwords do provide better security, so that's what you'll do here.

Here's the source code of the user registration script `register.php`. It'll be explained as you go along. To begin with, include the `common_db.inc` file:

```php
<?php
//register.php
include_once "./common_db.inc";
```

in_use()

The `in_use()` function queries the MySQL server about whether the typed-in userid is already in use, and returns 1 if it is:

```php
function in_use($userid)
{
    global $user_tablename;

    $query = "SELECT userid FROM $user_tablename WHERE userid = '$userid'";
    $result = mysql_query($query);
    if(!mysql_num_rows($result)){
        return 0;
    }else{
        return 1;
    }
}
```

register_form()

The `register_form()` function displays the form into which a user types in his membership details. You begin by connecting to the database and finding out which positions you can present as options to prospective players who want to be involved in the sport:

```php
function register_form()
{
    global $userposition;
    global $PHP_SELF;

    $link_id = db_connect();
    mysql_select_db("sample_db");
    $position_array = enum_options('userposition', $link_id);
    mysql_close($link_id);
?>
```

The array `$position_array` now holds all the positions from which the user can choose. Next, you create the table that will serve as the interface for the users—notice the use of the POST method for this example:

```php
<center><H3>Create your account!</H3></center>
<form method="post" action="<?php echo $PHP_SELF ?>">
<input type="hidden" name="action">
    <div align="center"><center><table border="1" width="90%">
```

```
          <tr>
            <th width="30%" nowrap>Desired ID</th>
            <td width="70%"><input type="text" name="userid"
                            size="8" maxlength="8"></td>
          </tr>
          <tr>
            <th width="30%" nowrap>Desired Password</th>
            <td WIDTH="70%"><input type="password"
                            name="userpassword" size="15"></td>
          </tr>
          <tr>
            <th width="30%" nowrap>Retype Password</th>
            <td width="70%"><input type="password"
                            name="userpassword2" size="15"></td>
          </tr>
          <tr>
            <th width="30%" nowrap>Full Name</th>
            <td width="70%"><input type="text" name="username" size="20"></td>
          </tr>
          <tr>
            <th width="30%" nowrap>Position</th>
            <td width="70%"><select name="userposition" size="1">
  <?php
```

There are two password fields rather than one. Because you specify TYPE = "PASSWORD", the value entered is masked by asterisks, so that not even the user can see what he's typing in. Having him type it in twice will catch any mistyping later when you check that the two values match.

The userposition drop-down menu is constructed on-the-fly from the values held in the $position_array variable, which you populated at the beginning of the function:

```
    for($i=0; $i < count($position_array); $i++) {
        if(!isset($userposition) && $i == 0) {
            echo "<OPTION SELECTED VALUE=\"". $position_array[$i] .
            "\">" . $position_array[$i] . "</OPTION>\n";
        }else if($userposition == $cposition_array[$i]) {
            echo "<OPTION SELECTED VALUE=\"". $position_array[$i] . "\">" .
            $position_array[$i] . "</OPTION>\n";
        }else{
            echo "<OPTION VALUE=\"". $position_array[$i] . "\">" .
            $position_array[$i] . "</OPTION>\n";
        }
    }
  ?>
```

Now you continue with the other options in the table:

```
        </select></td>
      </tr>
      <tr>
        <th width="30%" nowrap>Email</th>
        <td width="70%"><input type="text" name="useremail" size="20"
        </td>
      </tr>
```

```
          <tr>
            <th width="30%" nowrap>Profile</th>
            <td WIDTH="70%"><textarea rows="5" cols="40"
                                      name="userprofile"></textarea></tr>
          </tr>
          <tr>
            <th width="30%" colspan="2" nowrap>
              <input type="submit" value="Submit">
              <input type="reset" value="Reset"></th>
          </tr>
        </table>
        </center></div>
      </form>
      <?php
      }
```

create_account()

The `create_account()` function inserts the new record into the user table. It can be called only when the Submit button created in `register_form()` is clicked. As a result, you know that the `$_POST` array will be populated, and you can use those values like so:

```
function create_account()
{
    $userid = $_POST['userid'];
    $username = $_POST['username'];
    $userpassword = $_POST['userpassword'];
    $userpassword2 = $_POST['userpassword2'];
    $userposition = $_POST['userposition'];
    $useremail = $_POST['useremail'];
    $userprofile = $_POST['userprofile'];

    global $default_dbname, $user_tablename;
```

The user-submitted values are verified, to check that what's been entered correctly:

```
if(empty($userid)){
    error_message("Enter your desired ID!");
}
if(empty($userpassword)){
    error_message("Enter your desired password!");
}
if(strlen($userpassword) < 4 ){
    error_message("Password too short!");
}
if(empty($userpassword2)) {
    error_message("Retype your password for verification!");
}
if(empty($username)){
    error_message("Enter your full name!");
}
if(empty($useremail)){
    error_message("Enter your email address!");
}
```

```
if(empty($userprofile)){
    $userprofile = "No Comment.";
}

if($userpassword != $userpassword2){
    error_message("Your desired password and retyped password mismatch!");
}
```

Then, make a connection to the database and call the in_use() function to verify that the userid is unique (because it is the primary key):

```
$link_id = db_connect($default_dbname);

if(in_use($userid)){
    error_message("$userid is in use. Please choose a different ID.");
}
```

When querying to insert a new user's details, you pass NULL to usernumber to auto-increment it. You also use the password() server function to encrypt the user-specified password:

```
$query = "INSERT INTO user VALUES(NULL, '$userid', password('$userpassword'),
                '$username', '$userposition', '$useremail', '$userprofile')";
$result = mysql_query($query);
if(!$result){
    error_message(sql_error());
}
```

You report the newly incremented user number with mysql_insert_id():

```
    $usernumber = mysql_insert_id($link_id);
    html_header();
?>
```

And you display a table showing the user his membership information:

```
<center><h3>
<?php echo $username ?>, thank you for registering with us!
</h3></center>

<div align="center"><center><table border="1" width="90%">
  <tr>
    <th width="30%" nowrap>User Number</TH>
    <td width="70%"><?php echo $usernumber ?></td>
  </tr>
  <tr>
    <th width="30%" nowrap>Desired ID</th>
    <td width="70%"><?php echo $userid ?></td>
  </tr>
  <tr>
    <th width="30%" nowrap>Desired Password</th>
    <td width="70%"><?php echo $userpassword ?></td>
  </tr>
```

```
  <tr>
    <th width="30%" nowrap>Full Name</th>
    <td width="70%"><?php echo $username ?></td>
  </tr>
  <tr>
    <th width="30%" nowrap>Position</th>
    <td width="70%"><?php echo $userposition ?></td>
  </tr>
  <tr>
    <th width="30%" nowraP>Email</th>
    <td width="70%"><?php echo $useremail ?></td>
  </tr>
  <tr>
    <th width="30%" nowrap>Profile</th>
    <td width="70%"><?php echo htmlspecialchars($userprofile) ?></td>
  </tr>
</table>
</center></div>
<?php
    html_footer();
}
```

Choosing Actions to Take

Finally, you use action to specify the appropriate functions to call. In case $_POST is unset, give it a default value that takes you to the registration_form() function:

```
if (empty($_POST)){
    $_POST['action'] = "";
}
switch($_POST['action']) {
    case "register":
        create_account();
    break;
    default:
        html_header();
        register_form();
        html_footer();
    break;
}
?>
```

Let's see how that looks in action. First, register_form() displays a form (see Figure 11-7) into which the user can enter his details.

The user can then fill in his details as he sees fit. As the last step, the script displays a thank you note plus a table showing the information the user entered and that was used to create his account. Figure 11-8 shows the resulting page of creating an account for a player called Darren:

You should note that it's not a good idea to display a user's password like this. A relatively secure way to confirm this information is to include it in an e-mail sent to the user's specified account.

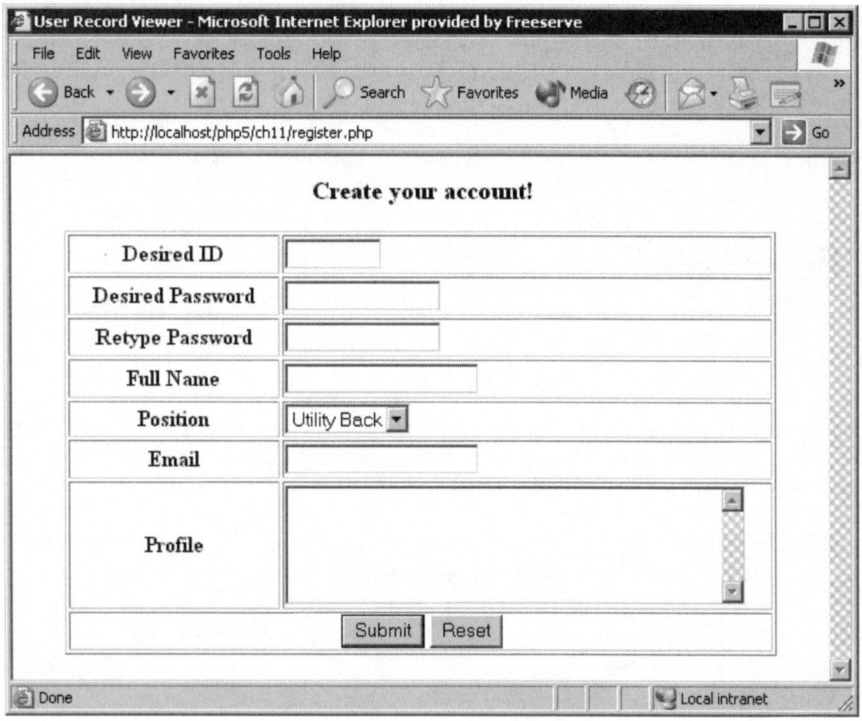

Figure 11-7

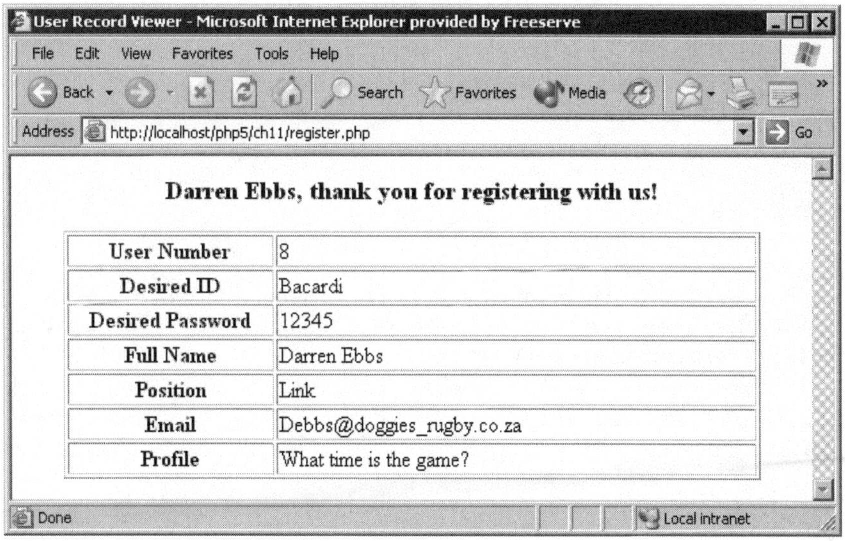

Figure 11-8

Now you've seen how you can use PHP to add members to your database, and therefore the site. Obviously, if you wanted to build on this, or integrate it into your own site, you may want to add extra buttons to take you to different pages once you've confirmed a user's registration. This, however, suffices for the example.

Now let's move on to see how you can record users' accesses to your site.

Creating an Access Logger Script

To track users' activities, you need to know who has made a request for what, which is why users are required to log in to the site. Without a login process, there's no way for you to identify anyone requesting a Web page.

The most convenient way of authenticating users is to specify a unique ID and associated password for each one. When a user logs in, all you need to do is to check the values (username and password) he submits against the ones you have stored.

The following script makes a query to the table user for user authentication. You start by including common_db.inc and specifying a link to the registration page:

```php
<?php
include_once "./common_db.inc";
$register_script = "./register.php";
```

auth_user.php

Next, define the functions auth_user() and login_form()—more on these in a moment—but the main story begins with a session_start() call. You're going to store the user-entered values for ID and password as session variables, thereby saving the user from having to re-enter the values every time he accesses a new page.

If $userid has not been defined, call the login_form() function, which displays (surprise, surprise!) a login form, into which the user can enter ID and password:

```php
if(!isset($userid)) {
    login_form();
    exit;
```

If $userid is defined (as will be the case if the script has been called from the login form), register the user-provided values userid and userpassword as session variables for later use, and use them as arguments to call the auth_user() function:

```php
}else{
    session_start();
    session_register("userid", "userpassword");
    $username = auth_user($_POST['userid'], $_POST['userpassword']);
```

The value returned by auth_user() is either:

❑ The user's name as stored in the user table. This is returned only if the submitted ID/password values correspond to those stored in a specific record in the table.

❑ 0. This is returned when no match is found.

Store this value in $username, and use it to determine a response:

```
if(!$username) {
    $PHP_SELF = $_SERVER['PHP_SELF'];
    session_unregister("userid");
    session_unregister("userpassword");
    echo "Authorization failed. " .
        "You must enter a valid userid and password combo. " .
        "Click on the following link to try again.<BR>\n";
    echo "<A HREF=\"$PHP_SELF\">Login</A><BR>";
    echo "If you're not a member yet, click " .
        "on the following link to register.<BR>\n";
    echo "<A HREF=\"$register_script\">Membership</A>";
    exit;
}else{
    echo "Welcome, $username!";
}
}
```

If authentication fails, unregister the session variables to ensure that login_form() is called whenever an unauthenticated user tries to access a password-protected area. login_form() is just a table that enables the user to enter his userid and password so that you can use the values in the auth_user() function:

```
function login_form()
{
    global $PHP_SELF;
?>
<html>
<head>
<title>login</title>
</head>
<body>
<form method="post" action="<?php echo "$PHP_SELF"; ?>">
    <div align="center"><center>
        <h3>Please log in to access the page you requested.</h3>
    <table border="1" width="200" cellpadding="2">
        <tr>
            <th width="18%" align="right" nowrap>id</th>
            <td width="82%" nowrap>
                <input type="text" name="userid" size="8">
            </td>
        </tr>
        <tr>
            <th width="18%" align="right" nowrap>Password</th>
            <td width="82%" nowrap>
                <input type="password" name="userpassword" size="8">
            </td>
        </tr>
```

```
        <tr>
            <td width="100%" colspan="2" align="center" nowrap>
                <input type="submit" value="login" name="Submit">
            </td>
        </tr>
    </table>
    </center></div>
</form>
</body>
</html>
<?
}
```

The real meat of the script lies in the auth_user() function, which takes $userid and $userpassword as arguments, and validates them against the values stored in the user table:

```
function auth_user($userid, $userpassword)
{
    global $default_dbname, $user_tablename;

    $link_id = db_connect($default_dbname);
```

After you're connected to the database, query for a record whose userid and password entries correspond to the user-provided arguments, and SELECT the username value for that record:

```
$query = "SELECT username FROM $user_tablename WHERE userid = '$userid'
                        AND userpassword = password('$userpassword')";
$result = mysql_query($query);
```

If no records match both criteria, return 0; otherwise fetch and return the username value:

```
    if(!mysql_num_rows($result)){
        return 0;
    }else{
        $query_data = mysql_fetch_row($result);
        return $query_data[0];
    }
}
```

Make certain that you encrypt $userpassword *before* comparing it with the value in the user table so that you're comparing two encrypted values that have been derived by exactly the same process, and are therefore identical. Not all types of encryption would enable you to do this, but MySQL's encryption algorithm is one-way. In other words, two identical strings always produce two identically encrypted strings.

Figure 11-9 shows how the interface should look.

When a user successfully logs in, he's greeted by name, as Figure 11-10 shows.

access_logger.php

You can develop the last script so that it authenticates users and logs their visits to Web pages. Call this modified version access_logger.php. You'll log user accesses by automatically attaching access_logger.php to the beginning of all your Web pages. You can do this very simply, by setting

Figure 11-9

Figure 11-10

`auto_prepend_file` in the `php.ini` configuration file so that it specifies the absolute location of the script. For example:

```
auto_prepend_file = /home/james/access_logger.php
```

Another option is to include the logging script at the top of each of the Web pages that you want to password-protect. You'd need to be sure to include it at the top of the page, before sending out any HTML tags or text, otherwise the `header()` function won't work.

Assuming you use the blanket approach and set `auto_prepend_file`, you're going to attach the access logging script to every `.php` page on the server. If you want to exclude certain files and directories from the authentication process, you can list them respectively in a pair of arrays. When a user tries to access a Web page, the access logging script can check the page's name and path against the arrays' contents, and demand authentication only if there's no match.

Start off by including the `common_db.inc` file, and defining the exclusion arrays and table names:

```php
<?php
require_once ('common_db.inc');
$exclude_dirs = array('/info', '/contact');
```

```
$exclude_files = array('index.html', 'info.html', 'register.php');
$user_tablename = 'user';
$access_log_tablename = 'access_log';
$PHP_SELF = $_SERVER['PHP_SELF'];
```

Because someone is logging on to your site, you can start the session and register his userid as a session variable. You'll use the userid and password to authenticate the user in your do_authenticate() function in a moment. When you first start the session and register the userid and password, they have no values, so you check to see if the page is on your exclude list. If it isn't, you call the do_authenticate() function:

```
session_start();
session_register('userid', 'userpassword');
if (!$_SESSION['userid']){
    $filepath = dirname($_SERVER['SCRIPT_FILENAME']);
    $filename = basename($_SERVER['SCRIPT_FILENAME']);
    if($filepath == ''){
        $filepath = '/';
    }

    $auth_done = 0;

    for($j=0; $j < count($exclude_dirs); $j++) {
        if($exclude_dirs[$j] == $filepath){
            break;
        }else{
            for($i=0; $i< count($exclude_files); $i++) {
                if($exclude_files[$i] == $filename){
                    break;
                }
                if ($i == (count($exclude_files) - 1)){
                    do_authentication();
                    $auth_done = 1;
                    break;
                }
            }
        }
        if($auth_done){
            break;
        }
    }
}
?>
```

How do you track the page accesses of a user who's already logged onto the site and submitted his userid and password information? You don't want to recall do_authenticate(), of course, but you do know that if the user is successfully logged on, then both the userid and userpassword session variables are defined, so you can say the following:

```
if ($_SESSION['userid'] && $_SESSION['userpassword']){
    $userid = $_SESSION['userid'];
    $filename = basename($_SERVER['SCRIPT_FILENAME']);
    $link_id = db_connect($default_dbname);
```

```
        $query = "SELECT userid FROM $access_log_tablename
        WHERE page = '$filename' AND userid = '$userid'";
        $result = mysql_query($query);

        if(!mysql_num_rows($result)){
            $query = "INSERT INTO $access_log_tablename
            VALUES ('$filename', '$userid', 1, NULL)";
        }else{
            $query = "UPDATE $access_log_tablename
            SET visitcount = visitcount + 1, accessdate = NULL
            WHERE page = '$filename' AND userid = '$userid'";
        }

        mysql_query($query);

        $num_rows = mysql_affected_rows($link_id);
        if($num_rows != 1){
            die(sql_error());
        }
    }
```

Now all of your page visits will faithfully be logged as users navigate around the site.

Declare the authentication function, checking to see if the user has sent her userid. If not, send her to the login_form() function, the same one you saw in auth_user.php (you just need to cut and paste it into this file in order for the call to work—it isn't shown here again):

```
function do_authentication()
{
    global $default_dbname, $user_tablename, $access_log_tablename;
    global $MYSQL_ERROR, $MYSQL_ERRNO;
    global $filename;
    global $PHP_SELF;

    if(!isset($_POST['userid'])) {
        login_form();
        exit;
```

If you've obtained a userid and password from the user, use the submitted values to query the database. You're also defining the session variables here—remember that these session variables persist between pages:

```
    }else {
        $_SESSION['userpassword'] = $_POST['userpassword'];
        $_SESSION['userid'] = $_POST['userid']; }
        $userid = $_POST['userid'];
        $userpassword = $_POST['userpassword'];
        $link_id = db_connect($default_dbname);
        $query = "SELECT username FROM $user_tablename
        WHERE userid = '$userid' AND userpassword = password('$userpassword')";
        $result = mysql_query($query);
    }
```

If your query fails (perhaps the user tried to be sneaky and entered only his username), unregister the session and tell the user that he's failed authorization:

```
if(!mysql_num_rows($result)) {
    session_unregister("userid");
    echo "Authorization failed. " .
    "You must enter a valid userid and password combo. " .
    "Click on the following link to try again.<BR>\n";
    echo "<A HREF=\"$PHP_SELF\">Login</A><BR>";
    echo "If you're not a member yet, click on the " .
    "following link to register.<BR>\n";
    echo "<A HREF= \"register.php\">Membership</A>";
    exit;
```

If our query is successful then check whether the user has accessed the page before, and either insert values or update the table appropriately:

```
}else{
    $query = "SELECT userid FROM $access_log_tablename
    WHERE page = '$filename' AND userid = '$userid'";
    $result = mysql_query($query);
    if(!mysql_num_rows($result)) {
        $query = "INSERT INTO $access_log_tablename
        VALUES ('$filename', '$userid', 1, NULL)";
    }else{
        $query = "UPDATE $access_log_tablename
        SET visitcount = visitcount + 1, accessdate = NULL
        WHERE page = '$filename' AND userid = '$userid'";
    }
    mysql_query($query);

    $num_rows = mysql_affected_rows($link_id);
    if($num_rows != 1) die(sql_error());
    }
}
```

If you try running just this script, you'll see just a blank page in your browser (assuming you used a correct userid and password). However, if you take a look at the contents of the access_log table, you'll see that your activity has been logged. In the example, the site administrator browsed to access_logger.php to ensure it works:

```
mysql> select * from access_log;
+------------------+--------+------------+----------------+
| page             | userid | visitcount | accessdate     |
+------------------+--------+------------+----------------+
| stats.html       | Brian  |          1 | 20040304143102 |
| score.html       | Pads   |          2 | 20040312160114 |
| refs.html        | Nicrot |          5 | 20040124122744 |
| log.html         | Nicrot |          3 | 20040124122642 |
| log.html         | Greeny |          4 | 20040124112654 |
| access_logger.php | Dodge |          1 | 20040314192430 |
+------------------+--------+------------+----------------+
6 rows in set (0.00 sec)
```

Creating a User Manager

At last you can put all the examples together, and upgrade your user record viewer (built in the previous chapter) so that it can manipulate data in the related tables. Using the following script, userman.php, you can edit and delete user records and/or corresponding access log records.

userman.php

Start as you did with register.php, by fetching ENUM options on the userposition field:

```
<?php
//userman.php
include_once "./common_db.inc";

$link_id = db_connect();
mysql_select_db("sample_db");
$position_array = enum_options('userposition', $link_id);
mysql_close($link_id);
```

user_message()

The user_message() function reports the result of a given operation. If fed an optional URL argument, it loads the specified page:

```
function user_message($msg, $url ='')
{
    html_header();

    if(empty($url)){
        echo "<SCRIPT>alert(\"$msg\");history.go(-1)</SCRIPT>";
    }else{
        echo "<SCRIPT>alert(\"$msg\");self.location.href='$url'</SCRIPT>";
    }

    html_footer();
    exit;
}
```

list_records()

The revised list_records() function adds an option to delete a chosen record. The rest of the function is the same as in the previous version (in Chapter 10):

```
function list_records()
{
...
        echo "<td WIDTH=\"25%\" ALIGN=\"CENTER\">
            <a href=\"javascript:open_window('$PHP_SELF?action=view_record&
                                                userid=$userid');\">
            View</a>
            <a href=\"$PHP_SELF?action=delete_record&userid=$userid\"
                onClick=\"return confirm('Are you sure?');\">
            Delete</a>
            </td>\n";
        echo "</tr>\n";
...
}
```

delete_record()

The `delete_record()` function deletes a given user's record from the user table, along with corresponding records in the access_log table:

```
function delete_record()
{
    global $default_dbname, $user_tablename, $access_log_tablename;
    $userid = $_GET['userid'];

    if(empty($userid)){
        error_message('Empty User ID!');
    }

    $link_id = db_connect($default_dbname);
    if(!$link_id){
        error_message(sql_error());
    }

    $query = "DELETE FROM $user_tablename WHERE userid = '$userid'";
    $result = mysql_query($query);
    if(!$result){
        error_message(sql_error());
    }

    $num_rows = mysql_affected_rows($link_id);
    if($num_rows != 1){
        error_message("No such user: $userid");
    }

    $query = "DELETE FROM $access_log_tablename WHERE userid = '$userid'";
    $result = mysql_query($query);

    user_message("All records regarding $userid have been trashed!");
}
```

edit_record()

The `edit_record()` function updates a given user's record in the user table. If a userid is changed, it also updates the related records in the access_log table to reflect that change:

```
function edit_record()
{
    global $default_dbname, $user_tablename, $access_log_tablename;
    $PHP_SELF = $_SERVER['PHP_SELF'];
    $userid = $_GET['userid'];
    $newuserid = $_GET['new_userid'];
    $username = $_GET['username'];
    $userpassword = $_GET['userpassword'];
    $userposition = $_GET['userposition'];
    $useremail = $_GET['useremail'];
    $userprofile = $_GET['userprofile'];
```

```
    if(empty($userid)){
        $userid = $_GET['new_userid'];
    }

    $link_id = db_connect($default_dbname);
    if(!$link_id){
        error_message(sql_error());
    }

    $field_str = '';
```

Yes, the userid field itself can be changed. From a database manager's point of view though, it's generally unacceptable for a user to alter his userid because it acts like his Social Security number in that it's both unique and unchangeable. Nevertheless, if a user were to insist on changing his userid, every record in every related table, no matter how many there were, would have to be changed, or you'd end up with a bunch of useless, orphan records that had lost their owner.

You must compare the new userid with the existing one, and update $field_str if necessary:

```
    if($userid != $new_userid) $field_str = " userid = '$newuserid', ";
```

Unless the $userpassword variable is empty, the userpassword field is updated:

```
    if(!empty($userpassword)) {
        $field_str .= " userpassword = password('$userpassword'), ";
    }
```

Check like this to prevent an administrator from accidentally putting empty values into the userpassword field. Then update the other fields and check that everything's gone to plan:

```
    $field_str .= " username = '$username', ";
    $field_str .= " userposition = '$userposition', ";
    $field_str .= " useremail = '$useremail', ";
    $field_str .= " userprofile = '$userprofile'";

    $query = "UPDATE IGNORE $user_tablename SET $field_str WHERE
    userid = '$userid'";
    $result = mysql_query($query);
    if(!$result){
        error_message(sql_error());
    }

    $num_rows = mysql_affected_rows($link_id);
    if(!$num_rows){
        error_message("Nothing changed!");
    }
```

Notice the IGNORE statement in this query. userid is part of the primary key and mysql balks at having to change it, so adding the IGNORE statement enables you to go ahead and make the change. You're updating all the other tables to reflect the changes so your database will be okay.

If the userid field is to be changed, edit_record changes all the related records in the access_log table too and refreshes the view:

```
if($userid != $new_userid){
    $query = "UPDATE $access_log_tablename SET userid = '$newuserid'
    WHERE userid = '$userid'";
    $result = mysql_query($query);
    if(!$result){
        error_message(sql_error());
    }

    user_message("All records regarding $userid have been changed!",
    "$PHP_SELF?action=view_record&userid=$newuserid");
}else{
    user_message("All records regarding $userid have been changed!",
    "$PHP_SELF?action=view_record&userid=$userid");
}
}
```

If the userid field has been changed, you call user_message() with the second URL argument specifying userid=$new_userid because falling back to the script with the old userid value would produce an unexpected result: an edit form for a nonexistent user.

edit_log_record()

The edit_log_record() function updates a given user's access records in the access_log table:

```
function edit_log_record()
{
    global $default_dbname, $access_log_tablename;
    $userid = $_GET['userid'];
    $newpage = $_GET['new_page'];
    $visitcount = $_GET['visitcount'];
    $accessdate = $_GET['accessdate'];
    $orgpage = $_GET['org_page'];
    $PHP_SELF = $_SERVER['PHP_SELF'];

    if(empty($userid)){
        error_message('Empty User ID!');
    }

    $link_id = db_connect($default_dbname);
    if(!$link_id){
        error_message(sql_error());
    }

    $field_str = '';

    $field_str .= " page = '$newpage', ";
    $field_str .= " visitcount = '$visitcount', ";
    $field_str .= " accessdate = '$accessdate' ";
```

This function works much like edit_record(), with one major difference: it uses both userid and page fields to select relevant access log records.

You preserve the existing value of the page field in the $org_page variable just in case the administrator changes its value in an edit form:

```
$query = "UPDATE $access_log_tablename SET $field_str WHERE userid = '$userid'
AND page = '$orgpage'";

$result = mysql_query($query);
if(!$result){
    error_message(sql_error());
}
```

If no record has been updated, that means the administrator has pressed the Submit button without changing anything in the corresponding edit form.

The mysql_affected_rows() function returns 0 because the previous UPDATE operation resulted in no changed rows. An UPDATE command does nothing if the new record has the same values as the ones in the existing record:

```
$num_rows = mysql_affected_rows($link_id);
if(!$num_rows){
    error_message("Nothing changed!");
}

user_message("All records regarding $userid have been changed!",
"$PHP_SELF?action=view_record&userid=$userid");
}
```

view_record()

The revised view_record() function lets the administrator edit user records:

```
function view_record()
{
    global $default_dbname, $user_tablename, $access_log_tablename;
    global $position_array;
    $userid = $_GET['userid'];
    $PHP_SELF = $_SERVER['PHP_SELF'];

    if(empty($userid)){
        error_message('Empty User ID!');
    }

    $link_id = db_connect($default_dbname);

    if(!$link_id){
        error_message(sql_error());
    }
    $query = "SELECT usernumber, userid, username, userposition, useremail,
    userprofile FROM $user_tablename WHERE userid = '$userid'";
    $result = mysql_query($query);
    if(!$result){
        error_message(sql_error());
    }
```

```
$query_data = mysql_fetch_array($result);
$usernumber = $query_data["usernumber"];
$userid = $query_data["userid"];
$username = $query_data["username"];
$userposition = $query_data["userposition"];
$useremail = $query_data["useremail"];
$userprofile = $query_data["userprofile"];
```

Finally, you display a number of forms from which the administrator can edit the user's record and his access log data:

```
    html_header();
    echo "<center><H3>
    Record for User No.$usernumber - $userid($username)
    </h3></center>";
?>

<form method="get" action="<?php echo $PHP_SELF ?>">
<input type="hidden" name="action" value="edit_record">
<input type="hidden" name="userid" value="<? echo $userid ?>">
<div align="center"><center>
<table border="1" width="90%" cellpadding="2">
    <tr>
        <th width="30%" nowrap>User ID</th>
```

The hidden field new_userid is being used in case an administrator changes the userid of a given user:

```
<td width="70%">
        <input type="text" name="new_userid"
                        value="<?php echo $userid ?>"
                        size="8" maxlength="8"></td>
    </tr>
    <tr>
        <th width="30%" nowrap>User Password</th>
```

You don't echo out the encrypted password because it's of no use:

```
<td width="70%"><input type="text" name="userpassword" size="15"></td>
    </tr>
    <tr>
        <th width="30%" nowrap>Full Name</th>
        <th width="70%"><input type="text" name="username"
                                value="<?php echo $username ?>" SIZE="20"></td>
    </tr>
    <tr>
        <th width="30%" nowrap>Position</th>
        <td width="70%"><select name="userposition" size="1">
<?php
```

Use the $position_array variable to construct a droplist of positions:

```
for($i=0; $i < count($position_array); $i++) {
    if(!isset($userposition) && $i == 0) {
```

```
            echo "<OPTION SELECTED VALUE=\"". $position_array[$i] . "\">" .
               $position_array[$i] . "</OPTION>\n";
         }else if($userposition == $position_array[$i]) {
            echo "<OPTION SELECTED VALUE=\"". $position_array[$i] . "\">" .
               $position_array[$i] . "</OPTION>\n";
         }else{
            echo "<OPTION VALUE=\"". $position_array[$i] . "\">" .
               $position_array[$i] . "</OPTION>\n";
         }
      }
?>
      </select></td>
    </tr>
    <tr>
      <th width="30%" nowrap>Email</th>
      <td width="70%"><input type="text" name="useremail" size="20"
                        value="<?php echo $useremail ?>"></td>
    </tr>
    <tr>
      <th width="30%" nowrap>Profile</th>
```

The `htmlspecialchars()` function ensures that any HTML special characters in the `$userprofile` variable are echoed as HTML entities and can't do any damage to the surrounding markup:

```
<td width="70%">
        <textarea rows="5" cols="40" name="userprofile">
          <?php echo htmlspecialchars($userprofile) ?>
        </textarea>
      </td>
    </tr>
    <tr>
      <th width="100%" colspan="2" nowrap>
        <input type="submit" value="Change User Record">
        <input type="reset" value="Reset">
      </th>
    </tr>
  </table>
  </center></div>
</form>
<?php
   echo "<HR SIZE=\"2\" WIDTH=\"90%\">\n";
```

Each access log record is presented in a separate form:

```
$query = "SELECT page, visitcount, accessdate, date_format(accessdate, '%M, %e,
   %Y') as formatted_accessdate FROM $access_log_tablename WHERE
userid = '$userid'";
$result = mysql_query($query);

   if(!$result){
      error_message(sql_error());
   }
```

```php
    if(!mysql_num_rows($result)){
        echo "<center>No access log record for $userid ($username).</center>";
    }else{
        echo "<center>Access log record(s) for $userid ($username).</center>";
    }
?>
<div align="center"><center>
<table border="1" width="90%" cellpadding="2">
  <tr>
    <th width="20%" nowrap>Page</th>
    <th width="20%" nowrap>Hits</th>
    <th width="30%" nowraP>Last Access</th>
    <th width="30%" nowrap>Action</th>
  </tr>
<?php
```

You show the results of the query in a nice table that the administrator can use to modify the access_log values:

```php
    while($query_data = mysql_fetch_array($result)){
        $page = $query_data["page"];
        $visitcount = $query_data["visitcount"];
        $accessdate = $query_data["accessdate"];
        $formatted_accessdate = $query_data["formatted_accessdate"];

        echo "<FORM METHOD=\"GET\" ACTION=\"$PHP_SELF\">";
        echo "<INPUT TYPE=\"HIDDEN\" NAME=\"action\"VALUE=\"edit_log_record\">";
        echo "<INPUT TYPE=\"HIDDEN\" NAME=\"userid\" VALUE=\"$userid\">";
        echo "<INPUT TYPE=\"HIDDEN\" NAME=\"org_page\" VALUE=\"$page\">";
        echo "<TR>\n";
        echo "<TD WIDTH=\"20%\"><INPUT TYPE=\"TEXT\"NAME=\"new_page\" SIZE=\"30\"
        VALUE=\"$page\"></TD>\n";
        echo "<TD WIDTH=\"20%\" ALIGN=\"CENTER\">
        <INPUT TYPE=\"TEXT\" NAME=\"visitcount\" SIZE=\"3\"
        VALUE=\"$visitcount\"></TD>\n";
        echo "<TD WIDTH=\"30%\" ALIGN=\"CENTER\">
        <INPUT TYPE=\"TEXT\" NAME=\"accessdate\" SIZE=\"14\"
        MAXLENGTH=\"14\" VALUE=\"$accessdate\">
        <BR>$formatted_accessdate</TD>\n";
        echo "<TD WIDTH=\"30%\" ALIGN=\"CENTER\">
        <INPUT TYPE=\"SUBMIT\" VALUE=\"Change\">
        <INPUT TYPE=\"RESET\" VALUE=\"Reset\"></TD>\n";
        echo "</TR>\n";
        echo "</FORM>\n";
    }
?>
  </tr>
</table>
</center></div>
<?php
    html_footer();
}
```

Choosing an Action to Take

Finally, you use $action to specify which functions to call:

```
if (empty($_GET['action'])){
    $_GET['action'] = "";
}
switch($_GET['action']) {
    case "edit_record":
        edit_record();
        break;
    case "edit_log_record":
        edit_log_record();
        break;
    case "delete_record":
        delete_record();
        break;
    case "view_record":
        view_record();
        break;
    default:
        list_records();
        break;
}
?>
```

Assuming you want your records listed by usernumber, Figure 11-11 shows the screen you get after clicking the relevant field header.

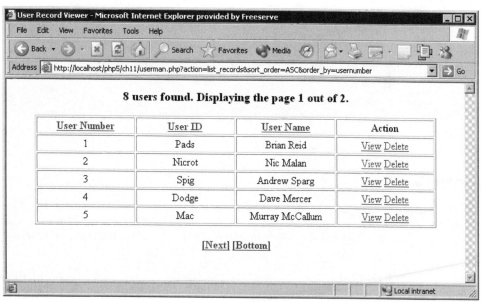

Figure 11-11

When you click a View link, it opens up a new window displaying the records of the user associated with the link, as Figure 11-12 shows.

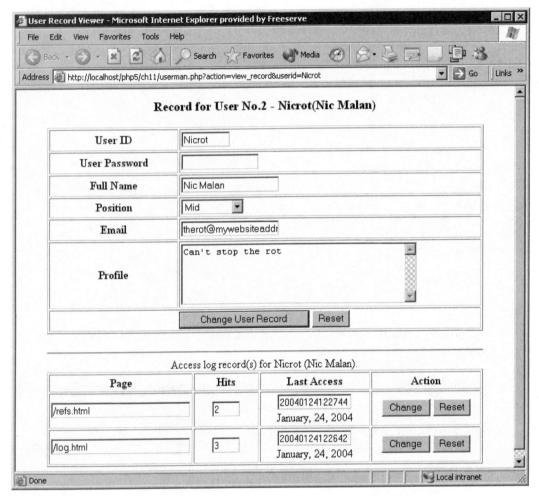

Figure 11-12

Summary

In this chapter, you walked through the process of manipulating existing data in database tables, building a user registration script and an access logger script that can be used together to track user accesses to your Web site. You also learned how easily user authentication can be done in PHP using its session management feature.

The three-chapter MySQL series ended with a user manager script. With MySQL as the backend for your data storage, the extent to which you can develop high-performance applications is restricted only by your imagination. Let your imagination fly!

Exercises

1. Make a list of suitable field descriptors for each of the columns in this table. *Hint: Remember that restaurants generally have many individual orders in any given day.*

First name	Order _ID	User _ID	Resturaunt	Password	Last name	Total Price ($)	Email
David	2	1	Nandos	12345	Mercer	21.45	davidm@contechst.com
David	4	1	Mimos	12345	Mercer	20.95	davidm@contechst.com
Nic	3	2	St Elmos	23212	Malan	15.45	therot@doggiestouch.co.za
Brian	5	4	Spur	32123	Reid	22.00	pads@doggiestouch.co.za
Darren	1	3	Home	43212	Ebbs	11.85	Bacardi@doggiestouch.co.za

2. The site manager decides to have a page for users to view their past orders and their totals. Using principles of normalization, create new tables to represent one entity each. Give each table a suitable name, and a primary key. (Check that your changes would reduce redundancy in large amounts of data.)

3. Create these tables in your database using SQL statements.

4. After the Web site's been in business for six months, customers begin to complain that the site is going slowly when they want to view their previous orders. The site administrator looks at the Orders table and finds that there are now thousands of records. Why is the site slow, and how can the administrator speed things up? Update the table accordingly.

5. The boss decides he wants to see how popular Nandos is with his customers. What query could the administrator build to obtain the totals for all the orders (a) made by one customer and (b) made to Nandos. *Hint: Try* `Select SUM(column) from table.`

6. Create a script that enables a user to enter his details into the database by registering at the site. The database should be set up so that the user ID is assigned automatically. Once the user is registered he should be able to place an order with any of the five restaurants. (Just complete one to begin with. Don't worry about creating a full interface—being able to enter a price is the important thing.) Clicking an order button should create a new entry in the Orders table, with an incremented Order_ID, and the correct User_ID inserted for the customer. *Hint: You may want to use a session to store the users User_ID upon registration.*

An Introduction to Object-Oriented Programming

Object-oriented (OO) software development can be a confusing topic for developers who create primarily procedural code. But it doesn't need to be. In this chapter we explore some of the basic theory behind OO and cover the (sometimes daunting) multisyllabic terminology. You'll learn why you should be interested in OO techniques, how they can really improve the speed with which you develop complex applications, and the ease with which you can modify those applications.

In the next chapter, we'll look at how to implement these techniques in PHP5 and show you the power of this technique by building a real application.

What Is Object-Oriented Programming?

Object-oriented programming (OOP) is a different way of thinking about the way you construct your applications. Objects enable you to more closely model the real world things, processes, and ideas that your application is designed to handle. Instead of thinking about an application as a thread of control that passes chunks of data from one function to the next, an OOP approach allows you to model the application as a set of collaborating objects that independently handle certain activities.

For example, when a house is being constructed, the plumbers deal with the pipes, and the electricians deal with the wires. The plumbers don't need to know whether the circuit in the bedroom is 10 amps or 20. They need only concern themselves with their own activities. A general contractor ensures that each subcontractor is completing the work that needs to be accomplished but isn't necessarily interested in the particulars of each task. An OO approach is similar in that each object hides from the others the details of its implementation. How it does its job is irrelevant to the other components of the system. All that matters is the service that the object is able to provide.

The concepts of classes and objects, and the ways in which you can leverage these ideas in the development of software, are the fundamental ideas behind object-oriented programming. This is, in a sense, the opposite of procedural programming, which is programming using functions and global data structures. As you'll see, an object-oriented approach gives you some big benefits over procedural programming, and with the new implementation of OO support in PHP5, some large performance boosts, as well.

Let's take a look at some of the enormous advantages that an OOP approach to software development gives you.

First is the ease with which you can map business requirements to code modules. Because an OOP approach enables you to model your application based on the idea of real world objects, you can often create a direct mapping of people, things, and concepts to PHP classes. These classes have the same properties and behaviors as the real-world concepts they represent, which helps you to quickly identify what code needs to be written and how different parts of the application need to interact.

A second benefit of OOP is code reuse. You frequently need the same types of data in different places in the same application. For example, an application that enables a hospital to manage its patient records would definitely need a class called `Person`. There are a number of people involved in patient care—the patient, the doctors, the nurses, hospital administrators, insurance claims people, and so on. At each step in the care of the patient, that patient's record requires a note about which person was performing a given action (such as prescribing medicine, cleaning wounds, or sending a bill to an insurance carrier) and verifying that person is allowed to perform that action. By defining a class called `Person` that encompasses all the properties and methods common to all of these people, you get an enormous amount of code reuse that isn't always possible in a procedural programming approach.

What about other applications? How many applications can you think of that at some point handle information about individuals? Probably quite a few. A well-written `Person` class could easily be copied from one project to another with little or no change, instantly giving you all the rich functionality for dealing with information about people that you developed previously. This is one of the biggest benefits of an OO approach—the opportunities for code reuse within a given application as well as across different projects.

Another OOP advantage comes from the modularity of classes. If you discover a bug in your `Person` class or you want to add to or change the way that class functions, you have only one place to go. All the functionality of that class is contained in a single PHP file. Any processes of the application that rely on the `Person` class are immediately affected by changes to it. This can vastly simplify the search for bugs and makes the addition of features a relatively painless task.

It might seem trivial in a smaller application, but in a more complex software architecture the benefits of modularity can be enormous. I once worked on a project involving more than 200,000 lines of procedural PHP code. Easily 65 percent of the time spent fixing bugs was devoted to uncovering where certain functions were located and determining which data interacted with which functions. A rewrite of that software in an OO architecture resulted in dramatically less code, which would have meant not only less work (if it had been done that way in the first place) but also fewer bugs (the less code there is, the fewer the opportunities for problems) and a faster turnaround time on bug fixes.

Because an OO approach forces you to think about how the code is organized, it's a lot easier to discover the structure of an existing application when you are new to the development team; you have a framework to guide the location of new functions you develop.

On larger projects, there is often a multimember software development team, usually composed of programmers with varying skill levels. Here, too, an OO approach has significant benefits over procedural code. Objects hide the details of their implementation from the users of those objects. Instead of needing to understand complex data structures and all of the quirks of the business logic, junior members of the team can, with just a little documentation, begin using objects created by senior members of the team. The objects themselves are responsible for triggering changes to data or the state of the system.

When the large application I mentioned previously was still using procedural code, it could often take up to two months for new members of the software development team to learn enough about the application to be productive. Once the software was rebuilt using objects, it usually took no more than a couple of days for new members of the team to begin making substantial additions to the code base. They were able to use even the most complex objects quickly because they did not need to fully understand the particulars of how the functionality contained within those objects was implemented.

Now you have a good idea about why you should consider using an OO paradigm as your programming method of choice. The following sections offer you a better understanding of the fundamental concepts behind OO. Within the next couple of chapters, you'll probably come to see the benefits of this approach for yourself.

Understanding OOP Concepts

This section introduces the primary concepts of object-oriented programming and explores how they interact. (Chapter 13 looks at the specifics of implementing them in PHP5.) You'll learn about:

❑ Classes, which are the "blueprints" for an object and are the actual code that defines the properties and methods.

❑ Objects, which are running instances of a class and contain all the internal data and state information needed for your application to function.

❑ Inheritance, which is the ability to define a class of one kind as being a sub-type of a different kind of class (much the same way a square is a kind of rectangle).

❑ Interfaces, which are contracts between unrelated objects to perform a common function.

❑ Encapsulation, which is the capability of an object to protect access to its internal data.

Along the way, we'll discuss polymorphism, which allows a class to be defined as being a member of more than one category of classes (just like a car is "a thing with an engine" and "a thing with wheels").

Classes

In the real world, objects have characteristics and behaviors. A car has a color, a weight, a manufacturer, and a gas tank of a certain volume. Those are its characteristics. A car can accelerate, stop, signal for a turn, and sound the horn. Those are its behaviors. Those characteristics and behaviors are common to all cars. Although different cars may have different colors, all cars have a color. OOP enables you to establish the idea of a car as being something with all of those characteristics through the use of a construct known as a *class*. A class is a unit of code, composed of variables and functions, which describes the characteristics and behaviors of all the members of a set. A class called Car, for example, would describe the properties and methods common to all cars.

In OO terminology, the characteristics of a class are known as its *properties*. Properties have a name and a value. Some allow that value to be changed while others do not. For example, the Car class would probably have such properties as color and weight. Although the color of the car can be changed by giving it a new paint job, the weight of the car (without cargo or passengers) is a fixed value.

Some properties represent the state of the object. State refers to those characteristics that change due to certain events but are not necessarily directly modifiable on their own. In an application that simulates vehicle performance, the Car class might have a property called `velocity`. The velocity of the car is not a value that can be changed on its own, but rather is a byproduct of the amount of fuel being sent to the engine, the performance characteristics of that engine, and the terrain over which the car is traveling.

The behaviors of a class—that is, the actions associated with the class—are known as its *methods*. Methods are implemented as functions. Like functions, methods can accept parameters of any valid data type. Some methods act on external data passed to them as parameters but they can also act on the properties of their object either using those properties to inform actions made by the method, such as when the `accelerate` method examines the remaining amount of fuel to determine whether the car is capable of accelerating, or to change the state of the object by modifying values such as the velocity of a car.

Objects

To begin with, you can think of a class as a blueprint for constructing an object. In much the same way that many houses can be built from the same blueprint, you can build multiple instances of an object from its class. But the blueprint doesn't specify things like the color of the walls, or type of flooring. It merely specifies that those things will exist. Classes work much the same way. The class specifies the behaviors and characteristics the object will have, but not necessarily the values of those characteristics. An *object* is a concrete entity constructed using the blueprint provided by a class. So although the idea of a house is analogous to a class, your house (a specific instance of the idea of a house) is analogous to an object.

With a blueprint in hand and some building materials, you can construct a house. In OOP, you use the class to build an object, a process known as *instantiation*. Instantiating an object requires two things:

❏ A memory location into which to load the object. This is automatically handled for you by PHP.

❏ The data that will populate the values of the properties. This data could come from a database, a flat text file, another object, or some other source.

A class never has property values or state. Only objects can. You have to use the blueprint to build the house before you can give it wallpaper or vinyl siding. Similarly, you have to instantiate an object from the class before you can interact with its properties or invoke its methods. When to use the word class and when to use the word object is often confusing to those new to OOP. Just remember that classes are manipulated at design-time when you make changes to the methods or properties, and objects are manipulated at runtime when values are assigned to their properties and their methods are invoked.

Once an object is instantiated, it can be put to work implementing the business requirements of the application. Let's look at exactly how to do that in PHP.

Creating a Class

Let's start with a simple example. Save the following in a file called `class.Demo.php`:

```php
<?php

   class Demo {

   }

?>
```

And there you have it—the `Demo` class. Not terribly exciting just yet, but this is the basic syntax for declaring a new class in PHP. Use the keyword `class` to let PHP know you're about to define a new class. Follow that with the name of the class and braces to indicate the start and end of the code for that class.

You can instantiate an object of type `Demo` like this:

```php
<?php

  require_once('class.Demo.php');

  $objDemo = new Demo();

?>
```

To instantiate an object, first make sure PHP knows where to find the class declaration by including the file containing your class (`class.Demo.php` in this example). Then invoke the `new` operator, and supply the name of the class and opening and closing parentheses. The return value of this statement is assigned to a new variable, `$objDemo` in this example. Now you can invoke the `$objDemo` object's methods and examine or set the value of its properties—if it actually has any.

> It's important to have a clearly defined convention for organizing your source code files. A good rule to follow is to put each class into its own file and to name that file `class.[ClassName].php`.

Even though the class you've created doesn't do much of anything yet, it's still a valid class definition.

Adding a Method

The `Demo` class isn't particularly useful if it isn't able to do anything, so let's look at how you can create a method. Remember, a method of a class is basically just a function. If you read Chapter 6, "Writing High-Quality Code," (and you did read Chapter 6, right?) you already know how to create a function. By adding a function inside the braces of your class, you're adding a method to that class. Here's an example:

```php
<?php

  class Demo {

    function sayHello($name) {
      print "Hello $name!";
    }

  }

?>
```

An object derived from your class is now capable of printing out a greeting to anyone who invokes the `sayHello` method. To invoke the method on your `$objDemo` object, you need to use the operator `->` to access the newly created function. Save the following code in a file called `testdemo.php`:

```php
<?php

  require_once('class.Demo.php');

  $objDemo = new Demo();
  $objDemo->sayHello('Steve');

?>
```

The object is now capable of printing a friendly greeting! The -> operator is used to access all methods and properties of your objects.

For those who have had exposure to OOP in other programming languages, please note that the -> operator is always used to access the methods and properties of an object. PHP does not use the dot operator (.) in its OO syntax at all.

Adding a Property

Adding a property to your class is as easy as adding a method. You just declare a variable inside the class to hold the value of the property. In procedural code, if you want to store a value, you assign that value to a variable. In OOP, if you want to store the value of a property, you also use a variable. This variable is declared at the top of the class declaration, inside the braces that bracket the class's code. The name of the variable is the name of the property. If the variable is called $color, you have a property called color.

Open the class.Demo.php file and add the highlighted code:

```php
<?php

   class Demo {

      public $name;

      function sayHello() {
         print "Hello $this->name!";
      }
   }

?>
```

Adding this new variable, called $name, is all you have to do to create a name property of the Demo class. To use this property, the same -> operator that you saw earlier is used, along with the name of the property. The rewritten sayHello method shows how to access the value of this property.

Create a new file called testdemo1.php and add the following:

```php
<?php

   require_once('class.Demo.php');

   $objDemo = new Demo();
   $objDemo->name = 'Steve';

   $objAnotherDemo = new Demo();
   $objAnotherDemo->name = 'Ed';

   $objDemo->sayHello();
   $objAnotherDemo->sayHello();

?>
```

Save the file and then open it in your Web browser. The strings "Hello Steve!" and "Hello Ed!" print to the screen.

The keyword `public` is used to let the class know that you want to have access to the following variable from outside the class. Some member variables of the class exist only for use by the class itself and should not be accessible to external code. In this example, you want to be able to set and retrieve the value of the property name. Note that the way the `sayHello` method works has changed. It now fetches the `name` value from the property instead of taking a parameter.

You use the variable `$this` so that an object can get information about itself. You might have multiple objects of a class, for instance, and because you don't know in advance what the name of an object variable will be, the `$this` variable enables you to refer to the current instance.

In the example, the first call to `sayHello` prints `Steve` and the second call prints `Ed` because the `$this` variable enables each object to talk to itself without having to know the name of the object variable currently referencing it. Remember that some properties influence the action of certain methods, such as when the `accelerate` method of the `Car` class, for example, needs to examine the amount of fuel remaining. The code inside `accelerate` would use code such as `$this->amountOfFuel` to access that property.

When accessing properties, you only need one $. The syntax is `$obj->property`, not `$obj->$property`. This often causes confusion for those new to PHP. The property variable is *declared* as `public $property;` and *accessed* using `$obj->property`.

In addition to the variables that store the values for the properties of the class, there may be other variables declared for use by the internal operations of the class. Both kinds of data are collectively referred to as the class's *internal member variables*. Some of these are accessible to code outside the class in the form of properties. Others are not accessible and are strictly for internal housekeeping. For example, if the `Car` class needed to get information from a database for whatever reason, it might keep a database connection handle in an internal member variable. This database connection handle is obviously not a property of the car, but it is something the class needs to carry out certain operations.

Protecting Access to Member Variables

There are three different levels of visibility that a member variable or method can have: public, private, and protected. Public members are accessible to any and all code. Private members are only accessible to the class itself. These are typically items used for internal housekeeping, such as the database connection handle in the `Car` class that I mentioned earlier. Protected members are available to the class itself, and to classes that inherit from it. Inheritance is defined and discussed in detail later in this chapter.

> *Public is the default visibility level for any member variables or functions that do not explicitly set one, but it is good practice to always explicitly state the visibility of all the members of the class.*

By creating `get` and `set` functions for all your properties it becomes much easier to add data validation, new business logic or other changes to your objects in the future. Even if the current business requirements for your application involve no data validation of a given property, you should still implement that property with get and set functions so you can add validation or business logic functionality in the future.

As the preceding example shows, you can set the value of the `name` property to just about anything you want—including an object, an array of integers, a file handle, or any other nonsensical value. However, you don't get an opportunity to do any sort of data validation or update any other values when the `name` property is set.

To work around this problem, always implement your properties in the form of functions called get[property name] and set[property name] as you'll see in the following *Try It Out* section.

Try It Out   Access Properties with get and set Methods

Make the changes highlighted in the following to class.Demo.php:

```php
<?php

  class Demo {

    private $_name;

    public function sayHello() {
      print "Hello {$this->getName()}!";
    }

    public function getName() {
      return $this->_name;
    }

    public function setName($name) {
      if(!is_string($name) || strlen($name) == 0) {
          throw new Exception("Invalid name value");
      }

      $this->_name = $name;
    }

  }

?>
```

Edit testdemo.php as shown here:

```php
<?php

  require_once('class.Demo.php');

  $objDemo = new Demo();
  $objDemo->setName('Steve');
  $objDemo->sayHello();

  $objDemo->setName(37); //would trigger an error

?>
```

How It Works

As you can see, the member access level of name has changed from public to private and been prefixed it with an underscore. The underscore is a recommended naming convention to indicate private member variables and functions, however it is just a convention and is not required by PHP. The keyword private protects code outside the object from modifying this value. Private internal member variables are not accessible from outside the class. Because you can't access these variables directly, you're forced to use the getName() and setName() methods to access this information, ensuring that your class can examine the value before allowing it to be set. In this example, an exception is thrown if an invalid value is supplied for the name property. Additionally, the public access specifier for the functions has been added.

Always use get and set functions for your properties. Changes to business logic and data validation requirements in the future will be much easier to implement.

Using _get and _set

The imperative to use get and set methods for all of your properties is advice you should take. However large objects with dozens of properties are going to take a fairly large amount of code to implement. This effort is especially unwelcome if there are no immediate business logic requirements for most of the properties. This is where methods called __get and __set come in handy.

If you try to access a property of an object, but there is no public member variable with that name, PHP looks to see if a function called __get has been defined for the object. If it has, PHP automatically calls __get to try to determine the value for the property. Similarly, when setting a property that does not exist, PHP invokes a function called __set, if it's has been defined.

Try It Out   Use _get and _set

This example shows how to use the __get and __set functions to make handling properties easier. Create a file called class.PropertyObject.php and enter the following code into it:

```php
<?php

class PropertyObject {

  private $_properties = array(
                  'name' => null,
                  'dateofbirth' => null
              );

  function __get($propertyName) {
    if(!array_key_exists($propertyName, $this->_properties))
      throw new Exception('Invalid property value!');

    if(method_exists($this, 'get' . $propertyName)) {
      return call_user_func(array($this, 'get' . $propertyName));
    } else {
      return $this->_properties[$propertyName];
    }
  }

  function __set($propertyName, $value) {
    if(!array_key_exists($propertyName, $this->_properties))
      throw new Exception('Invalid property value!');

    if(method_exists($this, 'set' . $propertyName)) {
```

```
        return call_user_func(
                array($this, 'set' . $propertyName),
                $value
                );
    } else {
      $this->_properties[$propertyName] = $value;
    }
  }

  function setDateOfBirth($dob) {
    if(strtotime($dob) == -1) {
      throw new Exception("The date of birth must be a valid date!");
    }
    $this->_properties['dateofbirth'] = $dob;
  }

  function sayHello() {
      //$this->_properties['name'] and $this->_properties['dateofbirth']
      //will be retrieved by __get
      print "Hi! My name is $this->name. I was born on $this->dateofbirth";
  }

}
?>
```

To test this new class, create a file called `testpropertyobject.php` and enter the following:

```
<?php
  require_once('class.PropertyObject.php');

  $obj = new PropertyObject();
  $obj->name = 'Bob'; //"Bob" is assigned to $_properties['name'] by __set
  $obj->dateofbirth = 'March 5, 1977'; //setDateOfBirth is invoked by __set
  $obj->sayHello();

  $obj->dateofbirth = 'blue'; //throws an exception

?>
```

Run `testpropertyobject.php` in your Web browser. You should see the sayHello message, "Hi! My name is Bob. I was born on March 5, 1977," followed by a rather ugly error message letting you know that the value `'blue'` is invalid for the `dateofbirth` property.

How It Works

This enables you to define all the valid properties that this object can have in an array, whose values you initialize to some sort of reasonable default value (in this case null). Any attempts to access properties for which there is no public member variable are automatically passed by PHP to the __get function.

The implementation of __get in this example first validates that the property has been defined in the private $_properties array. If it hasn't been defined, an exception is thrown. If the property has been defined, you examine the object itself to see if a function called get[property name] has been defined. If that function exists, you call it by using the call_user_func method. The method calls a procedural function if the first parameter is a string (where the string contains the name of the function to be called). If the first parameter is an array, in the form array($object, $methodName), then __get invokes the method $methodName on the object $object. In this case, you tell it to call the function get[property name] on $this. If there's no function called get[property name], then you just return the value of the item in the $_properties array at the array index corresponding the property name.

You do the same with the __set method. First, validate that the property has been defined, and then look for a function called set[property name], invoking it if it exists, and passing to it the value to be set. If that method doesn't exist, simply set the value of the item in the properties array having the key equal to the name of the property.

In this example, the setDateOfBirth method validates the date supplied to this property. The attempt to set the date of birth to the string 'blue' throws an exception.

The power of this technique is that it lets you use simple variables to store property values, but by simply creating a new function, you can easily add business logic and data validation without having to rewrite any of the code that might be using your class. It's also worth mentioning that the syntax of setting properties with $obj->myProperty = 'foo' is more intuitive than calling a function to set a simple property. You'll see the PropertyObject class a few more times in this chapter and the next (Chapter 13) to look at ways of improving it. By the end of the next chapter, you'll have a powerful utility class that you can use in all your projects.

Initializing Objects

For many of the classes you create, you'll need to do some special set up when an object of that class is first instantiated. You might need to fetch some information from a database, or initialize some property values, for example. By creating a special function called __construct(), you can perform any activities required to instantiate the object. PHP automatically calls this special function when instantiating the object.

For example, you could rewrite PropertyObject class in the following way:

```php
<?php

class PropertyObject {

    private $_properties;

    public function __construct() {
        $this->_properties = array();
        $this->_properties['name'] = null;
        $this->_properties['dateofbirth'] = null;
}

. . . //remaining code omitted for brevity
```

The __construct function is invoked automatically when you instantiate a new object of class PropertyObject.

For PHP4 users: In PHP4, object constructors were functions with the same name as the class. PHP5 changed this to use a unified constructor scheme. For backward compatibility, PHP first looks for a function called __construct, but if none is found, it still looks for a function with the same name as the class.

You can also pass parameters to the constructor. These parameters could be used to initialize the values of the properties with data, or to fetch some information from a database. The following example shows the use of the PostgreSQL functions to get some information about a user from a database. This class reuses the same __get and __set methods from the PropertyObject class.

Try It Out   Populate An Object in its Constructor

Save the following in a file called class.User.php. The unhighlighted code can be copied from class.PropertyObject.php. You will need a running MySQL database to use this example. If you have a different database available to you, feel free to substitute the mysql_ functions for those appropriate to your database platform. Be sure to change the connection string to match that required by your environment.

```php
<?php

class User {

    private $_properties;
    private $_hDB;

    public function __construct($userID) {
        $this->_properties = array();
        $this->_changedProperties = array();
        $this->_properties['id'] = null;
        $this->_properties['username'] = null;
        $this->_properties['realname'] = null;

        $this ->_hDB = mysql_connect('localhost', 'dbuser', 'mypassword');
        if(! is_resource($this->_hDB)) {
          throw new Exception("Unable to connect to the database!");
        }

        $connected = mysql_select_db('mydatabase', $this ->_hDB);
        if(! $connected) {
          throw new Exception("Unable to use the database 'mydatabase'!");
        }

        $sql = "select * from users where id = $userID";
        $rs = mysql_query($sql, $this->_hDB);

        if(! mysql_num_rows($rs)) {
          throw new Exception("No user exists with id $userID!");
        }

        $row = mysql_fetch_assoc($rs);

        $this->_properties['id'] = $row['id'];
        $this->_properties['username'] = $row['username'];
        $this->_properties['realname'] = $row['realname'];

    }

    // __get and __set omitted for brevity
```

```
        //don't allow the user ID value to be altered
        function setID($value) {
            throw new Exception('The user ID value may not be modified!');
    }

    function sayHello() {
        print "Hi! My name is {$this->realname}. My userid is {$this->id}";
    }


}
?>
```

Create a file called `testuser.php` and enter the following:

```
<?php
    require_once('class.User.php');

    $obj = new User(27); //User Bob Smith
    $obj->sayHello();
    //Prints "Hi! My name is Bob Smith. My userid is 27"

?>
```

If you have a working MySQL database to test against, run the following SQL statement to create the users table.

```
CREATE TABLE users (
    id int NOT NULL AUTO_INCREMENT PRIMARY KEY,
    username varchar(50),
    realname varchar(255)
);
```

You can also create a dummy value to test the example against by using the following INSERT statement:

```
mysql> INSERT INTO users (id, username, realname) VALUES(
    -> 27,
    -> 'bsmith',
    -> 'Bob Smith');
```

If the user ID supplied to the constructor does not exist in the database and you don't wrap the instantiation of `$obj` in a `try...catch...` block, you'll see something like the following printed to the screen:

Fatal *error:* Uncaught exception *'exception'* with *message* 'No user *exists* with *id* 12345!' in /path/to/class.User.php:28 Stack *trace:* #0 /path/to/testuser. php(4): User->__construct() #1 {main} thrown *in* /path/to/class.User.php on line 28

How It Works

You created a private member variable $_hDB to store the resource handle to your database connection. You then added the constructor function __construct and gave it a parameter $userID. When creating new objects of type User, you pass in the ID of the user you want to fetch. This value represents the primary key of a table in the database where you store information about the user.

The constructor opens a connection to the database and stores the resource handle in `$this->_hDB`. Call `mysql_select_db` to specify the name of the database to which you want to connect. You then issue a `SELECT` statement to the database to fetch all the information about the user. The values you're interested in are written to the `$_properties` array where they will be used by `__get`, `__set`, and any `get[property name]` or `set[property name]` functions you might create.

> *In a real-world application, you'd store the database connection information in a globally included file (see Chapters 9, 10, and 11) to make it easier to change the connection parameters or database name, should that become necessary. That way there's only one place where that information is kept, making it easier to change rather than having to revisit many different files to update the information.*

By using a constructor with a parameter, you can initialize all the property values by fetching them from the database. In this case you retrieve information about this user. Of course in a real-world application, you'd make sure line 4 of `testuser.php` is wrapped in a `try...catch...` block to catch any errors that might occur when connecting to the database or fetching this user.

Also note that the `setID` function throws an exception if you attempt to change the ID property. Because the ID is the primary identifier of this user, you should not allow modifications to that value.

If you have a class that does not require any special initialization code to be run, there is no need to create a constructor. As we saw in the very simple preceding `Demo` class, PHP automatically does what it needs to do to create that object. Create a constructor function only when you need one.

Destroying Objects

The object variables that you create are removed from system memory when the requested page has completed running, when the variable falls out of scope, or when it is explicitly set to null. In PHP5 you can trap the destruction of the object and take actions when that happens. To do so, create a function called `__destruct` with no parameters. Before the object is destroyed, this function, if it exists, is called automatically.

This gives you the opportunity to perform any last minute clean up, such as closing file handles or database connections that might have been opened by the class, or any other last-minutes housekeeping that might need to be done before the object is destroyed.

Try It Out   Create a Destructor

The following example uses the code from the earlier `User` class with a destructor added to demonstrate a really powerful technique. The following code changes allow `User` objects to automatically save their own changes to the database. When one of the object's properties is changed, you make a note of that change. When the object is destroyed, you look to see which properties, if any, were altered, and then update the database with these new values.

Make the following changes to `class.User.php`:

```php
<?php

class User {

    private $_properties;
```

```php
    private $_changedProperties; //keeps a list of the properties
                                 //that were altered
  private $_hDB;

 // __construct and __get omitted for brevity

    function __set($propertyName, $value) {
      if(!array_key_exists($propertyName, $this->_properties))
        throw new Exception('Invalid property value!');

      if(method_exists($this, 'set' . $propertyName)) {
        return call_user_func(
                   array($this, 'set' . $propertyName),
                   $value
                    );
      } else {
        //If the value of the property really has changed
        //and it's not already in the changedProperties array,
        //add it.
        if($this->_properties[$propertyName] != $value &&
           !in_array($propertyName, $this->_changedProperties)) {
          $this->_changedProperties[] = $propertyName;
        }

        //Now set the new value
      $this->_properties[$propertyName] = $value;
    }
  }
}

//don't allow the user ID value to be altered
function setID($value) {
  throw new Exception('The user ID value may not be modified!');
}

function sayHello() {
  print "Hi! My name is {$this->realname}. My userid is {$this->id}";
}

 function __destruct() {

  //Check to see if anything was changed. If
  //so, save the changes back to the database.
  if(sizeof($this->_changedProperties)) {

    $sql = "UPDATE users SET ";

  //Build up the SQL statement by creating
  //an array of set statements then join them
  //with commas at the end.
    $setStatements = array();
    foreach($this->_changedProperties as $prop) {
      $setStatements[] = "$prop = '{$this->_properties[$prop]}'";
    }

    //create the string
```

```
    $sql .= join(', ', $setStatements);

    //append the WHERE clause
    $sql .= " WHERE userid = $this->id";

    $hRes = mysql_query($sql);
    }

    //Close the connection to the database -- you're done.
    mysql_close($this->_hDB);
  }
}
```

Alter `testuser.php` as shown here:

```php
<?php
  require_once('class.User.php');

  $obj = new User(27); //User Robert Smith
  $obj->realname = 'Bob Smith';
  $obj->sayHello();

  $obj2 = new User(34); //Jane Doe
  $obj2->sayHello();

?>
```

How It Works

You first create a new private member variable called `$_changedProperties`. The __set method is changed to keep track of any properties that might have been modified in this variable. When __set is called, you look at both the name of the property being changed and its value. If the new value is different from the old value, you make a note of the change and set the new value. There's no need to make note of the change more than once, so you also check to see that this property has not already been added to the `$_changedProperties` array.

Then add the destructor by creating the __destruct method. In this example, __destruct has two responsibilities:

1. To see if anything was changed in this object. If any changes were made, it constructs an UPDATE statement to be issued to the database. The UPDATE statement updates only those values that were actually modified.

2. It closes your connection to the database server. After writing any changes back to the database, you still have an open database connection resource that needs to be closed. This was the connection initially opened in the constructor. By keeping that connection open throughout the lifetime of the object, you can use that connection to perform other database queries without having to incur the overhead of opening a new connection each time you need it. By closing the connection when you're done with the object, you save system resources.

After `$obj2` has said hello, the script is done executing and PHP begins the process of cleaning up any unused variables, including `$obj` and `$obj2`. Part of that clean-up process checks to see if a __destruct method has been defined. If so, that method is invoked on the object prior to removing it from system memory. In this example, that happens at the end of testuser.php.

Look at how powerful this technique can be. You can fetch a user from the database, change a property of that user and automatically write the changed information back to the database with only two lines of code in testuser.php. If nothing is changed, as was the case for $obj2, you don't need to go back to the database, saving load on the database server and improving the performance of the application.

Users of the object do not necessarily need to understand its internals. If a senior member of the software development team wrote the User class, she would be able to give this object to a junior member, who perhaps doesn't understand SQL as well, and the junior member of the team would be able to put this object to use without any knowledge whatsoever of where the data comes from or how to save changes to it. In fact, you could change the data source from a MySQL database to a PostgreSQL database or even to an XML file without the junior team member ever knowing, and without ever having to touch any of the code that uses this class.

Inheritance

If you were creating an application to handle inventory at a car dealership, you'd probably need classes such as Sedan, PickupTruck, and MiniVan that would correspond to the same types of automobiles in the dealer's inventory. Your application would need to show not only how many of these items were in stock, but also report on the characteristics of these vehicles so the salespeople could ably give the information to customers.

A sedan is a four-door car and you'd want to record the back seat space and the trunk capacity. A pickup truck doesn't have a trunk, but it has a cargo bed with a certain capacity, and a towing capacity. A minivan has a number of sliding doors (either one or two) and a number of seats inside.

But each of these vehicles is really just a different type of automobile and as such would share a number of characteristics in your application, such as color, manufacturer, model, year, vehicle identification number, and so on. To ensure that each of the classes has these same properties, you could copy the code that creates those properties into each of the files containing your class definitions. As mentioned earlier, though, one of the benefits of an OOP approach is code reuse, so of course you don't need to copy code, but instead can reuse the properties and methods of these classes through a process called *inheritance*. Inheritance is the capability of a class to assume the methods and properties of a parent class.

Inheritance enables you to define a base class—in this case, Automobile—and say that other classes are a type of Automobile and as such have all the same properties and methods that all Automobiles have. You can say that a Sedan is an Automobile, and the Sedan would automatically inherit everything defined by the Automobile class without your having to copy any code. Then you only need to write the additional properties and methods of the Sedan class that are not shared by all automobiles. The only work left for you to do is define the differences; the similarities between the classes are inherited from the base class.

The capability to reuse code is one benefit, but there's a second major advantage to using inheritance. Let's say you have a class called Customer with a method buyAutomobile. This method would take one parameter, an object of class Automobile, and its internal operations would print the paperwork needed to document the sale and would decrement the car in question from the inventory system. Because all Sedans, PickupTrucks, and MiniVans are Automobiles, you can pass objects of these classes to a function expecting an Automobile. Because the three specific types inherit from the more generic parent class, you know that they will all have the same base set of properties and methods. As long as you only need the methods and properties common to all Automobiles you can accept objects of any class that inherits from Automobile.

Here's another example: cats. All cats share some properties. They eat, sleep, purr, and hunt. They also have shared properties—weight, fur color, whisker length, and running speed. However, lions have a mane of a certain length (at least the male lions do) and they growl. Cheetahs have spots. Common house cats have neither of these things, yet all of these animals are cats.

In PHP you specify that a class is a subset of another by using the keyword `extends`, which tells PHP that the class you are declaring should inherit all the properties and methods from its parent class, and that you are adding functionality or providing some additional specialization to that class.

If you had to design an application to handle zoo animals, you'd probably need to have classes `Cat`, `Lion`, and `Cheetah`. Before writing any code, plan your class hierarchy in UML diagrams so you have something to work from when you write the code and the documentation of those classes. (We'll take a closer look at UML in Chapter 13, so don't worry if you can't completely understand what's shown here.) Your class diagram should indicate a parent class `Cat` with subclasses `Lion` and `Cheetah` inheriting from it. Figure 12-1 shows that diagram.

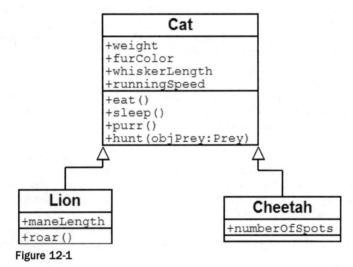

Figure 12-1

Both the `Lion` and `Cheetah` classes inherit from `Cat`, but the `Lion` class also implements the property `maneLength` and the method `roar()`, whereas `Cheetah` adds the property `numberOfSpots`.

The `Cat` class can be implemented as follows:

```php
<?php

class Cat {
    public $weight;         //in kg
    public $furColor;
    public $whiskerLength;
    public $maxSpeed;       //in km/hr
```

```php
    public function eat() {
      //code for eating...
    }

    public function sleep() {
      //code for sleeping...
    }

    public function hunt(Prey $objPrey) {
      //code for hunting objects of type Prey
      //which we will not define...
    }

    public function purr() {
      print "purrrrrrr...";
    }

  }
?>
```

This simple class sets up all the properties and methods common to all cats. To create the `Lion` and `Cheetah` classes, you could copy all the code from the `Cat` class to classes called `Lion` and Cheetah, but that generates two problems. First, if you find a bug in the `Cat` class, you have to know to fix it in the `Lion` and `Cheetah` classes, as well. This creates more work for you, not less (and creating less work is supposed to be one of the primary advantages of an OO approach).

Second, imagine you had a method of some other object that looked like this:

```php
//. . .additional code cut
public function petTheKitty(Cat $objCat) {
  $objCat->purr();
}
```

Although it may not be a terribly safe idea to pet a lion or cheetah, they will purr if they let you get close enough to do so. You should be able to pass an object of class `Lion` or `Cheetah` to the `petTheKitty()` function.

So you need to take the other route to creating the `Lion` and `Cheetah` classes, and that's to use inheritance. By using the keyword `extends` and specifying the name of the class that is extended, you can easily create two new classes that have all the same properties as a regular cat but provide some additional features. For example:

```php
<?php
  require_once('class.Cat.php');

  class Lion extends Cat {
    public $maneLength; //in cm

    public function roar() {
      print "Roarrrrrrrr!";
    }
  }
?>
```

And that's it! With the `Lion` class extending `Cat` you can now do something like the following `testlion.php` file:

```php
<?php
include('class.Lion.php');

$objLion = new Lion();
$objLion->weight = 200; //kg = ~450 lbs.
$objLion->furColor = 'brown';
$objLion->maneLength = 36; //cm = ~14 inches
$objLion->eat();

$objLion->roar();
$objLion->sleep();
?>
```

So you can invoke the properties and methods of the child class `Cat` without having to rewrite all that code. Remember that the `extends` keyword tells PHP to automatically include all of the functionality of a `Cat` along with any `Lion`-specific properties or methods. It also tells PHP that a `Lion` object is also a `Cat` object and you can now call the `petTheKitty()` function with an object of class `Lion`, even though the function declaration uses `Cat` as the parameter hint:

```php
<?php
include('class.Lion.php');
$objLion = new Lion();
$objLion->petTheKitty($objLion);
?>
```

In this way, any changes you make to the `Cat` class are automatically inherited by the `Lion` class. Bug fixes, changes to function internals, or new methods and properties are all passed along to the subclasses of a parent class. In a large, well-designed object hierarchy, this can make bug fixing and the addition of enhancements very easy. A small change to one parent class can have a large effect on the entire application.

Try It Out   Create the Cheetah Class

In this example, you'll see how a custom constructor can be used to extend and specialize a class. Create a new file called `class.Cheetah.php` and enter the following:

```php
<?php
require_once('class.Cat.php');

class Cheetah extends Cat {
  public $numberOfSpots;

  public function __construct() {
    $this->maxSpeed = 100;
  }
}
?>
```

Enter the following code into `testcheetah.php`:

```php
<?php
require_once('class.Cheetah.php');

    function petTheKitty(Cat $objCat) {
      if($objCat->maxSpeed < 5) {
        $objCat->purr();
      } else {
          print "Can't pet the kitty - it's moving at " .
                $objCat->maxSpeed . " kilometers per hour!";
      }
    }

    $objCheetah = new Cheetah();
    petTheKitty($objCheetah);

    $objCat = new Cat();
    petTheKitty($objCat);
?>
```

How It Works

The Cheetah class adds a new public member variable called numberOfSpots and a constructor that did not exist in the parent Cat class. Now when you create a new Cheetah, the maxSpeed property (inherited from Cat) is initialized to 100 kilometers per hour (roughly 60 miles per hour), which is the approximate maximum speed of a cheetah over short distances. Because a default value for the Cat class isn't specified, the maxSpeed evaluates as 0 (actually, null) in the petTheKitty() function. Given how much house cats sleep, their maximum speed probably is approaching 0!

By adding new functions, properties, or even constructors and destructors, the functionality of subclasses of a parent class can easily be extended. In other words, you can add new features and capabilities to your application with a minimum amount of code. You'll see a much more powerful example of this toward the end of the chapter when you extend the PropertyObject class to the classes of the contact manager application.

When you can say that a class is a special type of another class, use inheritance to maximize the potential for code reuse and increase the flexibility of your application.

Overriding Methods

Just because a child class inherits from a parent doesn't mean that the child class necessarily needs to use the parent class's implementation of a function. For example, if you were designing an application that needed to calculate the area of different geometric shapes, you might have classes called Rectangle and Triangle. Both of these shapes are polygons, and as such these classes will inherit from a parent class called Polygon.

The Polygon class will have a property called numberOfSides and a method called getArea. All polygons have a calculable area, although the methods for calculating that area can be different for different types of polygons. The formula for the area of a rectangle, for example, is w*h where w is the width of the rectangle and h is the height. The area of a triangle is calculated as (h/2)*b where h is the height of a triangle with base b. Figure 12-2 shows both of these examples.

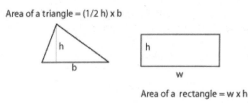

Area of a triangle = (1/2 h) x b

Area of a rectangle = w x h

Figure 12-2

For each subclass of `Polygon` that you create, you probably need an area method different from the default implementation. By simply redefining that method for the specific class you can provide your own implementation.

In the case of the `Rectangle` class, for example, you create two new properties, `height` and `width`, and override the `Polygon` class's implementation of the `getArea` method (the general formula for the area of a noncomplex polygon—which would be the `Polygon` class's `getArea` method—is rather complicated, and because you're going to override it for all of your subclasses, there's really no need to go into that formula here). For the `Triangle` class, you would probably add properties to store information about the three angles, the height, and length of the base segment, and use the height and base length to override the `getArea` method. By using inheritance and overriding methods of the parent class, you can allow the subclasses to specialize their implementations of those methods.

A function that takes `Polygon` as a parameter and needs to print the area of that polygon automatically calls the `getArea` method of the subclass of `Polygon` that was passed to it (that is, `Rectangle` or `Triangle`). This capability for an OO programming language to automatically determine at runtime which `getArea` method to call is known as *polymorphism*. Polymorphism is the capability of an application to do different things based on the particular object it is acting on. In this case, that means invoking a different `getArea` method.

> *Override a method in a subclass when the parent class's implementation is different from that required by the subclass. This enables you to specialize the activities of that subclass.*

Sometimes you want to retain the implementation provided by the parent class but also perform some additional activities in the method of the subclass. Let's say, for example, that you have an application that manages a nonprofit organization, and that you have a class called `Volunteer` that has a method called `signUp`. This method enables volunteers to sign up for a community service project, and then adds the users to the list of volunteers for that activity.

However, you might have some users with restrictions, such as a criminal background, that should prevent them from signing up for certain projects. In this case, polymorphism enables you to create a class called `RestrictedUser` with an overridden `signUp` method that first checks the restrictions on the user account against the properties of the project and prevents users from signing up if their restrictions do not permit them to volunteer for a particular activity. If their restrictions do not prohibit them from participating, then you invoke the actions of the parent class to complete their registration.

When you override methods of the parent class, you do not necessarily need to completely rewrite the method. You can continue to use the implementation provided by the parent but add additional specialization for your subclass. In this way, you can reuse code and also provide customizations as required by the business rules.

The capability for one class to inherit the methods and properties of another class is one of the most compelling features of an object-oriented system and enables you to gain an incredible level of efficiency and flexibility in your applications.

Override Inherited Methods

In this example, you create two classes—Rectangle and Square. A square is a special kind of rectangle. Anything you can do with a rectangle you can do with a square, but a rectangle has two different side lengths and a square has only one, you need to do some things differently.

Create a file called class.Rectangle.php and add the following code:

```php
<?php

  class Rectangle {
    public $height;
    public $width;

    public function __construct($width, $height) {
      $this->width = $width;
      $this->height = $height;
      }

      public function getArea() {
       return $this->height * $this->width;
      }
    }
?>
```

This is a fairly straightforward implementation of a class to model a rectangle. The constructor takes parameters for the width and height and the area function calculates the area of the rectangle by multiplying them together.

Here's class.Square.php:

```php
<?php
  require_once('class.Rectangle.php');

  class Square extends Rectangle {
    public function __construct($size) {
      $this->height = $size;
      $this->width = $size;

    }

    public function getArea() {
      return pow($this->height, 2);
    }

  }
?>
```

This code overrides both the constructor and the getArea() method. In order for a square to be a square, both sides must be of the same length. As a result, you need only one parameter for the constructor. If more than one parameter is passed to the function, any values after the first are ignored.

Test it using the following script (testsquare.php):

```php
<?php
require_once ('class.Square.php');
$obj = new Square(7);
$a = $obj->getArea();
echo "$a";
?>
```

This code echoes out the expected value for the area of a square with sides of length 7.

> *PHP does not raise an error if the number of parameters passed to a user-defined function is greater than the number of parameters established in the function declaration. There are a few cases where this is actually desired behavior. If you'd like to learn more, see the documentation of the built-in* func_get_args() *function.*

It also overrides the getArea() function. The implementation in the Rectangle class would have returned a perfectly correct result for Square objects, but the method was overridden to improve application performance (although in this case the performance benefit is miniscule). It is faster for PHP to fetch one property and compute its square than to fetch two properties and multiply them together.

By overriding constructors, destructors, and methods you can alter aspects of how subclasses operate.

Preserving the Functionality of the Parent

Sometimes, you want to preserve the functionality provided by the parent. You don't need to completely override the function, you just need to add something to it. You could copy all the code from the parent method into the subclass' method, but as you've already seen, OOP offers you better ways of doing this than just copying lines of code.

To call the functionality provided by the parent, use the syntax parent::[function name]. To just add additional behavior to a method, first call parent::[function name] and then add your additional code. When extending a function in this way, always call the method on the parent before doing anything else. This ensures that any changes to the operation of the parent won't break your code.

> *Because the parent class may be expecting the object to be in a certain state, or may alter the state of the object, overwrite property values, or manipulate the objects internal data, always invoke the parent method before adding your own code when extending an inherited method.*

Let's take a look at how this works.

Try It Out   Preserve the Functionality of a Parent Method

This example has two classes—Customer and SweepstakesCustomer. A supermarket has an application that from time to time switches which class is being used in the cash register application when certain promotions are run. Each customer who comes in has his own ID value (which comes from a database) as well as a customer number, which indicates how many customers have come to the supermarket before him. For this sweepstakes, the one millionth customer wins a prize.

Create a file called `class.Customer.php` and add the following:

```php
<?php

  class Customer {
    public $id;
    public $customerNumber;
    public $name;

    public function __construct($customerID) {
      //fetch customer infomation from the database
      //
      //This obviously doesn't come from a database, but in a
      //real application it would.
      $data = array();
      $data['customerNumber'] = 1000000;
      $data['name'] = 'Jane Johnson';

      //Assign the values from the database to this object
      $this->id = $customerID;
      $this->name = $data['name'];
      $this->customerNumber = $data['customerNumber'];
    }
  }

?>
```

Create a file called `class.SweepstakesCustomer.php` and type in this code:

```php
<?php
  require_once('class.Customer.php');

  class SweepstakesCustomer extends Customer {
    public function __construct($customerID) {
      parent::__construct($customerID);

      if($this->customerNumber == 1000000) {
        print "Congratulations $this->name! You're our millionth
customer! " .
              "You win a year's supply of frozen fish sticks! ";
      }
    }
  }

?>
```

To see how to use this class, create a file called `testCustomer.php` and enter the following code:

```php
<?php

  require_once('class.SweepstakesCustomer.php');
  //since this file already includes class.Customer.php, there's
  //no need to pull that file in, as well.
```

```
function greetCustomer(Customer $objCust) {
  print "Welcome back to the store $objCust->name!";
}


//Change this value to change the class used to create this customer object
$promotionCurrentlyRunning = true;

if($promotionCurrentlyRunning) {
  $objCust = new SweepstakesCustomer(12345);
} else {
  $objCust = new Customer(12345);
}

greetCustomer($objCust);

?>
```

Run `testCustomer.php` in your browser with the `$promotionCurrentlyRunning` variable set first to `false`, then to `true`. When the value is `true`, the prize message is displayed.

How It Works

The `Customer` class initializes values from the database based on the customer ID. You would most likely retrieve the customer ID from a loyalty program swipe card like the type available at most larger grocery store chains. With the customer ID, you can fetch his personal data from the database (just hard coded in this example) along with an integer value representing how many customers have entered the store before him. Store all of this information in public member variables.

The `SweepstakesCustomer` class adds a bit of extra functionality to the constructor. You first invoke the parent class's constructor functionality by calling `parent::_construct` and pass to it the parameters it expects. You then look at the `customerNumber` property. If this customer is the one-millionth customer, you inform him that he's won a prize.

Interfaces

There are times when you have a group of classes that are not necessarily related through an inheritance-type relationship. You may have totally different classes that just happen to share some behaviors in common. For example, both a jar and a door can be opened and closed, and are in no other way related. No matter the kind of jar or the kind of door, they both can carry out these activities, but there is no other common thread between them.

In OOP, an *interface* enables you to specify that an object is capable of performing a certain function but it does not necessarily tell you how the object does so. An interface is a contract between unrelated objects to perform a common function. An object that implements the interface is guaranteeing to its users that it is capable of performing all of the functions defined by the interface specification. Bicycles and footballs are totally different things, yet objects representing those items in a sporting goods store inventory system must be capable of interacting with that system.

By declaring an interface and then implementing it in your objects, it's possible to hand completely different classes to common functions. The following example shows the door-and-jar analogy.

Try It Out   **Use Interfaces**

Create a file called interface.`Openable.php`:

```php
<?php

  interface Openable {
    abstract function open();
    abstract function close();
  }

?>
```

Just as you name your class files `class.[class name].php`, you should use the same convention with interfaces and call them `interface.[interface name].php`.

You declare the interface `Openable` using syntax similar to that of a class, except you substitute the word interface for the word class. Generally, an interface does not have member variables or specify an implementation of its member functions.

Because no implementation is specified, you declare these functions to be `abstract`. This tells PHP that any class implementing this interface is responsible for providing an implementation of the functions. If you fail to provide an implementation of *all* of the abstract methods of an interface, PHP raises a runtime error. You can't selectively choose some of the abstract methods to implement—you must provide implementations of all of them.

An abstract method is one for which no implementation is provided. Abstract methods can appear in interfaces and classes. If a method in a class is declared abstract, then the class itself must be declared abstract by placing the keyword `abstract` before the word `class` in the class declaration. An abstract class is one that cannot be instantiated on its own, but must have subclasses that provide a concrete implementation of the abstract methods. Note that abstract method declarations do not involve braces and end with a semicolon.

How It Works

The `Openable` interface is a contract with other parts of the application that says any class implementing this interface will provide two methods—`open()` and `close()`—that take no parameters. With this agreed-upon set of methods you can allow very different objects to pass into the same function without their needing to be an inherited relationship between them.

Create the file `class.Door.php`:

```php
<?php

require_once('interface.Openable.php');

class Door implements Openable {

  private $_locked = false;
```

```
      public function open() {
        if($this->_locked) {
          print "Can't open the door. It's locked.";
        } else {
          print "creak...<br>";
        }
      }

      public function close() {
        print "Slam!!<br>";
      }

      public function lockDoor() {
        $this->_locked = true;
      }

      public function unlockDoor() {
        $this->_locked = false;
      }

  }

  ?>
```

And the file `class.Jar.php`:

```
  <?
  require_once('interface.Openable.php');

  class Jar implements Openable {
    private $contents;

    public function __construct($contents) {
        $this->contents = $contents;
    }

    public function open() {
      print "the jar is now open<br>";
    }

    public function close() {
      print "the jar is now closed<br>";
    }
  }
  ?>
```

To use them, create a new file called `testOpenable.php` in the same directory:

```
<?php
  require_once('class.Door.php');
  require_once('class.Jar.php');

  function openSomething(Openable $obj) {
    $obj->open();
  }
```

```
    $objDoor = new Door();
    $objJar = new Jar("jelly");

    openSomething($objDoor);
    openSomething($objJar);

?>
```

Because both the Door class and the Jar class implement the Openable interface, you can pass both to the openSomthing() function. Because that function accepts only something that implements the Openable interface, you know that you can call the functions open() and close() within it. However, you should not attempt to access the contents property of the Jar class or utilize the lock() or unlock() functions of the Door class within the openSomething() function because that property and those methods are not part of the interface. The interface contract guarantees that you have open() and close() methods and nothing else.

By using interfaces in your application, you can allow completely different and unrelated objects to talk to each other with a guarantee that they will be able to interact on the terms specified in the interface.

Encapsulation

As mentioned earlier in this chapter, objects enable you to hide the details of their implementation from users of the object. For example, a user doesn't need to know whether the Volunteer class stores information in a database, a flat text file, an XML file, or other data storage mechanism to be able to invoke the signUp method. Similarly, he doesn't need to know whether the information about the volunteer contained within the object is implemented as single variables, an array, or even another object. This ability to hide the details of implementation is known as *encapsulation*. Generally speaking, encapsulation refers to these two concepts: the protection of a class's internal data from code outside that class, and the hiding of the details of implementation.

The word encapsulate literally means to place in a capsule, or outer container. A well-designed class provides a complete outer shell around its internals and presents an interface to code outside the class that is wholly separated from the particulars of those internals. By doing this, you gain two advantages: you can change the implementation details at any time without affecting code that uses your class and, because you know that nothing outside your class can inadvertently modify the state or property values of an object built from your class without your knowledge, you can trust the state of the object and the value of its properties to be valid and to make sense.

You'll recall from earlier in the chapter that the member variables of a class and its functions have a *visibility*, which refers to what can be seen by code outside the class. Private member variables and functions are not accessible to code outside the class and are used for the class's internal implementation. Protected member variables and functions are only visible to the subclasses of the class. Public member variables and functions are usable by any code, inside or outside of the class.

Generally speaking, all internal member variables of a class should be declared private. Any access needed to those variables by code outside the class should be done through a public method. When someone wants you to try a new food, you don't allow him to insert it directly into your stomach for a good reason—you need to be able to examine the food and determine if it's something you want to allow into your body. The method for giving you food involves handing it to you and allowing you to decide to eat it or not. Similarly, when an object wants to allow code outside of it to change properties or in some other way affect its internal data, by encapsulating access to that data in a public function (and by keeping the internal data private) you have the opportunity to validate the changes and accept or reject them.

For example, if you're building a banking application that handles details of customer accounts, you might have an `Account` object with a property called `totalBalance` and methods called `makeDeposit` and `makeWithdrawal`. The `totalBalance` property should be read-only. The only way to affect the balance is to make a withdrawal or a deposit. If the `totalBalance` property is implemented as a public member variable, you can write code that would increase the value of that variable without having to actually make a deposit. Obviously, this would be bad for the bank. Instead, you implement this property as a private member variable and provide a public method called `getTotalBalance`, which returns the value of that private member variable. With the variable storing the value of the account balance made private, it can't be manipulated directly. Because the only public methods that affect the account balance are `makeWithdrawal` and `makeDeposit`, a user has to actually make a deposit if he wants to increase the value of his account.

Encapsulation of internal data and method implementations allows an object-oriented software system to protect and control access to data and to hide the details of implementation, giving you flexible, stable applications.

Changes to OO in PHP5

Support for objects in PHP goes all the way back to PHP3. There was never any intention of supporting the idea of classes or objects, but some limited support was added, almost as an afterthought, to provide "syntactic sugar" (to use Zeev Suraski's phrase) for associative arrays. Object support in PHP was originally designed as a convenient way of grouping data and functions, but only a small subset of the features traditionally associated with a full-blown object oriented-programming language was included.

As PHP grew in popularity, the use of an OO approach became increasingly common in large applications. However, the poor internal implementation became limiting. Most notably, there was no support for real encapsulation. You could not specify member variables or methods to be private or protected. Everything was public which, as you've seen, can be problematic.

Additionally, there was no support for abstract interfaces or methods. Methods and member variables could not be declared static. There were no destructors. All of these are concepts that are familiar to anyone with a background in other object-oriented programming languages and the lack of these features in PHP's object model could make that transition from a language like Java (which does support all of these ideas) to PHP difficult.

PHP5 introduces a number of major changes to the object-oriented features in the language that addresses these problems and others, giving PHP real OO capabilities and providing increased performance when using the OO capabilities:

❑ Keywords for controlling the visibility of member variables and methods allowing for private, protected, and public members.

❑ PHP5 provides dereferencing support such that you can write code such `$obj->getObj()->doSomething()`. In previous versions of PHP, dereferencing support was limited.

❑ Static methods and class constants are now supported, allowing for greater compile-time and runtime checking. Static methods are invoked with the `::` operator.

❑ Unified constructors, using the `__construct()` method, instead of a method with the same name as the class makes it easier to alter inheritance when multiple classes are involved in a tree of inheritance.

❑ Classes in PHP can now have destructors, through the `__destruct()` method. This allows actions to be taken when the object is destroyed.

❑ Support for abstract classes and interfaces has been added. This gives you the capability to define required methods in a parent class while deferring implementation to a subclass. Abstract classes can't be instantiated, only their nonabstract subclasses can.

❑ Functions and methods can use type hints on their parameters. It's now possible to specify the class for function parameters that are expecting an object. `function foo(Bar $objBar) { ...` enables you to be sure that the data type of the parameter $objBar will be an object of class `Foo`.

Summary

In this chapter you explored the concept of object-oriented programming. A class was seen as a blueprint for creating objects. Objects are runtime bundles of data and functions created from a class definition. Objects have characteristics, called properties, and behaviors, called methods. Properties can be thought of as variables and methods are functions.

Some classes share a common parent type. When you declare a class to be a subtype of a parent class, it inherits the methods and properties of the parent. You have the option to override inherited methods. You can completely reimplement the method, if you so choose, or continue to use the parent's implementation but also add specializations particular to the subclass (or not override the method at all).

Encapsulation is an important concept in object-oriented programming. It refers to the capability of a class to protect access to its internal member variables and shield users of that class from the particulars of its implementation. There are three levels of visibility of data and functions: private members that can only be used by the class's internal operations; protected members that are visible to subclasses; and public members that be used by code outside the class.

Object-oriented support in PHP received a major overhaul with the introduction of PHP5 and the Zend Engine 2. New features and significant performance improvements make PHP a real OO programming language.

Exercises

1. Define the difference between a class and an object.

2. Explain inheritance and give an example of when it should be used. Don't repeat any of the examples already provided in this chapter!

3. Describe the utility of an interface and its practical application in a software architecture. How is an interface different from an inherited class? Can you come up with additional examples of when this might be useful?

Working with UML and Classes

One of the most useful tools for modeling object-oriented programs is UML, Unified Modeling Language. This chapter introduces you to UML and discusses why you should use it, what software is available to PHP programmers to create UML, and how the various UML diagrams you create help you build your applications. The UML diagrams you produce at the start of the chapter will develop into a full example application: the contact manager.

The contact manager is intended to manage data about individuals and organizations and enable users to look up and edit the contact information about these entities. The discussion about the sample program provides a good discourse on the issues behind creating working object-oriented applications. Along the way, it also demonstrates the major principles behind the object-oriented paradigm such as code reuse, encapsulation, and of course, abstraction.

The Unified Modeling Language

With the cumbersome vocabulary of OOP, it can be difficult to get your head around a written description of a set of objects. However, carefully planning and clearly documenting your objects is crucial to the successful delivery of an application. This is especially true in a large application that's using dozens of objects. But how do you generate this documentation in a manner that will be accessible to those who need to read it? As the saying goes, a picture is worth a thousand words. The Unified Modeling Language (UML) is a specification that describes standard processes for generating a visualization of object-oriented software systems.

UML isn't a language—not in the usual sense of the word, anyway. It's a system for representing classes and the interactions between them in a visual way, using standardized symbols to build a complete graphical model of the application. You use images to clearly communicate complex class relationships and provide a document that others can use to understand your software and how to use it (or that you can use to understand your own software when you need to make changes to it long after the initial build). Prior to the publication of the UML specification, there were a number of competing symbologies for representing these concepts. The UML spec took the best features from each of these other systems and combined them into a single standard that deprecated the previous systems and established a common visual language.

The current version of the UML specification defines 12 different types of diagrams that describe the structure, behavior, or organization of an application, depending on which diagram you are creating. This chapter covers only one of those diagrams in detail, the class diagram, although you'll get a peek at a few other kinds of UML diagrams. A complete discussion of UML is beyond the scope of this book; if you want to learn more about UML, there are a number of excellent resources available, including *UML 2 Toolkit*, published by Wiley & Sons (ISBN: 0-471-46361-2).

Why Would You Want to Use UML?

Many software developers complain about having to write documentation. Often these documents are meant for consumption by clients, business development people, and other nontechnical staff, and creating them distracts from what you really want to be doing—writing code. Even the developer-oriented documents, such as a technical specification, often go untouched and unread after first being generated. UML diagrams are meant to be a working tool for describing your project and the act of creating them really, truly benefits the developer *during* the software development process, not just in the planning stages.

UML diagrams enable you to put to paper the ideas you have in your head about how to architect your application without all the time-wasting fuss of having to write text to describe your ideas. While you're still in the planning stages of a project, the diagrams make it easy for you to render large-scale changes to the software architecture without having to worry about the code. They provide a vehicle by which software architects can communicate their ideas to those who will be helping them to implement those ideas. And, most impressively, depending on the tools you're using to create your diagrams, you can actually generate much of the code for your classes from the diagrams. You can literally draw your code!

UML Software

There are dozens of different application out there that are capable of generating UML diagrams, both open-source and commercial software. Unfortunately, support for automatic code generation for PHP is fairly limited at time of writing. Here are a just a few of the tools you might want to consider:

❑   Dia (www.lysator.liu.se/~alla/dia/): A GPL'ed gtk+-based tool that has support for UML diagrams along with a wide variety of other diagram types. It has a precompiled binary available for Windows. Has no support for automatic code generation. All the UML diagrams in this book were generated using Dia.

❑   Visio (www.microsoft.com/office/visio): Part of the Microsoft Office suite of applications, it is used for everything from UML diagrams, to network diagrams, to floor plans and organization charts. Dia was meant to be the open-source alternative to Visio. Visio also has no facility for automatic code generation.

❑   IBM Rational Rose (www.rational.com): Long the gold standard for UML development, Rational provides not only software, but also a complete methodology for software development. Code generators are available for Java and .NET, but there's no support for PHP.

❑   ArgoUML (http://argouml.tigris.org): ArgoUML itself is written in Java but it currently has experimental support for PHP code generation. It is free and covered by a BSD-style license (see the ArgoUML Web site for more information).

❑ Umbrello (http://uml.sourceforge.net): A Unix-only (no Windows binaries) UML tool with full PHP code generation support. Open source.

❑ Poseidon For UML, Professional Edition (www.gentleware.com/products/): Commercial UML tool with full support for PHP code generation.

Although you won't need any of these tools to follow along with the book, it's recommended that you download one of them so that you can create UML diagrams of your own as you work through the chapter. Dia is used in this book, so you may want to download that one—simply go to the site and follow the instructions. There's very little required in the way of initialization and installation, so you should have no problems there.

There are two reasons why PHP code generation support is limited or nonexistent in most of these tools. Traditionally, software developers in scripting languages such as PHP rarely used the rigorous software development processes common to Java and C++ developers. UML is a process tool and as a result, PHP support was overlooked. The other reason is that until PHP5, there was only rudimentary OO support in PHP. Now that PHP has real OO support, I expect to see more of these UML tools providing PHP code generation facilities.

Class Diagrams

Ready to get started? As mentioned earlier, this book covers only one of the 12 diagrams defined by the UML specification in detail—the class diagram. A class diagram shows the classes in an application and the relationships among them.

The basic class symbol (see Figure 13-1) is a rectangle divided into three parts. The first part shows the class name, the second shows its properties, and the third shows its methods. The sections are separated by a horizontal line.

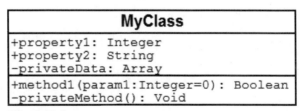

Figure 13-1

This example has a class called MyClass, with two public properties (property1, an Integer, and property2, a String) and one private member variable (privateData, an Array). There are also two methods. method1() is a public method that takes one Integer param1 as its parameter with a default value of 0 and returns a Boolean value. The private method privateMethod() takes no parameters and has no return value (Void). You can see that a plus sign next to a property or method indicates a public item, whereas a minus sign indicates a private member. Protected items are indicated by an octothorpe (#, also called the hash or pound symbol).

Obviously all of this is a lot easier to get from looking at the diagram than from reading the text description. This is why you use UML to describe your objects. It took me nearly three times as long to type up and format that description than it did to create the diagram in Dia.

Of course, if all you had was one class, the diagram isn't all that useful. It's only useful in a hierarchy of objects. The next section will walk you through the creation of a UML diagram for a real-world application that you will actually begin building here.

Creating the Contact Manager

The sample application you'll deal with in the rest of this chapter is a contact manager. A contact management application enables the user to track individuals and organizations; their contact information, such as address, email and phone number; and the relationships between them. This is basically what Microsoft's Outlook address book does.

The application needs to be able to track information about individuals and organizations in a database and display it on a Web page. Contacts can have zero or more addresses, e-mail addresses, and phone numbers. An individual has an employer (which is an organization) and an organization has employees (which are individuals).

The Contact Manager UML Diagrams

Fire up the UML diagramming application of your choice and create a new file called `ContactManager.[extension]` where `[extension]` is the default file extension for your application (that is, `.dia` for diagrams created using Dia).

You first create classes to represent the three different kinds of contact information—address, email address, and phone number. Here are their properties:

Class	Properties
Address	street1 street2 city state zipcode type (that is, Home, Work, etc.)
EmailAddress	email type
PhoneNumber	number extension type

These classes just store and display data, so you don't need to define any methods at this time, and the third sections of the class symbols are empty. The properties are all public so they're prefixed with a plus sign. Figure 13-2 shows the UML representation of these classes.

Now you map out the `Individual` and `Organization` classes. An Individual has a first name, a last name, a unique identifier (the id field from the database), a collection of emails, addresses, and phone

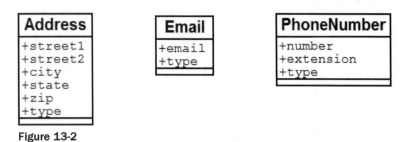

Figure 13-2

numbers, an employer, and a job title. You also need to be able to add contact types. Figure 13-3 shows a UML diagram of the Individual class.

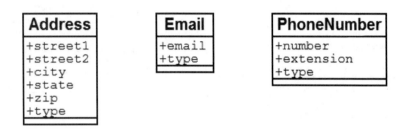

Individual
+firstname
+lastname
+employer: Organization
+title
+id
+addresses: Address[]
+emails: EmailAddress[]
+phonenumbers: PhoneNumber[]
+addEmail(objEmail:Email)
+addAddress(objAddress:Address)
+addPhone(objPhone:PhoneNumber)

Figure 13-3

An Organization has a name, an id, the same collections of contact types, methods to add them, and a collection of employees. Figure 13-4 shows a UML diagram of the Organization class.

The diagram shows the Individual and Organization classes sharing a lot of the same properties and methods. This is generally an indication that you could save yourself a lot of work and improve the flexibility of your application by using inheritance. You can create another class (Entity in this example) in which you combine the features common to the Individual and Organization classes and allow them to share the same code. In a UML diagram, you only indicate properties and methods on the class that actually implements them. In this case, you need to move all the common properties and methods of the Individual and Organization classes to the symbol representing the Entity class (see Figure 13-5). You repeat them in the child class only if the child overrides the implementation.

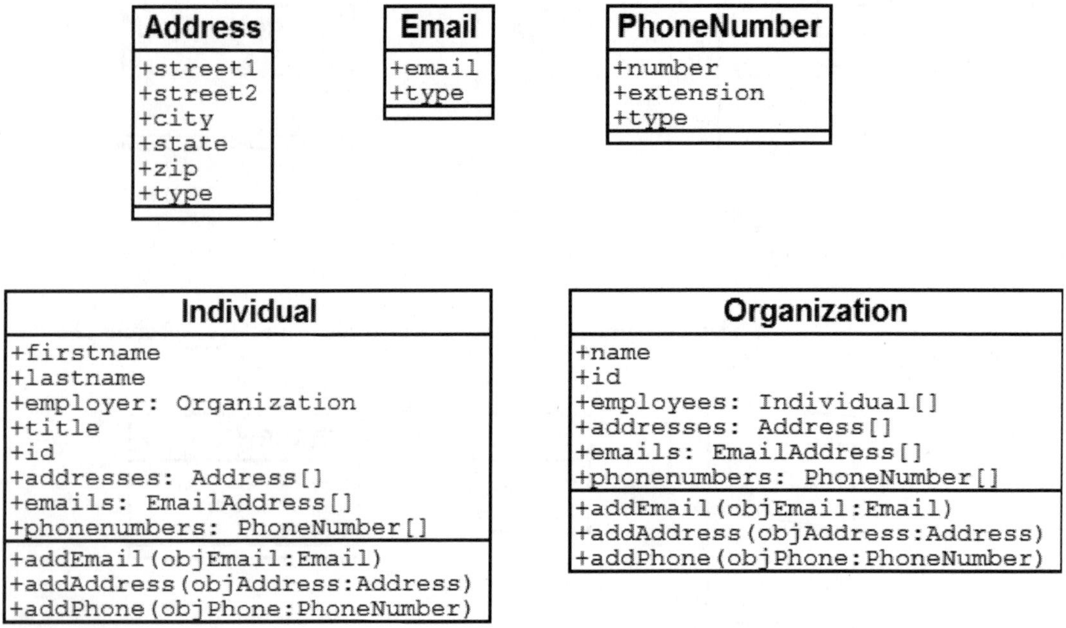

Address

+street1
+street2
+city
+state
+zip
+type

Email

+email
+type

PhoneNumber

+number
+extension
+type

Individual

+firstname
+lastname
+employer: Organization
+title
+id
+addresses: Address[]
+emails: EmailAddress[]
+phonenumbers: PhoneNumber[]

+addEmail(objEmail:Email)
+addAddress(objAddress:Address)
+addPhone(objPhone:PhoneNumber)

Organization

+name
+id
+employees: Individual[]
+addresses: Address[]
+emails: EmailAddress[]
+phonenumbers: PhoneNumber[]

+addEmail(objEmail:Email)
+addAddress(objAddress:Address)
+addPhone(objPhone:PhoneNumber)

Figure 13-4

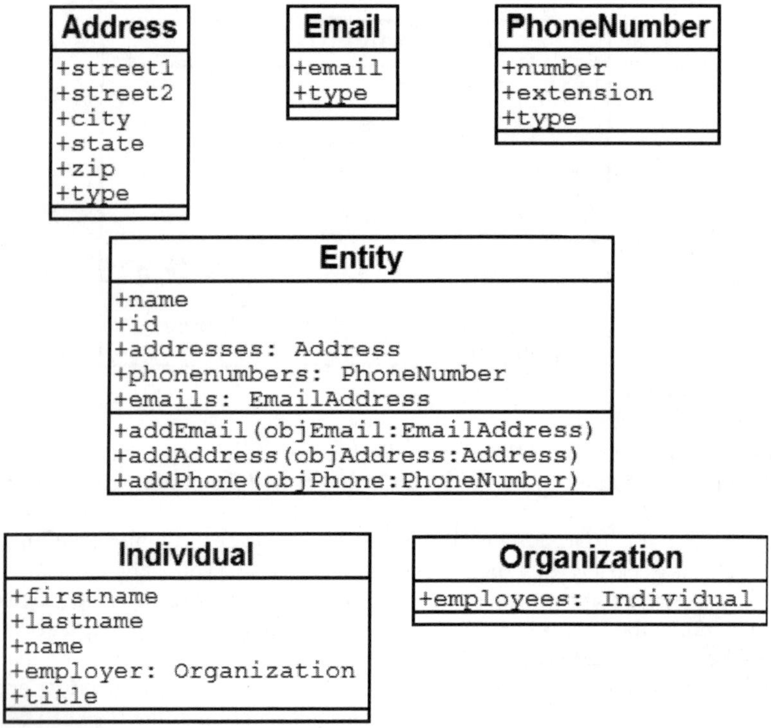

Address

+street1
+street2
+city
+state
+zip
+type

Email

+email
+type

PhoneNumber

+number
+extension
+type

Entity

+name
+id
+addresses: Address
+phonenumbers: PhoneNumber
+emails: EmailAddress

+addEmail(objEmail:EmailAddress)
+addAddress(objAddress:Address)
+addPhone(objPhone:PhoneNumber)

Individual

+firstname
+lastname
+name
+employer: Organization
+title

Organization

+employees: Individual

Figure 13-5

In this case, the name property of the Entity class is overridden in the Individual class. When you retrieve the name property of an Individual later, you'll return "lastname, firstname." This way, you can hand the Organization or Individual classes to a function that will just print a name without having to use separate functions.

UML also defines symbols to indicate relationships. In this example, you need something to show that the Individual and Organization classes inherit from the Entity class. The UML specification calls this relationship *generalization* and indicates it by an open-headed arrow that points from the child class(es) to the parent class, as shown in Figure 13-6.

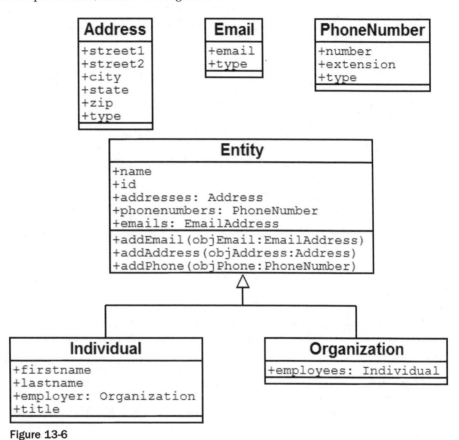

Figure 13-6

Now it's clear that the Individual and Organization classes inherit from the Entity class. Using connectors to indicate inheritance makes it easy to glance at the diagram and see how the classes relate to one another.

There's another type of connection you need to show: the Entity class uses the Address, Email, and PhoneNumber classes. The UML specification calls this relationship *aggregation,* and you indicate it by using a black diamond on the end of the line attached to the user of the class (see Figure 13-7). The classes being used also have a property called multiplicity, that is, how many of them are used. In this example, an Entity may have zero, one, or more of any of the contact types, so you write 0..* on the connector line closest to the item being used to indicate that an class may have 0 or more of the class pointed to. Figure 13-7 also shows that notation. By revealing this relationship in the diagram, you can clearly see which parts of the application will be affected by a change to another part. Here, a change to the Email, Address, or PhoneNumber classes will have an impact on the Entity, Individual, and Organization classes.

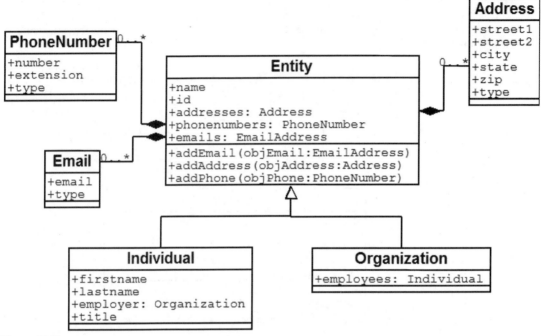

Figure 13-7

An Entity has a PhoneNumber, an Email, and an Address and that in all three cases it may have zero or more of that item. Because Individual and Organization inherit from Entity, both of these also have zero or more of the contact types.

With the completed UML diagram in place, you can begin to actually write the software that will drive this application. If your UML tool can generate PHP code, you could have the initial skeletons of these classes automatically generated for you. Then you'd only have to add data-access and business logic.

Other Useful UML Diagrams

Class diagrams aren't the only UML diagrams that you can use when designing or describing your application. In fact, there are 11 others that you can leverage. Let's just briefly look at a few of the most commonly used diagrams. Consult online and print UML resources to learn more about these types of diagrams, the symbols they use, and the other diagrams defined by the UML specification.

Activity Diagrams

Activity diagrams are used to map out business logic and decisions that the software needs to make. They are especially helpful in documenting complex decision-making processes. Figure 13-8 shows an activity diagram of the fairly simple decision-making process that you encountered with the `Volunteer` and `RestrictedVolunteer` classes in Chapter 12.

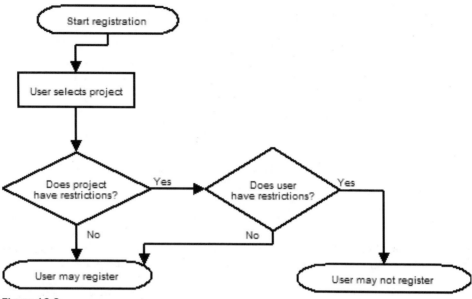

Figure 13-8

The diagram shows where decisions are being made (the diamonds), the activities involved (rectangles), and beginning and final state (ellipses) of that process. When you find yourself writing complex conditional code in your application, generate an activity diagram to plan and document that code.

Use Case Diagrams

A use case diagram illustrates the business processes that take place and who uses those processes. It's nontechnical diagram, making it a great tool for use in client meetings.

The two basic symbols of a use case diagram are the actor (the user of a process) and the use case (the process). An actor is usually a class of user of your application. For example, a large Web site typically has a public-facing component, and an administration system that allows certain users to manipulate the content of that Web site. So you have two actors: system administrator and user. System administrators change and view content, and run reports. Users only view content. Figure 13-9 shows a use case diagram of this situation.

The diagram shows two actors, three use cases, and an indication of which actors participate in which use cases. These diagrams help you understand roles and responsibilities of the application and to enumerate the business processes that the application will handle.

Sequence Diagram

A sequence diagram shows the order of operations for a given process in an application. The horizontal axis represents the life cycle of the objects involved in the process. The vertical axis represents the order of operations, with the first activities appearing on the top. It shows you, from the start of an activity to the

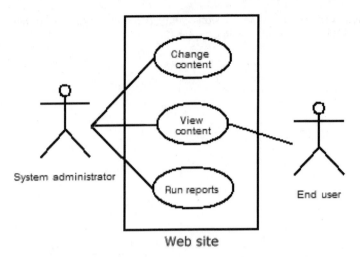

Figure 13-9

end of that activity, which objects are talking to each other and the messages they are passing back and forth. Figure 13-10 shows an example of sequence diagram for a content change.

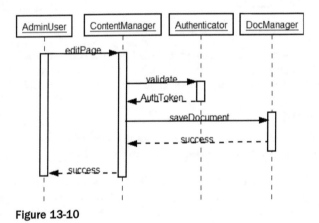

Figure 13-10

The solid lines show the messages being sent to the objects listed at the top. Each dashed line shows the response from an object. The rectangular boxes indicate the beginning and end of an object's participation in a particular part of the sequence. This diagram shows that when an administrator edits a page, the ContentManager class validates the user's credentials by creating an instance of the Authenticator class and invoking the validate() method. That method returns an authentication token in the form of an AuthToken object. The content manager then asks the DocManager class to save the document. The saveDocument() method returns success or failure (success in this example) and this result is passed on to the admin user.

A sequence diagram helps you map out the communications between objects and document the steps involved in the execution of an activity.

These examples have shown how useful UML can be when architecting an application. By providing a common visual language for representing various concepts in a software system, you can communicate complex ideas and document intricate processes in an easy-to-understand manner. The standardization of the symbols used ensures that other software developers can understand your diagrams and use them to build the application documented by those diagrams

Creating the Entity Class

Time to put everything you've learned so far to bear on the contact manager application designed earlier. To review the project, you've been contracted to build a contact management system for a client. The application is to manage individuals and organizations and enable users to look up and edit contact information. Figure 13-11 recaps the contact manager UML diagram.

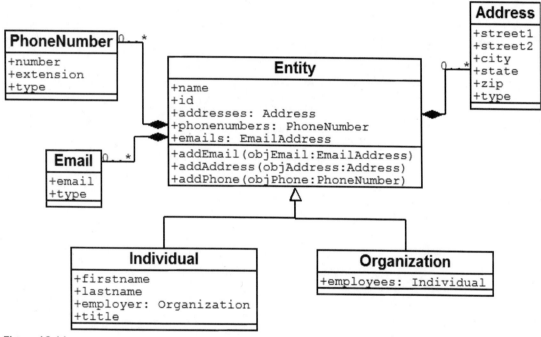

Figure 13-11

The Entity class is fairly straightforward. It needs to store the name and id of the entity along with arrays of addresses, phone numbers, and e-mail addresses. It won't be used directly, instead, it'll be the parent class of the Individual and Organization classes. The User class that you developed in Chapter 12 makes a good foundation for the Entity class.

Create a new text file called class.Entity.php and enter the following code, much of which is borrowed from the User class, although there are a number of important changes. Although this is a long code sample, much of it should be fairly clear to you now. A complete explanation of the class follows the code.

```php
<?php

class Entity {

    private $_properties;
    private $_changedProperties;
    private $_hDB;
    private $_emails;
    private $_addresses;
    private $_phonenumbers;

    public function __construct($entityID)
    {
        $this->_properties = array();
        $this->_changedProperties = array();

        $this->_properties['id'] = $entityID;
        $this->_properties['name'] = null;
        $this->_properties['type'] = null;
        $this->_properties['addresses'] = array();
        $this->_properties['phonenumbers'] = array();
        $this->_properties['emails'] = array();
        $this->_properties['numberOfEmails'] = 0;
        $this->_properties['numberOfPhonenumbers'] = 0;
        $this->_properties['numberOfAddresses'] = 0;

        $this->_hDB = mysql_connect('localhost', 'dbuser', 'mypassword');

        $this->_init();

    }

    private function _init()
    {
        $this->_initUser();
        $this->_initEmails();
        $this->_initAddresses();
        $this->_initPhones();
    }

    private function _initUser()
    {
        $sql = "select * from entities where entityid = $this->id";

        $rs = mysql_query($sql, $this->_hDB);
        $row = mysql_fetch_assoc($rs);

        $this->_properties['id'] = $row['entityid'];
        $this->_properties['name1'] = $row['name1'];
        $this->_properties['name2'] = $row['name2'];
        $this->_properties['type'] = $row['type'];

    }
```

```php
    private function_initEmails()
    {
        //fetch email data...
    }

    private function_initPhones()
    {
        //fetch phone data...
    }

    private function_initAddresses()
    {
        //fetch address data...
    }

    function __get($propertyName)
    {
        if(!array_key_exists($propertyName, $this->_properties)){
            throw new Exception('Invalid property value!');
        }
    }

    if(method_exists($this, 'get' . $propertyName)){
        return call_user_func(array($this, 'get' . $propertyName));
    } else {
        return $this->_properties[$propertyName];
    }
}

    function __set($propertyName, $value)
    {
        if(!array_key_exists($propertyName, $this->_properties)){
            throw new Exception('Invalid property value!');
        }
    }

    if(method_exists($this, 'set' . $propertyName)) {
        return call_user_func(array($this, 'set' . $propertyName), $value);
    } else {
        //If the value of the property really has changed
        //and it's not already in the changedProperties array,
        //add it.
        if($this->_properties[$propertyName] != $value &&
        !in_array($propertyName, $this->_changedProperties)) {
            $this->_changedProperties[] = $propertyName;
        }

        //Now set the new value
        $this->_properties[$propertyName] = $value;

        }
    }

    function __toString()
```

```
{
    return $this->name;
}

function getName()
{
    return $this->_properties['name1'];
}

function setID($val)
{
    throw new Exception('You may not alter the value of the ID field!');
}

function phonenumbers($index)
{
    if(!isset($this->_phonenumbers[$index])) {
        throw new Exception('Invalid phone number specified!');
    } else {
        return $this->_phonenumbers[$index];
    }
}

function getNumberOfPhoneNumbers()
{
    return sizeof($this->_phonenumbers);
}

function addPhoneNumber(PhoneNumber $phone)
{
    $this->_phonenumbers[] = $phone;
}

function addresses($index)
{

    if(!isset($this->_addresses[$index])) {
        throw new Exception('Invalid address specified!');
    } else {
        return $this->_addresses[$index];
    }
}

function getNumberOfAddresses()
{
    return sizeof($this->_addresses);
}

function addAddress(Address $address)
{
    $this->_addresses[] = $address;
}

function emails($index)
```

```php
{
   if(!isset($this->_emails[$index])) {
      throw new Exception('Invalid email specified!');
   } else {
      return $this->_emails[$index];
   }
}

function getNumberOfEmails()
{
   return sizeof($this->_emails);
}

function addEmail(Email $email)
{
   $this->_emails[] = $email;
}

function_updateEntity()
{
   $sql = "UPDATE entities SET ";

   //Build up the SQL statement by creating
   //an array of set statements then join them
   //with commas at the end.
   $setStatements = array();
   foreach($this->_changedProperties as $prop) {
      $setStatements[] = "$prop = '{$this->_properties[$prop]}'";
   }
   //create the string
   $sql .= join(', ', $setStatements);

   //append the WHERE clause
   $sql .= " WHERE entityid = $this->id";
   print $sql;
   $hRes = mysql_query($sql, $this->hDB);
   $intAffected = mysql_affected_rows($hRes);
}

function_createEntity()
{

   $data = array();
   $data['name1'] = "'" . mysql_escape_string($this->name1) . "'";
   $data['name2'] = "'" . mysql_escape_string($this->name2) . "'";
   $data['type'] = "'" . mysql_escape_string($this->type) . "'";

   $sql = "INSERT INTO entities (" . join(',' array_keys($data)). ") ";
   $sql .= " (" . join(', ', array_values($data)) . ")";
   $res = mysql_query($sql, $this->hDB);
   if (!$res) {
       //Note that we cannot trap exceptions thrown from the
       //destructor (which is what will call this function),
```

```
            //so we need to use trigger_error to indicate a problem.
            trigger_error("An error occurred saving an entity object!",
            E_USER_WARNING);
        }
    }

    function __destruct()
    {
        //Check to see if anything was changed.
        if(sizeof($this->_changedProperties)) {
            if($this->id) {
                //we are updating an existing record;
                $this->_updateEntity();
            } else {
            //this must be a new record
            $this->_createEntity();
            }
        }

        //Close our connection to the database -- we're done.
        mysql_close($this->_hDB);
    }
}

?>
```

To create the MySQL table `entities`, run the following SQL statement:

```
CREATE TABLE entities (
    entityid INT NOT NULL AUTO_INCREMENT PRIMARY KEY,
    name1 varchar(100) NOT NULL,
    name2 varchar(100) NOT NULL,
    type char(1) NOT NULL
);
```

A number of additions and modifications are made to the original User class to allow the Entity class to handle its requirements for addresses, phone numbers, and e-mail addresses. There are now three private member variables named $_emails, $_addresses, and $_phonenumbers. These member variables are initialized to empty arrays in the constructor and will store the Address, Email, and PhoneNumber objects associated with this entity.

Next, a private initialization function named_init(), which is called by the constructor, is added. This function then invokes the four private init functions that handle the population of data for the entity. The_initUser() function does the same database lookup and data assignment functions that used to happen in the User class's constructor. Init functions for the three contact type objects also are added. Those functions are empty for now, but will contain the code to create the Address, Email, and PhoneNumber objects that will be stored in the arrays mentioned in the preceding paragraph.

Three functions are added to each contact type: getNumberOf[x], add[x], and respectively, emails, addresses, or phonenumbers. getNumberOf[x] tells you how many objects exist in the private arrays, and add[x] enables you to add new ones. The other functions are not quite as obvious, but eventually they enable you to write code like this:

```
for($x = 0; $x < $obj->numberOfEmails; $x++ ) {
  print "<a href=\"mailto:{$obj->emails($x)->email}\">" .
        $obj->emails($x)->email .
        "</a> (" . $obj->emails($x)->type . ")<br>\n";
}
```

Basically, they give you a nice syntax for iterating over the collection of contact types and accessing individual members of those arrays. Although they are marked as properties in the UML diagram, implementing them as functions allows you to write cleaner, easier to understand code when using the Entity class.

Also worth noting are the database fields name1 and name2 and the new function getName(). Organizations have only one name field whereas individuals need two (first name and last name). To accommodate this, the Entity class fetches both values; by default, however, the name property returns only name1 (which is where you will store the name of the organization). When you develop the Individual class, that property will return the first name and the last name.

Because each object should be responsible for its own housekeeping, you do not update the $_changedProperties array when a new contact type is added. Instead, those classes will be responsible for their own database inserts and updates.

Which brings you to the new and improved destructor. This object now has the ability to save any changes made to it as well to create a brand new record. Depending on whether you have an existing record or a new entity, either _updateEntity() or _saveEntity() is called. A new record will be created if upon destruction of the object there is no id value. You may assume that if the id is null, the object does not yet have an entry in the entities table (because entityid is marked NOT NULL in the database) and so you execute an INSERT statement to create the new record. Note that you also have the setID() function that throws an error on any attempt to alter the value of the id property.

Putting It All Together

You'll recall from the encapsulation discussion in Chapter 12 that it's always a good idea to protect your data in private member variables and use functions to access all of the properties of your classes. You also looked at using __get and __set to make this process a bit easier. You can see just by looking at the class diagrams shown earlier that all of your classes have fairly simple property requirements and that most of them could benefit from the approach you took in implementing the Entity class earlier.

Because you know about inheritance and how to use it to your advantage in PHP, let's remove all that clever functionality from being tied to just the Entity class and create a class that will enable you to reuse the code in other classes. You originally called this class PropertyObject.

The PropertyObject Class

The original PropertyObject class and the Entity class that followed it had no unified facility for data validation, so you need an interface for anything that can be validated. Here's the code:

```php
<?php
  interface Validator {
    abstract function validate();
  }
?>
```

Name the file interface.Validator.php. Now put it to some use with the new and improved PropertyObject class. The code that follows shows how to integrate the Validator interface with the PropertyObject class. Enter the code in a file called class.PropertyObject.php.

```php
<?php
   require_once('interface.Validator.php');

   abstract class PropertyObject implements Validator {

      protected $propertyTable = array();      //stores name/value pairs
                                               //that hook properties to
                                               //database field names

      protected $changedProperties = array();  //List of properties that
                                               //have been modified

      protected $data;                         //Actual data from
                                               //the database

      protected $errors = array();             //Any validation errors
                                               //that might have occurred

      public function __construct($arData) {
         $this->data = $arData;
      }

      function __get($propertyName) {
         if(!array_key_exists($propertyName, $this->propertyTable))
            throw new Exception("Invalid property\"$propertyName\"!");

         if(method_exists($this, 'get' . $propertyName)) {
            return call_user_func(array($this, 'get' . $propertyName));
         } else {
            return $this->data[$this->propertyTable[$propertyName]];
         }
      }

      function __set($propertyName, $value) {
         if(!array_key_exists($propertyName, $this->propertyTable))
            throw new Exception("Invalid property\"$propertyName\"!");

         if(method_exists($this, 'set' . $propertyName)) {
            return call_user_func(
                     array($this, 'set' . $propertyName),
                     $value
                     );
         } else {

            //If the value of the property really has changed
            //and it's not already in the changedProperties array,
            //add it.
            if($this->propertyTable[$propertyName] != $value &&
               !in_array($propertyName, $this->changedProperties)) {
```

```
                $this->changedProperties[] = $propertyName;
            }

            //Now set the new value
            $this->data[$this->propertyTable[$propertyName]] = $value;

        }
    }

    function validate()
    {}

  }
?>
```

Take a closer look at what's happening here. You've created four protected member variables. Protected member variables are only visible to subclasses of a class; they aren't visible to the code that uses those objects.

$propertyTable will contain a mapping of real property names to field names in your database. Often the names of database fields have been prefixed with a naming convention to indicate their data type. For example, entities.sname1 might be a field in the table entities of type string, containing the first name. However, sname1 isn't a terribly friendly name for an object property, so you need to provide a mechanism to translate database field naming conventions to friendly property names.

$changedProperties serves the same purpose as in previous implementations of this class. It's an array that stores a list of the names of the properties that have been modified.

$data will be an associative array of database field names and values. The array will be supplied to the constructor with the data structure coming directly from pg_fetch_assoc() (or mysql_fetch_assoc(), or any of the other [x]_fetch_assoc() database functions). This makes constructing a useful object directly from a database query a lot easier, as you'll see shortly.

The last member variable, $errors, will contain an array of field names and error messages in the event that the validate method (required by the Validate interface) should fail.

The class is declared abstract for two reasons. The first is that the PropertyObject class on its own is not very useful. The classes that extend PropertyObject still have some work to do before you can use them. The second is that you have not provided an implementation of the required method validate(). Because you are still labeling that method abstract in PropertyObject, you must also label the class itself abstract, forcing all inheriting classes to implement that function. Any attempts to use classes that extend PropertyObject but not implement that function will cause a runtime error.

Next, you see the greatly simplified constructor. All the constructor does is accept the associative array that will most likely be populated from a database query and assign it to the protected member variable $data. Most subclasses of PropertyObject will need to override the constructor and do something a little more interesting.

The other major change is in the internals of the __get() and __set() functions. Because you are storing data in the $data member, you need to be able to map property names to the actual field names

in the database. The lines that contain the code `$this->data[$this->propertyTable`
`[$ propertyName]]` are doing just that. By fetching and assigning values to the `$data` member using
their database field names, rather than their property names you can easily implement the sort of
automatic database persistence that you saw previously in the Entity class.

If the workings of the `$data` and `$propertyTable` members aren't clear to you yet, don't worry. They
will be as soon as you see an example.

The Contact Type Classes

Now that you have the handy-dandy `PropertyObject` class, you can start putting it to some use. The
files that follow are for the `Address`, `EmailAddress`, and `PhoneNumber` classes.

In the code you'll see a reference to a class called `DataManager`, which is going to be a wrapper class for
all the database functions you need to use. That enables you to have one central place for all your
data-interaction code. You'll examine that class in just a bit.

Enter the code that follows (the `Address` class) into a file called `class.Address.php`:

```php
<?php
  require_once('class.PropertyObject.php');

  class Address extends PropertyObject {

    function __construct($addressid) {
      $arData = DataManager::getAddressData($addressid);

      parent::__construct($arData);

      $this->propertyTable['addressid'] = 'addressid';
      $this->propertyTable['id'] = 'addressid';
      $this->propertyTable['entityid'] = 'entityid';
      $this->propertyTable['address1'] = 'saddress1';
      $this->propertyTable['address2'] = 'saddress2';
      $this->propertyTable['city'] = 'scity';
      $this->propertyTable['state'] = 'cstate';
      $this->propertyTable['zipcode'] = 'spostalcode';
      $this->propertyTable['type'] = 'stype';
    }

    function validate() {
      if(strlen($this->state) != 2) {
        $this->errors['state'] = 'Please choose a valid state.';
      }

      if(strlen($this->zipcode) < 5 ||
        strlen($this->zipcode) > 10) {
```

```
                $this->errors['zipcode'] = 'Please enter a 5 or 9 digit zipcode';
        }

        if(!$this->address1) {
                $this->errors['address1'] = 'Address 1 is a required field.';
        }

        if(!$this->city) {
                $this->errors['city'] = 'City is a required field.';
        }

        if(sizeof($this->errors)) {
          return false;
        } else {
          return true;
        }
    }

    function __toString() {
      return $this->address1 . ', ' .
              $this->address2 . ', ' .
              $this->city . ', ' .
              $this->state . ' ' . $this->zipcode;
    }
  }
?>
```

Because the `PropertyObject` class took care of so much of the work, only two methods in the `Address` class needed to be implemented (a `__toString()` implementation was thrown in just for fun). In the constructor, you see for the first time how the `$propertyTable` array works. The list of properties required in the class was specified in the UML diagram created during the initial architecture of the application (in the beginning of this chapter). Based on the properties this object has, you can also make some decisions about the structure of the database table. Generally, you need one field for each property and because this class has to relate back to the `Entity` class, you also need to store some reference to the parent `Entity`. Let's assume that you have the following SQL statement to create the `Address` table:

```
CREATE TABLE entityaddress (
  addressid int NOT NULL AUTO_INCREMENT PRIMARY KEY,
  entityid int,
  saddress1 varchar(255),
  saddress2 varchar(255),
  scity varchar(255),
  cstate char(2),
  spostalcode varchar(10),
  stype varchar(50),
  CONSTRAINT fk_entityaddress_entityid
    FOREIGN KEY (entityid) REFERENCES entity(entityid)
);
```

A properly named database field indicates its data type by using a one-character prefix, letting you know what kind of data goes in the field. Having naming conventions is just as important for database design as it is for your code.

The `propertyTable` array is set up in the `Address` class to map friendly property names (like city, state, and ZIP code) to the less friendly database field names (like scity, cstate, and spostalcode). Note that you can map multiple property names to the same database field name in `propertyTable`. This enables you to refer to the primary key of the address by either `$objAddress->addressid` or `$objAddress->id`.

What's incredibly exciting about the `Address` class is that the overwhelming majority of the code is spent implementing business logic and data validation. There's almost no extraneous code here. Its sole responsibility is to populate itself and validate its own contents. Everything else is left up to the `DataManager` class (which you'll see in detail shortly) and the `PropertyObject`.

The code for the `Email` class, which looks very similar, follows. Enter it into a file called `class.EmailAddress.php`.

```php
<?php
  require_once('class.PropertyObject.php');

  class EmailAddress extends PropertyObject {

    function __construct($emailid) {
      $arData = DataManager::getEmailData($emailid);

      parent::__construct($arData);

      $this->propertyTable['emailid'] = 'emailid';
      $this->propertyTable['id'] = 'emailid';
      $this->propertyTable['entityid'] = 'entityid';
      $this->propertyTable['email'] = 'semail';
      $this->propertyTable['type'] = 'stype';
    }

    function validate() {
      if(!$this->email) {
          $this->errors['email'] = 'You must set an email address.';
      }

      if(sizeof($this->errors)) {
        return false;
      } else {
        return true;
      }
    }

    function __toString() {
      return $this->email;
    }
  }
?>
```

There's very little ancillary code here, just fetching the code from the database and setting up the `propertyTable`. Everything else is data validation. Again, the UML diagram was the guide to deciding on the properties of the `Email` class and the structure of the corresponding database table.

The database table for the entityemail table looks like this:

```sql
CREATE TABLE entityemail (
  emailid int NOT NULL AUTO_INCREMENT PRIMARY KEY,
  entityid int,
  semail varchar(255),
  stype varchar(50),
  CONSTRAINT fk_entityemail_entityid
    FOREIGN KEY (entityid) REFERENCES entity(entityid)
);
```

The `PhoneNumber` class works very much like `Address` and `Email`. Here's the code to enter the code into `class.PhoneNumber.php`:

```php
<?php
  require_once('class.PropertyObject.php');

  class PhoneNumber extends PropertyObject {

    function __construct($phoneid) {
      $arData = DataManager::getPhoneNumberData($phoneid);

      parent::__construct($arData);

      $this->propertyTable['phoneid'] = 'phoneid';
      $this->propertyTable['id'] = 'phoneid';
      $this->propertyTable['entityid'] = 'entityid';
      $this->propertyTable['number'] = 'snumber';
      $this->propertyTable['extension'] = 'sextension';
      $this->propertyTable['type'] = 'stype';
    }

    function validate() {
      if(!$this->number) {
          $this->errors['number'] = 'You must supply a phone number.';
      }

      if(sizeof($this->errors)) {
        return false;
      } else {
        return true;
      }
    }

    function __toString() {
      return $this->number .
              ($this->extension ? ' x' . $this->extension : '');
    }
  }
?>
```

And here's the SQL statement to create the entityphone table:

```
CREATE TABLE entityphone (
  phoneid int NOT NULL AUTO_INCREMENT PRIMARY KEY,
  entityid int,
  snumber varchar(20),
  sextension varchar(20),
  stype varchar(50),
  CONSTRAINT fk_entityemail_entityid
    FOREIGN KEY (entityid) REFERENCES entity(entityid)
);
```

The DataManager is used to self-populate the data, set up the propertyTable, and define some validation rules. A __toString implementation is created to make it easier to print out complete phone numbers with their extensions later on.

The DataManager Class

Let's have a look at that DataManager class. It and the other database code samples in this chapter have been using MySQL, although a class like it would work just as well with PostgresSQL, Oracle, or any other RDBMS. The primary responsibility of the DataManager class is to put all the data access code into a single location, making it much easier to change the database type or connection parameters later on. All of the class's methods have been declared static because the class doesn't rely on any member variables. Note the use of the static function variable in getConnection(). This is done to ensure that only one database connection is open during a single page request. There's a lot of overhead associated with establishing a database connection so eliminating unnecessary connections helps improve performance. Create a file class.DataManager.php: and enter the following class code:

```php
<?php
require_once('class.Entity.php'); //this will be needed later
require_once('class.Individual.php');
require_once('class.Organization.php');

class DataManager {
  private static function_getConnection() {
    static $hDB;

    if(isset($hDB)) {
      return $hDB;
    }

    $hDB = mysql_connect('localhost', 'phpuser', 'phppass')
      or die("Failure connecting to the database!");
$Link = mysql_select_db('sample_db') or die('Failure selecting the
database!');
    return $hDB;
  }

  public static function getAddressData($addressID) {
    $sql = "SELECT * FROM entityaddress WHERE addressid = $addressID";
```

```
      $res = mysql_query($sql, DataManager::_getConnection());
      if(! ($res && mysql_num_rows($res))) {
        die("Failed getting address data for address $addressID");
      }

      return mysql_fetch_assoc($res);
    }

    public static function getEmailData($emailID) {
      $sql = "SELECT * FROM entityemail WHERE emailid = $emailID";
      $res = mysql_query($sql, DataManager::_getConnection());

      if(! ($res && mysql_num_rows($res))) {
        die("Failed getting email data for email $emailID");
      }

      return mysql_fetch_assoc($res);
    }
  }
?>
```

The DataManager class provides the data structures used to populate the $data member of your PropertyObject subclasses. There are separate functions to return the data for each of the types. You'll be adding a few new functions to this class a bit later.

All of the methods of this class are declared to be static. Remember, static methods are those requiring all member variables to be static. You don't need to instantiate static classes to use their methods. There are several cases where this makes sense. Consider a class called Math that exposes methods such as squareRoot(), power(), and cosine(), and has properties including the mathematical constants e and pi. All instances of this class perform the same math. The square root of 2 doesn't change, 4 raised to the 3rd power is always going to be 64, and the two constants are, well, constant. There's no need to create separate instances of this class because its state and properties never change. A class called Math implemented in this manner should allow for all its functions to be called statically.

The DataManager class is much the same. All of the functions are self-contained, and all of the member variables they interact with are static. The class exposes no properties. You can invoke the methods of the class using the static method operator :: as a result. Because all the methods you've created are static, you never need to instantiate an object with $obj = new DataManager(); you can use the syntax DataManager::getEmail() instead.

Note the use of a static function variable in the private method _getConnection(). The use of static function variables was discussed in Chapter 6.

The Entity, Individual, and Organization Classes

With all the supporting classes in place, you can move on to the core of the application: the Entity class and its subclasses.

First, make sure you're updating your UML diagram as you make changes to the object hierarchy. You've created the PropertyObject class and made all of your classes subclasses of it with one exception—the new `DataManager` class, which does not inherit from anything. The `PropertyObject` implements an abstract interface called `Validator`. Figure 13-12 shows the updated diagram.

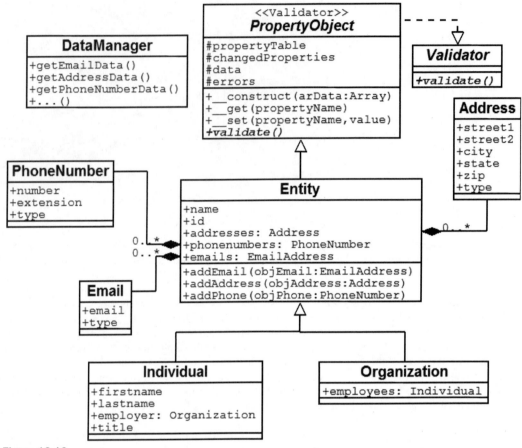

Figure 13-12

Now you can begin to develop the `Entity`, `Individual`, and `Organization` classes. The following code shows the fully implemented `Entity` class:

```php
<?php

require_once('class.PropertyObject.php');
require_once('class.PhoneNumber.php');
require_once('class.Address.php');
require_once('class.EmailAddress.php');

abstract class Entity extends PropertyObject {

  private $_emails;
  private $_addresses;
  private $_phonenumbers;
```

```php
public function__construct($entityID) {
  $arData = DataManager::getEntityData($entityID);

  parent::__construct($arData);

  $this->propertyTable['entityid'] = 'entityid';
  $this->propertyTable['id'] = 'entityid';
  $this->propertyTable['name1'] = 'sname1';
  $this->propertyTable['name2'] = 'sname2';
  $this->propertyTable['type'] = 'ctype';

  $this->_emails = DataManager::getEmailObjectsForEntity($entityID);
  $this->_addresses = DataManager::getAddressObjectsForEntity($entityID);
  $this->_phonenumbers = DataManager::getPhoneNumberObjectsForEntity
  ($entityID);

}

  function setID($val) {
    throw new Exception('You may not alter the value of the ID field!');
  }

  function setEntityID($val) {
    $this->setID($val);
  }

  function phonenumbers($index) {
    if(!isset($this->_phonenumbers[$index])) {
      throw new Exception('Invalid phone number specified!');
  } else {
      return $this->_phonenumbers[$index];
    }
  }

  function getNumberOfPhoneNumbers() {
    return sizeof($this->_phonenumbers);
  }

  function addPhoneNumber(PhoneNumber $phone) {
    $this->_phonenumbers[] = $phone;
  }

  function addresses($index) {
    if(!isset($this->_addresses[$index])) {
      throw new Exception('Invalid address specified!');
    } else {
      return $this->_addresses[$index];
    }
  }

  function getNumberOfAddresses() {
    return sizeof($this->_addresses);
  }
```

```
        function addAddress(Address $address) {
          $this->_addresses[] = $address;
        }

        function emails($index) {
          if(!isset($this->_emails[$index])) {
            throw new Exception('Invalid email specified!');
          } else {
            return $this->_emails[$index];
          }
        }

        function getNumberOfEmails() {
          return sizeof($this->_emails);
        }

        function addEmail(Email $email) {
          $this->_emails[] = $email;
        }

        public function validate() {
          //Add common validation routines
        }

    }
?>
```

By moving all of the property getting and setting functionality to the parent `PropertyObject` class, you simplify the `Entity` class and ensure that it is focused only on the code required to implement an entity.

The `Entity` class is declared abstract because it isn't useful on its own. All entities are either `Individuals` or `Organizations`. You do not want to be able to instantiate objects of class `Entity`. Declaring it abstract prevents the class from being instantiable.

You've added requests to a few new functions of the `DataManager: getEntityData()` and `get[x]ObjectsForEntity. getEntityData()` returns the data required to instantiate an entity, just like functions you've already seen for the contact types. The following shows the code for the new functions in `class.DataManager.php`:

```
// top of file omitted for brevity
    ...
        die("Failed getting phone number data for phone $phoneID");
    }

    return pg_fetch_assoc($res);
  }

public static function getEntityData($entityID) {
    $sql = "SELECT * FROM entities WHERE entityid = $entityID";
    $res = mysql_query($sql, DataManager::_getConnection());
    if(! ($res && mysql_num_rows($res))) {
      die("Failed getting entity $entityID");
    }
```

```
      return mysql_fetch_assoc($res);
  }

?>
```

To add the get[x]ObjectsForEntity functions, place the following code at the end of class
.DataManager.php, just after the getEntityData function:

```
public static function getAddressObjectsForEntity($entityID) {
  $sql = "SELECT addressid from entityaddress WHERE entityid = $entityID";
  $res = mysql_query($sql, DataManager::_getConnection());
  if(!$res) {
    die("Failed getting address data for entity $entityID");
  }

  if(mysql_num_rows($res)) {
    $objs = array();
    while($rec = mysql_fetch_assoc($res)) {
      $objs[] = new Address($rec['addressid']);
    }
    return $objs;
  } else {
    return array();
  }
}

public static function getEmailObjectsForEntity($entityID) {

  $sql = "SELECT emailid from entityemail WHERE entityid = $entityID";
  $res = mysql_query($sql, DataManager::_getConnection());
    if(!$res) {
    die("Failed getting email data for entity $entityID");
  }

  if(mysql_num_rows($res)) {
    $objs = array();
    while($rec = mysql_fetch_assoc($res)) {
      $objs[] = new EmailAddress($rec['emailid']);
    }
    return $objs;
  } else {
    return array();
  }
}

public static function getPhoneNumberObjectsForEntity($entityID) {
  $sql = "SELECT phoneid from entityphone WHERE entityid = $entityID";
  $res = mysql_query($sql, DataManager::_getConnection());

  if(!$res) {
    die("Failed getting phone data for entity $entityID");
  }
```

```
    if(mysql_num_rows($res)) {
      $objs = array();
      while($rec = mysql_fetch_assoc($res)) {
        $objs[] = new PhoneNumber($rec['phoneid']);
      }

      return $objs;
    } else {
      return array();
    }
  }
```

These functions take an entity ID value. They query the database to determine if any e-mails, addresses, or phone numbers exist for the entity in question. If so, they build an array of `EmailAddress`, `Address`, or `PhoneNumber` objects by passing each id to the constructor for the appropriate object type. This array is then passed back to the `Entity` object where it is stored in the appropriate private member variable.

With the `Entity` class doing all the heavy lifting, the remaining work is fairly simple. You just need to implement the `Individual` and `Organization` classes. Create a file called `class.Individual.php` and enter the following:

```php
<?php
  require_once('class.Entity.php');
  require_once('class.Organization.php');

  class Individual extends Entity {

    public function __construct($userID) {
      parent:: __construct($userID);

      $this->propertyTable['firstname'] = 'name1';
      $this->propertyTable['lastname'] = 'name2';

    }

    public function __toString() {
      return $this->firstname . ' ' . $this->lastname;
    }

    public function getEmployer() {
      return DataManager::getEmployer($this->id);
    }

    public function validate() {
      parent::validate();

      //add individual-specific validation

    }

  }
?>
```

Short and sweet. Inheritance makes this easy. The Individual class sets up a few new properties that make it easier to access the first and last name of the individual, instead of having to use the rather ugly name1 and name2 properties defined in the Entity class. It also defines a new method, getEmployer(),which requires a new function in the DataManager. You get to that function as soon as you have your Organization class, which is shown in the following code. Create a file called class.Organization.php, and enter this code into it:

```php
<?php
  require_once('class.Entity.php');
require_once('class.Individual.php');

  class Organization extends Entity {

    public function __construct($userID) {
      parent: __construct($userID);

      $this->propertyTable['name'] = 'name1';

    }

    public function __toString() {
      return $this->name;
    }

    public function getEmployees() {
      return DataManager::getEmployees($this->id);
    }

    public function validate() {
      parent::validate();
      //do organization-specific validation
    }

  }

?>
```

Again, a fairly simple class, thanks to the power of inheritance. You declare a property called name that makes it easier to obtain the one and only name that an organization has (the sname2 property goes unused for organizations).

To add the functions getEmployer() and getEmployee() to the DataManager class, append the following code to the end of class.DataManager.php:

```php
public static function getEmployer($individualID) {
    $sql = "SELECT organizationid FROM entityemployee " .
        "WHERE individualid = $individualID";
    $res = mysql_query($sql, DataManager::_getConnection());
    if(! ($res && mysql_num_rows($res))) {
      die("Failed getting employer info for individual $individualID");
    }

    $row = mysql_fetch_assoc($res);
```

```
      if($row) {
        return new Organization($row['organizationid']);
      } else {
        return null;
      }
  }

  public static function getEmployees($orgID) {
    $sql = "SELECT individualid FROM entityemployee " .
           "WHERE organizationid = $orgID";
    $res = mysql_query($sql, DataManager::_getConnection());
    if(! ($res && mysql_num_rows($res))) {
      die("Failed getting employee info for org $orgID");
    }

    if(pg_num_rows($res)) {
      $objs = array();
      while($row = mysql_fetch_assoc($res)) {
        $objs[] = new Individual($row['individualid']);
      }
      return $objs;
    } else {
      return array();
    }
  }
```

These two functions rely on the presence of a table entityemployee, shown here:

```
CREATE TABLE entityemployee (
  individualid int NOT NULL,
  organizationid int NOT NULL,
  CONSTRAINT fk_entityemployee_individualid
    FOREIGN KEY (individualid) REFERENCES entity(entityid),
  CONSTRAINT fk_entityemployee_organizationid
    FOREIGN KEY (organizationid ) REFERENCES entity(entityid)
);
```

The table relates individuals to the organizations by which they are employed. The DataManager functions are similar to code you've already seen.

There's one last function needed to make the entire system work—the DataManager method for listing all the entities in the database. It's called getAllEntitiesAsObjects() and it finishes all the work you need to do on your objects:

```
public static function getAllEntitiesAsObjects() {
    $sql = "SELECT entityid, type from entities";
    $res = mysql_query($sql, DataManager::_getConnection());

    if(!$res) {
      die("Failed getting all entities");
    }
```

```
    if(mysql_num_rows($res)) {
      $objs = array();
      while($row = mysql_fetch_assoc($res)) {
        if($row['type'] == 'I') {
          $objs[] = new Individual($row['entityid']);
        } elseif ($row['type'] == 'O') {
          $objs[] = new Organization($row['entityid']);
        } else {
          die("Unknown entity type {$row['type']} encountered!");
        }
      }
      return $objs;
    } else {
      return array();
    }
  }
}
```

DataManager enables you to enumerate over all of the contacts in your system. It examines the value of the ctype field in the entity table to determine if the entry is an Individual or an Organization, and then instantiates an object of the appropriate type and adds it to the array that the function returns.

Making Use of the System

By now you can see the real power of an OOP approach. The following code (test.php) will display a view, albeit a rather ugly view, of all of the contacts in your database with all of their contact details:

```php
<?php
  require_once('class.DataManager.php'); //everything gets included by it

function println($data) {
  print $data . "<br>\n";
}

$arContacts = DataManager::getAllEntitiesAsObjects();
foreach($arContacts as $objEntity) {

  if(get_class($objEntity) == 'individual') {
    print "<h1>Individual - {$objEntity->__toString()}</h1>";
  } else {
    print "<h1>Organization - {$objEntity->__toString()}</h1>";
  }

  if($objEntity->getNumberOfEmails()) {
    //We have emails! Print a header
    print "<h2>Emails</h2>";

    for($x=0; $x < $objEntity->getNumberOfEmails(); $x++) {
      println($objEntity->emails($x)->__toString());
    }
  }

  if($objEntity->getNumberOfAddresses()) {
    //We have addresses!
```

```
    print "<h2>Addresses</h2>";

    for($x=0; $x < $objEntity->getNumberOfAddresses(); $x++) {
      println($objEntity->addresses($x)->__toString());
    }
  }

  if($objEntity->getNumberOfPhoneNumbers()) {
    //We have phone numbers!
    print "<h2>Phones</h2>";

    for($x=0; $x < $objEntity->getNumberOfPhoneNumbers(); $x++) {
      println($objEntity->phonenumbers($x)->__toString());
    }
  }
  print "<hr>\n";

}
?>
```

If you navigate to this file, you'll see something like Figure 13-13 (of course, the data in your tables will be different):

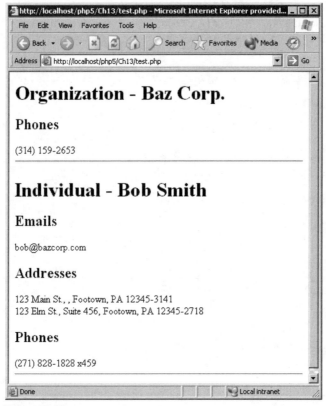

Figure 13-13

In only 36 lines of code you can display nearly everything there is to show about the entities in your system. Employer and employees aren't shown here, but are left as an exercise for the reader. The line that calls the `get_class` function should give you some ideas for figuring out which class you're dealing with so you'll know whether to call `getEmployer()` on an `Individual`, or `getEmployees()` on an `Organization`.

Summary

UML diagrams are an essential tool for planning complex (and even not-so-complex) applications. Properly designed diagrams enable you to document intricate systems in a clearer way than text alone allows. When you use class diagrams as part of your routine software development process, it's a lot easier to see how your classes and database tables should be designed.

Take full advantage of the OO features in PHP5 to help you rapidly develop applications and establish a code base that's easier to maintain, offers a greater degree of flexibility and extensibility, and reduces the total volume of code required to implement the business requirements.

By separating the software architecture into a business logic layer, like the `Individual` class, and a data access layer, like the `DataManager` class, you make it easy to change the underlying data source, table structure, or queries without disrupting the rest of the application. Objects that are responsible for implementing business logic aren't cluttered with the data access mechanism, the presence of which can confuse and obfuscate the business rules.

PEAR

There'll be times when, as an aspiring PHP developer faced with a new project, you'll think that the mountain ahead of you seems almost impossible to climb.

Finding the right psychological starting point can be tricky for the best of us, but one of the most satisfying things to discover at the start of the project is that half of what you figured you'd have to write has already been written.

As your portfolio of PHP projects matures, you'll find that you can reuse much of your own code from previous projects (yet another reason why taking a modular, object-oriented approach to your work is highly recommended). So-called "search-and-replace" development has saved thousand of engineer hours over the years.

There will be times, of course, when you simply have nothing to fall back on. Some components can be immensely time-consuming to develop without actually contributing to the core ethos of your project. That is when the "blank canvas" syndrome can kick in, and the urge to make just *one* more cup of coffee before you get started takes hold.

Thankfully, there is an answer: a repository of thousands of useful, fully tested, re-usable PHP components, all of which are broadly free to use and include in your own application.

In this chapter, you explore this repository; and discover why it exists, and how it can help you. You find out when—and when not—to use it. Most importantly, you learn how to identify the components most relevant to your project, and how to integrate them into your application.

What Is PEAR?

PEAR—the PHP Extension and Application Repository—was set up in 1999 by one of the PHP project's most respected and longest-serving contributors, Norwegian Stig Sæther Bakken. Its principal purpose is to provide an officially sanctioned library of open-source components contributed by PHP architects from all over the world, as well as an integrated means for installing those components into installations of PHP.

Those with experience of PERL may well draw similarities to the Comprehensive Perl Archive Network (CPAN), and would be right to do so. PEAR borrows many of the excellent features offered by CPAN, including the detection and automatic installation of dependent components when installing modules.

The components—or *packages*—within the PEAR network cover a myriad of functionality, including database connectivity, support for reading and writing unusual file formats, and widgets for generating complex HTML. Many components feature XML support, meaning you can put to use the skills you learned in Chapter 11.

In addition, PEAR provides a set of coding standards to which its contributors must adhere, which we examine shortly.

How Is PEAR Structured?

The PEAR Project is divided into a number of missions:

❑   A library of packages, each representing a discrete area of functionality.

❑   The PEAR Package Manager, used for installing and removing these packages from an installation of PHP.

❑   The PHP Foundation Classes (PFC), a subset of the PEAR repository consisting of modules of a highly stable and thoroughly tested nature, which are included in a standard PHP installation.

❑   The PHP Extension Community Library—PECL—a library of components written in C (rather than native PHP), which has just recently become a project in its own right (see http://pear.php.net for more information).

❑   The PEAR Coding Standards, which we'll explore later in the chapter.

Any single package found in the PEAR repository is almost always distributed as a class, a concept to which you've been introduced in the preceding two chapters. Because the packages are designed as reusable, modular components, an object-oriented methodology makes a great deal of sense.

This does mean that if you haven't yet read Chapters 12 and 13, now would be a good time to do so.

The PHP Foundation Classes

The PHP Foundation Classes (PFC), which are included by default in a normal installation of PHP, offer a number of essential toolkit routines beyond the basic intrinsic functionality of PHP. Although still, strictly speaking, unofficial, their common use in PHP applications is considered standard and accepted.

Packages within PFC generally have large scopes of use, rather than concerning themselves with, for example, obscure database platforms or file formats. Furthermore, such packages are always considered stable. At the time of this writing, some of the foundation classes distributed with PHP5 include the Mail class, an OS Guess class for determining the host operating system in PHP, and classes for making socket connections to other network hosts. Some of these classes may seem a little obscure in their own right, but nonbundled PEAR classes often make substantial use of them. By distributing them with PHP, the Package Manager does not have to install them on your behalf when you install a PEAR class that requires them. The PFC classes are always optimized for the version of PHP with which they are bundled; were it left to the Package Manager to download a copy, obscure incompatibilities between versions of PHP and versions of the PFC classes might start to cause problems. Explicitly tying PFC classes to distributions provides a common interface to the core of PHP such that non-PFC PEAR classes do not have to concern themselves with any differences between PHP versions.

If you are curious to know which modules are included as part of the Foundation Classes, check out the `/usr/local/lib/php` (Unix) or `C:\PHP\PEAR` (Windows) folder on your fresh PHP installation. Documentation for usage of these classes resides, like any other PEAR class, on the PEAR Web site at `http://pear.php.net`.

As these packages are included in a standard installation of PHP, you should not need to install them by hand, unless you explicitly requested they not be installed when you set up your development environment.

In theory, you can keep them up-to-date by using the PEAR Package Manager (more on this shortly), but in practice they are upgraded as and when new versions of PHP become available.

The PHP Extension Community Library

The PHP Extension Community Library or PECL (pronounced *pickle*) was originally a subset of the PEAR repository consisting of components written in C, rather than in native PHP. The rationale behind such components is usually the need for speed; compiled C often works out a lot quicker than PHP, particularly for mathematically intensive operations. PECL offers a means for component developers to avail themselves of the speed and power of C, whilst continuing to provide an interface to those components through standard PHP syntax.

PECL has recently evolved into a project in its own right, completely separate from PEAR—although it does retain the layout and politics of PEAR.

PECL is outside the scope of this chapter; however, familiarity with PEAR should leave you in good stead to tackle PECL should you want to do so. A good starting point is the project's Web site: `http://pecl.pear.net`.

The PEAR Package Manager

Many of the packages in the PEAR repository have *dependencies*. A dependency is the existence of a requirement for one class to be installed in order for another to function successfully. For example, a PEAR component that provides the capability to perform HTTP POST requests may depend on the existence of a generic HTTP functionality package. That package may in turn depend on a TCP/IP abstraction package, and so on.

As you can tell, starting with a fresh PHP installation and installing all necessary dependencies to make your class of choice function correctly could be immensely difficult to do by hand. The process is made much easier by means of the PEAR Package Manager.

The Package Manager provides a wealth of functionality for managing the insurgence of PEAR into your PHP setup, but its principal purpose is to allow you to install and remove PEAR packages with ease.

It is dependency-aware, which means that when you ask it to install a particular package that depends on one or more other packages, it kindly installs those dependent packages for you. It's also aware of the hierarchy of dependency, so it ensures that those packages are installed in the correct order.

Installing packages using the PEAR Package Manager is covered later in this chapter.

Recapping PEAR Standards

We discussed coding standards in Chapter 6, but let's just review the stylistic conventions used in this book's sample code.

The "correct" way to write code is something that's been debated for the last 30 years or so, without any particular common consensus having been reached. PHP is somewhat fortunate in that as a relatively youthful language, there has not been time for the kind of stylistic divergence witnessed in other languages. In this book, all of the authors decided that any example code we write would follow the standards set out by PEAR—known as the PEAR coding standards (PCS); that is to say, we'd stick to the same standards in our code as that to which authors of packages submitted to PEAR are required to adhere.

Indeed, should you ever want to try your hand at submitting your own work to PEAR so that others might benefit from it, you will need to adhere to them, too, so it's not a bad thing to get into the habit straightaway.

The PEAR Web site goes into great detail on the subject of coding standards, so we'll just explore some of those here. The following sections should get you into the right habits, in case you aren't already in them.

Control Structures, Comments, and Indenting

PEAR dictates that all code should be indented appropriately according to its context by using a suitable number of spaces (not tabs). In the case of PEAR, it's four spaces.

> You may be able to configure your editor of choice such that when the tab key is pressed, four spaces are rendered instead of an actual tab character.

As well as being indented, PEAR requires that constructs err on the side of verbosity. For example, if a parenthesis is optional but its inclusion improves clarity, then its inclusion is required. White space should be used only to separate out distinct lines and thoughts, and where it is included for reason of clarity, it should be kept as minimal as possible.

Curly braces should always be used in control structures (while/if/switch/for/foreach) even when there is only a single line within the block, and that's why the use of braces is not required by the PHP interpreter. This improves clarity immeasurably. The opening brace should always begin on the same line as the start of the control block. The closing brace should fall on a new line. PEAR does not comment on whether it is appropriate to suffix the closing brace with a semicolon.

Starting and finishing blocks of PHP by means of the <?php and ?> operators should always include the optional letters php for reasons of clarity.

Comments are encouraged wherever it would improve readability to include them. Avoid using the # comment predicate, even though PHP allows it; instead, opt for C-style // (for a single-line comment) or /* and */ (to begin and end a multiline comment).

Here is an example of a PEAR-compliant control structure:

```php
<?php
if ((($x == 14) && ($y == 19)) || $z = 24) {
    print($strMyVal. "\n");
```

```
        // This is a meaningful comment
};
?>
```

Function Calls and Definitions

When calling a function, there should be no space placed between the name of the function and its opening parenthesis prior to its argument list. If there are no arguments to be passed, a blank list should be used by opening and then immediately closing parentheses, as this example shows:

```php
<?php
    $strMyVar = myFunction($strA, $strB, $strC);
    $strAnotherVar = anotherFunctionWithNoParameters();
?>
```

When declaring your own functions, the rules for braces in control structures are changed slightly; the starting brace for the block should begin on a new line, immediately after the function name and argument list definition. Here's an example of that syntax:

```php
<?php
    function myFunction($strArg1, $strArg2)
    {
        return($strMyResult);
    };
?>
```

In the argument list, arguments that are optional should be designated by using the $strArg = " methodology. Optional arguments should always be last in the argument lists.

Finally, functions should always return a value if it is meaningful to do so. At the very least, a function should return whether or not it was successful in its designed endeavors.

Naming Conventions

Naming of variables, classes, and functions in languages that have weak typing (are loosely typed), such as PHP, is of immense importance.

PEAR conventions require the following:

❑ Classes should begin with a capital letter, such as Publisher. If the class has hierarchical placement within PEAR, this should be reflected in the name, such as HTML_TreeMenu, where TreeMenu is a component within the HTML hierarchy of PEAR.

❑ Functions should be named using the name of their parent package followed by an underscore (if applicable), and then a descriptive name without underscores; the descriptive name should have its first word or syllable lowercase, with the first letter of each subsequent word or syllable (as appropriate) capitalized (XML_RPC_serializeData) Private member functions or variables of classes accessed only from inside other methods of that class should be prefixed with an underscore ($this->_currentStatus).

❑ Constants should be capitalized, with underscores used to separate words, such as $HOME_DIRECTORY.

PEAR does not voice an opinion about naming convention for working variables. Many PEAR authors have adopted Hungarian Notation whereby the expected contents of a variable are alluded to in its name; for example, `$strMyVariable` is designed to hold a string, and `$intMyNumber` is for holding a number.

The authors strongly suggest you adopt this method, except where it is awkward to do so; for example, counter variables for `for` loops might reasonably make use of `$x`, `$y`, and `$z`, but these should never be used for variables holding meaningful integers.

Installing PEAR Packages

Installing PEAR packages is remarkably easy. Far trickier is tracking down the right package for your project. Often, there is a steep learning curve in simply familiarizing yourself with a package's interface to the point that you can play with it to assess its feasibility. As PEAR matures, however, so will its packages, and the documentation supplied with them will improve immeasurably.

Finding Your Way Around pear.php.net

A good starting point for finding PEAR packages is to visit the PEAR home page, `http://pear.php.net`.

If you know what package you want to install, you can jump right to "*Using the PEAR Package Manager,*" but if you're just after a certain bit of functionality, you can use the PEAR site to browse through available packages, or even search based on a keyword.

To browse packages, click the Packages link at the top-right of the screen. If you've ever used Yahoo! or any other hierarchical directory engine, this should look pretty familiar. Select the category in which you're interested, and you get a list of all the packages stored under that category.

Unlike Yahoo!, however, PEAR never goes more than one level deep; click HTML, for example, and you see every single package under the HTML organizational structure, there's no such thing as a subcategory. Pagination buttons keep screen flood to a minimum.

Sadly, the search page on PEAR is rather lacking—it currently only searches the package names, not their descriptions. Whether you can find anything in this manner is anyone's guess. If you want to play, however, there's an integrated search form at the top of every page on PEAR. Type a few words there and click the button.

Exploring PEAR Classes and Applications

Once you've found a package to look at, click its name and you are taken to its home page. From there, you can view the package's revision history, see what dependencies (either parent or child) it has, and browse some fascinating package statistics.

Importantly, many packages here have a link to View Documentation, which takes you to a well-laid reference detailing the package's various classes, methods and routines. If you have ever used the PHP Web site reference at `www.php.net`, this will probably seem comfortingly familiar.

The one thing you probably shouldn't try to do from this page is download a release of the package. Unless you're absolutely stuck, you're far better off using the PEAR Package Manager. Manual installation is possible, of course, but is outside the scope of this chapter—the PEAR Web site details the process for this.

Knowing when to turn your back on PEAR is every bit as important as knowing when to greet it with open arms. Although the repository is home to some great software, a handful of the packages are unfinished or unstable in some way—and some may simply not be your cup of tea. Planning your PHP project involves identifying where repositories like PEAR can help and where they can't well in advance, so don't be afraid to play with components in a sandbox environment before you commit to any deadlines. If you do find yourself forced to author a component from scratch, why not offer it to PEAR for incorporation into the repository? Not only will thousands of others get to benefit from your programming prowess, but you yourself will benefit from a warm, fuzzy feeling for weeks to come.

Installing and Using the PEAR Package Manager

The PEAR Package Manager is bundled with all modern versions of PHP, and certainly all v5 releases.

For Linux and UNIX installations, the Package Manager should already be installed, unless you explicitly requested it not be installed when you first set up PHP.

For Windows installations, however, there is an extra step you need to follow. Linux users can skip this section.

Keep in mind that if you're deploying your finished application to a live server, such as a Web server hosted by an Internet services provider (ISP), the ISP must install any PEAR packages required by your application before it will work correctly. If your ISP won't do this for you, you can install the PEAR packages by hand, although you won't benefit from the automatic detection of missing dependencies. There's more information about installing PEAR packages by hand on the PEAR Web site.

Setting up the PEAR Package Manager on Windows

In this example installation, it's assumed that you have installed PHP in C:\PHP (the default). If this is not the case, simply change the syntax to fit your own installation directory.

Open a command prompt and run the following:

```
C:\>cd php\pear

C:\php\PEAR>..\php go-pear.php
Welcome to go-pear!
```

The script on screen guides you through the process of setting up the Package Manager. Its ultimate aim is to simply create an executable called pear that you can run, just like those on Linux/UNIX distributions.

The script asks you for an HTTP proxy server because it needs to download and update the PEAR Foundation Classes from the Internet. This setting is recorded and used in any subsequent downloads of PEAR packages, so it's important to be precise here. Most users won't need to specify anything here; if you're unsure, ask your ISP or your Systems Administrator, as appropriate.

The default installation directories are fine for most users, so just hit the Enter key when prompted.

When asked if you want to install the PEAR packages bundled with PHP, say yes.

The packages will download, unpack, and barring any problems with your Internet connection, install into your normal PHP library path. The pear executable is created in C:\PHP; run it to start the PEAR Package Manager. If you specified a proxy server, this setting is retained.

You're now ready to use the Package Manager!

Using the PEAR Package Manager

To run the Package Manager, open up a command prompt (Windows) or command shell (UNIX).

Ideally, you need to be an administrator or root (as appropriate) to use the Package Manager, otherwise you may find that you don't have permission to write to the PHP library folder.

There're a myriad of different commands, but the most useful ones are likely to be install, uninstall, and upgrade. Here's the syntax for them:

```
pear install component_name

pear uninstall component_name

pear upgrade component_name
```

Make sure you enter the component name carefully, keeping any capitalization, spacing, and underscores intact. With a bit of luck, you should see output that looks something like the following:

```
root@genesis:~# pear install HTML_TreeMenu
downloading HTML_TreeMenu-1.1.9.tgz ...
...done: 49,213 bytes
install ok: HTML_TreeMenu 1.1.9
root@genesis:~#
```

This indicates everything went okay—the PEAR Package Manager managed to connect to PEAR, download the package (and any dependent packages), and install the lot.

If you see a large number of warnings about things being "deprecated," don't panic. Some packages on PEAR are written for PHP4, and version 5 sometimes complains if the syntax of the package you are installing isn't particularly version 5-friendly. Most of the time, these warnings can be safely ignored; if the package installs successfully, all is well. It's worth checking the PEAR Web site, which you'll meet later, to see if there are any useful compatibility notes about the package you're installing.

Generally speaking, PEAR has to put the module in your PHP library directory, which is usually something that's defined on a per-server instead of a per-user basis, hence the need to have administrative privileges.

There may be (such as with the HTML_TreeMenu component described later) additional steps before you can usefully incorporate the package in your code. Refer to the package documentation to determine what these might be. You may, for example, be required to copy data files (such as GIFs and JPEGs, XML configuration files etc) to a more meaningful location for your project.

Nine times out of ten, however, using the Package Manager is the hassle-free way to add PEAR packages to your PHP installation. It's truly a friend indeed.

Try It Out — Check Out a PEAR Component

One of the best ways to explore the PEAR repository and assess the suitability of a component for your application is to install the component and try it out.

Let's say, for example, that you are developing a staff intranet for a small company. A huge array of documents—health and safety, holiday procedures, sick leave forms—is to be made accessible to your users, and you have decided that a Dynamic HTML (DHTML) collapsible hierarchical navigation—such as the kind you may have seen on Microsoft's MSDN reference—may be the best approach.

As a savvy PHP developer, you realize that the path to enlightenment lies in code reuse; so you consult the PEAR Web site for a suitable component, using the steps set out earlier, eventually stumbling across HTML_TreeMenu.

> You can find full details of the HTML_TreeMenu package on the PEAR site at http://pear.php .net/package/HTML_TreeMenu.

Install the package on your PHP installation using the PEAR Package Manager. The following example is much the same whether you are running your PHP installation on a UNIX or Windows setup. Simply type what is shown at a command prompt (if using UNIX, you should, of course, be root):

```
pear install HTML_TreeMenu
  downloading HTML_TreeMenu-1.1.9.tgz ...
  ...done: 49,213 bytes
  install ok: HTML_TreeMenu 1.1.9
```

If everything looks good, go ahead and try out your newly installed package.

The HTML_TreeMenu class can be used out-of-the-box for generating a tree navigation using pure PHP statements. However, a much more useful piece of functionality would be if it could generate a tree navigation from a piece of XML. This would allow the navigation to be updated frequently without having to change your PHP at all. In bigger projects, this would even mean that non-PHP-literate staff could update the navigation without bothering the PHP developers.

HTML_TreeMenu does not natively support rendering a navigation tree from XML. In its version 4 incarnation, it recommended the installation of a supplementary class (not from PEAR), which would add this support. However, this support class has not been updated to support the radically altered XML support in PHP5. Accordingly, we've added our own support class to enable this functionality; it's introduced later in the chapter. You shouldn't shy away from adapting or extending PEAR classes this way to meet your own needs a little better; it doesn't hurt to make a good thing even better!

The first step, obviously, is to read the documentation. Browsing to the project's home page on PEAR, you'll notice that this particular class does not have that all-important Documentation link (not all PEAR packages do). Do not fear—all is not lost.

Take a look on the server in /usr/local/lib/php/docs/HTML_TreeMenu, under UNIX, or C:\PHP\ PEAR\pear\DOCS\HTML_TreeMenu under Windows. You'll find, very helpfully, a file named HTML_TreeMenu.pdf, which you can open in Adobe Acrobat. The file goes into some detail about the class's various exposed properties and methods—its API (Application Programming Interface), in effect—and also provides examples to get you up and running. Because of the incompatibilities mentioned earlier, you'll have to disregard its recommendations about how to parse XML.

Go ahead and create the following file, call it treemenutest.xml. For simplicity, use the XML DTD (Document Type Definition) alluded to in the HTML_TreeMenu documentation, it's all quite straightforward. Make sure you save the file where PHP can get to it, such as C:\inetpub\wwwroot\xml on Windows, or ~/public_html/xml on UNIX, although it doesn't necessarily have to reside where your site visitors can retrieve it with their Web browsers, if you'd prefer to keep it private.

```xml
<?xml version="1.0"?>
<treemenu>
    <node text="Home" icon="folder.gif" link="treemenutest.php" />
    <node text="Health and Safety" icon="folder.gif">
        <node text="About Health and Safety" icon="document.gif" link="#" />
        <node text="Accident Policy" icon="document.gif" link="#" />
        <node text="Sickness Policy" icon="document.gif" link="#" />
        <node text="Long Term Sickness" icon=" document.gif" link="#" />
    </node>
</treemenu>
```

Because all you're doing is assessing the feasibility of the component at this stage, there's no need to include a vast number of items in the XML—just enough to take it for a test drive.

Note the reference to a couple of .GIF files. HTML_TreeMenu uses a few more of its own that haven't been explicitly mentioned in the XML to draw plus and minus signs and so forth. These files are included with the distribution, and if you can muster the energy to dig them out and copy them to a folder called images underneath the root of where you're saving the following code, feel free to do so.

Now construct your navigation display page. Create a file, enter the following code in it, and name the file treemenutest.php:

```php
<HTML>
    <HEAD>
        <SCRIPT LANGUAGE="Javascript" SRC="TreeMenu.js"></SCRIPT>
    </HEAD>
    <BODY>
        <?php
            require_once('HTML/TreeMenu.php');
            require_once('xmlhtmltree.phpm');
            $objXMLTree = new XMLHTMLTree("treemenutest.xml");
            $objXMLTree->GenerateHandOffs();
            $objXMLTree->ParseXML();
            $objTreeMenu = $objXMLTree->GetTreeHandoff();
        ?>
            <H1>Tree Menu Test</H1>
```

```
            <HR>
            <?php
                $objTreeMenu->printMenu();
            ?>
        </BODY>
    </HTML>
```

The PEAR package HTML_TreeMenu is included, but so is a seemingly brand new package called xmlhtmltree.phpm. This is the "helper" class alluded to earlier; it converts XML into PHP statements to feed into the HTML_TreeMenu class.

Following is the code for the "helper" component. Save it as xmlhtmltree.phpm in the same folder you saved treemenutest.php. Don't worry about how it works, yet—you'll see that shortly.

```
<?
class XMLHTMLTree {
 private $xml_content;
 private $hanTreeHandoff;
 private $objHTMLTreeMenu;

 function __construct($strXMLSourceFile = "", $strXMLSource = "") {
   if ($strXMLSourceFile) {
     $this->xml_content = implode('', @file($strXMLSourceFile));
   } else {
     $this->xml_content = $strXMLSource;
   };
   $this->objHTMLTreeMenu  = new HTML_TreeMenu();
   $this->depth = 0;
 }

 function ParseXML() {
   $strXML = $this->xml_content;
   $objDOM = simplexml_load_string($strXML);
   foreach ($objDOM->node as $thisNode) {
     $this->_ParseNode($thisNode);
   };
 }

 private function_ParseNode(&$objNode, & $arPoint = "") {
   # Add this node
   if (!$arPoint) {
     $objNewNode = new HTML_TreeNode(array('text' => $objNode['text'], 'link' =>
$objNode['link'], 'icon' => 'folder.gif', 'expandedIcon' =>
'folder-expanded.gif', 'expanded' => false));
       $newArPoint = &$objNewNode;
     } else {
       $newArPoint = &$arPoint->addItem(new HTML_TreeNode(array('text' =>
$objNode['text'], 'link' => $objNode['link'], 'icon' => 'folder.gif',
'expandedIcon' => 'folder-expanded.gif')));
     };
   # See if the original has any child nodes
   foreach ($objNode->node as $thisNode) {
```

```
            if ($thisNode['text']) {
               $this->_ParseNode($thisNode, $newArPoint);
            };
      };
      if (!empty($objNewNode)) {
         $this->objHTMLTreeMenu->addItem($objNewNode);
      };
   }

   function GenerateHandOffs() {
      // Create the presentation class
      $this->hanTreeHandoff = &new HTML_TreeMenu_DHTML($this->objHTMLTreeMenu,
array('defaultClass' => 'treeMenuDefault'));
         $this->hanTreeHandoff->images = 'images';
   }

   function GetTreeHandoff() {
      return($this->hanTreeHandoff);
   }


}
?>
```

The only thing you might want to change in this code is the location for the images used in rendering the navigation. Should you want (or need) to save these somewhere other than a subdirectory called images, change the line

```
$this->hanTreeHandoff->images = 'images';
```

to wherever you have saved the images. The images used in the example screenshot came with the HTML_TreeMenu distribution and can be found in the images subdirectory of /usr/local/lib/php/data/HTML_TreeMenu (UNIX) or C:\PHP\PEAR\PEAR\DATA\HTML_TreeMenu (Windows) should you want to copy them out.

There's one final step before you can see the class in action. You might notice that a JavaScript library called TreeMenu.js included. This comes bundled with the package, but is kept in a place where PHP can see it just fine, but where your Web browser can't (JavaScript files are simply requested by the Web browser—PHP doesn't get involved). To overcome this, copy the JavaScript file out of /usr/local/lib/php/data/HTML_TreeMenu (or the Windows equivalent) and pop it in the same folder as the PHP file treemenutest.php you just created.

Fire up a Web browser and point it at treemenutest.php. Figure 14-1 shows the result.

Go ahead and play with the navigation. Expand and collapse the Health and Safety section. If it works, congratulations! You just used your first PEAR module.

If you have problems, the first place to look is the PHP error log. Depending on how you have PHP set up, this may either be straight to the screen, or to your Web server's own error log. In either case, look for any clues that might help you diagnose the problem, which is likely to be simple typographical error, which is easily fixed, or it might be that PHP cannot find the HTML_TreeMenu class. In the latter case, something's probably amiss in your PEAR setup, and it's time to retrace your steps from earlier in the chapter.

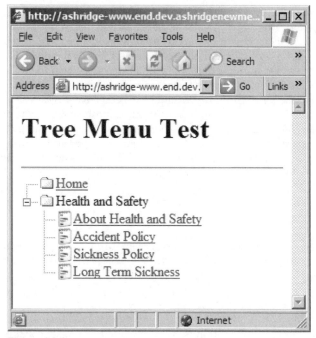

Figure 14-1

How It Works

Let's work through the code to see how the HTML_TreeMenu package transforms your simple XML into a working navigation tree.

Including the Package

First, you use the require_once function to tell PHP that you want to include the code from the HTML_TreeMenu PEAR library.

You must also include the xmlhtmltree.phpm helper class for now, which enables you to simply hand a piece of XML to the HTML_TreeMenu class.

There are a couple of reasons for using require_once instead of any of PHP's other inclusion functions

❑   If the package cannot be found, PHP throws a fatal exception and stops execution.

❑   If the package has already been included by some other piece of code in the execution of this particular script, it won't be included a second time, which greatly improves performance.

Working with the Classes

Then, you instantiate the classes.

To begin, create an instance of the HTML_TreeMenu class itself:

```
$objXMLTree = new XMLHTMLTree("treemenutest.xml");
```

If you use include rather than require to include the package, PHP doesn't abort the script execution until it reaches this line. This may not seem like a big deal in this example, when the line happens to immediately follow the inclusion. In the real world, however, where a whole bunch of database entries are being created between inclusion and usage, it is a very big deal indeed. For example, imagine an e-commerce Web site where multiple database entries are placed as part of a single order. If you didn't use the exposed PEAR class until, say, half way through making those database entries then, upon abortion, only half of the database entries would have been created. As well as being technically unclean, this could provide a true real-world administrative mess for the company running the site in terms of figuring out how far the order had progressed, whether the customer had paid, and so forth. In practice, database transactions can be used to stop this from happening, but it is far cleaner to ensure that if a component you know will be required later on in the script is missing from the word go, an error is thrown and the rest of the script isn't executed in vain.

Note that you aren't using the PEAR class directly but are instantiating the helper class with the path to your input XML document.

You instruct the helper class to create the necessary DHTML HTML_TreeMenu object—the "handoff." This object is inextricably linked to the class's own member HTML_TreeMenu object, so that when a node is added to the tree object, it is also added to the handoff.

```
$objXMLTree->GenerateHandOffs();
```

You'll learn more about the inner workings of this method in a few pages' time when you examine the helper class in more detail.

Next, the helper class is instructed to actually parse the XML of your input document. It does this using SimpleXML, which conveniently presents the XML it has parsed as an object hierarchy that you can easily traverse. Although the helper class traverses that hierarchy, it uses methods provided by the original PEAR class HTML_TreeMenu to add nodes (essentially items on the list) to its member HTML_TreeMenu object.

The helper class now has an object ready to produce dynamic HTML to render an attractive navigation at a moment's notice. You could simply tell it to do so straightaway, but it will wait for the lifetime of the script for the order. This enables you to render the rest of the page first. In the example, all you have are some basic HTML headers. In a real-world application, a great deal more is likely going on before the navigation is required.

First, you must retrieve the DHTML HTML_TreeMenu object from the helper class:

```
$objTreeMenu = $objXMLTree->GetTreeHandoff();
```

When you want the object to produce the necessary HTML, you simply need to call one method:

```
$objTreeMenu->printMenu();
```

And it produces the necessary output to render the menu.

The more curious among you may have already done a view source from within your Web browser to try to figure out what it's doing to generate the clickable menu. In fact, as you'll notice, the PHP isn't producing any HTML at all—only JavaScript. The PHP in this case is used to populate a JavaScript array—its own tree object, if you will—that your Web browser uses on the client side to render the menu. The actual logic for rendering the DHTML is kept well to the side in the treeMenu.js file. Using dynamic server-side logic to produce static client-side logic through JavaScript is proving increasingly popular these days, and this package provides an excellent example of why that is; you not only can take advantage of PHP's immensely powerful XML parsing techniques to determine exactly what is to be rendered in Web browsers, but you also can take full advantage of the rendering capabilities of today's generation of Web browsers to determine *how* it is displayed. This separation of layers hints at a more advanced technique of programming known as the MVC Design Pattern—MVC standing for Model View, Controller. This is a little way off yet, but getting into the habit now is no bad thing.

How the DHTML itself works is outside the scope of this book, but the excellent Dynamic Duo Web site run by Dan Steinman at www.dansteinman.com/dynduo/provides ample explanation.

The Helper Class—Only for the Curious!

Let's take a few minutes to explore the helper class xmlhtmltree.phpm in a bit more detail. As mentioned earlier, this class is necessary to enable you to use XML as the data source for your tree menu instead of having to populate it using PHP statements for each item.

The task for this helper class, therefore, is to take a piece of well-formatted XML, instantiate an HTML_TreeMenu class into an object, and then traverse that XML, calling the exposed methods of that object along the way to populate it based solely on the content of that XML.

This helper class is used throughout the chapter wherever you meet HTML_TreeMenu, so let's examine each of its methods that you can see for yourself how it works its magic!

First, let's look at the member variables:

```
private $xml_content;
private $hanTreeHandoff;
private $objHTMLTreeMenu;
```

The first represents your XML content, stored as a string, the second is your handoff—a reference to the DHTML version of your HTML_TreeMenu object, and the third is the HTML_TreeMenu object itself.

In the constructor, one of two parameters is accepted, either, the path to the XML source file, or a string containing the XML itself. By using the = " " operator, you can inform PHP that both parameters are optional. In the event that a source file has been specified, you retrieve its contents. Either way, the XML source itself is then stored in the xml_content member variable, ready to be parsed.

```
function __construct($strXMLSourceFile = "", $strXMLSource = "") {
  if ($strXMLSourceFile) {
    $this->xml_content = implode('', @file($strXMLSourceFile));
  } else {
    $this->xml_content = $strXMLSource;
  };
  $this->objHTMLTreeMenu = new HTML_TreeMenu();
}
```

Also in the constructor, the HTML_TreeMenu class is instantiated into an object, which is stored as a member variable of the class.

The `GenerateHandOffs` method creates the exposed DHTML `HTML_TreeMenu` object, which then can be retrieved using the `GetTreeHandoff` method.

```
function GenerateHandOffs() {
   // Create the presentation class
   $this->hanTreeHandoff = &new HTML_TreeMenu_DHTML($this->objHTMLTreeMenu,
array('defaultClass' => 'treeMenuDefault'));
   $this->hanTreeHandoff->images = 'images';
}
```

The syntax for exposing the DHTML representation of the member tree menu object is lifted directly from the `HTML_TreeMenu` documentation. The images path property is set here such that the various images used by the rendered tree navigation can be found correctly.

The `ParseXML` method commences the parsing of the XML content of the helper class.

```
function ParseXML() {
  $strXML = $this->xml_content;
  $objDOM = simplexml_load_string($strXML);
  foreach ($objDOM->node as $thisNode) {
    $this->_ParseNode($thisNode);
  };
}
```

First, you retrieve your XML content from your class, and localize it within the method. This isn't strictly necessary, but it makes your code a little cleaner.

Next, use the SimpleXML method `simplexml_load_string` to load your XML structure and present it as a pseudo-object model, which you store in $objDom.

Because all the nodes in your XML are called node, simply call the `foreach` method to traverse this collection of node "objects," which has been made available to you by SimpleXML. You pass a reference for each of these objects to a method called _ParseNode, which is a private method inaccessible from outside the helper class.

```
private function_ParseNode($objNode, & $arPoint = "") {
  # Add this node
  if (!$arPoint) {
    $objNewNode = new HTML_TreeNode(array('text' => $objNode['text'],
'link' => $objNode['link'], 'icon' => 'folder.gif', 'expandedIcon' =>
'folder-expanded.gif', 'expanded' => false));
    $newArPoint = &$objNewNode;
  } else {
    $newArPoint = &$arPoint->addItem(new HTML_TreeNode(array('text' =>
$objNode['text'], 'link' => $objNode['link'], 'icon' => 'folder.gif',
'expandedIcon' => 'folder-expanded.gif')));
  };
  # See if the original has any child nodes
  foreach ($objNode->node as $thisNode) {
    if ($thisNode['text']) {
```

```
        $this->_ParseNode($thisNode, $newArPoint);
      };
    };
    if ($objNewNode) {
      $this->objHTMLTreeMenu->addItem($objNewNode);
    };
  }
```

The _ParseNode method calls itself recursively. Recursion is best described as a means for a given method to make selective calls to itself for the purpose of traversing an unknown degree of nesting in some data structure. If you had a two-dimensional grid of numbers, you would traverse it using two for loops—probably one using the counter variable x, and the other using the counter variable y. Similarly, if you had a three-dimensional cube of numbers, you would use three for loops—x, y and z, nested within each other. But in these two examples, the number of dimensions is constant and known. In XML, any given structure can have any number of child nodes, each of which can have any number of child nodes, and so on. By using recursion, you ensure that every individual node is processed by launching a new instance of the method whenever a new set of children is found; once that set of children has been processed, the parent instance picks up where it left off.

This works quite neatly and simply for you in the example code. For each node in the XML, a corresponding node is created in the HTML_TreeMenu object, using the methods described in the component's documentation. Then a check is made to see if any child nodes exist under the node currently being rendered. If they do, each one in turn is then passed into a new instance of the _ParseNode method, which then carries out the exact same process with that child node. A reference to the parent node (if any) is also passed into the method, so that the method knows to which node it should add a child object in the hierarchy it has been creating.

Finally, let's look at the GetTreeHandoff() method.

```
function GetTreeHandoff() {
  return($this->hanTreeHandoff);
}
```

Quite simply, this returns the reference to the DHTML HTML_TreeMenu rendering made available by the GenerateHandOffs() method used earlier. What is returned by this method can have its printMenu method called at will to render the HTML and JavaScript to make the menu visible on the user's browser screen.

Helper classes are inevitable from time to time. If you do find yourself repeatedly using a class you've written, you may want to look at submitting it to PEAR yourself, with the original PEAR class on which it is based listed as a dependency. You can find more information on to do this on the PEAR Web site.

Using PEAR Packages

By now you should have a good grasp of how to identify a good PEAR package to use in your project, how to install it and any of its dependencies, and how to incorporate it into your own code. Let's put that knowledge to work to build a working application using a single PEAR component and a few more common built-in PHP routines.

Try It Out   **Build an Application Using a Single PEAR Component**

The application you're going to write is designed for use on a personal Web site to show site visitors what kind music you've been listening to lately. It works by ferreting through your MP3 collection. Many people collect MP3s—it is still by far the most popular format for encoding music for computer-based listening despite proprietary offerings from some enormous industry players—many people have MP3 collections running to thousands of songs.

This particular bit of PHP is designed to be run on your desktop computer simply because it needs access to wherever you keep your MP3 files for day-to-day listening. This may not be practical for any number of reasons, but as a working example of a stand-alone application, it will suffice.

Let's assume that you keep your MP3s in C:\MP3—if that isn't the case (or you're running under UNIX), you can change the $MY_MP3_DIR constant in the code.

The PEAR Package: MP3_ID

The MP3_ID package is used to read what is known as the IDv3 Tag information from an MP3 file. This tag contains information on the song's genre, date, and country of origin, and much more. The tag is present in every MP3 file, but may be blank—it all depends on what was used to produce the MP3 in the first place. For the purposes of this project, assume all your MP3s are properly tagged up!

> More information on the package can be found at `http://pear.php.net/package/MP3_ID`.

The package provides methods for both reading and writing the IDv3 Tags, but in this example you are only going to be using its read methods to discover certain information about the MP3 files in your collection—namely the artist and title of the song.

It is installed in the usual manner:

```
root@genesis:~# pear install MP3_ID
downloading MP3_Id-1.0.tgz ...
...done: 7,517 bytes
install ok: MP3_Id 1.0
root@genesis:~#
```

The Application

You'll build this application as a single PHP page that, when accessed, produces a list of the top five MP3 files in the directory, ordered by the last time each file was accessed (which should be, in theory, the same order they were last played). If more than five files are found in the directory, only the first five will be shown.

Create a PHP file named mp3id.php, and place it where your Web server can see it. Enter the following code in that file. Don't forget to change the constant $MY_MP3_DIR to the path to where your MP3s are actually kept (make sure there are some MP3s in that folder). Don't worry if anything doesn't make sense—we'll pick it apart straight after.

```php
<?php
    require_once 'MP3/Id.php';

    static $MY_MP3_DIR = "/home/ed/mp3"; # Change this to your MP3 directory!
```

```php
    $objDir = dir($MY_MP3_DIR);
    $intNumFiles = 0;
    $arFileTimeHash = Array();
    # Loop through all the files we've found
    while (false !== ($strEntry = $objDir->read())) {
        # Check this is actually an MP3 file, and not a directory entry or similar!
        if (eregi("\.mp3$", $strEntry)) {
            $arFileTimeHash[$strEntry] = fileatime($MY_MP3_DIR . "/" . $strEntry);
            $intNumFiles++;
        };
    };

    # Now sort into order of date accessed and put into a traditional array
structure for display later
    arsort($arFileTimeHash);
    $arFileList = Array();
    $intThisArrayIndex = 0;
    foreach ($arFileTimeHash as $strFilename => $intAccessTime){
        $arFileList[$intThisArrayIndex]["FILENAME"] = $strFilename;
        $arFileList[$intThisArrayIndex]["ACCESSED"] = $intAccessTime;
        $intThisArrayIndex ++;
    };

    # If we found more than 5 MP3s, just show the first 5
    if ($intNumFiles > 5) {
        $intNumFiles = 5;
    };
?>
<!DOCTYPE HTML PUBLIC "-//W3C//DTD HTML 4.01 Transitional//EN">
<html>
    <head>
        <title>My MP3 Collection</title>
    </head>
    <body>
    <H1>My MP3 Collection</H1>
    <HR>
    Here's the top 5 songs I've been listening to lately!
    <BR><BR>
    <table border="1" cellpadding="3" cellspacing="3">
        <tr>
            <td>Position</td>
            <td>Artist</td>
            <td>Name</td>
            <td>Last listened to on:</td>
        </tr>
    <?php
        $objMP3ID = new MP3_Id();
        for ($i = 0; $i<=($intNumFiles)-1; $i++) {
    ?>
        <tr>
    <?php
        $strThisFile = $arFileList[$i]["FILENAME"];
        $strPath = $MY_MP3_DIR . "/" . $strThisFile;
        $intResult = $objMP3ID->read ($strPath);
```

```
        $strArtist = $objMP3ID->getTag ("artists", "Unknown Artist");
        $strName = $objMP3ID->getTag ("name", "Unknown Track");
        $intAccessTime = $arFileList[$i]["ACCESSED"];
    ?>
        <td><?=$i+1?></td>
        <td><?=$strArtist?></td>
        <td><?=$strName?></td>
        <td><?=date("m/d/Y H:i", $intAccessTime)?></td>
    </tr>
    <?php
        };
    ?>
    </body>
</html>
```

Fire up your Web browser, and point it at the PHP you've just created. Your output should look similar to Figure 14-2.

Figure 14-2

How It Works

Just like the HTML_TreeMenu example, this little application does the bulk of the clever stuff right at the top, and then displays the information when it is needed, neatly embedded within the HTML. MP3_ID is neat in that it has no real dependencies; it's very much plug'n'go.

The first line—the `require` line—loads the module:

```
require_once 'MP3/Id.php';
```

You don't instantiate it because you don't need it yet.

The first job is to traverse the MP3 directory and build up an associative array of every MP3 file in it along with its access time:

```
static $strMyMP3Directory = "/home/ed/mp3";
$objDir = dir($strMyMP3Directory);
$intNumFiles = 0;
$arFileTimeHash = Array();
# Loop through all the files we've found
while (false !== ($strEntry = $objDir->read())) {
    # Check this is actually an MP3 file, and not a directory entry or similar!
    if (eregi("\.mp3$", $strEntry)) {
        $arFileTimeHash[$strEntry] = fileatime($strMyMP3Directory . "/"
        . $strEntry);
            $intNumFiles++;
    };
};
```

The helpful `Dir` object lets you traverse your directory of choice. Unfortunately, it doesn't enable you to filter its output. When listing the contents of the directory, there's a good chance that you're going to get a bunch of results you don't want.

The workaround is to pass every result you get back from the `Dir` object through a regular expression. Regular expressions are a huge topic and handled briefly back in Chapter 5. The regular expression used here is `.mp3$`, which is passed into the case-insensitive regular expression match check method `eregi` that checks whether the entry ends with the four-character string `.mp3`. If it does, you can be fairly sure it's an MP3 file and include it in your associative array.

The associative array is keyed with the filename (minus the path) of each file, the value is the time that file was last accessed, which is retrieved by using the `fileatime` function. The value of `$intNumFiles` is incremented with each file successfully found, and will be of use to you later.

With the associative array intact, you can make use of PHP's `arsort` function, which sorts an associative array, in reverse, by the values of its key-value pairs:

```
# Now sort into order of date accessed and put into a traditional array
structure for display later
    arsort($arFileTimeHash);
```

In this example, the key is the filename, and the value is the access time, so in effect, you're sorting the array by most-recently-accessed first.

You translate the sorted array into a traditional numbered array, each component of which is an associative array in its own right, with just two keys: FILENAME (the name of the file) and ACCESSED (when it was accessed):

```php
$intThisArrayIndex = 0;
foreach ($arFileTimeHash as $strFilename => $intAccessTime)
{
    $arFileList[$intThisArrayIndex]["FILENAME"] = $strFilename;
    $arFileList[$intThisArrayIndex]["ACCESSED"] = $intAccessTime;
    $intThisArrayIndex ++;
};
```

This step isn't strictly necessary—it just makes the logic a bit easier to follow when it comes to display the files.

Finally, you add a simple rule to limit our output—if there are more than five MP3s in the array, show only the first 5, if there are fewer than five, show all of them:

```php
# If we found more than 5 MP3s, just show the first 5
if ($intNumFiles > 5)
{
    $intNumFiles = 5;
};
```

Now you're ready to kick off the HTML. With a table in place to display the results, you cycle through your array from 0 (the first MP3) to the value of intNumFiles—the number of files you determined earlier. Of course, because you start counting at zero, you deduct one from the total to work out your upper limit.

With each cycle, you make use of the instantiated MP3_ID class by feeding it a filename to process, and extracting the "artists" and "name" tags from the MP3, using the read and getTag methods, respectively:

```php
<?php
  $objMP3ID = new MP3_Id();
  for ($i = 0; $i<=($intNumFiles)-1; $i++)
  {
?>
    <tr>
<?php
    $strThisFile = $arFileList[$i]["FILENAME"];
    $strPath = $strMyMP3Directory . "/" . $strThisFile;
    $intResult = $objMP3ID->read ($strPath);
    $strArtist = $objMP3ID->getTag ("artists", "Unknown Artist");
    $strName = $objMP3ID->getTag ("name", "Unknown Track");
    $intAccessTime = $arFileList[$i]["ACCESSED"];
?>
        <td><?=$i+1?></td>
        <td><?=$strArtist?></td>
        <td><?=$strName?></td>
```

```
        <td><?=date("m/d/Y H:i", $intAccessTime)?></td>
    </tr>
<?php
    };
?>
```

Note that you display the access time here, too. That information isn't derived from the IDv3 tag of the file, but from the file list array itself. You retrieve and record this information when you actually perform the directory listing, and you can simply refer back to it here.

You display the access time, which was presented as an "epoch timestamp" (a value in seconds relative to January 1, 1970) in a more friendly format using PHP's excellent date function.

And so, in a few simple steps, you created an original diversion for your home page (and it's certainly a bit more engaging than "Sign my guestbook!").

Spotted a Problem?

Some of you may have experienced a small problem with this lovely application. Run it once, and all works fine. Run it a second time (hit Refresh), and the "last listened to" column seems strangely . . . recent.

It's not a bug, but more of an accidental feature. By reading the ID tag of the MP3, you are in fact—you guessed it—accessing the file. By accessing the file, you are updating its last accessed attribute on the file system. As a result, when you next go to run your app, the last accessed property of your MP3 reflects the last time you ran the script, *not* the last time you listened to the MP3.

There is a clever way around this, using a native PHP function called touch. The principle is that after accessing the file to retrieve its IDv3 contents, you immediately use the touch function to set its access time back to what it was previously. If you feel strongly about access times, and want to experiment adding this functionality as an exercise, please do so. Unfortunately, this method only works if the "owner" of the MP3 files is the same as the "owner" of the Web server process, which is rarely the case in a production environment.

A more sophisticated workaround involves periodically indexing your MP3 files into a database, so that it isn't necessary to read the IDv3 tags every time somebody hits the Web page; instead, the database can be consulted, leaving the access time of the file intact. Again, this is left as an exercise!

> *A file's access time is a property that is offered to PHP by the operating system. Depending on the operating system you're running, and the file system with which your server's disk is formatted, this property may not be available to PHP. In that case, the operating system may offer up the last modified time instead. This means the data returned by the script in such cases will not be wholly accurate, so if you are planning to deploy this onto a real-world production environment, you may want to sanity check the results you get before you open it up to general access.*

Building an Application Using Two PEAR Components

Let's put all your PEAR skills together now, and build a fresh application from the ground up. Let's see if you can combine the use of the two PEAR components you've met so far—HTML_TreeMenu and MP3_ID—to build a genuinely useful application.

The Application

Some of the more enlightened Internet radio stations these days, as well as traditional broadcast radio stations with an online presence, offer some facility for its listeners to request music via the station's Web site.

With a limited play list, it would be unwise for a station to allow a free-text request form because many of its listeners' requests would have to go unfulfilled. Generally speaking, such stations would normally want to offer a list of all tracks in the station archive, and let the listener to choose from that list.

Constant new additions to that archive, which is normally made up of MP3 files, could make maintaining the request part of the Web site pretty tricky. As a result, some means for the request list to be generated dynamically and be arranged in some sensible manner would be just swell.

This application permits just that. It presents all the MP3 files in a server's directory in a hierarchical list (using the HTML_TreeMenu PEAR component), ordered by artist. It enables the submitting user to click a particular song to request it, and then render an e-mail to the DJ of the radio station instructing him to play that file.

You'll use PHP's built-in `mail()` function to send this e-mail. This is a very simple way to send e-mail, and in most real-world applications, you'll need something a little chunkier. In the next chapter, you'll hook up with some PEAR classes that can help you out.

Because you've used XML to drive the contents of the output of the HTML_TreeMenu component so far, let's stick with that method. You'll still need to use the helper class, however, to turn the XML into PHP methods that HTML_TreeMenu can understand.

Architecture

The application can be divided into two distinct PHP files, just to make things a bit neater. The first, `radiogeneratexml.php`, generates an XML representation of the MP3 folder on the server, organized and ordered by artist. The second, `radiorequest.php`, actually displays that list, and handles any form submissions by the user.

The XML gets from one script to the other by means of an HTTP request. Yes, your script will cause your server to make a request from itself! If you've ever played with the idea of XML-based Web services, this might not seem so crazy. The idea is to allow the feed of XML data to come from practically any source, in practically any location. For example, in a real live radio station you might use one Web server to serve the public Web site, but a totally separate server to hold the MP3 files. The server holding the MP3s might not even be accessible to the outside world. Instead of trying to read over any kind of network share, which is incredibly inefficient, you could place `radiogeneratexml.php` on the server with the MP3s, and keep `radiorequest.php` on the public Web server, and tell it to request the XML straight off the other server.

Should you ever decide to extend your application so that third-party Web sites could access the data, you just might make that XML feed public.

> *The XML, for the purposes of this application, conforms to the standards required by the HTML_TreeMenu component, which you have already seen. With the possibility of some kind of secondary use of the XML feed in mind, it may be wise to consider, as a project for a rainy day, upgrading the application to produce XML in a more service-driven than display-driven format. You could then use a simple XSL style sheet to convert the service-driven XML into XML that the PEAR component could understand.*

Generating the XML

`radiogeneratexml.php` not only is in charge of producing XML that can be used by the make-a-request page, but also is in charge of reading the MP3 directory, extracting the useful artist and title data from each MP3 file, and then grouping and sorting the list of MP3s in an appropriate way.

Let's just quickly review the kind of XML you want to produce for the HTML_TreeMenu component. Take a look at this example output:

```
<?xml version="1.0"?>
<treemenu>
    <node text="Extreme Metal Grinding" icon="folder.gif">
        <node text="Extreme Noises" icon="document.gif"
link="radiorequest.php?requestfile=9991885931034.mp3" />
        <node text="Extreme Temper Loss" icon="document.gif"
link="radiorequest.php?requestfile=9991885931035.mp3" />
    </node>
    <node text="Massive Pitch Correction" icon="folder.gif">
        <node text="How long ago" icon="document.gif"
link="radiorequest.php?requestfile=9991885931036.mp3" />
        <node text="Ten minutes to Sunrise" icon="document.gif"
link="radiorequest.php?requestfile=9991885931037.mp3" />
    </node>
</treemenu>
```

In this output, you can see that two artists have been identified in the MP3 collection: "Extreme Metal Grinding" and "Massive Pitch Correction" (this isn't the greatest radio station in the world). The available songs by each of these two fine artists have been placed under their nodes in the hierarchy.

The name of each song is the caption for the link itself—to `radiorequest.php`—passing a GET parameter called `requestFile`. The actual MP3 filename is passed because it is of more use to the DJ than the information from the IDv3 tag of the file. PHP's `urlencode()` function will make sure the MP3 filename is URL-friendly before it's passed, of course.

If you want to see what this will look like when rendered by HTML_TreeMenu, use your code from the first "Try It Out" example in this chapter and paste this XML into `treemenutest.xml`. You then need to modify `treemenutest.php` to look at the correct XML file:

```
$objXMLTree = new XMLHTMLTree("treemenutest.xml");
```

Fire up your Web browser, and point it to `treemenutest.php` again, to see how your new XML looks (see Figure 14-3).

Now we're happy with the output of our request page (we'll probably want to fiddle with surrounding HTML a bit, though), we just have to figure out how we're going to produce some similar output—dynamically, of course—from the contents of our MP3 collection folder.

Try It Out   **Build a Two-Tier, Two-Component PEAR Application**

If this looks pretty tough at first, try not to panic too much—we'll go through all the code for both components in some detail after the listings.

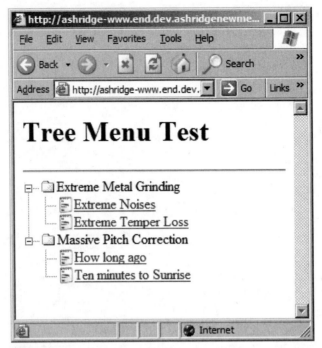

Figure 14-3

radiogeneratexml.php

Create a new file, insert the following code, and save it as `radiogeneratexml.php`. This particular tier of the application generates the XML for your tree navigation component automatically from the MP3 folder on your own computer. Place it on your server where you can reach it easily.

```php
<?php
    header("Content-Type: text/xml\n\n");

    require_once 'MP3/Id.php';

    static $strMyMP3Directory = "/home/ed/mp3";
    $objDir = dir($strMyMP3Directory);
    $intNumFiles = 0;
    $arMP3Files = Array();

    // Loop through all the files we've found and put them into an array
    while (false !== ($strEntry = $objDir->read())) {
        // Check this is actually an MP3 file, and not a directory entry or
similar!
        if (eregi("\.mp3$", $strEntry)) {
            $arMP3Files[] = $strMyMP3Directory . "/" . $strEntry;
        };
    };
```

```
    // Instantiate our MP3_ID Class
    $objMP3ID = new MP3_Id();

    // Set up an array of unique artists
    $arArtists = Array();
    $arTestArtists = Array();
    for ($i=0; $i<=sizeof($arMP3Files)-1; $i++) {
        $strPath = $arMP3Files[$i];
        $intResult = $objMP3ID->read ($strPath);
        $strArtist = $objMP3ID->getTag ("artists", "Unknown Artist");
        $strTestArtist = strtoupper(preg_replace("/[^A-Za-z0-9]
/", "", $strArtist));
        // Check to see if this artist (when uncommon characters are made
irrelevant and all letters are capitalized) is in our array of artists - if
not, add them
        if (in_array($strTestArtist, $arTestArtists) == false) {
            array_push($arArtists, $strArtist);
            // Note we use the original spacing and capitalization for our
addition to $arArtists ...
            array_push($arTestArtists, $strTestArtist);
        };
    };

    // For each artist, create an array containing all the song filenames
written by that artist, and their titles
    $arTracks = Array();
    // We'll also create an array of all the song indices we've already
accounted for, to save reading their details more than once
    $arAlreadyAccountedForSongIndices = Array();
    for ($i=0; $i<=sizeof($arArtists)-1; $i++) {
        $strArtistName = $arArtists[$i];
        $strTestArtistName = $arTestArtists[$i];
        $arTracks[$strArtistName] = Array();
        // See which songs are written by this artist
        for ($j=0; $j<=sizeof($arMP3Files)-1; $j++) {
            if (in_array($j, $arAlreadyAccountedForSongIndices) == false) {
                $strPath = $arMP3Files[$j];
                $intResult = $objMP3ID->read ($strPath);
                $strThisArtist = $objMP3ID->getTag ("artists", "Unknown Artist");
                $strThisTestArtist = strtoupper(preg_replace("/[^A-Za-z0-9]/", "",
$strThisArtist));
                if ($strThisTestArtist == $strTestArtistName) {
                    // This song is indeed by the artist we're testing, so slap its
index into $arAlreadyAccountedForSongIndices so we won't ever test it again
                    array_push($arAlreadyAccountedForSongIndices, $j);
                    // Get its title and request link and push them into a temporary hash
                    $arSongHash["TITLE"] = $objMP3ID->getTag ("name", "Unknown Title");
                    $strSongFilename = str_replace("$strMyMP3Directory" . "/", "",
$arMP3Files[$j]);
                    // Create a link based on the filename by making the filename
URL friendly using urlencode
                    $arSongHash["LINK"] = "radiorequest.php?requestfile=" .
urlencode($strSongFilename);
```

```
                    // Push this hash as the result of the next available index of
$arTracks[name of artist]
                    array_push($arTracks[$strArtistName], $arSongHash);
            };
        };
    };

    // Sort this hash by artist name, ascending A-Z - use ksort rather than
asort to sort by key
    ksort($arTracks);

    // Now output this in the appropriate XML format
?>
<treemenu>
<?php foreach ($arTracks as $artist_name => $arHash) { ?>
    <node text="<?=$artist_name?>" icon="folder.gif">
<?php for ($i=0; $i<=sizeof($arHash)-1; $i++) { ?>
        <node text="<?=htmlentities($arHash[$i]["TITLE"])?>" icon="document.gif"
link="<?=htmlentities($arHash[$i]["LINK"])?>" />
<?php }; ?>
    </node>
<?php }; ?>
</treemenu>
```

radiorequest.php

Create a new file and enter the following code. Save it as `radiogeneratexml.php` and put it in the same folder on your server as `radiogeneratexml.php`. This script displays the tree navigation of the MP3 tracks available to request generated by `radiogeneratexml.php`, and handles the requests submitted by the user.

```
<?php
    static $strMyMP3Directory = "/home/ed/mp3";
    static $strMyDJsEmailAddress = "ed@example.com";

    // Require our necessary PEAR objects
            require_once('HTML/TreeMenu.php');
            require_once('xmlhtmltree.phpm');

    // Define XML URL for retrieval and retrieve it - you can modify this if
you have the XML generator on another server!
    $strXMLURL = "http://" . $_SERVER["SERVER_NAME"] . str_replace("request",
"generatexml", $_SERVER["SCRIPT_NAME"]);

    $strXML = implode (false, file($strXMLURL));

        $objXMLTree = new XMLHTMLTree("", $strXML);
        $objXMLTree->GenerateHandOffs();
        $objXMLTree->ParseXML();
        $objTreeMenu = $objXMLTree->GetTreeHandoff();

    // Let's see if we've made a request - if we do, we should alter our output
slightly
```

```php
    $requestMade = false;
    $requestSuccessful = false;


if (!empty($_GET['requestfile'])) {
    $requestMade = true;
    // Get the filename
        $strRequestFilename = $_GET['requestfile'];
    // Check this file actually exists
    $strFullPath = $strMyMP3Directory . "/" . $strRequestFilename;
    }
    if (@filesize($strFullPath) > 0) {
        $requestSuccessful = true;
        // It's all worked - let's email the DJ
        mail($strMyDJsEmailAddress, "New song request", "A request has been
made for: " . $strFullPath);
    } else {
        $requestSuccessful = false;
    }

?>
<HTML>
    <HEAD>
        <SCRIPT LANGUAGE="Javascript" SRC="TreeMenu.js"></SCRIPT>
    </HEAD>
    <BODY>
        <H1>Radio PHP</H1>
        <?php
            if ($requestMade) {
        ?>
        <B>Thanks for your request!</B>
        <BR><BR>
            <?php
                if ($requestSuccessful) {
            ?>
            You'll be pleased to hear your request was successful, and we'll
try and play your song as soon as we can.

            <?php
                } else {
            ?>
            Unfortunately we weren't able to play the song you
requested. We may have just recently removed it from our collection.
Please feel free to try again!
            <?php
                };
            ?>
        <BR><BR>
        <?php
            };
        ?>
        <?php
            if (!($requestSuccessful)) {
        ?>
```

```
        Request your song from our list below and it will be emailed to our
DJ - if we've not played it too recently we'll try and incorporate it for
you as soon as we can!
        <HR>
        <?php
            $objTreeMenu->printMenu();
        ?>
    <?php
        };
    ?>
  </BODY>
</HTML>
```

Navigate to `radiorequest.php`, and you'll see something like what's shown in Figure 14-4.

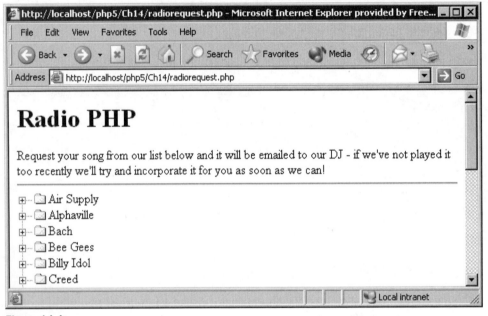

Figure 14-4

Expanding one of the links and clicking it displays the message shown in Figure 14-5, assuming you have your mail settings in order (`sendmail_path` setting in your `php.ini` file).

How It Works: radiogeneratexml.php

Now you've seen the source in full, so let's now go through `radiogeneratexml.php` step by step.

Strictly speaking, you're sending XML, not HTML, to the client, so you should tell the client to expect it (not that PHP's built-in HTTP request object really cares) by using the correct Content Type HTTP header:

```
header("Content-Type: text/xml\n\n");
```

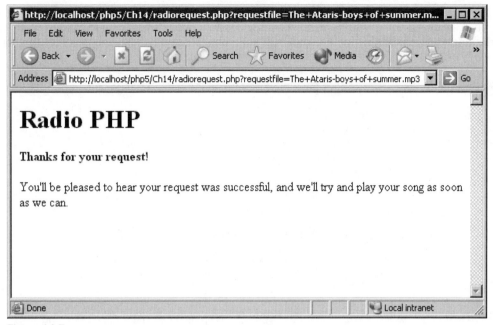

Figure 14-5

It's very important that no white space outside of delimiting <?php and ?> tags comes before this header, because the second you incorporate any non-PHP code—even a space or carriage return—PHP helpfully sends a text/html content type header, and you're committed to using it.

Then, include your PEAR class (MP3_ID):

```
require_once 'MP3/Id.php';
```

In this file you're simply outputting plain XML so you don't need to include the HTML_TreeMenu class.

Now let's start listing the contents of your MP3 folder. Change the constant to reflect wherever you keep your MP3s (for this example to work, you need to have at least three in there). Then use a slightly modified version of your code from the earlier MP3_ID project to create a one-dimensional array of all the MP3s—by filename—in that folder:

```
static $strMyMP3Directory = "/home/ed/mp3"; # Change this to your MP3 directory!
$objDir = dir($strMyMP3Directory);
$intNumFiles = 0;
$arMP3Files = Array();

while (false !== ($strEntry = $objDir->read())) {
    if (eregi("\.mp3$", $strEntry)) {
        $arMP3Files[] = $strMyMP3Directory . "/" . $strEntry;
    };
};
```

So far, so good.

You're ready to put your linear collection of MP3 files to use. Because the physical structure of what you're creating is going to be on an artist-by-artist basis, it makes sense to try to amass a single array of all the individual artists that comprise your MP3 collection. There may be thousands of files in there, but with a bit of luck, there should only a hundred or so distinct artists.

Retrieving the artist name of each file is your first use of the MP3_ID class:

```
$objMP3ID = new MP3_Id();
$arArtists = Array();
$arTestArtists = Array();
for ($i=0; $i<=sizeof($arMP3Files)-1; $i++) {
    $strPath = $arMP3Files[$i];
        $intResult = $objMP3ID->read ($strPath);
        $strArtist = $objMP3ID->getTag ("artists", "Unknown Artist");
        $strTestArtist = strtoupper(preg_replace("/[^A-Za-z0-9]/", "",
$strArtist));
        if (in_array($strTestArtist, $arTestArtists) == false) {
                array_push($arArtists, $strArtist);
                array_push($arTestArtists, $strTestArtist);
        };
};
```

Note that you create two arrays —arArtists, which holds the actual artist names, and arTestArtists, which holds a mangled version of each artist's name, whereby we have made it all-capitals, and stripped out any characters (including spaces) other than A–Z and 0–9. You do this for a very good reason: you want to make certain each MP3 file's artist appears only once. By stripping away spaces and punctuation, and standardizing capitalization, you can test the artist name extracted from the IDv3 tag against those we have already witnessed in the lifespan of the loop, with a great deal of certainty.

Consider the fictional artist Extreme Metal Grinding for a moment. Let's say that you have three MP3 files purportedly by this artist, which have been encoded on three separate dates, by three separate pieces of software. The artist could easily be represented by three slightly different ways in the tag, such as Extreme Metal Grinding, EXTREME 'Metal' Grinding, and Extreme Metalgrinding. By performing the regular expression and conversion to uppercase in the statement $strTestArtist = strtoupper (preg_replace("/[^A-Za-z0-9]/", "", $strArtist)) on each of these tags, you always arrive at the same result: EXTREMEMETALGRINDING. This may not look too nice on screen, but it's great to test against to establish membership of this particular group of artists.

So you loop through each MP3 file, retrieving the artist tag and applying the regular expression to it. You check to see whether this mangled artist name appears in your test array. If it doesn't, you add to both the test array (using the mangled artist name) and the real artist array (using the unsullied artist name). If it does, there's no need to add it again.

Now you get to the clever bit, which is where you push every song you've captured into a single hash. The output you want to create is going to be keyed by unique artists, so it makes sense to have an associative array with those artist names as keys. In terms of what to use as a value, there will almost certainly be more than one song by each artist, so the value of your hash is another linear array, with each slot in the array representing a single song. Because you want to store both the actual title and the filename of each song, you split each slot using another hash. The resulting data structure is quite complex (take a look with var_dump() if you're curious), but it is perfect for producing XML, and it makes the code in radiorequest.php very simple indeed.

You loop through each of the artists you established in the array you have just created, as shown in the following code:

```
$arTracks = Array();
$arAlreadyAccountedForSongIndices = Array();
for ($i=0; $i<=sizeof($arArtists)-1; $i++) {
    $strArtistName = $arArtists[$i];
    $strTestArtistName = $arTestArtists[$i];
    $arTracks[$strArtistName] = Array();
    for ($j=0; $j<=sizeof($arMP3Files)-1; $j++) {
        if (in_array($j, $arAlreadyAccountedForSongIndices) == false) {
            $strPath = $arMP3Files[$j];
            $intResult = $objMP3ID->read ($strPath);
            $strThisArtist = $objMP3ID->getTag ("artists", "Unknown Artist");
            $strThisTestArtist = strtoupper(preg_replace("/[^A-Za-z0-9]/", "",
$strThisArtist));
            if ($strThisTestArtist == $strTestArtistName) {
                array_push($arAlreadyAccountedForSongIndices, $j);
                $arSongHash["TITLE"]=$objMP3ID->getTag("name","UnknownTitle");
                $strSongFilename = str_replace("$strMyMP3Directory" . "/", "",
$arMP3Files[$j]);
                $arSongHash["LINK"] = "radiorequest.php?requestfile=" .
urlencode($strSongFilename);
                array_push($arTracks[$strArtistName], $arSongHash);
            };
        };
    };
};
```

Essentially, you loop through your list of artists (the proper list instead of the test list) and establish a key in your hash based on the artist name.

Then for each key, you loop through your entire list of MP3s and test to see whether each MP3 is authored by that artist. You use the artist name held at the corresponding index of your test list, and test it against the artist name of the MP3 file, passing it through the regular expression first. Again, this means that deviations in spacing, punctuation, and capitalization are ignored.

Because you're looping through the entire collection to determine what each artist has and hasn't written, this script could become quite resource-intensive, even slow. So a clever feature is introduced to improve performance. Each index of the MP3 array ($arMP3Files) needs to be linked to an artist just once—after all, an MP3 can be written only by a single artist—at least insofar as an IDv3 tag is concerned. A check is made of the index you're searching, and if it's already linked to an artist, there's no point wasting time on that index. As soon as you positively establish a given MP3 file (at index j in your original $arMP3Files array), you add that index j to a further array, called $arAlreadyAccountedForSongIndices. The result is that you can choose not to test that MP3 file on subsequent iterations if you've already established that it's been written by a given artist. This greatly increases performance by limiting the number of IDv3 reads that have to be performed throughout the script.

If the artist name of the track you're testing matches the artist whose authorship you're currently assessing, you add a suitable hash representing that track to the array of the current artist's key of the hash. The hash that you add consists of the title of the song, and a link to radiorequest.php offering its filename (less its path), the idea being that when that link is clicked, the user is positively asserting that she wants to hear that song. You use the `urlencode` function to ensure that the URL you generate is Web-browser friendly.

Finally, you use `ksort` to sort the array by its keys into alphabetical order. Much like `arsort`, which you used in the previous MP3_ID application, this sort maintains the intrinsic link between each key in an associative array and its value.

```
ksort($arTracks);
```

With your data structure in place, it's time to output it as XML.

Because the XML you're producing is incredibly simple, you won't take advantage of PHP5's built-in libxml-provided XML support to produce it. Instead, you're going to cheat and code it just as if it were HTML. If you feel strongly about this, feel free to rewrite the relevant routine to use libxml2 (see Chapter 8).

Quite simply, you recurse through the structure and output directly to the browser. Justification for the seemingly awkward data structure in the previous block of code should now be evident, in that you can convert your data structure to XML in just a few lines of code. In effect, you've made life slightly more complicated for yourself so that life can be slightly easier in producing your XML. This is a good thing; should you need to tweak the XML later for some reason, because you can easily do so without disrupting many lines of complex logic.

The following code prints the XML to the browser:

```
<treemenu>
<? foreach ($arTracks as $artist_name => $arHash) { ?>
    <node text="<?=$artist_name?>" icon="folder.gif">
<? for ($i=0; $i<=sizeof($arHash)-1; $i++) { ?>
        <node text="<?=htmlentities($arHash[$i]["TITLE"])?>" icon="document.gif"
link="<?=htmlentities($arHash[$i]["LINK"])?>" />
<? }; ?>
    </node>
<? }; ?>
</treemenu>
```

You use `htmlentities` when rendering both values (title and link) to ensure that you are fully XML-compliant. This might screw up the link URL in literal terms, but the parser in the HTMLTree_Menu component will fix this for you.

If you like, go ahead and request `radiogeneratexml.php` using your Web browser. If you want to force Internet Explorer to render it as XML (which makes it prettier to read, and lets you expand and collapse individual nodes) you can use the following URL trick:

```
http://your_server_name/radiogeneratexml.php/.xml
```

The Web server ignores the extraneous /.xml at the end, but Internet Explorer thinks you're definitely requesting an XML page, and so does its pretty rendering. (Quite why it doesn't just look at the MIME header that you took so much trouble to issue at the start of your script is beyond me.)

If you want to be really sure things are working, you can copy and paste the XML output here into `treemenutest.xml` and check out `treemenutest.php` again. To retrieve it, simply open the preceding URL in your own Web browser. You should see XML rendered in your browser window, and you should be able to pick out some of your own MP3 files within the XML data structure. If all looks good, you're more than half way there.

How it Works: radiorequest.php

`radiorequest.php` is by far the simpler of the two files. If you can get your head around how `radiogeneratexml.php` works, you'll probably be fine here.

Let's go through it together just to be on the safe side.

You kick off with some constants:

```php
<?php
    static $strMyMP3Directory = "/home/ed/mp3";     # Change to your MP3 dir!
    static $strMyDJsEmailAddress = "ed@example.com";
?>
```

You should probably replace the e-mail address with something sensible here, and insert the directory on your Web server where you keep your MP3s, as you did in the XML generation script.

If you really don't have any MP3s anywhere, and you'd like to download some to play with (within copyright limitations, of course) check out www.iuma.com. If you want to play with the MP3s' IDv3 tags, download Winamp (www.winamp.com), which is an MP3 player that also enables you to edit the IDv3 tags of the songs in your play list.

Next, you include your PEAR objects. No need to mess with MP3_ID here—just the HTML_Treemenu and helper components:

```php
require_once('HTML/TreeMenu.php');
require_once('xmlhtmltree.phpm');
```

You use some trickery to work out the URL of the XML generator script. In the example script, you can assume it's on your own server, in the same folder as wherever you saved the generator script. You know the URL of the request script, because it's being called by the user. The correct URL for the generator script is going to be identical to that, except the word `request` will be replaced with `generatexml`. You use a bit of search and replace to make that word change, and get the URL of your generator script as a result.

Once you have the URL, you retrieve its contents just as you would a file on your own file system—PHP is smart enough to request the URL for you. You then feed the output XML you receive straight into the HTML_TreeMenu object just as you did at the beginning of the chapter. Here's a code snippet demonstrating this:

```php
$strXMLURL = "http://" . $_SERVER["SERVER_NAME"] . str_replace("request",
"generatexml", $_SERVER["SCRIPT_NAME"]);

$strXML = implode ('', file($strXMLURL));

$objXMLTree = new XMLHTMLTree("", $strXML);
$objXMLTree->GenerateHandOffs();
```

```
$objXMLTree->ParseXML();
$objTreeMenu = $objXMLTree->GetTreeHandoff();
```

Next, you include the conditional logic telling the script what to do if you are passed a chosen song to request. Remember in our output XML, how we generated links for our tree that looked like:

```
/radiorequest.php?requestfile=9991885931037.mp3
```

The `radiorequest.php` script actually fulfills two functions: it displays the tree of MP3 files, and it displays your "thank you" message if the request is successful. You must account for requests for this PHP script that include the parameter `requestfile`, which specifies the filename of the MP3 being requested. Not only do you want to know if a request has been made, but you want to know if that request was valid. You do this through a fairly cursory check to see whether the file exists:

```
$requestMade = false;
$requestSuccessful = false;
if (!empty($_GET['requestfile']))
{
    $requestMade = true;
    $strRequestFilename = $_GET["requestfile"];
    $strFullPath = $strMyMP3Directory . "/" . $strRequestFilename;
    if (@filesize($strFullPath) > 0) {
```

Notice that you test for the existence of the file by calculating what its full path would be were you to open it, and then using the `filesize` function to test its size. A size greater than one indicates that the file does exist. You use the @ operator because PHP considers a nonexistent file in calls to `filesize` to be a critical error, worthy of ceasing script execution—which, of course, isn't something you particularly want to happen.

If the file exists, you mark the request as successful and go ahead and e-mail the DJ, using the constant you defined at the top of the file as the target e-mail address:

```
            $requestSuccessful = true;
            // It's all worked - let's email the DJ
            mail($strMyDJsEmailAddress, "New song request", "A request has been
made for: " .
$strFullPath);
        } else {
            $requestSuccessful = false;
        };
    };
```

The `mail()` function lets you specify a target e-mail address, subject line, and message body—and much more, which you'll learn about in Chapter 15.

With your logic taken care of, you can commence your display logic—that is, rendering something that the user can actually see.

Notice that a combination of $requestMade and $requestSuccessful is used to determine what to display. If no request has been made, you invite the user to make a request and show the HTML_TreeMenu component. If a request has been made and it is not successful, you explain that to the user and invite him to try again, showing the HTML_TreeMenu component. If a request has been made and it is successful, you thank the user, but don't show the HTML_TreeMenu component because, for the sake of this exercise, we assume that the user does not want to request another title. In practice, some greater security, perhaps using cookies, would be required should the radio station genuinely want to limit the number of requests that an individual user is able to make each day.

Here's the display logic:

```
<HTML>
    <HEAD>
        <SCRIPT LANGUAGE="Javascript" SRC="TreeMenu.js"></SCRIPT>
    </HEAD>
    <BODY>
        <H1>Radio PHP</H1>
        <?php
            if ($requestMade) {
        ?>
        <B>Thanks for your request!</B>
        <BR><BR>
            <?php
                if ($requestSuccessful) {
            ?>
            You'll be pleased to hear your request was successful, and we'll
try to play your song as soon as we can.
            <?php
                } else {
            ?>
            Unfortunately we weren't able to play the song you requested.
We may have just recently removed it from our collection. Please feel
free to try again!
            <?php
                };
            ?>
        <BR><BR>
        <?php
            };
        ?>
        <?php
            if (!($requestSuccessful)) {
        ?>
            Request your song from our list below and it will be emailed to our
DJ - if we've not played it too recently we'll try to incorporate it for you
as soon as we can!
            <HR>
            <?php
                $objTreeMenu->printMenu();
            ?>
        <?php
            };
        ?>
    </BODY>
</HTML>
```

The menu is rendered exactly the same way that it was in the example at the start of the chapter.

Finally, don't forget to include the JavaScript file required by the HTML_TreeMenu component at the top of your HTML—it's a prerequisite.

Summary

In this chapter, you were introduced to PEAR, the PHP Extension and Application Repository.

You discovered how to browse the PEAR Web site to identify suitable packages for use in your applications, and how to download and add those packages into an installation of PHP. You also picked up a decent grasp of how the PEAR project is structured, which should make it easier for you to find what you're looking for in the future.

You also found out how to explore the interface of a new PEAR component and assess its feasibility for incorporation in your project—and you've been forewarned about some of the idiosyncrasies of PEAR packages and how to overcome them.

You refreshed your knowledge of the PEAR coding standards adhered to throughout this book, as well as examining the rationale behind them.

Finally, you met the challenge of producing a functional, useful application using a number of PEAR packages.

In the next chapter, you look at PHP's built-in e-mail functionality, and put your newfound knowledge of PEAR to use as you examine a handful of packages that provide some sophisticated mail processing and dispatch functions.

PHP5 and E-Mail

One of the simplest and most common requirements for a PHP application is to send e-mail. E-mail has become, in a very short space of time, one of the most popular means of communication and naturally PHP provides the functionality to implement e-mail within your applications. The nitty-gritty of how Internet mail works can be quite complex, and much of the complexity doesn't even come from your PHP programs, but rather the various technologies, platforms and protocols that are used to get mail from one point to the next. Luckily, you can begin using PHP and e-mail with just a few simple functions.

In this chapter you explore some of the technical background behind sending e-mail before learning the basic setup required for sending mail from Windows and Linux platforms. Of course, understanding how PHP5 communicates with your mail server is pretty important, and to help you understand this, you create a simple mail sending application, utilizing the mail() function. Finally, you examine a method of producing different types of content within your e-mails using MIME (Multipurpose Internet Mail Extension).

E-Mail Background

To use the most common PHP functions, PHP must be running on an operating system (such as Windows or Linux), and have the services of Web server software available. For e-mail functions, PHP must also have access to an MTA (Mail Transport Agent) such as Sendmail, server software that sends and receives e-mail.

> *Although there is a mail() function in PHP that sends e-mail, there is not (as yet) a released version of any PHP functions or extensions that receive e-mail. A mailparse extension is in the works.*

The most common MTA used with PHP is Sendmail; if your server administrator is using Sendmail, you might not even be aware of it—you just use the mail() function and it works. As a prelude to a discussion of mail(), the following section covers some of the technical issues associated with Internet mail protocols, but if your interest is primarily sending mail and the mail function works, you might want to skip straight to the *"Building a Simple PHP E-Mail Application"* section.

Internet Mail Protocols

Like any other communications across the Internet, there are protocols involved in mail transmission. Internet protocols are based on Requests For Comment (RFCs) that, when adopted, form a mutually-agreed-upon language for effecting the communications in question. Sending e-mail on the Internet is based on Simple Mail Transfer Protocol (SMTP), RFC 821, by Jonathan B. Postel. RFC 821 was later updated as RFC 2821 by the Network Working Group, edited by J. Klensen of AT&T Laboratories, in 2001.

The communications model (the conceptual structure for communications) is that the user (and the user's file system) uses a client (an e-mail program such as Outlook or Eudora) to hook up (in technical terms, establish a two-way transmission channel) with an SMTP server. The server then relays the message to the appropriate receiving SMTP server (based on a domain name lookup of the ending portion of the e-mail address). It is the responsibility of the receiving SMTP server to place the message in the appropriate spot (commonly called a mailbox or popbox) or otherwise perform the appropriate functions.

That gets your mail from one server to the next. What about actually retrieving your mail from the server? There are a couple of protocols that are used in this case—POP3 and IMAP servers are the most common. These perform some sort of authentication before retrieving mail from a remote mail server. It's like your having a post office box, giving someone your mailbox key, and having him fetch your mail—if you give him the right key, he brings you your mail.

Structure of an E-Mail Message

An appropriately structured e-mail message has headers followed by the body of the message, and may also include separate files as attachments. The headers include the e-mail address to which the message is being sent, the e-mail address from which the message is being sent, the subject of the message, a list of recipients to be sent copies of the message, a message ID, and a message body. Not all of these headers are required, and some may be user-defined, making them easy to forge.

RFC 2822 provides definition for the composition of Internet e-mail messages. (If you would like to look through some of the RFCs, you can find them at www.faqs.org/rfcs/.) It defines a message as being composed of US-ASCII characters divided into lines of characters with each line ending in a carriage return and line feed (CRLF). The header fields are lines of characters separated by a special syntax, and the body of the message follows the headers, separated by a blank line (a line with nothing before the CRLF).

A header field is a line of characters containing the field name, a colon, and the field body. Header fields don't have to be in any particular order. The only required field is From, which contains the origination date and originator address. Available header fields include:

Header Field	Description
Trace	Includes resent-date, resent-from, resent-to, and so on, and is used when a message is resent (For example, when the first delivery attempt is made but not completed, your mail server may attempt to resend at a later time)
From	Required. It contains the address of the sender, but note that even if this field is included, there's no guarantee of its accuracy. If this field contains

Header Field	Description
	more than one address, the sender field is required with a single address. The origination date is included in the data for this field. Note that this is not the same as the optional From: field
Sender	Contains a single address from which mail is being sent
Reply-to	Contains an optional reply-to address
To	Contains a comma-separated list of addresses to which the message is sent
Cc	Contains a comma-separated list of addresses to which copies of the messages are sent
Bcc	Contains a comma-separated list of addresses to which copies of the message are sent, while preventing other recipients from seeing or knowing that any particular Bcc recipient received the message (may be handled with various levels of security)
Message-id	Optional, but every message should have one. It contains a unique message identifier
In-reply-to	Optional. One or more message identifiers
References	Optional. One or more message identifiers
Subject	Optional. Contains a short string identifying the subject of the message
Comments	Optional. Comments about the body of the message
Keywords	Optional. Keywords, comma-separated, that the user might find important
Optional	Optional. It only needs to comply with the formatting instructions included in RFC 2822. Its content is unspecified

Here's an example message with headers and body (the body has been truncated to save space), in text format. This message was received and displayed as a Web page, in HTML, although only the text is included here. Note the From header line, with the name of the mailing program user (in this case it's mailer@mailer.lindows.com) and the origination date; the Received: line, which shows the IP address and lineage of the e-mail message; and the To:, Date:, From:, and Subject: lines (the From:, with the colon, is not the same as the beginning From line).

```
From mailer@mailer.lindows.com Thu Jan 22 17:52:58 2004
Received: from [130.94.123.236] (helo=mailer.lindows.com)
    by mail1.servata.com with esmtp (Exim 3.35 #1 (Debian))
    id 1AjqVG-0005LN-00
    for <info@servata.com>; Thu, 22 Jan 2004 17:52:58 -0800
Received: (qmail 30557 invoked by uid 99); 23 Jan 2004 01:23:04 -0000
To: info@servata.com
Date: Thu, 22 Jan 2004 16:23:43 -0800
From: Michael Robertson <mailer@mailer.lindows.com>
Subject: Michael's Minute: Disagree with Linus
MIME-Version: 1.0
Content-Type: multipart/alternative;
```

```
        boundary="-----=_LINDOWS_34a8357a5a341381f6a48042673dcb9c"
Message-Id: <E1AjqVG-0005LN-00@mail1.servata.com>

Lindows.com Michael's MinuteFrom: Michael Robertson [mailer@mailer.lindows.com]
Sent: Thursday, January 22, 2004 4:24 PM
To: info@servata.com
Subject: Michael's Minute: Disagree with Linus
        If this message is not displaying properly, click here to launch it in
your browser.

        Michael's Minute: Disagree with Linus

I've never personally met Linus Torvalds, the much heralded man behind Linux.
...
some computer manufacturers are now shipping computers preinstalled with
desktop Linux through major retailers, making it practical for average or
even new computer users to embrace Linux.
...
```

Sending E-Mail with PHP

There are few settings to deal with on both Windows and Linux installs before you can take a more practical look at how to implement e-mail.

For Windows, you will need to have access to an SMTP server—this can be your ISP's server if you are working on a personal machine. Open your php.ini file and go to the section entitled [mail function]. Set your SMTP setting like so:

```
SMTP = smtp.my.server.net
```

Then set your sendmail_from setting to reflect your e-mail address, like so:

```
sendmail_from = davidm@doggiestouch.co.za
```

Linux users need only set their sendmail_path option in php.ini like this:

```
sendmail_path = smtp.my.server.net
```

That's it. Now you can use the mail() function to send an e-mail.

Using the mail() Function

The mail() function is Boolean, meaning that you can use an if statement to check whether it performed its function successfully. It takes as arguments an address to send to, a subject, a body, and any additional mail headers you want to send. Code such as this, in which you send the e-mail address to send to, the subject, and a message body composed of three lines separated by newline characters (the \n) will work:

```
If (mail("joeblow@example.com", "The Subject", "First line\nSecond line
\nThird line")) {
    //tell the user the email was sent
} else {
    //tell the user there was an error
}
```

Send an E-Mail

The mail() function sends e-mail through the default MTA when called in your PHP application. Logically, it requires at least a To e-mail address, a Subject, and a message (commonly called body). To add a From e-mail address (or other additional information), you can include additional headers when formatting your e-mail. Try this out in a little script called mail.php (remember to substitute an appropriate e-mail address in the $to variable—send this one to yourself):

```php
<?php
$to = "edit@contechst.com";
$subject = "Your email has been sent!";
$body = "This is a test";
if(mail($to,$subject,$body)){
    echo "<b>PHP has sent your email<b>";
}
?>
```

Assuming your connection and SMTP server are all up and running correctly, a confirmation message is printed to your screen. Bear in mind, that just because the e-mail was sent successfully doesn't mean it will be received. There are a number of things that could prevent the mail from arriving—the e-mail address you sent to may not be an actual address on the receiving server, the receiving server could be temporarily down, and so on.

How It Works

PHP5's mail() function enables you to send e-mail messages by calling the function and specifying several arguments (such as the e-mail address to send to). It is a Boolean function, meaning it returns true if successful (the mail was sent) and false if not. You can specify the arguments as text strings or as variables containing the appropriate data.

Assuming all went well, you receive the e-mail you sent. Figure 15-1 shows the result.

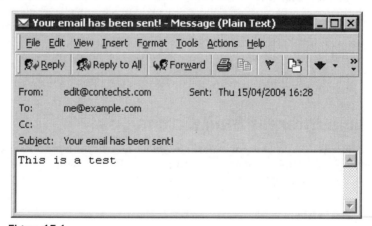

Figure 15-1

Let's take a look at each argument accepted by the mail() function.

The To: header is automatically added by the function, and the data inserted is taken from the first argument. You can hard code this in, accept it as a variable generated by a form submission (you'll see this a little later), or capture it from entries in a database or other data source. You can specify more than one recipient in this field by putting a comma (no space) between the e-mail addresses (the comma must be inside the quotes containing the e-mail addresses, otherwise it would be interpreted by the mail() function as the next argument).

The subject of your e-mail message is automatically taken from the second argument in the function. Again, you can hard code it in, accept it as a variable generated by a form submission, or insert it from any data source. Of course, it would be a little strange to send each recipient a different subject (unless perhaps you are a spammer), but it could certainly be done.

The body of your message is composed of text, and you might want to add a salutation and an ending (such as regards and your name/title). But the body is just text, and any beginnings, endings, or other components you add can be done just using the concatenation operator (.) to build a larger body.

Additional headers, such as the From: field, can be added as text strings as a fourth argument to the mail() function. Each argument takes the form of a header beginning with the appropriate keyword followed by a colon, such as From:. After that, a string containing the sender's name and the sender's e-mail address (in angle brackets) is inserted, followed by a carriage return and line feed. The following code shows how to assemble the From: header:

```
"From: $sender_name <$from>\r\n"
```

If other headers are to be added, they can each be assembled in a variable named $headers, so long as they end with the carriage return and line feed.

Some UNIX MTAs may work with just a single newline (\n).

The simple mail-sending application you develop later in this chapter uses e-mail addresses inserted one at a time, but for more sophisticated applications (such as an e-mail newsletter manager) you might use a looping structure such as a for loop or do while loop to process many e-mails at a time. The source of your e-mail address list could be entries in a database, an .xml file, or even a simple text file.

So far, so good. But what if you want to add an attachment to your e-mail—or send something other than plain text? Well, there are ways to do these, so read on.

Multipurpose Internet Mail Extensions

Multipurpose Internet Mail Extensions (MIME) extends e-mail beyond plain text by enabling you to specify the content type and encoding for your messages. RFC 2045 defines MIME, and you can read about it at www.faqs.org/rfcs/rfc2045.html.

MIME Header Fields

Like the basic text e-mail protocol, MIME includes header fields to define the content and structure of e-mail messages that contain nonstandard text content, as well as attached files. Header fields include:

❏   MIME Version: Indicates that the overall message complies with this RFC if version is 1.0.

❏   Content-Type: Indicates the media type of the message body or attached file. Lack of content-type header indicates the type is plain text. For example, to send e-mail messages in HTML format (very popular these days), you need to set the headers for MIME-version and Content-type as follows:

```
$headers .= "MIME-Version: 1.0 \n";

$headers .= "Content-type: text/html; charset=iso-8859-1 \n";
```

❏   Content-Transfer-Encoding: Indicates the encoding mechanism for the data, such as base64 for image file data.

❏   Content-Id (optional, with exceptions): Uniquely identifies MIME identities, allowing one body to identify the other.

❏   Content-Description (optional): Text description of the content.

❏   Content-Disposition Header: Recommends to the client application how to treat the part of the message for which the current headers apply. This header can be set to `attachment` or `inline`, and as these terms imply, that part of the message will either be presented as an attached file or will be displayed inline. Inline display is useful for HTML e-mails with included images.

Multipart MIME

MIME also provides for sending e-mails with attachments. These are known as multipart MIME messages, because the MIME section is split into multiple parts, each with its own MIME headers. The overall MIME Content-Type is multipart/mixed, but each subsection may be individually set for its own type, such as text/html and so on.

Boundary Marker

Part of building multipart MIME e-mail messages is the construction of a boundary marker. When composing a message, a parameter (called *boundary*) in the Content-Type header is set equal to an arbitrarily defined text string. This text string is simply made up, but you should not create a boundary that might logically be found in the body of the message (such as a common word). You may want to incorporate the md5 () function into the construction of your boundary marker, perhaps using the value of the current time and some arbitrary text. This is highly unlikely to ever be encountered as part of the body of the message.

Just examine the multipart MIME message sections that are shown here. Note how the boundary is defined and then used to separate the various parts of the overall message.

```
//beginning header

MIME-Version: 1.0
Content-Type: multipart/mixed; boundary="0000_PHP5_0000";
Content-Transfer-Encoding: 7bit

This part of the E-mail should not be visible to the reader of the email, so
long as they are using a MIME-compatible email client.

--0000_PHP5_0000
```

```
//text header

Content-Type: text/plain; charset="iso-8859-1"
Content-Transfer-Encoding: 7bit

This is the body of the message, and should be readable in plain text.

--0000_PHP5_0000

//attached image header

Content-Type: image/jpeg; name="myimage.jpg";
Content-Transfer-Encoding: base64
Content-Disposition: attachment

<base64 encoded data for the myimage.jpg image>

--0000_PHP5_0000

//inline image header

Content-Type: image/jpeg; name="myimage.jpg";
Content-Transfer-Encoding: base64
Content-Disposition: inline

<base64 encoded data for the myimage.jpg image>

--0000_PHP5_0000
```

HTML E-Mails

Although ordinary e-mail message bodies are plain text, you can set the MIME headers so that your message body is sent in HTML format. In the application you create later in this chapter, a radio button is provided so that the user can choose to send plain text or HTML messages. If HTML format is selected, the application sets the MIME headers to properly specify a Content-Type of text\html.

In addition to properly setting the headers for HTML format, the application includes a very nice tool for the user to create HTML code interspersed with text and images. This tool is a JavaScript named htmlArea, created and freely distributed by interactivetools.com, Inc. A little bit of the code for inserting this tool is shown in the Web page side of the application, although the main source code for the tool isn't included. However, you can easily download all the code and images that make up the tool from www.interactivetools.com. It isn't related to any PHP mail functions, but it's very handy for enabling users to visually create HTML-formatted e-mail message bodies.

PEAR Mail Libraries

The PEAR repository contains several classes that can be used to create objects for working with e-mail. You may need to install the PEAR libraries to get them to work with your PHP scripts (see Chapter 14 for more information on PEAR).

Once they are installed, you can dabble with new instances of PEAR mail objects. The PEAR mail classes include:

- ❏ `Mail`: Sends e-mail using the built-in PHP `mail()` function.
- ❏ `Mail_IMAP`: Provides a c-client backend for Web mail.
- ❏ `Mail_Mbox`: Mbox PHP class to Unix MBOX parsing and using.
- ❏ `Mail_Mime`: Provides classes to create and decode mime messages.
- ❏ `Mail_Queue`: Enables mail to be put in queues and sent later in background.

Building a Simple PHP E-Mail Application

The application you build in this section is capable of composing and sending e-mail using the PHP `mail()` function and MIME—assuming Sendmail is installed. In order for the application to send e-mails with multiple files attached, the files must reside on the local server. Because you created a simple application that lets users upload files to the server in Chapter 7, it's assumed that the file upload portion of the application has already been run by the user, and that the necessary files have been placed in the `atts` folder.

With that done, the application reads the files and enables the user to pick (from a list) one or more files to send with the e-mail. When sending HTML-formatted e-mail, the user can specify filenames that are present in the `atts` folder and send those along with the e-mail for display inline in the message.

When the application opens in your browser, it displays a Web page constructed with HTML. JavaScript is added in the `<head>` element of the page to help create a visual HTML editing text area. After the `</head>`, the `<body>` element begins, and a `<table>` encompasses the entire form. Later, as you'll see, another chunk of JavaScript in the form element actually calls this first script to create the text area if the user is using Internet Explorer 5.5 or better. So fire up your HTML editor and begin entering the following code. You'll be adding to it as you explore the functions of the various parts of the application:

```
<html>
  <head>
    <title>PHP Mail Functions</title>
      <meta http-equiv="Content-Type" content="text/html; charset=iso-8859-1">
      <script language="Javascript1.2"><!-- // load htmlarea
      _editor_url = "http://www.bigtip.com/php5/Chapter15/htmlarea/"; // URL to
      htmlarea files var win_ie_ver =
      parseFloat(navigator.appVersion.split("MSIE")[1]);
if (navigator.userAgent.indexOf('Mac')         >= 0) { win_ie_ver = 0; }
if (navigator.userAgent.indexOf('Windows CE')>= 0) { win_ie_ver = 0; }
if (navigator.userAgent.indexOf('Opera')       >= 0) { win_ie_ver = 0; }
if (win_ie_ver >= 5.5) {
   document.write('<scr' + 'ipt src="' +_editor_url+ 'editor.js"');
   document.write(' language="Javascript1.2"></scr' + 'ipt>');
} else { document.write('<scr'+'ipt>function editor_generate() {
         return false; }</scr'+'ipt>');
}
// --></script>

</head>
```

```
<body bgcolor="#FFFFFF">
<table width="100%" border="0" cellpadding="10">
  <tr>
    <td>
      <h2>Using PHP to Send Email</h2>
```

This is the logical place to begin the form within the HTML. Because the form needs to display a list of files ready to be sent as attachments from the `atts` folder to which they've been uploaded, you need to initialize the `$default_directory` variable to contain the folder name. You do this in PHP:

```
<?php
$default_dir = "atts";
```

You don't want the main PHP processing code to run unless the user has already seen the form, filled it out, and submitted it, so you use the `$_POST[posted]` variable within an `if` statement condition to test whether the form has been submitted; if it has, the PHP code can begin formatting an e-mail message to be sent.

If the form hasn't been posted, the `if` statement condition is `false` (`$_POST[posted]` is not set), and the entire PHP processing code is bypassed, displaying the HTML form to the user instead. It should be clear that the first time the user opens the page, and anytime the user refreshes the page without clicking the Submit button, the form will be displayed and the main PHP processing code will not run.

Check to see if the form was submitted, and if so, compose the sender's name into a single variable:

```
if (!empty($_POST)) {
    $sender_name = $_POST['first_name'] . " " . $_POST['last_name'];
```

Check to see what type of e-mail is being sent (an HTML message or with attachments or the default plain text) using the value of the radio button named `html_or_text`:

```
if ($_POST['html_or_text'] == "html") {
```

If the `html` value has been selected in the radio button, check to see if there are any attached files by examining the count value of the `$attachments` array:

```
if (count($_POST['attachments']) > 0) {
```

If there are attachments to send, initialize a counter variable (`$cnt`) to zero and create a boundary marker value for separating MIME headers:

```
$cnt = 0;
$boundary = "0000_PHP5_0000";
```

Then run through all the attached files, opening each of them, extracting the content, and creating the appropriate MIME header while splitting the content into chunks before closing the file:

```
for ($i = 0; $i < count($_POST['attachments']); $i++) {

    $fp = fopen($default_dir . "\\" .
            $_POST['attachments'][$i],"rb");
    $file_name = basename($_POST['attachments'][$i]);
    $content[$cnt] = fread($fp,filesize($default_dir . "/" .
            $_POST['attachments'][$i]));
    $files_attached = "";
    $files_attached.="--$boundary\n"
    ."Content-Type: image/jpeg; name=\"$file_name\"\n"
    ."Content-Transfer-Encoding: base64\n"
    ."Content-Disposition: inline; filename=\"$file_name\"\n\n"
    .chunk_split(base64_encode($content[$cnt]))."\n";
    $cnt++;
    fclose($fp);
}
```

With the attached files set up, create the From:, CC:, BCC:, and Reply-To: headers; the salutation, body and regards portion; and then the main MIME header (although an HTML-formatted e-mail may also contain attachments, ignore this possibility and just assume the main message is plain text):

```
$from_header = "From: $sender_name <$_POST[from]>\nCC:
    $_POST[cc] \nBCC: $_POST[bcc]\nReply-To: $_POST[from]\n";
$salutation = $_POST['salutation'] . "\n\n";
$body = $salutation . $_POST['body'] . "\n\n" . $_POST['regards'];

// Create the main MIME header, then add the body message and the
        //files attached
$files_attached .= "--".$boundary."\n";
$add_header = "";
$add_header .="MIME-Version: 1.0\n"   ."Content-Type:
        multipart/mixed; boundary=\"$boundary\"; Message-ID:
        <".md5($_POST['from'])."@example.com>";
$mail_content="--".$boundary."\n"
."Content-Type: text/plain; charset=\"iso-8859-1\"\n"
."Content-Transfer-Encoding: 8bit\n\n"
.$body."\n\n".$files_attached;

$body = $mail_content;
```

Notice that the $body variable is set to equivalent to all the $mail_content (because the $mail_content variable at this point actually contains the data in the $body and the $files_attached variables) with attached files. This is simply so you can insert the $body into the mail() function later.

If the e-mail message is formatted as HTML, use the following code to set up a few headers before sending the e-mail:

```
} else {
    $salutation = $_POST['salutation'];
    $salutation = $salutation . "<br><br>";
    $body = $salutation . stripslashes($_POST['body']) . "<br><br>" .
            $_POST['regards'];
```

```
      //Set HTML Headers
      $from_header = "From: $sender_name <$_POST[from]>\nCC:
          $_POST[cc]\nBCC: $_POST[bcc]\nReply-To: $_POST[from]\n";
      $add_header = "MIME-Version: 1.0\n";
      $add_header .= "Content-type: text/html; charset=iso-8859-1\n";
   }
```

If the e-mail is formatted as plain text, you also set up a few headers:

```
   } else {
      //for plain text with no attachments
      $from_header = "From: $sender_name <$_POST[from]> \nCC: $_POST[cc]\nBCC:
          $_POST[bcc]\nReply-To: $_POST[from]\n";
      $salutation = $_POST['salutation'];
      $salutation = $salutation . "\n\n";
      $body = $_POST['body'];
      $body = $salutation . $body . "\n\n" . $_POST['regards'];
   }
```

Compose the To: addresses into a single variable named $to:

```
$to = "$_POST[to]";

do{
     next($_POST);
}while (key($_POST) !== 'to');
for ($i = 1; $i <=7; $i++) {
   $next = next($_POST);
     if(!empty($next)){
     $to = $to . ", " . $next;
     }
}
```

Then do a minimal check to validate the e-mail address and send the e-mail, returning an error message if not sent or a bad e-mail address was encountered:

```
if (strpos($_POST['to'],"@") >= 0) {

      //Send the mail
      echo "<BR>To: $to<P>";
      echo "Subject: $_POST[subject]<P>";
      echo "Body: $body<P>";
      echo "$from_header<P>";
      echo "$add_header<P>";
      if(!isset($add_header)){
         if (mail($to, $_POST['subject'], $body)){
            echo "<h3>Your email has been sent</h3>";
         } else {
            echo "An error occurred, and your email has not been sent";
         }
         }else if (mail($to, $_POST['subject'], $body, "$from_header".
         "$add_header")) {
```

```
            echo "<h3>Your email has been sent</h3>";
        } else {
            echo "An error occurred, and your email has not been sent";
        }

        } else {
    echo "A bad email address was encountered";
        }
```

If you haven't posted any information, simply display the form that allows the user to enter his e-mail details:

```
} else {
?>

    <form method="POST" action="php_mail.php">
    <input type="hidden" name="posted" value="true">
        <table width="100%" border="1">
            <tr>
                <td width="16%" valign="top"><font face="Arial, Helvetica,
                sans-serif"
                size="-1"><b>Your Name:</b></font></td>
                <td width="84%"><font size="-1" face="Arial, Helvetica,
sans-serif"><b>First</b></font>
                    <input type="text" name="first_name">
                    <b><font size="-1" face="Arial, Helvetica, sans-
                    serif">Last</font></b>
                    <input type="text" name="last_name">
                </td>
            </tr>
            <tr>
                <td width="16%" valign="top"><b><font face="Arial,
                Helvetica, sans-serif" size="-1">From:</font></b></td>
                <td width="84%">
                    <input type="text" name="from">
                </td>
            </tr>
            <tr>
                <td width="16%" valign="top"><b><font face="Arial,
                Helvetica, sans-serif" size="-1">To:</font></b></td>
                <td width="84%">
                    <input type="text" name="to">
                    <input type="text" name="to01">
                    <input type="text" name="to02">
                    <input type="text" name="to03">
                    <input type="text" name="to04">
                    <input type="text" name="to05">
                    <input type="text" name="to06">
                    <input type="text" name="to07">
                </td>
            </tr>
            <tr>
```

```
                <td width="16%" valign="top"><b><font face="Arial,
                Helvetica, sans-serif" size="-1">CC:</font></b></td>
                <td width="84%">
                   <input type="text" name="cc">
                </td>
              </tr>
              <tr>
                <td width="16%" valign="top"><b><font face="Arial,
                Helvetica, sans-serif" size="-1">BCC:</font></b></td>
                <td width="84%">
                   <input type="text" name="bcc">
                </td>
              </tr>
              <tr>
                <td width="16%" valign="top"><b><font face="Arial,
                Helvetica, sans-serif" size="-1">Subject:</font></b></td>
                <td width="84%">
                   <input type="text" name="subject">
                </td>
              </tr>
              <tr>
                <td width="16%" valign="top"><b><font face="Arial,
                Helvetica, sans-serif" size="-1">Attachments:<br>
                   Use Ctrl-Click to remove selections</font></b></td>
                <TD width="84%">
                   <select name="attachments[]" size="4" multiple>
<?php

//fill the list box with available filenames
if(!($dp = opendir($default_dir))) {
   die("Cannot open $default_dir.");
} else {
   while($file = readdir($dp)) {
      if($file != '.' && $file != '..') {

?>
      <OPTION value="<?php echo $file; ?>"><?php echo $file; ?></option>
<?php

      }
   }
closedir($dp);
}
?>

                   </select>
                </td>
              </tr>
              <tr>
                <td width="16%" valign="top"><b><font face="Arial, Helvetica,
                sans-serif" size="-1">Salutation:</font></b></td>
                <td width="84%">
```

```
               <input type="text" name="salutation">
            </td>
         </tr>
         <tr>
            <td width="16%" valign="top"><b><font face="Arial,
            Helvetica, sans-serif" size="-1">Body:</font></b></td>
            <td width="84%">
               <textarea name="body" cols="40" rows="10"></textarea>
<script language="javascript1.2">
editor_generate('body');
</script>
            </td>
         </tr>
         <tr>
            <td width="16%" valign="top"><b><font face="Arial,
            Helvetica, sans-serif" size="-1">Regards:</font></b></td>
            <td width="84%">
               <input type="text" name="regards">
            </td>
         </tr>
         <tr>
            <td width="16%" valign="top"> </td>
            <td width="84%"> <font face="Arial, Helvetica, sans-serif"><b>
            <font
            size="-1">HTML
               or Attached Files
               <input type="radio" name="html_or_text" value="html">
               Plain Text
               <input type="radio" name="html_or_text" value="text" checked>
               <input type="submit" name="Submit" value="Send Email">
               </font> </b> </font> </td>
         </tr>
      </table>
</form>
<?php
}
?>
   </td>
  </tr>
</table>
</body>
</html>
?>
```

Save your file as php_mail.php and then open it in your browser. Figure 15-2 shows the initial screen.

Figure 15-3 shows the confirmation message you receive after you click Send Email.

Well, that's it, isn't it? Not quite...

You may notice that you kick up an error if you don't fill in certain fields—CC, or BCC and so on. In the exercises at the end of the chapter, you will need to modify the script so that you produce well-formed headers regardless of whether the user provides input.

Figure 15-2

Figure 15-3

Summary

You explored Internet e-mail protocols, the structure of e-mail messages, the `mail()` function and the arguments it takes, and how to send multipart and HTML-formatted e-mail messages with PHP. The example application serves as a good beginning for you to build on if you decide to implement some form of e-mail functionality on your own sites. This chapter has served as a basic grounding from which you can explore the intricacies of Internet mail.

You can find more information on e-mail at the International Mail Consortium, `www.imc.org`.

Exercise

The application you've created works well for composing and sending individual e-mails. For this exercise, modify the application so that it sends the e-mail to a list of e-mail addresses retrieved from a database.

Generating Graphics

Up to this point you've seen how the PHP language works—how to use the language to interact with the user, connect and manipulate databases, and e-mail your information off. There is, however, one aspect of the Web that we haven't yet touched on—adding graphics to your pages. I'm not talking about creating an image for your page using a graphics program, but rather using PHP to generate the graphic for you when the script runs. After all, you've just learned how to use data from a database to make your pages more dynamic, so why not make your images more dynamic as well?

PHP contains a range of functions that enable you to open, manipulate, and output graphics—both to the Web browser and to disk. In the course of this chapter you'll see how these functions work and how you can use them to create graphics for your pages. To begin, you'll explore some of the basic concepts that you need to understand before you create images: color theory and how image coordinate systems work in PHP, for example. Then using PHP's drawing tools, you'll learn to build own images from scratch, drawing lines, curves and other shapes on your images. You'll also see how you can work with existing images, such as applying watermarks to images, creating thumbnails, and adding text.

The image functions that PHP uses are based on the GD image library that is developed by Boutell.Com at (not surprisingly) www.boutell.com. In previous versions of PHP the GD library was used as-is within PHP, but since PHP4.3 the code for the GD library has been bundled with the PHP installation and includes some enhancements to the original code such as alpha blending. The bundled GD installation is better maintained for PHP and will therefore be more stable. The version of GD that is bundled along with PHP5 is version 2.0.15, and now that the patents for LZW compression are expiring, read-only support for the GIF file format is included. Besides the read-only GIF support, you also can read and write JPEG, PNG, and WBMP format files.

Basics of Computer Graphics

First, you need to explore some basic image-related concepts. You should understand some basics of color theory and the RGB color model, how you can position things within an image using the GD libraries, and a little bit about different image types.

Color Theory

Computers create colors using a color theory model called the RGB model. RGB stands for red, green and blue, the three basic colors that are combined to create color that you see on your monitors. The RGB model is known as an *additive color model* because different amounts of red, green, and blue are combined together to create the final color. Each of the values of red, green, and blue can range from a minimum of 0 to a maximum of 255, and colors are defined by the three values. A pure blue color would have an RGB value of 0,0,255—the red and green values are empty (0) and the blue value is set to the maximum of 255. The maximum number of colors that you can therefore find in an RGB image is 16.7 million colors—$256 \times 256 \times 256$.

When each of the red, green, and blue components is set to 0, you have a complete absence of color—black. Conversely, setting each of the value to the maximum of 255 results in white.

Each of the individual values for red, green, and blue is stored in an 8-bit number—255 is the decimal value of the 8-digit binary number 11111111—combining these three 8-bit numbers together give you the bit depth of an RGB image—24-bit. Typical image bit depths range from 1 to 64—a bit depth of 1 allows you black and white, a bit depth of 8 for the image would allow 256 colors, although a bit depth of 64 would allow a huge number of colors in the image.

As you will see a bit later, we can create both 8- and 24-bit images with the GD libraries.

Coordinate Systems

As soon as you start drawing shapes and text within an image, you want to be able to position that shape or text within the image. If you have a mathematical background, you're already familiar with a graph type layout where the x and y coordinates radiate to the right and upward from the bottom left corner, as Figure 16-1 shows.

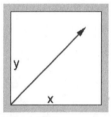

Figure 16-1

With the PHP image functions, the coordinates radiate to the right and down from the top-left corner, as Figure 16-2 shows.

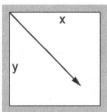

Figure 16-2

The first pixel in the top left-hand corner is position 0,0. This means that the last pixel across the image is the width of the image less 1, and the last pixel at the bottom of the image is the height of the image less 1. Figure 16-3 shows an image 300 pixels wide by 200 pixels high and its corner pixel coordinates in PHP.

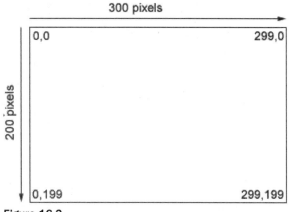

Figure 16-3

Image Types

You typically encounter two types of images: vector and raster. A vector image uses mathematical equations to describe the shapes that make up the image. The SVG (Scalable Vector Graphics) format is a good example of a vector image. Vector images are great for diagrams that include lines and curves and blocks of color, but are not suitable for photographic-type images. Raster images are made up of pixel data—in a 20-pixel-wide by 20-pixel-high image there will be 400 individual pixels making up the image, and each of these pixels will have its own RGB color value.

The current GD image libraries enable you to output three main Web image file formats—JPEG and PNG for desktop Web browsers, and WBMP images for PDA browsers. All three are raster images. The GD functions in PHP do not output vector image file formats.

These are compressed file formats, which means that they use mathematical algorithms to reduce the amount of data required to completely describe the image. They play a very important role in keeping your file sizes small and download times short!

It's important to be able to recognize when you should use each of these file formats, and it's their compression that shows you. Although both are raster images, they use quite different compression techniques, and most images are better suited to one or the other.

The JPEG format uses *lossy* compression, in which some of the data in the original image is lost during compression. The format is designed to work best with images like photographs, where there's a lot of subtle shading and not too much fine detail. It's the format to use when a slight loss in quality won't be too apparent to the viewer.

The PNG format on the other hand is compressed in a *lossless* fashion. It works best with images that contain lines and large blocks of color, cartoons for example. When the image is uncompressed, it will contain all of its original information. This means that sharp edges and straight lines (which suffer under JPEG compression) will be reproduced faithfully.

Early versions of GD (and thus PHP) contained support for GIF files, which are similar in many respects to PNG. However, Unisys held a patent on the algorithm used to create fully compressed GIFs, and consequently GIF support had been completely replaced by that for PNG files since GD version 1.6. Although the JPEG and PNG image encoding formats should be sufficient for all your graphics needs, PHP also includes read-only GIF support.

Working with Raster Images

Let's get started generating and refining images. There are four steps for creating and working with an image in PHP:

1. Create a blank image canvas for PHP to work with. This is basically an area of memory that is set aside, within which the PHP image functions will draw your image data.

2. Work through the steps involved in drawing the image that you want. This includes setting up the colors and drawing the shapes and text that you want within your image.

3. Send your finished image to the Web browser or save it to disk.

4. Remove your image from the server's memory

Creating a New Image

The first thing to do is to create a new blank image canvas for PHP to work in. To do this you can use either the vimagecreate() function, which creates a palette-based image with a maximum of 256 colors, or use the imagecreatetruecolor() function, which creates a true color image capable of including up to 16.7 million colors. Both the imagecreate() and imagecreatetrucolor() functions take two parameters—the width and height of the blank image that you want to create:

```
resource imagecreate (int x_size, int y_size)
```

```
$myImage = imagecreate(200, 150);
```

The new blank image that this line creates is 200 pixels wide and 150 pixels high. As you can see, the function also returns a value—after the function has been called, $myImage contains an image identifier that refers to the new blank image in memory. You'll use this image identifier with other image functions so that they know which image in memory you're working with. You can think of the image identifier as being similar to the file handle or database link ID that you used in previous chapters.

Allocating Colors

Before you can start drawing on your blank image, you need to decide what colors you want and then use the imagecolorallocate() function, which takes four parameters:

```
int imagecolorallocate (resource image, int red, int green, int blue)
```

You would do this in PHP using the following code:

```php
$myGreen = imagecolorallocate($myImage, 51, 153, 51);
```

The first parameter is the image identifier of the image that you want to allocate this color for. This is the image identifier that was returned to you by the `imagecreate()` or `imagecreatetruecolor()` functions. If you are working with two images at the same time, and want to allocate the same green color to use in each of them, you have to call the `imagecolorallocate()` function twice, once for each image. Each time you call the `imagecolorallocate()` function you need to pass it the unique image identifier for that image.

The next three parameters are the red, green and blue values for the color that you want. As you saw earlier, each of these can range from 0 to 255 and define the color using the RGB color model.

The `imagecolorallocate()` function returns a color identifier to the newly allocated color within the image palette, or a value of -1 if it could not allocate the color to the palette. This happens if your image palette already contains 256 colors and there's no space to allocate a new color. In this case, you can use the `imagecolorresolve()` function which always returns a valid color identifier.

The `imagecolorresolve()` function takes the same parameters as the `imagecolorallocate()` function (an image identifier and the red, green and blue values of the color that you want), but unlike the `imagecolorallocate()` function which simply tries to allocate the requested color into the image palette, the `imagecolorresolve()` function first tries to find if the color that you are requesting already exists in the palette. If it does, the function simply returns the color index for that color. If it doesn't exist, the function tries to allocate the color that you requested. If successful, it returns the color identifier within the palette. If it fails then it looks at all of the existing colors in your palette, and returns the color identifier of the color in the palette that is the closest to the color that you want.

The first color that you allocate to a palette based image (one created with the `imagecreate()` function) is used as the background color for that image. Images created using the `imagecreatetrucolor()` function are created with a black background and it is then up to you to color it as you need to.

Basic Drawing Functions

Once you have allocated the colors that you want to draw with, you can start using them to draw on your blank canvas. The PHP image library provides functions for drawing points, lines, rectangles, ellipses, arcs and polygons.

All of the drawing functions in PHP have a similar pattern in the parameters that you need to pass them. The first parameter is always the image identifier of the image that you want to draw on. The next set of parameters vary in number, but are always the x and y pixel positions that you need to draw the shape that you want. If you are drawing only a single pixel, you only have to provide one x and one y coordinate, but if you are drawing a line you need to provide x and y coordinates for both the start and end positions of the line. The last parameter is always the color with which you want to draw.

Drawing Individual Pixels

To color a single pixel on your canvas, use the `imagesetpixel()` function:

```php
int imagesetpixel (resource image, int x, int y, int color)

imagesetpixel($myImage, 120, 60, $myBlack);
```

This colors a single pixel that is 121 pixels across and 61 pixels down in the image $myImage the color within the palette of $myImage identified by $myBlack. Figure 16-4 shows the layout of this single pixel in the image.

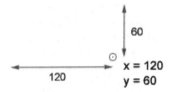

Figure 16-4

Remember, the first pixel in the top left-hand corner of the image is 0, 0, which is why the position x = 120 is actually 121 pixels across to the right.

Drawing Lines

To draw a line in an image use the `imageline()` function. Because the `imageline()` function is drawing a line, it needs to have start and end points, so you must do it with an extra set of coordinates as parameters:

```
int imageline (resource image, int x1, int y1, int x2, int y2, int color)
```

Try It Out   **Drawing a Line**

1. Open your text editor and add the following code:

```php
<?php
$myImage = imagecreate(200,100);
$myGrey = imagecolorallocate($myImage,204,204,204);
$myBlack = imagecolorallocate($myImage, 0, 0, 0);
imageline($myImage, 15, 35, 120, 60, $myBlack);
header("Content-type: image/png");
imagepng($myImage);
imagedestroy($myImage);
?>
```

2. Save the file as `line.php`.

3. Open `line.php` in a Web browser. Figure 16-5 shows the output.

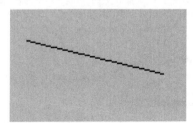

Figure 16-5

You will receive an error message if you have not added the GD extension to your PHP installation by uncommenting the following line in your php.ini *file:*

```
extension=php_gd2.dll
```

Remember to restart your server after you've made this change.

How it Works

You first create a new blank image. The imagecreate() function returns an image identifier that you store in the $myImage variable. Then allocate two colors—a gray and a black. Because the gray is allocated first, it will be used as the background color of the image.

Use the imageline() function to draw the line. The first parameter is always the image identifier of the image. The next two parameters tell the imageline() function where the line starts—in this example, 16 pixels across and 36 pixels down. The next two parameters then tell the function where the line should end —121 pixels across and 61 pixels down in the example. The last parameter is, of course, the color in which to draw the line.

After the image is drawn, you need to output it to the Web browser. This is done in two steps:

1. Use the header() function to send a header to the Web browser telling it the type of data that it is about to receive. This ensures that the browser displays the content correctly.

2. Use the imagepng() function, passing it the image identifier as parameter. This sends the image data stored in $myImage as a PNG image to the Web browser.

Finally, you remove the image from memory using the imagedestory() function.

Drawing Rectangles

To be able to draw a rectangle you really only need two positions on the stage—the two opposite corners of your rectangle. Because of this, the syntax for the imagerectangle() function is exactly the same as the imageline() function. In the case of the imagerectangle() function, the two coordinates you provide are used as opposite corners of the rectangle rather than a line joining the two together:

```
int imagerectangle (resource image, int x1, int y1, int x2, int y2, int col)
```

Open the line.php file that you just created and save it as rectangle.php. Replace the line

```
imageline($myImage, 15, 35, 120, 60, $myBlack);
```

with the line

```
imagerectangle($myImage,15,35,120,60,$myBlack);
```

As you can see, the parameter values passed in this imagerectangle() function are exactly the same as those used in the line-drawing example. Save the file and preview it in a Web browser. Figure 16-6 shows the image generated by this code.

Figure 16-6

The imagerectangle() function uses the first set of coordinates as the top-left corner of the rectangle and the second set of coordinates as the bottom-right corner. If you had left in both the imageline() and imagerectangle() functions, you'd get the output shown in Figure 16-7.

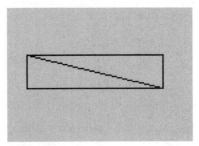

Figure 16-7

Drawing Circles and Ellipses

To draw circles and ellipses in PHP, use the imageellipse() function. It works differently from the imagerectangle() and imageline() functions, in that you do not provide the outer limits of the shape. Rather, the ellipse is described by providing its center point, and then telling the imageellipse() function how high and how wide the ellipse has to be. Here's what the function syntax looks like:

```
imageellipse(resource image, int x, int y, int width, int height, int col);
```

Here's an example:

```
imageellipse($myImage, 90, 60, 160, 50, $myBlack);
```

The example ellipse, shown in Figure 16-8, has its center on the pixel where x = 90 and y = 60. The width of the ellipse is 160 pixels and the height is 50 pixels.

To draw a circle, simply describe an ellipse that has the same width and height (see Figure 16-9):

```
imageellipse($myImage,90,60,70,70,$myBlack);
```

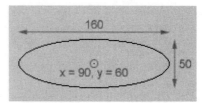

Figure 16-8

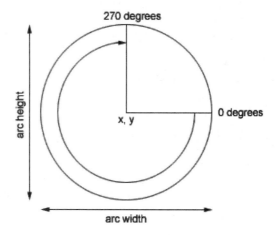

Figure 16-9

Drawing an Arc

An arc is a partial ellipse—one that doesn't join up. You describe an arc in the same way as an ellipse, except that you need to add additional parameters to describe where the arc starts and ends. The start and end points are provided in degrees, there being 360 degrees in a complete ellipse. 0 degrees is at the far-righthand side of the ellipse, the 3 o'clock position on a clock face, as shown in Figure 16-10. The degrees progress in a clockwise position:

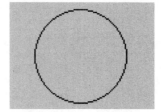

Figure 16-10

Here's the syntax for an arc:

```
imagearc(resource image, int x, int y, int width, int height, int
start_degree, int end_degree, int col)
```

And here's an example of using the `imagearc()` function to draw a partial ellipse:

```
imagearc($myImage,90,60,160,50,45,200,$myBlack);
```

The first parameter (`$myImage`) identifies the image in which you're drawing. The next two parameters (`90,60`) specify the center point of the ellipse that the arc follows. The parameters `160,50` are the same as in the ellipse example earlier. It's the next two parameters that really create the arc: `45` tells the `imagearc()` function to start the arc at the 45-degree position (at 4:30 if it was a clock) and `200` is the position in degrees where the arc is to end. Remember, the `200` is the degree position, not the number of degrees to rotate around the ellipse. Figure 16-11 shows the arc drawn from 45 to 200 degrees.

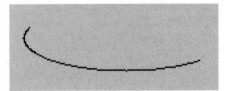

Figure 16-11

The arc in the figure may look strange, but remember, the arc is drawn along the ellipse described by the width and height you provide. Compare this arc with the ellipse you drew earlier (see Figure 16-8) using the same width and height parameters.

Drawing Polygons

A polygon is a shape that has three or more corners or apexes. Because the function to draw a polygon can handle shapes with a varying number of apexes, the `imagepolygon()` function takes different parameters to the preceding image functions. Besides passing parameters for the image identifier, you also need to pass the points that define the corners or apexes of your polygon as an array of points, alternating between x and y coordinates. A second parameter tells the function how many apexes there are in the polygon.

int imagepolygon (resource image, array points, int num_points, int color)

Take a look at the following code:

```
$myPoints = array(20,20,185,55,70,80);
imagepolygon($myImage,$myPoints,3,$myBlack);
```

You first create an array of points. In this example, there are six elements in the array, in sets of x and y coordinates of a point. This means that there are three apexes to this polygon: at `20,20`, `185,55`, and `70,80`.

You then call the `imagepolygon()` function, passing it the following parameters:

1. The image resource identifier.
2. The array of points.
3. The number of apexes in the polygon.
4. The color with which you want to draw the shape.

Figure 16-12 shows the example polygon.

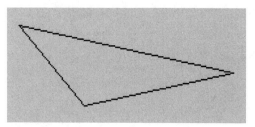

Figure 16-12

Try It Out   **Draw a Rectangle with Rounded Corners**

1.   Open your text editor and enter the following code:

```php
<?php
function roundrect($image, $x1, $y1, $x2, $y2, $curvedepth, $color) {
   imageline($image, ($x1 + $curvedepth), $y1, ($x2 - $curvedepth), $y1, $color);
   imageline($image, ($x1 + $curvedepth), $y2, ($x2 - $curvedepth), $y2, $color);
   imageline($image, $x1, ($y1 + $curvedepth), $x1, ($y2 - $curvedepth), $color);
   imageline($image, $x2, ($y1 + $curvedepth), $x2, ($y2 - $curvedepth), $color);
   imagearc($image, ($x1 + $curvedepth), ($y1 + $curvedepth), (2 * $curvedepth),
(2 * $curvedepth), 180, 270, $color);
   imagearc($image, ($x2 -$curvedepth), ($y1 + $curvedepth), (2  * $curvedepth),
(2 * $curvedepth), 270, 360, $color);
   imagearc($image, ($x2 - $curvedepth), ($y2 - $curvedepth), (2 * $curvedepth),
(2 * $curvedepth), 0, 90, $color);
   imagearc($image, ($x1 + $curvedepth), ($y2 -      $curvedepth), (2  * $curvedepth),
(2 * $curvedepth), 90, 180, $color);
}
$myImage = imagecreate(200,100);
$myGrey = imagecolorallocate($myImage,204,204,204);
$myBlack = imagecolorallocate($myImage,0,0,0);
roundrect($myImage, 20, 10, 180, 90, 20, $myBlack);
header("Content-type: image/png");
imagepng($myImage);
imagedestroy($myImage);
?>
```

2.   Save the file as roundrect.php.

3.   Open roundrect.php in a Web browser. Figure 16-13 shows the script's output.

How It Works

Let's take a look at the code that creates that rounded rectangle. There's nothing there that you haven't seen in the last few pages, the only trick to creating a rounded rectangle is in understanding how you combine the lines and arcs to get the effect that you want.

The first thing that you do in the script is create a function to draw the rounded rectangle for you. Rather than write the code to do it as part of the script itself, you separate the code into its own function so that

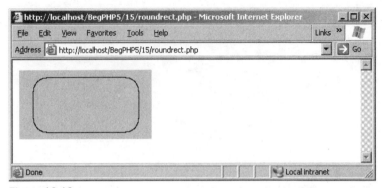

Figure 16-13

you can reuse the code later if you want to draw another rectangle with rounded corners. The function is defined with seven parameters:

```php
<?php
function roundrect($image, $x1, $y1, $x2, $y2, $curvedepth, $color) {
```

The first parameter is the image resource identifier of the image within which you want to draw the rectangle. The next two parameters are for the top left corner of the rectangle (because you're drawing a rectangle that has rounded corners you won't actually be drawing anything on this point, but you'll use it as an anchor point for the one corner of the rectangle). The next two parameters are for the bottom-right corner of the rectangle. The sixth parameter, $curvedepth, is the number of pixels before the end of rectangle that you want the curve to begin. The last parameter is, of course, the color that you want to draw in. Figure 16-14 shows how the parameters passed to the roundrect() function are used.

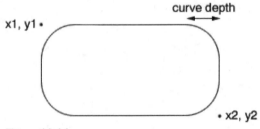

Figure 16-14

Depending on which line and corner you're drawing, you use different combinations of $x1, $x2, $y1, $y2, and $curvedepth.

You first draw the line across the top of the rectangle. You won't want to draw the line all the way from $x1 to $x2 because you have to take the curve of the corner into account. That's why you need to add the $curvedepth value to the $x1 position, and subtract it from the $x2 position:

```php
imageline($image, ($x1 + $curvedepth), $y1, ($x2 - $curvedepth), $y1, $color);
```

Because the line is horizontal, both points use the same *y* position. The next line goes along the bottom of the rectangle. Again, you need to alter the width of the line by the depth of the curve and use the same *y* values for each point:

```
imageline($image, ($x1 + $curvedepth), $y2, ($x2 - $curvedepth), $y2, $color);
```

The next two lines are the vertical lines that go down the left and right-hand sides of the rectangle. This time we will use the same x values for each of the lines ($x1 for the left hand line and $x2 for the right hand side), and will have to alter the y values appropriately so that the height of the curve fits in with our curved corners.

```
imageline($image, $x1, ($y1 + $curvedepth), $x1, ($y2 - $curvedepth), $color);
imageline($image, $x2, ($y1 + $curvedepth), $x2, ($y2 - $curvedepth), $color);
```

The top-left corner of the rectangle is the first curve you're drawing. You need to provide the center point of the arc (see Figure 16-15), so you add the value of $curvedepth to both the $x1 and the $y1 values. You also provide the width and height for the arc. Because the curve depth is actually the radius of the arc, you will need to double the curve depth to get the arc's width and height.

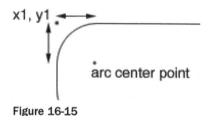

Figure 16-15

The arc starts at 180 degrees (9 o'clock position) and curves around to 270 degrees.

```
imagearc($image, ($x1 + $curvedepth), ($y1 + $curvedepth), (2 * $curvedepth),
(2 * $curvedepth), 180, 270, $color);
```

The rest of the corners are created in exactly the same way, except that you either add or subtract the curve depth from different values of x and y to get the correct center points for each arc. Also remember that the start and end positions of the arcs change for each corner.

```
imagearc($image, ($x2 - $curvedepth), ($y1 + $curvedepth), (2 * $curvedepth),
(2 * $curvedepth), 270, 360, $color);
imagearc($image, ($x2 - $curvedepth),
($y2 - $curvedepth), (2 * $curvedepth), (2 * $curvedepth), 0, 90, $color);
 imagearc($image, ($x1 + $curvedepth), ($y2 - $curvedepth), (2 * $curvedepth),
(2 * $curvedepth), 90, 180, $color);
```

That's all you need to do to draw the rounded rectangle, so close off the function and begin drawing the image.

```
}
```

You create the blank image and allocate two colors to the image. The first color allocated is the background color for the image:

```
$myImage = imagecreate(200,100);
$myGrey = imagecolorallocate($myImage,204,204,204);
$myBlack = imagecolorallocate($myImage,0,0,0);
```

You call the `roundrect()` function, passing it the parameters previously discussed:

```
roundrect($myImage, 20, 10, 180, 90, 20, $myBlack);
```

To send the image to the Web browser viewing the page, you first send a header to the browser telling it what type of data it's about to receive. This lets the browser use the correct viewer to display the data. In this case you're saying that a PNG image is on its way.

```
header("Content-type: image/png");
```

Then use the `imagepng()` function to send the actual image data. The function takes a single parameter, the image resource identifier of the image that you want to output. To finish up, use the `imagedestroy()` function to clean up memory.

```
imagepng($myImage);
imagedestroy($myImage);
?>
```

Manipulating Raster Images

So far in this chapter you've seen how to create and build images using the drawing functions of the GD image library, and you've created some images of basic shapes of flat color and text. But what happens if you want to work with existing raster images that aren't made up of flat color but have millions of colors dotted all over the image—just like in a photograph? Well, the GD image libraries don't restrict you to creating new images—you can just as easily produce a new image that is based on an existing JPEG, PNG, or GIF image.

Opening an Existing Image

To create a new image you used the `imagecreate()` and `imagecreatetruecolor()` functions. To create a new image based on an existing image, you use the `imagecreatefrom` series of functions. The most common of these are `imagecreatefromjpeg()`, `imagecreatefromgif()`, and `imagecreatefrompng()`. There are a number of other functions that enable you to create new images in memory from existing image formats, but they aren't as widely used as these.

The `imagecreatefromjpeg()` function works in the same way as the `imagecreate()` function, except instead of passing it the width and height of the new image as parameters, you only pass the filename of the existing image as a string. The function returns an image resource identifier with which you can work.

The line

```
$myImage = imagecreatefromjpeg('moegie.jpg');
```

opens the JPEG file called `moegie.jpg` that is in the same directory in which my script is running. The image resource identifier `$myImage` contains the image data of the JPEG file. You can test this by outputting the image data without first doing anything to the actual data.

Try It Out   **Out Display a JPEG**

1. Type the following code in your text editor:

```php
<?php
$myImage = imagecreatefromjpeg('moegie.jpg');
header("Content-type: image/jpeg");
imagejpeg($myImage);
imagedestroy($myImage);
?>
```

2. Save it as `showjpeg.php`. Make sure that the filename that you provide as the parameter to the `imagecreatefromjpeg()` function is a JPEG file and exists in the same directory from which the `showjpeg.php` script is running.

3. Browse to `showjpeg.php` in your Web browser. Figure 16-16 shows the output in my browser—you'll have a different image, of course.

Figure 16-16

How It Works

The code is relatively straightforward and shouldn't pose any problems. You first use the `imagecreatefromjpeg()` function to create a new image resource from your existing image:

```
$myImage = imagecreatefromjpeg('moegie.jpg');
```

Then you send a header to the Web browser, telling it that you are about to send it image data:

```
header("Content-type: image/jpeg");
```

And all that's left to do is send the data and clean up the image from memory:

```
imagejpeg($myImage);
imagedestroy($myImage);
```

Of course, you haven't done anything that you couldn't have done yourself using straight HTML, so you may be wondering what the point is. Well, being able to open existing images and manipulating them before sending them to the browser is useful for a number of reasons. Some of the things that we will be able to do to images using the GD image functions are:

❑   Resize the image dimensions to create a thumbnail for display, or drop the image quality for faster load speed.

❑   Annotate the image with some descriptive text or a caption.

❑   Copy a portion of another image into it to use a watermark for copyright purposes.

Let's take a look at how you can apply a watermark to an image, and also how to create thumbnails of your images.

Applying a Watermark

If you are working on a Web site that displays original art or photographs, you may want to protect your or your clients' intellectual property from being stolen. A common way of doing this is to apply a watermark to the image in such a way that it is still recognizable, but stops someone else from using it as his own. Let me show you how I did this, and why don't you follow along with your own images?

First, I created a simple copyright image (see Figure 16-17) that I could use on my other images. I added some black text to white background image and saved it as a PNG with an 8-color palette. (I'll explain why I saved the file like this a bit later.)

©Allan Kent, 2004

Figure 16-17

Copying the Copyright into the Image

Now, I open the original image that I want to watermark:

```
<?php
$myImage = imagecreatefromjpeg('moegie.jpg');
```

I then open my copyright notice or logo. Because it's a PNG file I use the `imagecreatefrompng()` function to open the file.

```
$myCopyright = imagecreatefrompng('copyright.png');
```

You may want to position your copyright notice in the top-left hand corner of the image, in which case you don't need the next set of steps. But if you want to position your notice on the right, bottom, or center of the image you have to know the dimensions of each of your images. The function `imagesx()` returns the width of an image, although the function `imagesy()` returns the image height. Both functions take a single parameter of the image resource identifier of the image that you would like to get the width or height of. In this example, I'll position the copyright in the center of my image, so I must get the width and height of both the original image and the copyright notice:

```
$destWidth = imagesx($myImage);
$destHeight = imagesy($myImage);
$srcWidth = imagesx($myCopyright);
$srcHeight = imagesy($myCopyright);
```

You need to work out the top-left corner position of where the copyright notice needs to be placed. This is a simple matter of subtracting the width of the copyright notice from the width of the image to be watermarked, and then dividing the difference by two. To get the y position, perform the same calculation but using the image heights:

```
$destX = ($destWidth - $srcWidth) / 2;
$destY = ($destHeight - $srcHeight) / 2;
```

If you wanted to position your copyright notice against the right edge of your image, you'd simply subtract the width of the copyright notice from the width of the image to be watermarked to get the x position for the copyright.

Once you know where you need to put the copyright notice, you can go ahead and copy it into the image to be watermarked. The function to do this is `imagecopy()`:

```
imagecopy($myImage, $myCopyright, $destX, $destY, 0, 0, $srcWidth,
$srcHeight);
```

It takes eight parameters that tell the function what to copy from the source image and where to place it in the destination image. The first parameter is the image resource identifier of the image into which the data is to be copied—the image that you want to watermark. The second parameter is the image resource identifier of the image from where the image data is being copied—the copyright image. The third and fourth parameters are the x and y position in the destination image where the image data is to be copied. They mark the top-left corner of the block of data that is being copied across. The next two parameters ($0, 0$, in the example) are the x and y position in the source image to start copying from. The function uses these two parameters along with the next two, the width and height of the data to copy, to work out where and how much to copy from the source image. In this case, I want the entire image to be copied across, so I use $0, 0$ as the top-left position of the block to be copied, and the width and height are the same as the width and height of my copyright image.

After the data is copied across, you can output the image as usual. Remember to clean up the memory that the copyright image has used:

```
header("Content-type: image/jpeg");
imagejpeg($myImage);
imagedestroy($myImage);
imagedestroy($myCopyright);
?>
```

Figure 16-18 shows the result of my first attempt at a watermark.

Figure 16-18

One of the goals that I had for my watermark was that the image still be recognizable. As you can clearly see in the figure, a large portion of that image is now obscured. I'm going to refine the script so that we can see more of the image.

Working with Transparency

Rather than display the entire copyright image as is, I can copy only the text across. To do this, I have to make the white area of the copyright image transparent. The function I need to use works with color identifiers, so before I can make the area transparent, I have to retrieve the color index of white. There are a number of ways of doing this—I could use the imagecolorat() function that will retrieve the palette index of the color of the pixel at the exact pixel location that I provide, or I could provide the exact color itself and try retrieve the palette index for that color. The only drawback to the latter is that if the color does not exist in my images color palette I won't get a valid image resource returned to me. Earlier, I saved my copyright image as an 8-color PNG—this was so that I only had a small palette to work with and I could be sure that the white background of my image was uniform throughout the image. If I'd saved the image as a JPEG with millions of colors, the dither in the image might have created slight variations in the white background, making it very difficult for me to pinpoint the white that I wanted to be transparent. (Dither refers to a method in which you create the appearance of a color by putting 2 pixels of different colors next to one another). By saving the image as a PNG with a small number of colors, you don't get that dither effect.

I use the imagecolorexact() function to return the color index of the white. (You can see the syntax for this function in Appendix B, *PHP Functions Reference*.) imagecolorexact() takes four parameters—the image resource identifier that you're working with and then the red, green, and blue values for the color that you want to find. Because my image has only eight colors in it, I can be sure that I'll get a color index returned.

Once I have the color index, I use the imagecolortransparent() function to make the specified color transparent in the image. The function takes two parameters: the image resource identifier and the color index that I want to make transparent. The following two highlighted lines of code fit into an earlier part of the script—they go right after I worked out the destination x and y positions and before I copy the data from one image to the other.

```
$destY = ($destHeight - $srcHeight) / 2;
$white = imagecolorexact($myCopyright, 255, 255, 255);
imagecolortransparent($myCopyright, $white);
imagecopy($myImage, $myCopyright, $destX, $destY, 0, 0, $src width,
$srcHeight);
```

Now the script's output (see Figure 16-19) looks more promising.

Figure 16-19

The whitish area that you can see around the 2004 in the image is the effect of anti-aliasing the font. If you don't want that kind of effect, just turn off the anti-aliasing of your font in your graphics program, or save the image as a 2-color PNG. As you might expect, trying to get a smooth curve into the small pixel range that a font character has is quite a difficult task. Anti-aliasing a font uses shades of the font color to blend the curves of the font into the background image, so that you don't get a jagged curve. This does mean that the curves of the font are made up of a number of different shades of the font color, and when applying a transparency to the background color of the image, you see the anti-aliasing of the font showing up as it has in Figure 16-19. Removing the anti-aliasing or forcing the font to be two colors only makes the font look choppier, but removes that effect from around the 2004. To lessen the effect and also make the watermark less intrusive, I could also change the opacity of the data that is copied into the image.

Working with Opacity

The *opacity* of an image defines a degree of transparency. This can range from completely see-through or transparent, to opaque, where you cannot see through the image at all. In the `imagecopy()` function in the previous section, the black text of my copyright was opaque although its white background was transparent. To make the watermark less obvious, I use the `imagecopymerge()` function to give the copied data a degree of transparency. The function works in the exact same way as the `imagecopy()` function, except that I now provide a ninth parameter, which controls how transparent or opaque it is. In this parameter, a value of 0 means that the color is completely transparent and you won't see the data is copied across, although a value of 100 means that the data is completely opaque—in which case the function operates like the `imagecopy()` function. I simply change this script line:

```
imagecopy($myImage, $myCopyright, $destX, $destY, 0, 0, $srcWidth,
$srcHeight);
```

to read:

```
imagecopymerge($myImage, $myCopyright, $destX, $destY, 0, 0, $srcWidth,
$srcHeight, 50);
```

That is, I change the `imagecopy()` function to `imagecopymerge()` and provide the extra parameter with a value of 50—halfway between transparent and opaque. The output of the script now looks a lot more like a watermark, as Figure 16-20 shows.

If playing with transparency effects in images appeals to you, take a look at the `imagecolorallocatealpha()` and `imagealphablending()` functions in the PHP Manual. Although you won't be able to reproduce all of the effects that you can get with a professional graphics program, you can create some interesting effects nonetheless.

The next section also deals with manipulating an existing image, but this time you're going to reduce it to a thumbnail.

Creating Thumbnails

Creating a thumbnail of an image uses a similar method to applying a watermark, except that you copy in the other direction—instead of copying the smaller image into the larger image, you copy the larger image into a new smaller image, scaling it down as you go.

Figure 16-20

Choose an image of your own, save it as thumbnail.php, and follow these steps to create a thumbnail:

1. Open the image of which you want to create a thumbnail:

```php
<?php
$mainImage = imagecreatefromjpeg('moegie.jpg');
```

2. Use the imagesx() and imagesy() functions to get the width and height of the original image. You need these to work out the size of the new thumbnail image:

```php
$mainWidth = imagesx($mainImage);
$mainHeight = imagesy($mainImage);
```

3. In this example, you want the thumbnail to be a quarter the size of the original image, so divide the original width and height by 4. Return those values as integers because you can't have a half a pixel:

```php
$thumbWidth = intval($mainWidth / 4);
$thumbHeight = intval($mainHeight / 4);
```

You aren't limited to scaling the image down this way. You could scale it down to within specific dimensions, requiring that the both the width and the height of the new thumbnail fit within a given size. Or, you could say that all your thumbnails must be the same width, and scale them down accordingly.

The important thing is that you want to change your width and height proportionately to one another so you don't end up with a thumbnail that's all squashed out of proportion.

4. Create a new blank image with the thumbnail width and height. Typically you'll be copying photo type images, so you want an image with a large number of colors. So use the `imagecreatetruecolor()` function to create the blank thumbnail:

```
$myThumbnail = imagecreatetruecolor($thumbWidth, $thumbHeight);
```

Now you need to scale down the original image and copy it into the new thumbnail image. There are two functions that can do this—`imagecopyresized()` and `imagecopyresampled()`. The difference between the two is that `imagecopyresized()` is slightly faster, but does not anti-alias the image at all. If you use `imagecopyresized()` to create a thumbnail and then zoom in, you'll see a pixilation effect much like that shown in Figure 16-21.

Figure 16-21

The `imagecopyresampled()` function, although slightly slower, interpolates the pixels so that you do not get that blocky effect. Both the `imagecopyresized()` and the `imagecopyresampled()` functions take the same 10 parameters. The first two are the destination image resource identifier and then the image resource identifier of the image from which you're copying the image data. The second two parameters are the *x* and *y* positions of the top-left corner of the block of data that you're copying in the destination image, which is used to position the data in the image that it is being copied into. This example uses 0, 0, which will fill the thumbnail with the image. The next two parameters tell the function where it needs to start copying the image data from in the source image. Again, this example uses all of the data, so it starts in the top left corner at position 0, 0. The following two parameters tell the function how wide and how high to resize the data in the destination image. This is where you use the new width and height that you calculated earlier: the width and height of the thumbnail image. The last two parameters specify the width and height of the block of image data that is copied out of the original image. In this example, it's the width and height of the original image because you're copying the entire image into the new thumbnail.

You don't have to copy all of the image, you can rather specify just a small part of the image to copy. Because you can specify any width or height for the data in the destination image, you could easily copy the data out of proportion, so be very careful when working out your image widths and heights.

5. Use the `imagecopyresampled()` function to copy the image data to the thumbnail image:

```
imagecopyresampled($myThumbnail, $mainImage, 0, 0, 0, 0, $thumbWidth,
$thumbHeight, $mainWidth, $mainHeight);
```

6. Send the image data to the browser (see Figure 16-22) and clean up the memory that the script used:

```
header("Content-type: image/jpeg");
imagejpeg($myThumbnail);
imagedestroy($myThumbnail);
imagedestroy($mainImage);
?>
```

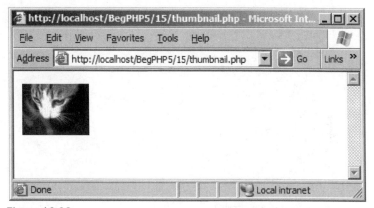

Figure 16-22

Using Text in Images

Adding text to images with the PHP image functions enables you to annotate images or draw dynamic charts and graphs. The quickest and easiest way of adding text to an image is to use the `imagestring()` function, which lets you draw a string of text on your image at the location you specify.

Adding Standard Text

It's easy to draw on your image with `imagestring()` because the function can use a set of built-in system fonts for your text, so you don't have to have your font in a suitable format and loaded on your server.

Here's the syntax for `imagestring()`:

```
imagestring (image, font, x, y, text, color)
```

As always, the first parameter is the image resource identifier. The second parameter specifies the font to use to draw the string. This is an integer value and ranges from 1 upward. Values of 1 to 5 are built-in system fonts, any fonts you load subsequently are increasing numbers above 5.

To load a font for the imagestring() *function, use the* imageloadfont() *function. It loads a bitmap font that is architecture dependent—this means the font needs to be generated on the same type of system that you want to use it on. A far easier solution is to use True Type fonts—which we'll get to in just a bit.*

The x and y parameters enable you to position the font within the image. They are the top-left corner of the rectangle within which your text will appear. The last two parameters are the actual text that you want to draw in the image and the color with which to draw it.

Try It Out **Display System Fonts**

Follow this script (drawstring.php) to display how these system fonts look.

```php
<?php
$textImage = imagecreate(200,100);
$white = imagecolorallocate($textImage, 255, 255, 255);
$black = imagecolorallocate($textImage, 0, 0, 0);
$yOffset = 0;
for ($i = 1; $i <=5; $i++) {
  imagestring($textImage, $i, 5, $yOffset, "This is system font $i", $black);
  $yOffset += imagefontheight($i);
}
header("Content-type: image/png");
imagepng($textImage);
imagedestroy($textImage);
?>
```

Figure 16-23 shows the output of this script.

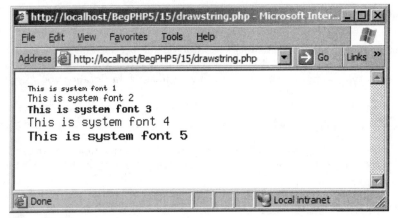

Figure 16-23

How It Works

First, you create a blank image for the text and then allocate the colors white and black. Because you allocate white first, it will be the background color of the image.

```
<?php
$textImage = imagecreate(200,100);
$white = imagecolorallocate($textImage, 255, 255, 255);
$black = imagecolorallocate($textImage, 0, 0, 0);
```

Then, set a variable to store the y position (how far down the image) for you to draw the string. In this example, you start at the top of the image, so this variable is set to 0.

```
$yOffset = 0;
```

Loop around five times—once for each of the built-in system fonts.

```
for ($i = 1; $i <=5; $i++) {
```

Draw the string in the image using $i as the font—this will range from 1 to 5 as you work your way through the loop. It's positioned 5 pixels from the left edge of the image and the $yOffset variable (as the y position) positions it vertically in the image.

```
imagestring($textImage, $i, 5, $yOffset, "This is system font $i", $black);
```

The imagefontheight() function is passed to the font identifier and returns the height of the font in pixels. Add this function to the $yOffset variable so that the text strings are drawn one underneath another and don't overlap. (If you want to get the width of the font, use the imagefontwidth() function.)

```
$yOffset += imagefontheight($i);
```

Finally, you output the image and clean up.

```
}
header("Content-type: image/png");
imagepng($textImage);
imagedestroy($textImage);
?>
```

Using True Type Fonts

When drawing basic charts and graphs you may prefer to use the built-in system fonts because they are nonproportional fonts—all of the character widths are the same—so it makes layout and positioning easier. However, if you'd like your text to look more elegant, you probably want to use a True Type font.

For Windows users, the GD library that comes with PHP includes support for True Type fonts, but UNIX users have to install the FreeType library before compiling PHP. The FreeType library is available from www.freetype.org.

Using a True Type font offers a lot more versatility—not only can you control what your text looks like by choosing a suitable font, but you can also specify the size of the font and an angle at which to draw it. The preferred function to do this is imagefttext(), which uses the FreeType 2 library to draw the True Type text. The function take similar parameters to the imagestring() function, but the order is different and some are used in different ways.

True Type Font

Take a look at the following script entitled `truetype.php`:

```php
<?php
$textImage = imagecreate(200,100);
$white = imagecolorallocate($textImage, 255, 255, 255);
$black = imagecolorallocate($textImage, 0, 0, 0);
imagefttext($textImage, 16, 0, 10, 50, $black,"C:\ Windows\fonts\arial.ttf",
"Arial, 16 pixels");
header("Content-type: image/png");
imagepng($textImage);
imagedestroy($textImage);
?>
```

Figure 16-24 shows the text drawn in Arial font, 16 pixels in size. The degrees of 0 specifies that the text is drawn from the left to the right—in the direction of the 0 degree.

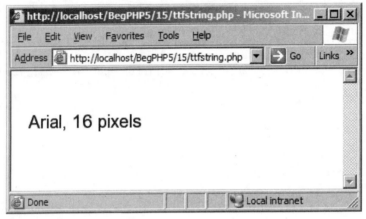

Figure 16-24

How It Works

First, you create a blank image and allocate two colors.

```php
<?php
$textImage = imagecreate(200,100);
$white = imagecolorallocate($textImage, 255, 255, 255);
$black = imagecolorallocate($textImage, 0, 0, 0);
```

Then, go ahead and draw your string on the image:

```php
imagefttext($textImage, 16, 0, 10, 50, $black,"C:\Windows\fonts\arial.ttf",
"Arial, 16 pixels");
```

The first parameter is, of course, the image resource in which you're working. The second parameter is the size of the font—this is pixels and determines the height of the font. The next parameter is the angle at which you want to draw the text. The angle works in the same way as the imagearc() function, but the angle specifies the direction in which the text is drawn. This means that because 0 degrees is at the 3 o'clock position, the text will be drawn in a left to right direction. A big difference between this function and imagearc() is that the direction of rotation is counterclockwise. You'll see this demonstrated a bit later. The next two parameters are the x and y position of where you want the font to start. That's the bottom-left hand position of the bounding block around the text—this is different from the imagestring() function, where the coordinates are the top-left corner of the bounding block. Next, you have to provide the full system path to the font (TTF) file on your disk. The last parameter is the actual string that you want to draw.

And you close it out as usual:

```
header("Content-type: image/png");
imagepng($textImage);
imagedestroy($textImage);
?>
```

To demonstrate how you can draw rotated text, change the line

```
imagefttext($textImage, 16, 0, 10, 50, $black,"C:\Windows\fonts\arial.ttf",
"Arial, 16 pixels");
```

to

```
imagefttext($textImage, 16, -30, 10, 30, $black,"C:\Windows\fonts\arial.ttf",
"Arial, 16 pixels");
```

All that has changed is that you're now drawing the text in a –30-degree direction, rather than 0 degrees. I said that the direction of rotation was counterclockwise, so a negative number would angle the text in a clockwise direction. If 0 degrees is 3 o'clock, then 30 degrees in a clockwise direction would be the 4 o'clock position on a clock. As you can see in Figure 16-25 the text is drawn at an angle down toward the 4 o'clock position.

Figure 16-25

Summary

This chapter discussed how to create and output images with PHP. You saw how to combine two images together to watermark images, and you learned how to open existing images and manipulate them to create thumbnail images. This enables you to add a new dimension to the scripts and Web pages that you already know how to create.

You also discovered how the PHP image functions work with color and how you can draw different shapes and text in your images.

Exercises

Here are some exercises to help you practice some of the techniques that you learned in this chapter and extend them to apply to real-world examples. You'll find solutions to these exercises in Appendix A.

1. Create a PHP script that opens an image file and adds a one-pixel black border to the image.

2. Using the `disk_total_space()` and `disk_free_space()` functions show how much disk space you have used on your hard drive in a graphical way.

17

Case Study:
A PHP Logging Agent

By now you have a good grounding in the basics of PHP programming! You've explored a wide range of topics and concepts including good programming techniques, object-oriented programming, PEAR, and fundamentals such as conditional statements, data types, scope, and code structure. In this, the final chapter, you pull together the various different aspects of PHP programming that you've learned in the book to create a more substantial application.

Of course, creating a reasonably sized application doesn't entail sitting down and simply writing out reams of code. There is plenty of planning and thought that goes into creating high-quality software, as you've learned. So this chapter presents the case study in a kind of software design lifecycle format. And as a bonus, you're introduced to Smarty templates, what they can do, and how to use them.

First, you'll get a look at the application in terms of a problem statement and explore how to solve the problem. After a suitable method of implementing a solution is decided, you design the program. This entails examining how the classes and objects that you create work together to produce the solution. Remember using UML in Chapter 13? You use it again in the design part of this application.

Then, you dive into the nitty-gritty of code implementation, looking into all of the important code that you'll use to perform the necessary tasks. A complete code listing isn't provided in this chapter because it would be prohibitively long, but the entire working application is available to download at the Wrox Web site.

Before any programmer can port her application to a production environment, she must first test the code rigorously. This chapter provides an in-depth look at a suite of tests that you'll use to prove that this application is production ready. After you've ensured that the code works and is robust, you'll see the whole application in action. You'll also take a look at the type of improvements you could implement if you decide to use this code as the basis for an application of your own.

That's about it! I'm sure you're eager to get on with it, so without further ado, go ahead, check out the case study.

Why a Logging Agent?

Nowadays, it's not particularly unusual for companies, and even individuals, to have several Web sites. Many publishers, for example, create different Web sites for each of their imprints. The reasons for doing this sort of thing are varied, but the important thing is that these companies often find it necessary to collect information from several different Web sites. If a publisher wanted to offer a discount on all its books to registered users at all of its Web sites, for instance, then the marketing department would probably need a list of all the users who were eligible for this discount to make the budget balance.

There's a huge number of permutations regarding the types of technologies used to create Web sites, so it's likely that information stored in the databases or server logs of each of these Sites varies wildly in format or even, on a more fundamental level, data type. Trying to pull registration details (or whatever) from each different site by looking at the server logs and database entries could prove to be quite a time-consuming task.

Assuming that some poor soul did, in fact, need to perform this task, then just retrieving all the information is probably not good enough for the people in the marketing department. Quite rightly, the people who requested the information probably want it in a uniform format to make it easy for them to read. Receiving server log reports mixed with database output from several different databases could be quite confusing because there's bound to be extraneous information in the reports of the required information spread over different tables. Manually formatting all this data would take a goodly amount of work to be sure.

This already quite daunting task could be made worse for the hapless person charged with performing this duty. He or she may be required to do this every few months to coincide with new book launches or conventions and so on. This type of repetitive work is definitely a candidate for automation, but how do you go about solving this problem?

The short answer is to log the information you want from each person at each Web site as and when she adds her information. That'll certainly help you locate the required information and, with a bit of communication, each site could probably ensure that it collects the information in a standard format—CSV files, for example. Not a bad solution, but it still means that each site needs to be visited to collect the required data. Even then, CSV files are not the prettiest to read through and the marketing department folks would probably complain if they were presented with a single, massive CSV file containing all the information they wanted.

You run the risk of duplicating a lot of information as well because it isn't unheard of for one person to be registered at more than one site. Making a check on each of the other site's logs before inserting a record seems ridiculous. So, it looks like the solution is really going to require a central server to log the information to—this means that you would only need to make one check before inserting a new record.

Okay, it's decided: what's needed is an application that receives information from various Web sites, logs that information, and then spits it out in a nice friendly format. How to solve the formatting part of the problem hasn't been discussed yet, but those of you who have used Smarty templates will probably be saying to yourselves that this is the perfect place to use a template to give the output a good consistent feel. And you'd be right! The application will enable you to query the central database server, which in this case will be implemented using SQLite. Then it'll serve up the results in a number of predefined formats—you'll see a couple in this chapter to illustrate the principle, but you are free to explore how to present reports in as much detail as you want. Bear in mind that you can also use Smarty for a number of other things, but you'll see those possibilities as they turn later in the chapter.

Part of the case study presentation is a quick introduction to Smarty because some of you may not have encountered it before. You'll be using `PHPUnit` to help test out the application, so there's a short section covering `PHPUnit`, too. If you already have a good working knowledge of Smarty and `PHPUnit`, feel free to skip those sections.

Smarty

"Why are we even covering Smarty?" some of you may be asking. Well, if you've ever worked on a Web-based application as either a page designer or a programmer, you might well be familiar with the frustration of having to modify your code every time someone else modified his or hers. For example, you receive the html pages for a given site and spend a week adding the PHP code to the presentation layer so that users can perform table lookups or send information (whatever the site is designed to do).

A week later, your clients decide they don't like the look of the site. The page designer goes into conniptions but redesigns everything according to the new mandate. He then goes on a week's vacation at the most remote golf course he can find, leaving a good looking but utterly broken Web site for you to fix. Because the entire HTML has been modified, none of your embedded PHP works properly, so all that's left is for you to go through it piece by piece to get it up and running again.

Wouldn't it be nice to separate the presentation logic from the business logic? It sure would, and this is where Smarty comes in.

Getting Smarty Set Up

Because you'll use Smarty in the case study, you want to make sure that you have it installed. When you complete the installation process, you'll run a quick example to make sure everything is working as it should, and then you can begin designing our case study.

Here's how to install Smarty:

1. Get a copy of the Smarty template engine from the Smarty Web site, `http://smarty.php.net`.

2. Unpack the download to a folder of your choice

3. You need to ensure that PHP can find the classes provided by Smarty. These are in the `libs` folder in your Smarty install. Add the absolute path to your `include_path` variable in your `php.ini` file:

```
includepath = ".;c:\php5\includes;c:\php5\pear;C:\Program
Files\Smarty-2.6.2\libs"
```

4. Of course, you can also treat the Smarty classes like any other and include them in your `.php` files on an individual basis like this:

```
require('C:\Program Files\Smarty-2.6.2\libs');
$smarty = new Smarty;
```

That's almost it. There are, however, a couple of things that you will need to bear in mind when trying to run Smarty. Smarty requires four directories which are (by default) named templates, templates_c, configs, and cache. You can explicitly define these values in the `Smarty.class.php` file—each is contained within the following variables, respectively: $template_dir, $compile_dir, $config_dir, $cache_dir. Please make sure that your Web server has permission to write to the $compile_dir (templates_c by default).

The documentation recommends that you set up a separate set of these directories for each application that will use Smarty.

For security reasons, it's recommended that you place these directories outside of the document root. The Web browser should never access them.

Next up is a quick example to ensure that everything is working fine.

Try It Out   **Use Smarty**

This example creates a template that presents the information you collect from a mysql table in a nicely formatted list. You make one .php file that's responsible for making a database connection, querying the table, and returning the results to the Smarty template. The template then formats the information gathered by the PHP script using one of the Smarty built-in functions.

1. Save the following code in a file called index.php. You either need access to the user table that you created in the database chapters, or you can create your own table to run this script against:

```php
<?php
require 'Smarty.class.php';
$smarty = new Smarty;

$hostname = "localhost";
$db_user = "me";
$db_pass = "mypassword";
$db_name = "sample_db";

// connect to the database
$conn = mysql_connect($hostname, $db_user, $db_pass);
if (!$conn){
    die ("Could not connect to the database!");
}

mysql_select_db($db_name);

$sql = "SELECT DISTINCT userposition FROM user";

$res = mysql_query($sql);
$results = array();
$i=0;
while ($pos=mysql_fetch_row($res)) {
    $results[$i++] = $pos[0];
}

$smarty->assign('results', $results);
$smarty->display('index.tpl');
?>
```

2. Now open up a new file, call it `index.tpl`, and save the following code in it:

```
<HTML>
<BODY>
<B>Here's a list of Player's position: </B><BR><BR>
{section name=position loop=$results}
  {$results[position]}<BR>
{/section}
</BODY>
</HTML>
```

3. Navigate to the `index.php` page, and the result should look like Figure 17-1

Figure 17-1

How It Works

The PHP script begins by including the `Smarty` class, and instantiating a new `Smarty` object to work with:

```
<?php
require 'Smarty.class.php';
$smarty = new Smarty;
```

The rest of the code really presents little that you haven't already seen. You create a mysql connection, making sure to exit the program with an error message if you cannot connect to the database properly:

```
$hostname = "localhost";
$db_user = "me";
$db_pass = "mypassword";
$db_name = "sample_db";

// connect to the database
$conn = mysql_connect($hostname, $db_user, $db_pass);
if (!$conn){
    die ("Could not connect to the database!");
}

mysql_select_db($db_name);
```

Next, create the SQL query that you'll use to query the database for the results you want. Because you want to present a list of the userpositions, and not every occurrence of a userposition in the table, you use the `DISTINCT` keyword. Then pop the results into an array:

```
$sql = "SELECT DISTINCT userposition FROM user";
$res = mysql_query($sql);
$results = array();
$i=0;
while ($pos=mysql_fetch_row($res)) {
    $results[$i++] = $pos[0];
}
```

The final part of this script is the interesting bit! You assign the results to a template variable (in this case the variable is called `results`) and then display the template (entitled `index.tpl`):

```
$smarty->assign('results', $results);
$smarty->display('index.tpl');
?>
```

That's the end of the PHP script, so turn your attention to the template file `index.tpl`. You begin with the standard HTML tags, and a short note explaining the results:

```
<HTML>
<BODY>
<B>Here's a list of Player's position: </B><BR><BR>
```

The business part of the template uses a `section` function to loop over the array of results. For this particular function, the `name` and `loop` attributes are required. In the example, the function loops as long as there are values in the `$results` array. As you can probably deduce, the section's name must be given next to variable name within brackets as follows:

```
{section name=position loop=$results}
    {$results[position]}<BR>
{/section}
```

Finish with the closing HTML tags:

```
</BODY>
</HTML>
```

The only other thing to note is that you will see a generated PHP file in your templates_c directory. This is what your template file produces. You don't have to worry about all the code contained in here—it's presented only for interest's sake:

```
<?php /* Smarty version 2.6.2, created on 2004-04-12 21:22:51
         compiled from index.tpl */ ?>
<HTML>
<BODY>
<B>Here's a list of Player's position: </B><BR><BR>
<?php if (isset($this->_sections['position']))
```

```
    unset($this->_sections['position']);
    $this->_sections['position']['name'] = 'position';
    $this->_sections['position']['loop'] = is_array($_loop=$this-
    >_tpl_vars['results']) ?
    count($_loop) : max(0, (int)$_loop); unset($_loop);
    $this->_sections['position']['show'] = true;
    $this->_sections['position']['max'] =
    $this->_sections['position']['loop'];
    $this->_sections['position']['step'] = 1;
    $this->_sections['position']['start'] =
    $this->_sections['position']['step'] > 0 ? 0 :
    $this->_sections['position']['loop']-1;
    if ($this->_sections['position']['show']) {
        $this->_sections['position']['total'] =
        $this->_sections['position']['loop'];
        if ($this->_sections['position']['total'] == 0)
            $this->_sections['position']['show'] = false;
    } else
        $this->_sections['position']['total'] = 0;
    if ($this->_sections['position']['show']):

    for ($this->_sections['position']['index'] =
    $this->_sections['position']['start'],
    $this->_sections['position']['iteration'] = 1;
    $this->_sections['position']['iteration'] <=
    $this->_sections['position']['total'];
    $this->_sections['position']['index'] +=
    $this->_sections['position']['step'],
    $this->_sections['position']['iteration']++):
    $this->_sections['position']['rownum'] =
    $this->_sections['position']['iteration'];
    $this->_sections['position']['index_prev'] =
    $this->_sections['position']['index'] -
    $this->_sections['position']['step'];
    $this->_sections['position']['index_next'] =
    $this->_sections['position']['index'] +
    $this->_sections['position']['step'];
    $this->_sections['position']['first'] =
    ($this->_sections['position']['iteration'] == 1);
    $this->_sections['position']['last'] =
    ($this->_sections['position']['iteration'] ==
    $this->_sections['position']['total']);
    ?>
      <?php echo $this->_tpl_vars['results'][$this->_sections['position']
      ['index']]; ?>
    <BR>
    <?php endfor; endif; ?>
    </BODY>
    </HTML>
```

That concludes our introduction to the Smarty template engine. For more information on Smarty, you can view the documentation at http://smarty.php.net/manual/en/. Now that you know enough about Smarty to follow along with its use in the case study, move on to an in-depth look at the design of the Logging Agent application.

PHPUnit

You can download the latest version of PHPUnit from the following address: http://sourceforge
.net/projects/phpunit/. Once you have downloaded it and placed it in a folder of your choice, you
need to ensure that PHP can find the phpunit.php file, so place the path to this file in PHP's
include_path. If you don't want to do this, then installing it in the same directory as the
code-under-test will also work.

Ready to see how you can make use of PHPUnit?

Working with PHPUnit

Of course, not everything PHPUnit does can be covered here, but once you have the basics, you can
explore PHPUnit yourself and play around with the various classes it provides.

First, PHPUnit provides you with functions you can use to test certain conditions. Say, you want to
determine whether a given method returns true or false. To do so, you make an assertion about that
method and test whether your assertion is correct. To test whether your assertion is correct, PHPUnit
provides the assert() method:

```
function assert($boolean, $message=0) {
    if (! $boolean)
        $this->fail($message);
}
```

If you want to make an assertion about a database connection being open, for example, you could have a
function like this:

```
function isOpen($db){
    If ($db == null){
        Return false;
    }
    return true;
}
```

Knowing that isOpen() returns a Boolean value, you could use assert() like this:

```
$this->assert(isOpen($db)), "You don't have a connection! Sorry...");
```

That's not the only function you'll be using, and you will see a couple of ways in which assert() can be
used. For now, though, that's all you need to know about how PHPUnit methods can be put to work.

Some of you may be wondering how you actually get at these methods because obviously you need to
have instantiated a PHPUnit object of some sort. Well, that's where the value of PHPUnit comes into play.
Using PHPUnit makes it easy to run all your tests in one go in a uniform, intuitive manner. Here's how:

1. To provide a context in which you can run your tests, create a class that extends the PHPUnit
   TestCase class:

```
class MultiLogTestSuite extends TestCase
```

2. Give yourself a specific context in which to run tests by defining the setUp() method—you literally set up the environment in which you are going to test things. In this case study, you'll define values for and create a couple of UserLog objects in the setUp() method, which you then use to run your tests against. (You'll see this in action in the "Testing the Application" section toward the end of this chapter.)

3. Create the tests you want to run, naming them with the following convention:

```
testMeaningfulName()
testAnotherMeaningfulyName()
```

4. Create a new suite of tests:

```
$suiteOfTests = new TestSuite;
```

5. Add your tests to this suite

```
$suiteOfTests->addTest(New MultiLogTestSuite("testMeaningfulName");
$suiteOfTests->addTest(New MultiLogTestSuite("testAnotherMeaningfulName");
```

6. Create a new TestRunner object. The TestRunner class simply defines a run() function to run all the defined tests, and report them back to you.

```
$testRunner = new TestRunner();
```

7. Finally, call the run() function (defined in the preceding step):

```
$testRunner->run($suiteOfTests);
```

That's it! PHPUnit will now faithfully run all the tests in your suite, reporting back all the results. Remember, you'll be doing all this in far more detail later in the chapter; this section only suffices to get you started. Don't worry if all this seemed a bit quick. It is recommended that you spend some time going through the PHPUnit class yourself after you've completed this chapter, because there's certainly plenty of value in being able to use these unit tests.

You have all the background information you need to build and test the case study, so charge ahead on.

Designing the Logging Agent

There is quite a lot to think about before you jump straight into coding the solution. Questions such as the following should be first and foremost in your mind when you begin any new project:

❑   What are you trying to accomplish?

❑   How are you going to accomplish it?

There are also several different aspects of any proposed application to think about. For example, what type of validation and error collecting are you going to implement? Do you need to implement any kind of security? And so on.

In this case, you don't really need too much security because you aren't going to be logging credit card information or anything like that (as tempting as that may be). Basically, you're looking at logging data such as user details, the site ID, and whatever other information users may be sending on. Nothing too private there! You will, however, want to make sure that you perform good exception handling and to that end you'll implement a `DataValidation` interface for error handling (more about this later).

The application can nominally be split in two based on which way the data is travelling—into or out of the database. On the one side, you want to receive a `POST` or `GET` from each site and have the application faithfully log away the data. On the other, you need to be able to retrieve the captured data and report it back in a nice, readable format. That's about the highest level look at what you're going to need.

In keeping with the latest programming techniques, you'll use an object-oriented approach to the application. PHP5, as you now know, has good support for the object-oriented paradigm, so you should definitely make use of the power of objects. One big advantage of OOP is that you can create a visual representation of your intended solution by using UML in the design phase—you'll look at that in a moment.

During the testing phase of the design process, you'll need to create a whole bunch of tests to ensure that the application behaves in a predictable manner, and that it isn't going to break if it's used. Debugging small scripts is often relatively straightforward, and shouldn't be too time-consuming, but as the size and complexity of an application increases, so does the time it takes to debug it. As you have just seen, `PHPUnit` can help reduce that time, and provides some useful functions that you can use to create a structured uniform testing suite.

One other thing to bear in mind is that you probably want to separate the application into layers—in other words, create a tiered architecture. That aids in debugging and maintenance further down the line because loosely coupled architectures enable you to compartmentalize logically separate code. Smarty will help to keep application code out of the presentation layer. What about the other side of things—the data layer? The answer of course is to create a class to deal with the bulk of the database handling functionality (much like the `DataManager` class you saw in Chapter 13).

SQLite will be the database of choice, and the required databases will be generated in a couple of scripts. On the subject of databases, let's take a look at the tables you are going to use to store the information you want to gather on the users of the various sites. Knowing the structure of your database often forces you to think about the type of code you'll need to build, so it's a good place to start.

The sitelogs.db Database

To make sense of the tables for this project, you need to know the assumptions that were made to design the case study. There are two fictional sites for the project—a comic book site and a hardware site. Of course, you could expand this quite easily to any number of sites. Each site will provide a few questions to its registered users. The types of sites from which you collect information aren't important—to make a suitable database you just need to know the type of field descriptors you need for the data. For example, if you're logging access dates, you'd use a date type, or a string for names, and so on.

Of course, simply logging a user's personal details to a central site is still not that useful. More than likely, you'll need to know which site each user logged on to, when he logged on, and whatever other site-specific information could be useful.

The `sitelogs.db` database will contain three tables used to store user information and the questions and answers from the different sites. Don't worry about setting up the tables—scripts to do that for you are provided with the code download. For right now, just be concerned about understanding what information is going to be stored where.

SQLite comes bundled with PHP5 and isn't covered in this chapter. If you have any problems getting it to work, please see this book's "SQLite" appendix.

The first table you need is entitled `user_log` and is created with the following SQLite query:

```
CREATE TABLE user_log (
    user_log_id integer primary key,
    visit_date  date,
    visit_time  time,
    site_id     int,
    demo_id     int,
    login_id    string,
    session     string,
    firstname   string,
    lastname    string,
    address1    string,
    address2    string,
    city        string,
    state       string,
    zip         string
)
```

This table holds all the information you need for each user. As you can see, you're going to log the date and time of the visit, session and login information, and more. Note that you're logging the site ID; it will be important in determining which user has been answering which questions from which site.

The next table, user_demographics, is created with the following query:

```
CREATE TABLE user_demographics (
    user_log_id integer,
    seq         int,
    answer      string,
    primary key (user_log_id, seq)
)
```

This table holds the answers the user supplied to the questions provided by the site they were visiting. It is related to the user_log table by the `user_log_id` field.

The final table is called demographic_description and it's created like this:

```
CREATE TABLE demographic_description (
    demo_id     int,
    seq         int,
    question    string,
    primary key (demo_id, seq)
)
```

As you may have surmised, this table simply holds the questions that are given on each site. The demo_id field holds the identifier of the type of questions asked. For instance an ID of 1 represents comic books and an id of 2 is for hardware. Because the questions are asked in a specific order you store that information in the seq field.

To summarize, the demographic_description table is prepopulated with the questions that are to be answered. The user_log table will contain the basic information, and the answers (to the questions) will be stored in the user_demographic table, ordered by seq.

Using UML to Map Out the Logging Agent

Creating diagrams of what you intend to build is an excellent way to visualize an application. All the major aspects of the application should be discussed before visualizing the various parts of the proposed solution using class and sequence diagrams. Sequence diagrams will help you to understand the flow of information through the logging agent from the presentation layer all the way to the database and back.

UML class diagrams can help you understand how each class is constructed, and how each relates to the other. And a sequence diagram will show how everything is intended to work. Don't worry about the code implementation at the moment; that'll all be covered later.

Mapping the Data Handling Classes

To begin with, there are two main types of logs: UserLog, and UserDemographic. UserLog contains all the information about a given user. The database is set up to store the relevant information for the users. You just need some way to represent the information internally because you can't just shove your request array directly into the database. Well, strictly speaking I suppose you could, but the data you end up storing probably wouldn't be very useful.

The best way to represent the user information is an object so that you can perform any and all operations on the data that you'd conceivably need. You could create a class to handle user information by deciding on the properties and methods you'd need to take in information, perform some operations (like data validation), and store it in the database.

A contructor, `__construct()`, could be used to initialize your object, and populate an array that you would use to represent our data. So, you have a UserLog class that contains the following property:

```
#contentBase: array
```

and method:

```
+__construct(initdict)
```

What else will you need? You know you're going to have to be able to persist the data to a database, so you should really have a method to do that for you. Add a public `persist()` method, too. What else? What about the need to perform some validation on the object data? Add a `getInvalidData()` method! Actually, you'll implement validation using an interface, so the method will simply provide the functionality for the `DataValidation` interface.

Speaking of interfaces, there's another operation that all of your data-handling classes will need to implement: displaying information back to the user. For that, you could use a `DataOutput` interface, which will expose the abstract function `toHTML()`. This means that the UserLog would also need to have a `toHTML()` function defined in it.

That seems to be all you really need to do for the UserLog. Hang on, though! You're populating an array with the data captured from a request. You really only want this object to persist user information, but obviously the user demographics (answers) are going to be part of the $_REQUEST environment variable. You're definitely going to need some way of pulling the demographic information out of this array and feeding it to the UserDemographic object, which will be used to deal with this data. Easily done, in this case the constructor takes care of it for you.

Because the UserLog class is going to be taking in all the information you capture, the UserDemogrpahic class is simply going to be contained within it. In other words, the only place a UserDemographic object is instantiated from is UserLog. This makes sense because the only time you need to worry about user demographics is when you are referring to users anyway. (Don't confuse this with inheritance—think of it almost like an object within an object instead.)

Because of the relationship that the UserDemographic and UserLog classes have, you need to add a gatherUserDemographics() method to the UserLog class. It will be responsible for retrieving the unique demographic answers from the database for use by the Logcontainer class (discussed in a moment).

There's one more thing you need to think about in terms of storing the user logs. What will you use as the primary key? You should really have a private property to store the user log id, which will be captured and used as the primary key in the user_log table. So, you add a private property called id, and provide a default integer value of 0 for it.

The user demographics are also going to need to be persisted and acted upon so there should be a UserDemographic class to handle that. In this project, the class will store a single demographic, with the associated question. The question is easily enough stored in a private property, but one of the most important aspects of this class that you need to retain the association between the user, the questions, and the order in which the questions are given (obviously your information is useless if you retrieve only the wrong answers for the wrong users from the database). So you add two public functions to the UserDemographic class: getId(Id) and setSequence(sequence).

The UserDemographic class won't be responsible for persisting itself because it is contained within the UserLog class, but it wouldn't hurt to have it generate its own SQL queries for use by the UserLog class. (You wouldn't really want the UserLog class to implement a method specifically for another class anyway.) As a result, you also add a toSQL() function to the UserDemographics class.

Of course, the two classes also have functionality in common, and you wouldn't be performing your OO duty if you didn't realize that there is scope to create a parent class from which these two classes inherit. Enter the PersistableLog class!

PersistableLog is going to be responsible for implementing __get() and __set() methods, getProperty() and setProperty() methods, and of course a destructor __destruct(). It will, in effect, be a base class for the other two classes we're discussing.

Internally, the objects are going to store information in several different formats. One will be an array of keys and values pertaining to the database, another will contain keys and values in human readable format for output. The result is that the objects you use will contain an array that can be used to insert values to the database (using the field names) and an array that can be used to return output with names that humans can read easily.

625

Whew! Almost there. The last thing to consider is a `LogContainer` class. As the name implies, it is simply going to be used to contain a series of `UserLog` objects. Why do you need this? You may ask. When you query the database for a report, you want to be able to retrieve a bunch of `UserLog` objects based on certain criteria. For example, you might want to view all the logs from one site, in which case, the `LogContainer` class will be initialized by retrieving and holding all the `UserLog` objects that meet that criteria.

Internally, you're going to store these `UserLog` objects in an array, which you will keep as private. You also need a private connection to the database, as well as a couple of utility methods such as `getCount()` (which returns the number of logs that are retrieved on any given request) and `getUserLogs()`.

That's really about it. The UML diagram in Figure 17-2 represents what you've learned about the logging agent.

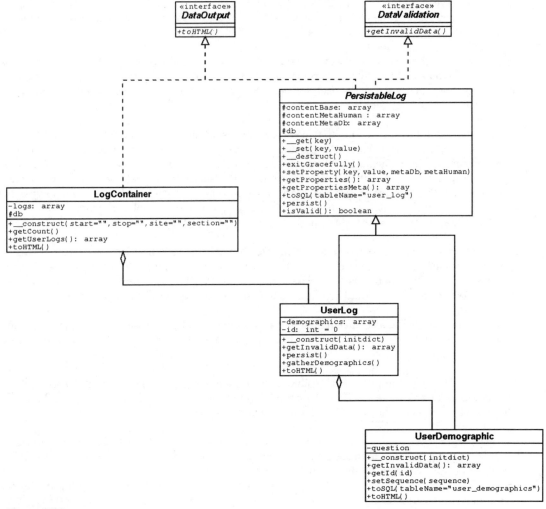

Figure 17-2

One thing worth is that there's a LogUtils class from which these classes inherit underlying database functionality and so on. The LogUtils class is part of good programming practice, promoting database abstraction. In other words, if you wanted to change databases, you wouldn't have too much to worry about because most of the changes would take place in the class. It isn't represented here because it isn't really part of the application business logic. You will see it in more detail in the code section.

Take a look at the exception handling class diagrams now.

Mapping the Exception Handling Classes

The base logging agent exception class, MultiLogException, extends the native PHP5 Exception class, in keeping with recommended practice. It holds a message as a protected property, which is assigned in the constructor, __constructor($message). Intuitively, it also provides two public functions, suggestedSolutions() and getErrorMessage().

An interesting thing to note here is that suggestedSolutions() is defined as abstract, so you're forcing the inheriting classes to implement it. This will make after you view the class diagram because there are a variety of different types of exceptions that will need to provide the user with different suggestions to rectify what has gone wrong.

Apart from that, the rest of the exception classes are designed to deal with specifics, like UserLog specific exceptions, LogContainer specific exceptions, invalid database, and simply invalid data exceptions. Figure 17-3 shows the diagram for these.

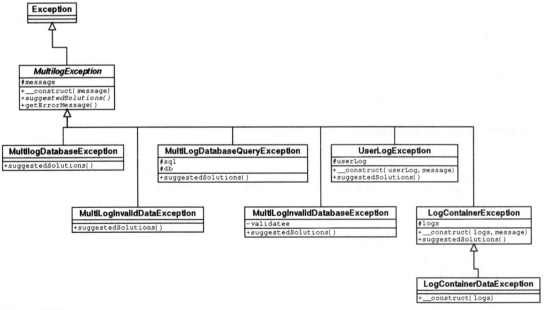

Figure 17-3

Finally, you should take a quick look at the application's sequence diagram to get a feel for how everything meshes together

The Logging Agent Sequence Diagram

From the Logging Agent sequence diagram in Figure 17-4 it should be apparent that most of the application revolves around the `UserLog` object. It is the `UserLog` class that's responsible for creating the `UserDemographic` objects, requesting and returning information from the database, as well as being involved with sending and retrieving information form the Smarty/presentation layer:

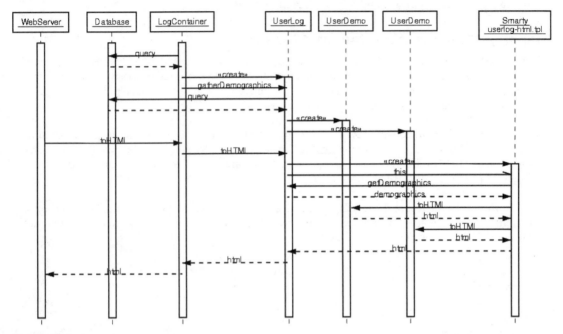

Figure 17-4

Coding the Solution

You've a good idea of how the logging agent is designed, you know what each class consists of, and you have a good notion of how they relate. In many ways, that's the most difficult part! All that's left for you now is to write out what's already in your head. Get started with the application's main classes.

Miscellaneous Scripts

Before you go any further, there are a couple of very small scripts that should be mentioned here. These files are not central to the way in which the application functions, but it's worth covering them here to avoid any confusion later on.

settings.php

The `settin common.php s.php` file holds a few global values that you'll need access to, and you should change these settings to reflect your set up:

```
<?
$GLOBALS['basepath'] = "/var/www/beginning-php/";
$GLOBALS['baseurl'] = "http://localhost/beginning-php/";
$GLOBALS['dbpath'] = "/var/www/beginning-php/logs/"; // keep out of webroot,
                                                     // final slash required
$GLOBALS['dbname'] = "sitelogs.db";
$GLOBALS['smarty-path']=$GLOBALS['basepath']."/lib/smarty/";
$GLOBALS['maxdemo'] = 1024;
?>
```

common.php

common.php just includes a few files that are needed most often by other classes:

```
<?
require_once ("class.exceptions.php");
require_once ("class.LogUtils.php");
?>
```

setup.php

The setup.php file is simply responsible for initializing the database, and returning one of the custom-made error messages in the event it fails:

```
<?
require_once ("settings.php");
require_once ("lib/common.php");

try {

    // will run it
    require_once ("logs/initialize.php");

} catch (MultiLogException $e) {
    print "<h3>An error has occured.</h3>";
    print $e->getErrorMessage();
}
?>
<h3>done</h3>
```

This class itself is not responsible for initializing the database. That is left for initialize.php.

initialize.php

The initialize.php script's function is simply to create the databases that you'll use. You've already looked at the databases so there's no need to spend much time analyzing the script, which begins by opening a connection to the database, creating the first table, user_log, and creating some indexes on it to expedite retrievals:

```
<?
$db = LogUtils::openDatabase ();

LogUtils::executeQuery($db, "drop table user_log");
```

```
LogUtils::executeQuery($db, "
CREATE TABLE user_log (
    user_log_id integer primary key,
    visit_date  date,
    visit_time  time,
    site_id     int,
    demo_id     int,
    login_id    string,
    session     string,
    firstname   string,
    lastname    string,
    address1    string,
    address2    string,
    city        string,
    state       string,
    zip         string
)");

LogUtils::executeQuery($db,
"CREATE INDEX index_user_log_site ON user_log (site_id)");
LogUtils::executeQuery($db,
"CREATE INDEX index_user_log_demo ON user_log (demo_id)");
LogUtils::executeQuery($db,
"CREATE INDEX index_user_log_login ON user_log (login_id);");
LogUtils::executeQuery($db,

"CREATE INDEX index_user_log_date ON user_log (visit_date);");
```

Next create the user_demographics table:

```
LogUtils::executeQuery($db, "drop table user_demographics");
LogUtils::executeQuery($db, "
CREATE TABLE user_demographics (
    user_log_id integer,
    seq         int,
    answer      string,
    primary key (user_log_id, seq)
)");
```

The demographic_description table is treated slightly differently because it won't contain information retrieved from a site:

```
LogUtils::executeQuery($db, "drop table demographic_description");

LogUtils::executeQuery($db, "
CREATE TABLE demographic_description (
    demo_id     int,
    seq         int,
    question    string,
    primary key (demo_id, seq)
)");
```

Instead, it stores the questions (demographics) for each site, so you need to initialize it with some data (in a production environment, you would know the questions provided on the site, and add them to this table separately). In fact, the demographics placed on a given site may even be drawn from this database—in other words, the questions are devised, approved, and placed into the database. When they are ready to be displayed, the site administrators upload them.

This table is critical to the application—it holds the data you need to associate with the answers you store in the user_demographics table. Without it, you wouldn't be able to tell which answer went with which question. You can verify what was said earlier about using a comic book store and a hardware store as the initial examples by looking at the following INSERT statements:

```
LogUtils::executeQuery($db,
"CREATE INDEX index_demographic_description_demo_pk ON
demographic_description (demo_id, seq)");

LogUtils::executeQuery($db,
"INSERT INTO demographic_description (demo_id, seq, question)
VALUES (1, 0, 'Comic books purchased in month period.' )");

LogUtils::executeQuery($db,
"INSERT INTO demographic_description (demo_id, seq, question)
VALUES (1, 1, 'Titles' )");

LogUtils::executeQuery($db,
"INSERT INTO demographic_description (demo_id, seq, question)
VALUES (1, 2, 'Dollar amount' )");

LogUtils::executeQuery($db,
"INSERT INTO demographic_description (demo_id, seq, question)
VALUES (1, 3, 'Credit amount' )");

LogUtils::executeQuery($db,
"INSERT INTO demographic_description (demo_id, seq, question)
VALUES (2, 0, 'Age of first use of screwdriver.' )");

LogUtils::executeQuery($db,
"INSERT INTO demographic_description (demo_id, seq, question)
VALUES (2, 1, 'Average number of months between screwdriver purchases.' )");

LogUtils::executeQuery($db,
"INSERT INTO demographic_description (demo_id, seq, question)
VALUES (2, 2, 'Total number of screwdrivers purchased during lifetime.' )");

LogUtils::executeQuery($db,
"INSERT INTO demographic_description (demo_id, seq, question)
VALUES (2, 3, 'Number of weeks between screwdrive uses.' )");
```

End by closing the database connection:

```
LogUtils::closeDatabase ($db);
?>
```

Data-Handling Scripts

The data-handling scripts form the core of the application, and are responsible for everything from opening and closing connections to the database, to converting incoming information into the correct internal format, to retrieving and manipulating data—basically everything you do with data happens in these. Specifically, you'll explore the following classes in this section:

- ❑ class.LogUtils.php
- ❑ class.PersistableLog.php
- ❑ class.UserLog.php
- ❑ class.LogContainer.php
- ❑ class.UserDemographic.php

class.LogUtils.php

class.LogUtils.php contains most of the functions that enable you to maintain database abstraction. It also contains a few other classes that are utility or convenience functions (useful to have around). You begin by including the exceptions class to implement the needed error handling. Then declare the class abstract because it doesn't need to do anything itself—it only contains methods needed by other classes, so you don't need to instantiate it:

```
<?
require_once ("class.exceptions.php");

abstract class LogUtils
{
```

You begin with a few utility classes that are used by the other classes. This returns a default value if a source is not present:

```
public static function getDef (&$source, $default)
{
    if (!empty ($source)) return $source;
    return $default;
}
```

It is used, for example, in the constructor of the UserLog class to assign a default user_log_id value (among other things), like this:

```
$this->id = LogUtils::getDef ($initdict["user_log_id"], 0);
```

The next utility function works just like the PHP implode function, except that it surrounds strings supplied to it with quotes, leaving numbers alone:

```
public static function implodeQuoted (&$values, $delimiter)
{
    $sql = "";
    $flagIsFirst = true;
    foreach ($values as $value) {
```

```
            if ($flagIsFirst) {
                $flagIsFirst = false;
            } else {
                $sql .= $delimiter;
            }

            if (gettype ($value) == "string") {
                $sql .= "'".$value."'";
            } else {
                $sql .= $value;
            }
        }
        return $sql;
    }
```

It is used by the `generateSQLInsert()` function later for formatting queries.

Next, there are a couple of date and time formatting functions:

```
public static function formattedDate ()
{
    return substr(date("c"), 0, 10);
}

public static function formattedTime ()
{
    return substr(date("c"), 11, 8);
}
```

Another utility function, required to flatten N-dimension arrays, is as follows:

```
public static function arrayNth ($a, $n)
{
    $out = array();
    foreach ($a as $item) {
        $out[$item[$n]]=$item[$n];
    }
    return $out;
}
```

Because you'd like to represent your data internally as arrays, the following function is pretty important. It takes a query, and pops the result into an array for you:

```
public static function queryToMultidimArray ($db, $sql)
{
    $out = array();

    $query = LogUtils::executeQuery ($db, $sql);

    if ( !$query ) {
    throw new MultiLogDatabaseQueryException ($sql);
    }
```

```
            while ($row = LogUtils::getQueryArray ($query)) {
                array_push ($out, $row);
            }

            return $out;
        }
```

There are a couple of functions included here for convenience. The first returns an array of all the distinct sites present within your database, and the second returns all the unique sections (or demo_ids):

```
        public static function gatherSites ($db)
        {
            return LogUtils::queryToMultidimArray(
                $db, "select distinct site_id from user_log order by site_id");
        }
        public static function gatherSections ($db)
        {
            return LogUtils::queryToMultidimArray (
                $db, "select distinct demo_id from user_log order by demo_id");
        }
```

One of the main functions you need to provide in this class is the capability to open your SQLite database. The following function does that for you. (It throws one of your own exceptions, `MultilogOpenDatabaseException()`, if there is a problem accessing the database):

```
        public static function openDatabase ()
        {
            $db = sqlite_popen($GLOBALS['dbpath'].$GLOBALS['dbname'], 0666, $err);
            if ( !$db ) {
                throw new MultiLogOpenDatabaseException ();
            }
            return $db;
        }
```

Generally, if you open a connection, you provide a close connection function. However, because this function opens a persistent connection, closing it may not be a good idea because you're sharing the connection between different parts of the application. If you decided to open individual connections each time you needed to access data, you'd close them with something like this:

```
        public static function closeDatabase ($db)
        {
            // this is what it might look like:
            if ( $db ) {
                sqlite_close ($db);
            }
        }
```

The next function makes use of the `implodeQuoted` function that you created earlier. It returns a generated SQL statement:

```
        public static function generateSqlInsert ($tableName, &$metas, &$values)
        {
            return "insert into ".$tableName.
```

```
"            ( ".implode            ($metas, ", ").") ) ".
" values ( ".LogUtils::implodeQuoted ($values, ", ").") ) ";
}
```

You need to think about errors that may be generated by the database. You can provide a function to return the last error generated by the database. This is actually used in the exceptions class to print out an error message to the screen in the event that your SQL goes horribly wrong.

Some of you may be frowning at this, because the last thing you should print to the browser is an error message that hands out a map of what's going on "under the hood." Here, though, you do it as an exercise in development, with the understanding that you never do this in a production environment:

```
public static function databaseError ($db)
{
    $err = "";

    if ( $db ) {
        $err = "error #".sqlite_last_error($db).
            " : ".sqlite_error_string (sqlite_last_error($db));
    }
    return $err;
}
```

Round off this class with a few functions that promote database abstraction:

```
public static function executeQuery ($db, $sql)
{
    return sqlite_query($sql, $db);
}
public static function getLastInsertedRowId ($db)
{
    return sqlite_last_insert_rowid($db);
}

public static function getQueryArray ($query)
{
    return sqlite_fetch_array ($query);
}
}
?>
```

Now you can move on to class.PersistableLog.php from which the remaining three classes inherit.

class.PersistableLog.php

The main function of class.PersistableLog.php is to expose the tools and functionality that the other data classes need to ensure you persist an object to the database. It should come as no surprise that it relies quite heavily on the LogUtils class (just discussed) to implement the connections it requires—this represents one layer of database abstraction.

To begin with, you declare the class abstract (because you won't need to instantiate it) and also declare a few arrays that you'll use to store human and database meta information about the data with which you're working. In other words, $contentBase will contain the actual values you insert into the database, whereas $contentMetaDb contains the names of the fields into which you insert the values. The $contentMetaHuman array contains the human-readable values.

```
abstract class PersistableLog implements DataValidation
{

    protected $contentBase = array();
    protected $contentMetaHuman = array();
    protected $contentMetaDb = array();

    protected $db = null;
```

Next, declare a __get() function:

```
function __get ($key)
{
    if (array_key_exists ($key, $this->contentBase)) {
        return $this->contentBase[$key];
    }
    return null;
}
```

Of course, you could also declare a destructor to close any open resources, like so:

```
function __destruct ()
{
    $this->exitGracefully();
}

function exitGracefully ()
{
    LogUtils::closeDatabase ($this->db);
    $this->db = null; // generic way of testing an open db connection
}
```

You create a setProperty() function to populate your local state, as well as getProperties() and getPropertiesMeta() to return the populated arrays:

```
function setProperty ($key, $value, $metaDb, $metaHuman)
{
    $this->contentBase[$key] = $value;
    $this->contentMetaHuman[$key] = $metaHuman;
    $this->contentMetaDb[$key] = $metaDb;
}

function getProperties () {
    return $this->contentBase;
}

function getPropertiesMeta () {
    return $this->contentMetaHuman;
}
```

Now convert it to an SQL statement with the following function (note the use of the `Logutils` function `generateSqlInsert()` in here):

```
function toSQL ($tableName = "user_log")
{
    return LogUtils::generateSqlInsert (
        $tableName, $this->contentMetaDb, $this->contentBase);
}
```

You've reached the business part of this class. The `persist()` function is responsible for inserting the data into the database, or exiting gracefully. First, check whether the object is valid; if it isn't, throw an exception:

```
function persist ()
{
    $rowid = 0;

    // do not bother to continue if this object is not valid.
    if (!$this->isValid()) {
        throw new MultiLogInvalidDataException ($this);
    }
```

Because you're going to close the connection after you've persisted the data, check first whether the connection is alive. If not, say so:

```
if ($this->db == null) {
    throw new MultiLogInvalidDatabaseException($this);
}
```

Assuming all has gone well, generate the necessary SQL and then close the connection:

```
if (LogUtils::executeQuery($this->db, $this->toSQL())) {
    $rowid = LogUtils::getLastInsertedRowId ($this->db);
    $this->exitGracefully();
} else {
    throw new MultiLogDatabaseQueryException ($this->toSQL(),
                                              $this->db);
}
```

Utilizing the primary key is often a handy thing because it's essentially the unique [database] identifier. If you have it, return it:

```
    return $rowid;
}
```

Finally, you define the `isValid()` function which was used in `persist()`—this is merely a Boolean version of `getInvalidData()`:

```
function isValid ()
{
    if (count ($this->getInvalidData()) == 0) {
```

```
            return true;
        }

        return false;
    }
}

?>
```

class.UserLog.php

The main purpose of class.UserLog.php is to map user log data to the database. It also associates the answers to the questions that are from a specific site. It implements DataValidation and can store itself (effectively, the captured data) to the SQLite database using the PersistableLog class, which was just covered. Like the other data classes it relies on the LogUtils class to deal with SQLite connections.

To begin with, include the files you need. Notice that the Smarty class is included here. That's because one of the utility functions you provide in this class demonstrates how you can use Smarty to output data in HTML format. Remember that you use the LogUtils class in here, but it's included via the common.php file:

```
<?
require_once ("common.php");
require_once ("class.PersistableLog.php");
require_once ("class.UserDemographic.php");
require_once ("interface.DataValidation.php");
require_once ('Smarty.class.php');
```

Next, you declare the private variables that you'll need, and create the constructor. The purpose of the constructor is to map the incoming data to your internal state, and database level names. This works because the data that is passed to UserLog on instantiation is in the form of an array:

```
class UserLog extends PersistableLog implements DataValidation
{
    private $demographics = array();
    private $id = 0;

    function __construct ($initdict) // pass by value on purpose
    {
        $key = "";
        $this->db = LogUtils::openDatabase ();
        $this->id = LogUtils::getDef ($initdict["user_log_id"], 0);
```

To get a clear understanding of precisely what's happening in here, take a look at how you work on one value in particular. You'll see how the visit_date property is set, a process that's repeated for all other keys. First, you assign the database level field name:

```
$key="visit_date";
```

Using the setProperty() function, which is contained in the PersistableLog class, you associate the key with its corresponding value as well as the human readable description (which can be used for output and so on). Recall that setProperty() takes the following form:

```
function setProperty ($key, $value, $metaDb, $metaHuman)
```

Knowing this, you can see that $value, in this case, is given by the following expression:

```
LogUtils::getDef ($initdict[$key], LogUtils::formattedDate())
```

You already know that getDef() simply returns the second argument in the event that the first does not exist. So, in effect, you're using the following statement to provide your internal representation of the data with default values in the event that certain values were not submitted from the site:

```
$this->setProperty ($key,
    LogUtils::getDef ($initdict[$key], LogUtils::formattedDate()),
    $key, "Date of visit");
```

The rest of the assignments are dealt with in exactly the same way. You merely run through each key value and call setProperty():

```
$key="visit_time";
$this->setProperty ($key,
    LogUtils::getDef ($initdict[$key], LogUtils::formattedTime()),
    $key, "Time of visit");

$key="site";
$this->setProperty ($key,
    LogUtils::getDef ($initdict[$key], 0),
    "site_id", "Site ID");

$key="site_id";
$this->setProperty ("site",
    LogUtils::getDef ($initdict[$key], $this->site),
    $key, "Site ID");

$key="section";
$this->setProperty ($key,
    LogUtils::getDef ($initdict[$key], 0),
    "demo_id", "Section ID");

$key="section_id";
$this->setProperty ("section",
    LogUtils::getDef ($initdict["demo_id"], $this->section),
    "demo_id", "Section ID");

$key="login";
$this->setProperty ($key,
    LogUtils::getDef ($initdict[$key], ""),
    "login_id","Login ID");

$key="login_id";
$this->setProperty ("login",
    LogUtils::getDef ($initdict[$key], $this->login),
    $key, "Login ID");

$key="session";
$this->setProperty ($key,
```

```
        LogUtils::getDef ($initdict[$key], ""),
        $key, "Session");

$key="firstname";
$this->setProperty ($key,
    LogUtils::getDef ($initdict[$key], ""),
    $key, "First Name");

$key="lastname";
$this->setProperty ($key,
    LogUtils::getDef ($initdict[$key], ""),
    $key, "Last/Sur Name");

$key="address1";
$this->setProperty ($key,
    LogUtils::getDef ($initdict[$key], ""),
    $key, "Address Line 1");

$key="address2";
$this->setProperty ($key,
    LogUtils::getDef ($initdict[$key], ""),
    $key, "Address Line 2");

$key="city";
$this->setProperty ($key,
    LogUtils::getDef ($initdict[$key], ""),
    $key, "City");

$key="state";
$this->setProperty ($key,
    LogUtils::getDef ($initdict[$key], ""),
    $key, "State/Province");

$key="zip";
$this->setProperty ($key,
    LogUtils::getDef ($initdict[$key], ""),
    $key, "ZIP/Postal Code");
```

Before you finish with the constructor, you need to deal with the answers (demographics) to each site's questions, which are also submitted in the request along with the UserLog information. You have a separate table to deal with these demographics, so you call the UserDemographics class to create objects that you can send to that table. You don't know how many demographics could be contained within the request, so iterate through them until you either reach a limit, or run out. Included at the top of this class is the class.UserDemographic.php file, and this is where it comes in.

For each demographic (submitted in the request in the form demo1=>value1, demo2=>value2 and so on), create a new UserDemographic object and populate its internal state with the values sent in the request. Don't worry too much about UserDemographic at the moment; you'll get to it later.

```
for ($i=0; $i <= $GLOBALS['maxdemo']; $i++) {
    $key = 'demo'.$i;
    if (array_key_exists($key, $initdict)) {
```

```
                $d = new UserDemographic (
                   array("id"=>$this->id, "demo"=>$initdict[$key]));
                array_push ($this->demographics, $d);
            } else {
                break;
            }
        }
    }
}
```

You also need a function to associate the unique answers with the predefined questions. This leads you to the rather ugly SQL statement that you place in a function called gatherDemographics():

```
function gatherDemographics ()
{
    if (!$this->db) $this->db = LogUtils::openDatabase ();
    $sql = "SELECT ud.user_log_id AS id, ud.answer AS demo,
    dd.question AS question FROM user_demographics ud
    LEFT JOIN user_log ul ON
       ud.user_log_id = ul.user_log_id
    LEFT OUTER JOIN demographic_description dd ON (
       ul.demo_id = dd.demo_id and ud.seq = dd.seq ) WHERE
       ul.user_log_id =
       '".$this->id."' AND ul.site_id = '". $this->site."' AND
       ul.demo_id =
       ".$this->section." ORDER BY ud.seq";

    $query = LogUtils::executeQuery ($this->db, $sql);
    if ( !$query ) {
       throw new MultiLogDatabaseQueryException ($sql);
    }

    while ($row = LogUtils::getQueryArray($query)) {
        $demo = new UserDemographic ($row);
        if ($demo->isValid()) {
            array_push ($this->demographics, $demo);
        }
    }

    LogUtils::closeDatabase ($this->db);
}
```

You should also provide some checks that the data you have is valid. This could be extended to whatever you want really, but three tests are provided here. You actually use this class from PersistableLog::isValid() and the exception classes (which are discussed a little later on):

```
function getInvalidData ()
{
    $badDataEntries = array();
    if ($this->site == 0) {
        array_push ($badDataEntries, "'site' is zero");
    }
```

```
        if ($this->section == 0) {
            array_push ($badDataEntries, "'section' is zero");
        }

        if ($this->login == "") {
            array_push ($badDataEntries, "'login' is missing");
        }

        return $badDataEntries;
    }
}
?>
```

Finally, you define your own persist function so that you have `UserDemographic` data, which you need to persist to the Demographics table. You also need to associate it with the UserLog entities, so you need access to the user_log_id, which you can only grab after the UserLog object has been persisted:

```
function persist()
{
    // persist ourself
    $this->id = parent::persist();
    // persist our demographics, order matters
    $i=0;
    foreach ($this->demographics as $demo) {
        $demo->setId($this->id);
        $demo->setSequence($i++);
        $demo->persist();
    }
}
}
?>
```

class.LogContainer.php

As its name implies, `class.LogContainer.php` merely acts as a container for `UserLog` objects. As usual, you begin by including the necessary files, and declaring your class:

```
<?php
require_once ("common.php");
require_once ("class.UserLog.php");

class LogContainer
{
    private $sql;
    private $logs = array();
    protected $db = null;
```

The constructor initializes an SQL query that will be used to obtain the UserLog information you want to return. (In case you are wondering, this class is called when you want to make a report of the logs that are contained within the database.)

```
function__construct ($start = "",
                     $stop = "",
                     $site = "",
                     $section = "")
```

```
    {
        $initsql = "SELECT * FROM user_log WHERE 1=1 and";
        if ($site <> "")     $initsql .= " site_id = '".$site."' and";
        if ($section <> "")  $initsql .= " demo_id = '".$section."' and";
        if ($start <> "")    $initsql .= " visit_date >= '".$start."' and";
        if ($stop <> "")     $initsql .= " visit_date <= '".$stop."'";
```

You ensure that your SQL query doesn't trail an "and", and then use the statement to query the database:

```
// remove final and?
if (substr($initsql, strlen($initsql)-4, 4) == " and") {
    $initsql = substr($initsql, 0, strlen($initsql) - 4);
}

// query database
$this->db = LogUtils::openDatabase();
$query = LogUtils::executeQuery ($this->db, $initsql);

if ( !$query ) {
    throw new MultiLogDatabaseQueryException ($initsql);
}
```

Now, you go through the results and if they are valid, reassociate them with their questions. If they aren't, populate the $badLogs array, which can be used to give you an error message (at the bottom of the constructor):

```
$badLogs = array();
while ($row = LogUtils::getQueryArray($query)) {
    $ul = new UserLog ($row);
    if ($ul->isValid()) {
        $ul->gatherDemographics(); // reassociate demo questions
        array_push ($this->logs, $ul);
    } else {
        array_push ($badLogs, $ul);
    }
}

LogUtils::closeDatabase ($this->db);
if (count ($badLogs) > 0) {
    throw new LogContainerInvalidDataException($badLogs);
}
}
```

The rest of the class provides a couple of functions that come in handy here and there. For example, getCount() enables you to capture the number of logs you have; you can use this to report back to the browser:

```
function getCount ()
{
    return count ($this->logs);
}
```

643

```
        function toHTML ()
        {
            $html = '<table border="0" class="LogContainerTable">';
            foreach ($this->logs as $ul) {
                $html .= $ul->toHTML();
            }
            $html .= "</table>";
            return $html;
        }
        function getUserLogs ()
        {
            return $this->logs;
        }
}
?>
```

class.UserDemographic.php

The final data class in the logging agent—class.UserDemographic.php—is actually used solely from within UserLog (which makes sense because all the demographic information is supplied to UserLog anyway). It holds a single user demographic, its associated question, and the UserLog identifier for persistence. Here's how to begin:

```
<?
require_once ("common.php");
require_once ("class.PersistableLog.php");

class UserDemographic extends PersistableLog
{
    private $question = "";
```

Notice that you inherit from PersistableLog so that you can expose some of its functionality in this class. Make use of it in the constructor, like this:

```
    function__construct ($initdict) // pass by value on purpose
    {
        $key = "";
        $this->db = LogUtils::openDatabase ();

        $this->setId(LogUtils::getDef ($initdict["id"],0));
        $this->setId(LogUtils::getDef ($initdict["user_log_id"], $this->id));
        $this->setProperty ("demo",
            LogUtils::getDef ($initdict["demo"], 0),
            "answer",
            LogUtils::getDef ($initdict["question"], "Demographic Answer"));
        $this->setProperty ("demo",
            LogUtils::getDef ($initdict["answer"], $this->demo),
            "answer",
            LogUtils::getDef ($initdict["question"], "Demographic Answer"));
        $this->question = LogUtils::getDef($initdict["question"], "");
    }
```

The `setId()` function used in the constructor is defined next, as follows:

```
function setId ($id)
{
    $this->setProperty ("id", $id, "user_log_id", "User ID");
}
```

The order in which you sequence the answers is very important:

```
function setSequence ($seq)
{
    $this->setProperty ("seq", $seq, "seq", "Sequence");
}
```

You should perform some validation on the `UserLog` object, so define a `getInvalidDate()` function here. Don't check the demographic because "nothing" may be a valid answer:

```
function getInvalidData ()
{
    $badDataEntries = array();

    if ($this->id == null || $this->id <= 0) {
        array_push ($badDataEntries, "'id' is zero");
    }

    return $badDataEntries;
}
```

Redefine the toSQL function like so:

```
function toSQL ($tableName = "user_demographics")
{
    return LogUtils::generateSqlInsert ($tableName,
                            $this->contentMetaDb,
                            $this->contentBase);
}
```

Validation and Error-Handling Scripts

Right from the start it's important to think about how to validate data, and deal with the various errors that can be kicked up. In this application, you've seen how you can implement validation using an interface, and also how to provide a base error-handling class that all other classes can make use of. This is another example of how good programming technique enables you to separate functionality out so that you maximize code reuse and provide a single point of contact to modify specific functionality.

This section presents two scripts. One is simply the interface for data validation, and the other is the exceptions class from which all the data classes inherit. Obviously, you've already seen these scripts in action by virtue of the fact that you've made many calls to functions like `MultiLogException()` and `getInvalidData()` from our data scripts.

It won't hurt to give you a quick bird's eye view of one of the ways in which you've used the `DataValidation` interface in the logging agent, so let's do that before you dive into the code.

The interface is implemented by `class.exceptions.php`, which is the base class for all exceptions, and provides several different classes to cater to the various errors that you may or may not encounter. You'll recall from the UML diagrams presented earlier in the chapter that `class.exceptions.php` contains the following classes:

- `MultiLogException`
- `MultiLogOpenDatabaseException`
- `MultiLogDatabaseQueryException`
- `MultiLogInvalidDatabaseException`
- `MultiLogInvalidDataException`
- `UserLogException`
- `LogContainerException`
- `LogContainerInvalidDataException`

Some of these exception classes force the class throwing the exception to implement the `getInvalidData()` function for themselves. For example, `MultiLogInvalidDataException` declares the following function:

```
function suggestedSolutions ()
{
    return $this->validatee->getInvalidData();
}
```

The `UserDemographic` class, you remember, defines a `getInvalidData()` function like so:

```
function getInvalidData ()
{
    $badDataEntries = array();

    if ($this->id == null || $this->id <= 0) {
        array_push ($badDataEntries, "'id' is zero");
    }

    // nothing may be a valid answer, don't check the demo
    return $badDataEntries;
}
```

The constructor of the `UserDemographic` class contains the following statement:

```
$this->db = LogUtils::openDatabase ();
```

If you go to the `LogUtils` class, you see that it inherits from the exceptions base class, and this is required because `openDatabase()` has the following structure:

```
public static function openDatabase ()
{
    $db = sqlite_popen($GLOBALS['dbpath'].$GLOBALS['dbname'], 0666, $err);
    if ( !$db ) {
```

```
            throw new MultiLogOpenDatabaseException ();
        }
        return $db;
    }
```

In case you are wondering how the suggestedSolutions() function in the MultiLogOpenData-baseException class gets called, remember that this class extends MultiLogException, which declares its suggestedSolutions() function as abstract, meaning that any call made to this function has to be implemented by the calling class. As luck would have it, MultiLogException does make a call to suggestedSolutions() like this:

```
function getErrorMessage()
{
    $message = "<h3>Error</h3>".$this->message."<br>";
    $message .= "<ul>";
    foreach ($this->suggestedSolutions() as $solution) {
        $message .= "<li>".$solution;
    }
    $message .= "</ul>";
    return ($message);
}
}
```

Okay, that should give you an idea of the many ways in which you can use the interface. Now let's look at the code.

Pretty simple declaration here—nothing you haven't seen before. The function is basically used to define the validity of the current state of the given object:

```
<?
interface DataValidation
{
    abstract function getInvalidData();
}
?>
```

You already know that class.exceptions.php is the base exception class from which all other classes inherit, so you don't need to include anything other than the interface to begin with:

```
<?
require_once ("interface.DataValidation.php");
```

The first class you declare is MultiLogException, which is used by many of the other exception classes. You must declare this class abstract because you implement one abstract function. The abstract function is used to force subclasses to implement their own suggested solutions to the problem as an array:

```
abstract class MultiLogException extends Exception
{
    protected $message = ""; // every exception has a reason

    /**
     * Initialize self with an error message
     */
```

```
function__construct ($msg)
{
    $this->message = $msg;
}

abstract function suggestedSolutions ();
```

You also provide a function for returning the error message. As you can see, this relies on the calling function to implement the suggestedSolutions() function as discussed earlier:

```
function getErrorMessage()
{
    $message = "<h3>Error</h3>".$this->message."<br>";
    $message .= "<ul>";
    foreach ($this->suggestedSolutions() as $solution) {
        $message .= "<li>".$solution;
    }
    $message .= "</ul>";
    return ($message);
}
}
```

The next class you define is called MultiLogOpenDatabaseException and it extends the MultiLogException class you just defined. The constructor simply passes a message to the parent constructor in MultiLogException:

```
class MultiLogOpenDatabaseException extends MultiLogException
{
    function__construct ()
    {
        parent::__construct ("Open Database Error");
}
```

In this instance you implement suggestedSolutions() right here, because you won't expect the calling class to do it for you—this is called only when you have an error opening the database, so you just need to echo out a standard message. (Remember, in a production environment you would not report these errors to the browser. Doing so would constitute a great security risk to your system.)

```
function suggestedSolutions ()
{
    return array ("Has the initization script been run yet?",
                "Is the directory (".$GLOBALS['dbpath'].") readable and
                writeable? ...by the webserver?",
                "Is the file (".$GLOBALS['dbname'].") readable and
                writable? ...by the webserver?",
                "Was the database pre-existing and created with the same
                version of sqlite as php?"
                );
}
}
```

Now declare `MultiLogDatabaseQueryException` to deal with query exceptions. It also inherits from the parent class `MultiLogException` and passes a message to the parent constructor. You'll implement `suggestedSolutions()` in this class so you allow the constructor to accept two arguments that can be used in that function:

```
class MultiLogDatabaseQueryException extends MultiLogException
{
    protected $sql = "";
    protected $db = null;

    function_construct ($sql = "(no sql supplied)", $db = null)
    {
    parent::__construct ("Database Query Exception");
    $this->sql = $sql;
    $this->db = $db;
}
```

Then implement the `suggestedSolutions()` method, which uses the `$db` and `$sql` (the database connection and SQL query) values, if they have been passed, to print out some hopefully helpful messages:

```
function suggestedSolutions ()
{
    $err = array();

    if ($this->db) {
        array_push (
            $err, "Database error: ".LogUtils::databaseError ($this->db));
    }
    array_push ($err, "Database error, suspect SQL = ".$this->sql);
    array_push ($err, "Do you have write permission?");
    array_push ($err, "Is there sufficient space for the database?");

    return $err;
    }
}
```

The next class simply returns some insightful messages if you find that you're using a bad database connection:

```
class MultiLogInvalidDatabaseException extends MultiLogException
{
    function__construct ()
    {
        parent::__construct ("Invalid Database");
    }

    function suggestedSolutions ()
    {
        return array ("Was the database correctly opened?",
                "Was it perhaps closed twice or are you trying to
                save the same thing twice?");
    }
}
```

649

The next class is quite important because it's responsible for telling you why you have invalid data. Pass it an object that implements `DataValidation`—this is necessary because you don't define `getInvalidData()` here. You throw this exception before persisting an object to the database. Recall that you check to see if an object is valid before bothering to write it to the database in the `PersistableLog` class. If it isn't, you pass that object to this function to find out why it's invalid and to let you know:

```php
class MultiLogInvalidDataException extends MultiLogException
{
    private $validatee = null;

    function __construct ($v)
    {
        parent::__construct ("Invalid Data");
        $this->validatee = $v;

    }

    function suggestedSolutions ()
    {
        return $this->validatee->getInvalidData();
    }
}
```

You define a couple of `UserLog` specific exception classes. After displaying a short error message, you call the `exitGracefully()` method to release the database connection—remember that `exitGracefully()` is defined in PersistableLog, UserLog's base class:

```php
abstract class UserLogException extends MultiLogException
{
    protected $userLog = null;

    function __construct ($userLog, $message)
    {
        parent::__construct ($message);
        $this->userLog = $userLog;
        $this->userLog->exitGracefully(); // defined in PersistableLog
    }
}
```

The `LogContainer` class also will need to implement some exception handling, so define the following class to go through each and every `UserLog` defined within the container, and retrieve the invalid data from each and every one of them:

```php
abstract class LogContainerException extends MultiLogException
{
    protected $logs = null;

    function __construct ($logs, $message) {
        parent::__construct ($message);
        $this->logs = $logs;
    }
```

```
        function suggestedSolutions ()
        {
            $solutions = array();
            foreach ($this->logs as $log) {
                $solutions = array_merge (
                    $solutions, $log.DataValitation::getInvalidData());
            }
            return $solutions;
        }
    }
```

That exception doesn't really tell you which logs contain invalid data, so you do that by defining a class that inherits from `LogContainerException()` like this:

```
class LogContainerInvalidDataException extends LogContainerException
{
    function__construct ($logs)
    {
        parent::__construct ($logs, "UserLogs contain invalid data.");
    }
}

?>
```

With that, you're done. You've implemented exception handling for the various data classes using a variety of different object-oriented methods ranging from a straight invocation of a class to more complex uses of inheritance and interfaces. Obviously, there is scope to increase the amount of exception handling you implement, but this is a good base from which to start.

Having an exception class makes it quite easy to define a new exception (dealing with whatever issue you need) and call it from the class which throws the exception. This is one good demonstration for the power of encapsulation which is one of the cornerstones of the object-oriented design paradigm.

Presentation Scripts and Templates

With the bulk of the application completed, take a brief look at the interface of the Logging agent. An index page will enable you to initialize the database, run all the tests (which are created in the next section), post information to the logging agent, and view reports. In this section the focus is on the Smarty template files, but you'll also explore the index page because it's the main point of contact with the application.

index.php

The index file, `index.php`, really just serves as a drop-in point for the rest of the application. As you can see from the following code, it provides you with a set of links pointing to the main test files as well as the `userlog.php` script, which is responsible for making use of the data-handling classes:

```
<H3>Options</H3>
<UL>
<LI><A HREF="setup.php">Initialize database</A> (warning, will delete data!)
<LI><A HREF="lib/test.UserLog.php">Run UserLog test suite</A>
```

```
<LI><A HREF="lib/test.LogContainer.php">Run LogContainer test suite</A>
<LI><A HREF="lib/test.UserDemographic.php">Run UserDemographic test suite</A>
<LI><A HREF="post.php">Post logging data</A>
<lLI<A HREF="report.php">View reports</A>
</UL>
```

The final link in this code is to `report.php`, which is responsible for displaying an interface for users to query for the logs they would like to have displayed.

report.php

Because you'll be using Smarty templates in this script (`report.php`), one of the first things you need to do is include the `Smarty` class along with any others you'll need. If you have your own distribution of Smarty, change the path to your `Smarty` class:

```
<?

require_once ("settings.php");
require_once ("lib/common.php");
require_once ($GLOBALS["smarty-path"].'Smarty.class.php');
```

Next, create the Smarty object and assign the page title to the Smarty title variable:

```
$smarty = new Smarty;
$smarty->assign ('title', "MultiLog Reporting");
```

You need to declare a function that will be used to format the site and section items suitable for display in an HTML drop-down control. First, make the array larger at the beginning and insert a blank string for the default selection. The `arrayNth()` function is used to flatten the associative array into a simple one-dimensional array:

```
function optionMassage (&$a) {
    $a = array_pad ($a, count($a)*(-1)-1,""); // enlarge array at front
    $a[0][0] = ""; // insert blank in front
    $a = LogUtils::arrayNth($a,0); // flatten array to include only values
    return $a;
}
```

You now need to decide which report you want to display. Initially, you need to display `report.tpl` because that's what enables you to make your selection of criteria for retrieving logs:

```
if ($_REQUEST['action'] <> "html") {

    // display input
    $db = LogUtils::openDatabase();

    $smarty->assign ('sites', optionMassage(LogUtils::gatherSites($db)));
    $smarty->assign ('sections', optionMassage(LogUtils::gatherSections($db)));

    LogUtils::closeDatabase($db);

    $smarty->display ("report.tpl");
```

If you've made a selection, then you use the `report-html.tpl` template to display the results of the request. To do this, first create a new `LogContainer` object and populate it with the values retrieved from the request made using the `report.tpl` template. Displaying the results is then just a matter of assigning the results to the next template:

```
} else {

    // display results
    require_once ("lib/class.UserLog.php");
    require_once ("lib/class.LogContainer.php");

    $logs = new LogContainer ($_REQUEST["start_Year"].
    "-".$_REQUEST["start_Month"]."-".$_REQUEST["start_Day"],
    $_REQUEST["stop_Year"]."-".$_REQUEST["stop_Month"]."-".
    $_REQUEST["stop_Day"],
    $_REQUEST["site"], $_REQUEST["section"]);

    $smarty->assign ('logs', $logs);
    $smarty->display ("report-html.tpl");
}

?>
```

You'll see these scripts in action toward the end of the chapter. For now, take look at the actual template files.

report.tpl

The `report.tpl` template simply displays a few drop-down lists that you can use to create a query to retrieve and display the desired logs. Notice that the form returns `html` as the value for the action key. That enables you to decide which report to display in the `report.php` script:

```
<html><title>MultiLog Report</title>
<body>

<h3>{$title}</h3>

<form action="report.php" method="post">
<table>
<tr><td align="right">Start Date:</td><td>{html_select_date prefix="start_"
start_year="-2"}</td></tr>
<tr><td align="right">End Date:</td>  <td>{html_select_date prefix="stop_"
start_year="-2"}</td></tr>
<tr><td align="right">Site:</td>      <td><select name=site> {html_options
options=$sites} </select> </td></tr>
<tr><td align="right">Section:</td>   <td><select name=section> {html_options
options=$sections} </select></td></tr>
<tr><td align="right"></td>           <td><input type="submit" value="Show
Report"></td></tr>
</table>
<input type="hidden" name="action" value="html">
</form>

</body>
</html>
```

report-html.tpl

If you have logs to display, use the `report-html.tpl` template to print them out to the screen. This is a pretty basic output, but you could extend it as you see fit. Simply put, it displays the results in a table, and reports back the number of logs returned. You may recall from the sequence diagram presented earlier you'd see the Smarty template actually makes a request—in this case, it is to the `toHTML()` and `getCount()` methods of the `UserDemographic` class:

```
<html><title>MultiLog Report</title>
<body>

<h3>{$title}</h3>

<table width="2048"><tr><td>
{$logs->toHTML ()}
</td></tr></table>

<h3>Log Count: {$logs->getCount()}</h3>

</body>
</html>
```

You're basically done creating the application. All the business logic is in place, and like good programmers, you've implemented data validation and exception handling throughout. You'd think that you're more or less ready to sign off on everything and go to lunch. Almost....

Testing the Application

There is, in fact, quite a lot yet to do. How do you know that everything actually works? Sure, you may have run it a few times and everything held together, but what you need is a sophisticated approach to putting the program through its paces. PHPUnit was discussed early in the chapter, and here's where it comes in. Now, you'll build a set of tests to check that that application is robust, and acts the way you expect it to act.

Three sets of unit tests will serve to verify the expected behavior of the `UserLog`, `UserLogContainer`, and `UserDemographic` classes. For each class, you will set a specific context in which to run the tests, and then show a variety of ways in which you can make use of the functionality provided by PHPUnit.

To check out the behavior of the `UserLog` class, you're going to develop a series of 11 tests. In this section you also meet a new `PHPUnit` function called `assertEquals()` that will help test out a few conditions along the way.

The class declaration begins as normal. Recall that any test class must inherit from `PHPUnit`'s `TestCase` class so that it can set a context as well as perform other operations. The two variables declared in the `TestUserLog` class act as array containers for the objects against which you'll run your tests.

Of important notice is that the tests get their settings from `settings-test.php` (a separate settings file) because the various tests empty and fill various database tables for a complete end-to-end test. `PHPUnit` is also now included in the required files:

```php
<?php

require_once ("../settings-test.php");
require_once ("class.UserLog.php");
require_once ("phpunit/phpunit.php");

class TestUserLog extends TestCase {
    private $ulGood = null;
    private $ulBad = null;
```

Now, you define a specific context in which to run the tests by defining values in the setUp() function provided by PHPUnit. In this case, you create two UserLog objects, like so:

```php
function setUp()
{
    $this->ulGood = new UserLog (
        array ('site'      => 1,
               'section'   => 2,
               'login'     => "3",
               'session'   => "1E23553",
               'firstname' => "Alice",
               'lastname'  => "AppleGate",
               'address1'  => "123Main",
               'city'      => "Sandusky",
               'state'     => "OH",
               'zip'       => "44870",
               'demo0'     => "21",
               'demo1'     => "15",
               'demo2'     => "22",
               'demo3'     => "26"));

    $this->ulBad = new UserLog (
        array ('site'      => 0,
               'section'   => 0,
               'login'     => "",
               'session'   => "1E23553",
               'firstname' => "Alice",
               'lastname'  => "AppleGate",
               'address1'  => "123Main",
               'city'      => "Sandusky",
               'state'     => "OH",
               'zip'       => "44870",
               'demo0'     => "21",
               'demo1'     => "15",
               'demo2'     => "22",
               'demo3'     => "26"));
}
```

Begin defining the test functions.

The first, testValid0(), uses PHPUnit's assertEquals() function to verfiy that:

❑   Sandusky is the city present in the $ulGood UserLog object.

- ❑ $ulGood is a valid log.
- ❑ $ulGood has no invalid data.

These tests give you a bit of peace of mind because you know that if the tests pass, the context in which you are running the tests—at least for $ulGood—is running correctly. If you want to view the code for assertEquals(),view the phpunit.php file in your PHPUnit: installation:

```php
function testValid0()
{
        $this->assertEquals("Sandusky", $this->ulGood->city, "invalid city");
        $this->assertEquals(true, $this->ulGood->isValid(), "valid log");
        $this->assertEquals(0, count ($this->ulGood->getInvalidData()),
                        "valid count");
}
```

The next test creates a new UserLog object, $ul, and populates the array with some invalid data— namely the site value. Assert that this will cause the isValid() function to return false, and also that the number of invalid items is 1. If these tests execute correctly, you can be sure that you're correctly picking up invalid data within your objects:

```php
function testInvalid0()
{
        $ul = new UserLog (array ('site'        => 0,
                                'section'    => 9,
                                'login'      => "user101",
                                'session'    => "1E23553",
                                'firstname' => "Alice",
                                'lastname'  => "AppleGate",
                                'address1'  => "123Main",
                                'city'       => "Sandusky",
                                'state'      => "OH",
                                'zip'        => "44870",
                                'demo0'      => "21",
                                'demo1'      => "15",
                                'demo2'      => "22",
                                'demo3'      => "26"));
        $this->assertEquals(false, $ul->isValid(), "valid ul");
        $this->assertEquals(1, count ($ul->getInvalidData()), "valid site");
}
```

The third test gives $ulBad the once over. You assert that it is not valid, and further that the number of invalid items is three:

```php
function testInvalid1()
{

        $this->assertEquals(false, $this->ulBad->isValid(), "invalid ul");
        $this->assertEquals(3, count ($this->ulBad->getInvalidData()),
                        "invalid site, section, and login");
}
```

The preceding tests have all dealt with the actual data contained within the objects. What if you want to test the next part of the process, which is persisting the objects to the database? Well, you develop a couple of tests, of course. The next one makes use of a try catch block as well as the assert()

method. In it you attempt to send the information contained in $ulGood to the database—if successful, there are no errors thrown and your assertion is true. If it is unsuccessful, the assertion is set to false and an error message is printed.

Notice that assert() is not being used to display an error message. That's because you'd ideally like a slightly better idea of what type of error occurred, so in this case, use the error thrown by the try block:

```
function testGoodPersist0()
{
    try {
        $this->ulGood->persist();
        $this->assert(true);
    } catch (MultiLogException $e) {
        $this->assert(false);
        print ($e->getErrorMessage());
    }
}
```

Now do exactly the same thing with $ulBad. Of course, you expect it to fail, so the assertions change accordingly:

```
function testBadPersist0()
{
    try {
        $this->ulBad->persist();
        $this->assert(false); // it should fail
    } catch (MultiLogInvalidDataException $e) {
        $this->assert(true);
    }
}
```

Of course, you shouldn't be able to persist the same object twice in a row. If you test for it, obviously you should assert that the second persist call fails. Then the second persist will cause an exception to occur, and you can use it to make the correct assertion:

```
function testBadPersist1()
{
    try {
        $this->ulGood->persist();
        $this->assert(true);
        $this->ulGood->persist();
        $this->assert(false); // it should fail
    } catch (MultiLogInvalidDatabaseException $e) {
        $this->assert(true);
    } catch (MultiLogDatabaseQueryException $e) {
        $this->assert(false); // wrong one
    }
}
```

What if things don't go according to plan? Perhaps you accidentally made a typo somewhere along the line. For this test, the word "where" has "accidentally" been inserted into our session value. If you try to persist this, you're going to throw an exception.

In the catch block $ul->persist() is mistakenly asserted to be true. This should cause the test to fail and you'll see the output when you run the tests at the end of this section:

```
function testBadPersist2_fail()
{
    $ul = new UserLog (array ('site'      => "1",
                              'section'   => "9",
                              'login'     => "user101",
                              'session'   => "1' where '1' and '1"));
    try {
        $ul->persist();
        $this->assert(false); // it should fail
    } catch (MultiLogDatabaseQueryException $e) {
        $this->assert(true);
    }
}
```

Of course, this isn't the only way to go about making assertions. The following example shows how to insert any statement into the assert() method—provided it returns a Boolean value. It also uses the assert() method to output an error message in the event you fail.

Fiddle around with the values to see for yourself the results of an improper SQL statement. For example, you may want to modify the word "insert" to "inert":

```
function testSqlGeneration0()
{
    $this->assert(
        strpos (" ".$this->ulGood->toSQL(),
                "insert into user_log(visit_date,
                visit_time, site_id, demo_id, login_id, session,
                firstname,
                lastname, address1, address2, city, state, zip )") > 0,
                "invalid SQL generation first");

    $this->assert(
        strpos (" ".$this->ulGood->toSQL(), "1, 2, '3', '1E23553', 'Alice',
                'AppleGate', '123Main', '', 'Sandusky', 'OH', '44870' )")
        > 0, "invalid SQL generation last");
}
```

Now test a couple other methods—the toHTML() and getDemographics() functions. Nothing particularly new here in terms of the assertions you make:

```
function testHtmlGeneration0 ()
{
    $this->assert(strpos (" ".$this->ulGood->toHTML(), "<tr") > 0);
    $this->assert(strpos ($this->ulGood->toHTML(), ">AppleGate</td><td")
        > 0);
}

function testDemo0 ()
```

```
        {
            $this->assertEquals(4, count($this->ulGood->getDemographics()));
            $this->assertEquals(4, count($this->ulBad->getDemographics()));
        }
```

The final test recreates the database, persists the $ulGood object again, and then manually queries the database to determine the number of values returned. This confirms the result from the preceding test:

```
        function testDemo1 ()
        {
            include ("../logs/initialize.php"); // re-create db

            try {
                $this->ulGood->persist();
                $this->assert(true);
            } catch (MultiLogException $e) {
                $this->assert(false);
                print ($e->getErrorMessage());
                return;
            }

            $this->db = LogUtils::openDatabase();
            $query = LogUtils::executeQuery ($this->db,
            "SELECT COUNT(*) FROM user_demographics");

            $row = LogUtils::getQueryArray($query);
            $this->assertEquals ("4", $row[0]);
        }
    }
```

All the tests are completed, so it's time to bundle them into the test suite that will run them all together:

```
$suite = new TestSuite;
$suite->addTest(new TestUserLog("testValid0"));
$suite->addTest(new TestUserLog("testInvalid0"));
$suite->addTest(new TestUserLog("testInvalid1"));
$suite->addTest(new TestUserLog("testGoodPersist0"));
$suite->addTest(new TestUserLog("testBadPersist0"));
$suite->addTest(new TestUserLog("testBadPersist1"));
$suite->addTest(new TestUserLog("testBadPersist2_fail"));
$suite->addTest(new TestUserLog("testSqlGeneration0"));
$suite->addTest(new TestUserLog("testHtmlGeneration0"));
$suite->addTest(new TestUserLog("testDemo0"));
$suite->addTest(new TestUserLog("testDemo1"));
```

With that, you create a new TestRunner object, and invoke the run() method, which will execute all the tests and display the results:

```
$testRunner = new TestRunner();
$testRunner->run( $suite );
```

The first suite of tests is now complete, so take a look at the results. Navigate to test.UserLog.php (see Figure 17-5) scroll down to the bottom of the page, you'll see the error thrown by testBadPersist2_fail(). Notice that PHPUnit prints out default messages of ok and FAIL in green and red, respectively, depending on whether the test has run as expected or not.

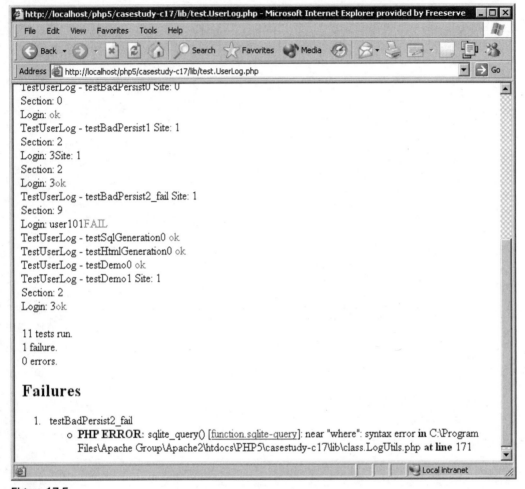

Figure 17-5

Begin the next class in the same way as the last, by declaring the classes you need to access to:

```php
<?php

require_once ("../settings-test.php"); // this is important!
require_once ("class.UserLog.php");
require_once ("class.LogContainer.php");
require_once ("phpunit/phpunit.php");
```

Because you're testing the LogContainer class, you need to include several UserLogs to work with within the test context. For this example, three new UserLog objects are created and persisted to the database:

```
class TestLogContainer extends TestCase
{
    function setUp()
    {
        include ("../logs/initialize.php"); // re-create db

        $ul0 = new UserLog (
            array ('site'      => "1",
                   'section'   => "111",
                   'login'     => "aapple",
                   'session'   => "1E23553",
                   'firstname' => "Aurthor",
                   'lastname'  => "Andersen",
                   'address1'  => "123 Main St.",
                   'city'      => "Sandusky",
                   'state'     => "OH",
                   'zip'       => "44870",
                   'demo0'     => "21",
                   'demo1'     => "15",
                   'demo2'     => "22",
                   'demo3'     => "26"));
        $ul0->persist();

        $ul1 = new UserLog (
            array ('site'      => "1",
                   'section'   => "112",
                   'login'     => "bbarker",
                   'session'   => "3F398",
                   'firstname' => "Blob",
                   'lastname'  => "Barker",
                   'address1'  => "100 Hollywood Blvd.",
                   'city'      => "LA",
                   'state'     => "CA",
                   'zip'       => "90036",
                   'demo0'     => "78",
                   'demo1'     => "21",
                   'demo2'     => "12",
                   'demo3'     => "7"));
        $ul1->persist();

        $ul2 = new UserLog (
            array ('site'      => "2",
                   'section'   => "200",
                   'login'     => "ccabbage",
                   'session'   => "L33T",
                   'firstname' => "Capitan",
                   'lastname'  => "Cabbage",
                   'address1'  => "55 Broadway",
                   'city'      => "NYC",
                   'state'     => "NY",
                   'zip'       => "10001",
                   'demo0'     => "14",
                   'demo1'     => "15",
                   'demo2'     => "41",
```

```
                    'demo3'      => "0"));
        $ul2->persist();

    }
```

With the specific context set, you can go ahead and create the test. For this example, only one test is included; it creates a new `LogContainer` object, which contains all the UserLogs coming from site 1:

```
    function testContainerValid0 ()
    {
        try {
            $lc = new LogContainer ("", "", "1", "");
```

Knowing your context, assert that there are only two UserLogs contained within this LogContainer:

```
        $this->assertEquals (2, $lc->getCount (), "count");
```

Then assert that the two UserLogs that exist within the LogContainer have the logins aapple and bbarker, respectively:

```
            $logs = $lc->getUserLogs ();
            $this->assert(strcmp ($logs[0]->getLogin, "aapple"),
            "login_id incorrect a");
            $this->assert(strcmp ($logs[0]->getLogin, "bbarker"),
            "login_id incorrect b");
        } catch (MultiLogException $e) {
            $this->assert(false);
            print $e->getErrorMessage ();
        }
    }
}
```

Finish off by creating and running the test suite as usual:

```
$suite = new TestSuite;
$suite->addTest(new TestLogContainer("testContainerValid0"));

$testRunner = new TestRunner();
$testRunner->run( $suite );
```

Navigating to the script should give you the output shown in Figure 17-6.

The final test class deals with the demographics part of the `UserLog` objects. Begin by including the files you need:

```
<?php

require_once ("../settings-test.php");
require_once ("class.UserDemographic.php");
require_once ("phpunit/phpunit.php");
```

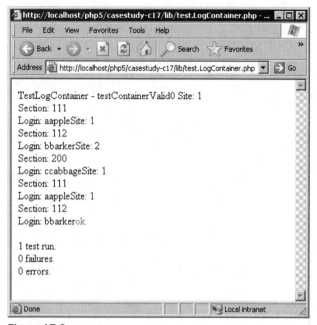

TestLogContainer - testContainerValid0 Site: 1
Section: 111
Login: aappleSite: 1
Section: 112
Login: bbarkerSite: 2
Section: 200
Login: ccabbageSite: 1
Section: 111
Login: aappleSite: 1
Section: 112
Login: bbarkerok

1 test run.
0 failures.
0 errors.

Figure 17-6

Start the class declaration by declaring the variables that will hold the UserDemographic objects. Also declare an `intializeDb()` function that you'll use to repopulate the database so you can reset the context:

```php
class TestUserDemographic extends TestCase
{
    private $demoGood = null;
    private $demoBad = null;

    function initializeDb () {
        include "../logs/initialize.php";
    }
}
```

Next, initialize your specific context—recall the demographics occupy only the tail end of the array, so you can effectively ignore the first part of the UserLog objects:

```php
function setUp()
{
    $this->demoGood = new UserDemographic (
        array ('id'        => 1,          // ignored
               'site'      => 1,          // ignored
               'section'   => 2,          // ignored
               'login'     => "3",        // ignored
               'session'   => "1E23553",  // ignored
               'firstname' => "Alice",    // ignored
               'lastname'  => "AppleGate", // ignored
```

```
                        'address1'     => "123Main",      // ignored
                        'city'         => "Sandusky",     // ignored
                        'state'        => "OH",           // ignored
                        'zip'          => "44870",        // ignored
                        'demo'         => "21",
                        'demo1'        => "15",
                        'demo2'        => "22",
                        'demo3'        => "26"));

            $this->demoBad = new UserDemographic (
                array ('site'          => 1,              // ignored
                        'section'      => 2,              // ignored
                        'login'        => "3",            // ignored
                        'session'      => "1E23553",      // ignored
                        'firstname'    => "Alice",        // ignored
                        'lastname'     => "AppleGate",    // ignored
                        'address1'     => "123Main",      // ignored
                        'city'         => "Sandusky",     // ignored
                        'state'        => "OH",           // ignored
                        'zip'          => "44870",        // ignored
                        'demo1'        => "15",
                        'demo2'        => "22",
                        'demo3'        => "26"));
    }
```

The first test you perform on the `UserDemographic` objects is:

```
function testValid0()
{
    $this->assertEquals(null, $this->demoGood->city, "invalid city");
    $this->assertEquals("21", $this->demoGood->demo, "invalid demo0");
    $this->assertEquals(null, $this->demoGood->demo1, "invalid demo1");
    $this->assertEquals(null, $this->demoGood->demo2, "invalid demo2");
    $this->assertEquals(null, $this->demoGood->demo3, "invalid demo3");
    $this->assertEquals(null, $this->demoGood->demo4, "invalid demo4");
    $this->assertEquals(true, $this->demoGood->isValid(), "valid log");
    $this->assertEquals(0, count ($this->demoGood->getInvalidData()),
                    "valid count");
}
```

You ensure that the alleged invalid data is in fact invalid in the following test:

```
function testInvalid0()
{
    $this->assertEquals(false, $this->demoBad->isValid(), "invalid log");
    $this->assertEquals(1, count ($this->demoBad->getInvalidData()),
                    "expecting 1 invalid item");
}
```

Finally, you create a test to ensure that you can save the object into the database:

```
function testGoodPersist0()
{
    $this->initializeDb();
```

```
        try {
            $this->demoGood->persist();
            $this->assert(true);
        } catch (MultiLogException $e) {
            $this->assert(false);
            print ($e->getErrorMessage());
        }
    }
}
```

And finish with this familiar code:

```
$suite = new TestSuite;
$suite->addTest(new TestUserDemographic("testValid0"));
$suite->addTest(new TestUserDemographic("testInvalid0"));
$suite->addTest(new TestUserDemographic("testGoodPersist0"));

$testRunner = new TestRunner();
$testRunner->run( $suite );
```

Figure 17-7 shows the results of running the tests.

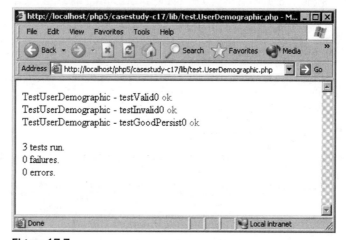

Figure 17-7

It's worth noting that PHPUnit has plenty more functionality to play around with. You've learned enough to begin with, but there are plenty of other checks you can create—all left to you as an exercise.

Working with the Logging Agent

At last, the moment you've all been waiting for. The logging agent is finally ready to be rolled out. For your convenience, I've provided an index page from which you can initialize the database, run all the tests, post some information to the database, and view the reports. Before you do that, however, you need to look at the one file that brings everything together: the userlog.php script.

userlog.php

userlog.php is responsible for actually capturing the request data. It takes a request string and creates a new UserLog object, which it then logs to the database—provided the information supplied in the URL passes the validation functions. This is all done within a try...catch block, which you use to throw one of your own MultiLogExceptions() in the event something goes awry:

```php
<?

require_once ("settings.php");
require_once ("lib/class.UserLog.php");

try {
    $ul = new UserLog ($_REQUEST);
    $ul->persist();
} catch (MultiLogException $e) {
    print $e->getErrorMessage();
    print "<h3>Environment:</h3>";
    phpinfo(); // insecure
}

?>
```

Each site could GET the information to you by using a URL string like this:

```
http://logging_site/userlog.php?site=101&section=1&login=user101&sessionid
=1E23553&firstname=Alice&lastname=AppleGate&address1=123Main&city
=Sandusky&state=OH&zip=44870
```

You can invoke methods to act on the data, and because you really want to persist this data (send it to the database), you simply call the persist() method on it.

Viewing the Logging Agent

Open your browser and navigate to the logging agent program's index page (see Figure 17-8).

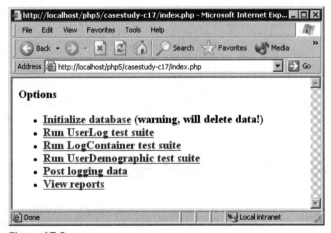

Figure 17-8

Clicking the Initialize Database link simply reports the message "Done" on success. You've already seen the results of running the three tests, so there's no need to check those links now. So click the Post Logging Data link.

You get a full printout of the two UserLog objects, as well as the UserDemographic objects, and the option to view the reports (to prove that you really have persisted the objects to the database). See Figure 17-9.

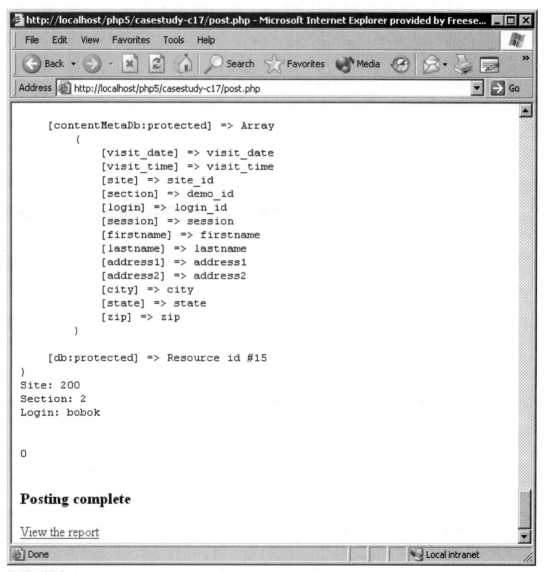

Figure 17-9

Go ahead and click the View the Report link at the bottom. Select the dates, sites, and section for which you would like to view reports. Figure 17-10 shows an example.

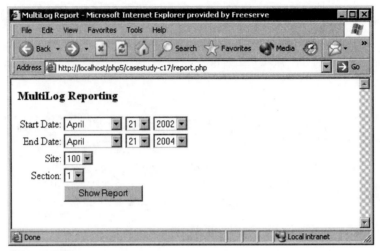

Figure 17-10

Your results should print out much like those in Figure 17-11.

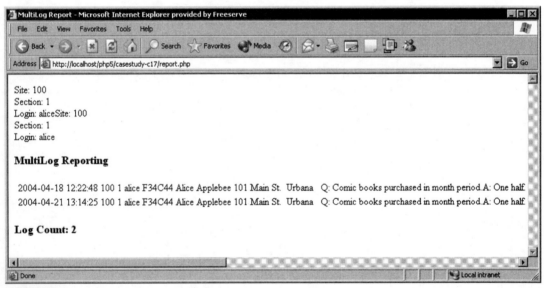

Figure 17-11

You can check that you can post information to the database by sending your captured information in a request. Remember the demonstration URL in the "*userlog.php*" section? Modify that URL to reflect some personally identifiable information, and GET it in your browser. Here's what I did:

```
http://logging_site/userlog.php?site=100&section=1&login=user101&sessionid
=2D56553&firstname=David&lastname=Mercer&address1=65SomePlace&city
=CapeTown&state=WP&zip=8001
```

On success, you should get a terse confirmation note, as shown in Figure 17-12.

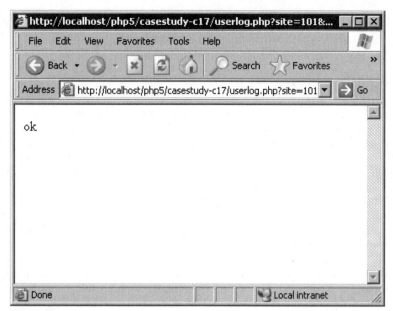

Figure 17-12

Now go back to the reports page and check whether the log has been successfully entered into the database. Figure 17-13 shows the expected results.

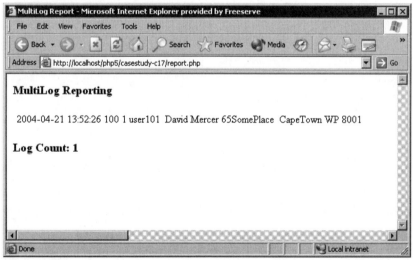

Figure 17-13

You've done it! You can now bundle off requests to the logging agent from whichever sites you care to collect information from. Of course, you can modify this quite easily to:

❑ Retrieve different types of data—not necessarily user demogrpahics.

❏   Display more complex reports.

❏   Implement more exception handling and data validation.

Summary

Unlike the other chapters in this book, which concentrated on a single aspect of PHP programming, this one presented a good look at a more rounded application, giving you the opportunity to become more aware of the various issues that need to be considered and dealt with to create a more complex application. Good programming practices were fostered, and an object-oriented approach—with emphasis on good validation techniques and exception handling—was demonstrated.

You saw the entire development cycle for creating a single case study application, the logging agent, and you were introduced to some new technologies that PHP developers can use to augment various aspects of their programs. Specifically, you looked at Smarty for abstracting the presentation layer, and at PHPUnit to provide unit testing.

UML class diagrams helped you visualize the major classes involved in the case study, and sequence diagrams showed the intended flow of information and demonstrated the different layers of abstraction. You also examined the actual code implementation—putting the design into practice—and looked at all of the code, piece by piece, to get an in-depth understanding of the application. You tested everything and then toured the final product, trying out everything and enjoying your success.

Having completed this final chapter, you're ready to take on more complex projects. Of course, the learning curve never ends (and often gets steeper), but the rewards are good and the work is satisfying. Enjoy!

Answers

Most of the chapters in this book provide an exercise (or more) to help you reinforce your new knowledge and/or hone your new skills. This appendix provides the solutions for the exercises by chapter. Here you'll find the full text of each exercise and its solution. Code solutions may be provided here or as a download from www.wrox.com. Of course, the code provided here also is available at that site.

Many of the exercises are flexible; meaning that there may be several workable solutions, so you may arrive at a different solution than the one shown here. The solution provided is designed to be generic, and in some cases the code has been written for readability, not necessarily to show the fastest or most abstracted method for providing the result. And some of the exercises, especially in the earlier chapters, may not involve code at all, or may include parts that require writing pseudo code or planning-type documents. The exercises are important because they encourage familiarity with the process by which programming projects are actually done, something you'll definitely want to know.

Chapter 1

Exercise

You'll find this exercise helpful whenever you have to install with or work with PHP on a new platform. To complete this exercise, do the following:

Create a document that summarizes all of the following:

- ❑ What are the hardware capabilities of the computer on which PHP is running? Describe the CPU, hard drive, RAM, and so on, and any particular limitations you perceive.

- ❑ What operating system is running on the hardware? List the version and any current patches and known bugs.

- ❑ What Web server software is running on the machine? List the version, patches, and known bugs. Also, list how the Web server is configured, the root folder, how PHP is set up to work with the server, and any file permissions you've set.

- ❑ What version of PHP was installed? List the version, the files installed, the folders in which they were installed, and any Registry settings that were set or created to support the PHP installation.

- ❏ What configuration settings were set or changed (from the default) to install PHP? List them.
- ❏ What extensions were enabled? List them all, and why you enabled them.

Having a document such as this makes it much easier for the next programmer to understand why PHP programs behave in a particular way, as well as make it easier for you to find all the information you need in one place later, rather than having to examine everything again when you get stuck.

Solution

Create a document like the following for your own system:

Documentation—Server 01	
CPU – Hard drive – RAM	Pentium 4, 1.7 Ghz – 120GB – 512MB
Operating System	Red Hat Linux Fedora
Web Server Software	Apache 2.0
Scripting Software	PHP 5.0
Php configuration settings	register_globals = off, default development settings

Chapter 2

Exercise 1

Create a PHP program that rearranges sentence one into sentence two, and outputs what it is doing (and the result) to the user. The two sentences are:

"now is the time for all good men to come to the aid of their country"
"the time is now to come to the aid of good men in the country"

Solution

Write a PHP script such as this:

```php
<?php
$my_array = explode(" ","now is the time for all good men to come to the aid of
their country");
echo $my_array[2] . $my_array[3] . $my_array[1] . $my_array[0] . $my_array[8] .
$my_array[9] . $my_array[8] . $my_array[2] . $my_array[12] . $my_array[13] .
$my_array[6] . $my_array[7] . "in" . $my_array[2] . $my_array[15];
?>
```

Exercise 2

Create a PHP program that creates two arrays of numbers and adds the values in each array to their corresponding values by index number. The two arrays should have the following values:

2,4,6,8,10
3,5,7,9,11

Solution

Write a PHP script such as this:

```
<?
$arr01 = array(2,4,6,8,10);
$arr02 = array(3,5,7,9,11);

for ($counter = 0; $counter <= 4; $counter ++){
    $arr03[] = $arr01[$counter] + $arr02[$counter];
    echo "The answer is now " . "$arr03[$counter]" . "<br>";
}
?>
```

Chapter 3

Exercise

PHP contains a very useful function named isset(), which tells your PHP program whether a particular variable has been set. For example, suppose you have a page with a form containing a submit button named login and another one named logout. When your user submits the form, you can tell which button he clicked by using the isset() function, like this:

```
if (isset($login)) {
//do this
} elseif (isset($logout)) {
//do this
}
```

For this exercise, create a Web page containing a form that submits to itself, and make your PHP program using the isset() function to tell when a form submission has occurred. If a form submission has not occurred, make your program display a form asking for the user's first and last name (but not the answer), and if a form submission has occurred, make your program not display the form but instead display the answer (a short statement such as: "Your first name is XX and your last name is XX.").

Hints: Use a hidden form field to determine if the form has been submitted, and use the $PHP_SELF variable to make the form submit back to itself.

Solution

```
<html><head><title>My Title</title></head>
<body>
<?php
if (isset($_POST['posted'])) {
    echo "Thanks. Your first name is $_POST[first_name] and your last name is
$_POST[last_name]";
} else {
?>
<h2>Please fill out this form</h2>
<form method="POST" action="<?php echo "$_SERVER[PHP_SELF]"; ?>">
<input type="hidden" name="posted" value="true">
```

```
First Name<input type="text" name="first_name"><br>
Last Name<input type="text" name="last_name">
<input type="submit" value="Send Info">
</form>
<?php
}
?>
</body>
</html>
```

The full code for the solution is a file named ch03ex01.php.

Chapter 4

Exercise

"We have a Web site, and it's outdated. It doesn't look very nice, but we're having a graphic artist redo the logo, so we'll probably be getting a lot more traffic once it's done. We'll be hiring more people to keep up with demand, and we want to have a way to gather resumes online.

"It should be easy for people to find the job listings, but the link shouldn't be the biggest thing on the page. We'll want to have their contact information, of course, and a search for jobs. If they don't have a college degree, they might as well not apply unless they're looking for entry-level jobs in the sales department or the shipping department. None of the jobs pays more than $20,000 to start, but management positions do offer incentive bonuses. They should send their salary requirements and at least 2 years of work experience, except for management positions (management positions must have at least 5 years experience, unless they have a Ph.D.). We'd like people to be able to search for jobs and apply for the ones they think would be a good fit for them, and also to be able to submit their resume and find out what jobs they qualify for."

Whew! Well, that's often exactly how the requirements for an application are first presented: someone who probably doesn't know much about what programmers do asks you to devise a program to do a particular function.

This exercise will definitely give you some practice in how to go from the statement of the problem all the way to the finished product. Your job is to decipher what's been said, use the capabilities of PHP to perform the processing, and collect the data and respond to the user with Web pages. To complete this exercise, you should include the following in addition to your finished program:

❑   A list of all required information, in addition to what has been presented.

❑   A description of the screens that you'll make, why you'll make them (why they are needed), and how the user will interact with them.

❑   A short description of how you'll integrate the screens with the existing Web site.

There's no one single PHP programming solution for this exercise, although all solutions will perform similar processing and use similar steps. Because databases or file system haven't been discussed yet, there's no way for you to store the resumes long-term, and the resume information will be lost once processing is complete.

You've got your assignment. Go on, get started!

Hint: To build a solution, try to lay out the problem as a series of screens first, and ask yourself what you'd expect to see. The, review the PHP capabilities that have been discussed so far to see which ones might be able to provide the data, and exactly what data must be present to complete the next step. It's much easier to arrive at a workable solution by breaking down the execution of the solution into small steps.

Solution

First, write a list of the information required. Essentially, the client wants to collect resumes. He doesn't seem to be concerned about making users log in, so the following basic categories of information are required:

1. Contact information, such as name, address, phone numbers, and so on. For many jobs, social security number will also be required.

2. Work experience

3. Education

4. Special qualifying information, such as degrees, certificates, and so on

5. Miscellaneous information

The requirements also describe the capability for people to search for jobs, and that implies that there will be a list of jobs internal to the system, maintained by a person within the client's company, and that person will enter search terms (keywords) that apply to each job. You should also ask whether the client wants jobs to be searchable by salary range.

There are a few conditions that may (or may not) apply to the job search and resume submission. One is that people without a degree should not even be able to apply for jobs except for entry-level jobs in sales or shipping. This prompts the question of whether they should even be able to begin their job search before entering some of their qualifications (why display jobs for which they can't qualify?).

Another condition is that they must have at least two years experience for all jobs except management positions, for which they may have 5 years' experience or a Ph.D.

The mention of salary does not seem to have a programming implication, other than to notify prospective employees that this company does not pay very well, although managers could make bonuses.

The next step is to begin devising the process by which users will interact with the system. Altogether, it would seem that a good process would be to first display a request for some basic information to prequalify job hunters, and then allow them to search for jobs or simply submit their resume and then view a list of any jobs for which they qualify.

You could do this by displaying a welcome screen asking for basic prequalification information, and then a screen providing a choice of searching for jobs or submitting a resume. When users reach the point of applying online, the resume screen could be broken into sections so they don't end up submitting all their data in one giant form on one screen.

As each form is filled out and submitted, the application should have a means of storing the information across page requests, and filling in the fields again in case the user wants to go back and edit.

So the pages you might have would be:

1. Welcome screen, with a form for entering pre-qualifying information, and a link to the Search/Resume screen.

2. The Search/Resume screen, with a form for submitting resume information (broken into logical chunks), and a search text field with search button.

The programming logic in PHP would then:

❏ Display the welcome screen.

❏ Request the user enter some prequalifying information, such as years of experience, level of education, and anything else that might be pertinent (most jobs have age and residency requirements, and that sort of thing, and you may have to ask a few questions to get these from the client).

❏ Store the prequalifying information, unless they don't qualify for any jobs at all (in which case this would be a good point to tell them that). Because you're handicapped by lack of any long-term storage device (which would not be the case in a real application), you'll have to store the data in hidden form fields.

❏ Depending upon which qualification requirements the user meets, display the appropriate resume submission form and the search form.

❏ As each part of the resume is submitted, store the data in hidden form fields, and provide the user a navigation link so previously entered data could be called up and revised as desired.

❏ Provide a search function that can display a list of jobs, with links, based on search terms entered by the user. This function would depend on pulling up the list of jobs from a database or file of some kind, but you can assume that the information is available in an array, so all you'd need to do is search the array using a `for` or `foreach` loop, and identify a keyword in the array by using a PHP function such as `substr()` to match up search terms entered with keywords found.

❏ Finally, if the user successfully enters a resume and applies for a particular job, the application would display a thank-you screen.

A relatively simple application with the process described here could be made all as one file using plain HTML forms and Web pages, a `switch` statement for each case when a form is submitted, and hidden form fields to store data across page requests.

A full solution, `ch04ex01.php`, is available at this book's Web site.

Chapter 5

Exercise

Create at least three regular expressions and insert them into the appropriate spots in the most recent form validation example. Suggested regular expressions are:

❏ 7– and 10–digit U.S. phone numbers

❏ Social Security numbers

❏ Gender using M and F for male and female

Solution

There are a number of ways to match telephone numbers, and the Regular Expression Library provides several examples that match U.S. phone numbers. The simplest is to look only for 7 or 10 digits in a row, excluding alphabetic characters. So you start by matching the beginning of the line with the carat, followed by one character from 2 to 9, two characters from 0 to 9, a dash, then one character from 2 to 9 and two characters from 0 to 9, a dash, and finally four characters from 0 to 9. That matches a 10-character phone number with dashes in between the segments, so you put in the "or" symbol (|) and repeat the second two portions of the first pattern so that you can also match a 7-character phone number. Then end the whole thing with the dollar sign ($) to match the end of the line.

```
^([2-9][0-9]{2}-[2-9][0-9]{2}-[0-9]{4}|[2-9][0-9]{2}-[0-9]{4})$
```

For Social Security numbers, you specify exactly three characters from 0 to 9, a dash, exactly two characters from 0 to 9, a dash, and exactly four characters from 0 to 9. The simplest expression is:

```
^[0-9]{3}-[0-9]{2}-[0-9]{4}$
```

Although this expression correctly evaluates the digit format for SSNs, it also accepts all zeros or 666, neither of which is found in a valid SSN. For extra credit, find a way to exclude character combinations with all zeros or 666.

For male and female gender, character classes may be used:

```
^([M]|[F])$
```

This `regexp` uses the carat and dollar sign to match the beginning and end of the line, and character cases for uppercase M or (using the "or" symbol |) uppercase F.

The full code for this solution is a file named `ch05ex01.php`.

Chapter 6

Exercise

Write a function that enables the user to construct his own Web form, with the capability to choose field names and field types, and then allow the users to submit the form to the page and see what they submitted echoed back to them. Use a `switch..case` statement to select various functions within your main function.

Solution

This solution involves writing HTML tags with PHP. You might start by constructing a Web form that lets users enter a predetermined number of field names and field types, and then define a number of variables that contain the HTML for those field names and types. When the user submits the form, another form will be generated based on the data entered by the user. The `switch..case` statement could be placed inside the function that generates the completed new form, selecting the HTML to produce the field name and type within a predefined HTML form.

There should also be a means of asking the user to provide extra information when a drop-down list (the <select> tag) has been chosen because these tags operate by means of multiple <option> tags inside them.

Here's an example of creating a function to write HTML tags:

```
//create the function to write the HTML tags
function createTags($field_name,$field_type)
{
    global $option_text01,$option_text02,$option_text03;
    global $option_value01,$option_value02,$option_value03;
    switch ($field_type) {
        case "text";
            $next_field = "<tr><td>$field_name:</td><td><input type='$field_type'
name='$field_name'></td></tr>";
            break;
        case "radio";
            $next_field = "<tr><td>$field_name:</td><td><input type='$field_type'
name='$field_name'></td></tr>";
            break;
        case "checkbox";
            $next_field = "<tr><td>$field_name:</td><td><input type='$field_type'
name='$field_name'></td></tr>";
            break;
        case "hidden";
            $next_field = "<tr><td>$field_name:</td><td><input type='$field_type'
name='$field_name'></td></tr>";
            break;
        case "textarea";
            $next_field = "<tr><td>$field_name:</td><td><textarea cols='40'
name='$field_name'></textarea></td></tr>";
            break;
        case "select";
            $next_field = "<tr><td>$field_name:</td><td>
<select name='$field_name'>"
                    ."<option value='$option_value01'>$option_text01</option>"
                    ."<option value='$option_value02'>$option_text02</option>"
                    ."<option value='$option_value03'>$option_text03</option>"
                    ."</select></td></tr>";
            break;
        default;
            break;
    }
    return $next_field;
}
```

For the full solution, see the code file ch06ex01.php.

Chapter 7

Exercise

Create a PHP application that can be used to find a particular directory when given a valid parent directory to search. Make the application look through the given directory and all directories under the given directory.

Solution

This application can make use of the PHP file system functions to search for the directory and to simply iterate through all directories and subdirectories given a valid parent directory. The first step might be to list all the directories in the parent directory, go through all of those directories identifying any subdirectories that have the name you're looking for, and then to go through all of them, and so on. Here's some code that finds a folder by name within the default folder.

```
//get the folder to search for
$folder_to_find = "$_POST[folder]";
//set the default directory
$default_dir = "C:";
//create the function to find the folder if it exists
function find_folder($default_dir,$folder_to_find) {
    if (!($dp = opendir($default_dir))) {
        die("Cannot open $default_dir.");
    } else {
        while ($file = readdir($dp)) {
            if ($file == $folder_to_find){
                return ($file);
            }
        }
    }
    closedir($dp);
    }
}
    $folder = find_folder($default_dir,$folder_to_find);
if ($folder != "") {
    echo "Found folder named " . $folder;
} else {
    echo "Folder not found.";
}
```

This code finds a folder in the default directory by name, but does not search subfolders. For the full solution, see the code file ch07ex01.php.

Chapter 8

Exercise

Create an application that reads an XML file with multiple elements and attributes into a simpleXML object, changes the values of some or all of its elements or attributes, and then returns the modified document back into the file.

Solution

You've already seen how to change values in XML files, and this solution is an extension of that. Here's an example of the code that can change element values based on their array index number:

```
//capture which element to change
$element_to_change = $_POST[element_to_change];
$change_value = $_POST[change_value];

if ($element_to_change == 0) {
```

```
    $first_xml_string->program[0]->price = $change_value;
} elseif ($element_to_change == 1) {
    $first_xml_string->program[1]->price = $change_value;
}
```

Naturally, the drawback to this code is that the element index numbers must be hard-coded in, and it doesn't show how to save the resulting XML document back into a file. For the full solution, including the ability to make changes to attribute values, see the code file ch08ex01.php.

Chapter 11

Exercise 1

Make a list of suitable field descriptors for each of the columns in this table. *Hint: Remember that restaurants generally have many individual orders in any given day.*

First name	Order _ID	User _ID	Resturaunt	Password	Last name	Total Price ($)	Email
David	2	1	Nandos	12345	Mercer	21.45	davidm@contechst.com
David	4	1	Mimos	12345	Mercer	20.95	davidm@contechst.com
Nic	3	2	St Elmos	23212	Malan	15.45	therot@doggiestouch.co.za
Brian	5	4	Spur	32123	Reid	22.00	pads@doggiestouch.co.za
Darren	1	3	Home	43212	Ebbs	11.85	Bacardi@doggiestouch.co.za

Solution

Here's a list of suitable field descriptors:

```
VARCHAR(30)
MEDIUMINT(7)
MEDIUMINT(7)
VARCHAR(30)
VARCHAR(20)
VARCHAR(50)
FLOAT(7)
VARCHAR(60)
```

Exercise 2

The site manager decides to have a page for users to view their past orders and their totals. Using principles of normalization, create new tables to represent one entity each. Give each table a suitable name, and a primary key. (Check that your changes would reduce redundancy in large amounts of data.)

Solution

Here's the Customer table:

User_ID	Firstname	Lastname	Password	Email
1	David	Mercer	12345	davidm@contechst.com
2	Nic	Malan	23212	therot@doggiestouch.co.za
3	Darren	Ebbs	43212	Bacardi@doggiestouch.co.za
4	Brian	Reid	32123	pads@doggiestouch.co.za

Here's the Orders table:

Order_ID	User_ID	Resturaunt	TotalPrice
1	3	Home	11.85
2	1	Nandos	21.45
3	2	St Elmos	15.45
4	1	Mimos	20.95
5	4	Spur	22.00

Exercise 3

Create these tables in your database using SQL statements.

Solution

The following SQL statements will create the Customer table in your database:

```
CREATE TABLE Customer (
User_ID MEDIUMINT(7) NOT NULL AUTO_INCREMENT,
Firstname VARCHAR(30) BINARY NOT NULL,
Lastname VARCHAR(50) BINARY NOT NULL,
Password VARCHAR(20) BINARY NOT NULL,
Email VARCHAR(60),
PRIMARY KEY (User_ID),
UNIQUE (Email)
);
```

These SQL statements will create the Orders table in your database:

```
CREATE TABLE Orders (
Order_ID MEDIUMINT (7) NOT NULL AUTO_INCREMENT,
User_ID MEDIUMINT (7) NOT NULL,
Resturaunt VARCHAR (30) NOT NULL,
Total_Price FLOAT (7) NOT NULL,
PRIMARY KEY (Order_ID)
);
```

Exercise 4

After the Web site's been in business for six months, customers begin to complain that the site is going slowly when they want to view their previous orders. The site administrator looks at the Orders table and finds that there are now thousands of records. Why is the site slow, and how can the administrator speed things up? Update the table accordingly.

Solution

The site is slow because there are now a large number of records in the Orders table. The lookup is being performed using the User_ID field because that is how you identify which records to return to a given user. To prevent full table accesses while performing these look ups, add an index to the User_ID field. (Remember, that while this will speed up SELECT statements, it slows down INSERT and UPDATE statements. In this case, it's probably worth your while to make the site faster for customers.) The administrator can speed things up by issuing the following query:

```
ALTER TABLE Orders ADD INDEX (User_ID);
```

Exercise 5

The boss decides he wants to see how popular Nandos is with his customers. What query could the administrator build to obtain the totals for all the orders (a) made by one customer and (b) made to Nandos. *Hint: Try Select SUM(column) from table.*

Solution

(a):

```
SELECT SUM(Total_price) FROM Orders WHERE User_ID = 1;
```

(b):

```
SELECT SUM(Total_price) FROM Orders WHERE Resturaunt = 'Nandos';
```

Exercise 6

Create a script that enables a user to enter his details into the database by registering at the site. The database should be set up so that the user ID is assigned automatically. Once the user is registered he should be able to place an order with any of the five restaurants. (Just complete one to begin with. Don't worry about creating a full interface—being able to enter a price is the important thing.) Clicking an order button should create a new entry in the Orders table, with an incremented Order_ID, and the correct User_ID inserted for the customer. *Hint: You may want to use a session to store the users User_ID upon registration.*

Solution

common_db.inc:

```php
<?php
$dbhost = 'localhost';
$dbusername = 'phpuser';
$dbuserpassword = 'phppass';
```

```
    $default_dbname = 'sample_db';
    $max_menu_items = 10;
    $MYSQL_ERRNO = '';
    $MYSQL_ERROR = '';

    function db_connect($dbname='') {
       global $dbhost, $dbusername, $dbuserpassword, $default_dbname;
       global $MYSQL_ERRNO, $MYSQL_ERROR;

       $link_id = mysql_connect($dbhost, $dbusername, $dbuserpassword);
       if(!$link_id) {
          $MYSQL_ERRNO = 0;
          $MYSQL_ERROR = "Connection failed to the host $dbhost.";
          return 0;
       }
       else if(empty($dbname) && !mysql_select_db($default_dbname)) {
          $MYSQL_ERRNO = mysql_errno();
          $MYSQL_ERROR = mysql_error();
          return 0;
       }
       else if(!empty($dbname) && !mysql_select_db($dbname)) {
          $MYSQL_ERRNO = mysql_errno();
          $MYSQL_ERROR = mysql_error();
          return 0;
       }
       else return $link_id;
    }

    function sql_error() {
       global $MYSQL_ERRNO, $MYSQL_ERROR;
       if(empty($MYSQL_ERROR)) {
          $MYSQL_ERRNO = mysql_errno();
          $MYSQL_ERROR = mysql_error();
       }
       return "$MYSQL_ERRNO: $MYSQL_ERROR";
    }
    ?>
```

Takeaway.php:

```
    <?php
    include_once "./common_db.inc";

    function login_form() {
    global $PHP_SELF;
    ?>
    <HTML>
    <HEAD>
    <TITLE>Login</TITLE>
    </HEAD>
    <BODY>
    <INPUT TYPE="HIDDEN" NAME="action" VALUE="register">
```

```
      <DIV ALIGN="CENTER"><CENTER>
         <H2>Welcome to Speedy Deliveries!</H2>
         <H3>Please take the time to register your details.</H3>
      <TABLE BORDER="1" WIDTH="400" CELLPADDING="2">
         <TR>
            <TH WIDTH="25%" ALIGN="RIGHT" NOWRAP>Firstname</TH>
            <TD WIDTH="82%" NOWRAP>
               <INPUT TYPE="Input" NAME="userfirstname" SIZE="30">
            </TD>
         </TR>
            <TR>
            <TH WIDTH="25%" ALIGN="RIGHT" NOWRAP>Lastname</TH>
            <TD WIDTH="82%" NOWRAP>
               <INPUT TYPE="Input" NAME="userlastname" SIZE="30">
            </TD>
         </TR>
         <TR>
            <TH WIDTH="25%" ALIGN="RIGHT" NOWRAP>Password</TH>
            <TD WIDTH="82%" NOWRAP>
               <INPUT TYPE="PASSWORD" NAME="userpassword" SIZE="30">
            </TD>
         </TR>
         <TR>
            <TH WIDTH="25%" ALIGN="RIGHT" NOWRAP>Email</TH>
            <TD WIDTH="82%" NOWRAP>
               <INPUT TYPE="Input" NAME="useremail" SIZE="30">
            </TD>
         </TR>
         <TR>
            <TD WIDTH="100%" COLSPAN="2" ALIGN="CENTER" NOWRAP>
               <INPUT TYPE="SUBMIT" NAME="Submit">
            </TD>
         </TR>
      </TABLE>
      </CENTER></DIV>
</FORM>
</BODY>
</HTML>
<?
}

function register_user() {
   global $default_dbname;
   $PHP_SELF = $_SERVER['PHP_SELF'];

   $link_id = db_connect($default_dbname);
    $query = "INSERT INTO Customer
       VALUES('','$_GET[userfirstname]','$_GET[userlastname]',
       $_GET[userpassword],
       '$_GET[useremail]')";
     $result = mysql_query($query);
   if(!$result) {
      Echo "Please go to the Home page and register.";
```

```
        ?>
    <FORM method="GET" action="<?php echo $PHP_SELF ?>">
      <INPUT type="submit" value="Home">
    </FORM>
<?php
  exit;
      }
  return $result;
}

function get_userid(){
      global $default_dbname;
    $link_id = db_connect($default_dbname);

    $query = "SELECT User_ID from Customer WHERE Password =
    '$_GET[userpassword]'";

    $result = mysql_query($query);
    $result_array = mysql_fetch_row($result);
    $userid = $result_array[0];
    if(!$userid) $userid = "";
    return $userid;
}
function order_menu(){
    $PHP_SELF = $_SERVER['PHP_SELF'];

?>
<HTML>
  <HEAD><TITLE>Resturaunts</TITLE></HEAD>
    <BODY>
      <DIV ALIGN="CENTER"><CENTER>
      <H2>Welcome to Nandos, <?php echo $_GET['userfirstname']; ?>!</H2>
        </CENTER></DIV>
    <FORM method="GET" action="<?php echo $PHP_SELF ?>">
        <INPUT TYPE="HIDDEN" NAME="action" VALUE="order">
Winglets Starter: $1.50
        <INPUT name="Choice1" type="checkbox" value="1.50">
          <BR>
Chicken Burger:    $3.00
        <INPUT name="Choice2" type="checkbox" value="3.00">
          <BR>
Softdrink:         $0.75
        <INPUT name="Choice3" type="checkbox" value="0.75">
          <BR>
          <BR>
        <INPUT type="submit" value="Order My Food">
    </FORM>
  </BODY>
</HTML>

<?php
}

function place_order(){
```

```php
    global $default_dbname, $max_menu_items;
    $PHP_SELF = $_SERVER['PHP_SELF'];
    $link_id = db_connect($default_dbname);
    $total = 0;
    for ($counter = 1; $counter <= 10; $counter ++)
    {
        $a = "Choice" . "$counter";
        if (isset($_GET[$a])){
        $total += $_GET[$a];
    }

}

$query = "INSERT INTO Orders VALUES ('', '$_SESSION[userid]', 'Nandos',
$total)";

$result = mysql_query($query);
if(!$result) die ("Could not place your order, please try again!");
  else {
     //On a live system, this should take you to a confirmation page, as
        simply refreshing the page as it is will cause the order to be
        duplicated.
     echo "Your order has been taken! You can expect delivery within the hour.
            The total came to \$$total";
?>
   <FORM method="GET" action="<?php echo $PHP_SELF ?>">
     <INPUT type="submit" value="Home">
   </FORM>
 <?php
  }
}

function customer_session(){
    $_SESSION['useremail'] = $_GET['useremail'];
    register_user();
    $userid = get_userid();
    $_SESSION['userid'] = $userid;
}

session_start();
session_register("userid", "useremail");
if (empty($_GET['action'])){
    $_GET['action'] = "";
  }

switch($_GET['action']) {
   case "order":
      place_order();
      break;
   case "register":
       customer_session();
      order_menu();
      break;
   default:
```

```
        login_form();
        break;
    }

?>
```

Chapter 12

Exercise 1

Define the difference between a class and an object.

Solution

A class is like a blueprint. It only provides the instructions for creating an object. An object is an instance of a class. Classes are manipulated at design time when you alter the code in a PHP file. Objects are manipulated at runtime when properties are accessed or changed and methods are invoked. A class is represented by text in a text file. An object exists as instructions in memory.

Exercise 2

Explain inheritance and give an example of when it should be used. Don't repeat any of the examples already provided in this chapter!

Solution

Inheritance is the capability of an object to acquire properties or methods of a parent object. Inheritance implies a related hierarchy and reuse of code. The child class is a more specialized version of the parent class, having additional methods and properties and/or different implementations of the same methods and properties. A child cannot have fewer methods or properties than its parent. An example of inheritance could be the relationship between Vertebrates and Mammals. All vertebrates have a spinal column composed of some number of segmented bony vertebrae surrounding a spinal cord, and a large brain encased in a skull. Mammals are a more specialized type of vertebrate. Although they have all of the properties of vertebrates, they also have hair or fur, are warm blooded, and lactate. A class Vertebrate might have properties such as numberOfVertebrae and skeletonType (values for the latter being cartilaginous as in sharks, or bony as with mammals and reptiles). Mammals would inherit all those properties and add furColor and normalBodyTemperature.

Exercise 3

Describe the utility of an interface and its practical application in a software architecture. How is an interface different from an inherited class? Can you come up with additional examples of when this might be useful?

Solution

An interface is an abstract construct that defines a "contract"—a mandate requiring implementing classes to have certain methods. Although an inherited class implies that there's a direct relationship between the parent class and the inheriting subclasses, an interface implies no such relationship, but is used to identify classes that are capable of performing the same functions. Because all classes that implement the interface must, by definition, have at least the set of methods defined in the interface (they may have additional methods, but not fewer) you can use an interface to pass otherwise unrelated objects to the same functions. For example, PHP comes with two interfaces—Iterator and IteratorAggregate—that enable you to pass objects into a foreach construct if and only if those objects implement one of these two interfaces. These interfaces allow objects that contain other objects to be looped through using foreach. You can have any class implement these interfaces, so you can use totally unrelated objects in the same foreach construct.

Chapter 15

Exercise

The application you created in this chapter works well for composing and sending individual e-mails. For this exercise, modify the application so that it sends the e-mail to a list of e-mail addresses retrieved from a database.

Solution

The first step in creating an application that sends e-mails to a list of e-mail addresses is to create a list of e-mail addresses in an array. Typically, when records are retrieved from a database such as MySQL or Postgres, the retrieval process begins by executing some type of SQL SELECT statement using the pg_exec() function or the mysql_query() function. The retrieved records are stored in a PHP variable (often named $res for result). The number of records in such an array can then be determined using the pg_numrows() or the mysql_numrows() function, and a for loop provides the means to retrieve individual rows (records) from the $res variable using the pg_fetch_array() or the mysql_fetch_array() function.

So you might run a SELECT query against a database holding customer information (including e-mail address), and then if there are multiple records in the result, use a for loop to fetch each e-mail address and insert it into a function such as the following to send it out (with a very little bit of e-mail address validation thrown in for good measure):

```
$query = "SELECT email FROM customers;";
$res = pg_exec($conn,$query);
if(pg_numrows($res) >= 1) {
    for ($i=0; $i<=pg_numrows($res)-1; $i++) {
        $rec = pg_fetch_array($res,$i);
        if ($rec[email] !== "") {
            if (strpos($rec[email],"@") >= 0) {
                $body = "This is the body"\n\n";
                //Set the From:
                $headers .= "From: Example <info@example.com>\n";
                //Send the mail
                $to = "$rec[email]";
                $subject = "Example Email";
                mail($to, $subject, $body, $headers);
            } else {
                echo = "The $i email address is no good.<br>";
            }
        }
    }
}
```

The full code for the solution is ch15ex01.php.

Chapter 16

Exercise 1

Create a PHP script that opens an image file and adds a one-pixel black border to the image.

Solution

The only trick to successfully complete this exercise is that the top-left corner of an image is x=0, y=0. This means that you must remember to subtract 1 from the width and height of the image to get the rightmost position and bottommost positions of the image, respectively. Here's the code (exercise1.php) to achieve Exercise 1:

```php
<?php
$myImage = imagecreatefromjpeg('cape_point.jpg');
$black = imagecolorallocate($myImage,0,0,0);
$width = imagesx($myImage);
$height = imagesy($myImage);
imagerectangle($myImage, 0, 0, $width-1, $height-1, $black);
header("Content-type: image/jpeg");
imagejpeg($myImage);
imagedestroy($myImage);
?>
```

If your script was similar to this one, your output should include a nice clean border around the image, like the one shown in Figure A-1.

Figure A-1

Exercise 2

Using the `disk_total_space()` and `disk_free_space()` functions show how much disk space you have used on your hard drive in a graphical way.

Solution

There are two obvious ways that you can graphically display the results for of this exercise. The quickest and easiest way is to create a simple sliding scale: a rectangular shape that is made up of two blocks of color, one color representing the used space on the disk, and the other representing the free space. This gives you a nice quick overview of your disk usage. Following is the code (`exercise2a.php`) for doing this.

It's always good practice to store the width and height of your images in variables within the script. Then if you want to change the size of the image you can do so easily at the beginning of the script and any calculations you do with the image width and height are automatically updated.

```php
<?php
$iWidth = 500;
$iHeight = 50;
```

Create the image and allocate black and white. Because white is the first color allocated, it will be the background color of the image. Black will be used to add a border to the image.

```php
$myImage = imagecreate($iWidth, $iHeight);
$white = imagecolorallocate($myImage,255,255,255);
$black = imagecolorallocate($myImage,0,0,0);
```

In this example solution, red and green are used to represent used disk space and free disk space respectively. You can use any colors you like.

```php
$red = imagecolorallocate($myImage, 255,0,0);
$green = imagecolorallocate($myImage,0,255,0);
```

Get the total amount of space on the disk and the amount of space that you have free. Both of these values are returned in bytes. The actual values are irrelevant—all you need them for is to get a proportion so that you can draw the bar.

```php
$diskTotal = disk_total_space('/');
$diskFree = disk_free_space('/');
```

Then draw a one-pixel black border around the outside of the image.

```php
imagerectangle($myImage, 0, 0, $iWidth - 1, $iHeight - 1, $black);
```

The `$threshold` variable will be used to mark the position along the x axis where you move from the used disk space to the free disk space in your diagram. Because used disk space is usually represented on the left side of such diagrams, you first need to calculate that space—it is the total disk space minus the free disk space. Divide that by the total amount of disk space to get a number between 0 and 1, which you then multiply by the width of the image. Remove 2 from the width of the image because you already used 2 pixels drawing the image border. And then add 1 because pixels start at 0.

```
$threshold = intval((($diskTotal - $diskFree) / $diskTotal) * ($iWidth-2))
+ 1;
```

For example, if your disk was 400 bytes in size and you had used 200 bytes, 200 divided by 400 equals 0.5. If your image width were 500 pixels, then you'd multiply the 0.5 and 498 (width minus 2 for the border) to get 249. Then you'd add 1 to get 250 the x pixel position that is halfway across the image.

Fill the image with a red rectangle that goes to the point of your threshold to represent the used disk space:

```
imagefilledrectangle($myImage, 1, 1, $threshold, ($iHeight-2), $red);
```

And a green rectangle from the threshold onward for the free disk space:

```
imagefilledrectangle($myImage, ($threshold + 1), 1, ($iWidth - 2),
$iHeight-2, $green);
```

Close it out in the usual manner.

```
header("Content-type: image/png");
imagepng($myImage);
imagedestroy($myImage);
?>
```

Figure A-2 shows the result of running this example on my machine.

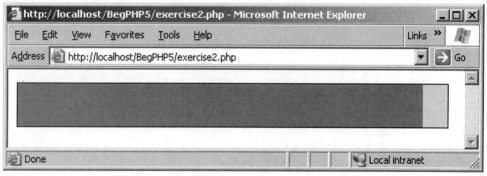

Figure A-2

The alternative solution to this exercise is to draw the space as a pie chart. The file exercise2b.php contains the code for this solution. Here's how it's done.

Instead of working out a threshold, you work out a number of degrees. The calculation works in the same way except you don't multiply by the width of the image, you multiply by 360—the number of degrees in a circle.

```
<?php
$iWidth = 200;
$iHeight = 200;
$myImage = imagecreate($iWidth, $iHeight);
```

```
$white = imagecolorallocate($myImage,255,255,255);
$red = imagecolorallocate($myImage, 255,0,0);
$green = imagecolorallocate($myImage,0,255,0);
$diskTotal = disk_total_space('/');
$diskFree = disk_free_space('/');
$usedDegrees = intval((($diskTotal - $diskFree) / $diskTotal) * 360);
```

The imagefilledarc() function works in the same way as the imagearc() function, except that it takes an additional argument specifying how that arc should be filled. The PHP constant IMG_ARC_EDGED causes PHP to connect the two end points of the arc to the center point of the arc and fill it with the color specified. You start at 0 degrees and draw the arc through to the degree that you worked out for $usedDegrees.

```
imagefilledarc($myImage, ($iWidth/2), ($iHeight/2), $iWidth - 2,
$iHeight - 2, 0, $usedDegrees, $red, IMG_ARC_EDGED);
```

To draw the arc that represents the free space, you simply start where the used space left off at $usedDegree and draw the arc through to 360 degrees, the end of the circle:

```
imagefilledarc($myImage, ($iWidth/2), ($iHeight/2), $iWidth - 2, $iHeight - 2,
$usedDegrees, 360, $green, IMG_ARC_EDGED);
```

And then finish up as usual:

```
header("Content-type: image/png");
imagepng($myImage);
imagedestroy($myImage);
?>
```

Figure A-3 shows the result on my machine.

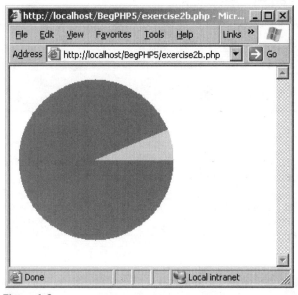

Figure A-3

PHP Functions Reference

This appendix cannot provide an exhaustive list of all of the PHP functions (or it would be hundreds of pages long!) but it presents a subset of functions that the authors think you will encounter in your everyday use of PHP along with brief descriptions of what those functions do. The core language functions are included, as well as the functions for PHP extensions that are in popular use.

This appendix is meant as a quick reference for you to check the input and return types of parameters—more of a reminder of how the function works than a verbose description of how to use the function in your scripts. If you need to see how a particular function should be used, or to read up on a function that isn't covered here, check out the PHP documentation online at www.php.net/docs.php.

Apache

Function	Returns	Description
apache_child_terminate(void)	Bool	Terminates Apache process after this request
apache_note(string note_name [, string note_value])	String	Gets and sets Apache request notes
virtual(string filename)	Bool	Performs an Apache sub-request
getallheaders(void)	Array	Alias for apache_request_headers()
apache_request_headers(void)	Array	Fetches all HTTP request headers
apache_response_headers(void)	Array	Fetches all HTTP response headers
apache_setenv(string variable, string value [, bool walk_to_top])	Bool	Sets an Apache subprocess_env variable

Continues

Function	Returns	Description
apache_lookup_uri(string URI)	Object	Performs a partial request of the given URI to obtain information about it
apache_get_version(void)	String	Fetches Apache version
apache_get_modules(void)	Array	Gets a list of loaded Apache modules

Arrays

Function	Returns	Description
krsort(array array_arg [, int sort_flags])	Bool	Sorts an array by key value in reverse order
ksort(array array_arg [, int sort_flags])	Bool	Sorts an array by key
count(mixed var [, int mode])	Int	Counts the number of elements in a variable (usually an array)
natsort(array array_arg)	Void	Sorts an array using natural sort
natcasesort(array array_arg)	Void	Sorts an array using case-insensitive natural sort
asort(array array_arg [, int sort_flags])	Bool	Sorts an array and maintains index association
arsort(array array_arg [, int sort_flags])	Bool	Sorts an array in reverse order and maintains index association
sort(array array_arg [, int sort_flags])	Bool	Sorts an array
rsort(array array_arg [, int sort_flags])	Bool	Sorts an array in reverse order
usort(array array_arg, string cmp_function)	Bool	Sorts an array by values using a user-defined comparison function
uasort(array array_arg, string cmp_function)	Bool	Sort an array with a user-defined comparison function and maintains index association
uksort(array array_arg, string cmp_function)	Bool	Sort an array by keys using a user-defined comparison function

Function	Returns	Description
end(array array_arg)	Mixed	Advances array argument's internal pointer to the last element and returns it
prev(array array_arg)	Mixed	Moves array argument's internal pointer to the previous element and returns it
next(array array_arg)	Mixed	Moves array argument's internal pointer to the next element and returns it
reset(array array_arg)	Mixed	Sets array argument's internal pointer to the first element and returns it
current(array array_arg)	Mixed	Returns the element currently pointed to by the internal array pointer
key(array array_arg)	Mixed	Returns the key of the element currently pointed to by the internal array pointer
min(mixed arg1 [, mixed arg2 [, mixed...]])	Mixed	Returns the lowest value in an array or a series of arguments
max(mixed arg1 [, mixed arg2 [, mixed...]])	Mixed	Returns the highest value in an array or a series of arguments
array_walk(array input, string funcname [, mixed userdata])	Bool	Apply a user function to every member of an array
array_walk_recursive(array input, string funcname [, mixed userdata])	Bool	Apply a user function recursively to every member of an array
in_array(mixed needle, array haystack [, bool strict])	Bool	Checks if the given value exists in the array
array_search(mixed needle, array haystack [, bool strict])	Mixed	Searches the array for a given value and returns the corresponding key if successful
extract(array var_array [, int extract_type [, string prefix]])	Int	Imports variables into symbol table from an array
compact(mixed var_names [, mixed...])	Array	Creates a hash containing variables and their values

Continues

Function	Returns	Description
`array_fill(int start_key, int num, mixed val)`	Array	Creates an array containing num elements starting with index start_key each initialized to val
`range(mixed low, mixed high[, int step])`	Array	Creates an array containing the range of integers or characters from low to high (inclusive)
`shuffle(array array_arg)`	Bool	Randomly shuffles the contents of an array
`array_push(array stack, mixed var [, mixed...])`	Int	Pushes elements onto the end of the array
`array_pop(array stack)`	Mixed	Pops an element off the end of the array
`array_shift(array stack)`	Mixed	Pops an element off the beginning of the array
`array_unshift(array stack, mixed var [, mixed...])`	Int	Pushes elements onto the beginning of the array
`array_splice(array input, int offset [, int length [, array replacement]])`	Array	Removes the elements designated by offset and length and replaces them with a supplied array
`array_slice(array input, int offset [, int length])`	Array	Returns elements specified by offset and length
`array_merge(array arr1, array arr2 [, array...])`	Array	Merges elements from passed arrays into one array
`array_merge_recursive(array arr1, array arr2 [, array...])`	Array	Recursively merges elements from passed arrays into one array
`array_keys(array input [, mixed search_value])`	Array	Returns just the keys from the input array, optionally only for the specified search_value
`array_values(array input)`	Array	Returns just the values from the input array
`array_count_values(array input)`	Array	Returns the value as key and the frequency of that value in input as value
`array_reverse(array input [, bool preserve keys])`	Array	Returns input as a new array with the order of the entries reversed

Function	Returns	Description
array_pad(array input, int pad_size, mixed pad_value)	Array	Returns a copy of input array padded with pad_value to size pad_size
array_flip(array input)	Array	Returns array with key <-> value flipped
array_change_key_case(array input [, int case=CASE_LOWER])	Array	Returns an array with all string keys lowercased (or uppercased)
array_unique(array input)	Array	Removes duplicate values from array
array_intersect(array arr1, array arr2 [, array...])	Array	Returns the entries of arr1 that have values that are present in all the other arguments
array_uintersect(array arr1, array arr2 [, array...], callback data_compare_func)	Array	Returns the entries of arr1 that have values that are present in all the other arguments. Data is compared by using a user-supplied callback
array_intersect_assoc(array arr1, array arr2 [, array...])	Array	Returns the entries of arr1 that have values that are present in all the other arguments. Keys are used to do more restrictive check
array_uintersect_assoc(array arr1, array arr2 [, array...], callback data_compare_func)	Array	Returns the entries of arr1 that have values that are present in all the other arguments. Keys are used to do more restrictive check. Data is compared by using an user-supplied callback
array_intersect_uassoc(array arr1, array arr2 [, array...], callback key_compare_func)	Array	Returns the entries of arr1 that have values that are present in all the other arguments. Keys are used to do more restrictive check and they are compared by using a user-supplied callback
array_uintersect_uassoc(array arr1, array arr2 [, array...], callback data_compare_func, callback key_compare_func)	Array	Returns the entries of arr1 that have values that are present in all the other arguments. Keys are used to do more restrictive check. Both data and keys are compared by using user-supplied callbacks

Continues

Function	Returns	Description
`array_diff(array arr1, array arr2 [, array...])`	Array	Returns the entries of arr1 that have values that are not present in any of the others arguments
`array_udiff(array arr1, array arr2 [, array...], callback data_comp_func)`	Array	Returns the entries of arr1 that have values that are not present in any of the other arguments. Elements are compared by a user-supplied function
`array_diff_assoc(array arr1, array arr2 [, array...])`	Array	Returns the entries of arr1 that have key value pairs that are not present in any of the other arguments
`array_diff_uassoc(array arr1, array arr2 [, array...], callback data_comp_func)`	Array	Returns the entries of arr1 that have key value pairs that are not present in any of the other arguments. Elements are compared by a user-supplied function
`array_udiff_assoc(array arr1, array arr2 [, array...], callback key_comp_func)`	Array	Returns the entries of arr1 that have key value pairs that are not present in any of the other arguments. Keys are compared by a user-supplied function
`array_udiff_uassoc(array arr1, array arr2 [, array...], callback data_comp_func, callback key_comp_func)`	Array	Returns the entries of arr1 that have key value pairs that are not present in any of the others arguments. Keys and elements are compared by user supplied functions
`array_multisort(array ar1 [, SORT_ASC|SORT_DESC [, SORT_REGULAR|SORT_NUMERIC| SORT_STRING]] [, array ar2 [, SORT_ASC|SORT_DESC [, SORT_REGULAR|SORT_NUMERIC| SORT_STRING]], ...])`	Bool	Sorts multiple arrays at once (similar to how ORDER BY clause works in SQL)
`array_rand(array input [, int num_req])`	Mixed	Returns key/keys for random entry/entries in the array
`array_sum(array input)`	Mixed	Returns the sum of the array entries
`array_reduce(array input, mixed callback [, int initial])`	Mixed	Iteratively reduces the array to a single value via the callback

Function	Returns	Description
array_filter(array input [, mixed callback])	Array	Filters elements from the array via the callback
array_map(mixed callback, array input1 [, array input2, ...])	Array	Applies the callback to the elements in given arrays
array_key_exists(mixed key, array search)	Bool	Checks if the given key or index exists in the array
array_chunk(array input, int size [, bool preserve_keys])	Array	Splits array into chunks
array_combine(array keys, array values)	Array	Creates an array by using the elements of the first parameter as keys and the elements of the second as corresponding keys
each(array arr)	Array	Returns the currently pointed key value pair in the passed array, and advances the pointer to the next element
error_reporting(int new_error_level=null)	Int	Returns the current error_reporting level and, if an argument was passed, changes to the new level

BCMath

Function	Returns	Description
bcadd(string left_operand, string right_operand [, int scale])	String	Returns the sum of two arbitrary precision numbers
bcsub(string left_operand, string right_operand [, int scale])	String	Returns the difference between two arbitrary precision numbers
bcmul(string left_operand, string right_operand [, int scale])	String	Returns the multiplication of two arbitrary precision numbers
bcdiv(string left_operand, string right_operand [, int scale])	String	Returns the quotient of two arbitrary precision numbers (division)
bcmod(string left_operand, string right_operand)	String	Returns the modulus of the two arbitrary precision operands (remainder)

Continues

Function	Returns	Description
`bcpowmod(string x, string y, string mod [, int scale])`	String	Returns the value of an arbitrary precision number raised to the power of another reduced by a modulus
`bcpow(string x, string y [, int scale])`	String	Returns the value of an arbitrary precision number raised to the power of another
`bcsqrt(string operand [, int scale])`	String	Returns the square root of an arbitray precision number
`bccomp(string left_operand, string right_operand [, int scale])`	Int	Compares two arbitrary precision numbers
`bcscale(int scale)`	Bool	Sets default scale parameter for all bc math functions

BZip2

Function	Returns	Description
`bzopen(string|int file|fp, string mode)`	resource	Opens a new BZip2 stream
`bzread(int bz [, int length])`	String	Reads up to length bytes from a BZip2 stream, or 1024 bytes if length is not specified
`bzwrite(int bz, string data [, int length])`	Int	Writes the contents of the string data to the BZip2 stream
`bzerrno(resource bz)`	Int	Returns the error number
`bzerrstr(resource bz)`	String	Returns the error string
`bzerror(resource bz)`	Array	Returns the error number and error string in an associative array
`bzcompress(string source [, int blocksize100k [, int workfactor]])`	String	Compresses a string into BZip2 encoded data
`bzdecompress(string source [, int small])`	String	Decompresses BZip2 compressed data
`bzclose((resource bz)`	Int	Close a bzip2 file pointer
`bzflush(resource bz)`	Int	Forces a write of all buffered BZip2 data

Calendar

Function	Returns	Description
unixtojd([int timestamp])	Int	Converts UNIX timestamp to Julian Day
jdtounix(int jday)	Int	Converts Julian Day to UNIX timestamp
cal_info(int calendar)	Array	Returns information about a particular calendar
cal_days_in_month(int calendar, int month, int year)	Int	Returns the number of days in a month for a given year and calendar
cal_to_jd(int calendar, int month, int day, int year)	Int	Converts from a supported calendar to Julian Day Count
cal_from_jd(int jd, int calendar)	Array	Converts from Julian Day Count to a supported calendarand returns extended information
jdtogregorian(int juliandaycount)	String	Converts a Julian Day Count to a Gregorian calendar date
gregoriantojd(int month, int day, int year)	Int	Converts a Gregorian calendar date to Julian Day Count
jdtojulian(int juliandaycount)	String	Converts a Julian Day Count to a Julian calendar date
juliantojd(int month, int day, int year)	Int	Converts a Julian calendar date to Julian Day Count
jdtojewish(int juliandaycount [, bool hebrew [, int fl]])	String	Converts a Julian Day Count to a Jewish calendar date
jewishtojd(int month, int day, int year)	Int	Converts a Jewish calendar date to a Julian Day Count
jdtofrench(int juliandaycount)	String	Converts a Julian Day Count to a French Republic calendar date
frenchtojd(int month, int day, int year)	Int	Converts a French Republic calendar date to Julian day count
jddayofweek(int juliandaycount [, int mode])	Mixed	Returns name or number of day of week from Julian Day Count
jdmonthname(int juliandaycount, int mode)	String	Returns name of month for Julian Day Count

Continues

Function	Returns	Description
easter_date([int year])	Int	Returns the timestamp of midnight on Easter of a given year (defaults to current year)
easter_days([int year, [int method]])	Int	Returns the number of days after March 21 that Easter falls on for a given year (defaults to current year)

Class/Object

Function	Returns	Description
class_exists(string classname)	Bool	Checks if the class exists
get_class(object object)	String	Retrieves the class name
get_parent_class (mixed object)	String	Retrieves the parent class name for object or class
is_subclass_of(object object, string class_name)	Bool	Returns true if the object has this class as one of its parents
is_a(object object, string class_name)	Bool	Returns true if the object is of this class or has this class as one of its parents
get_class_vars(string class_name)	Array	Returns an array of default properties of the class
get_object_vars (object obj)	Array	Returns an array of object properties
get_class_methods (mixed class)	Array	Returns an array of method names for class or class instance
method_exists(object object, string method)	Bool	Checks if the class method exists
Get_class_vars(string class_name)	Array	Returns an array of default properties of the class
get_declared_classes (string class_name)	Array	Returns an array with the names of the declared classes in the current script

Character Type

Function	Returns	Description
ctype_alnum(string text)	Bool	Checks for alphanumeric character(s)
ctype_alpha(string text)	Bool	Checks for alphabetic character(s)
ctype_cntrl(string text)	Bool	Checks for control character(s)
ctype_digit(string text)	Bool	Checks for numeric character(s)
ctype_graph(string text)	Bool	Checks for any printable character(s) except space
ctype_lower(string text)	Bool	Checks for lowercase character(s)
ctype_print(string text)	Bool	Checks for printable character(s)
ctype_punct(string text)	Bool	Checks for any printable character that is not whitespace or an alphanumeric character
ctype_space(string text)	Bool	Checks for whitespace character(s)
ctype_upper(string text)	Bool	Checks for uppercase character(s)
ctype_xdigit(string text)	Bool	Checks for character(s) representing a hexadecimal digit

Curl

Function	Returns	Description
curl_version([int version])	Array	Returns cURL version information
curl_init([string url])	resource	Initializes a CURL session
curl_setopt(resource ch, string option, mixed value)	Bool	Sets an option for a CURL transfer
curl_exec(resource ch)	Bool	Performs a CURL session
curl_getinfo(resource ch, int opt)	Mixed	Gets information regarding a specific transfer
curl_error(resource ch)	String	Returns a string contain the last error for the current session
curl_errno(resource ch)	Int	Returns an integer containing the last error number

Continues

Function	Returns	Description
curl_close(resource ch)	Void	Closes a CURL session
curl_multi_init(void)	resource	Returns a new CURL multi handle
curl_multi_add_handle (resource multi, resource ch)	Int	Adds a normal CURL handle to a CURL multi handle
curl_multi_remove_handle (resource mh, resource ch)	Int	Removes a multi handle from a set of CURL handles
curl_multi_select(resource mh[, double timeout])	Int	Gets all the sockets associated with the CURL extension, which can then be selected
curl_multi_exec(resource mh)	Int	Runs the sub-connections of the current CURL handle
curl_multi_getcontent (resource ch)	String	Returns the content of a CURL handle if CURLOPT_RETURNTRANSFER is set
curl_multi_info_read (resource mh)	Array	Gets information about the current transfers
curl_multi_close (resource mh)	Void	Closes a set of cURL handles

Date and Time

Function	Returns	Description
time(void)	Int	Returns current UNIX timestamp
mktime(int hour, int min, int sec, int mon, int day, int year)	Int	Gets UNIX timestamp for a date
gmmktime(int hour, int min, int sec, int mon, int day, int year)	Int	Gets UNIX timestamp for a GMT date
date(string format [, int timestamp])	String	Formats a local time/date
gmdate(string format [, int timestamp])	String	Formats a GMT/UTC date/time
idate(string format [, int timestamp])	Int	Formats a local time/date as integer

Function	Returns	Description
`localtime([int timestamp [, bool associative_array]])`	Array	Returns the results of the C system call local time as an associative array if the associative_array argument is set to 1 (otherwise it's a regular array)
`getdate([int timestamp])`	Array	Gets date/time information
`checkdate(int month, int day, int year)`	Bool	Returns true(1) if it is a valid date in gregorian calendar
`strftime(string format [, int timestamp])`	String	Formats a local time/date according to locale settings
`gmstrftime(string format [, int timestamp])`	String	Formats a GMT/UTC time/date according to locale settings
`strtotime(string time, int now)`	Int	Converts string representation of date and time to a timestamp
`microtime(void)`	String	Returns a string containing the current time in seconds and microseconds
`gettimeofday(void)`	Array	Returns the current time as array
`getrusage([int who])`	Array	Returns an array of usage statistics
`date_sunrise(mixed time [, int format [, float latitude [, float longitude [, float zenith [, float gmt_offset]]]]])`	Mixed	Returns time of sunrise for a given day and location
`date_sunset(mixed time [, int format [, float latitude [, float longitude [, float zenith [, float gmt_offset]]]]])`	Mixed	Returns time of sunset for a given day and location

Directory

Function	Returns	Description
`opendir(string path)`	Mixed	Opens a directoryand returns a dir_handle
`dir(string directory)`	Object	Directory class with properties handle and path, and methods read, rewind, and close

Continues

Function	Returns	Description
`closedir([resource dir_handle])`	Void	Closes directory connection identified by the dir_handle
`chroot(string directory)`	Bool	Changes root directory
`chdir(string directory)`	Bool	Changes the current directory
`getcwd(void)`	Mixed	Gets the current directory
`rewinddir([resource dir_handle])`	Void	Rewinds dir_handle back to the start
`readdir([resource dir_handle])`	String	Reads directory entry from dir_handle
`glob(string pattern [, int flags])`	Array	Finds pathnames matching a pattern
`scandir(string dir [, int sorting_order])`	Array	Lists files and directories inside the specified path
`dl(string extension_filename)`	Int	Loads a PHP extension at runtime

Error Handling

Function	Returns	Description
`error_log(string message [, int message_type [, string destination [, string extra_headers]]])`	Bool	Sends an error message somewhere
`debug_print_backtrace(void) */`	Void	Prints a backtrace
`debug_backtrace(void)`	Array	Returns backtrace as array
`restore_error_handler(void)`	Void	Restores the previously defined error handler function
`set_exception_handler(string exception_handler)`	String	Sets a user-defined exception handler function. Returns the previously defined exception handler, or false on error
`restore_exception_handler(void)`	Void	Restores the previously defined exception handler function
`trigger_error(string messsage [, int error_type])`	Void	Generates a user-level error/warning/notice message

Function	Returns	Description
set_error_handler(string error_handler)	String	Sets a user-defined error handler function. Returns the previously defined error handler, or false on error
leak(int num_bytes=3)	Void	Causes an intentional memory leak, for testing/debugging purposes

Filesystem

Function	Returns	Description
flock(resource fp, int operation [, int &wouldblock])	Bool	Portable file locking
file_get_contents(string filename [, bool use_include_path [, resource context]])	String	Reads the entire file into a string
file_put_contents(string file, mixed data [, int flags [, resource context]])	Int	Writes/Creates a file with contents data and returns the number of bytes written
file(string filename [, int flags [, resource context]])	Array	Reads entire file into an array
tempnam(string dir, string prefix)	String	Creates a unique filename in a directory
tmpfile(void)	resource	Creates a temporary file that will be deleted automatically after use
fopen(string filename, string mode [, bool use_include_path [, resource context]])	resource	Opens a file or a URL and returns a file pointer
fclose(resource fp)	Bool	Closes an open file pointer
popen(string command, string mode)	resource	Executes a command and opens either a read or a write pipe to it
pclose(resource fp)	Int	Closes a file pointer opened by popen()
feof(resource fp)	Bool	Tests for end-of-file on a file pointer
fgets(resource fp [, int length])	String	Gets a line from file pointer
fgetc(resource fp)	String	Gets a character from file pointer

Continues

Function	Returns	Description
`fgetss(resource fp [, int length, string allowable_tags])`	String	Gets a line from file pointer and strips HTML tags
`fscanf(resource stream, string format [, string...])`	Mixed	Implements a mostly ANSI-compatible fscanf()
`fwrite(resource fp, string str [, int length])`	Int	Binary-safe file write
`fflush(resource fp)`	Bool	Flushes output
`rewind(resource fp)`	Bool	Rewinds the position of a file pointer
`ftell(resource fp)`	Int	Gets file pointer's read/write position
`fseek(resource fp, int offset [, int whence])`	Int	Seeks on a file pointer
`mkdir(string pathname [, int mode [, bool recursive [, resource context]]])`	Bool	Creates a directory
`rmdir(string dirname[, resource context])`	Bool	Removes a directory
`readfile(string filename [, bool use_include_path [, resource context]])`	Int	Outputs a file or a URL
`umask([int mask])`	Int	Returns or change the umask
`fpassthru(resource fp)`	Int	Outputs all remaining data from a file pointer
`rename(string old_name, string new_name[, resource context])`	Bool	Renames a file
`unlink(string filename[, context context])`	Bool	Deletes a file
`ftruncate(resource fp, int size)`	Bool	Truncates file to size length
`fstat(resource fp)`	Int	Performs stat() on a filehandle
`copy(string source_file, string destination_file)`	Bool	Copies a file
`fread(resource fp, int length)`	String	Binary-safe file read

Function	Returns	Description
fgetcsv(resource fp [,int length [, string delimiter [, string enclosure]]])	Array	Gets line from file pointer and parses for CSV fields
realpath(string path)	String	Returns the resolved path
fnmatch(string pattern, string filename [, int flags])	Bool	Matches filename against pattern
disk_total_space(string path)	Float	Gets total disk space for filesystem that path is on
disk_free_space(string path)	Float	Gets free disk space for filesystem that path is on
chgrp(string filename, mixed group)	Bool	Changes file group
chown (string filename, mixed user)	Bool	Changes file owner
chmod(string filename, int mode)	Bool	Changes file mode
touch(string filename [, int time [, int atime]])	Bool	Sets modification time of file
clearstatcache(void)	Void	Clears file stat cache
fileperms(string filename)	Int	Gets file permissions
fileinode(string filename)	Int	Gets file inode
filesize(string filename)	Int	Gets file size
fileowner(string filename)	Int	Gets file owner
filegroup(string filename)	Int	Gets file group
fileatime(string filename)	Int	Gets last access time of file
filemtime(string filename)	Int	Gets last modification time of file
filectime(string filename)	Int	Gets inode modification time of file
filetype(string filename)	String	Gets file type
is_writable(string filename)	Bool	Returns true if file can be written
is_readable(string filename)	Bool	Returns true if file can be read
is_executable(string filename)	Bool	Returns true if file is executable

Continues

Function	Returns	Description
`is_file(string filename)`	Bool	Returns true if file is a regular file
`is_dir(string filename)`	Bool	Returns true if file is directory
`is_link(string filename)`	Bool	Returns true if file is symbolic link
`file_exists(string filename)`	Bool	Returns true if filename exists
`lstat(string filename)`	Array	Gives information about a file or symbolic link
`stat(string filename)`	Array	Gives information about a file
`readlink(string filename)`	String	Returns the target of a symbolic link
`linkinfo(string filename)`	Int	Returns the st_dev field of the UNIX C stat structure describing the link
`symlink(string target, string link)`	Int	Creates a symbolic link
`link(string target, string link)`	Int	Creates a hard link
`is_uploaded_file(string path)`	Bool	Checks if file was created by RFC1867 upload
`move_uploaded_file(string path, string new_path)`	Bool	Moves a file if and only if it was created by an upload
`parse_ini_file(string filename [, bool process_sections])`	Array	Parses configuration file

FTP

Function	Returns	Description
`ftp_connect(string host [, int port [, int timeout]])`	resource	Opens a FTP stream
`ftp_ssl_connect(string host [, int port [, int timeout]])`	resource	Opens a FTP-SSL stream
`ftp_login(resource stream, string username, string password)`	Bool	Logs into the FTP server
`ftp_pwd(resource stream)`	String	Returns the present working directory

Function	Returns	Description
`ftp_cdup(resource stream)`	Bool	Changes to the parent directory
`ftp_chdir(resource stream, string directory)`	Bool	Changes directories
`ftp_exec(resource stream, string command)`	Bool	Requests execution of a program on the FTP server
`ftp_raw(resource stream, string command)`	Array	Sends a literal command to the FTP server
`ftp_mkdir(resource stream, string directory)`	String	Creates a directory and returns the absolute path for the new directory or false on error
`ftp_rmdir(resource stream, string directory)`	Bool	Removes a directory
`ftp_chmod(resource stream, int mode, string filename)`	Int	Sets permissions on a file
`ftp_alloc(resource stream, int size[, &response])`	Bool	Attempts to allocate space on the remote FTP server
`ftp_nlist(resource stream, string directory)`	Array	Returns an array of filenames in the given directory
`ftp_rawlist(resource stream, string directory [, bool recursive])`	Array	Returns a detailed listing of a directory as an array of output lines
`ftp_systype(resource stream)`	String	Returns the system type identifier
`ftp_fget(resource stream, resource fp, string remote_file, int mode[, int resumepos])`	Bool	Retrieves a file from the FTP server and writes it to an open file
`ftp_nb_fget(resource stream, resource fp, string remote_file, int mode[, int resumepos])`	Int	Retrieves a file from the FTP server asynchronly and writes it to an open file
`ftp_pasv(resource stream, bool pasv)`	Bool	Turns passive mode on or off
`ftp_get(resource stream, string local_file, string remote_file, int mode[, int resume_pos])`	Bool	Retrieves a file from the FTP server and writes it to a local file

Continues

Function	Returns	Description
`ftp_nb_get(resource stream, string local_file, string remote_file, int mode[, int resume_pos])`	Int	Retrieves a file from the FTP server nbhronly and writes it to a local file
`ftp_nb_continue(resource stream)`	Int	Continues retrieving/sending a file nbronously
`ftp_fput(resource stream, string remote_file, resource fp, int mode[, int startpos])`	Bool	Stores a file from an open file to the FTP server
`ftp_nb_fput(resource stream, string remote_file, resource fp, int mode[, int startpos])`	Int	Stores a file from an open file to the FTP server nbronly
`ftp_put(resource stream, string remote_file, string local_file, int mode[, int startpos])`	Bool	Stores a file on the FTP server
`ftp_nb_put(resource stream, string remote_file, string local_file, int mode[, int startpos])`	Int	Stores a file on the FTP server
`ftp_size(resource stream, string filename)`	Int	Returns the size of the file, or -1 on error
`ftp_mdtm(resource stream, string filename)`	Int	Returns the last modification time of the file, or -1 on error
`ftp_rename(resource stream, string src, string dest)`	Bool	Renames the given file to a new path
`ftp_delete(resource stream, string file)`	Bool	Deletes a file
`ftp_site(resource stream, string cmd)`	Bool	Sends a SITE command to the server
`ftp_close(resource stream)`	Bool	Closes the FTP stream
`ftp_set_option(resource stream, int option, mixed value)`	Bool	Sets an FTP option
`ftp_get_option(resource stream, int option)`	Mixed	Gets an FTP option

Function Handling

Function	Returns	Description
call_user_func(string function_name [, mixed parmeter] [, mixed...])	Mixed	Calls a user function that is the first parameter
call_user_func_array(string function_name, array parameters)	Mixed	Calls a user function that is the first parameter with the arguments contained in array
call_user_method(string method_name, mixed object [, mixed parameter] [, mixed...])	Mixed	Calls a user method on a specific object or class
call_user_method_array(string method_name, mixed object, array params)	Mixed	Calls a user method on a specific object or class using a parameter array
register_shutdown_function (string function_name)	Void	Registers a user-level function to be called on request termination
register_tick_function (string function_name [, mixed arg [, mixed...]])	Bool	Registers a tick callback function
unregister_tick_function (string function_name)	Void	Unregisters a tick callback function
create_function(string args, string code)	String	Creates an anonymous function, and returns its name (funny, eh?)
function_exists(string function_name)	Bool	Checks if the function exists
func_num_args(void)	Int	Gets the number of arguments that were passed to the function
func_get_arg(int arg_num)	Mixed	Gets the $arg_num'th argument that was passed to the function
func_get_args()	Array	Gets an array of the arguments that were passed to the function

HTTP

Function	Returns	Description
header(string header [, bool replace, [int http_response_code]])	Void	Sends a raw HTTP header

Continues

Function	Returns	Description
setcookie(string name [, string value [, int expires [, string path [, string domain [, bool secure]]]]])	Bool	Sends a cookie
setrawcookie(string name [, string value [, int expires [, string path [, string domain [, bool secure]]]]])	Bool	Sends a cookie with no URL encoding of the value
headers_sent([string &$file [, int &$line]])	Bool	Returns true if headers have already been sent, false otherwise
headers_list(void)	String	Returns a list of headers to be sent/already sent

Iconv Library

Function	Returns	Description
iconv(tring in_charset, string out_charset, string str)	String	Returns str converted to the out_charset character set
ob_iconv_handler (string contents, int status)		Returns str in output buffer converted to the iconv.output_encoding character set
iconv_get_encoding ([string type])	Mixed	Gets internal encoding and output encoding for ob_iconv_handler()
iconv_set_encoding (string type, string charset)	Bool	Sets internal encoding and output encoding for ob_iconv_handler()

Image

Function	Returns	Description
exif_tagname(index)	String	Gets headername for index or false if not defined
exif_read_data(string filename [, sections_needed [, sub_arrays[, read_thumbnail]]])	Array	Reads header data from the JPEG/TIFF image filename and optionally reads the internal thumbnails

Function	Returns	Description
exif_thumbnail(string filename [, &width, &height [, &imagetype]])	String	Reads the embedded thumbnail
exif_imagetype(string imagefile)	Int	Gets the type of an image
gd_info()	Array	Retrieves information about the currently installed GD library
imageloadfont(string filename)	Int	Loads a new font
imagesetstyle(resource im, array styles)	Bool	Sets the line drawing styles for use with imageline and IMG_COLOR_STYLED
imagecreatetruecolor(int x_size, int y_size)	resource	Creates a new true color image
imageistruecolor(resource im)	Bool	Returns true if the image uses truecolor
imagetruecolortopalette (resource im, bool ditherFlag, int colorsWanted)	Void	Converts a true color image to a palette based image with a number of colors, optionally using dithering
imagecolormatch(resource im1, resource im2)	Bool	Makes the colors of the palette version of an image more closely match the true color version
imagesetthickness(resource im, int thickness)	Bool	Sets line thickness for drawing lines, ellipses, rectangles, polygons, etc
imagefilledellipse(resource im, int cx, int cy, int w, int h, int color)	Bool	Draws an ellipse
imagefilledarc(resource im, int cx, int cy, int w, int h, int s, int e, int col, int style)	Bool	Draws a filled partial ellipse
imagealphablending(resource im, bool on)	Bool	Turns alpha blending mode on or off for the given image
imagesavealpha(resource im, bool on)	Bool	Includes alpha channel to a saved image
imagelayereffect(resource im, int effect)	Bool	Sets the alpha blending flag to use the bundled libgd layering effects
imagecolorallocatealpha (resource im, int red, int green, int blue, int alpha)	Int	Allocates a color with an alpha level. Works for true color and palette-based images

Continues

Function	Returns	Description
`imagecolorresolvealpha (resource im, int red, int green, int blue, int alpha)`	Int	Resolves/allocates a color with an alpha level. Works for true color and palette based images
`imagecolorclosestalpha (resource im, int red, int green, int blue, int alpha)`	Int	Finds the closest matching color with alpha transparency
`imagecolorexactalpha(resource im, int red, int green, int blue, int alpha)`	Int	Finds exact match for color with transparency
`imagecopyresampled(resource dst_im, resource src_im, int dst_x, int dst_y, int src_x, int src_y, int dst_w, int dst_h, int src_w, int src_h)`	Bool	Copies and resizes part of an image using resampling to help ensure clarity
`imagerotate(resource src_im, float angle, int bgdcolor)`	resource	Rotates an image using a custom angle
`imagesettile(resource image, resource tile)`	Bool	Sets the tile image to $tile when filling $image with the IMG_COLOR_TILED color
`imagesetbrush(resource image, resource brush)`	Bool	Sets the brush image to $brush when filling $image with the IMG_COLOR_BRUSHED color
`imagecreate(int x_size, int y_size)`	resource	Creates a new image
`imagetypes(void)`	Int	Returns the types of images supported in a bitfield - 1=GIF, 2=JPEG, 4=PNG, 8=WBMP, 16=XPM
`imagecreatefromstring (string image)`	resource	Creates a new image from the image stream in the string
`imagecreatefromgif(string filename)`	resource	Creates a new image from GIF file or URL
`imagecreatefromjpeg(string filename)`	resource	Creates a new image from JPEG file or URL
`imagecreatefrompng(string filename)`	resource	Creates a new image from PNG file or URL
`imagecreatefromxbm(string filename)`	resource	Creates a new image from XBM file or URL

Function	Returns	Description
imagecreatefromxpm(string filename)	resource	Creates a new image from XPM file or URL
imagecreatefromwbmp(string filename)	resource	Creates a new image from WBMP file or URL
imagecreatefromgd(string filename)	resource	Creates a new image from GD file or URL
imagecreatefromgd2(string filename)	resource	Creates a new image from GD2 file or URL
imagecreatefromgd2part (string filename, int srcX, int srcY, int width, int height)	resource	Creates a new image from a given part of GD2 file or URL
imagexbm(int im, string filename [, int foreground])	Int	Outputs XBM image to browser or file
imagegif(resource im [, string filename])	Bool	Outputs GIF image to browser or file
imagepng(resource im [, string filename])	Bool	Outputs PNG image to browser or file
imagejpeg(resource im [, string filename [, int quality]])	Bool	Outputs JPEG image to browser or file
imagewbmp(resource im [, string filename, [, int foreground]])	Bool	Outputs WBMP image to browser or file
imagegd(resource im [, string filename])	Bool	Outputs GD image to browser or file
imagegd2(resource im [, string filename, [, int chunk_size, [, int type]]])	Bool	Outputs GD2 image to browser or file
imagedestroy(resource im)	Bool	Destroys an image
imagecolorallocate(resource im, int red, int green, int blue)	Int	Allocates a color for an image
imagepalettecopy(resource dst, resource src)	Void	Copies the palette from the src image onto the dst image
imagecolorat(resource im, int x, int y)	Int	Gets the index of the color of a pixel

Continues

Function	Returns	Description
`imagecolorclosest(resource im, int red, int green, int blue)`	Int	Gets the index of the closest color to the specified color
`imagecolorclosesthwb(resource im, int red, int green, int blue)`	Int	Gets the index of the color that has the hue, white, and blackness nearest to the given color
`imagecolordeallocate(resource im, int index)`	Bool	De-allocates a color for an image
`imagecolorresolve(resource im, int red, int green, int blue)`	Int	Gets the index of the specified color or its closest possible alternative
`imagecolorexact(resource im, int red, int green, int blue)`	Int	Gets the index of the specified color
`imagecolorset(resource im, int col, int red, int green, int blue)`	Void	Sets the color for the specified palette index
`imagecolorsforindex(resource im, int col)`	Array	Gets the colors for an index
`imagegammacorrect(resource im, float inputgamma, float outputgamma)`	Bool	Apply a gamma correction to a GD image
`imagesetpixel(resource im, int x, int y, int col)`	Bool	Sets a single pixel
`imageline(resource im, int x1, int y1, int x2, int y2, int col)`	Bool	Draws a line
`imagedashedline(resource im, int x1, int y1, int x2, int y2, int col)`	Bool	Draws a dashed line
`imagerectangle(resource im, int x1, int y1, int x2, int y2, int col)`	Bool	Draws a rectangle
`imagefilledrectangle(resource im, int x1, int y1, int x2, int y2, int col)`	Bool	Draws a filled rectangle
`imagearc(resource im, int cx, int cy, int w, int h, int s, int e, int col)`	Bool	Draws a partial ellipse
`imageellipse(resource im, int cx, int cy, int w, int h, int color)`	Bool	Draws an ellipse

Function	Returns	Description
imagefilltoborder(resource im, int x, int y, int border, int col)	Bool	Flood fills to specific color
imagefill(resource im, int x, int y, int col)	Bool	Flood fills with given color col
imagecolorstotal(resource im)	Int	Finds out the number of colors in an image's palette
imagecolortransparent(resource im [, int col])	Int	Defines a color as transparent
imageinterlace(resource im [, int interlace])	Int	Enables or disables interlace
imagepolygon(resource im, array point, int num_points, int col)	Bool	Draws a polygon
imagefilledpolygon(resource im, array point, int num_points, int col)	Bool	Draws a filled polygon
imagefontwidth(int font)	Int	Gets font width
imagefontheight(int font)	Int	Gets font height
imagechar(resource im, int font, int x, int y, string c, int col)	Bool	Draws a character
imagecharup(resource im, int font, int x, int y, string c, int col)	Bool	Draws a character rotated 90 degrees counter-clockwise
imagestring(resource im, int font, int x, int y, string str, int col)	Bool	Draws a string horizontally
imagestringup(resource im, int font, int x, int y, string str, int col)	Bool	Draws a string vertically rotated 90 degrees counter-clockwise
imagecopy(resource dst_im, resource src_im, int dst_x, int dst_y, int src_x, int src_y, int src_w, int src_h)	Bool	Copies part of an image
imagecopymerge(resource src_im, resource dst_im, int dst_x, int dst_y, int src_x, int src_y, int src_w, int src_h, int pct)	Bool	Merges one part of an image with another

Continues

Function	Returns	Description
`imagecopymergegray(resource src_im, resource dst_im, int dst_x, int dst_y, int src_x, int src_y, int src_w, int src_h, int pct)`	Bool	Merges one part of an image with another while preserving hue of source
`imagecopyresized(resource dst_im, resource src_im, int dst_x, int dst_y, int src_x, int src_y, int dst_w, int dst_h, int src_w, int src_h)`	Bool	Copies and resizes part of an image
`imagesx(resource im)`	Int	Gets image width
`imagesy(resource im)`	Int	Gets image height
`imageftbbox(int size, int angle, string font_file, string text[, array extrainfo])`	Array	Gives the bounding box of a text block using fonts via freetype2
`imagefttext(resource im, int size, int angle, int x, int y, int col, string font_file, string text, [array extrainfo])`	Array	Writes text to the image using fonts via freetype2
`imagettfbbox(int size, int angle, string font_file, string text)`	Array	Gives the bounding box of a text block using TrueType fonts
`imagettftext(resource im, int size, int angle, int x, int y, int col, string font_file, string text)`	Array	Writes text to the image using a TrueType font
`imagepsloadfont(string pathname)`	resource	Loads a new font from specified file
`Imagepscopyfont(int font_index)`	Int	Makes a copy of a font for purposes like extending or re-enconding
`imagepsfreefont(resource font_index)`	Bool	Frees memory used by a font
`imagepsencodefont(resource font_index, string filename)`	Bool	Change the character encoding vector of a font
`imagepsextendfont(resource font_index, float extend)`	Bool	Extends or condenses (if extend < 1) a font
`imagepsslantfont(resource font_index, float slant)`	Bool	Slants a font

Function	Returns	Description
imagepstext(resource image, string text, resource font, int size, int xcoord, int ycoord [, int space, int tightness, float angle, int antialias])	Array	Rasterizes a string over an image
imagepsbbox(string text, resource font, int size [, int space, int tightness, int angle])	Array	Returns the bounding box needed by a string if rasterized
image2wbmp(resource im [, string filename [, int threshold]])	Bool	Outputs WBMP image to browser or file
jpeg2wbmp (string f_org, string f_dest, int d_height, int d_width, int threshold)	Bool	Converts JPEG image to WBMP image
png2wbmp (string f_org, string f_dest, int d_height, int d_width, int threshold)	Bool	Converts PNG image to WBMP image
imagefilter(resource src_im, int filtertype, [args])	Bool	Applies Filter an image using a custom angle
imageantialias(resource im, bool on)	Bool	Should antialiased functions be used or not
image_type_to_mime_type (int imagetype)	String	Gets Mime-Type for image-type returned by getimagesize, exif_read_data, exif_thumbnail, exif_imagetype
image_type_to_extension (int imagetype [, bool include_dot])	String	Gets file extension for image-type returned by getimagesize, exif_read_data, exif_thumbnail, exif_imagetype
getimagesize(string imagefile [, array info])	Array	Gets the size of an image as 4-element array
iptcembed(string iptcdata, string jpeg_file_name [, int spool])	Array	Embeds binary IPTC data into a JPEG image
iptcparse(string iptcdata)	Array	Parses binary IPTC-data into associative array

IMAP

Function	Returns	Description
imap_open(string mailbox, string user, string password [, int options])	resource	Opens an IMAP stream to a mailbox
imap_reopen(resource stream_id, string mailbox [, int options])	Bool	Reopens an IMAP stream to a new mailbox
imap_append(resource stream_id, string folder, string message [, string options])	Bool	Appends a new message to a specified mailbox
imap_num_msg(resource stream_id)	Int	Gives the number of messages in the current mailbox
imap_ping(resource stream_id)	Bool	Checks if the IMAP stream is still active
imap_num_recent(resource stream_id)	Int	Gives the number of recent messages in current mailbox
imap_get_quota(resource stream_id, string qroot)	Array	Returns the quota set to the mailbox account qroot
imap_get_quotaroot(resource stream_id, string mbox)	Array	Returns the quota set to the mailbox account mbox
imap_set_quota(resource stream_id, string qroot, int mailbox_size)	Bool	Sets the quota for qroot mailbox
imap_setacl(resource stream_id, string mailbox, string id, string rights)	Bool	Sets the ACL for a given mailbox
imap_getacl(resource stream_id, string mailbox)	Array	Gets the ACL for a given mailbox
imap_expunge(resource stream_id)	Bool	Permanently deletes all messages marked for deletion
imap_close(resource stream_id [, int options])	Bool	Closes an IMAP stream
imap_headers(resource stream_id)	Array	Returns headers for all messages in a mailbox
imap_body(resource stream_id, int msg_no [, int options])	String	Reads the message body

Function	Returns	Description
imap_mail_copy(resource stream_id, int msg_no, string mailbox [, int options])	Bool	Copies the specified message to a mailbox
imap_mail_move(resource stream_id, int msg_no, string mailbox [, int options])	Bool	Moves the specified message to a mailbox
imap_createmailbox(resource stream_id, string mailbox)	Bool	Creates a new mailbox
imap_renamemailbox(resource stream_id, string old_name, string new_name)	Bool	Renames a mailbox
imap_deletemailbox(resource stream_id, string mailbox)	Bool	Deletes a mailbox
imap_list(resource stream_id, string ref, string pattern)	Array	Reads the list of mailboxes
imap_getmailboxes(resource stream_id, string ref, string pattern)	Array	Reads the list of mailboxes and returns a full array of objects containing name, attributes, and delimiter
imap_scan(resource stream_id, string ref, string pattern, string content)	Array	Reads a list of mailboxes containing a certain string
imap_check(resource stream_id)	Object	Gets mailbox properties
imap_delete(resource stream_id, int msg_no [, int options])	Bool	Marks a message for deletion
imap_undelete(resource stream_id, int msg_no)	Bool	Removes the delete flag from a message
imap_headerinfo(resource stream_id, int msg_no [, int from_length [, int subject_length [, string default_host]]])	Object	Reads the headers of the message
imap_rfc822_parse_headers (string headers [, string default_host])	Object	Parses a set of mail headers contained in a string,and returns an object similar to imap_headerinfo()
imap_lsub(resource stream_id, string ref, string pattern)	Array	Returns a list of subscribed mailboxes

Continues

Function	Returns	Description
`imap_getsubscribed(resource stream_id, string ref, string pattern)`	Array	Returns a list of subscribed mailboxes, in the same format as imap_getmailboxes()
`imap_subscribe(resource stream_id, string mailbox)`	Bool	Subscribes to a mailbox
`imap_unsubscribe(resource stream_id, string mailbox)`	Bool	Unsubscribes from a mailbox
`imap_fetchstructure(resource stream_id, int msg_no [, int options])`	Object	Reads the full structure of a message
`imap_fetchbody(resource stream_id, int msg_no, int section [, int options])`	String	Gets a specific body section
`imap_base64(string text)`	String	Decodes BASE64 encoded text
`imap_qprint(string text)`	String	Converts a quoted-printable string to an 8-bit string
`imap_8bit(string text)`	String	Converts an 8-bit string to a quoted-printable string
`imap_binary(string text)`	String	Converts an 8-bit string to a base64 string
`imap_mailboxmsginfo(resource stream_id)`	Object	Returns info about the current mailbox
`imap_rfc822_write_address (string mailbox, string host, string personal)`	String	Returns a properly formatted e-mail address given the mailbox, host, and personal info
`imap_rfc822_parse_adrlist (string address_string, string default_host)`	Array	Parses an address string
`imap_utf8(string mime_encoded_text)`	String	Converts mime-encoded text to UTF-8
`imap_utf7_decode(string buf)`	String	Decodes a modified UTF-7 string
`imap_utf7_encode(string buf)`	String	Encodes a string in modified UTF-7
`imap_setflag_full(resource stream_id, string sequence, string flag [, int options])`	Bool	Sets flags on messages
`imap_clearflag_full(resource stream_id, string sequence, string flag [, int options])`	Bool	Clears flags on messages

Function	Returns	Description
imap_sort(resource stream_id, int criteria, int reverse [, int options [, string search_criteria [, string charset]]])	Array	Sorts an array of message headers, optionally including only messages that meet specified criteria
imap_fetchheader(resource stream_id, int msg_no [, int options])	String	Gets the full unfiltered header for a message
imap_uid(resource stream_id, int msg_no)	Int	Gets the unique message id associated with a standard sequential message number
imap_msgno(resource stream_id, int unique_msg_id)	Int	Gets the sequence number associated with a UID
imap_status(resource stream_id, string mailbox, int options)	Object	Gets status info from a mailbox
imap_bodystruct(resource stream_id, int msg_no, int section)	Object	Reads the structure of a specified body section of a specific message
imap_fetch_overview (resource stream_id, int msg_no [, int options])	Array	Reads an overview of the information in the headers of the given message sequence
imap_mail_compose(array envelope, array body)	String	Creates a MIME message based on given envelope and body sections
imap_mail(string to, string subject, string message [, string additional_headers [, string cc [, string bcc [, string rpath]]]])	Bool	Sends an e-mail message
imap_search(resource stream_id, string criteria [, int options [, string charset]])	Array	Returns a list of messages matching the given criteria
imap_alerts(void)	Array	Returns an array of all IMAP alerts that have been generated since the last page load or since the last imap_alerts() call, whichever came last. The alert stack is cleared after imap_alerts() is called

Continues

Function	Returns	Description
imap_errors(void)	Array	Returns an array of all IMAP errors generated since the last page load, or since the last imap_errors() call, whichever came last. The error stack is cleared after imap_errors() is called
imap_last_error(void)	String	Returns the last error that was generated by an IMAP function. The error stack is not cleared after this call
imap_mime_header_decode (string str)	Array	Decodes mime header element in accordance with RFC 2047and returns an array of objects containing charset encoding and decoded text
imap_thread(resource stream_id [, int options])	Array	Returns are threaded by REFERENCES tree
imap_timeout(int timeout_type [, int timeout])	Mixed	Sets or fetches IMAP timeout

Mail

Function	Returns	Description
ezmlm_hash(string addr)	Int	Calculates EZMLM list hash value
mail(string to, string subject, string message [, string additional_headers [, string additional_parameters]])	Int	Sends an e-mail message

Math

Function	Returns	Description
abs(int number)	Int	Returns the absolute value of the number
ceil(float number)	Float	Returns the next highest integer value of the number

Function	Returns	Description
`floor(float number)`	Float	Returns the next lowest integer value from the number
`round(float number [, int precision])`	Float	Returns the number rounded to specified precision
`sin(float number)`	Float	Returns the sine of the number in radians
`cos(float number)`	Float	Returns the cosine of the number in radians
`tan(float number)`	Float	Returns the tangent of the number in radians
`asin(float number)`	Float	Returns the arc sine of the number in radians
`acos(float number)`	Float	Returns the arc cosine of the number in radians
`atan(float number)`	Float	Returns the arc tangent of the number in radians
`atan2(float y, float x)`	Float	Returns the arc tangent of y/x, with the resulting quadrant determined by the signs of y and x
`sinh(float number)`	Float	Returns the hyperbolic sine of the number, defined as (exp(number) – exp(–number))/2
`cosh(float number)`	Float	Returns the hyperbolic cosine of the number, defined as (exp(number) + exp(–number))/2
`tanh(float number)`	Float	Returns the hyperbolic tangent of the number, defined as sinh(number)/cosh(number)
`asinh(float number)`	Float	Returns the inverse hyperbolic sine of the number, that is, the value whose hyperbolic sine is number
`acosh(float number)`	Float	Returns the inverse hyperbolic cosine of the number, that is, the value whose hyperbolic cosine is number
`atanh(float number)`	Float	Returns the inverse hyperbolic tangent of the number, that is, the value whose hyperbolic tangent is number

Continues

Function	Returns	Description
`pi(void)`	Float	Returns an approximation of pi
`is_finite(float val)`	Bool	Returns whether argument is finite
`is_infinite(float val)`	Bool	Returns whether argument is infinite
`is_nan(float val)`	Bool	Returns whether argument is not a number
`pow(number base, number exponent)`	Number	Returns base raised to the power of exponent. Returns integer result when possible
`exp(float number)`	Float	Returns e raised to the power of the number
`expm1(float number)`	Float	Returns exp(number) – 1, computed in a way that's accurate even when the value of number is close to zero
`log1p(float number)`	Float	Returns log(1 + number), computed in a way that's accurate even when the value of number is close to zero
`log(float number, [float base])`	Float	Returns the natural logarithm of the number, or the base log if the base is specified
`log10(float number)`	Float	Returns the base-10 logarithm of the number
`sqrt(float number)`	Float	Returns the square root of the number
`hypot(float num1, float num2)`	Float	Returns sqrt(num1*num1 + num2*num2)
`deg2rad(float number)`	Float	Converts the number in degrees to the radian equivalent
`rad2deg(float number)`	Float	Converts the radian number to the equivalent number in degrees
`bindec(string binary_number)`	Int	Returns the decimal equivalent of the binary number
`hexdec(string hexadecimal_number)`	Int	Returns the decimal equivalent of the hexadecimal number

Function	Returns	Description
octdec(string octal_number)	Int	Returns the decimal equivalent of an octal string
decbin(int decimal_number)	String	Returns a string containing a binary representation of the number
decoct(int decimal_number)	String	Returns a string containing an octal representation of the given number
dechex(int decimal_number)	String	Returns a string containing a hexadecimal representation of the given number
base_convert(string number, int frombase, int tobase)	String	Converts a number in a string from any base <= 36 to any base <= 36
number_format(float number [, int num_decimal_places [, string dec_seperator, string thousands_seperator]])	String	Formats a number with grouped thousands
fmod(float x, float y)	Float	Returns the remainder of dividing x by y as a float
srand([int seed])	Void	Seeds random number generator
mt_srand([int seed])	Void	Seeds Mersenne Twister random number generator
rand([int min, int max])	Int	Returns a random number
mt_rand([int min, int max])	Int	Returns a random number from Mersenne Twister
getrandmax(void)	Int	Returns the maximum value a random number can have
mt_getrandmax(void)	Int	Returns the maximum value a random number from Mersenne Twister can have

MIME

Function	Returns	Description
mime_content_type(string filename|resource stream)	String	Returns content-type for file

Miscellaneous

Function	Returns	Description
get_browser([string browser_name [, bool return_array]])	Mixed	Gets information about the capabilities of a browser
constant(string const_name)	Mixed	Given the name of a constant this function returns the constant's associated value
getenv(string varname)	String	Gets the value of an environment variable
putenv(string setting)	Bool	Sets the value of an environment variable
getopt(string options [, array longopts])	Array	Gets options from the command line argument list
flush(void)	Void	Flushes the output buffer
sleep(int seconds)	Void	Delays for a given number of seconds
usleep(int micro_seconds)	Void	Delays for a given number of micro seconds
time_nanosleep(long seconds, long nanoseconds)	Mixed	Delays for a number of seconds and nano seconds
highlight_file(string file_name [, bool return])	Bool	Syntax highlights a source file
php_strip_whitespace(string file_name)	String	Returns source with stripped comments and whitespace
php_check_syntax(string file_name [, &$error_message])	Bool	Checks the syntax of the specified file
highlight_string(string string [, bool return])	Bool	Syntax highlights a string or optionally return it
uniqid([string prefix , bool more_entropy])	String	Generates a unique ID
version_compare(string ver1, string ver2 [, string oper])	Int	Compares two PHP-standardized version number strings
connection_aborted(void)	Int	Returns true if client disconnected
connection_status(void)	Int	Returns the connection status bitfield
ignore_user_abort(bool value)	Int	Sets whether we want to ignore a user abort event or not

Function	Returns	Description
define(string constant_name, mixed value, case_sensitive=true)	Bool	Defines a new constant
defined(string constant_name)	Bool	Checks whether a constant exists

MS SQL

Function	Returns	Description
mssql_connect([string servername [, string username [, string password]]])	Int	Establishes a connection to a MS-SQL server
mssql_pconnect([string servername [, string username [, string password]]])	Int	Establishes a persistent connection to a MS-SQL server
mssql_close([resource conn_id])	Bool	Closes a connection to a MS-SQL server
mssql_select_db(string database_name [, resource conn_id])	Bool	Select a MS-SQL database
mssql_fetch_batch(resource result_index)	Int	Returns the next batch of records
mssql_query(string query [, resource conn_id [, int batch_size]])	resource	Performs an SQL query on a MS-SQL server database
mssql_rows_affected(resource conn_id)	Int	Returns the number of records affected by the query
mssql_free_result(resource result_index)	Bool	Frees a MS-SQL result index
mssql_get_last_message(void)	String	Gets the last message from the MS-SQL server
mssql_num_rows(resource mssql_result_index)	Int	Returns the number of rows fetched in from the result id specified
mssql_num_fields(resource mssql_result_index)	Int	Returns the number of fields fetched in from the result id specified
mssql_fetch_row(resource result_id)	Array	Returns an array of the current row in the result set specified by result_id

Continues

Function	Returns	Description
`mssql_fetch_object(resource result_id [, int result_type])`	Object	Returns a psuedo-object of the current row in the result set specified by result_id
`mssql_fetch_array(resource result_id [, int result_type])`	Array	Returns an associative array of the current row in the result set specified by result_id
`mssql_fetch_assoc(resource result_id)`	Array	Returns an associative array of the current row in the result set specified by result_id
`mssql_data_seek(resource result_id, int offset)`	Bool	Moves the internal row pointer of the MS-SQL result associated with the specified result identifier to point to the specified row number
`mssql_fetch_field(resource result_id [, int offset])`	Object	Gets information about certain fields in a query result
`mssql_field_length(resource result_id [, int offset])`	Int	Gets the length of a MS-SQL field
`mssql_field_name(resource result_id [, int offset])`	String	Returns the name of the field given by offset in the result set given by result_id
`mssql_field_type(resource result_id [, int offset])`	String	Returns the type of a field
`mssql_field_seek(int result_id, int offset)`	Bool	Seeks to the specified field offset
`mssql_result(resource result_id, int row, mixed field)`	String	Returns the contents of one cell from a MS-SQL result set
`mssql_next_result(resource result_id)`	Bool	Moves the internal result pointer to the next result
`mssql_min_error_severity(int severity)`	Void	Sets the lower error severity
`mssql_min_message_severity(int severity)`	Void	Sets the lower message severity
`mssql_init(string sp_name [, resource conn_id])`	Int	Initializes a stored procedure or a remote stored procedure
`mssql_bind(resource stmt, string param_name, mixed var, int type [, int is_output [, int is_null [, int maxlen]]])`	Bool	Adds a parameter to a stored procedure or a remote stored procedure

Function	Returns	Description
mssql_execute(resource stmt [, bool skip_results = false])	Mixed	Executes a stored procedure on a MS-SQL server database
mssql_free_statement (resource result_index)	Bool	Frees a MS-SQL statement index
mssql_guid_string(string binary [, int short_format])	String	Converts a 16-byte binary GUID to a string

MySQL

Function	Returns	Description
mysql_connect([string hostname[:port] [:/path/to/socket] [, string username [, string password [, bool new [, int flags]]]]])	resource	Opens a connection to a MySQL Server
mysql_pconnect([string host-name[:port] [:/path/to/socket] [, string username [, string password [, int flags]]]])	resource	Opens a persistent connection to a MySQL Server
mysql_close([int link_identifier])	Bool	Closes a MySQL connection
mysql_select_db(string database_name [, int link_identifier])	Bool	Selects a MySQL database
mysql_get_client_info(void)	String	Returns a string that represents the client library version
mysql_get_host_info([int link_identifier])	String	Returns a string describing the type of connection in use, including the server host name
mysql_get_proto_info([int link_identifier])	Int	Returns the protocol version used by current connection
mysql_get_server_info([int link_identifier])	String	Returns a string that represents the server version number
mysql_info([int link_identifier])	String	Returns a string containing information about the most recent query

Continues

Function	Returns	Description
`mysql_thread_id([int link_identifier])`	Int	Returns the thread id of current connection
`mysql_stat([int link_identifier])`	String	Returns a string containing status information
`mysql_client_encoding([int link_identifier])`	String	Returns the default character set for the current connection
`mysql_create_db(string database_name [, int link_identifier])`	Bool	Creates a MySQL database
`mysql_drop_db(string database_name [, int link_identifier])`	Bool	Drops (deletes) a MySQL database
`mysql_query(string query [, int link_identifier])`	resource	Sends an SQL query to MySQL
`mysql_unbuffered_query (string query [, int link_identifier])`	resource	Sends an SQL query to MySQL, without fetching and buffering the result rows
`mysql_db_query(string database_name, string query [, int link_identifier])`	resource	Sends an SQL query to MySQL
`mysql_list_dbs([int link_identifier])`	resource	Lists databases available on a MySQL server
`mysql_list_tables(string database_name [, int link_identifier])`	resource	Lists tables in a MySQL database
`mysql_list_fields(string database_name, string table_name [, int link_identifier])`	resource	Lists MySQL result fields
`mysql_list_processes([int link_identifier])`	resource	Returns a result set describing the current server threads
`mysql_error([int link_identifier])`	String	Returns the text of the error message from the previous MySQL operation
`mysql_errno([int link_identifier])`	Int	Returns the number of the error message from the previous MySQL operation
`mysql_affected_rows([int link_identifier])`	Int	Gets number of affected rows in the previous MySQL operation

Function	Returns	Description
`mysql_escape_string(string to_be_escaped)`	String	Escapes string for mysql query
`mysql_real_escape_string (string to_be_escaped [, int link_identifier])`	String	Escapes special characters in a string for use in a SQL statement, taking into account the current charset of the connection
`mysql_insert_id([int link_identifier])`	Int	Gets the ID generated from the previous INSERT operation
`mysql_result(resource result, int row [, mixed field])`	Mixed	Gets result data
`mysql_num_rows(resource result)`	Int	Gets number of rows in a result
`mysql_num_fields(resource result)`	Int	Gets number of fields in a result
`mysql_fetch_row(resource result)`	Array	Gets a result row as an enumerated array
`mysql_fetch_object(resource result [, int result_type])`	Object	Fetches a result row as an object
`mysql_fetch_array(resource result [, int result_type])`	Array	Fetches a result row as an array (associative, numeric or both)
`mysql_fetch_assoc(resource result)`	Array	Fetches a result row as an associative array
`mysql_data_seek(resource result, int row_number)`	Bool	Moves internal result pointer
`mysql_fetch_lengths(resource result)`	Array	Gets max data size of each column in a result
`mysql_fetch_field(resource result [, int field_offset])`	Object	Gets column information from a resultand returns as an object
`mysql_field_seek(resource result, int field_offset)`	Bool	Sets result pointer to a specific field offset
`mysql_field_name(resource result, int field_index)`	String	Gets the name of the specified field in a result
`mysql_field_table(resource result, int field_offset)`	String	Gets name of the table the specified field is in
`mysql_field_len(resource result, int field_offset)`	Int	Returns the length of the specified field

Continues

Function	Returns	Description
`mysql_field_type(resource result, int field_offset)`	String	Gets the type of the specified field in a result
`mysql_field_flags(resource result, int field_offset)`	String	Gets the flags associated with the specified field in a result
`mysql_free_result(resource result)`	Bool	Frees result memory
`mysql_ping([int link_identifier])`	Bool	Pings a server connection. If no connection, it reconnects

Network Functions

Function	Returns	Description
`define_syslog_variables(void)`	Void	Initializes all syslog-related variables
`openlog(string ident, int option, int facility)`	Bool	Opens connection to system logger
`closelog(void)`	Bool	Closes connection to system logger
`syslog(int priority, string message)`	Bool	Generates a system log message
`ip2long(string ip_address)`	Int	Converts a string containing an (IPv4) Internet Protocol dotted address into a proper address
`long2ip(int proper_address)`	String	Converts an (IPv4) Internet network address into a string in Internet standard dotted format
`getservbyname(string service, string protocol)`	Int	Returns port number associated with service. Protocol must be tcp or udp
`getservbyport(int port, string protocol)`	String	xxxReturns service name associated with port. Protocol must be tcp or udp
`getprotobyname(string name)`	Int	Returns protocol number associated with name as per /etc/protocols
`getprotobynumber(int proto)`	String	Returns protocol name associated with protocol number

ODBC

Function	Returns	Description
odbc_close_all(void)	Void	Closes all ODBC connections
odbc_binmode(int result_id, int mode)	Bool	Handles binary column data
odbc_longreadlen(int result_id, int length)	Bool	Handles LONG columns
odbc_prepare(resource connection_id, string query)	resource	Prepares a statement for execution
odbc_execute(resource result_id [, array parameters_array])	Bool	Executes a prepared statement
odbc_cursor(resource result_id)	String	Gets cursor name
odbc_data_source(resource connection_id, int fetch_type)	Array	Returns information about the currently connected data source
odbc_exec(resource connection_id, string query [, int flags])	resource	Prepares and executes an SQL statement
odbc_fetch_object(int result [, int rownumber])	Object	Fetches a result row as an object
odbc_fetch_array(int result [, int rownumber])	Array	Fetches a result row as an associative array
odbc_fetch_into(resource result_id, array result_array, [, int rownumber])	Int	Fetches one result row into an array
odbc_fetch_row(resource result_id [, int row_number])	Bool	Fetches a row
odbc_result(resource result_id, mixed field)	Mixed	Gets result data
odbc_result_all(resource result_id [, string format])	Int	Prints result as HTML table
odbc_free_result(resource result_id)	Bool	Frees resources associated with a result
odbc_connect(string DSN, string user, string password [, int cursor_option])	resource	Connects to a datasource

Continues

Function	Returns	Description
`odbc_pconnect(string DSN, string user, string password [, int cursor_option])`	resource	Establishes a persistent connection to a datasource
`odbc_close(resource connection_id)`	Void	Closes an ODBC connection
`odbc_num_rows(resource result_id)`	Int	Gets number of rows in a result
`odbc_next_result(resource result_id)`	Bool	Checks if multiple results are avaiable
`odbc_num_fields(resource result_id)`	Int	Gets number of columns in a result
`odbc_field_name(resource result_id, int field_number)`	String	Gets a column name
`odbc_field_type(resource result_id, int field_number)`	String	Gets the datatype of a column
`odbc_field_len(resource result_id, int field_number)`	Int	Gets the length (precision) of a column
`odbc_field_scale(resource result_id, int field_number)`	Int	Gets the scale of a column
`odbc_field_num(resource result_id, string field_name)`	Int	Returns column number
`odbc_autocommit(resource connection_id [, int OnOff])`	Mixed	Toggles autocommit mode or gets autocommit status
`odbc_commit(resource connection_id)`	Bool	Commits an ODBC transaction
`odbc_rollback(resource connection_id)`	Bool	Rolls back a transaction
`odbc_error([resource connection_id])`	String	Gets the last error code
`odbc_errormsg([resource connection_id])`	String	Gets the last error message
`odbc_setoption(resource conn_id| result_id, int which, int option, int value)`	Bool	Sets connection or statement options
`odbc_tables(resource connection_id [, string qualifier, string owner, string name, string table_types])`	resource	Calls the SQLTables function

Function	Returns	Description
odbc_columns(resource connection_id, string qualifier, string owner, string table_name, string column_name)	resource	Returns a result identifier that can be used to fetch a list of column names in specified tables
odbc_columnprivileges (resource connection_id, string catalog, string schema, string table, string column)	resource	Returns a result identifier that can be used to fetch a list of columns and associated privileges for the specified table
odbc_foreignkeys(resource connection_id, string pk_qualifier, string pk_owner, string pk_table, string fk_qualifier, string fk_owner, string fk_table)	resource	Returns a result identifier to either a list of foreign keys in the specified table or a list of foreign keys in other tables that refer to the primary key in the specified table
odbc_gettypeinfo(resource connection_id [, int data_type])	resource	Returns a result identifier containing information about data types supported by the data source
odbc_primarykeys(resource connection_id, string qualifier, string owner, string table)	resource	Returns a result identifier listing the column names that comprise the primary key for a table
odbc_procedurecolumns (resource connection_id [, string qualifier, string owner, string proc, string column])	resource	Returns a result identifier containing the list of input and output parameters, as well as the columns that make up the result set for the specified procedures
odbc_procedures(resource connection_id [, string qualifier, string owner, string name])	resource	Returns a result identifier containing the list of procedure names in a datasource
odbc_specialcolumns(resource connection_id, int type, string qualifier, string owner, string table, int scope, int nullable)	resource	Returns a result identifier containing either the optimal set of columns that uniquely identifies a row in the table or columns that are automatically updated when any value in the row is updated by a transaction
odbc_statistics(resource connection_id, string qualifier, string owner, string name, int unique, int accuracy)	resource	Returns a result identifier that contains statistics about a single table and the indexes associated with the table

Continues

Function	Returns	Description
odbc_tableprivileges (resource connection_id, string qualifier, string owner, string name)	resource	Returns a result identifier containing a list of tables and the privileges associated with each table

Output Buffering

Function	Returns	Description
ob_list_handlers()	false|array	* Lists all output_buffers in an array
ob_start([string| array user_function [, int chunk_size [, bool erase]]])	Bool	Turns on Output Buffering (specifying an optional output handler)
ob_flush(void)	Bool	Flushes (sends) contents of the output buffer. The last buffer content is sent to next buffer
ob_clean(void)	Bool	Cleans (deletes) the current output buffer
ob_end_flush(void)	Bool	Flushes (sends) the output buffer, and deletes current output buffer
ob_end_clean(void)	Bool	Cleans the output buffer, and deletes current output buffer
ob_get_flush(void)	Bool	Gets current buffer contents, flushes (sends) the output buffer, and deletes current output buffer
ob_get_clean(void)	Bool	Gets current buffer contents and deletes current output buffer
ob_get_contents(void)	String	Returns the contents of the output buffer
ob_get_level(void)	Int	Returns the nesting level of the output buffer
ob_get_length(void)	Int	Returns the length of the output buffer

Function	Returns	Description
ob_get_status([bool full_status])	false|array	Returns the status of the active or all output buffers
ob_implicit_flush([int flag])	Void	Turns implicit flush on/off and is equivalent to calling flush() after every output call
output_reset_rewrite_vars(void)	Bool	Resets (clears) URL rewriter values
output_add_rewrite_var (string name, string value)	Bool	Adds URL rewriter values

PCRE

Function	Returns	Description
preg_match(string pattern, string subject [, array subpatterns [, int flags [, int offset]]])	Int	Performs a Perl-style regular expression match
preg_match_all(string pattern, string subject, array subpatterns [, int flags [, int offset]])	Int	Performs a Perl-style global regular expression match
preg_replace(mixed regex, mixed replace, mixed subject [, int limit])	String	Performs Perl-style regular expression replacement
preg_replace_callback (mixed regex, mixed callback, mixed subject [, int limit])	String	Performs Perl-style regular expression replacement using replacement callback
preg_split(string pattern, string subject [, int limit [, int flags]])	Array	Splits string into an array using a Perl-style regular expression as a delimiter
preg_quote(string str, string delim_char)	String	Quotes regular expression characters plus an optional character
preg_grep(string regex, array input)	Array	Searches an array and returns entries that match regex

PHP Options and Info

Function	Returns	Description
assert(string|bool assertion)	Int	Checks if assertion is false
assert_options(int what [, mixed value])	Mixed	Sets/gets the various assert flags
phpinfo([int what])	Void	Outputs a page of useful information about PHP and the current request
phpversion([string extension])	String	Returns the current PHP version
phpcredits([int flag])	Void	Prints the list of people whove contributed to the PHP project
php_logo_guid(void)	String	Returns the special ID used to request the PHP logo in phpinfo screens
php_real_logo_guid(void)	String	Returns the special ID used to request the PHP logo in phpinfo screens
php_egg_logo_guid(void)	String	Returns the special ID used to request the PHP logo in phpinfo screens
zend_logo_guid(void)	String	Returns the special ID used to request the Zend logo in phpinfo screens
php_sapi_name(void)	String	Returns the current SAPI module name
php_uname(void)	String	Returns information about the system PHP was built on
php_ini_scanned_files(void)	String	Returns comma-separated string of .ini files parsed from the additional ini dir
getmyuid(void)	Int	Gets PHP script owners UID
getmygid(void)	Int	Gets PHP script owners GID
getmypid(void)	Int	Gets current process ID
getmyinode(void)	Int	Gets the inode of the current script being parsed
getlastmod(void)	Int	Gets time of last page modification

Function	Returns	Description
`set_time_limit(int seconds)`	Bool	Sets the maximum time a script can run
`ini_get(string varname)`	String	Gets a configuration option
`ini_get_all([string extension])`	Array	Gets all configuration options
`ini_set(string varname, string newvalue)`	String	Sets a configuration option, returns false on error and the old value of the configuration option on success
`ini_restore(string varname)`	Void	Restores the value of a configuration option specified by varname
`set_include_path(string varname, string newvalue)`	String	Sets the include_path configuration option
`get_include_path()`	String	Gets the current include_path configuration option
`restore_include_path()`	Void	Restores the value of the include_path configuration option
`get_current_user(void)`	String	Gets the name of the owner of the current PHP script
`get_cfg_var(string option_name)`	String	Gets the value of a PHP configuration option
`set_magic_quotes_runtime(int new_setting)`	Bool	Sets the current active configuration setting of magic_quotes_runtimeand returns previous setting
`get_magic_quotes_runtime(void)`	Int	Gets the current active configuration setting of magic_quotes_runtime
`get_magic_quotes_gpc(void)`	Int	Gets the current active configuration setting of magic_quotes_gpc
`get_declared_classes()`	Array	Returns an array of all declared classes
`get_declared_interfaces()`	Array	Returns an array of all declared interfaces
`get_defined_functions(void)`	Array	Returns an array of all defined functions
`get_defined_vars(void)`	Array	Returns an associative array of names and values of all currently defined variable names (variables in the current scope)

Continues

Function	Returns	Description
`get_resource_type(resource res)`	String	Gets the resource type name for a given resource
`get_loaded_extensions(void)`	Array	Returns an array containing names of loaded extensions
`get_defined_constants(void)`	Array	Returns an array containing the names and values of all defined constants
`extension_loaded(string extension_name)`	Bool	Returns true if the named extension is loaded
`get_extension_funcs(string extension_name)`	Array	Returns an array with the names of functions belonging to the named extension
`get_included_files(void)`	Array	Returns an array with the names of included or required files
`zend_version(void)`	String	Gets the version of the Zend Engine

Program Execution

Function	Returns	Description
`exec(string command [, array &output [, int &return_value]])`	String	Executes an external program
`system(string command [, int &return_value])`	Int	Executes an external program and displays output
`passthru(string command [, int &return_value])`	Void	Executes an external program and displays raw output
`escapeshellcmd(string command)`	String	Escapes shell metacharacters
`escapeshellarg(string arg)`	String	Quotes and escapes an argument for use in a shell command
`shell_exec(string cmd)`	String	Executes command via shelland returns complete output as string
`proc_nice(int priority)`	Bool	Changes the priority of the current process
`proc_terminate(resource process [, long signal])`	Int	Kills a process opened by proc_open
`proc_close(resource process)`	Int	Closes a process opened by proc_open

Function	Returns	Description
proc_get_status(resource process)	Array	Gets information about a process opened by proc_open
proc_open(string command, array descriptorspec, array &pipes [, string cwd [, array env [, array other_options]]])	Resource	Runs a process with more control over its file descriptors

Regular Expressions

Function	Returns	Description
ereg(string pattern, string string [, array registers])	Int	Matches a regular expressions
eregi(string pattern, string string [, array registers])	Int	Matches a case-insensitive regular expression
ereg_replace(string pattern, string replacement, string string)	String	Replaces regular expression
eregi_replace(string pattern, string replacement, string string)	String	Replaces a case-insensitive regular expression
split(string pattern, string string [, int limit])	Array	Splits string into array by regular expression
spliti(string pattern, string string [, int limit])	Array	Splits a string into an array by regular case-insensitive expression
sql_regcase(string string)	String	Creates a regular expression for a case insensitive match on string

Sessions

Function	Returns	Description
session_set_cookie_params(int lifetime [, string path [, string domain [, bool secure]]])	Void	Sets session cookie parameters
session_get_cookie_params(void)	Array	Returns the session cookie parameters

Continues

Function	Returns	Description
`session_name([string newname])`	String	Returns the current session name. If newname is given, the session name is replaced with newname
`session_module_name([string newname])`	String	Returns the current module name used for accessing session data. If newname is given, the module name is replaced with newname
`session_set_save_handler(string open, string close, string read, string write, string destroy, string gc)`	Void	Sets user-level functions
`session_save_path([string newname])`	String	Returns the current save path passed to module_name. If newname is given, the save path is replaced with newname
`session_id([string newid])`	String	Returns the current session id. If newid is given, the session id is replaced with newid
`session_regenerate_id()`	Bool	Updates the current session id with a newly generated one
`session_cache_limiter([string new_cache_limiter])`	String	Returns the current cache limiter. If new_cache_limiter is given, the current cache_limiter is replaced with new_cache_limiter
`session_cache_expire([int new_cache_expire])`	Int	Returns the current cache expire. If new_cache_expire is given, the current cache_expire is replaced with new_cache_expire
`session_register(mixed var_names [, mixed...])`	Bool	Adds varname(s) to the list of variables which are freezed at the session end
`session_unregister(string varname)`	Bool	Removes varname from the list of variables which are freezed at the session end
`session_is_registered(string varname)`	Bool	Checks if a variable is registered in session
`session_encode(void)`	String	Serializes the current setup and returns the serialized representation

Function	Returns	Description
session_decode(string data)	Bool	Deserializes data and reinitializes the variables
session_start(void)	Bool	Begins session—reinitializes freezed variables, registers browsers, etc
session_destroy(void)	Bool	Destroys the current session and all data associated with it
session_unset(void)	Void	Unsets all registered variables
session_write_close(void)	Void	Writes session data and ends session

Simple XML

Function	Returns	Description
simplexml_load_file(string filename)	simplemxml_element	Loads a filenameand returns a simplexml_element object to allow for processing
simplexml_load_string(string data)	simplemxml_element	Loads a stringand returns a simplexml_element object to allow for processing
simplexml_import_dom(domNode node)	simplemxml_element	Gets a simplexml_element object from dom to allow for processing

Sockets

Function	Returns	Description
socket_select(array &read_fds, array &write_fds, &array except_fds, int tv_sec[, int tv_usec])	Int	Runs the select() system call on the sets mentioned with a timeout specified by tv_sec and tv_usec
socket_create_listen(int port[, int backlog])	Resource	Opens a socket on port to accept connections
socket_accept(resource socket)	Resource	Accepts a connection on the listening socket fd

Continues

Function	Returns	Description
`socket_set_nonblock(resource socket)`	Bool	Sets nonblocking mode on a socket resource
`socket_set_block(resource socket)`	Bool	Sets blocking mode on a socket resource
`socket_listen(resource socket[, int backlog])`	Bool	Sets the maximum number of connections allowed to be waited for on the socket specified by fd
`socket_close(resource socket)`	Void	Closes a file descriptor
`socket_write(resource socket, string buf[, int length])`	Int	Writes the buffer to the socket resource, length is optional
`socket_read(resource socket, int length [, int type])`	String	Reads a maximum of length bytes from socket
`socket_getsockname(resource socket, string &addr[, int &port])`	Bool	Queries the remote side of the given socket which may either result in host/port or in a UNIX filesystem path, dependent on its type
`socket_getpeername(resource socket, string &addr[, int &port])`	Bool	Queries the remote side of the given socket which may either result in host/port or in a UNIX filesystem path, dependent on its type
`socket_create(int domain, int type, int protocol)`	Resource	Creates an endpoint for communication in the domain specified by domain, of type specified by type
`socket_connect(resource socket, string addr [, int port])`	Bool	Opens a connection to addr:port on the socket specified by socket
`socket_strerror(int errno)`	String	Returns a string describing an error
`socket_bind(resource socket, string addr [, int port])`	Bool	Binds an open socket to a listening port. Port is only specified in AF_INET family
`socket_recv(resource socket, string &buf, int len, int flags)`	Int	Receives data from a connected socket
`socket_send(resource socket, string buf, int len, int flags)`	Int	Sends data to a connected socket
`socket_recvfrom(resource socket, string &buf, int len, int flags, string &name [, int &port])`	Int	Receives data from a socket, connected or not

Function	Returns	Description
socket_sendto(resource socket, string buf, int len, int flags, string addr [, int port])	Int	Sends a message to a socket, whether it is connected or not
socket_get_option(resource socket, int level, int optname)	Mixed	Gets socket options for the socket
socket_set_option(resource socket, int level, int optname, int|array optval)	Bool	Sets socket options for the socket
socket_create_pair(int domain, int type, int protocol, array &fd)	Bool	Creates a pair of indistinguishable sockets and stores them in an array
socket_shutdown(resource socket [, int how])	Bool	Shuts down a socket for receiving, sending, or both
socket_last_error([resource socket])	Int	Returns the last socket error (either the last used or the provided socket resource)
socket_clear_error([resource socket])	Void	Clears the error on the socket or the last error code
fsockopen(string hostname, int port [, int errno [, string errstr [, float timeout]]])	Int	Opens Internet or Unix domain socket connection
pfsockopen(string hostname, int port [, int errno [, string errstr [, float timeout]]])	Int	Opens persistent Internet or Unix domain socket connection

SQLite

Function	Returns	Description
sqlite_popen(string filename [, int mode [, string &error_message]])	Resource	Opens a persistent handle to a SQLite database. Will create the database if it does not exist
sqlite_open(string filename [, int mode [, string &error_message]])	Resource	Opens a SQLite database. Will create the database if it does not exist
sqlite_factory(string filename [, int mode [, string &error_message]])	Object	Opens a SQLite database and creates an object for it. Will create the database if it does not exist

Continues

Function	Returns	Description
`sqlite_busy_timeout(resource db, int ms)`	Void	Sets busy timeout duration. If ms <= 0, all busy handlers are disabled
`sqlite_close(resource db)`	Void	Closes an open sqlite database
`sqlite_unbuffered_query(string query, resource db [, int result_type ])`	Resource	Executes a query that does not prefetch and buffer all data
`sqlite_query(string query, resource db [, int result_type ])`	Resource	Executes a query against a given database and returns a result handle
`sqlite_fetch_all(resource result [, int result_type [, bool decode_binary]])`	Array	Fetches all rows from a result set as an array of arrays
`sqlite_fetch_array(resource result [, int result_type [, bool decode_binary]])`	Array	Fetches the next row from a result set as an array
`sqlite_fetch_object(resource result [, string class_name [, NULL|array ctor_params [, bool decode_binary]]])`	Object	Fetches the next row from a result set as an object
`sqlite_array_query(resource db, string query [, int result_type [, bool decode_binary]])`	Array	Executes a query against a given database and returns an array of arrays
`sqlite_single_query(resource db, string query [, bool first_row_only [, bool decode_binary]])`	Array	Executes a query and returns either an array for one single column or the value of the first row
`sqlite_fetch_single(resource result [, bool decode_binary])`	String	Fetches the first column of a result set as a string
`sqlite_current(resource result [, int result_type [, bool decode_binary]])`	Array	Fetches the current row from a result set as an array
`sqlite_column(resource result, mixed index_or_name [, bool decode_binary])`	Mixed	Fetches a column from the current row of a result set
`sqlite_libversion()`	String	Returns the version of the linked SQLite library
`sqlite_libencoding()`	String	Returns the encoding (iso8859 or UTF-8) of the linked SQLite library

Function	Returns	Description
sqlite_changes(resource db)	Int	Returns the number of rows that were changed by the most recent SQL statement
sqlite_last_insert_rowid (resource db)	Int	Returns the rowid of the most recently inserted row
sqlite_num_rows(resource result)	Int	Returns the number of rows in a buffered result set
sqlite_has_more(resource result)	Bool	Returns whether more rows are available
sqlite_has_prev(resource result)	Bool	* Returns whether a previous row is available
sqlite_num_fields(resource result)	Int	Returns the number of fields in a result set
sqlite_field_name(resource result, int field_index)	String	Returns the name of a particular field of a result set
sqlite_seek(resource result, int row)	Bool	Seeks to a particular row number of a buffered result set
sqlite_rewind(resource result)	Bool	Seeks to the first row number of a buffered result set
sqlite_next(resource result)	Bool	Seeks to the next row number of a result set
sqlite_prev(resource result)	Bool	* Seeks to the previous row number of a result set
sqlite_escape_string(string item)	String	Escapes a string for use as a query parameter
sqlite_last_error(resource db)	Int	Returns the error code of the last error for a database
sqlite_error_string(int error_code)	String	Returns the textual description of an error code
sqlite_create_aggregate(resource db, string funcname, mixed step_func, mixed finalize_func[, long num_args])	Bool	Registers an aggregate function for queries
sqlite_create_function(resource db, string funcname, mixed callback[, long num_args])	Bool	Registers a regular function for queries

Continues

Function	Returns	Description
`sqlite_udf_encode_binary` `(string data)`	String	Applies binary encoding (if required) to a string to return from an UDF
`sqlite_udf_decode_binary` `(string data)`	String	Decodes binary encoding on a string parameter passed to an UDF

Streams

Function	Returns	Description
`stream_socket_client(string remoteaddress [, long &errcode, string &errstring, double timeout, long flags, resource context])`	Resource	Opens a client connection to a remote address
`stream_socket_server(string localaddress [, long &errcode, string &errstring, long flags, resource context])`	Resource	Creates a server socket bound to localaddress
`stream_socket_accept(resource serverstream, [ double timeout, string &peername])`	Resource	Accepts a client connection from a server socket
`stream_socket_get_name(resource stream, bool want_peer)`	String	Returns either the locally bound or remote name for a socket stream
`stream_socket_sendto(resouce stream, string data [, long flags [, string target_addr]])`	Long	Sends data to a socket stream. If target_addr is specified it must be in dotted quad (or [ipv6]) format
`stream_socket_recvfrom(resource stream, long amount [, long flags [, string &remote_addr]])`	String	Receives data from a socket stream
`stream_get_contents(resource source [, long maxlen ])`	Long	Reads all remaining bytes (up to maxlen bytes) from a stream and returns them as a string
`stream_copy_to_stream(resource source, resource dest [, long maxlen ])`	Long	Reads up to maxlen bytes from source stream and writes them to destination stream
`stream_get_meta_data(resource fp)`	Resource	Retrieves header/meta data from streams/file pointers

Function	Returns	Description
stream_get_transports()	Array	Retrieves list of registered socket transports
stream_get_wrappers()	Array	Retrieves list of registered stream wrappers
stream_select(array &read_streams, array &write_streams, array &except_streams, int tv_sec[, int tv_usec])	Int	Runs the select() system call on the sets of streams with a timeout specified by tv_sec and tv_usec
stream_context_get_options (resource context|resource stream)	Array	Retrieves options for a stream/wrapper/context
stream_context_set_option (resource context|resource stream, string wrappername, string optionname, mixed value)	Bool	Sets an option for a wrapper
stream_context_set_params (resource context|resource stream, array options)	Bool	Sets parameters for a file context
stream_context_create([array options])	Resource	Creates a file context and optionally sets parameters
stream_filter_prepend(resource stream, string filtername[, int read_write[, string filterparams]])	Bool	Prepends a filter to a stream
stream_filter_append(resource stream, string filtername[, int read_write[, string filterparams]])	Bool	Appends a filter to a stream
stream_get_line(resource stream, int maxlen, string ending)	String	Reads up to maxlen bytes from a stream or until the ending string is found
stream_set_blocking(resource socket, int mode)	Bool	Sets blocking/nonblocking mode on a socket or stream
set_socket_blocking(resource socket, int mode)	Bool	Sets blocking/nonblocking mode on a socket
stream_set_timeout(resource stream, int seconds, int microseconds)	Bool	Sets timeout on stream read to seconds + microseonds

Continues

Function	Returns	Description
`stream_set_write_buffer(resource fp, int buffer)`	Int	Sets file write buffer
`stream_wrapper_register(string protocol, string classname)`	Bool	Registers a custom URL protocol handler class
`stream_bucket_make_writeable (resource brigade)`	Object	Returns a bucket object from the brigade for operating on
`stream_bucket_prepend(resource brigade, resource bucket)`	Void	Prepends bucket to brigade
`stream_bucket_append(resource brigade, resource bucket)`	Void	Appends bucket to brigade
`stream_bucket_new(resource stream, string buffer)`	Resource	Creates a new bucket for use on the current stream
`stream_get_filters(void)`	Array	Returns a list of registered filters
`stream_filter_register(string filtername, string classname)`	Bool	Registers a custom filter handler class

Strings

Function	Returns	Description
`crc32(string str)`	String	Calculates the crc32 polynomial of a string
`crypt(string str [, string salt])`	String	Encrypts a string
`convert_cyr_string(string str, string from, string to)`	String	Converts from one Cyrillic character set to another
`lcg_value()`	Float	Returns a value from the combined linear congruential generator
`levenshtein(string str1, string str2)`	Int	Calculates Levenshtein distance between two strings
`md5(string str, [ bool raw_output])`	String	Calculates the md5 hash of a string
`md5_file(string filename [, bool raw_output])`	String	Calculates the md5 hash of given filename
`metaphone(string text, int phones)`	String	Breaks English phrases down into their phonemes

Function	Returns	Description
pack(string format, mixed arg1 [, mixed arg2 [, mixed...]])	String	Takes one or more arguments and packs them into a binary string according to the format argument
unpack(string format, string input)	Array	Unpacks binary string into named array elements according to format argument
sha1(string str [, bool raw_output])	String	Calculates the sha1 hash of a string
sha1_file(string filename [, bool raw_output])	String	Calculates the sha1 hash of given filename
soundex(string str)	String	Calculates the soundex key of a string
bin2hex(string data)	String	Converts the binary representation of data to hex
strspn(string str, string mask [, start [, len]])	Int	Finds length of initial segment consisting entirely of characters found in mask. If start or/and length is provided, works like strspn(substr($s, $start,$len), $good_chars)
strcspn(string str, string mask [, start [, len]])	Int	Finds length of initial segment consisting entirely of characters not found in mask. If start or/and length is provided, works like strcspn(substr($s, $start,$len)$bad_chars)
nl_langinfo(int item)	String	Queries language and locale information
strcoll(string str1, string str2)	Int	Compares two strings using the current locale
trim(string str [, string character_mask])	String	Strips whitespace from the beginning and end of a string
rtrim(string str [, string character_mask])	String	Removes trailing whitespace
ltrim(string str [, string character_mask])	String	Strips whitespace from the beginning of a string
wordwrap(string str [, int width [, string break [, boolean cut]]])	String	Wraps buffer to selected number of characters using string break char

Continues

Function	Returns	Description
explode(string separator, string str [, int limit])	Array	Splits a string on string separatorand returns array of components
join(array src, string glue)	String	An alias for implode function
implode([string glue,] array pieces)	String	Joins array elements placing glue string between itemsand returns one string
strtok([string str,] string token)	String	Tokenizes a string
strtoupper(string str)	String	Makes a string uppercase
strtolower(string str)	String	Makes a string lowercase
basename(string path [, string suffix])	String	Returns the filename component of the path
dirname(string path)	String	Returns the directory name component of the path
pathinfo(string path)	Array	Returns information about a certain string
stristr(string haystack, string needle)	String	Finds first occurrence of a string within another, case insensitive
strstr(string haystack, string needle)	String	Finds first occurrence of a string within another
strchr(string haystack, string needle)	String	An alias for strstr
strpos(string haystack, string needle [, int offset])	Int	Finds position of first occurrence of a string within another
stripos(string haystack, string needle [, int offset])	Int	Finds position of first occurrence of a string within another, case insensitive
strrpos(string haystack, string needle [, int offset])	Int	Finds position of last occurrence of a string within another string
strripos(string haystack, string needle [, int offset])	Int	Finds position of last occurrence of a string within another string
strrchr(string haystack, string needle)	String	Finds the last occurrence of a character in a string within another
chunk_split(string str [, int chunklen [, string ending]])	String	Returns split line

Function	Returns	Description
`substr(string str, int start [, int length])`	String	Returns part of a string
`substr_replace(mixed str, mixed repl, mixed start [, mixed length])`	Mixed	Replaces part of a string with another string
`quoted_printable_decode (string str)`	String	Converts a quoted-printable string to an 8-bit string
`quotemeta(string str)`	String	Quotes (escapes with \) meta characters
`ord(string character)`	Int	Returns ASCII value of character
`chr(int ascii)`	String	Converts ASCII code to a character
`ucfirst(string str)`	String	Makes a string's first character uppercase
`ucwords(string str)`	String	Uppercases the first character of every word in a string
`strtr(string str, string from, string to)`	String	Translates characters in str using given translation tables
`strrev(string str)`	String	Reverses a string
`similar_text(string str1, string str2 [, float percent])`	Int	Calculates the similarity between two strings
`addcslashes(string str, string charlist)`	String	Escapes all chars mentioned in charlist with backslash. It creates octal representations if asked to backslash characters with 8-bit set or with ASCII<32 (except '\n', '\r', '\t', etc)
`addslashes(string str)`	String	Escapes single quote, double quotes, and backslash characters in a string with backslashes
`stripcslashes(string str)`	String	Strips backslashes from a string. Uses C-style conventions
`stripslashes(string str)`	String	Strips backslashes from a string
`str_replace(mixed search, mixed replace, mixed subject [, int &replace_count])`	Mixed	Replaces all occurrences of search in haystack with replace
`str_ireplace(mixed search, mixed replace, mixed subject [, int &replace_count])`	Mixed	Replaces all (case-insensitive) occurrences of search in haystack with replace

Continues

Function	Returns	Description
hebrev(string str [, int max_chars_per_line])	String	Converts logical Hebrew text to visual text
hebrevc(string str [, int max_chars_per_line])	String	Converts logical Hebrew text to visual text with newline conversion
nl2br(string str)	String	Converts newlines to HTML line breaks
strip_tags(string str [, string allowable_tags])	String	Strips HTML and PHP tags from a string
setlocale(mixed category, string locale [, string...])	String	Sets locale information
parse_str(string encoded_string [, array result])	Void	Parses GET/POST/COOKIE data and sets global variables
str_repeat(string input, int mult)	String	Returns the input string repeat mult times
count_chars(string input [, int mode])	Mixed	Returns info about what characters are used in input
strnatcmp(string s1, string s2)	Int	Returns the result of string comparison using 'natural' algorithm
localeconv(void)	Array	Returns numeric formatting information based on the current locale
strnatcasecmp(string s1, string s2)	Int	Returns the result of case-insensitive string comparison using 'natural' algorithm
substr_count(string haystack, string needle)	Int	Returns the number of times a substring occurs in the string
str_pad(string input, int pad_length [, string pad_string [, int pad_type]])	String	Returns input string padded on the left or right to specified length with pad_string
sscanf(string str, string format [, string...])	Mixed	Implements an ANSI C-compatible sscanf
str_rot13(string str)	String	Performs the rot13 transform on a string
str_shuffle(string str)	Void	Shuffles string. One permutation of all possible is created

Function	Returns	Description
str_word_count(string str, [int format])	Mixed	Counts the number of words inside a string. If format of 1 is specified, it returns an array containing all the words found. A format of 2 returns an associative array where the key is the numeric position of the word
money_format(string format , float value)	String	Converts monetary value(s) to string
str_split(string str [, int split_length])	Array	Converts a string to an array. If split_length is specified, breaks the string down into chunks each split_length characters long
strpbrk(string haystack, string char_list)	Array	Searches a string for any of a set of characters
substr_compare(string main_str, string str, int offset [, int length [, bool case_sensitivity]])	Int	Binary safe optionally case-insensitive comparison of 2 strings from an offset, up to length characters
uuencode(string data)	String	Unencode a string
uudecode(string data)	String	Decode a uuencoded string
sprintf(string format [, mixed arg1 [, mixed...]])	String	Returns a formatted string
vsprintf(string format, array args)	String	Returns a formatted string
printf(string format [, mixed arg1 [, mixed...]])	Int	Outputs a formatted string
vprintf(string format, array args)	Int	Outputs a formatted string
fprintf(resource stream, string format [, mixed arg1 [, mixed...]])	Int	Outputs a formatted string into a stream
vfprintf(resource stream, string format, array args)	Int	Outputs a formatted string into a stream
htmlspecialchars(string string [, int quote_style][, string charset])	String	Converts special characters to HTML entities
html_entity_decode(string string [, int quote_style][, string charset])	String	Converts all HTML entities to their applicable characters

Continues

Function	Returns	Description
htmlentities(string string [, int quote_style][, string charset])	String	Converts all applicable characters to HTML entities
get_html_translation_table([int table [, int quote_style]])	Array	Returns the internal translation table used by htmlspecialchars and htmlentities
strlen(string str)	Int	Gets string length
strcmp(string str1, string str2)	Int	Binary safe string comparison
strncmp(string str1, string str2, int len)	Int	Binary safe string comparison
strcasecmp(string str1, string str2)	Int	Binary safe case-insensitive string comparison
strncasecmp(string str1, string str2, int len)	Int	Binary safe string comparison

URL

Function	Returns	Description
http_build_query(mixed formdata [, string prefix])	String	Generates a form-encoded query string from an associative array or object
parse_url(string url)	Array	Parses a URLand returns its components
get_headers(string url)	Array	Fetches all the headers sent by the server in response to an HTTP request
urlencode(string str)	String	URL-encodes all nonalphanumeric characters except -_
urldecode(string str)	String	Decodes URL-encoded string
rawurlencode(string str)	String	URL-encodes all nonalphanumeric characters
rawurldecode(string str)	String	Decodes URL-encoded string
base64_encode(string str)	String	Encodes string using MIME base64 algorithm
base64_decode(string str)	String	Decodes string using MIME base64 algorithm
get_meta_tags(string filename [, bool use_include_path])	Array	Extracts all meta tag content attributes from a file and returns an array

Variable Functions

Function	Returns	Description
gettype(mixed var)	String	Returns the type of the variable
settype(mixed var, string type)	Bool	Sets the type of the variable
intval(mixed var [, int base])	Int	Gets the integer value of a variable using the optional base for the conversion
floatval(mixed var)	Float	Gets the float value of a variable
strval(mixed var)	String	Gets the string value of a variable
is_null(mixed var)	Bool	Returns true if variable is null
is_resource(mixed var)	Bool	Returns true if variable is a resource
is_bool(mixed var)	Bool	Returns true if variable is a Boolean
is_long(mixed var)	Bool	Returns true if variable is a long (integer)
is_float(mixed var)	Bool	Returns true if variable is float point
is_string(mixed var)	Bool	Returns true if variable is a string
is_array(mixed var)	Bool	Returns true if variable is an array
is_object(mixed var)	Bool	Returns true if variable is an object
is_numeric(mixed value)	Bool	Returns true if value is a number or a numeric string
is_scalar(mixed value)	Bool	Returns true if value is a scalar
is_callable(mixed var [, bool syntax_only [, string callable_name]])	Bool	Returns true if var is callable
var_dump(mixed var)	Void	Dumps a string representation of variable to output
debug_zval_dump(mixed var)	Void	Dumps a string representation of an internal zend value to output
var_export(mixed var [, bool return])	Mixed	Outputs or returns a string representation of a variable

Continues

Function	Returns	Description
serialize(mixed variable)	String	Returns a string representation of variable (which can later be unserialized)
unserialize(string variable_representation)	Mixed	Takes a string representation of variable and recreates it
memory_get_usage()	Int	Returns the allocated by PHP memory
print_r(mixed var [, bool return])	Mixed	Prints out or returns information about the specified variable
import_request_variables(string types [, string prefix])	Bool	Imports GET/POST/Cookie variables into the global scope

XML

Function	Returns	Description
xml_parser_create([string encoding])	Resource	Creates an XML parser
xml_parser_create_ns([string encoding [, string sep]])	Resource	Creates an XML parser
xml_set_object(resource parser, object &obj)	Int	Sets up object which should be used for callbacks
xml_set_element_handler(resource parser, string shdl, string ehdl)	Int	Sets up start and end element handlers
xml_set_character_data_handler (resource parser, string hdl)	Int	Sets up character data handler
xml_set_processing_instruction_ handler(resource parser, string hdl)	Int	Sets up processing instruction (PI) handler
xml_set_default_handler (resource parser, string hdl)	Int	Sets up default handler
xml_set_unparsed_entity_decl_ handler(resource parser, string hdl)	Int	Sets up unparsed entity declaration handler
xml_set_notation_decl_ handler(resource parser, string hdl)	Int	Sets up notation declaration handler
xml_set_external_entity_ref_ handler(resource parser, string hdl)	Int	Sets up external entity reference handler

Function	Returns	Description
xml_set_start_namespace_decl_handler(resource parser, string hdl)	Int	Sets up character data handler
xml_set_end_namespace_decl_handler (resource parser, string hdl)	Int	Sets up character data handler
xml_parse(resource parser, string data [, int isFinal])	Int	Starts parsing an XML document
xml_parse_into_struct(resource parser, string data, array & struct, array & index)	Int	Parses an XML document
xml_get_error_code(resource parser)	Int	Gets XML parser error code
xml_error_string(int code)	String	Gets XML parser error string
xml_get_current_line_number (resource parser)	Int	Gets current line number for an XML parser
xml_get_current_column_number (resource parser)	Int	Gets current column number for an XML parser
xml_get_current_byte_index (resource parser)	Int	Gets current byte index for an XML parser
xml_parser_free(resource parser)	Int	Frees an XML parser
xml_parser_set_option(resource parser, int option, mixed value)	Int	Sets options in an XML parser
xml_parser_get_option(resource parser, int option)	Int	Gets options from an XML parser
utf8_encode(string data)	String	Encodes an ISO-8859-1 string to UTF-8
utf8_decode(string data)	String	Converts a UTF-8 encoded string to ISO-8859-1

ZLib

Function	Returns	Description
gzfile(string filename [, int use_include_path])	Array	Reads and uncompress entire .gz-file into an array
gzopen(string filename, string mode [, int use_include_path])	Resource	Opens a .gz-fileand returns a .gz-file pointer

Continues

Function	Returns	Description
`readgzfile(string filename [, int use_include_path])`	Int	Outputs a .gz-file
`gzcompress(string data [, int level])`	String	Gzip-compresses a string
`gzuncompress(string data [, int length])`	String	Unzips a gzip-compressed string
`gzdeflate(string data [, int level])`	String	Gzip-compresses a string
`gzinflate(string data [, int length])`	String	Unzips a gzip-compressed string
`zlib_get_coding_type(void)`	String	Returns the coding type used for output compression
`gzencode(string data [, int level [, int encoding_mode]])`	String	GZ encodes a string
`ob_gzhandler(string str, int mode)`	String	Encodes str based on accept-encoding setting; designed to be called from ob_start() as a callback function

Using SQLite

As of PHP5, the SQLite library is bundled with the PHP distribution, effectively giving users a complete server-side scripting/relational database management system in a single, free, easy-to-use tool. How, or even if, you use this option is up to you. Briefly, this appendix provides the information you need to decide how SQLite fits into your Web development plans; but the primary purpose is to arm you with the tools necessary to make use of SQLite.

What Is SQLite?

SQLite is a basic library, written in C, which makes an embeddable SQL database engine available to the applications that use it. Of course, you can use SQLite as a stand-alone database system—and we'll get to that—but its primary value is as the back end to a more feature rich application that you develop yourself using PHP. SQLite is not a client-server RDBMS system such as MySQL, nor even just one part of such a system. Instead, SQLite reads and writes from locally stored disk files that contain the databases you create and manage. This may sound a lot like a flat file system such as DBM; but don't be fooled. SQLite is a fairly complete RDBMS with a many of the attendant features that the label suggests, as well as a substantial SQL implementation based on SQL 92.

SQLite is the baby of D. Richard Hipp of Wyrick & Company, Inc., and has been publicly developed since December of 2000. Despite its apparent commercial connotations, SQLite is free and has been placed completely in the public domain, relieving users of the responsibility implied by a license, even one as liberal as the GPL.

How Do You Get SQLite?

If you have not explicitly disabled SQLite, then you already have everything you need to write SQLite-based applications. If you would like to experiment with SQLite independently of PHP, before going to the trouble learning a new PHP extension, you need the command line tool, which you can obtain from www.sqlite.org/download.html. The SQLite Web site, www.sqlite .org/, has more information about SQLite than can plausibly be included in this appendix; although there is not much information about its use with PHP. Of course, SQLite is due to get much more attention as a result of this new bundling; and so that is likely to change in the near future. In the interim, your best source of information on that topic is still the PHP site at www.php.net/.

Why (or Why NOT) Use SQLite?

One coder's pro is another coder's con. It is in this spirit that the following notions about SQLite are offered not as benefits or disadvantages; but rather as facts you can evaluate to make your own decision based on your particular application requirements.

1. SQLite is "serverless": As already mentioned; the SQLite system does not consist of client and server components, as do many other databases. Instead, SQLite is a simple C library that handles all the data manipulation tasks passed to it. On the one hand, this makes for easy bundling and deployment of applications. On the other hand, remote database access is virtually out of the question.

2. SQLite is "typeless": There's an interesting discussion of this fact at the SQLite Web site. It boils down to the creator's concerted defense of this choice. To quote the site: *"This behavior is a feature, not a bug. A database is supposed to store and retrieve data and it should not matter to the database what format that data is in. The strong typing system found in most other SQL engines and codified in the SQL language spec is a misfeature—it is an example of the implementation showing through into the interface. SQLite seeks to overcome this misfeature by allowing you to store any kind of data into any kind of column and by allowing flexibility in the specification of datatypes."*

   You don't have to be a programming purist or even a masochist to appreciate what strict typing does for performance on larger relational databases. However, this "typelessness" greatly simplifies table design and creation and in the case of SQLite, smaller tables are really just about as small as they can possibly be. This fact is of consequence when resources such as disk space and memory are at a minimum. Because PHP also largely uses loose typing, this presents no real conflict

3. Missing SQL: SQLite's creator, Hipp, acknowledges several missing parts of the SQL standard. A few of the key items include FOREIGN KEY constraints not being enforced, incomplete support for triggers, single concurrent transactions only, and a handful of JOIN types not fully implemented—particularly RIGHT and FULL OUTER JOIN. And the big one: there's no ALTER TABLE syntax available, although he suggests that this is forthcoming. For now, structural changes require saving data to a temporary table, deleting the old table and recreating it from scratch with the new structure, and then importing the temporary data.

4. Permissions scheme: Also on the list of missing SQL are GRANT and REVOKE commands. The Hipp explains this away as meaningless in an embedded database engine; but you may disagree. Permissions are essentially controlled by the file's disk permissions—an element not easily implemented in PHP running with `safe_mode = on`. If you have any permission control needs whatsoever, you are basically forced to develop a permissions control system native to your application.

A few other points of interest:

❑ Data files are easily shared independent of platform.

❑ Binary data must be text encoded before insert and decoded for display. PHP natively supports SQLite's internal implementation for this or you can roll your own using other standard PHP functions.

❑ Databases as big as 2 terabytes are supported.

❑ Speed benchmarks are favorable on smaller databases; but information on larger databases is not publicly available yet.

If you've decided, based on this information, not to use SQLite, the rest of this appendix won't have anything you can't get elsewhere in this book. If, however, you think SQLite may be a good fit for your needs, then move on to the next section.

Using SQLite with PHP

PHP offers a host of functions for working with PHP databases, so let's take a look at them. If you've already used PHP with another database, you may even find that you can intuit how to work with SQLite databases pretty easily. There are some gotchas, however, mostly having to do with working with disk file databases, so read on to familiarize yourself more thoroughly with those things you might want to do differently.

Connection and Maintenance

The following table describes the general database connection and maintenance functions:

Function	Syntax	Description
sqlite_open()	resource sqlite_open (string filename [, int mode [, string &error_message]])	Opens or creates a SQLite database. Takes as a parameter a relative or absolute filename of the database. The mode parameter is not currently supported by the SQLite library but is intended to control the way the database is accessed
		Read-Only permissions can be set at runtime for operations that don't require a write such as a SELECT query
		error_message is a pass-by-reference variable set to contain a descriptive error message passed by SQLite as to why a database could not be opened
sqlite_popen()	resource sqlite_popen (string filename [, int mode [, string &error_message]])	The persistent connection version of sqlite_open. It looks for an existing handle and returns that information, or failing to find one, creates a new persistent connection
sqlite_close()	void sqlite_close (resource dbhandle)	Closes the specified database handle
sqlite_libencoding()	string sqlite_libencoding (void)	Returns the encoding used by the active SQLite library

Continues

Function	Syntax	Description
sqlite_libversion()	string sqlite_libversion (void)	Returns the version number of the active SQLite library
sqlite_query()	resource sqlite_query (resource dbhandle, string query)	Although you would mostly use this for data manipulation and read operations, you will of course need it to create your data tables. This function returns a result handle for results bearing queries and a BOOLEAN true or false for all other types of queries Unlike what you may be used to from MySQL functions, the resource handle is required. This function is discussed again in the next table, with more attention to how it functions in data manipulation

Data Manipulation

Functions for reading, manipulating, and storing data are described in the following table:

Function	Syntax	Description
sqlite_query()	resource sqlite_query (resource dbhandle, string query)	Returns a seekable result handle for the query it runs against the database specified by dbhandle
sqlite_unbuffered_query()	resource sqlite_unbuffered_query (resource dbhandle, string query)	Same as sqlite_query() except the results are returned as a sequential forward-only result set
sqlite_seek()	bool sqlite_seek (resource result, int rownum)	Looks for the row given by rownum, and returns False if it is not found and True if it is
sqlite_next()	bool sqlite_next (resource result)	Moves the result handle to the next row. Returns False if there is none
sqlite_rewind()	bool sqlite_rewind (resource result)	Moves back to the first row in the result set. If there are no results in the set, it returns False
sqlite_current	array sqlite_current (resource result [, int result_type [, bool decode_binary]])	Fetches the current row in the result set as an array, but unlike sqlite_fetch_array() it doesn't move to the next row

Function	Syntax	Description
sqlite_fetch_array()	array sqlite_fetch_array (resource result [, int result_type [, bool decode binary]])	Same as sqlite_current() but advances one row after returning a result. Returns False if there are no more rows
sqlite_has_more()	bool sqlite_has_more (resource result)	Returns True if there are more rows available in the result set
sqlite_fetch_single()	string sqlite_fetch_single (resource result [, int result_type [, bool decode binary]])	Returns the first column of the result set
sqlite_column()	mixed sqlite_column (resource result, mixed index_or_name [, bool decode_binary])	Returns the column specified by the index or name
sqlite_array_query()	array sqlite_array_query (resource dbhandle, string query [, int result_type [, bool decode_binary]])	Returns the result of a given query as a set of arrays

Data about Data

This table covers the functions dealing in SQLite metadata:

Function	Syntax	Description
sqlite_changes()	int sqlite_changes (resource dbhandle)	Returns the number of rows that were changed by the last SQL statement
sqlite_field_name()	string sqlite_field_name (resource result, int field_index)	Returns the name of the column specified by field_index number
sqlite_last_insert_rowid()	int sqlite_last_insert _rowid (resource dbhandle)	Returns the assigned primary key value of the last inserted record. This will only work on columns designated as INTEGER PRIMARY KEY
sqlite_num_fields()	int sqlite_num_fields (resource result)	Returns the number of fields in an SQLite result set. It will not work with sqlite_unbuffered_query()
sqlite_num_rows()		Returns the number of rows in a result set. Will not work with unbuffered result sets

Grab Bag

Although they'll come in handy at some stage, the functions in the following table don't fall into any one category.

Function	Syntax	Description
sqlite_busy_ timeout()	void sqlite_busy_timeout (resource dbhandle, int milliseconds)	PHP uses a default of 60 seconds to wait for a busy SQLite resource handle to become available. This value expects milliseconds if specified, and a value of 0 results in an immediate return of SQLITE_BUSY status code. Generally, the default is more than adequate and not so long as to make debugging tedious
sqlite_create_ aggregate()	bool sqlite_create_aggregate (resource dbhandle, string function_name, mixed step_func, mixed finalize_func [, int num_args])	Implements secondary functions, generally user defined, to calculate a result aggregated based on an entire query result set. step_func performs an operation on each row of the result set, and then finalize_func returns the aggregate value after all rows are processed. func_name specifies the function you will use in your SQL statement
sqlite_create_ function()	bool sqlite_create_ function (resource dbhandle, string function_name, mixed callback [, int num_args])	function_name specifies the name of the function that you will use in your SQL statements; callback can be any PHP callback to specify the PHP function that will handle the SQL function. The optional num_args specifies the number of parameters expected by the function
sqlite_error_ string()	string sqlite_error_string (int error_code)	Returns a human-readable string corresponding to the supplied error_code, which generally will have been retrieved by sqlite_last_error()

Function	Syntax	Description
`sqlite_escape_string()`	string sqlite_escape_string (string item)	Properly quotes and escapes a string for use in a SQL statement; and is even useable on binary data, although that function is probably better handled by `sqlite_udf_encode_binary()`
`sqlite_last_error()`	int sqlite_last_error (resource dbhandle)	Returns the error code returned from the last function performed using the specified handle
`sqlite_udf_decode_binary()`	string sqlite_udf_decode_binary (string data)	A great SQLite-specific function for decoding binary data stored in a SQLite table using its companion function (described next)
`sqlite_udf_encode_binary()`	string sqlite_udf_encode_binary (string data)	Applies binary encoding to your data so that it can be safely returned by queries

SQLite in Practice

Most of the key features of PHP's other database APIs are duplicated in SQLite. You may have some doubts about employing an unfamiliar tool that has no documented large-scale real-world testing on your critical, high-volume sites; and you'd be justified in feeling that way. Some appropriate applications for you to experiment on while you get your SQLite legs might be a guest book, a small inventory manager, a site user management system, or a forms manager.

For now, go ahead and try SQLite out with a simple application to manage the contents of your personal library.

A Personal Library Application

This library application can't get too complicated in the space provided, so you won't get into accounting for things like multiple authors, multiple editions, and so on; but you will explore enough topics to get you up and running with confidence. Individual code snippets used as examples in this section will have to be typed; however, all of the code used in the final product is available for download from www.wrox.com.

To begin, you need a place to store your SQLite databases. A good spot would be somewhere outside of the Web tree; but owned by the Web server user so that it can be freely written to and read from. For purposes of this example, use /var/sqlite, or create a sqlite folder in an appropriate place if you are using Windows.

Next, decide on a table structure. You might want to store the following information about your books:

❑ Title
❑ Author

- ❑ Year of publication
- ❑ Publisher
- ❑ Read date
- ❑ Score
- ❑ Loaned to

And now let's use SQLite to do this for you.

Creating the Database and Tables

You'll use a short script called `books_table_create.php` to create the required database structure. This script should look pretty familiar by now—it's similar to the mysql scripts you created in Chapters 9, 10, and 11. Here's the script:

```
<html>
<head>
<title>Create Library Database and Table</title>
</head>
<body>
<?php
echo ( '<p>Creating Personal Library Database and Table with SQLite Version: '
  . sqlite_libversion() . '</p>' );
```

Obviously, the first line of PHP in the script is not necessary to its functionality; however, as this is your first run with SQLite on this machine, it can certainly provide useful information. Failure of this line, of course, would explain any subsequent problems. If it executes correctly, it tells you how current you are, which is useful information if you have anything to debug.

Next, you define the database that you want to use, and then open up a handle with `sqlite_open()`. Remember that this creates the database if it doesn't already exist:

```
$libraryDB = "/var/sqlite/library";
if ($db = @sqlite_open($libraryDB, 0666, $error)) {
    print ( '<p>Successfully created SQLite database called library</p>' );
    $sql = "CREATE TABLE books (
        book_id INTEGER PRIMARY KEY,
        book_title VARCHAR,
        book_author VARCHAR,
        book_pub_year INTEGER,
        book_publisher VARCHAR,
        book_read VARCHAR,
        book_score VARCHAR,
        book_loan VARCHAR
    )";
```

Finally, assuming you've been successful, print out some friendly messages explaining the current state of affairs:

```
    if ( @sqlite_query($db, $sql) ) {
        print ( '<p>Successfully created SQLite table called books</p>' );
    } else {
        print ( '<p>Failed creating SQLite table called books because of error:
    <br />' . sqlite_error_string(sqlite_last_error($db)) . '</p>' );
    }
} else {
    print ( '<p>Failed creating SQLite database called library because
of error:
        <br />' . $error . '</p>' );
}
?>
</body>
</html>
```

There are a few things to note here. First, when you catch the error, you use `sqlite_error_string()` directly on `sqlite_last_error()`. This sort of shorthand can be a real time saver over the long haul.

Second, despite the "typelessness" of SQLite, you've included types (albeit very loose ones) in your table definition. SQLite accepts (and returns) most common SQL data typing information, even though it doesn't actually use it. This makes it easier for other programmers to discern your intent, and even works well as a reminder to yourself should you want to port your application to another database later.

Finally, observe a notable exception to SQLite's usual position on types. The `book_id` column is set up as `INTEGER PRIMARY KEY`, which signals to SQLite that this field is intended to be a unique index. You can also accomplish this with the SQL words `PRIMARY KEY` by themselves for a non-numeric primary key or `UNIQUE` to enforce the constraint of nonrepetition on any field that is not keyed. Although the net effect of any of these three combinations is the same, setting this `PRIMARY KEY` as an `INTEGER` has the side effect of designating it as an auto increment field.

When SQLite receives an SQL `INSERT` statement on the table and the `book_id` field is `NULL` or undefined, it inserts a sequential integer value into this field. If you don't like auto increment types, you can easily circumvent this by inserting your own value. SQLite passes it in and blithely moves on to the next meaningful instruction.

Run this script from your browser. Figure C-1 shows the messages you should see.

A Data Entry Form

It would be rather nice to jump right in and start browsing your personal library; but of course, SQLite doesn't know about your library yet. Therefore, your first reusable code will gather book data from the user and insert it into the books table.

If you've been through the earlier database chapters, nothing here should surprise you. The main difference is the substitution of `sqlite_` for `mysql_` in the function name. The SQL statement itself is identical to what you would expect for MySQL. That's part of the beauty of standards. The implications of this kind of interoperability are staggering. Of course there are some differences from one SQL implementation to the next; but once you've learned on a nice compliant system, the others will fall into your grasp easily.

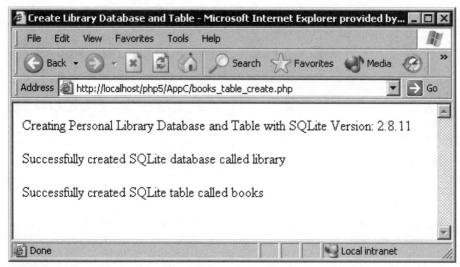

Figure C-1

Here's the script, called `books_insert.php`:

```
<html>
<head>
<title>Personal Library: Add a Book</title>
</head>
<body>
<h1 align="center">Welcome to the Library</h1>
<?php
```

You use exactly the same control structure and error reporting method that you used when creating the table; in fact, that part of the script is pure cut-and-paste:

```
   if ($_POST['action'] == "Insert") {
      $libraryDB = "/var/sqlite/library";
      if ($db = @sqlite_open($libraryDB, 0666, $error)) {
         // Library opened, on with the insert SQL
         $sql = "INSERT INTO books(book_title, book_author, book_pub_year,
                  book_publisher, book_read, book_score, book_loan)
                  values('$_POST[form_title]', '$_POST[form_author]',
                  '$_POST[form_pub_year]', '$_POST[form_publisher]',
                  '$_POST[form_read]', '$_POST[form_score]',
'$_POST[form_loan]')";
         if ( @sqlite_query($db, $sql) ) {
            print ( '<p>Successfully added '. $_POST[form_title] . ' to table
books.</p>' );
            print ( '<p>Add another book if you wish.</p>' );
         } else {
            print ( '<p>Failed adding '. $_POST['form_title'] . ' because
of error:
```

```
            <br />' . sqlite_error_string(sqlite_last_error ($db)) . '</p>' );
        }
    } else {
        print ( '<p>Failed opening SQLite database called library because
of error:
        <br />' . $error . '</p>' );
    }
} else {
    print ( '<p>Please enter book information below. Include at least a title
and author</p>') ;
}
?>
```

Next, a form is written out in straight HTML whether or not an insert is performed. This gives the user the capability to easily enter several books consecutively. A link is added back to your main page, even though it hasn't been created yet, so you won't have to revisit this script later:

```
<p><form action="books_insert.php" method="post"><br />
Enter a book title:<br />
<input type="text" name="form_title"><br />
Enter the author (last, first) of this book:<br />
<input type="text" name="form_author"><br />
Enter the year of publication<br />
<input type="text" name="form_pub_year"><br />
Enter the publisher:<br />
<input type="text" name="form_publisher"><br>
Have you read this book yet?<br />
<select name="form_read"><br />
<option value="Yes" SELECTED>Yes</option><br />
<option value="No">No</option><br />
</select><br />
Give this book a rating (1 to 5)<br />
<input type="text" name="form_score"><br />
Currently loaned to:<br />
<input type="text" name="form_loan"><br />
<input type="submit" name="action" value="Insert"><br />
</form></p>
<p><a href="index.php">Back to the main library page.</a></p>
</body>
</html>
```

Figure C-2 shows what the initial page looks like just before you submit your data.

Go ahead and pump in a few books so you'll have some data to test your subsequent scripts on.

A Switchboard and Book Listing

On to the main page, which actually serves a dual purpose. First, it contains an interface to the rest of the application functions, which you can call the switchboard. And second, it lists the books contained in the database along with options to edit or delete them. This is an important step to take at this time because while the absence of errors in your previous script is all very well, nothing is as reassuring as seeing your

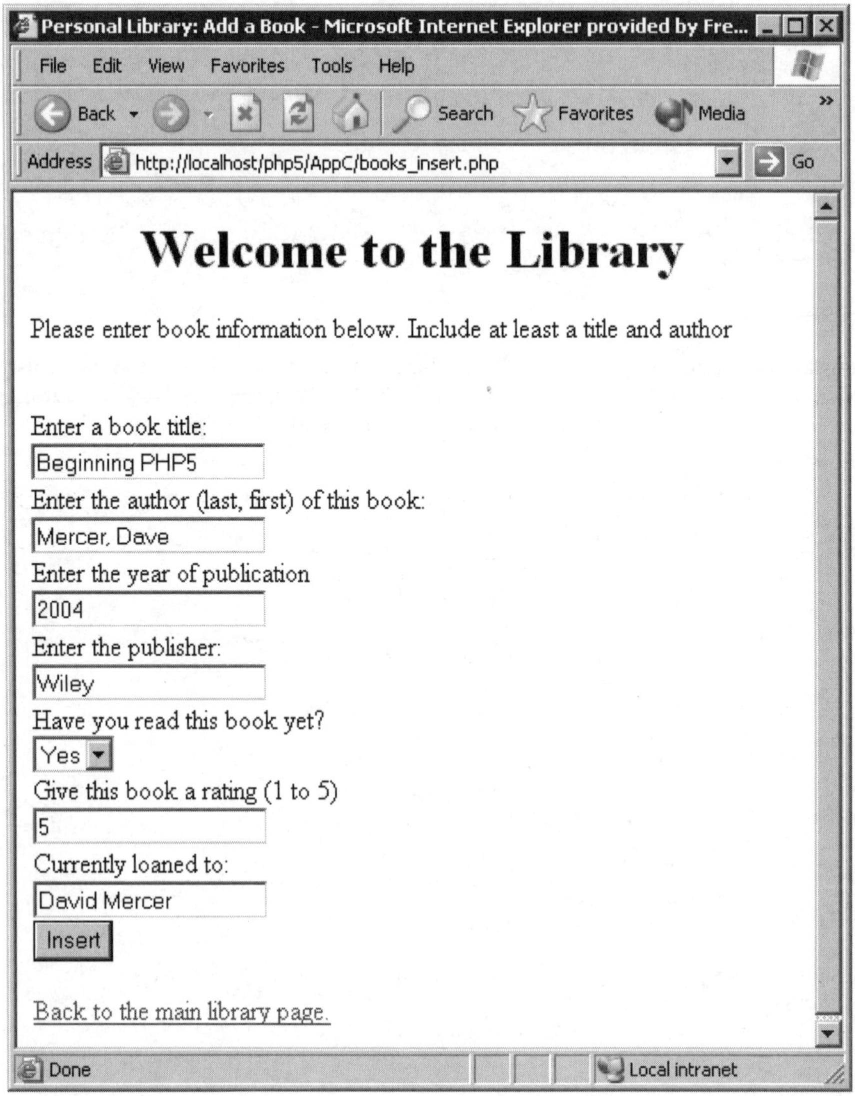

Figure C-2

data returned by the database. `index.php` is the name implied for this script in your preceding script, so just call it that:

```
<html>
<head>
<title>Personal Library: Switchboard</title>
</head>
<body>
<h1 align="center">Welcome to the Library</h1>
<p><a href="books_insert.php">Add a book</a></p>
```

You've inserted the option to add a book to your database.

Then, the first couple of lines of PHP set up the database connection, as usual, taking into account failed connections:

```php
<?php
$libraryDB = "/var/sqlite/library";
if ($db = @sqlite_open($libraryDB, 0666, $error)) {
```

The next lines look to see if the script is called with a book id number, which signals to the script that you want to perform a delete operation. If this page is called directly—that is, without a GET request—nothing in this block executes. The delete function calls the same page with a book id number, triggering the delete function.

```php
if ($_GET['id']) {
    $sql = "DELETE FROM books where book_id = '$_GET['id']'";
    if ( @sqlite_query($db, $sql)) {
        print ( '<p>Succeeded deleting record ' . $_GET['id'] . '</p>' );
    } else {
        print ( '<p>Failed deleting record ' . $_GET['id'] . ' because of error:
        <br />' . sqlite_error_string(sqlite_last_error($db)) . '</p>' );
    }
}
```

Assuming you've made it this far with no errors, your next step is print out a listing of the books. Once again, the SQL is the same as you'd see with MySQL. You pull each successive record into an array with a while loop and print out the listings:

```php
// Library opened, on with the insert SQL
$sql = "SELECT * FROM books";
if ( $result = sqlite_query($db, $sql) ) {
    print ( '<p>There are ' . sqlite_num_rows($result) .
    ' books in the library.</p>');
    while ($book = sqlite_fetch_array($result)) {
        print ( '<p><strong>Book:</strong> ' . $book[book_title] .
        ' <strong>Author</strong>: ' . $book[book_author] . '<br />' .
        ' <strong>Publishing:</strong> ' . $book[book_publisher] . '; ' .
        $book[book_pub_year] . ' <strong>Read:</strong> ' . $book[book_read] .
        ' <strong>Score:</strong> ' . $book[book_score] . '<br />' .
        '<strong>Loaned to:</strong> ' . $book[book_loan] . '<br />' .
```

Add in the links to edit and delete records:

```php
        '<a href="books_edit.php?id=' . $book[book_id] . '">Edit</a> | ' .
        '<a href="index.php?id=' . $book[book_id] . '">Delete</a></p>' );
    }
} else {
    print ( '<p>Failed reading table books because of error:
    <br />' . sqlite_error_string(sqlite_last_error($db)) . '</p>' );
}
} else {
    print ( '<p>Failed opening SQLite database called library because of error:
    <br />' . $error . '</p>' );
}
?>
```

Conclude with a final link to add books, and then close your html:

```
<p><a href="books_insert.php">Add a book</a></p>
</body>
</html>
```

Figure C-3 shows the result of running this script.

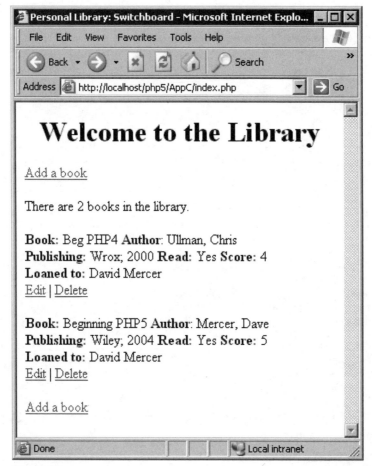

Figure C-3

Your application is coming along, but you won't be able to edit a record until you have completed the next section.

Editing a Record

This last script is the most involved; but even at that, there's not a whole lot to it. Here's the script for editing records, books_edit.php:

```
<html>
<head>
<title>Personal Library: Edit Record</title>
</head>
<body>
<h1 align="center">Welcome to the Library</h1>
<?php
$libraryDB = "/var/sqlite/library";
if ($db = @sqlite_open($libraryDB, 0666, $error)) {
    // Library opened, choose an operation
    if ($_GET['id']) {
```

You first set up the page.

The books_edit.php page is always called with an id value set so you can include that in your SQL query. When the query returns the required information, you can print it out in your form:

```
$sql = "SELECT * FROM books where book_id = '$_GET[id]'";
if ( $result = sqlite_query($db, $sql) ) {
    $book = sqlite_fetch_array($result);
    print("<p><form action=\"books_edit.php\" method=\"post\"><br />");
    print("<input type=\"text\" name=\"form_id\" value=\"$_GET[id]\"><br />");
    print("Enter a book title:<br />");
    print("<input type=\"text\" name=\"form_title\"
value=\"$book[book_title]\"><br />");
    print("Enter the author (last, first) of this book:<br />");
    print("<input type=\"text\" name=\"form_author\"
value=\"$book[book_author]\"><br />");
    print("Enter the year of publication<br />");
    print("<input type=\"text\" name=\"form_pub_year\"
value=\"$book[book_pub_year]\"><br />");
    print("Enter the publisher:<br />");
    print("<input type=\"text\" name=\"form_publisher\"
value=\"$book[book_publisher]\"><br />");
    print("Have you read this book yet?<br />");
    print("<select name=\"form_read\"><br />");
    print("<option value=\"Yes\"");
    if ($book[book_read] == 'Yes') { print("selected"); }
    print(">Yes</option><br />");
    print("<option value=\"No\"");
    if ($book[book_read] == 'No') { print("selected"); }
    print(">No</option><br />");
    print("</select><br />");
    print("Give this book a rating (1 to 5)<br />");
    print("<input type=\"text\" name=\"form_score\"
value=\"$book[book_score]\"><br />");
    print("Currently loaned to:<br />");
    print("<input type=\"text\" name=\"form_loan\"
value=\"$book[book_loan]\"><br />");
    print("<input type=\"submit\" name=\"action\"
value=\"Update\"><br />");
    print("</form></p>");
```

```
  } else {
    print ( '<p>Failed retrieveing record because of error:
      <br />' . sqlite_error_string(sqlite_last_error($db)) . </p>' );
  }
```

You use PHP to print out the entire form in this example. You could have just as easily used HTML and embedded our PHP calls within it, as you've done in other examples throughout the book:

Once the user has made any changes he needs to, you capture the values in the $_POST global array, and use them in an UPDATE statement which modifies the values in your database:

```
    } else if ($_POST[form_id]) {
        $sql = "update books set book_title = '$_POST[form_title]',
        book_author = '$_POST[form_author]',
        book_pub_year = '$_POST[form_pub_year]',
        book_publisher = '$_POST[form_publisher]',
        book_read = '$_POST[form_read]',
        book_score = '$_POST[form_score]',
        book_loan = '$_POST[form_loan]'
        where book_id = '$_POST[form_id]'";
        print $sql;
        if (sqlite_query($db, $sql)) {
            print ( '<p>Your edits were successfully posted.</p>' );
        } else {
            print ( '<p>Failed updating record because of error:
              <br />' . sqlite_error_string(sqlite_last_error($db)) . '</p>' );
        }
    }
} else {
    print ( '<p>Failed opening SQLite database called library because of error:
      <br />' . $error . '</p>' );
}
?>
<p><a href="index.php">Back to the main library page.</a></p>
</body>
</html>
```

So, your library application is functionally complete, although it lacks a few features that might make it a little more robust. Here are a few pointers for ways to flesh it out that you might want to follow up with, ordered from easiest to most complicated:

❑ Adjust the SQL in index.php to sort the records, or even offer the user a variable sort order.

❑ Use sqlite_escape_string() to make the insert and update statements more tolerant of special characters.

❑ Use sqlite_num_rows() in conjunction with SQL LIMIT clauses to write a simple pagination routine for index.php. Once a large number of records are entered, this first page could get pretty confusing.

SQLite is a nifty little tool. Despite its relative youth, it's a pretty stable, capable, and feature-complete technology. You may not yet want to port all your existing applications to it; but its mere inclusion in PHP is a strong endorsement of its qualities. You now have a good grounding in the basics of SQLite, and should be at the level where teaching yourself as much or as little as you need to know is easy.

ODBC

ODBC stands for Open DataBase Connectivity. It's a type of Application Programming Interface (API) for using Structured Query Language (SQL) to work with databases made by many different manufacturers. ODBC comprises a middle layer (called a *database driver*) between an application and a database, so that the application can send SQL commands (queries) to the database via ODBC, and the database will understand and correctly process the queries. For example, if you program a PHP application and want to use an Access database or a SQL Server database as the data store for your application, you can use an ODBC-compliant database driver to format your SQL commands so that either database understands them and responds correctly to them. The ODBC database driver essentially translates SQL into a format the database can understand.

This appendix provides a list of ODBC functions that can be used with ODBC-compliant databases (such as Access and Microsoft SQL Server). It also provides an example of creating a data source name (DSN) in Windows, as well as an example PHP app (odbc.php) on Windows that connects to a SQL Server database. You can use these examples for connecting to Access databases as well.

Common ODBC Functions

No matter how you access a database, there are some things you're going to need to do, such as open a connection, run a SQL query, and close a connection. If you've read through the database chapters in this book, you've seen and used functions for connecting to a database (SQLite, for instance). In PHP (if you've installed or loaded SQLite) there are functions available to open a database connection (sqlite_open()), run a SQL query against the database (sqlite_array_query()) via the open connection, and close the connection (sqlite_close()).

These functions, along with similar functions for the MySQL database and the PostgreSQL database, are built into PHP and are not ODBC functions. But they do the same things as ODBC functions (such as odbc_connect(), odbc_exec(), and odbc_close()), albeit a little faster than ODBC functions. So if PHP has built-in functions for running SQL against a particular database, make use of them; they'll probably be faster and more efficient, and they may give you access to database-specific functions that ordinary ODBC functions don't provide for. But if not, there's a high probability that the database you're using has an ODBC driver available so you can still use it with your PHP application.

PHP ODBC Functions

Following is a table of common PHP ODBC functions with a description of their functionality.

ODBC Function	Description
`odbc_connect()` and `odbc_pconnect()`	Assuming you have already created a database to connect to, one of the first things you'll want to do is make a connection to the database through which you can send commands and receive results. This function creates a connection by referencing a data source name (DSN), and providing the username, password, and optional cursor type. If the database you are connecting to requires no username and password then empty strings will work. The `odbc_pconnect()` function works like the `odbc_connect()` function except that the connection remains open persistently, so it can be used again later as needed, possibly shortening the time required to access the database
`odbc_close()`, `odbc_close_all()`, and `odbc_free_result()`	The `odbc_close()` and `odbc_close_all()` functions close the connection when you are through with it, when you send the `connection_id` (which you got from `odbc_connect()`). The `odbc_free_result()` function frees any recourses associated with the result returned, and is often used before closing a connection to make sure there is plenty of memory available for other parts of the script
`odbc_exec()`, `odbc_execute`, and `odbc_prepare`	Sending the connection_id and a SQL query formatted as a string with the `odbc_exec()` function prepares and executes the query. Some queries, such as INSERT, UPDATE, and DELETE, do not return result sets, and so may run this function by itself, although a SELECT query should return results, and therefore you might assign a variable to the result set, so you could use the results for further processing by your PHP application. Using the `odbc_prepare()` function before the `odbc_execute()` function does both parts of the odbc_exec() function separately. Note: `odbc_do()` is the same as `odbc_exec()`
`odbc_num_rows()`	Once you've obtained a result set from a database, you'll often want to know how many rows are in the result. For example, if you SELECT all the order records for a particular customer, you may want to know how many there are, and using the result set as an argument in this function returns that number
`odbc_fetch_row()`, `odbc_result()`, and `odbc_fetch_array()`	The `odbc_fetch_row()` function retrieves a row of data from a result set, and the `odbc_result()` function can then use that to get a value by fieldname from the row. The `odbc_fetch_array()` function, although undocumented, can retrieve a row from a result set an associative array, such

ODBC Function	Description
	that each spot in the array is named for the fieldname and contains the value for that row. Although the `odbc_fetch_array()` function needs a row number (the array returned is indexed starting at zero), each call to `odbc_fetch_row()`, if sent without a number, simply fetches the next row from the result set
`odbc_commit()`, `odbc_autocommit()`, and `odbc_rollback()`	Transactions are used to ensure that all portions of a particular operation on a database are performed completely, not just one or another of several SQL commands you may have sent. If the entire set of commands succeed, the transaction completes, and if not the transaction is rolled back. Disabling autocommit by sending the result id (which you got from making the connection) and `FALSE` via the `odbc_autocommit()` function is the same as starting a transaction. From there you can run SQL commands until you are ready to commit the transaction (using the `odbc_commit()` function); if you get an error you can run the `odbc_rollback()` function to put everything back as it was
`odbc_error()` and `odbc_errormsg()`	The `odbc_error()` function returns a code telling whether an error has occurred by getting the last error code for the connection. The `odbc_errormsg()` function gets the text of the message, if you'd like to see it. These functions are commonly used immediately following the execution of a query, to find out of the query was properly processed

Other ODBC Functions

The rest of the ODBC functions are used primarily for getting more data about a connection or the database being connected to, and for working with that data in specialized ways. For example:

❑   `odbc_tables()` returns a list of tables in the database.

❑   `odbc_tableprivileges()` returns the tables and privileges of each.

❑   `odbc_statistics()` returns information such as table owner and indexes.

❑   `odbc_procedures()` returns the stored procedures in a database.

❑   `odbc_field...` functions return information about fields (such as length, name, datatype, and so on).

Using ODBC on Windows or Linux

ODBC is part of PHP for Windows, but to run ODBC functions on a Linux installation of PHP you must either compile PHP with ODBC or load ODBC as an extension. The site www.iodbc.org has extensive instructions about how to successfully load ODBC for PHP on Linux.

PHP ODBC Configuration Options

Because ODBC is compiled with PHP, there's no need to change configuration settings in the php.ini file to get it to work. However, you should note that there are a number of settings that affect some PHP ODBC functions, including:

❑   odbc.default_db: Provides a string defining the default database to use if the odbc_connect() or odbc_pconnect() functions are used without specifying a database.

❑   odbc.default_user: Provides a string defining the user name to use if the odbc_connect() or odbc_pconnect() functions are used without specifying a username.

❑   odbc.default_pw: Provides a string defining the password to use if the odbc_connect() or odbc_pconnect() functions are used without specifying a password.

Configuration settings can also be used to specify whether to allow for or check persistent connections or set the maximum number of persistent connections (odbc.allow_persistent, odbc.check_persistent, and odbc.max_persistent), set the maximum number of connections, including persistent connections (odbc.max_links), and set handling of LONG fields or binary data (odbc.defaultlrl and odbc.defaultbinmode).

A PHP ODBC Example Running on Windows, Using SQL Server

To use ODBC with PHP with our example, you need a SQL Server database with at least one table in it (we use a table named "emails"), and a DSN. The DSN is simply a storage area for any connection information required (you can create a DSN-less connection by including all the connection information in a connection string, and if you don't have the ability to setup a DSN that's what you'll need to do).

Creating a SQL Server Database

To create a database with SQL Server, SQL Server must be installed and setup. Our example uses SQL Server 2000 running on Windows 2000. We use the Enterprise Manager to manipulate SQL Server. To mimic our example, use these steps:

1.   Open the SQL Server Enterprise Manager (Start ⇨ Programs ⇨ Microsoft SQL Server ⇨ Enterprise Manager).

2.   Open nodes until you reach the Local server, as shown in Figure D-1.

3.   Right-click the databases node and choose new database from the shortcut menu.

4.   Name your database (the example database is named BPHP5).

5.   Open the node of your new database and create a table within it by right-clicking the Tables node and choosing New Table from the shortcut menu.

6.   In design mode enter the field name email_id, and set the data type to int, and make this field an identity (this setting is at the bottom of the screen), and also make the field a primary key by selecting the entire field and clicking the Primary Key button.

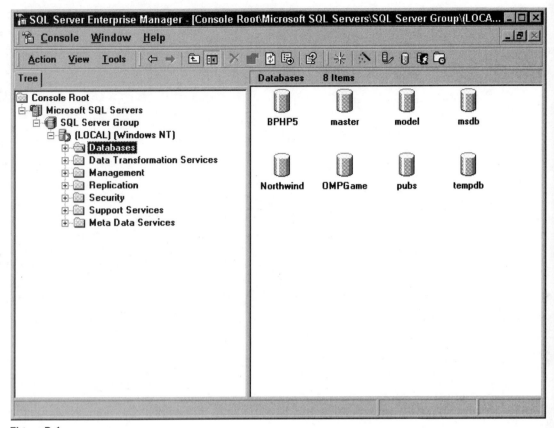

Figure D-1

7. Make another field named email, and set its data type to `varchar` with 100 characters.

8. Save the table as `emails`. Your table (in design mode) should resemble the one shown in Figure D-2.

9. Close SQL Server.

If you want to use an Access database instead, you can simply open Access on your computer, create a blank database and save it in a location you can find later (when you're creating the DSN), add a new table named emails with the same datatypes for its fields, and you're done. You can access it with the same ODBC functions as a SQL Server database.

Creating a System DSN

An ODBC database can be connected to so long as the required information is available. Required information includes such things as the name of the database server, the name of the database (or database file), the driver to use, username/password (if necessary), and so forth. This information can be present in a connection string, or can be stored (on Windows systems) in a Data Source Name (DSN). In this example we show how to create a DSN on Windows 2000.

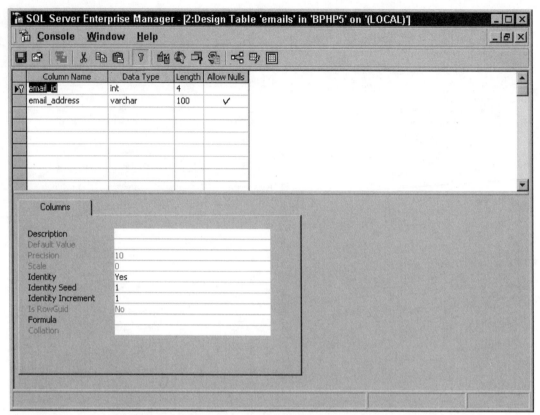

Figure D-2

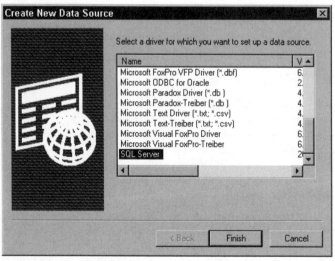

Figure D-3

1. Open Data Sources ODBC (Start ⇨ Programs ⇨ Administrative Tools ⇨ Data Sources (ODBC)).

2. Click the System DSN tab and then click the Add button. From the screen that appears choose the appropriate driver, as shown in Figure D-3.

3. Click the Finish button.

4. On the next screen, enter a name for the DSN (this is what you'll use to connect to the database in your PHP code later; we used "bphp5" as our DSN name), a short description, and the SQL Server you're going to connect to, as shown in Figure D-4.

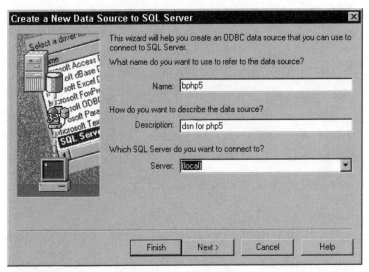

Figure D-4

5. Click the Next button. On the next screen (Figure D-5) leave the defaults as they are.

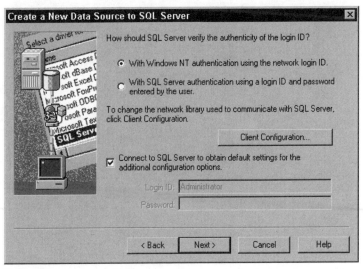

Figure D-5

6. Click the Next button. On the next screen change the default database to BPHP5 (see Figure D-6).

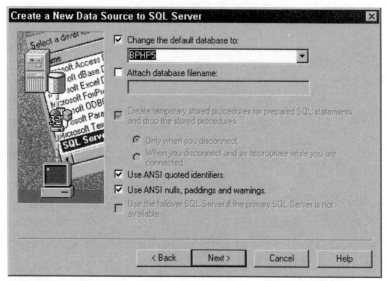

Figure D-6

7. Click the Next button. On the next screen (Figure D-7) leave the defaults as they are.

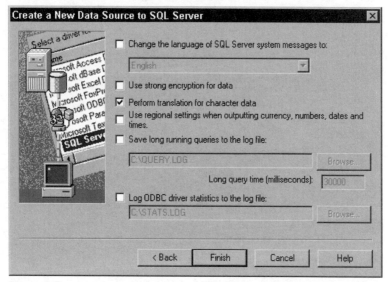

Figure D-7

8. Click the Finish button. You'll see a screen that shows your settings (see Figure D-8).

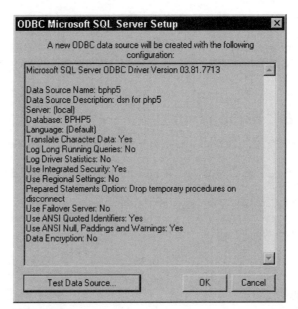

Figure D-8

9. Click the Test Data Source button. The results are displayed (see Figure D-9).

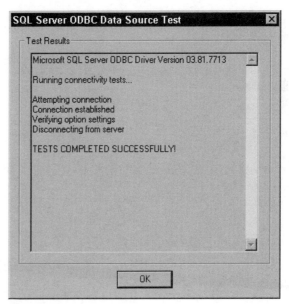

Figure D-9

10. If the test is successful, you're done.

To create a DSN for an Access database, just choose the Access database driver in step 2, rather than the SQL Server driver. You'll then have the opportunity to locate the Access database file you created previously, as well as provide a username and password if you've set one for the database. Now you can use this DSN to connect to the Access database, in the same way as you would use the DSN to connect to a SQL server database.

Using PHP ODBC Functions

There are more than 40 ODBC functions included in PHP, enabling you to do everything from creating a connection to executing a query to checking field names and data types to retrieving errors. In this example we demonstrate several of the key ODBC functions being used in a practical way.

The example, odbc.php, makes a connection to the database, selects records (if any), and enables you to add, edit, and delete records. It creates a single PHP Web page file. The example begins with the body of the page and includes a table to contain the page content:

```
<html>
  <head>
    <title>Beginning PHP5 - ODBC</title>
      <meta http-equiv="Content-Type" content="text/html; charset=iso-8859-1">
  </head>
  <body bgcolor="#FFFFFF">
    <form action="odbc.php" method="POST">
      <table>
        <tr>
          <td>
```

The odbc_connect() function sets a variable named $conn equal to the connection. Notice the name of the DSN ("bphp5") is used as the first parameter in the function, followed by empty parameters for username and password. If you wanted to specify a cursor type, you could use one of the constants defined for the cursortype (SQL_CUR_DEFAULT, SQL_CUR_USE_DRIVER, and so forth) as the optional fourth parameter of this function.

```
<?php
//make a connection
$conn = odbc_connect("bphp5", "", "");
```

When the user attempts to add a record by clicking the Add New Email Address button, the query specified as a string in $query is run against the database by using the odbc_exec() function. The $conn variable is the first parameter and the $query variable is the second parameter.

```
//add a record
if(isset($_POST['add'])) {
    $query = "INSERT INTO emails (email_address_) values('$_POST[email]');";
    odbc_exec($conn,$query);
    echo "<h3>Email Address Added</h3><br><br>";
}
```

Although this example is very simple and does not perform any error checking, you could use the odbc_error() function to check for the existence of an error, and get the error message with the odbc_errormsg() function.

An update is performed on the emails table. The record specified by the user is identified using the value inserted in the hidden field named $up_id (the value is inserted into the field in response to the user selecting an e-mail address from a drop-down list that is created later in the program):

```
//edit a record
if(isset($_POST['update'])) {
    $query = "UPDATE emails SET email_address = '$_POST[up_email]' WHERE
email_id=$_POST[up_id];";
    odbc_exec($conn,$query);
    echo "<h3>Email Address Updated</h3><br><br>";
}
```

A SELECT query runs against the emails table, retrieves the selected record, and then places the id value into the hidden field named "up_id":

```
//select a record from the drop-down list
if(isset($_POST['select'])) {
    $query = "SELECT * FROM emails WHERE email_id=$_POST[select_id];";
    $res = odbc_exec($conn,$query);
    $rec = odbc_fetch_array($res,0);

//insert the id value of the selected record into the hidden field
?>
<input type=hidden name="up_id" value="<? echo $rec[email_id];?>">
```

A form enables the user to see the current value of the email field (the email address) in the selected record, as well as Update and Delete buttons for modifying or eliminating the record. The bulk of the HTML table tags are used to provide formatting only:

```
<table border="0" cellspacing="0" cellpadding="2">
  <tr valign="top">
    <td bgcolor="#003399">
      <table width="619" height="11" bgcolor="#FFFFFF" cellpadding="4"
      cellspacing="0">
        <tr>
          <td colspan="2" class="tablecell">
          </td>
        </tr>
        <tr>
          <td width="150" class="tablecell">Email Address</td>
          <td width="469" class="tablecell">
            <input type="text" name="up_email" value="<? echo
            $rec[email_address];
            ?>" size="60">
          </td>
        </tr>
        <tr>
          <td width="150"></td>
          <td width="494">
            <table border="0" cellspacing="0" cellpadding="4">
              <tr>
                <td>
                  <input type="submit" value="Update" name="update">
```

```
                    </td>
                    <td>
                      <input type="submit" value="Delete" name="delete">
                    </td>
                  </tr>
                </table>
              </td>
            </tr>
          </table>
        </td>
      </tr>
    </table>
    <table border="0" cellspacing="0" cellpadding="4" align="center">
      <tr>
        <td height="10"></td>
      </tr>
      <tr>
        <td align="center">
          <?
}
```

PHP code runs a query for deleting a record. The record to delete is specified in the same manner as for editing a record (using the id value in the hidden field "up_id"):

```
//delete a record
if(isset($_POST['delete'])) {
    $query = "DELETE FROM emails WHERE email_id=$_POST[up_id];";
      odbc_exec($conn,$query);
      echo "<h3>Email Address Deleted</h3>";
}
```

Here's the default code that displays e-mail addresses from the emails table when the page first opens. It runs every time the page is displayed, and reflects the current records in the table. The odbc_exec() function sets $res equal to the contents returned from the query; the odbc_fetch_row() function fetches a row from $res; the odbc_result() function gets the value from the field named ($res is the first parameter in odbc_result(), and the actual name of the field is used as the second parameter in odbc_result()). A while() loop is used to iterate through the rows fetched, and because it is running inside an HTML <select> element, it echoes out an HTML <option> element for each e-mail address retrieved:

```
//retrieve all records and place in a drop-down list
$query = "SELECT * FROM emails ORDER BY email_id;";
$res = odbc_exec($conn,$query);
?>
<select name="select_id">
<?
while (odbc_fetch_row($res)) {
    $email_id = odbc_result($res,"email_id");
      $email = odbc_result($res,"email");
?>
    <option value="<? echo $email_id; ?>">
    <? echo "Email ID is " . $email_id . ":" . " and Email Address is "
```

```
      . $email; ?>
      </option>
      <?
      }
      ?>
      </select>
                  <input type="submit" name="select" value="Select Email Address">
                </td>
              </tr>
            </table>
```

This HTML code displays a form for adding new e-mail addresses:

```
                <table border="0" cellspacing="0" cellpadding="2" align="center">
                  <tr>
                    <td bgcolor="#003399">
                      <table width="619" cellpadding="4" cellspacing="0"
align="center"
                         bgcolor="#FFFFFF">
                       <tr>
                         <td colspan="2" class="tablecell">
                         </td>
                       </tr>
                       <tr>
                         <td width="150" height="29">Email Address</td>
                         <td width="494" height="29">
                           <input type="text" name="email" size="60">
                         </td>
                       </tr>
                       <tr>
                         <td width="130"></td>
                         <td width="477">
                           <input type="submit" value="Add New Email Address"
                           name="add">
                         </td>
                       </tr>
                      </table>
                    </td>
                  </tr>
                </table>
              </td>
            </tr>
        </table>
      </form>
    </body>
</html>
```

Navigate to odbc.php in your browser. The screen looks much like Figure D-10. Go ahead and add a few e-mail addresses.

Of course, you can select any of the addresses you have added to the database, and modify or delete them, as shown in Figure D-11.

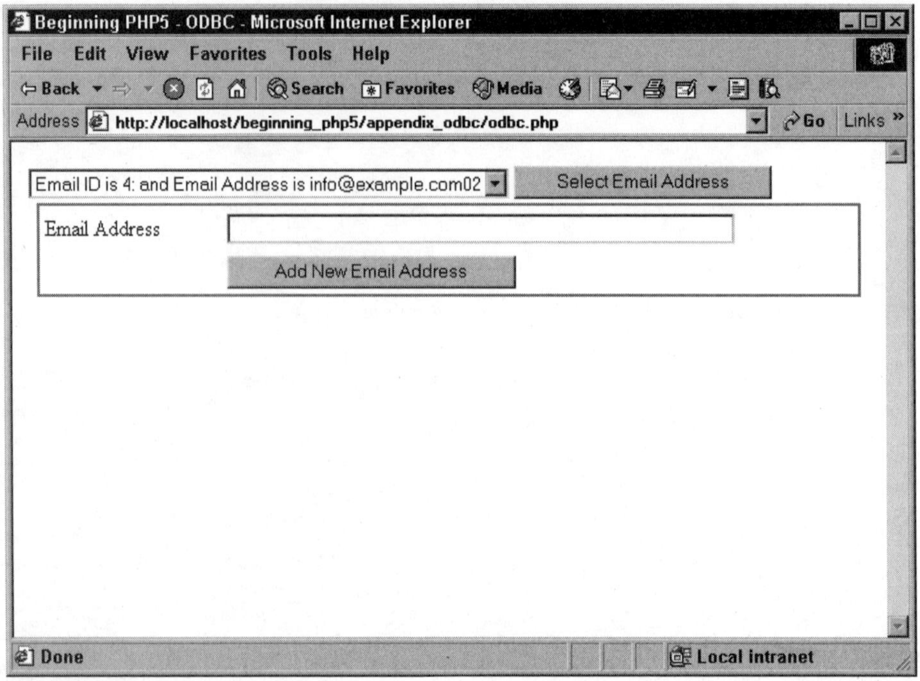

Figure D-10

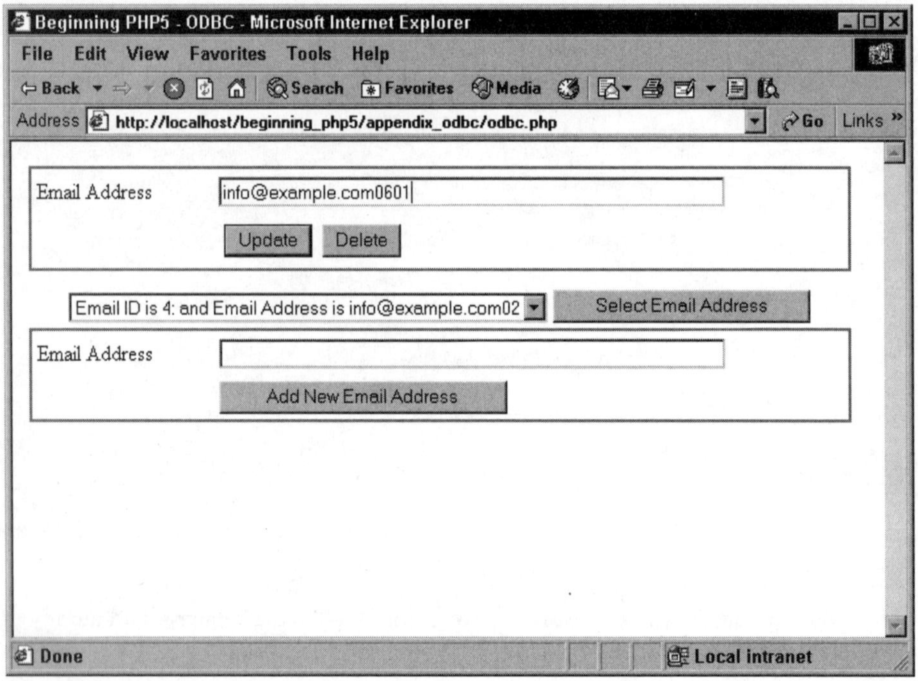

Figure D-11

PHP CLI

One of the nicest developments in PHP over the past year or so has been the introduction of PHP CLI, or Command Line Interpreter. The CLI enables you to put your PHP skills to use in an environment that is not Web-centric, such as system administration or even as an add-in to another application. This gives PHP the power to handle a lot of jobs that were traditionally handled by tools such as Perl, Bash, or DOS. This appendix introduces you to the CLI and shows you some of what can be done with it.

Because PHP CLI represents an evolutionary step, borrowing from several much older technologies, let's first take a quick look at some history.

In the Beginning

For a very long time, UNIX and DOS users have been familiar with the concept of a shell script, a usually quite simple program written in one of several available scripting languages or shells to handle routine system administration tasks. Your Linux box wouldn't get very far without a few shell scripts to move things along; and some very standard administrative tasks, such as log rotation and backups, are often handled by these deceptively simple-looking little pieces of programming prose. But these files are little more than dusty old recipe cards without an interpreter to mix the ingredients and heat them up—that is to say, carry out the instructions contained within.

An interpreter generally takes the form of one of two things: an interactive shell or an interpreted language. Some examples of the former are the infamous command.com of early MS-DOS fame and the wonderful variety of shells available to most Linux/UNIX users—Bash, Csh, Zsh, and a host of others. The latter category includes such widely recognized names as Perl, Python, and Tcl and more recently PHP. Shells generally have some simple constructs built in for things like flow control and conditional behavior; and they frequently borrow from the system tools for most of the rest. But for bigger, more complicated jobs, you need a more flexible tool, and that's where our interpreter friends come in. These tools typically offer more flexible typing, a wider variety of standard programming constructs, and better security features than their less potent counterparts.

Let's leave that thread there for a moment and pick up a different one. In the World Wide Web's early days, Web pages were largely static documents, indiscriminately served up by the http daemon to whoever requested them. Any necessary changes had to be made to the actual document and copied to any other locations that expected to have access to it. Web pages couldn't do all the nifty tricks they do now such as remembering users and delivering customized content based on saved preferences. If this book is your first venture into server-side scripting, you might be tempted to think that PHP is the solution to that problem; but in fact, PHP and its functional cousins such as Active Server Pages and Java Server Pages rode in on the back of another earlier technology called the Common Gateway Interface (CGI).

With the CGI, the Web server opens an interface to an external program, usually one of the interpreted languages mentioned earlier. The server passes the program some instructions for generating a page, which are then passed back to the Web server and delivered to the browser; and this is where the threads of this story rejoin each other.

CGI served its purpose quite well for a number of years before the idea of server modules came into being. PHP is one such; but even Perl can be run as an Apache module. This development was dictated by some of the problems of CGI, most notably in the area of security; but performance can also be problematic in this application.

Of course, CGI is still pretty widely used, even in many PHP installations. Although it's less than optimal, you may even be using it yourself. Users can still opt for a CGI-style installation simply by failing to pass any Web server-specific flags to the configuration script. The notion of using PHP for system administration is not necessarily new. Some system administrators can, and often do, use the old-style php executable for such things.

But these uses, even in very simple scripts, are obfuscated by the Web orientation of the CGI executable. In the PHP4.2.x series, the PHP CLI was introduced as an experimental feature; and by the 4.3.x series, and continuing in the 5.0 series, an installation of PHP CLI is the default behavior. If you absolutely, positively can't bear to have it on your system, you can pass -disable-cli to the configure script.

Some Points to Consider

For those of you who are an experienced shell users or system administrators already accustomed to tools such as Perl or Python, here are a few key differences in the PHP CLI behavior.

❑   The PHP CLI does not change the working directory to that of the script. You need to explicitly define full working paths or use constants or variables to accomplish this.

❑   Invoking the PHP CLI without any parameters does not start an interactive shell as do Python or Tcl.

❑   Unlike Perl, the code inside a PHP CLI script does still need to be inside <?php and ?> start and close tags, even if you've defined the interpreter with the usual #!/usr/local/bin/php syntax. Lines not enclosed in the scripts tags are returned to stdout unaltered.

The PHP CLI can take a few command line switches, described in the following table.

Switch	Description
-s	Display color syntax highlighted source of your script, for example: php -s myscript. This returns a syntax colored version of your script using HTML font tags, so it's not very pretty as console output; but you could easily pipe the output to a browser that displays the output nicely

Switch	Description
-w	Displays the script source with comments and whitespace characters removed
-f	Use to specify a file to pass to the interpreter, for example, php -f myscript. This flag is optional and simply using php myscript has an identical result. However, you might find that this flag is useful for achieving a higher degree of clarity in a crontab or scripts that call other scripts
-v	Print a version number and exit
-c	Specify a php.ini file other than the default
-a	Run interactively
-d	Define a php.ini variable, for example: php -d safe_mode=off. This value will not persist beyond the currently running instance
-e	Generate extended information for the debugger and code profiler
-z	Load a specific Zend extension. This extension will not stay loaded beyond the currently running instance
-l	Syntax check only. This can be useful for non-destructive testing of your scripts; and can incidentally also be used on your Web scripts. Very handy!
-m	This returns a list of compiled in php modules. This will not return dynamically loaded modules
-i	Returns general php configuration information. This is equivalent to phpinfo() without the html formatting. You'll want to pipe the output to a paging program such as more or less for convenient reading
-r	Run code entered on the command line without using script tags. You will need to enclose your code in a single quotes
-h	Returns a list of command line options and formatting parameters

Working with Arguments

Your PHP scripts on the Web can easily receive and incorporate arguments from a variety of sources such as cookies, Web forms, and database values. Database values are still fair game in a script that uses CLI; but there will be no browser from which to retrieve other. Nevertheless, you may want to pass values or arguments at runtime. PHP CLI uses $argc and $argv to handle command-line input. These constructs are already familiar to C/C++ programmers. For the uninitiated, $argc is scalar variable holding the number of arguments whereas $argv is a zero-based global array holding the arguments in the same order they were read in.

Arguments with PHP CLI

Here's a quick script that takes a few arguments and reads them back to you. Create a file named `myscript` and enter this script as shown (Windows users can omit the first line):

```
#!/usr/local/bin/php
<?php
print "Received $argc arguments\n";
for ($i = 0; $i <= $argc -1 ; $i++) {
    print "Hi, I'm argument $i and I am equal to $argv[$i]\n";
}
?>
```

Save the file, and then run it from the command line. You don't need to explicitly pass it to the interpreter, because that information is defined in the first line of the script. This method is used throughout the rest of this appendix. Just for fun, throw in a few arguments to see what happens. On Linux, type:

```
> ./myscript Dan David Alan Steven Clark Wankyu
```

For Windows, type:

```
> php myscript Dan David Alan Steven Clark Wankyu
```

The result should look something like the following:

```
Received 7 arguments
Hi, I'm argument 0 and I am equal to ./myscript
Hi, I'm argument 1 and I am equal to Dan
Hi, I'm argument 2 and I am equal to David
Hi, I'm argument 3 and I am equal to Alan
Hi, I'm argument 4 and I am equal to Steven
Hi, I'm argument 5 and I am equal to Clark
Hi, I'm argument 6 and I am equal to Wankyu
```

The first argument is the name of the script itself, even though it doesn't technically sit in an argument position. This is handy if you need your script to be self-referencing because you do not have `$_SERVER[SCRIPT_NAME]` available to you. As a result, the first index of all true arguments is 1, although the array itself is 0-based.

Now that you know how to read in arguments from the command line and have an idea how it works, let's try a slightly more involved application that actually does something useful.

Run a Shell Command

The `user` command on Linux, or for that matter on any UNIX like system, is a handy way for system administrators to see who is currently active and logged into the system. Its weakness, however, is that it turns out an unordered list of space-separated names that can be difficult to decipher on a colorless console. If you just want to quickly look for a specific user, you need something a little more flexible. The following short script takes a username as an argument and then matches it based on the list of users currently logged in, returning a message with that user's status. Place the contents of this script into a file and save it as check_user:

```
#!/usr/local/bin/php
<?php
$command = "users";
$logged_in = explode(' ', shell_exec($command));
for ($i = 0; $i < count($logged_in); $i++) {
    if ($argv[1] == trim($logged_in[$i])) {
        $found_user = 1;
    }
}
if($found_user) {
    print "User $argv[1] is currently logged in\n";
} else {
    print "User $argv[1] is NOT currently logged in\n";
}
?>
```

Run this script on the command line as:

```
> ./check_user someuser
```

and you should get a result somewhat like the following:

```
User someuser is logged in
```

Note the use of PHP's trim() function in this example. UNIX system commands notoriously use whitespace for formatting, especially in a console. Although separating spaces were removed by passing a space to explode() as a separator, the users command leaves a final trailing hard return at the end of the output that is necessary to get the match if it should occur on the last name in the list. The rim() function is non-destructive if there are no whitespace characters to remove, leaving the useful part of the output untouched.

Windows users can shorten the code and substitute in a DOS command. Name the new file directory:

```
<?php
$dir = shell_exec("dir");
echo "$dir";
?>
```

Run this form the command line by typing:

```
> php directory
```

The contents of your current directory are echoed out to the screen.

Automating PHP CLI

You've seen how CLI scripts can be executed as needed from the command line, but what about automating the running of these scripts? One possible use might be to e-mail reminders as part of a larger calendar system. In fact, this functionality already is part of the PHP WebCalendar project. Another possibility might be to track users on the system throughout the course of the day. In this section, you'll extend an earlier script to track the users on a hypothetical system every half hour, then e-mail a report to a the system administrator. The standard tool for automating tasks on Windows is the built-in Task Manager. This tool is fairly straightforward and easy to use. On Linux, the standard for this job is Cron, which is a little more complicated, and so the emphasis of this section is on that utility.

We'll look at a Windows example in a moment. For now, start with a version of the earlier script check_user. To it you add modifications to include the functionality just described:

```php
#!/usr/local/bin/php
<?php
$first_command = "users";
$second_command = "date";
$third_command = "hostname";
$logged_in = explode(' ', shell_exec($first_command));
for ($i = 0; $i <= count($logged_in); $i++) {
    $users .= trim($logged_in[$i]) . "\n";
}
$dt = shell_exec($second_command);
$subject = "Half-hourly logged-in users report.";
$body .= $subject . "\n\n";
$body .= "At " . trim($dt) . "; the following users are logged into "
. shell_exec($third_command) . ":";
$body .= $users;
mail("root@localhost", $subject, $body,
"From:root@localhost\r\n");
?>
```

There really isn't anything in this script that you haven't seen before. All of the functions employed are covered earlier in the book. The system commands are UNIX/Linux specific, but their names give strong clues as to their purpose. You start by turning the list returned by users into a single column with one name per row, for readability. Using the date command, you effectively time stamp the message, followed by a call to hostname, which could be useful if you want to run the same script on different machines.

You can (and should) test this script from the command line first. It should send an e-mail message something like the following:

```
Half-hourly logged-in users report

At Mon Jan 26 12:42:16 EST 2004; the following users were logged into ds3

akent
cmorgan
dmercer
dsquier
snowicki
wchoi
```

Good enough—that's more or less what you were expecting. We'll use Cron to automate the task every half-hour; but before the job is set up, let's explore how Cron works first. The Cron program has two basic parts. The actual program is crond, known more fully as the Cron daemon. On UNIX-like systems, a daemon is any program that runs constantly in the background, typically awaiting some sort of instructions. Web servers, ftp servers, and mail servers are all examples of daemons.

The Cron daemon generally starts with the rest of the servers on your system. It takes its instructions from the second part of this utility, the `crontab`, which is read in when the program is first started. A `crontab` is a simple text file that holds a list of jobs to perform and when to perform them. Each user on the system has a `crontab`, although it may be empty. You can see all the jobs in your `crontab` by typing `crontab -l`. This displays a list of Cron jobs to the console. The list may look something like this:

```
# Run hourly cron jobs at 47 minutes after the hour:
47 * * * * /usr/bin/run-parts /etc/cron.hourly 1> /dev/null
#
# Run daily cron jobs at 4:40 every day:
40 4 * * * /usr/bin/run-parts /etc/cron.daily 1> /dev/null
#
# Run weekly cron jobs at 4:30 on the first day of the week:
30 4 * * 0 /usr/bin/run-parts /etc/cron.weekly 1> /dev/null
#
# Run monthly cron jobs at 4:20 on the first day of the month:
20 4 1 * * /usr/bin/run-parts /etc/cron.monthly 1> /dev/null
```

The first five fields of any `crontab` entry are increments of time outlining when to execute the command supplied in the sixth field, which is everything up to the end of the line. As you might expect, a # sign precedes any comments. The time fields are, in order, minute, hour, day, month and weekday. This example gives you some idea how these fields are used, although it might not be immediately apparent how to schedule the stated goal of every half hour. Actually, the line for that Cron job would look something like this:

```
*/30 * * * * user_report 1> /dev/null
```

The default behavior of the Cron daemon is to mail a report on successful completion of the job, which can become a little annoying. The purpose of `1>/dev/null` is to simply redirect what would go to the standard output, to the cosmic UNIX garbage can.

An administrator may want to keep track of all the file changes in a certain directory each day. For example, Windows users can e-mail the current folder directory to a given e-mail address using the following code:

```php
<?php
$dir = shell_exec("dir");
$subject = "Daily file report.";
$body = "The following files are in the current directory : \n\n";
$body .= $dir;
mail("root@localhost", $subject, $body, "From:root@localhost\r\n");
?>
```

To automate this job in Windows, go to the control panel and select Scheduled Tasks ⇨ Add Scheduled Task. The wizard guides your setup and gives you whatever options you want. Type in the following as the Run option:

```
C:\PHP5\php.exe directory
```

Alternatively, you can browse to your php executable on the second page of the wizard, and add in the name of the file you want to run.

Depending on how you set things up, you will get an e-mail updating you with your directory's contents on schedule.

Interactivity with PHP CLI

PHP is as deft with interactivity on the command line as it is on the Web. You can easily create CLI scripts that accept consecutive bits of user input to perform a larger task using streams. PHP provides access to three streams that simulate the corresponding UNIX functionality. The following table explains these streams.

Stream	Corresponds to	To Access in PHP
Standard input	Keyboard	php://stdin
Standard output	Console	php://stdout
Standard error	Console or system log file	php://stderr

Now try a simple script that collects some user information and produces a signature file for use with an e-mail client. Create a file named `sigfile` and enter the following code:

```
#!/usr/local/bin/php
<?php
$stdin = fopen('php://stdin', 'r');
    echo "Welcome to our PHP Signature file generator.\n";
        echo "Please enter your Full Name: ";
$name = trim(fgets($stdin,100));
        echo "Please enter your Street Address: ";
$address = trim(fgets($stdin,100));
        echo "Please enter your City: ";
$city = trim(fgets($stdin,100));
        echo "Please enter your State: ";
$state = trim(fgets($stdin,100));
        echo "Please enter your Postal Code: ";
$zip = trim(fgets($stdin,100));
        echo "Please enter your Phone Number: ";
$phone = trim(fgets($stdin,100));
        echo "Please enter your Email Address: ";
$email = trim(fgets($stdin,100));
        echo "What do you want to call this signature: ";
$sig = trim(fgets($stdin,100));
fclose($stdin);
$data = "$name\n$address\n$city,
$state $zip\n$phone\n$email";
shell_exec("touch $sig");
if (!$sigfile = fopen($sig, 'w')) {
    print "Could not open file for writing\n";
```

```
    } else {
        if (!fwrite($sigfile,$data)) {
            print "\n\nFailed Writing Data\n";
        } else {
            print "\n\nYour signature is ready now\n";
        }
        fclose($sigfile);
    }
?>
```

You start by opening a stream from the standard input, which you'll keep open until your last entry is retrieved. Then you grab the first 100 characters from each successive user input. You subject this input to trim() because unfortunately the Enter key the user presses to submit it passes a hard return back to the script. When you have everything you need, you close the input stream and open a file with the name chosen by the user. Write your concatenated signature to the file and close that stream.

Windows users can use the same file, changing this line:

```
shell_exec("touch $sig");
```

To this:

```
'copy con $sig ^Z \n';
```

Save the file. Running this example produces output something like this:

```
> php sigfile
Welcome to our PHP Signature file generator.
Please enter your Full Name: David Mercer
Please enter your Street Address: 148 Mystreet
Please enter your City: Cape Town
Please enter your State: WP
Please enter your Postal Code: 8001
Please enter your Phone Number: 021 555-1234
Please enter your Email Address: davidm@doggiesrugby.co.za
What do you want to call this signature: MySig

Your signature is ready now
```

Wrapping Up

It's easy to see that PHP CLI has the same flexibility and power as PHP in a Web-centric environment. It would be safe to say that the potential uses are limited only by the power of PHP itself, which isn't much of a limitation at all. The capability to add interactivity by working with streams is a particularly nice feature. If you are already a system administrator, you might want to try using PHP CLI for your next administrative task. Experiment with using it for backups, system notifications, and anything else your imagination can conjure up. As a supplement to your Web applications, scheduled PHP CLI jobs can add features previously only dreamed of in PHP development.

Configuring PHP5

The configuration file named php.ini plays a major role in how PHP behaves. When PHP starts, the configuration file is read and the settings within it applied. If you've installed PHP as a server module, the file is read once; if PHP is running as a CGI, the file is read for each instance of PHP running.

This appendix covers all the configuration sections and settings in the php.ini file. Many of these settings were discussed throughout the book, so this appendix is a reference rather than completely new material.

Two versions of the php.ini file are delivered with the current distribution of PHP: php.ini-recommended and php.ini-dist. The dist file is suitable for development, whereas the recommended file is suitable for production, according to the makers of PHP. There are several settings in the recommended file that are said to improve performance, but may break older scripts right away, notably the register_global settings, which is turned off (and is deprecated in future versions of PHP). This appendix describes the contents of php.ini-dist.

php.ini-dist File Description

The initial description of the file mentions that it is suitable for development but not recommended for production sites, as well as where the file should be located, how PHP finds it when starting, and how the file is formatted (with lots of instructions about the allowable values and operators in settings).

```
;;;;;;;;;;;
; WARNING ;
;;;;;;;;;;;
; This is the default settings file for new PHP installations.
; By default, PHP installs itself with a configuration suitable for
; development purposes, and *NOT* for production purposes.
; For several security-oriented considerations that should be taken
; before going online with your site, please consult php.ini-recommended
; and http://php.net/manual/en/security.php.
```

```
;;;;;;;;;;;;;;;;;;;;
; About this file ;
;;;;;;;;;;;;;;;;;;;;
; This file controls many aspects of PHP's behavior. In order for PHP to
; read it, it must be named 'php.ini'. PHP looks for it in the current
; working directory, in the path designated by the environment variable
; PHPRC, and in the path that was defined in compile time (in that order).
; Under Windows, the compile-time path is the Windows directory. The
; path in which the php.ini file is looked for can be overridden using
; the -c argument in command line mode.
;
; The syntax of the file is extremely simple. Whitespace and Lines
; beginning with a semicolon are silently ignored (as you probably
guessed).
; Section headers (e.g. [Foo]) are also silently ignored, even though
; they might mean something in the future.
;
; Directives are specified using the following syntax:
; directive = value
; Directive names are *case sensitive* - foo=bar is different from
FOO=bar.
;
; The value can be a string, a number, a PHP constant (e.g. E_ALL or M_PI)
, one
; of the INI constants (On, Off, True, False, Yes, No and None) or an
expression
; (e.g. E_ALL & ~E_NOTICE), or a quoted string ("foo").
;
; Expressions in the INI file are limited to bitwise operators and
parentheses:
; |          bitwise OR
; &          bitwise AND
; ~          bitwise NOT
; !          boolean NOT
;
; Boolean flags can be turned on using the values 1, On, True or Yes.
; They can be turned off using the values 0, Off, False or No.
;
; An empty string can be denoted by simply not writing anything after the
equal
; sign, or by using the None keyword:
;
; foo =            ; sets foo to an empty string
; foo = none       ; sets foo to an empty string
; foo = "none"     ; sets foo to the string 'none'
;
; If you use constants in your value, and these constants belong to a
; dynamically loaded extension (either a PHP extension or a Zend
extension),
; you may only use these constants *after* the line that loads the
extension.
;
; All the values in the php.ini-dist file correspond to the builtin
; defaults (that is, if no php.ini is used, or if you delete these lines,
; the builtin defaults will be identical).
```

Language Options

Language options are configuration settings that directly affect how PHP behaves. For instance, setting short_open_tag to On means that you can use the <? and ?> tags to delimit your PHP code, rather than <?php and ?> (although all of the authors recommend using the longer version by convention).

This section also contains a special feature called *Safe mode*. Safe mode and other Safe mode options are designed to directly affect the security of your PHP applications. PHP includes functions that, if not used correctly or in concert with other security measures, can allow unlimited access to your system. That being the case, Safe mode is an option that's useful when you don't necessarily trust the person writing the PHP script. For instance, it enables you to limit the capability of the scripts to access the file system. If you are running a virtual hosting server, in which many different Web sites operate on the same server, it's highly recommended that you examine Safe mode and its relatives to provide a truly secure system.

Here's a example of Safe mode working in combination: safe_mode = on and safe_mode_exec_dir = my_safe_mode_exec_dir (this is not a real directory name, of course, but one that you would create). When Safe mode is on and you've created and set the Safe mode exec directory, only executables in that directory may be run using the PHP exec command.

Another good example of using Safe mode concerns environment variables. Enabling users to set environment variables may cause a security breach, so when Safe mode is on, the safe_mode_allowed_env_vars setting (such as the default PHP) restricts users to changing only those environment variables that begin with the prefix PHP. Eliminating this setting permits any environment variable to be changed. And the safe_mode_protected_env_vars option goes even further, protecting a comma-delimited list of variables from changes no matter what the prefix setting in safe_mode_allowed_env_vars is.

The bottom line is that Safe mode and other Safe mode options enable you to set security options in many ways, depending upon what you need your application to do. Review them carefully and read the online security material as well in order to protect your system and your users' data.

```
;;;;;;;;;;;;;;;;;;;
; Language Options ;
;;;;;;;;;;;;;;;;;;;

; Enable the PHP scripting language engine under Apache.
engine = On

; Allow the <? tag. Otherwise, only <?php and <script> tags are recognized.
; NOTE: Using short tags should be avoided when developing applications or
; libraries that are meant for redistribution, or deployment on PHP
; servers which are not under your control, because short tags may not
; be supported on the target server. For portable, redistributable code,
; be sure not to use short tags.
short_open_tag = On

; Allow ASP-style <% %> tags.
asp_tags = Off

; The number of significant digits displayed in floating point numbers.
precision = 12
```

```
; Enforce year 2000 compliance (will cause problems with non-compliant
browsers) y2k_compliance = On

; Output buffering allows you to send header lines (including cookies) even
; after you send body content, at the price of slowing PHP's output layer a
; bit. You can enable output buffering during runtime by calling the output
; buffering functions. You can also enable output buffering for all files by
; setting this directive to On. If you wish to limit the size of the buffer
; to a certain size - you can use a maximum number of bytes instead of 'On', as
; a value for this directive (e.g., output_buffering=4096).
output_buffering = Off

; You can redirect all of the output of your scripts to a function. For
; example, if you set output_handler to "mb_output_handler", character
; encoding will be transparently converted to the specified encoding.
; Setting any output handler automatically turns on output buffering.
; Note: People who wrote portable scripts should not depend on this ini
;          directive. Instead, explicitly set the output handler using
;          ob_start().
;          Using this ini directive may cause problems unless you know what script
;          is doing.
; Note: You cannot use both "mb_output_handler" with "ob_iconv_handler"
;          and you cannot use both "ob_gzhandler" and "zlib.output_compression".
;output_handler =

; Transparent output compression using the zlib library
; Valid values for this option are 'off', 'on', or a specific buffer size
; to be used for compression (default is 4KB)
; Note: Resulting chunk size may vary due to nature of compression. PHP
;          outputs chunks that are few hundreds bytes each as a result of
;          compression. If you prefer a larger chunk size for better
;          performance, enable output_buffering in addition.
; Note: You need to use zlib.output_handler instead of the standard
;          output_handler, or otherwise the output will be corrupted.
zlib.output_compression = Off

; You cannot specify additional output handlers if zlib.output_compression
; is activated here. This setting does the same as output_handler but in
; a different order.
;zlib.output_handler =

; Implicit flush tells PHP to tell the output layer to flush itself
; automatically after every output block. This is equivalent to calling the
; PHP function flush() after each and every call to print() or echo() and each
; and every HTML block. Turning this option on has serious performance
; implications and is generally recommended for debugging purposes only.
implicit_flush = Off

; The unserialize callback function will called (with the undefind class'
; name as parameter), if the unserializer finds an undefined class
; which should be instanciated.
; A warning appears if the specified function is not defined, or if the
; function doesn't include/implement the missing class.
```

```
; So only set this entry, if you really want to implement such a
; callback-function.
unserialize_callback_func=

; When floats & doubles are serialized store serialize_precision significant
; digits after the floating point. The default value ensures that when floats
; are decoded with unserialize, the data will remain the same.
serialize_precision = 100

; Whether to enable the ability to force arguments to be passed by reference
; at function call time. This method is deprecated and is likely to be
; unsupported in future versions of PHP/Zend. The encouraged method of
; specifying which arguments should be passed by reference is in the function
; declaration. You're encouraged to try and turn this option Off and make
; sure your scripts work properly with it in order to ensure they will work
; with future versions of the language (you will receive a warning each time
; you use this feature, and the argument will be passed by value instead of by
; reference).
allow_call_time_pass_reference = On

; Safe Mode
;
safe_mode = Off

; By default, Safe Mode does a UID compare check when
; opening files. If you want to relax this to a GID compare,
; then turn on safe_mode_gid.
safe_mode_gid = Off

; When safe_mode is on, UID/GID checks are bypassed when
; including files from this directory and its subdirectories.
; (directory must also be in include_path or full path must
; be used when including)
safe_mode_include_dir =

; When safe_mode is on, only executables located in the safe_mode_exec_dir
; will be allowed to be executed via the exec family of functions.
safe_mode_exec_dir =

; Setting certain environment variables may be a potential security breach.
; This directive contains a comma-delimited list of prefixes. In Safe Mode,
; the user may only alter environment variables whose names begin with the
; prefixes supplied here. By default, users will only be able to set
; environment variables that begin with PHP_ (e.g. PHP_FOO=BAR).
;
; Note:  If this directive is empty, PHP will let the user modify ANY
; environment variable!
safe_mode_allowed_env_vars = PHP_

; This directive contains a comma-delimited list of environment variables that
; the end user won't be able to change using putenv(). These variables will be
; protected even if safe_mode_allowed_env_vars is set to allow to change them.
safe_mode_protected_env_vars = LD_LIBRARY_PATH
```

```
; open_basedir, if set, limits all file operations to the defined directory
; and below. This directive makes most sense if used in a per-directory
; or per-virtualhost web server configuration file. This directive is
; *NOT* affected by whether Safe Mode is turned On or Off.
;open_basedir =

; This directive allows you to disable certain functions for security reasons.
; It receives a comma-delimited list of function names. This directive is
; *NOT* affected by whether Safe Mode is turned On or Off.
disable_functions =

; This directive allows you to disable certain classes for security reasons.
; It receives a comma-delimited list of class names. This directive is
; *NOT* affected by whether Safe Mode is turned On or Off.
disable_classes =

; Colors for Syntax Highlighting mode. Anything that's acceptable in
; <font color="??????"> would work.
;highlight.string   = #DD0000
;highlight.comment  = #FF9900
;highlight.keyword  = #007700
;highlight.bg       = #FFFFFF
;highlight.default  = #0000BB
;highlight.html     = #000000


;
; Misc
;
; Decides whether PHP may expose the fact that it is installed on the server
; (e.g. by adding its signature to the Web server header). It is no security
; threat in any way, but it makes it possible to determine whether you use PHP
; on your server or not.
expose_php = On
```

Resource Limits

Any application makes use of server resources to accomplish the tasks required of it. Resource limits include CPU cycles, hard drive space, and so on. PHP's configuration file includes options limiting PHP's use of these resources.

These options allow PHP to limit itself from excess resource usage per request. The default limits are acceptable for most applications. When a script actually reaches one of these limits, it is a good idea to examine your code for bugs, or explore other means of accomplishing the task.

```
;;;;;;;;;;;;;;;;;;;;
; Resource Limits ;
;;;;;;;;;;;;;;;;;;;;

max_execution_time = 30     ; Maximum execution time of each script, in seconds
max_input_time = 60     ; Maximum amount of time each script may spend parsing
request data
memory_limit = 8M       ; Maximum amount of memory a script may consume (8MB)
```

Error Handling and Logging

PHP can handle errors differently depending on how you configure this section. If you are still developing a Web application, it's useful to leave error reporting on the default setting because you'll notice the errors more quickly. However, with a production Web site, PHP errors could give end users information that you don't want them to have (potentially creating a security problem); if nothing else, errors on your Web application are embarrassing. In that case, we recommend that you use error logging, which silently lists the errors in a log file that end users can't see.

```
;;;;;;;;;;;;;;;;;;;;;;;;;;;;;;;
; Error handling and logging ;
;;;;;;;;;;;;;;;;;;;;;;;;;;;;;;;

; error_reporting is a bit-field. Or each number up to get desired error
; reporting level
; E_ALL            - All errors and warnings
; E_ERROR          - fatal run-time errors
; E_WARNING        - run-time warnings (non-fatal errors)
; E_PARSE          - compile-time parse errors
; E_NOTICE         - run-time notices (these are warnings which often result
;                    from a bug in your code, but it's possible that it was
;                    intentional (e.g., using an uninitialized variable and
;                    relying on the fact it's automatically initialized to an
;                    empty string)
; E_STRICT         - run-time notices, enable to have PHP suggest changes
;                    to your code which will ensure the best interoperability
;                    and forward compatability of your code
; E_CORE_ERROR     - fatal errors that occur during PHP's initial startup
; E_CORE_WARNING   - warnings (non-fatal errors) that occur during PHP's
;                    initial startup
; E_COMPILE_ERROR  - fatal compile-time errors
; E_COMPILE_WARNING - compile-time warnings (non-fatal errors)
; E_USER_ERROR     - user-generated error message
; E_USER_WARNING   - user-generated warning message
; E_USER_NOTICE    - user-generated notice message
;
; Examples:
;
;    - Show all errors, except for notices
;
;error_reporting = E_ALL & ~E_NOTICE
;
;    - Show only errors
;
;error_reporting = E_COMPILE_ERROR|E_ERROR|E_CORE_ERROR
;
;    - Show all errors except for notices and coding standards warnings
;
error_reporting = E_ALL & ~E_NOTICE & ~E_STRICT

; Print out errors (as a part of the output). For production web sites,
; you're strongly encouraged to turn this feature off, and use error logging
; instead (see below).  Keeping display_errors enabled on a production web site
```

```
; may reveal security information to end users, such as file paths on your Web
; server, your database schema or other information.
display_errors = On

; Even when display_errors is on, errors that occur during PHP's startup
; sequence are not displayed. It's strongly recommended to keep
; display_startup_errors off, except for when debugging.
display_startup_errors = Off

; Log errors into a log file (server-specific log, stderr, or error_log
(below))
; As stated above, you're strongly advised to use error logging in place of
; error displaying on production web sites.
log_errors = Off

; Set maximum length of log_errors. In error_log information about the
source is
; added. The default is 1024 and 0 allows to not apply any maximum length
at all.
log_errors_max_len = 1024

; Do not log repeated messages. Repeated errors must occur in same file
on same
; line until ignore_repeated_source is set true.
ignore_repeated_errors = Off

; Ignore source of message when ignoring repeated messages. When this setting
; is On you will not log errors with repeated messages from different files or
; sourcelines.
ignore_repeated_source = Off

; If this parameter is set to Off, then memory leaks will not be shown (on
; stdout or in the log). This has only effect in a debug compile, and if
; error reporting includes E_WARNING in the allowed list
report_memleaks = On

; Store the last error/warning message in $php_errormsg (boolean).
track_errors = Off

; Disable the inclusion of HTML tags in error messages.
; Note: Never use this feature for production boxes.
;html_errors = Off

; If html_errors is set On PHP produces clickable error messages that direct
; to a page describing the error or function causing the error in detail.
; You can download a copy of the PHP manual from http://www.php.net/docs.php
; and change docref_root to the base URL of your local copy including the
; leading '/'. You must also specify the file extension being used including
; the dot.
; Note: Never use this feature for production boxes.
;docref_root = "/phpmanual/"
;docref_ext = .html

; String to output before an error message.
;error_prepend_string = "<font color=ff0000>"
```

```
; String to output after an error message.
;error_append_string = "</font>"

; Log errors to specified file.
;error_log = filename

; Log errors to syslog (Event Log on NT, not valid in Windows 95).
;error_log = syslog
```

Data Handling

The most important option in this section, and perhaps the entire configuration, is `register_globals`. This feature automatically converts input data into variables, for example an input field named last_name in the HTML form would automatically create a variable `$last_name` that could be easily used in the script. This is a powerful feature that allows very rapid development. However, if used improperly, `register_globals` can cause confusion and serious security risks (this is perhaps the single most common cause of security problems for PHP applications), so use with caution, and always properly validate input if security is important. People who have used PHP for a long time will be accustomed to `register_globals=On`, because at one time it was not possible to disable the feature. Now, the default setting is `Off`.

`magic_quotes_gpc` is also a feature worth noting. It can help improve security by automatically escaping "dangerous" characters, usually to prevent a SQL injection attack. If your application already processes the input in this way, turn this feature off, because it could doubly escape the dangerous characters, leaving extra \ characters inside the input strings.

```
;;;;;;;;;;;;;;;;;;
; Data Handling ;
;;;;;;;;;;;;;;;;;;
;
; Note - track_vars is ALWAYS enabled as of PHP 4.0.3

; The separator used in PHP generated URLs to separate arguments.
; Default is "&".
;arg_separator.output = "&amp;"

; List of separator(s) used by PHP to parse input URLs into variables.
; Default is "&".
; NOTE: Every character in this directive is considered as separator!
;arg_separator.input = ";&"

; This directive describes the order in which PHP registers GET, POST, Cookie,
; Environment and Built-in variables (G, P, C, E & S respectively, often
; referred to as EGPCS or GPC). Registration is done from left to right, newer
; values override older values.
variables_order = "EGPCS"

; Whether or not to register the EGPCS variables as global variables. You may
; want to turn this off if you don't want to clutter your scripts' global scope
; with user data. This makes most sense when coupled with track_vars - in which
; case you can access all of the GPC variables through the $HTTP_*_VARS[],
; variables.
;
```

```
; You should do your best to write your scripts so that they do not require
; register_globals to be on; Using form variables as globals can easily lead
; to possible security problems, if the code is not very well thought of.
register_globals = Off

; Whether or not to register the old-style input arrays, HTTP_GET_VARS
; and friends. If you're not using them, it's recommended to turn them off,
; for performance reasons.
register_long_arrays = On

; This directive tells PHP whether to declare the argv&argc variables (that
; would contain the GET information). If you don't use these variables, you
; should turn it off for increased performance.
register_argc_argv = On

; Maximum size of POST data that PHP will accept.
post_max_size = 8M

; This directive is deprecated. Use variables_order instead.
gpc_order = "GPC"

; Magic quotes
;

; Magic quotes for incoming GET/POST/Cookie data.
magic_quotes_gpc = On

; Magic quotes for runtime-generated data, e.g. data from SQL, from exec(), etc.
magic_quotes_runtime = Off

; Use Sybase-style magic quotes (escape ' with '' instead of \ ').
magic_quotes_sybase = Off

; Automatically add files before or after any PHP document.
auto_prepend_file =
auto_append_file =

; As of 4.0b4, PHP always outputs a character encoding by default in
; the Content-type: header. To disable sending of the charset, simply
; set it to be empty.
;
; PHP's built-in default is text/html
default_mimetype = "text/html"
;default_charset = "iso-8859-1"

; Always populate the $HTTP_RAW_POST_DATA variable.
;always_populate_raw_post_data = On
```

Paths and Directories

PHP makes use of the file system for a number of tasks, and settings in this section affect how those tasks proceed. For example, if you want to bring a file into one of your scripts with require() or include(), you simply place the file in the same folder as the script. Alternatively, you can place the file in a special "includes" folder and then set the path to this folder using the include_path option. Doing so means you won't have to specify a separate whole path for the file to be found.

```
;;;;;;;;;;;;;;;;;;;;;;;;;;
; Paths and Directories ;
;;;;;;;;;;;;;;;;;;;;;;;;;;

; UNIX: "/path1:/path2"
;include_path = ".:/php/includes"
;
; Windows: "\ path1;\ path2"
;include_path = ".;c:\ php\ includes"

; The root of the PHP pages, used only if nonempty.
; if PHP was not compiled with FORCE_REDIRECT, you SHOULD set doc_root
; if you are running php as a CGI under any web server (other than IIS)
; see documentation for security issues. The alternate is to use the
; cgi.force_redirect configuration below
doc_root =

; The directory under which PHP opens the script using /~username used only
; if nonempty.
user_dir =

; Directory in which the loadable extensions (modules) reside.
extension_dir = "./"

; Whether or not to enable the dl() function. The dl() function does NOT work
; properly in multithreaded servers, such as IIS or Zeus, and is automatically
; disabled on them.
enable_dl = On

; cgi.force_redirect is necessary to provide security running PHP as a CGI under
; most web servers. Left undefined, PHP turns this on by default. You can
; turn it off here AT YOUR OWN RISK
; **You CAN safely turn this off for IIS, in fact, you MUST.**
; cgi.force_redirect = 1

; if cgi.force_redirect is turned on, and you are not running under Apache or
Netscape
; (iPlanet) web servers, you MAY need to set an environment variable name that PHP
; will look for to know it is OK to continue execution. Setting this variable MAY
; cause security issues, KNOW WHAT YOU ARE DOING FIRST.
; cgi.redirect_status_env = ;

; FastCGI under IIS (on WINNT based OS) supports the ability to impersonate
; security tokens of the calling client. This allows IIS to define the
; security context that the request runs under. mod_fastcgi under Apache
; does not currently support this feature (03/17/2002)
; Set to 1 if running under IIS. Default is zero.
; fastcgi.impersonate = 1;

; cgi.rfc2616_headers configuration option tells PHP what type of headers to
; use when sending HTTP response code. If it's set 0 PHP sends Status: header that
; is supported by Apache. When this option is set to 1 PHP will send
```

```
; RFC2616 compliant header.
; Default is zero.
;cgi.rfc2616_headers = 0
```

File Uploads

If your application is heavily dependent on file uploads, you'll need a good place to store the uploaded files temporarily. If you want to avoid excess disk access, you could even set this to a memory-based file system (although you have to create the memory-based file system from the operating system, and supply the path in upload_tmp_dir). The default upload_max_filesize setting is fairly conservative, so you may want to increase the value unless you expect end users to abuse the higher file size limit.

```
;;;;;;;;;;;;;;;;;
; File Uploads ;
;;;;;;;;;;;;;;;;;

; Whether to allow HTTP file uploads.
file_uploads = On

; Temporary directory for HTTP uploaded files (will use system default if not
; specified).
;upload_tmp_dir =

; Maximum allowed size for uploaded files.
upload_max_filesize = 2M
```

Fopen Wrappers

The most important configuration option in Fopen wrappers section is allow_url_fopen, which is a convenient way of treating a Web site as if it were a file. The default setting is On, and unless you want to restrict other programmers on your server from using this feature, it should remain on.

The significance of these options is that sometimes you may want PHP to open remote files using a URL. In such cases, being able to set a timeout (default_socket_timeout), or an anonymous username (from), and so on help you find and open the remote file you need.

```
;;;;;;;;;;;;;;;;;;;;
; Fopen wrappers ;
;;;;;;;;;;;;;;;;;;;;

; Whether to allow the treatment of URLs (like http:// or ftp://) as files.
allow_url_fopen = On

; Define the anonymous ftp password (your email address)
;from="john@doe.com"

; Define the User-Agent string
; user_agent="PHP"
```

```
; Default timeout for socket based streams (seconds)
default_socket_timeout = 60

; If your scripts have to deal with files from Macintosh systems,
; or you are running on a Mac and need to deal with files from
; unix or win32 systems, setting this flag will cause PHP to
; automatically detect the EOL character in those files so that
; fgets() and file() will work regardless of the source of the file.
; auto_detect_line_endings = Off
```

Dynamic Extensions

Extensions enable you to add functionality to PHP without recompiling the source code. A typical change you might make is to uncomment the extension for the database that you prefer, for example, extension=php_pgsql.dll, if you're on a Windows platform and want be able to connect to a PostgreSQL server (on a UNIX platform, you use .so instead of .dll).

```
;;;;;;;;;;;;;;;;;;;;;;
; Dynamic Extensions ;
;;;;;;;;;;;;;;;;;;;;;;
;
; If you wish to have an extension loaded automatically, use the following
; syntax:
;
;    extension=modulename.extension
;
; For example, on Windows:
;
;    extension=msql.dll
;
; ... or under UNIX:
;
;    extension=msql.so
;
; Note that it should be the name of the module only; no directory information
; needs to go here. Specify the location of the extension with the
; extension_dir directive above.

;Windows Extensions
;Note that MySQL and ODBC support is now built in, so no dll is needed for it.
;
;extension=php_bz2.dll
;extension=php_cpdf.dll
;extension=php_curl.dll
;extension=php_dba.dll
;extension=php_dbase.dll
;extension=php_dbx.dll
;extension=php_exif.dll
;extension=php_fdf.dll
;extension=php_filepro.dll
;extension=php_gd2.dll
;extension=php_gettext.dll
;extension=php_iconv.dll
```

```
;extension=php_ifx.dll
;extension=php_iisfunc.dll
;extension=php_imap.dll
;extension=php_interbase.dll
;extension=php_ldap.dll
;extension=php_mbstring.dll
;extension=php_mcrypt.dll
;extension=php_mhash.dll
;extension=php_mime_magic.dll
;extension=php_ming.dll
;extension=php_mssql.dll
;extension=php_msql.dll
;extension=php_mysql.dll
;extension=php_oci8.dll
;extension=php_openssl.dll
;extension=php_oracle.dll
;extension=php_pdf.dll
;extension=php_pgsql.dll
;extension=php_shmop.dll
;extension=php_snmp.dll
;extension=php_sockets.dll
;extension=php_sybase_ct.dll
;extension=php_w32api.dll
;extension=php_xmlrpc.dll
;extension=php_xsl.dll
;extension=php_yaz.dll
;extension=php_zip.dll
```

Module Settings

Module settings are, of course, settings passed to the modules loaded (see the *Dynamic Extensions* section for the modules you've loaded). This section contains options for a wide variety of modules, so you should examine the settings for each module you want to load and the rest can be safely ignored. For instance, if you choose not to load support for Oracle in favor of PostgreSQL, you need only examine the settings beginning with pgsql.

```
;;;;;;;;;;;;;;;;;;;;
; Module Settings ;
;;;;;;;;;;;;;;;;;;;;

[Syslog]
; Whether or not to define the various syslog variables (e.g. $LOG_PID,
; $LOG_CRON, etc.). Turning it off is a good idea performance-wise. In
; runtime, you can define these variables by calling define_syslog_variables().
define_syslog_variables = Off

[mail function]
; For Win32 only.
SMTP = localhost

; For Win32 only.
;sendmail_from = me@example.com
```

```
; For Unix only. You may supply arguments as well (default: "sendmail -t -i").
;sendmail_path =

; Force the addition of the specified parameters to be passed as extra
parameters
; to the sendmail binary. These parameters will always replace the value of
; the 5th parameter to mail(), even in safe mode.
;mail.force_extra_paramaters =

[SQL]
sql.safe_mode = Off

[ODBC]
;odbc.default_db = Not yet implemented
;odbc.default_user = Not yet implemented
;odbc.default_pw = Not yet implemented

; Allow or prevent persistent links.
odbc.allow_persistent = On

; Check that a connection is still valid before reuse.
odbc.check_persistent = On

; Maximum number of persistent links. -1 means no limit.
odbc.max_persistent = -1

; Maximum number of links (persistent + non-persistent). -1 means no limit.
odbc.max_links = -1

; Handling of LONG fields. Returns number of bytes to variables. 0 means
; passthru.
odbc.defaultlrl = 4096

; Handling of binary data. 0 means passthru, 1 return as is, 2 convert to
char.
; See the documentation on odbc_binmode and odbc_longreadlen for an explanation
; of uodbc.defaultlrl and uodbc.defaultbinmode
odbc.defaultbinmode = 1

[MySQL]
; Allow or prevent persistent links.
mysql.allow_persistent = On

; Maximum number of persistent links. -1 means no limit.
mysql.max_persistent = -1

; Maximum number of links (persistent + non-persistent). -1 means no limit.
mysql.max_links = -1

; Default port number for mysql_connect(). If unset, mysql_connect() will use
; the $MYSQL_TCP_PORT or the mysql-tcp entry in /etc/services or the
; compile-time value defined MYSQL_PORT (in that order). Win32 will only look
; at MYSQL_PORT.
mysql.default_port =
```

```
; Default socket name for local MySQL connects. If empty, uses the built-in
; MySQL defaults.
mysql.default_socket =

; Default host for mysql_connect() (doesn't apply in safe mode).
mysql.default_host =

; Default user for mysql_connect() (doesn't apply in safe mode).
mysql.default_user =

; Default password for mysql_connect() (doesn't apply in safe mode).
; Note that this is generally a *bad* idea to store passwords in this file.
; *Any* user with PHP access can run 'echo get_cfg_var("mysql.default_password")
; and reveal this password! And of course, any users with read access to this
; file will be able to reveal the password as well.
mysql.default_password =

; Maximum time (in secondes) for connect timeout. -1 means no limimt
mysql.connect_timeout = 60

; Trace mode. When trace_mode is active (=On), warnings for table/index scans
and
; SQL-Erros will be displayed.
mysql.trace_mode = Off

[mSQL]
; Allow or prevent persistent links.
msql.allow_persistent = On

; Maximum number of persistent links. -1 means no limit.
msql.max_persistent = -1

; Maximum number of links (persistent+non persistent). -1 means no limit.
msql.max_links = -1

[PostgresSQL]
; Allow or prevent persistent links.
pgsql.allow_persistent = On

; Detect broken persistent links always with pg_pconnect(). Need a little overhead.
pgsql.auto_reset_persistent = Off

; Maximum number of persistent links. -1 means no limit.
pgsql.max_persistent = -1

; Maximum number of links (persistent+non persistent). -1 means no limit.
pgsql.max_links = -1

; Ignore PostgreSQL backends Notice message or not.
pgsql.ignore_notice = 0

; Log PostgreSQL backends Noitce message or not.
; Unless pgsql.ignore_notice=0, module cannot log notice message.
pgsql.log_notice = 0
```

```
[Sybase]
; Allow or prevent persistent links.
sybase.allow_persistent = On

; Maximum number of persistent links. -1 means no limit.
sybase.max_persistent = -1

; Maximum number of links (persistent + non-persistent). -1 means no limit.
sybase.max_links = -1

;sybase.interface_file = "/usr/sybase/interfaces"

; Minimum error severity to display.
sybase.min_error_severity = 10

; Minimum message severity to display.
sybase.min_message_severity = 10

; Compatability mode with old versions of PHP 3.0.
; If on, this will cause PHP to automatically assign types to results according
; to their Sybase type, instead of treating them all as strings. This
; compatability mode will probably not stay around forever, so try applying
; whatever necessary changes to your code, and turn it off.
sybase.compatability_mode = Off

[Sybase-CT]
; Allow or prevent persistent links.
sybct.allow_persistent = On

; Maximum number of persistent links. -1 means no limit.
sybct.max_persistent = -1

; Maximum number of links (persistent + non-persistent). -1 means no limit.
sybct.max_links = -1

; Minimum server message severity to display.
sybct.min_server_severity = 10

; Minimum client message severity to display.
sybct.min_client_severity = 10

[dbx]
; returned column names can be converted for compatibility reasons
; possible values for dbx.colnames_case are
; "unchanged" (default, if not set)
; "lowercase"
; "uppercase"
; the recommended default is either upper- or lowercase, but
; unchanged is currently set for backwards compatibility
dbx.colnames_case = "unchanged"

[bcmath]
; Number of decimal digits for all bcmath functions.
bcmath.scale = 0
```

```
[browscap]
;browscap = extra/browscap.ini

[Informix]
; Default host for ifx_connect() (doesn't apply in safe mode).
ifx.default_host =

; Default user for ifx_connect() (doesn't apply in safe mode).
ifx.default_user =

; Default password for ifx_connect() (doesn't apply in safe mode).
ifx.default_password =

; Allow or prevent persistent links.
ifx.allow_persistent = On

; Maximum number of persistent links. -1 means no limit.
ifx.max_persistent = -1

; Maximum number of links (persistent + non-persistent). -1 means no limit.
ifx.max_links = -1

; If on, select statements return the contents of a text blob instead of its
id.ifx.textasvarchar = 0

; If on, select statements return the contents of a byte blob instead of its
id.
ifx.byteasvarchar = 0

; Trailing blanks are stripped from fixed-length char columns. May help the
; life of Informix SE users.
ifx.charasvarchar = 0

; If on, the contents of text and byte blobs are dumped to a file instead of
; keeping them in memory.
ifx.blobinfile = 0

; NULL's are returned as empty strings, unless this is set to 1. In that case,
; NULL's are returned as string 'NULL'.
ifx.nullformat = 0

[Session]
; Handler used to store/retrieve data.
session.save_handler = files

; Argument passed to save_handler. In the case of files, this is the path
; where data files are stored. Note: Windows users have to change this
; variable in order to use PHP's session functions.
;
; As of PHP 4.0.1, you can define the path as:
;
;       session.save_path = "N;/path"
;
; where N is an integer. Instead of storing all the session files in
```

```
; /path, what this will do is use subdirectories N-levels deep, and
; store the session data in those directories. This is useful if you
; or your OS have problems with lots of files in one directory, and is
; a more efficient layout for servers that handle lots of sessions.
;
; NOTE 1: PHP will not create this directory structure automatically.
;         You can use the script in the ext/session dir for that purpose.
; NOTE 2: See the section on garbage collection below if you choose to
;         use subdirectories for session storage
;
; The file storage module creates files using mode 600 by default.
; You can change that by using
;
;     session.save_path = "N;MODE;/path"
;
; where MODE is the octal representation of the mode. Note that this
; does not overwrite the process's umask.
session.save_path = "/tmp"

; Whether to use cookies.
session.use_cookies = 1

; This option enables administrators to make their users invulnerable to
; attacks which involve passing session ids in URLs; defaults to 0.
; session.use_only_cookies = 1

; Name of the session (used as cookie name).
session.name = PHPSESSID

; Initialize session on request startup.
session.auto_start = 0

; Lifetime in seconds of cookie or, if 0, until browser is restarted.
session.cookie_lifetime = 0

; The path for which the cookie is valid.
session.cookie_path = /

; The domain for which the cookie is valid.
session.cookie_domain =

; Handler used to serialize data. php is the standard serializer of PHP.
session.serialize_handler = php

; Define the probability that the 'garbage collection' process is started
; on every session initialization.
; The probability is calculated by using gc_probability/gc_divisor,
; e.g. 1/100 means there is a 1% chance that the GC process starts
; on each request.

session.gc_probability = 1
session.gc_divisor     = 100

; After this number of seconds, stored data will be seen as 'garbage' and
; cleaned up by the garbage collection process.
```

```
session.gc_maxlifetime = 1440

; NOTE: If you are using the subdirectory option for storing session files
;       (see session.save_path above), then garbage collection does *not*
;       happen automatically. You will need to do your own garbage
;       collection through a shell script, cron entry, or some other method.
;       For example, the following script would is the equivalent of
;       setting session.gc_maxlifetime to 1440 (1440 seconds = 24 minutes):
;            cd /path/to/sessions; find -cmin +24 | xargs rm

; PHP 4.2 and less have an undocumented feature/bug that allows you to
; to initialize a session variable in the global scope, albeit register_globals
; is disabled. PHP 4.3 and later will warn you, if this feature is used.
; You can disable the feature and the warning seperately. At this time,
; the warning is only displayed, if bug_compat_42 is enabled.

session.bug_compat_42 = 1
session.bug_compat_warn = 1

; Check HTTP Referer to invalidate externally stored URLs containing ids.
; HTTP_REFERER has to contain this substring for the session to be
; considered as valid.
session.referer_check =

; How many bytes to read from the file.
session.entropy_length = 0

; Specified here to create the session id.
session.entropy_file =

;session.entropy_length = 16

;session.entropy_file = /dev/urandom

; Set to {nocache,private,public,} to determine HTTP caching aspects
; or leave this empty to avoid sending anti-caching headers.
session.cache_limiter = nocache

; Document expires after n minutes.
session.cache_expire = 180

; trans sid support is disabled by default.
; Use of trans sid may risk your users security.
; Use this option with caution.
; - User may send URL contains active session ID
;   to other person via. email/irc/etc.
; - URL that contains active session ID may be stored
;   in publically accessible computer.
; - User may access your site with the same session ID
;   always using URL stored in browser's history or bookmarks.
session.use_trans_sid = 0

; Select a hash function
; 0: MD5    (128 bits)
```

```
; 1: SHA-1 (160 bits)
session.hash_function = 0
; Define how many bits are stored in each character when converting
; the binary hash data to something readable.
;
; 4 bits: 0-9, a-f
; 5 bits: 0-9, a-v
; 6 bits: 0-9, a-z, A-Z, "-", ","
session.hash_bits_per_character = 4

; The URL rewriter will look for URLs in a defined set of HTML tags.
; form/fieldset are special; if you include them here, the rewriter will
; add a hidden <input> field with the info which is otherwise appended
; to URLs. If you want XHTML conformity, remove the form entry.
; Note that all valid entries require a "=", even if no value follows.
url_rewriter.tags = "a=href,area=href,frame=src,input=src,form=,fieldset="

[MSSQL]
; Allow or prevent persistent links.
mssql.allow_persistent = On

; Maximum number of persistent links. -1 means no limit.
mssql.max_persistent = -1

; Maximum number of links (persistent+non persistent). -1 means no limit.
mssql.max_links = -1

; Minimum error severity to display.
mssql.min_error_severity = 10

; Minimum message severity to display.
mssql.min_message_severity = 10

; Compatability mode with old versions of PHP 3.0.
mssql.compatability_mode = Off

; Connect timeout
;mssql.connect_timeout = 5

; Query timeout
;mssql.timeout = 60

; Valid range 0 - 2147483647. Default = 4096.
;mssql.textlimit = 4096

; Valid range 0 - 2147483647. Default = 4096.
;mssql.textsize = 4096

; Limits the number of records in each batch. 0 = all records in one batch.
;mssql.batchsize = 0

; Specify how datetime and datetim4 columns are returned
; On => Returns data converted to SQL server settings
```

```
; Off => Returns values as YYYY-MM-DD hh:mm:ss
;mssql.datetimeconvert = On
; Use NT authentication when connecting to the server
mssql.secure_connection = Off

; Specify max number of processes. Default = 25
;mssql.max_procs = 25

[Assertion]
; Assert(expr); active by default.
;assert.active = On

; Issue a PHP warning for each failed assertion.
;assert.warning = On

; Don't bail out by default.
;assert.bail = Off

; User-function to be called if an assertion fails.
;assert.callback = 0

; Eval the expression with current error_reporting(). Set to true if you want
; error_reporting(0) around the eval().
;assert.quiet_eval = 0

[Ingres II]
; Allow or prevent persistent links.
ingres.allow_persistent = On

; Maximum number of persistent links. -1 means no limit.
ingres.max_persistent = -1

; Maximum number of links, including persistents. -1 means no limit.
ingres.max_links = -1

; Default database (format: [node_id::]dbname[/srv_class]).
ingres.default_database =

; Default user.
ingres.default_user =

; Default password.
ingres.default_password =

[Verisign Payflow Pro]
; Default Payflow Pro server.
pfpro.defaulthost = "test-payflow.verisign.com"

; Default port to connect to.
pfpro.defaultport = 443

; Default timeout in seconds.
pfpro.defaulttimeout = 30
```

```
; Default proxy IP address (if required).
;pfpro.proxyaddress =
; Default proxy port.
;pfpro.proxyport =

; Default proxy logon.
;pfpro.proxylogon =

; Default proxy password.
;pfpro.proxypassword =

[Sockets]
; Use the system read() function instead of the php_read() wrapper.
sockets.use_system_read = On

[com]
; path to a file containing GUIDs, IIDs or filenames of files with TypeLibs
;com.typelib_file =
; allow Distributed-COM calls
;com.allow_dcom = true
; autoregister constants of a components typlib on com_load()
;com.autoregister_typelib = true
; register constants casesensitive
;com.autoregister_casesensitive = false
; show warnings on duplicate constat registrations
;com.autoregister_verbose = true

[mbstring]
; language for internal character representation.
;mbstring.language = Japanese

; internal/script encoding.
; Some encoding cannot work as internal encoding.
; (e.g. SJIS, BIG5, ISO-2022-*)
;mbstring.internal_encoding = EUC-JP

; http input encoding.
;mbstring.http_input = auto

; http output encoding. mb_output_handler must be
; registered as output buffer to function
;mbstring.http_output = SJIS

; enable automatic encoding translation accoding to
; mbstring.internal_encoding setting. Input chars are
; converted to internal encoding by setting this to On.
; Note: Do _not_ use automatic encoding translation for
;       portable libs/applications.
;mbstring.encoding_translation = Off

; automatic encoding detection order.
; auto means
;mbstring.detect_order = auto

; substitute_character used when character cannot be converted
; one from another
```

```
;mbstring.substitute_character = none;

; overload(replace) single byte functions by mbstring functions.
; mail(), ereg(), etc are overloaded by mb_send_mail(), mb_ereg(),
; etc. Possible values are 0,1,2,4 or combination of them.
; For example, 7 for overload everything.
; 0: No overload
; 1: Overload mail() function
; 2: Overload str*() functions
; 4: Overload ereg*() functions
;mbstring.func_overload = 0

[FrontBase]
;fbsql.allow_persistent = On
;fbsql.autocommit = On
;fbsql.default_database =
;fbsql.default_database_password =
;fbsql.default_host =
;fbsql.default_password =
;fbsql.default_user = "_SYSTEM"
;fbsql.generate_warnings = Off
;fbsql.max_connections = 128
;fbsql.max_links = 128
;fbsql.max_persistent = -1
;fbsql.max_results = 128
;fbsql.batchSize = 1000

[exif]
; Exif UNICODE user comments are handled as UCS-2BE/UCS-2LE and JIS as JIS.
; With mbstring support this will automatically be converted into the encoding
; given by corresponding encode setting. When empty mbstring.internal_encoding
; is used. For the decode settings you can distinguish between motorola and
; intel byte order. A decode setting cannot be empty.
;exif.encode_unicode = ISO-8859-15
;exif.decode_unicode_motorola = UCS-2BE
;exif.decode_unicode_intel    = UCS-2LE
;exif.encode_jis =
;exif.decode_jis_motorola = JIS
;exif.decode_jis_intel    = JIS

; Local Variables:
; tab-width: 4
; End:
```

Index

SYMBOLS AND NUMERICS

anchor characters
($), 210
(^), 210
assignment operators
defined, 47
(=), 133
equality operators
(==), 133
(===), 133
in if statements, 133
using of, 134
inequality operators
(!=), 134
(<>), 134
using, 134
logical operators
AND (&&), 136
defined, 47
in MySQL, 397
NOT (!), 136
OR ((||)), 136
using, 137
working example, 139
NOT LIKE operator for data retrieving, 399
qualifiers symbols
(*), 211
(?), 211
(+), 211
special assignment operators
(+=), 53
(−=), 53
unary operators, 46
(<) less than operator, 130
(<>) inequality operator, 134
(=)
as assignment operator, 133
as comparison operator, 133
(==)
comparison operator, 52
equality operator, 133

(===)
comparison operator, 52
equality operator, 133
MySQL comparison operators
(!=), 397
(<), 397
(<=), 397
(=), 397
(>), 397
(>=), 397
(>) greater than operator, 130, 397
(.) concatenation operator, 48, 51
(*)
qualifier symbol, 211
multiplication operator, 47
(++) increment/decrement operator, 53
(+)
qualifier symbol, 211
addition operator, 47
logical operators
AND (&&), 136, 397
NOT (!), 136
OR ((||)), 136, 397
boolean operators
and, 126
defined, 130
in control-flow structures, 129
not, 126
or, 126
xor, 126
comparison operators
(==), 52
(===), 52
defined, 47
greater than (>) operator, 130
less than (<) operator, 130
using, 130
working example, 132
increment/decrement operators
++, 53
defined, 47, 53
$dir variable, 300
$GLOBALS predefined variable, 69

$userfile_size variable, 309
$_COOKIES variable, 112
$_POST array, 438
$_POST variable, 328
(dir) function, 292
(int) statement, 271
1NF normalization
  defined, 352
  example, 353
2NF normalization
  defined, 354
  foreign key, use of, 354
3NF normalization, 355

A

access logging concept. *See also* user manager;
    authenticating users
  defined, 444
  do_authenticate() function, use of, 446
  login_form() function, use of, 447
  password, 446
  user ID, use of, 446
accessed pages counting
  PHP sessions, 118
  session identifiers (SID), 118
action attribute
  defined, 76
  for PHP files uploading, 308
additive color model. *See* RGB color model
addslashes() function
  inserting records, 418
  string validation, 206
aggregation, 499
allow_url_fopen function for PHP5 configuring,
    816
ALTER query, 360
ALTER TABLE command, 383
ANSI C compiler, 9
anti-aliasing, 604
Apache Web Server on Linux, 4, 6, 9
API (Application Programming Interface)
  defined, 333, 538
  using SQL (structured query language),
    781
append_child() function, 333
arc drawing
  syntax, 593
  using imagearc() function, 593
ArgoUML, 494

arguments, working with, 797. *See also* PHP CLI
    arguments
arithmetic operator. *See also* special arithmetic
    operator
  defined, 47, 52
  increment/decrement, 53
  special assignment, 53
array() function, 59, 163
arrays functions, description of, 694
arrays
  associative, 161, 163, 168
  components
    element, 58
    keys, 58
    values, 58
  defined, 145, 161
  elements, 161
  hidden controls, 167
  indexes, 59
  initializing, 60, 162
  iterating aspects, 164, 167, 169,
    172
  multidimensional, 176
  non-sequential, 169
  operators, 47, 58
  practical demonstration, 176
  sorting, 62, 173
  string-indexed, 172
  working example, 178
  working with, 60
array_flip() function, 61
array_multisort() function, 181. *See also*
    multidimensional arrays
array_pop() function, 303
arsort() function, 175, 549
asort() function, 62, 174
assert() method for logging, 656, 658
assertEquals() function, 654, 655
associative arrays
  defined, 161, 163, 168
  for MP3_ID package building, 549
  references for files ownership and permissions
    settings, 282
asXML function, 335
attribute in HTML tag, 64
authenticating users. *See also* access logging
    concept
  auth_user() function, 442
  login_form() function, 442, 443
  password, 442

session_start() function, 442
user IDs, 442
auth_user() function, 442
avg() function, 400

B

basename() function, 287, 299
BCMath functions, description of, 699
binary (compiled) method for PHP5 installation
  advantages, 6
  disadvantages, 6
binary operators, 46
binary RPMs PHP5 installation method
  advantages, 6
  disadvantages, 6
bitwise operator, 47
boolean logic
  boolean terms, 125, 126
  boolean values, 125
  control-flow aspects, 125
  importance in control-flow structures, 125
boolean terms
  and, 125
  not, 125
  or, 125
  using, 125, 126
  xor, 125
boolean values
  FALSE, 125
  TRUE, 125, 126
  using, 126
boundary marker, 573, 576
branching statements. See also conditional
    statements
  decision-making aspects, 128
  example, 128
  if statement, 130
branching structures. See control-flow structures
break command in switch statement, 140, 141
BZip2 functions, description of, 700

C

caching, 29
calendar functions, description of, 701
calling functions, 237. See also nesting; recursion
carriage return and line feed (CRLF), 568
case block for XML document reading, 330
casting, 44

ceil() function, 408
CGI (Common Gateway Interface)
  for Web page development, 796
  using, 5
character classes
  digits (\d), 210
  non-blank character (\S), 210
  non-digit (\D), 210
  non-word character (\W), 210
  whitespace (\s), 210
  word character (\w), 210
character type functions, description of, 703
chdir() function, 292, 293, 294
check boxes. See also multiple check boxes; text
    area; text fields
  defined, 85
  using, 86
  working, 87
chr() function, 49
circles and ellipses drawing
  function syntax, 592
  using imageellipse() function, 592
class diagrams, 495
class relationships
  aggregation, 499
  generalization, 499
class.Entity.php, creating, 503
class.exceptions.php, 646
class.LogContainer.php, 642
class.LogUtils.php, 632
class.PersistableLog.php, 635
class.UserDemographic.php, 644
class.UserLog.php, 638
class/object functions, description of, 702
classes
  adding a property, 466
  adding method, 465
  creating, 464
  defined, 463
  generalization concept, 499
  member variables, 467
  PEAR standards, 533
  properties, 463
  UML, 493
  visibility
    private, 467, 489
    protected, 467, 489
    public, 467, 489
CLI (Command Line Interpreter). See PHP CLI
client-server relationship, 36

client/server databases
  MySQL, 346
  open source, 346
  PostgreSQL, 346
  using, 345
close() function, 487
closedir() function, 291, 292
code
  optimization, 234
  reusability, 462
coding standards. See PEAR coding standards
color theory. See RGB color model
Command Line Interpreter (CLI). See PHP CLI
Common Gateway Interface. See CGI
common.php for logging, 629
Comprehensive Perl Archive Network (CPAN), 529
compressed file formats, 587
computer graphics, basics
  coordinate systems, 586
  image types, 587
  RGB color model, 585
concatenation operator (.), 48, 51
conditional statements
  defined, 127
  if, 129
  switch, 140
configuration file, global variable setting in, 69
confirm() method, 302
constants, PEAR standards for, 533
constructors. See object constructors
contact manager application, creating, 496
contact manager UML diagrams, 496
Contact Type classes, 512
control, 79
control-flow structures
  boolean logic, using, 125
  if statement structure, 123
  if statements, 129
  if..then...else..end if structure, 125
  if..then..else/elseif..end if structure, 126
  in decision-making logic, 123
  in PHP programming, 123, 124
  using boolean operators, 129
Cookie variables, 69
cookies
  defined, 109
  deleting, 112
  for session management, 117
  for state maintenance, 110
  for storing user preferences, 112, 114
  implementation issues, 110
  retrieving, 111
  setting, 111
  using in Web sites, 110, 111
  working, 114
copy() function, 288, 289, 308
copyright image. See watermark applying
count() function, 400
CPAN (Comprehensive Perl Archive Network), 529
CREATE query, 360
CREATE TABLE command, 376, _378_, _379_
create_account() function, 438
create_element() function, 333
CRLF. See carriage return and line feed
CSV files, 614
CSV format, 271
curdate() function, 423
curl functions, description of, 703
current() function
  for iterating through non-sequential arrays, 169
  for iterating through string-indexed arrays, 172
curtime() function, 423

D

data entry validation, 213
data handling classes, 624
data manipulation
  date and time type fields, use of, 422
  DELETE command, use of, 420, 422
  UPDATE query, use of, 420, 422
data processing logic, 125
data source name (DSN) creating, 785
data types
  converting, 44
  defined, 42
  for SQL, 356
  PHP, 43
data-handling scripts, 632
database and tables creating
  with MySQL, 375
  with PHP, 379, _380_, _381_
database architectures
  client/server, 345
  embedded, 345
database engine
  for PHP, 344
  MySQL, 350
database file contents
  error_message() function, 407

global variables, 405
html_footer() function, 406
html_header() function, 406
database functions, 426, 427
Database Management System. *See* **DBMS**
database tables, 426
DATABASES statement for data retrieving, 391
databases
choosing aspects, 346
for PHP applications, 343, 344
for state maintenance, 110
MySQL, 346
with SQL, 355
DataManager class, 516
date and time functions, description of, 704
date and time type fields
DATE, 422
DATETIME, 422
for data manipulation, 422
TIME, 422
TIMESTAMP, 422
YEAR, 422
date() function, 33, 551
date_format() function, 423
date_str() function, 302
dayname() function, 425
DBMS. *See also* **RDBMS**
features, 345
for data modification, 344
for data retrieval, 344
for data storage, 344
for PHP applications, 344
debugging
in PHP, 189
in PHP5, 198
decision-making
boolean logic, 126
code, 123
structures, 125
define() function, 46
defined constants, 45
defining functions, 236, 237
del filename command, use of, 290
DELETE query, 359, 364
delete_record() function, 450
dependency, 531
DESCRIBE command, 362
DHTML (Dynamic HTML), 537, 542
DHTML object, 542, 544. *See also*
 HTML_TreeMenu object

Dia for UML diagrams generation, 494
dir object methods
close(), 294
read(), 294
rewind(), 294
directories
creating, 259
defined, 260
handling, 260
list directory, 291
directory functions, description of, 705
directory functions
(dir) function, 292
chdir() function, 292, 294
closedir() function, 291, 292
dirname() function, 292
dir_page() function, 298, 300
mkdir() function, 292
mkdir_form(), 297
opendir() function, 290
readdir() function, 291, 292
rewinddir(), 292
rmdir() function, 292
traverse_dir(), 294
directory hierarchy
recursion, 294
subdirectories holding, 294
traverse_dir() function, using, 294
traversing, 294
directory navigator, creating
defined, 295
dir_page() function, using, 298
display() function, using, 298
file extensions setting, 295
mkdir_form() function, using, 297
directory paths
defined, 287
for Linux systems, 260
for PHP on Windows, 260
for Windows systems, 260
directory tree, 290
dirname() function, 292, 293
display() function, 298
dist file, 3. *See also* **php.ini-dist**
DISTINCT keyword for data retrieving, 401
do while loop. *See also* **while loop**
defined, 152
using, 154
working, 154
DOCTYPE declaration for DTD referencing, 320

Document Object Model. *See* DOM
Document Type Definition. *See* DTD
DOM extension, 333
DOM objects
  creating, 333
  DOMDocument, 333
  DOMElement object, 333
  importing with simpleXML, 339, 340
DOM
  defined, 313, 323
  for XML document, 332
DOMDocument object, 333
DOMElement object, 333
domxml_new_doc function, 333
domxml_open_file() function, 333
domxml_open_mem() function, 333
dot operator. *See* concatenation
    operator
do_authenticate() function, 446
drawing
  arc, 593
  circles and ellipses, 592
  lines, 590
  pixels, 589
  polygons, 594
  rectangles with rounded corners, 595
  rectangles, 591
DROP query, 360
DSN. *See* data source name
DSO. *See* Dynamic Shared Object
DTD (Document Type Definition)
  defined, 64
  for defining XML attributes, 314, 315
  for XHTML, 318
DTDs referencing
  DOCTYPE declaration, using, 321
  in XML documents, 320
  limitation, 320
  using DOCTYPE declaration, 320
  using URL, 320
  using xmlns attribute, 320
dynamic extensions, 817
Dynamic Shared Object (DSO), 11
dynamic Web pages, 2

E

e-mail addresses validating. *See also* uniform
    resource locators (URLs) validating
  defined, 213

HTML e-mails, 578
  working example, 215
e-mail message structure
  header fields
    Bcc, 569
    Cc, 569
    Comments, 569
    From, 568
    In-reply-to, 569
    Keywords, 569
    Message-id, 569
    Optional, 569
    Reference, 569
    Reply-to, 568
    Sender, 568
    Subject, 569
    To, 568
    Trace, 568
  RFC 2822 definition, 568
e-mail sending with PHP
  on Linux, 570
  on Windows, 570
  PEAR mail libraries, using, 574
  using mail() function, 570, 571, 572
  using Multipurpose Internet Mail Extensions
      (MIME), 572
e-mail, background of, 567
each() function, 171
EBNF (Extended Backus Naur Format),
    318
echo function, 33
echo statement for PHP5 debugging, 198
echo() statement, 140
edit_existing_file case, 305, 306
edit_log_record() function, 452
edit_record() function, 450, 452
ELEMENT callout in XHTML document,
    319
element of array, 161
elements of XML documents, 315
embedded databases
  dBase, 345
  DBM, 345
  SQLite, 345
encapsulation, 463, 489, 491
entire files, reading of, 272
entities in normalization, 353
Entity class, creating, 503
ENUM type fields, 431, 432, 434
environment variables for PHP5, 807

ereg() function
  defined, 300
  for HTML form validation, 208
eregi() function, 434
eregi_replace() function, 434
error control operator, 47
error handling functions, overview of, 706
error handling
  in PHP, 190, 220
  in PHP5, 198
errors types. See also PHP code debugging
  logic, 189
  runtime, 189
  syntax, 189
error_message() function, 304, 407
error_reporting() function, 372
escaping quotes in MySQL, 386
exception handling
  classes, 627
  defined, 622
  try/catch, 222
execution operator, 47
exit command for infinite loops, 152
exit statement for HTML form validation, 200
explode() function
  defined, 434, 799
  for HTML form, 206
Extended Backus Naur Format (EBNF), 318
eXtensible Markup Language (XML), 313
Extreme Programming, 233. See also RAD

F

fatal errors, 190, 193
fclose() function
  defined, 263
  example, 265, 267
feof() function, 269, 270, 271
fgetc() function, 269, 270, 271
fgetcsv() function, 269, 271
fgets() function, 269, 271
field in RDBMS, 351
field types
  defaults, 431
  ENUM, 431
file and directory handling, 300
file closing, 261, 263
file extensions for PHP program running
  .htm, 34
  .html, 34

file functions, 278
file functions
  basename(), 287
  copy(), 288, 289
  fclose(), 263
  fgetc(), 269
  fgetcsv(), 269, 271
  fgets(), 269, 271
  file handle, 260
  file(), 272
  filectime(), 279
  filegroup(), 283
  filemtime(), 279
  fileowner(), 283
  filetime(), 279
  filetype(), 283
  file_exists(), 278
  file_info(), 285
  fopen(), 261
  fpassthru(), 272, 273
  fputs(), 269
  fread(), 265
  fread(), 271
  fseek(), 274, 275, 277
  ftell(), 274, 275
  fwrite(), 261
  fwrite(), 265
  readfile(), 272, 273
  rename(), 288
  unlink(), 288
file handle
  defined, 260
  use of, 261, 263
file navigating functions
  fseek(), 275
  ftell(), 275
  rewind(), 275
  working, 277
file opening
  defined, 261
  fopen() function, using, 261
file path, 287
file pointer. See file handle
file system for PHP, 814
File Transfer Protocol (FTP), 36
file uploads for PHP5 configuring, 816
file() function, 272
file() version, 272
fileatime function, 549
filectime() function, 279

filegroup() function, 283
filemtime() function, 279
filename strings, 260
fileowner() function, 283
files data, accessing of
    using fseek() function, 274
    using ftell() function, 274
files information retrieving, 264. *See also* stat()
    function
files ownership and permissions references
    for group users
        Gid, 283
        members, 283
        name, 283
    for users
        directory (Dir), 282
        Gecos, 282
        group ID (Gid), 282
        name, 282
        password (passwd), 282
        shell, 282
    user ID (uid), 282
files ownership and permissions
    filegroup() function, using, 283
    fileowner() function, using, 283
    filetype() function, using, 283
    NTFS, using, 282
    on UNIX system, 282
    on Windows system, 282
    to all users, 282
    to file owner, 282
    to group of users, 282
files permissions
    to execute, 282
    to read, 282
    to write, 282
files reading
    using file() function, 272
    using fpassthru() function, 272
    using readfile() function:, 272
files storage, 259
files uploading
    example, 309
    using action attribute, 308
    using form tag, 307
    working of, 310
files, copying, deleting, and renaming of
    copy() function, use of, 288, 289
    rename() function, use of, 288
    unlink() function, use of, 288

files, defined, 260
files, handling of, 260
files, information on
    defined, 278
    file_exists() function, use of, 278
files, reading and writing characters in
    feof() function, use of, 269
    fgetc() function, use of, 269
    fgetcsv() function, use of, 269
    fgets() function, use of, 269
    fputs() function, use of, 269
files, reading to
    example, 265
    use of fread() function, 265
files, time-related properties, 279
files, working with, 267
files, writing to
    example, 265
    use of fwrite() function, 265
filesize() function, 278
filesystem functions, description of, 707
filetime() function, 279
filetype() function, 283
file_exists() function, 278
file_get_contents() function, 329
file_info() function
    using, 285
    working, 285
First Normal Form (1NF), defined, 352
font anti-aliasing, 604
fonts displaying
    code, 608
    color allocation aspects, 608
fopen() function
    defined, 261, 262
    example, 265, 267
for loops
    defined, 156
    foreach, 182
    using, 156
    working, 159
foreach loops
    defined, 182
    formats, 182
    using of, 183
    working example, 183
foreign key, 354. *See also* primary key; 2NF
    (Second Normal Form)
form element, 65, 75, 76, 79
form submitting in HTML, 75

fpassthru() function, 272, 273
fputs() function, 269
fread() function
  defined, 265, 271
  use of, 267, 269
FROM clause, 360, 402
fseek() function, 274, 275, 277
ftell() function, 274, 275
FTP (File Transfer Protocol), 36
FTP functions, description of, 710
function handling functions, description of, 713
functions calling
  based on PEAR standards, 533
  defined, 237
  using recursion, 252
  via nesting, 251
functions visibility
  private, 489
  protected, 489
  public, 489
fwrite() function, 261, 265

G

GD image functions features
  image dimensions resizing, 600
  watermark applying, 600
GD image libraries, 585, 587
generalization, 499
GenerateHandOffs method, 544
generatexml, 563
get function, 467
get method. See also set method
  for accessing properties, 468
  get function using, 467, 469, 470
  working with, 468
GET method
  defined, 38
  for text fields, 82
  using of, 79
GET value, 77
getAllEntitiesAsObjects() function, 524
getConnection(), 516
getdate() function, 279, 280
getDemographics() functions, 658
getEntityData() function, 520
getErrorMessage() function, 627
getName() function, 509
getTag method, 550
GetTreeHandoff() method, 545

get[x]ObjectsForEntity function, 520
get_element_by_tagname function, 333
global keyword, 45
global variables
  $_COOKIES, 112
  as database file content, 405
  scope, 247, 248
GRANT query command, 366
GROUP BY clause, 401. See also ORDER BY clause

H

HAVING clause, 402
HEAD method, 38
header() function, 591
hidden controls in arrays, 167
hidden form fields
  defined, 97
  state maintenance concept, 109
  using of, 98
  working of, 99
hierarchical model, 332
href attribute, 72
HTML (Web) forms
  form elements, 74
  form fields (controls), 79
HTML attributes
  action, 76
  href, 72
  method, 75, 76
  multiple, 94
  type, 80
HTML code
  for PHP program, 2, 31
  testing and debugging, 188
HTML document for Web page displaying, 322
HTML Document Type Definition (HTML DTD), 65
HTML e-mails, 574, 575, 577
HTML elements
  form, 65, 75, 76
  IMG, 64, 65
  input, 65
  option, 93
  select, 93
HTML for web page designing, 64
HTML form elements
  form, 74, 75, 76
  input, 74, 75
  select, 74
  textarea, 74

HTML form fields (controls)
  and PHP, 79
  check boxes, 85
  hidden form fields, 109
  hidden, 97
  list boxes, 93
  multiple check boxes, 88
  password fields, 101
  radio buttons, 91
  reset buttons, 101
  submit buttons, 101
  text area, 83
  text areas, 83
  text fields (text boxes), 80
HTML form validation
  data entry validation, 213
  defined, 199
  e-mail addresses validating, 214, 215
  example, 200
  regular expressions, 204, 206, 209, 216
  sensitive file accessing, prevention of, 219
  string validation, 204
  use of HTMLSpecialChars() function, 203
  using exit statement, 200
  using explode() function, 206
  using special characters, 209
  using try/catch exception-handling, 222,
    225
  via file path parameters checking, 218
  working of, 203
HTML form
  for Web page creating, 66
  for Web server interaction, 67
  useful information, 76
  using arrays, 166
  using do while loop, 154
HTML headers for session management, 119
HTML links, 72
HTML source code errors, 199
HTML tags
  defined, 64
  for Web page creating, 66
  form, 75
HTML Web page header, creating of, 303
HTML Web page, 64, 69
**htmlspecialchars() function for inserting records,
    419**
HTMLSpecialChars() function, 203
htmlspecialchars() function, 455
HTMLTree_Menu component, 562

html_footer() function, 406
html_header() function, 406
HTML_TreeMenu class, 537, 539, 542, 543
HTML_TreeMenu class, instantiating, 541
HTML_TreeMenu component, 553
HTML_TreeMenu object
  creating, 542
  retrieving, 542
HTML_TreeMenu package, 537, 538
HTML_TreeMenu package, working with
  class instance, creating, 541
  require_once function, use of, 541
HTML_TreeMenu, 552
HTTP (HyperText Transfer Protocol) data
  browser interaction, 67
  Web server interaction, 67
HTTP functions, description of, 713
HTTP header for radiogeneratexml.php, 558
HTTP message sections
  HTTP body, 37
  HTTP header, 37
  request line, 37, 38
  response line, 37, 39
HTTP protocol
  for PHP scripts running, 41
  for web communications, 37
  HTTP request, 37, 38
  HTTP response, 37, 39
  PHP processing engine, 41
  stateless protocol, concept of, 108
  Web server, 41
HTTP request for
  PHP scripts running, 41
  radiogeneratexml.php, 558
HTTP request handling methods
  GET, 38
  HEAD, 38
  POST, 38
HTTP request header
  Entity, 39
  General, 39
  Request, 39
HTTP request line, 38
HTTP request variables, 69
HTTP request
  defined, 38
  for PEAR packages, 552
  request body, 39
  request header, 39
  request line, 38

HTTP response header types
Entity, 40
General, 40
Response, 40
HTTP response header, 40
HTTP response line, 39
HTTP response variables, 69
HTTP response
body, 41
code classes, 40
header, 40
HyperText Preprocessor. *See* **PHP**
HyperText Transfer Protocol. *See* **HTTP**

I

IBM Rational Rose for UML diagrams generation, 494
iconv library functions, overview, 714
IDv3 tag, 546, 551, 553. *See also* **MP3 files**
IDv3, 561
if statements
executing, 129
using boolean operators, 129
using comparison operators, 130
using equality operators, 133
using inequality operators, 134
using logical operators, 136, 137
if..then..else statements for form validation, 203
IGNORE statement, 451
IIS. *See* **Internet Information Server**
image functions, 585
image functions, overview of, 714
image types
raster, 587
vector, 587
imagealphablending() functions, 604
imagearc() function, 594
imagecolorallocatealpha() function, 604
imagecolorat() function, 602
imagecolorexact() function, 603
imagecolortransparent() function, 603
imagecopy() function, 604
imagecopymerge() function, 604
imagecopyresampled() function, 606
imagecopyresized() function, 606
imagecreate() function, 591, 598
imagecreatefrom() function, 598
imagecreatefromgif() function, 598
imagecreatefromjpeg() function, 598

imagecreatefromjpeg() function, working of, 600
imagecreatefrompng() function, 598, 601
imagecreatetruecolor() function, 598
imagedestroy() function, 598
imagefontwidth() function, 609
imagefttext() function, 609
imageline() function, 590
imageloadfont() function, 608
imagepng() function, 591, 598
imagepolygon() function, 594
imagerectangle() function, 591, 592
images using text
standard text adding
imageloadfont() function, use of, 608
imagestring() function, use of, 607
using True Type fonts, 609
imagesetpixel() function, 589
imagestring() function, 607
imagesx() function, 605
imagesy() function, 601, 605
IMAP functions, description of, 722
IMAP servers, 568
IMG element of HTML, 64
import_request_variables (), 69
include files, 255
include statements. *See also* **require statements**
defined, 254
important points, 257
working example, 257
writing, 254
include() function for PHP5 configuring, 814
includes, conditional, 255
indenting standards, 235
index in SQl, 357
index numbers, 161. *See also* **array indexes**
index values, 162
index.php, 651
Individual class, 517
infinite loops
defined, 151
example, 152
runtime errors, concept of, 196
information packets, 37. *See also* **TCP/IP protocol**
inheritance
class creating concept, 480
defined, 463, 477
methods overriding
defined, 481
example, 483

inheritance *(continued)*

parent functionality, preserving of, 484, 486

working of, 481

initialization of arrays, 162

initialize.php for logging, 629

initUser() function, 508

inodes, 290

input element

defined, 74, 75

for check boxes, 85

of HTML, 65

INSERT command

defined, 385

escaping quotes, 386

putting records into tables, 387

INSERT query, 359, 364

inserting new record in SQL, 364

inserting records using PHP

addslashes() function, use of, 418

defined, 417

htmlspecialchars() function, use of, 419

special characters, use of, 418

stripslashes() function, use of, 418

install command, 536

INSTALL files, 4

interfaces

defined, 463, 486

using of, 487

working

close() function, use of, 487

open() function, use of, 487

Internet Information Server (IIS), 3, 4, 19

Internet mail protocols

Requests For Comment (RFCs), 568

Simple Mail Transfer Protocol (SMTP), 568

Internet Protocol (IP). See TCP/IP protocol

interpreter forms

interactive shell, 795

interpreted language, 795

intializeDb() function, 663

in_use() function, 436, 439

isOpen() function, 620

isset ()function

defined, 120, 132

for HTML form validation, 225

for XML document reading, 329

is_dir() function, 284

is_file() function, 284

iterating through arrays, 164, 167

iterating through non-sequential arrays. *See also* iterating through string-indexed arrays

current() function, 169

defined, 169

each() function, 171

key() function, 169

list() function, 171

next() function, 170

prev() function, 170

iterating through string-indexed arrays

current() function, 172

defined, 172

key() function, 172

J

JavaScript for HTML-e-mails, 575

JavaScript library, 540

Javascript, 2

join operation, 404

JPEG file opening

code, 599

imagecreatefromjpeg() function, use of, 599

JPEG format, 587

K

key() function

for iterating through non-sequential arrays, 169

for iterating through string-indexed arrays, 172

keys. *See* array components

Konqueror, 9

ksort() function, 175

L

language options for PHP5 configuring, 807

less than (<) operator, 130

LIKE operator for data retrieving, 399

LIMIT clause for data retrieving, 396

LIMIT clause, 409

lines drawing

code, 590

using header() function, 591

using imagecreate() function, 591

using imageline() function, 590

using imagepng() function, 591

links

forWeb page designing, 72

with URL, 72

Linux version
Debian, 5
FreeBSD, 5
RedHat, 5
list boxes. *See also* **radio buttons; check boxes**
defined, 93
using of, 94
working of, 95
list directory, 291
list() function, 171
list_records() function, 407, 411, 449
loadXML function, 340
loan application form
example of, 103
possible form improvements, 107
working of, 105
local variables, scope of, 247, 248
LogContainer class, 650, 660
LogContainerException class, 646
LogContainerException() class, 651
LogContainerInvalidDataException class, 646
logging access. *See* **access logging concept**
logging agent, coding
data-handling scripts
class.LogContainer.php, 642
class.LogUtils.php, 632
class.PersistableLog.php, 635
class.UserDemographic.php, 644
class.UserLog.php, 638
miscellaneous scripts
common.php, 629
initialize.php, 629
settings.php, 628
setup.php, 629
presentation scripts and templates
index.php, 651
report-html.tpl, 654
report.php, 652
report.tpl, 653
presentation scripts and templates:, 651
validation and error-handling scripts, 645
logging agent, designing
defined, 621
exception handling, 622
object-oriented support, 622
PHPUnit, use of, 622
sitelogs.db database designing, 622
testing and debugging, 622

using UML, 624
data handling classes, mapping of, 624
exception handling classes, mapping of, 627
logging agent, working with
userlog.php, 665
viewing, 666
logging agent
exception class, 627
overview, 614
sequence diagram, 628
testing and application of, 654
logical errors
logical output errors, 197
runtime, 193
types, 193
logical output errors
defined, 197
functions with incorrect argumenmts ordering, 197
functions without return value, 197
login_form() function, 442, 443, 447
logs types
UserDemographic, 624
UserLog, 624
loops and arrays, using of, 145, 164, 167
loops
defined, 145
do while, 145, 152
for, 145, 156
infinite loops, 151
while, 145, 147
loosely typed languages. *See also* **strongly typed languages**
and PHP, 43
data type rules, 43
defined, 41, 43

M

magic_quotes_gpc feature og PHP5, 813
mail functions, description of, 726
mail servers
IMAP servers, 568
POP3 server, 568
SMTP server, 568
Mail Transport Agent. *See* **MTA**
mail() function, 552, 564, 567, 570-572
Math class, methods of
cosine(), 517
power(), 517
squareRoot(), 517

math functions, description of, 726. See also PHP
    math functions
max() function, 400
md5() function, 573
member variables visibility
  private, 467
  protected, 467
  public, 467
metacharacters
  $, 213
  (abc), 212
  *, 213
  +, 213
  ., 212
  ?, 212
  [a-z], 212
  [abc], 212
  [^abc], 212
  \b, 212
  \d and \D, 212
  \s and \S, 212
  \w and \W, 212
  ^, 213
  {,y}, 213
  {x,y}, 213
  {x,}, 213
  {x}, 213
method attribute
  for text fields, 82
  GET value, 77
  using GET method:, 76
  using POST method, 76
methods overriding, 481
MIME (Multipurpose Internet Mail Extensions)
  header fields, 572
  HTML e-mails, 574
  multipart MIME, 573
MIME functions, overview of, 729
MIME header fields
  Content-Disposition Header, 573
  Content-Id, 573
  Content-Transfer-Encoding, 573
  Content-Type, 573
  MIME Version, 572
MIME header, 576
min() function, 400
miscellaneous functions, description of, 730
mkdir() function, 292, 293
mkdir_form() function, 297
Model View, Controller (MVC), 543

module settings for PHP5, 818
move_uploaded_file() function, 308
MP3 files, 546, 549, 552, 560
mp3id.php file, creating, 546
MP3_ID package, 546
MP3_ID package, working of
  ACCESSED key, 550
  FILENAME key, 550
  use of associative array, 549
MS-SQL functions, description of, 731
msyql_field_name() function, 426, 428
MTA (Mail Transport Agent), 567, 571
multidimensional arrays, 176
MultiLogDatabaseQueryException class, 646,
    649
MultiLogException class
  defined, 627, 646, 648
  getErrorMessage() function, 627
  suggestedSolutions() function, 627
MultiLogInvalidDatabaseException class, 646
MultiLogInvalidDataException class, 646
MultiLogOpenDatabaseException class, 646
multiple arrays. See multidimensional arrays
multiple attribute, 94
multiple check boxes. See also check boxes
  using of, 88
  working of, 90
multiplication operator (*), 47
Multipurpose Internet Mail Extensions. See MIME
MVC (Model View, Controller), 543
MySQL attributes
  AUTO INCREMENT, 376
  BINARY, 376
  DEFAULT, 376
  NOT NULL, 376
  NULL, 376
MySQL clauses, 401
MySQL client for data retrieving, 394
MySQL client program, 360. See also MySQL server
    using client program
mysql command line, 378
MySQL commands
  ALTER TABLE, 383
  CREATE TABLE, 375, 376
  for data retrieving, 391
  INSERT, 385
  mysqlshow, 350
  startmysqld, 350
MySQL configuring, 350. See also MySQL installing
MySQL connecting from PHP

for Linux, 367
for Windows, 367
MySQL data manupulation
date and time type fields, use of, 422
inserting records, 417
updating and deleting records, 420
using PHP, 417
MySQL data types, 422
MySQL database engine, 350, 363
MySQL fields
KEY/INDEX keyword, 377
PRIMARY KEY, 377
TIMESTAMP, 378
UNIQUE, 377
MySQL functions, description of, 733
MySQL functions
avg(), 400
count(), 400
max(), 400
min(), 400
mysql_affected_rows(), 369
mysql_close(), 368
mysql_connect(), 368, 371
mysql_errno(), 372
mysql_error(), 372
mysql_fetch_row(), 369
mysql_list_dbs(), 368
mysql_list_tables(), 369
mysql_num_rows(), 369
mysql_select_db(), 369
password(), 364
sum(), 400
MySQL installing
on Linux
from source, 349
using RPMs, 348
on Windows, 347
MySQL logical operators
AND, 397
OR, 397
MySQL packages
MySQL-client, 349
MySQL-devel, 349
MySQL-shared, 349
MySQL program files, 350
MySQL queries. See query commands
MySQL server errors
coding, 372
handling of, 371, 372, 374
PHP functions, use of

error_reporting(), 372, 374
mysql_errno(), 372
mysql_error(), 372
MySQL server using client program
data manipulation, 364
database, selecting of, 361
DESCRIBE command, using of, 362
looking at data, 363
program coding, 360
SHOW TABLES command, using of, 362
MySQL server
connectivity in PHP, 370, 371
date and time field types, 423
MySQL setting up
configuring, 350
installing, 347
MySQL source code installing, 349
MySQL. *See also* **SQLite**
access privileges, 364
advantages, 346
as client/server database, 346
configuring, 350
data types, 356
encryption scheme, 364
for data retrieving, 394, 295
for databases and tables creating, 379
mysql_affected_rows() function, 453
mysql_data_seek() function, 393
mysql_fetch_array() function, 392
mysql_fetch_field() function, 428
mysql_fetch_field() function, use of, 429
mysql_fetch_field() function, working with, 430
mysql_fetch_object() function, 393
mysql_fetch_row() function, 392
mysql_field_flags() function, 426, 428
mysql_field_len() function, 426, 428, 430
mysql_field_type() function, 426, 428
mysql_insert_id function, 439
mysql_list_fields() function, 426, 427
mysql_num_fields() function, 426, 427
mysql_num_rows() function, 413
mysql_query() function, 379
mysql_result() function, 393

N

name/value pairs, 73, 74. *See also* **query strings**
namespace
defined, 320
for XHTML, 321

naming conventions, 235
naming variables, 42
navigation tree, 537
nesting, 251
network connections for PHP installing, 4
network functions, description of, 736
next() function, 170
nodes, 332
normalization
  1NF (First Normal Form), 352
  2NF (Second Normal Form), 354
  3NF (Third Normal Form), 355
  defined, 352
  other normal forms, 355
notice error condition, 190
now() function for data manipulation, 423
NTFS (NT File System), 282
NULL entry in SQL queries, 359

O

object constructors. See also object destructors
  for MySQL database, 472, 473
  in PHP4, 471
object destructors. See also object constructors
  creating, 474
  defined, 474
  working with, 476
  __destruct method, 476
object-oriented (OO) changes in PHP5
  abstract classes, 491
  class constants supporting, 491
  class destructors support, 491
  dereferencing support, 490
  interfaces support, 491
  keywords for controlling visbility, 490
  static methods, supporting of, 491
  unified constructors, 491
  use of type hints by functions and methods, 491
object-oriented programming (OOP) concepts
  classes, 461, 463
  encapsulation, 463, 489
  get methods, 468
  inheritance, 463, 477
  interfaces, 463, 486
  objects initializing, 471
  objects, 464
  set Methods, 468
object-oriented programming (OOP)
  advantages, 462

  code reuse, 462
  for software architecture, 462
  fundamentals, 461
  modularity of classes, 462
objects initializing
  object constructors, 471
  __construct() function, use of, 471
objects instantiation, 464
objects, defined, 463
ODBC (Open DataBase Connectivity)
  compliant databases, 781
  database driver, 781
  SQL Server database, connecting to, 781
  use of, 781
ODBC functions, description of, 737
ODBC functions
  other ODBC functions
    odbc_statistics(), 783
    odbc_tableprivileges(), 783
    odbc_tables(), 783
  PHP ODBC configuration
    ODBC prersistent connections, 784
    odbc.default_db, 784
    odbc.default_pw, 784
    odbc.default_user, 784
  PHP ODBC functions
    for PHP ODBC running on Windows, 790
    odbc_autocommit(), 783
    odbc_close(), 782
    odbc_close_all(), 782
    odbc_commit(), 783
    odbc_connect(), 782
    odbc_error(), 783
    odbc_errormsg(), 783
    odbc_exec(), 782
    odbc_execute, 782
    odbc_fetch_array(), 782
    odbc_fetch_row(), 782
    odbc_free_result(), 782
    odbc_num_rows(), 782
    odbc_pconnect(), 782
    odbc_prepare, 782
    odbc_result(), 782
    odbc_rollback(), 783
  using on Windows or Linux, 783
online PHP programs, 36
OOP. See object-oriented programming
opacity, 604
Open DataBase Connectivity. See ODBC
open() function, 487

opendir() function, 290
operator types. *See PHP operator types*
option element, 93
OR operator (}}), logical, 136
ORDER BY clause. *See also* Group By clause
  for data retrieving, 398
  query clause, 360
Organization class, 517
output buffering functions, description of, 740

P

page accesses. *See access logging concept*
parameters passing
  by reference, 245
  by setting default parameter values, 246
  by value, 245
  parameter ordering apsects, 246
parameters, 237
parse errors. *See syntax errors*
ParseXML method, 544
parsing, 32
password fields, 101
password() function, 364, 439
patterns of regular expressions, 206
PCRE functions, description of, 741
PCS (PEAR coding standards), 532
PEAR (PHP Extension and Add-on Repository)
    coding conventions, 234-235
PEAR (PHP Extension and Application Repository),
    529
PEAR classes and applications, 534
PEAR coding standards (PCS), 532
PEAR coding standards
  comments, 235
  control-flow structure formatting, 235
  defining functions, 236
  delimiters, 236
  function calls formatting, 235
  indenting, 235
  naming conventions
    classes, 235
    constants, 235
    functions, 235
    global variables, 235
    methods, 235
    predefined values, 235
PEAR components for application building
  single PEAR component, 546
  two PEAR components, 551

PEAR components. *See PEAR packages*
PEAR mail classes
  Mail, 575
  Mail_IMAP, 575
  Mail_Mbox, 575
  Mail_Mime, 575
  Mail_Queue, 575
PEAR mail libraries, 574
PEAR Package Manager, installing
  code, 537
  on Linux/UNIX, 535
  on Windows, 534, 535
PEAR Package Manager
  overview, 531
  using of, 536
PEAR packages
  for application building
    using single PEAR components, 545
    using two PEAR components, 551
  for PHP, 536
  HTML_TreeMenu class, 539
  HTML_TreeMenu, 537
  installing, 534, 535
  overview, 530
  xmlhtmltree.phpm, 539, 541
PEAR repository dependencies, 531
PEAR standards
  comments, 532
  control structures, 532
  function calls, 533
  function definitions, 533
  indenting, 532
  naming conventions
    for classes, 533
    for constants, 533
    for functions, 533
PEAR structure
  PEAR Package Manager, 531
  PECL (PHP Extension Community Library), 530, 531
  PFC (PHP Foundation Classes), 530
PEAR, overview of, 529
PECL (PHP Extension Community Library), 530
PERL (Practical Extraction and Reporting
    Language), 2
persist() method, 666
PersistableLog class, 650
persistent storage mechanism, 259
Personal Web Server (PWS)
  compatibility with PHP, 5
  installing aspects, 5

PFC (PHP Foundation Classes), overview of, 530

PHP CLI arguments
on Linux, 798
on Windows, 798
shell command running
on UNIX system, 798
on Windows system, 799

PHP CLI interactivity
defined, 802
using streams
standard error, 802
standard input, 802
standards output, 802

PHP CLI, automating of
defined, 799
on UNIX/Linux, 800
on Windows, 800

PHP CLI
behaviorial points, 796
command line switches, 796
for Web pages, 795
use of CGI, 796
using of, 795

PHP code debugging. *See also* **PHP script debugging**
basic error types, 189
code testing aspects, 188

PHP code markers, 35

PHP code running requirements
file extensions, 34
PHP delimiters, 34
syntactically correct PHP code, 35
Web page, 33, 34

PHP code
for random number generation, 132
for session management, 119
overview, 128
using arrays, 163
using while loop, 146

PHP codes
for logic designing, 123
high-quality code writing, 231
PEAR coding standards, 234
robust code writing, 187
testing and debugging, 188
testing, debugging, and maintenance, 233
user-defined functions, writing of, 236

PHP configuration file
php.ini, 1
php.ini-dist, 3
php.ini-recommended, 3

PHP configuring. *See also* **PHP installing; PHP running**
caching method, 29
configuration file settings, 3
of configuration file, 3
PHP extensions, 29
php.ini file modifying, 28

PHP data types
array, 43
boolean, 43
float, 43
integer, 43
NULL, 43
object, 43
resource, 43
string, 43

PHP delimiters, 34

PHP directories, working with, 290

PHP directory functions. *See directory functions*

PHP DOM extension functions
append_child(), 333
create_element(), 333
DOMDocument object, creating, 333
domxml_new_doc, 333
domxml_open_file(), 333
domxml_open_mem(), 333
get_element_by_tagname, 333
using of, 333

PHP e-mail application, building, 575

PHP embedding into HTML, 2

PHP error handling configuration
display_errors, 190
errors messages, suppressing of, 221
error_reporting, 190
log_errors, 190, 221
track_errors, 190

PHP error types
fatal, 190
notice, 190
warning, 190

PHP expressions, 47

PHP Extension and Add-on Repository (PEAR)
coding conventions, 234

PHP Extension and Application Repository. *See PEAR*

PHP Extension Community Library (PECL), overview of, 530, 531

PHP extensions, 29

PHP file contents, 407, 411

PHP file systems, types, 259
PHP files and directories handling, 259, 260
PHP Foundation Classes (PFC), overview of, 530
PHP functions
  arrays, 694
  BCMath, 699
  BZip2, 700
  calendar, 701
  character type, 703
  class/object, 702
  curl, 703
  date and time, 704
  directory, 705
  error handling, 706
  file system, 707
  for Apache, 693
  FTP, 710
  function handling, 713
  HTTP, 713
  iconv library, 714
  image, 714
  IMAP, 722
  mail(), 567, 571
  mail, 726
  math, 726
  MIME, 729
  miscellaneous, 730
  MS-SQL, 731
  MySQL, 733
  mysql_errno(), 372
  mysql_error(), 372
  network functions, 736
  ODBC, 737
  output buffering, 740
  PCRE, 741
  PHP options and info functions, 742
  program execution, 744
  regular expressions, 745
  sessions, 745
  simple XML, 747
  socket, 747
  SQLite, 749
  streams, 752
  strings, 754
  URL, 760
  variable functions, 761
  XML, 762
  ZLib, 763
PHP image library, 589
PHP installing. See also PHP configuring; PHP running
  automatic installer for Windows version, 4
  from Source files, 9
  Linux version using RPMs, 4
  network connections aspects, 4
  of server software, 3
  on Red Hat Linux machine, 1, 4, 9
  on Windows 2000 machine, 1
  on Windows 2000, 4, 19
  PEAR dependencies, 531
  system requirements, 2, 3
  testing and troubleshooting, 26, 27
  third-party installers
    FoxServ, 4
    PHPTriad, 4
  using RPM, 6
  with Linux and Apache, 6, 9
PHP language construct
  array(), 59
  echo, 33
  unset, 33
PHP logging agent, 613
PHP math functions
  defined, 54
  pi(), 54, 58
  rand(), 54, 58
PHP MySQL connectivity
  coding, 370
  functions used
    mysql_affected_rows(), 369
    mysql_close(), 368
    mysql_connect(), 368
    mysql_fetch_row(), 369
    mysql_list_dbs(), 368
    mysql_list_tables(), 369
    mysql_num_rows(), 369
    mysql_select_db(), 369
  server errors handling, 371
  steps involved, 368
  working of, 370
PHP ODBC configuration options, 784
PHP ODBC running on Windows, using SQL Server
  data source name (DSN) system creating, 785
  DSN, use of, 784
  SQL Server database, creating of, 784
  using PHP ODBC functions, 790

PHP operator types
arithmetic, 47, 52
arrays, 47, 58
assignment, 47
bitwise, 47
comparison, 47
error control, 47
execution, 47
increment/decrement, 53
incrementing/decrementing, 47
logical, 47
special assignment, 53
string, 47, 48
PHP operator, 46
PHP options and info functions, description of, 742
PHP program logic designing
boolean logic, 125
problem statement, 123
pseudo code writing, 124
PHP program
arrays, 145, 161
client-server relationship, 36
creating steps, 31
debugging, 187, 233
decision-making statements, 128
embedding in HTML Web page, 51
for creating UML, 493
for Web designing, 1
logic designing, 123
loops, 145
robust program, 187
running, 4, 5, 36
state maintenance aspects, 108
testing, 187, 233
using arrays, 162, 167
using database architectures, 345
using if statements, 129
using strings, 49
using switch statements, 141
using values returned from forms, 102
Web services aspects, 322
working, 51, 54, 58
XML features, 314
PHP programming language features
HTML codes, 2
working with HTML, 1
PHP programming
code optimization, 234
coding process, 233
control-flow structures, 123

defined, 74
Extreme Programming, 233
high-quality code writing, 231
logical operators, 136
RAD process, 233
software development processes, 232
specification writing, 232
using HTML forms, 75
PHP regular expressions, 208
PHP running. *See also* PHP installing; PHP configuring
as CGI binary, 5, 15
in conjunction with Web server, 5
on Red Hat Linux, 4
on Windows 2000, 4
online PHP programs running, 36
test machine setting up, 4
PHP script debugging. *See also* PHP code debugging
defined, 189
logic errors, 193
PHP configuring for error handling, 190, 220
PHP error messages, understanding of, 189
PHP error types, 190
runtime errors, 193
setting versus comparing values, 197
syntax errors, 190
PHP script
for Web, 797
running via HTTP request, 41
scope of variables, 247
using arrays, 162, 166
using database tables, 405
using for loop, 159
using if statement, 140
using infinite loop, 151
using Smarty, 616
using switch statements, 144
using values returned from forms, 102
PHP sessions
for access Web pages counting, 118
using session_register() function, 117
PHP string-handling functions, 323
PHP variables creating issues
data types, 42
global keyword, 45
naming, 41
static variable, 45
variable scope, 42, 44
PHP variables using, 41

PHP XML functions
  for PHP4, 323
  for PHP5, 334
  using of, 322
php.ini file for PHP5 configuring, 805
php.ini file versions
  php.ini-dist, 805
  php.ini-recommended, 805
php.ini
  php.ini-dist, 3, 23, 805
  php.ini-recommended, 3, 23, 28, 805
PHP/FI for web designing, 2
PHP4 XML functions
  features, 323
  xml_get_error_code, 323
  xml_parser_create, 323
  xml_parser_get_option_set_option, 323
  xml_parse_into_struct, 323
  xml_set_option, 323
PHP5 configuring
  data handling, 813
  error handling and logging, 811
  file uploading aspects, 816
  Fopen wrappers, 816
  language options, 807
  module settings, 818
  paths and directories, 814
  php.ini file, use of, 805
  resource limits
    CPU cycles, 810
    hard drive space, 810
PHP5 debugging and error handling. *See also* **PHP**
    script debugging
  HTML source code errors), 199
  own debugging tools, writing of, 198
  prevention of private information display, 198
  using echo(), 198
PHP5 error handling aspects, 222, 225
PHP5 installing on Windows 2000/Internet
    Information Server (IIS)
  php.ini and extensions, 22
  PHP5 downloading, 20
PHP5 installing on
  Linux and Apache, 9
  Red Hat Linux machine, 4, 9
  Windows 2000, 4, 19
PHP5 installing with Linux and Apache
  Apache configuring, 17
  Apache for DSO installation, 13
  Apache installing, 16

  Apache starting or restarting, 19
  configure options, 15
  configure options, running of, 15
  configure script
    commands, 14
    running, 14
  installation method, choosing of
    binary (compiled) method, 6
    binary RPMs method, 6
    source method, 6
  PHP5 compiling aspects, 14
  QUICK INSTALL (DSO) performing, 15
  running as CGI, 15
PHP5 XML functions
  features, 334
  simpleXML extension, 334
PHP5
  decision-making aspects, 123
  e-mail functions, 567
  for PHP installing, 3
  mail() function, 571
  overview, 1, 2
  problem statement, 124
  uilt-in libxml-provided XML support, 562
  using object-oriented programming (OOP) features,
    461
  using object-oriented programming (OOP), 490
  using SQLite, 765
  XML features, 313
PHP
  as HyperText Preprocessor, 1
  as loosly typed language, 43
  code markers, 35
  compatibility with Personal Web server (PWS), 5
  configuration file, 1, 3
  constants, 45
  data retrieval functions, 391
  data storing aspects, 344
  data types converting, 44
  database engine, use of, 344
  dynamic extensions, 817
  file and directory handling, 300
  file functions, 260, 284
  files uploading, 307, 309
  for databases and tables creating, 379
  for dynamic Web pages developing, 2
  for graphics creating, 585
  for MySQL data manupulation, 417
  for Web designing, 1
  image functions, 586

PHP *(continued)*
math functions, 54
on Linux server, 1
on Windows server, 1
operators and expressions, 46
paths and directories, 814
PEAR components, 529
predefined variables, 67
processing compatibility with HTML, 67
session identifier (SID) creating, 116
session management, 116
Web applications, creating and running of, 5
phpinfo() function, 68
PHPUnit, working with
assert() method, use of, 620
isOpen() function, 620
pi() function, 58
pixels drawing, 589. *See also* **imagesetpixel()**
function
PNG format, 587
polygons drawing
code, 594
parameter passing concept
apexes number, 594
array of points, 594
drawing color, 594
image resource identifier, 594
using imagepolygon() function, 594
POP3 server, 568
Poseidon for UML diagrams generation, 495
posix_getgrgid() function, 282
POST method
defined, 38, 75
for text area, 84
for user registration, 436
using of, 79
POST value, 79
Practical Extraction and Reporting Language
(PERL), 2
predefined arrays, 69
predefined variables, 67, 69
prev() function, 170
primary key. *See also* **foreign key**
for user registration, 435
in 1NF (First Normal Form), 354
in MySQL, 377
in SQL, 358
printMenu method, 545
print_r() function, 60, 69
private functions, 489

private member variables, 489
problem statement, 123
program execution functions, description
of, 744
program logic. *See* **PHP program logic designing**
PropertyObject class, 509
protected functions, 489
protected member variables, 489
pseudo code
defined, 35
for while loop execution, 146
writing, 124
public functions, 489
public member variables, 489

Q

quantifiers, 212
queries in SQL
NULL entry, use of, 359
query commands, use of, 358
query clauses
FROM, 360
ORDER BY, 360
WHERE, 360, 363, 364
query commands. *See also* **query clauses**
ALTER, 360
CREATE, 360
DELETE, 359, 364
DROP, 360
GRANT, 365
INSERT, 359, 364
REPLACE, 359, 365
REVOKE, 365
SELECT, 359
UPDATE, 359, 364
query string. *See also* **name/value pairs**
defined, 74
for state maintenance, 109
with URL, 73

R

RAD. *See* **Rapid Application Design**
radio buttons
defined, 91
using of, 91
working of, 92
radiogeneratexml.php, 552, 562
radiogeneratexml.php, working of, 558

radiorequest.php code, 560

radiorequest.php, 552

radiorequest.php, working

  display logic, 565

  filesize function, use of, 564

  HTML_Treemenu code, 563

  HTML_Treemenu component, 563

  URL of XML script, 563

rand() function

  defined, 58

  for random number generation, 132

random number generation code, 132

Rapid Application Design (RAD), 233. *See also*
      Extreme Programming

raster image file formats

  JPEG, 587

  PNG, 587

  WBMP, 587

raster images, creating and refining

  color allocation, 588

  drawing functions, use of, 589

  image creating steps, 588

  new image creating, 588

raster images, manipulating

  existing image opening

    imagecreate() function, use of, 598

    imagecreatefromjpeg() function, use of, 598,
      600

  thumbnails creating, 604

  watermark applying', 600

RDBMS benefits

  multiuser environment, 388

  performance, 388

  reliability, 388

  security, 388

RDBMS

  DB/2, 346

  defined, 351

  features, 346, 351

  field, 351

  for PHP, 345

  GRANT and REVOKE commands, using of,
    365

  MySQL, 346

  normalization, 352

  Oracle, 346

  record, 351

  redundancy concept, 352

  SQL Server, 346

  SQL, use of, 355

readdir() function, 291, 292

readfile() function, 272, 273

README files, 4

recommended file, 3

record in RDBMS, *351*

rectangles drawing

  code, 591

  using imagerectangle() function, 591

  with rounded corners

    coding, 595

    using imagedestroy() function, 598

    using imagepng() function, 598

    using roundrect() function, 595

recursion

  defined, 251

  function calling example, 252

Red Hat Package Manager. *See* **RPM**

redundancy in RDBMS, 352

regexps. *See* **regular expressions**

register_form() function, 436, 438

register_globals for PHP5 configuring, 813

register_globals setting, 69

registration_form() function, 440

regular expression functions, 204, 745

regular expressions

  defined, 206

  ereg() function, 208

  for file path parameters checking, 218

  for HTML form validation, 204, 206, 209, 216,
    218

  for URL validating, 216, 217

  special characters, 209

Relational Database Management Systems. *See*
    RDBMS

relational databases. *See* **RDBMS**

rename() function, 288

REPLACE and UPDATE queries, difference between,
    365

REPLACE query, 359, 365

report-html.tpl, 654

report.php, 652

report.tpl, 653

Requests For Comment (RFC), 568

require statements. *See also* **include statements**

  defined, 254

  important points, 257

  writing, 254

require() function, 304, 814

require_once function, 541

reset buttons, 101

retrieving data
  using PHP functions
    mysql_data_seek(), 393
    mysql_fetch_array(), 392
    mysql_fetch_object(), 392
    mysql_fetch_row(), 391
    mysql_query(), 391
    mysql_result(), 393
  using SQL statements
    FROM clause, 402
    GROUP BY, 401
    HAVING, 402
    LIKE operators, 399
    LIMIT, 396
    NOT LIKE operators, 399
    ORDER BY, 398
    SELECT, 394
    WHERE, 396
return statement, 238
REVOKE query command, 367
rewind() function, 275, 281
rewinddir() function, 292
RFC (Requests For Comment), 568
RGB color model, 586
RGB color value, 586, 587
rmdir() function, 292, 293
robust PHP program, 187
root account setting in MySQL,
    350
rounded rectangle drawing, 595
roundrect() function, 596
RPM (Red Hat Package Manager)
  abbreviated names, 7
  compatibility features, 7
  for MySQL installation, 348
  obtaining, 7
  PHP4 installation of, 6
RPM packages
  apache, 8
  gd, 8
  gd-devel, 8
  installation aspects, 8
  libjpeg, 8
  libpng, 8
  mod_php4, 8
  zlib, 8
rsort() function, 175
running as CGI, 15
runtime errors
  defined, 189, 193
  dividing by zero, 194
  infinite loops, 196

S

safe mode language option
  directory settings, 807
  environment variables, 807
  features, 807
  safe_mode = on, 807
SAPI (Server Application Programming Interface), 5
save_file case, 304, 306
Scalable Vector Graphics (SVG), 587
scope of variables
  defined, 247
  global variables, 247
  local variables, 247
  static variables, 247
  working example, 249
Second Normal Form (2NF), 354
SELECT queries for data retrieving, 391, 394
SELECT query, 359
select..case statement, 304, 307
Sendmail, 567
Server Application Programming Interface (SAPI), 5
server errors. *See* **MySQL server errors**
server software
  Linux, 3
  Windows 2000, 3
server-side scripting, 796
session identifier (SID)
  creating aspects, 116
  defined, 116
  session_register() function, 117, 118
  session_start() function, 117
session key, 109, 110
session management
  defined, 116
  using session_register() function, 119
  working of, 119
session variables, 446, 447
sessions functions, description of, 745
session_register() function
  for PHP sessions, 117
  for session identifier (SID), 117, 118
  for session management, 119
session_start() function, 116, 442
set function, creating, 467
set method. *See also* **get method**
  for accessing properties, 468

working with, 468
___set function using, 469, 470
setcookie() function parameters
secure integer, 112
string, 111
UNIX timestamp, 111
settings.php for logging, 628
setUp() method, 621
setup.php for logging, 629
SGML (Standard Generalized Markup Language), 63, 313
shell command, running of, 798
SHOW DATABASES query, 379
SHOW TABLES command, 362
SID. *See session identifier*
Simple Mail Transfer Protocol (SMTP), 568
Simple Object Access Protocol (SOAP), 322
simple XML functions, description of, 747
simpleXML extension functions
simplexml_element->asXML, 334
simplexml_element->attributes, 334
simplexml_element->children, 334
simplexml_element->xpath, 334
simplexml_import_dom, 334
simplexml_load_file, 334, 335
simplexml_load_string, 334
simpleXML extension, 323
simpleXML functions, 313
simpleXML method, 544
simpleXML object
DOM importing features, 339, 340
node value changing, 338
working example, 338
SimpleXML, 542
simplexml_element->asXML function, 334
simplexml_element->attributes function, 334
simplexml_element->children function, 334
simplexml_element->xpath function, 334
simplexml_import_dom function, 334
simplexml_load_file function, 334, 335
simplexml_load_string function, 334
simplexml_load_string method, 544
single PEAR component for application building.
See also MP3_ID package
sitelogs.db database designing, 622
Smarty class, 617
Smarty object, 617
Smarty
installing of, 615
overview, 615

using of, 616
working of
coding, 618
creating of mysql connection, 617
creating of SQL query, 618
SMTP (Simple Mail Transfer Protocol), 568
SMTP server, 568, 570
SOAP (Simple Object Access Protocol), 322
socket functions, description of, 747
software development processes for PHP, 232
sort functions
array_multisort(), 181
arsort(), 175
asort(), 174
ksort(), 175
rsort(), 175
sort(), 173
sort() function, 62
sorting arrays
asort(), 62
sort(), 62
Source method for PHP5 installation
advantages, 6
disadvantages, 6
special characters
anchors, 210
character classes, 210
defined, 204, 209
for inserting records into tables, 418
HTML entity, 420
metacharacters, 212
qualifiers, 211
quantifiers, 212
word boundaries, 211
specification writing, 232
SQL data types
character
BLOB, 357
CHAR, 357
ENUM, 357
LONGBLOB, 357
LONGTEXT, 357
MEDIUMBLOB, 357
MEDIUMTEXT, 357
SET, 357
TEXT, 357
TINYBLOB, 357
TINYTEXT, 357
VARCHAR, 357

SQL data types *(continued)*
date/time
  DATE, 356
  DATETIME, 356
  TIME, 356
  TIMESTAMP, 356
  YEAR, 356
numeric
  BIGINT, 356
  DECIMAL, 356
  DOUBLE/REAL, 356
  FLOAT, 356
  INT, 356
  MEDIUMINT, 356
  SMALLINT, 356
  TINYINT, 356
SQL features
  access privileges, 367
  data types, 356
  for RDBMS, 355
  queries, 358
SQL for PHP applications, 343
SQL statements for retrieving data
  DISTINCT keyword, use of, 401
  fields retrieving, 395
  LIKE operators, use of, 399
  LIMIT, 396
  MySQL server functions, use of, 394
  NOT LIKE operators, use of, 399
  ORDER BY, 398
  SELECT, 394
  summaries, reporting of, 400
  WHERE, 396
SQL statements, 358
SQLite databases
  connection and maintenance functions
    sqlite_close(), 767
    sqlite_libencoding()_open(), 767
    sqlite_open(), 767
    sqlite_poopen(), 767
    sqlite_query(), 768
    sqlite__libversion(), 768
  data manipulation functions
    sqlite_array_query(), 769
    sqlite_column(), 769
    sqlite_current, 768
    sqlite_fetch_array(), 769
    sqlite_fetch_single(), 769
    sqlite_has_more(), 769
    sqlite_next(), 768

sqlite_query(), 768
sqlite_rewind(), 768
sqlite_seek(), 768
sqlite_unbuffered_query(), 768
library application, 771
other functions
  sqlite_busy_timeout(), 770
  sqlite_create_aggregate(), 770
  sqlite_create_function(), 770
  sqlite_error_string(), 770
  sqlite_escape_string(), 771
  sqlite_last_error(), 771
  sqlite_udf_decode_binary(), 771
  sqlite_udf_encode_binary(), 771
SQLite facts, 766
SQLite functions, description of, 749
SQLite in practice, 771
SQLite library
  application, 771
  application:, 765
  book listing, 775
  comparison with MySQL, 773
  for database and tables creating, 772
  functions
    sqlite_error_string(), 773
    sqlite_last_error(), 773
    sqlite_open(), 772
  record editing, 778
  switchboard, 775
SQLite metadata functions
  sqlite_changes(), 769
  sqlite_field_name(), 769
  sqlite_last_insert_rowid(), 769
  sqlite_num_fields(), 769
  sqlite_num_rows(), 769
SQLite using with PHP, 767
**SQLite's INTEGER PRIMARY KEY field,
  773**
SQLite's record editing
  defined, 778
  sqlite_escape_string() function, 780
  UPDATE statement, use of, 780
  using SQL LIMIT clause, 780
  using sqlite_num_rows() function, 780
SQLite's SQL INSERT statement, 773
**Standard Generalized Markup Language (SGML),
  63, 313**
stat() function, 264
state maintenance, 108
state of application, 108

stateless protocol, 108
static function variables. *See also* static
    variables
  creating, 248
  defined, 248
static variables
  defined, 45, 247
  scope, 248
static Web pages, 2
streams functions, description of, 752
string formatting specifiers
  %a, 424
  %b, 424
  %D, 424
  %d, 424
  %e, 424
  %H, 424
  %h, 424
  %I, 424
  %M, 424
  %r, 424
  %s, 424
  %T, 424
  %W, 424
  %Y, 424
  %y, 424
string functions
  chr() function, 49
  strlen() function, 48
  strpos() function, 49
  strstr() function, 49
string operator
  concatenation operators, 48
  defined, 47, 48
string validation
  defined, 204
  for HTML forms, 204
  using addslashes() function, 206
  using stripslashes() function, 206
  using strlen() function, 205
  using strstr() function, 205
  using substr() function, 205
strings functions, description of, 754
strings
  as array indexes, 59
  for PHP program creating, 49
stripslashes() function
  for inserting records, 418
  for string validation, 206
strlen() function, 48, 51, 205

strongly typed languages. *See also* loosely typed
    languages
  data type rules, 43
  defined, 43
strpos() function, 49, 52
strstr() function, 49, 51, 205
Structured Query Language. *See* SQL
submit buttons
  defined, 101
  name and value attributes, 101
substr() function, 205, 413
suggestedSolutions() function, 627, 647
sum() function, 400
superglobal $_FILES array variable values
  $_FILES[userfile], 308
  $_FILES[userfile][name], 308
  $_FILES[userfile][size], 308
  $_FILES[userfile][type], 308
superglobal arrays
  $GLOBALS, 70
  $_COOKIE, 70
  $_ENV, 70
  $_FILES, 70
  $_GET, 70
  $_POST, 70
  $_REQUEST, 70
  $_SERVER, 70
  $_SESSION, 70
  defined, 69
superglobal variables. *See also* predefined variables
  defined, 67
  global keyword, using of, 69
SVG (Scalable Vector Graphics), 587
switch case block, 328, 329
switch statements
  defined, 140
  using break command, 140, 141
  using of, 142
  working example, 140, 144
switching functions, 243
syntax errors
  defined, 189, 190
  improper closing statements, 190
  improper code indentation, 191
  misspelling, 191
  typos errors, 190
system requirements for PHP installing
  PHP-compatible Web server, 3
  PHP5, 3
  relational database system, 3

system requirements for PHP installing *(continued)*
server software, 3
text editor, 3
Web browser, 3
system() function, 290

T

tables altering via ALTER TABLE, 383
tables creating via CREATE TABLE, 375
tables deleting via DELETE, 420, 422
tables inserting via INSERT, 385
tables updating via UPDATE query, 420, 422
tables using date and time type fields, 422
tables, retrieving data from, 394
TCP/IP protocol, 37
text area. *See also* **text fields**
defined, 83
element, 83
POST method, using of, 84
using of, 83
working of, 84
text boxes. *See* **text fields**
text editor
building, 300
for PHP installing, 3
for PHP program, 31
text fields. *See also* **text area**
example, 81, 82
GET method, using of, 82
method attribute, using of, 82
textarea element, 77, 83, 85
Third Normal Form (3NF), 355
thumbnails, creating
code, 604
using imagecopyresampled() function, 606, 607
using imagecopyresized() function, 606
using imagesx() function, 605
using imagesy() function, 605
time-related file functions
fileatime(), 281
filectime(), 279
filemtime(), 279
getdate() function, use of, 279, 280
working of, 280
TIMESTAMP as MySQL field, 378
timestamp, 111, 279
toHTML() function, 624
toHTML() method, 658

toSQL() function, 625
toString(), 513
to_days() function, 425
Transmission Control Protocol (TCP), 37
transparency applying
imagecolorat() function, 602
imagecolorexact() function, 603
imagecolortransparent() function, 603
transport protocol, 37
traverse_dir() function, 294
tree navigation, 538
TreeMenu.js, 540
treemenutest.php, 553
trim() function, 799, 803
True Type font (TTF)
color allocation aspects, 610
using code, 610
using imagefttext() function, 609
try/catch exception-handling
defined, 222
for PHP5, 222, 225
TTF. *See* **True Type font**
two-component PEAR application
radiogeneratexml.php creating, 553
radiorequest.php creating, 556
type attribute, 80

U

Umbrello for UML diagrams generation, 495
UML (Unified Modeling Language)
class relationships, 493
aggregation, 499
generalization, 499
for logging agent designing, 624
for object-oriented program (OOP) modeling, 493
working with, 493
UML diagrams generating tools, 494
ArgoUML, 494
Dia, 494
IBM Rational Rose, 494
Poseidon For UML, 495
Umbrello, 495
Visio, 494
UML diagrams. *See also* **contact manager application**
activity diagrams, 500
case diagrams, 501

defined, 493

sequence diagram, 501

UML software, 494

UML specification, 493

UML, using of, 494

Unified Modeling Language. See UML

uninstall command, 536

UNIX directory system, 290

UNIX file system, 290

UNIX timestamp, 111, 279

unlink() function, 288, 290

UPDATE and REPLACE queries, difference between, 365

UPDATE query, 359, 364

UPDATE statement for object destructor, 476

upgrade command, 536

URL (uniform resource locators) validating, 216, 217

URL encoded characters

!, 78

;, 78

#, 78

%, 78

&, 78

(, 78

), 78

+, 78

,, 78

., 78

/, 78

:, 78

;, 78

<, 78

=, 78

>, 78

?, 78

@, 78

space, 78

tab, 78

URL encoding, 77

URL functions, description of, 760

user interface for PHP program running, 34

user manager. See also access logging concept

action choosing aspects, 457

creating of, 449

delete_record() function, 450

edit_log_record() function, 452

edit_record() function, 450, 452

ENUM options, 449

htmlspecialchars() function, 455

IGNORE statement, 451

list_records() function, 449

mysql_affected_rows() function, 453

user_message() function, 452

user_message() function, use of, 449

view_record() function, 453

user registration script

create_account() function, use of, 438

creating steps, 435

for user registration, 436

in_use() function, use of, 436, 439

mysql_insert_id function, 439

password() function, 439

primary key, use of, 435

register_form() function, use of, 436, 438, 440

registration_form() function, use of, 440

using encrypted passwords, 436

using user ID, 435

user-defined functions

calling functions, 237

defining functions, 237

function calling, 251

functions structure, 237

functions writing steps, 237

parameter odering, 246

parameters passing aspects

by reference, 245

by setting default parameter values, 246

by value, 245

points to remember, 240

return statement, use of, 238

switching functions, 243

working example, 240, 243

writing of, 236

UserDemographic objects, 663, 664, 667

UserDemogrpahic class, 625

UserLog class, 625

UserLog object, 656

UserLog objects, 663, 667

userlog.php, 666

UserLogException class, 646

userviewer.php file building

created database file, use of, 404

database file contents, 405

database tables, viewing of, 405, 407

userviewer.php file contents. See PHP file contents

userviewer.php file, using of, 414

user_message() function, 449

V

valid HTML documents, 333
valid XML documents. *See also* well-formed XML
    documents
  defined, 318
  DTDs and XML Schemas, 318
  example of, 316
  syntax rules, 315
values. *See array components*
variable functions, description of, 761
variable scope
  local, 44
  variable creating issues, 44
var_dump function, 338, 560
vector images, 587
view_record() function, 411, 424, 453
Visio for UML diagrams generation,
    494

W

warning error condition, 190
watermark applying
  copyright copying into image
    using image functions, 600
    using imagecopy()function, 601
  image copyright, 600
  opacity, working with, 604
  transparency, working with, 602
Web browser for PHP installing, 3
web communications protocols
  HTTP, 37
  TCP/IP, 37
Web designing
  back-end programming functionality, 2
  HTML codes, using of, 2
  using Javascript, 2
  using PERL, 2
  using PHP/FI, 2
  using XML, 322
  via PHP programming, 1
Web image file formats
  JPEG, 587
  PNG, 587
  WBMP, 587
Web page creating
  using HTML forms, 66
  using HTML tags, 66
  via PHP program, 31

Web page designing
  using HTML, 64, 326
  using XML elements, 326
Web page displaying
  of HTML document, 318, 322
  of XHTML document, 318, 322
Web page
  access logging aspects, 444
  dynamic, 2
  for PHP program running, 34
  PHP CLI scripts, use of, 797
  static, 2
  user authentication, 442
Web server
  Apache, 3
  for PHP installing, 3
  Internet Information Server (IIS), 3
  use of cookies, 111
Web Service Description Language (WSDL),
    322
Web services
  SOAP protocol, using of, 322
  via XML, 322
  WSDL, using of, 322
Web sites
  logging features, 614
  use of cookies, 111
  user registration concept, 435
Web-hosting computers, 5
well-formed XML documents. *See also* valid XML
    documents
  code blocks, 328
  DOM extension, use of, 333
  example of, 316
  syntax rules, 315
  syntax rules, 316
WHERE clause
  for data retrieving, 396
  query clause, 360, 363, 364, 365
while loop
  example, 146
  execution of, 146
  for directory enteries sorting, 298
  using of, 147
  working example, 148
while statement, 271
wild cards for data retrieving, 399
wildcard (*) using in SQL, 364
with-dom=dom_dir, 333

word boundaries
defined, 211
symbols, 211
WSDL (Web Service Description Language), 322

X

XHTML document
ELEMENT callout, 319
namespace, 320, 321
rules, 319
using DOCTYPE declaration, 321
Web page displaying, 318, 322
XHTML DTD referencing. *See* **DTDs referencing**
XHTML DTD, 318, 320
XHTML namespace, 321
XML attributes. *See* **XML elements and attributes**
XML document parts
DTD, containing, 315
elements, 315
processing instructions (PI), 315
XML Schema, containing, 315
xml version line, containing, 315
XML document structure
valid, 315, 318
well-formed, 315, 316
XML documents
creating of, 323
DTDs referencing, 320
elements and attributes, 317
PHP functions, using, 322
reading of, 329, 330
referencing via XML keywords, 320
Schema, 318
simpleXML object, using, 334, 335, 338
with document object model (DOM), 332
working example, 326
writing with XHTML, 321
XML DTD, 538
XML elements and attributes
for Wen designing, 326
syntax rules, 317
using of, 317
XML elements. *See* **XML elements and attributes**
XML functions, description of, 762
XML functions. *See also* **PHP DOM extension
functions**
loadXML function, 340
simpleXML extension, 334

supported by PHP4, 323
supported by PHP5, 334
xml_get_error_code, 323
xml_parser_create, 323
xml_parse_into_struct, 323
xml_set_option, 323
XML generation for MP3 files, 553
XML parser functions
file_get_contents(), 329
xml_parser_create(), 329
xml_parse_into_struct(), 329
xml parser-related functions, 323
XML parsers, 323, 329
XML Schemas referencing. *See also* **DTDs
referencing**
code, 320
of external Schemas, 320
using URL, 320, 321
using xmlns attribute, 320, 321
XML Schemas, 315, 318
xml version line, 315
XML Web service, 322
XML
as data exchange standard, 313
elements and attributes, 317
features, 313, 314
for structured data storage, 313
navigation tree, 537
parsing capability, 313
similarities with HTML, 313
xmlhtmltree.phpm class, 543
xmlhtmltree.phpm, 541
xmlns attribute, 320, 321
xml_get_error_code function, 323
xml_parser_create() function, 329
**xml_parse_into_struct() function, 329,
331**
xml_set_option function, 323

Z

Zend Engine 2, 491
ZLib functions, description of, 763
__construct() function, 471
__destruct method, 476
__get() method, 625
__getConnection() function, 517
__ParseNode method, 544
__set() method, 625